Sir Walter Scott's Woodstock • Sir Wal[ter Scott's Woodstock]
Bliss Perry

Publisher's Note

The book descriptions we ask booksellers to display prominently warn that this is an historic book with numerous typos, missing text or index and is not illustrated.

We scanned this book using character recognition software that includes an automated spell check. Our software is 99 percent accurate if the book is in good condition. However, we do understand that even less than one percent can be a very annoying number of typos! And sometimes all or part of a page is missing from our copy of a book. Or the paper may be so discolored from age that you can no longer read the type. Please accept our sincere apologies.

After we re-typeset and design a book, the page numbers change so the old index and table of contents no longer work. Therefore, we usually remove them.

Our books sell so few copies that you would have to pay hundreds of dollars to cover the cost of proof reading and fixing the typos, missing text and index. Therefore, whenever possible, we let our customers download a free copy of the original typo-free scanned book. Simply enter the barcode number from the back cover of the paperback in the Free Book form at www.general-books.net. You may also qualify for a free trial membership in our book club to download up to four books for free. Simply enter the barcode number from the back cover onto the membership form on the same page. The book club entitles you to select from more than a million books at no additional charge. Simply enter the title or subject onto the search form to find the books.

If you have any questions, could you please be so kind as to consult our Frequently Asked Questions page at www.general-books.net/faqs.cfm? You are also welcome to contact us there. General Books LLC™, Memphis, USA, 2012. ISBN: 9780217791298.

INTRODUCTION

"For Human Delight, SJiakespeare, Cervantes, Boccaccio, and Scott!" — Edtasd Fitzgerald.

I.

For the scene of "Woodstock," the twenty-second Waverley novel, Scott chose, as in "Kenilworth," a spot in the very heart of England. The village of Woodstock, lying eight miles to the northwest of Oxford, in a fertile, lovely region, offered to the novelist a field rich in historical associations. Hero had stood, certainly since the time of Henry I.—and as legend affirms, since the days of Alfred —a favourite palace of the English sovereigns; here had been the bower of fair Rosamond, her refuge from the jealous hate of Henry the Second's queen; here Edward the Black Prince was born, and the Princess Elizabeth held a prisoner. The palace was half battered down by the Puritans in the Civil War. Ireland's "Tour of the Thames" contains a picturesque print of the ruins as they were in 1714, but nine years later they were entirely demolished, and two sycamore trees were planted to mark the site. In Scott's time, therefore, not a vestige of the great structure was to be seen, though Rosamond's well was no doubt trickling brightly, as it does to-day, through the shaded greensward of the park. The latter-day visitor to Woodstock is likely, as Scott hints in the opening of his tale, to neglect the more ancient features of the place in order " to view the magnificence of Blenheim," the splendid palace of the Dukes of Marlborough, whose park of twenty-seven hundred acres comprises a great portion of the former royal domain.

With the instinct of a practised writer of fiction, Scott selected an effective moment for the action of his story. "The busy period of the great Civil War," he notes in his Introduction, "was one in which ferent ... dis-played, and accordingly, the incidents which took place on either side were of a striking and extraordinary character, and afforded ample foundation for fictitious composition." One of these extraordinary incidents is narrated in the tract, "The Genuine History of the Good Devil of Woodstock, famous in the World in the year 1649, etc.," from which Scott quotes at second hand in his Introduction, and which is further illustrated in the Appendix. This Introduction was not published until 1832, the last year of Scott's life, when his mind was no longer entirely clear, and the account given of the tract is not quite consistent. It is sufficient for our purpose to note the free use he made of the material thus offered, and that by transferring these occurrences at the Woodstock Lodge to a period two years later than their actual date, he was able to combine with them an imaginary narrative dealing with the escape of the young Charles II. from his Roundhead enemies after the decisive battle of Worcester in September, 1651. The details of the King's wanderings and disguises, in those exciting weeks, are now well enough known. The "Merry Monarch" himself, after his restoration, was never weary of talking of them, and his Chancellor, Lord Clarendon, has written in the "History of the Great Rebellion" " the particulars of his escape as the Chancellor of the Exchequer had them from himself." The indebtedness of the author of "Woodstock " to Clarendon's "History " is pointed out more than once in the notes to the present edition, and in the following narrative of the King's stay at the house of Mr. Lane there are character-traits and situations which Scott certainly seems to have made use of.

"Within few days, a very lionest and discreet person, one Mr. Hndleston, a Benedictine Monk, who attended the service of the Roman Catholics in those parts, came to him, sent by Careless; and was a very great assistance and comfort to him. And when the places to which he carried him were at too great a distance to walk, he provided him a horse, and more proper habit than the rags he wore. This man told him, 'that the Lord Wilmot lay concealed likewise in a friend's house of his; which his Majesty was very glad of: and wished him to contrive some means how they might speak together; ' which the other easily did; and within a night or two. brought them into one place. Wilmot told the King, 'that he had by very good fortune fallen into the house of an honest gentleman, one Mr. Lane, a person of an excellent reputation for his fidelity to the King, but of so universal and general a good name, that, though he had a son, who had been a colonel in the King's service, during the late war, and was then upon his way with men to Worcester the very day of the defeat, men of all affections in the country, and of all opinions, paid the old man a very great respect: that he had been civilly treated there, and that the old gentleman had used some diligence to find out where the King was, that he might get him to his house; where, he was sure, he could conceal him till he might contrive a full deliverance.' He told him, 'he had withdrawn from that house in hope that he might, in some other place, discover where his Majesty was, and having now happily found him, advised him to repair to that house, which stood not near any other.'

"The King enquired of the monk of the reputation of this gentleman; who told him, that 'he had a fair estate; was exceedingly beloved; and the eldest justice of peace of that county of Stafford; and though he was a very zealous Protestant, yet he lived with so much civility and candour toward the Catholics, that they would all trust him, as much as they would do any of their own profession; and that he could not think of any place of so good repose and security for his Majesty's repair to.' The King liked the proposition, yet thought not fit to surprise the gentleman; but sent Wilmot thither again, to assure himself that he might be received there; and was willing that he should know what guest he received; which hitherto was so much concealed, that none of the houses, where he had yet been, knew, or seemed to suspect more than that he was one of the King's party that fled from Worcester. The monk carried him to a house at a reasonable distance, where he was to expect an account from the Lord Wilmot; who returned very punctually, with as much assurance of welcome as he could wish. And so they two went together to Mr. Lane's house; where the King found he was welcome, and conveniently accommodated in such places, as in a large house had been provided to conceal the persons of malignants, or to preserve goods of value from being plundered. Here he lodged, and eat very well; and begun to hope that he was in present safety. Wilmot returned under the care of the monk, and expected summons, when any farther motion should be thought to be necessary.

"In this station the King remained in quiet and blessed security many days, receiving every day information of the general consternation the kingdom was in, out of the apprehension that his person might fall into the hands of his enemies, and of the great diligence they used to enquire for him. He saw the proclamation that was issued out and printed; in which a thousand pounds were promised to any man who would deliver and discover the person of Charles Stuart, and the penalty of high treason declared against those who presumed to harbour or conceal him: by which he saw how much he was beholding to all those who were faithful to him. It was now time to consider how he might get near the sea, from whence he might find some means to transport himself: and he was now near the middle of the kingdom, saving that it was a little more northward, where he was utterly unacquainted with all the ports, and with the coast. In the West he was best acquainted, and that coast was most proper to transport him into France; to which he was inclined. Upon this matter lie communicated with those of this family to whom he was known, that is. with the old gentleman the father, a very grave and venerable person, the colonel his eldest son, a very plain man in his discourse and behaviour, but of a fearless courage, and an integrity superior to any temptation, and a daughter of the house, of a very good wit and discretion, and very fit to bear any part in such a trust."

To readers of "Woodstock," these characteristic paragraphs from Clarendon will reveal, in the plotting monk, the loyal old gentleman, the colonel his son, and the "daughter of the house, of a very good wit and discretion/' at least the analogues, if not the originals, of the personages in the household of Sir Henry Lee. Other personages and events, too, have been drawn into the circle where the story moves. Scott always preferred, if possible, to mingle, with the interest attaching to his characters as private individuals, the interest of the larger movement of history. The pause that followed upon the closing battle of the civil wars was a moment well calculated to exhibit the nature of the forces that had been so long at struggle: to show the fierce three-cornered animosity of Independents, Presbyterians, and Churchmen; the Soundhead and the Cavalier, victor and vanquished in the contest now terminated; the Parliament-men, jealous of the army, and the army-men, suspicious of the Parliament; the plain villagers and country-folk who were anxious only that the nation should be "settled" upon some permanent basis; and above all, that "man of men," as Milton called him, whose task it was to settle the nation, the great Oliver Cromwell himself. Such were the materials at Scott's disposal when he sat down to write "Woodstock." If his theme lacked, possibly, the freshness which still makes " Ivanhoe" turn all its readers into boys again, or the splendour that glows in "Kenilworth," certainly it was far more promising—to compare it with the two of Scott's English novels placed nearest it in time of action—than "Peveril of the Peak," or " The Fortunes of Nigel." Yet with all the wealth of incident which the plot of "

Woodstock" offers, with all its opportunities for the masterly display of character and dramatic situation, its appeal, on one side, to simple human feeling, and on the other, to the cultivated sense of the lover of history, there are few critics who place "Woodstock " in the very front rank of Sir Walter's works. Why is this? Was there anything in the circumstances of its composition that hindered Scott from doing himself full justice in his task? How far does it represent the best that there was in him? To answer these questions, we must turn to the record of what happened in 1826, the most significant year of Scott's life.

II.

Both as poet and novelist, Scott's career began late. He was thirty-four when "The Lay of the Last Minstrel" was published in 1805, and " Waverley," his first novel, did not appear until 1814, when he was forty-three. During that interval of nine years, his poetry gave him an assured fame, at least among his own countrymen; his salary as Sheriff of Selkirk, and later as Clerk of the Session at Edinburgh, gave him a steady income which was largely increased by the proceeds of his literary work; he had hosts of friends; he was happily married, and his children were growing up around him; and in 1812 he had realized his favourite dream by buying an estate at Abbotsford, the establishment and enlargement of which became the chief ambition of his life. In the summer of 1814 his genius suddenly took a new bent. He wrote at top speed a prose tale—the continuation of a story begun long before and laid aside—and published it anonymously under the title of "Waverley, or 'Tis Sixty Years Since." The immediate and extraordinary popularity of this book relieved Scott from the fear of financial embarrassment, which his expenditures at Abbotsford and a secret and most unlucky partnership with the Ballantynes, book publishers at Edinburgh, had threatened, and which had been weighing upon him for many months. More than this, it revealed to Scott himself the almost inexhaustible store of material for fiction which he had been laying up from boyhood: legend, history, family memoirs, court chronicles, country-side gossip, and shrewd, kindly observation of all sorts and conditions of men. Guarding strictly the secret of his authorship, and devoting to composition those hours only which he could spare from his official labors and his duties as head and host of the great establishment at Abbotsford, Scott poured forth volume after volume of the Waverley series. "They were faster written and better paid for than any other books in the world," says Carlyle, whose pen bites a little as he comments upon "Scott's career of writing impromptu novels to buy farms with." By the close of 1825 he had written twenty-one novels, besides doing much miscellaneous literary work; he had added a great many farms to his estate, had been knighted by George IV. , and had apparently realized his ambition to become the founder of a race of Scottish lairds.

But in the autumn of that year the tide of prosperity turned. Scott's secret partnership with the Ballantynes still continued, and a panic at London involved the firm in serious difficulties, which grew steadily worse as the year drew to its close. Fortunately for those who may wish to know the spirit with which a noble soul can face disaster, Scott began, on November 20th, to keep a journal in which he has set down the varying phases of the long struggle that was to fill his remaining years. Upon the 22d is noted the first intimation of the coming calamity, and it will be seen how quickly Scott's mind turned to " Woodstock" as a certain source of income in the expected crisis.

Nov. 22.—... Here is matter for a May morning, but much fitter for a November one. The general distress in the city has affected H. and R., Constable's' great agents. Should they *go,* it is not likely that Constable can stand, and such an event would lead to great distress and perplexity on the part of J. B. and myself. Thank God, I have enough at least to pay forty shillings in the pound, taking matters at the very worst. But much distress and inconvenience must be the consequence. I had a lesson in 1814 which should have done good upon me, but success and abundance erased it from my mind.... If W—st—k can be out by 25th January it will do much, and it is possible. *Nov. 25.*—... I here register my purpose to practise economics. I have little temptation to do otherwise. Abbotsford is all that I can make it. and too large for the property; so I resolve

No more building;

No purchases of land till times are quite safe;

No buying books or expensive trifles—I mean to any extent; and

Clearing off encumbrances, with the returns of this year's labour;—

Which resolutions, with health and my habits of industry, will make me "sleep in spite of thunder." *December 18.*—Ballantyne called on me this morning. *Venit ilia* 1 Hurst and Robinson, Booksellers, London.

Archibald Constable, who had long been Scott's publisher.

James Ballantyne.

Woodstock had been contracted for in 1823.

N *tuprema dies.* My extremity is come. Cadell1 has received letters from London which all but positively announce the failure of Hurst and Robinson, so that Constable & Co. must follow, and I must go with poor James Ballantyne for company. I suppose it will involve my all. But if they leave me £500, I can still make it £1000 or £1200 a year. And if they take my salaries of £1300 and £300, they cannot but give me something out of them. I have been rash in anticipating funds to buy land, but then I made from £5000 to £10,000 a year, and land was my temptation. I think nobody can lose a penny, that is one comfort. Men will think pride has had a fall. Let them indulge their own pride in thinking that my fall makes them higher, or seems so at least. I have the satisfaction to recollect that my prosperity has been of advantage to many, and that some at least will forgive my transient wealth on account of the innocence of my intentions, and my real wish to do good to the poor. This news will make sad hearts at Darnick. and in the cottages of Abbotsford, which I do not nourish the least hope of preserving. It has been my Delilah, and so I have often termed it; and now the recollection of the extensive woods I planted, and the walks I have formed, from which strangers must derive both the pleasure and profit, will excite feelings likely to sober my gayest moments I have half resolved never to see the place again. How could I tread my hall with such a diminished crest? How live a poor, indebted man where I was once the wealthy, the honoured? My children are provided; thank God for that. I was to have gone there on Saturday in joy and prosperity to receive my friends. My dogs will wait for me in vain. It is foolish—but the thoughts of parting from these dumb creatures have moved me more than any of the painful reflections I have put down. Poor things, I must get them kind masters; there may be yet those who loving me may love my dog because it has been mine. I must end this, or I shall lose the tone of mind with which men should meet distress.

December 29.—... Must go to W—k! yet am vexed by that humour of contradiction which makes me incline to do anything else in preference.... *January* 2. 1826.—I am pressed to get on with *Woodstock,* and must try. I wish I could open a good vein of interest which would breathe freely. I must take my old way, and write myself into goodhumour with my task. It is only when I dally with what I am about, look back, and aside, instead of keeping my eyes straight forward, that I feel these cold sinkings of the heart. All men I suppose do. less or more. They are like the sensation of a sailor when the ship is cleared for action, and all are at their places—gloomy enough; but the first broadside puts all to rights.... Robert Cadell, a partner in Constable & Co. The total liabilities of the three firms amounted in round numbers to nearly half a million pounds sterling Sir Walter, as the partner of Ballantyne & Co. , was held responsible for about £130,000. Before his death he succeeded in paying half this sum. and ultimately it was paid in full by his representatives, from the proceeds of copyrights. A hamlet near Abbotsford. *Woodstock. January* 3.—... J. B. writes me seriously on the carelessness of my style. I do not think I am more careless than usual; but I dare say he is right. I will be more cautious.

During the early part of January, Scott was induced to believe that the disaster might still be averted, but this belief was soon shown to be futile.

January 21.—... Things are so much worse with Constable than I apprehended that I shall neither save Abbotsford nor anything else. Naked we entered the world, and naked we leave it—blessed be the name of the Lord! *January* 22.—... There is just another die to turn up against me in this run of ill-luck; *i.e.* if I should break my magic wand in the fall from this elephant, and lose my popularity with my fortune. Then *Woodstock* and *Bony*1 may both go to the papermaker, and I may take to smoking cigars and drinking grog, or turn devotee, and intoxicate the brain another way. In prospect of absolute ruin, I wonder if they would let me leave the Court of Session. I would like, methinks, to go abroad, and lay my bones far from the *Tweed.* But I find my eyes moistening, and that will not do. I will not yield without a fight for it. It is odd, when I set myself to work *doggedly,* as Dr. Johnson would say, I am exactly the same man that I ever was, neither low-spirited nor *distrait.* In prosperous times I have sometimes felt my fancy and powers of language flag, but adversity is to me at least a tonic and a bracer.... *January* 2d.—... My powers of labour have not diminished during the last melancholy week. On Monday and Tuesday my exertions were suspended. Since Wednesday inclusive I have written thirty-eight of my close manuscript pages, of which seventy make a volume of the usual novel size. . . *January* 30. —... I laboured freely yesterday. The stream rose fast—if clearly, is another question; but there is bulk for it, at least—about thirty printed pages. "And now again, boys, to the oar." *January* 31.—There being nothing in the roll to-day, I stay at home from the Court, and add another day's perfect labour to *Woodstock,* which is worth five days of snatched intervals, when this current of thought and invention is broken in upon, and the mind shaken and diverted from its purpose by a succession of petty interruptions.

February 3.—... James Ballantyne is severely critical on what he calls imitations of Mrs Radcliffe in *Woodstock.* Many will think with him, yet I am of opinion he is quite wrong.... My object is not to excite fear of supernatural things in my reader, but to show the effect of such fear upon the agents in the story—one a 1The *Life of Napoleon Buonaparte,* begun in 1825. For the ordinary three-volume novel, in small octavo. Mrs. Ann Radcliffe (1764-1823), a romantic novelist belonging to what has been called the "School of Terror," author of *Tile Sicilian Romance, The Mysteries of Udolpho,* etc. man of sense and firmness—one a man unhinged by remorse—one a stupid uninquiring clown—one a learned and worthy, but superstitious divine. In the third place, the book turns on this hinge, and cannot want it.... From the 19th January to the 2d February inclusive is exactly fifteen days, during which time, with the intervention of some days' idleness, to let imagination brood on the task a little, I have written a volume. I think, for a bet, I could have done it in ten days.1 Then I must have had no Court of Session to take me up two or three hours every morning, and dissipate my attention and powers of working for the rest of the day. A volume, at cheapest, is worth £1000. This is working at the rate of £24,000 a year; but then we must not bake buns faster than people have appetite to eat them. They are not essential to the market, like potatoes. *February* 10.—... This morning I had some good ideas respecting *Woodstock* which will make the story better. The devil of a difficulty is, that one puzzles the skein in order to excite curiosity, and then cannot disentangle it for the satisfaction of the prying fiend they have raised.... *February* 12.— Having ended the second volume of *Woodstock* last night, I have to begin the third this morning. Now I

have not the slightest idea how the story is to be wound up to a catastrophe. I am just in the same case as I used to be when I lost myself in former days in some country to which I was a stranger. I always pushed for the pleasantest road, and either found or made it the nearest. It is the same in writing, I never could lay down a plan—or, having laid it down, I never could adhere to it; the action of composition always diluted some passages, and abridged or omitted others; and personages were rendered important or insignificant, not according to their agency in the original conception of the plan, but according to the success, or otherwise, with which I was able to bring them out. I only tried to make that which I was actually writing diverting and interesting, leaving the rest to fate. I have been often amused with the oritics distinguishing some passages as particularly laboured, when the pen passed over the whole as fast as it could move, and the eye never again saw them, except in proof. Verse I write twice and sometimes three times over. This may be called in Spanish the *Bar donde diere* mode of composition, in English *hab nab at a venture;* it is a perilous style, I grant, but I cannot help it. When I chain my mind to ideas which are purely imaginative—for argument is a different thing—it seems to me that the sun leaves the landscape, that I think away the whole vivacity and spirit of my original conception, and that the results are cold, tame, and spiritless. It is the difference between a written oration and one bursting from the unpremeditated exertions of the speaker, which have always something the air of enthusiasm and inspiration. I would not have young authors imitate my carelessness, however; *consilium, non currum cape.*
February 15.—Yesterday I did not write a line of *Woodstock.* Partly, I was a little out of spirits, though that would not have hindered. 1See Scott's letter of February 6, to Mr. Morrit (Lockhart's *Trife,* VII., 318). On the previous day his Edinburgh house, No. 39 Castle Street, which he had occupied since 1802, was placed on sale, with the furniPartly, I wanted to wait for some new ideas—

a sort of collecting of straw to make bricks of. Partly, I was a little too far beyond the press. I cannot pull well in long traces, when the draught is too far behind me. I love to hear the press thumping, clattering, and banging in my rear; it creates the necessity which almost always makes me work best....
For the next few weeks Scott occupied himself mainly with a series of political letters to the Edinburgh *Journal,* signed Malachi Malagrowther, "on the disposition to change everything in Scotland to an English model." But "Woodstock" was never long out of his mind.
March 12.—Resumed *Woodstock,* and wrote my task of six pages. I was interrupted by a slumberous feeling which made me obliged to stop once or twice. ... March 13.—Wrote to the end of a chapter, and knowing no more than the man in the moon what comes next, I will put down a few of Lord Elgin's remembrances, and something may occur to me in the mean while. *March* 17.—Abbotsford. Sent off a packet to J. B. ; only three pages copy, so must work hard for a day or two.... The conclusion will be luminous; we must try to make it dashing. Go spin, you jade, go spin.. . *March* 19.—I have a most melancholy letter from Anne. Lady S., the faithful and true companion of my fortunes, good and bad, for so many years, has, but with difficulty, been prevailed on to see Dr. Abercrombie, and his opinion is far from favourable.".. Really, these misfortunes come too close upon each other. *March* 26.—Here is a disagreeable morning, snowing and hailing, with gleams of bright sunshine between, and all the ground white and all the air frozen. I don't like this jumbling of weather.... No matter, it will serve as well as another day to finish *Woodstock.* Walked out to the lake, and coquetted with this disagreeable weather, whereby I catch chilblains in my fingers and cold in my head. Fed the swans.
Finished *Woodstock,* however, *cum Ma sequela* of title-page, introduction, etc., and so, as Dame Fortune says in *Quevedo,*

"Go wheel, and may the devil drive thee." ture, pictures, etc.. for the benefit

of his creditors. Scott was now living in lodgings in North St. David's Street. Lady Scott, whose health was rapidly failing, was at Abbotsford.
For the *Life of Napoleon.* Lady Scott died on May 15. She was now, with her daughter Anne, in Edinburgh, while Scott remained at Abbotsford, which, by a special arrangement with his creditors, had been left in his possession. *Fortune in her Wits, and the Hour of all Men.* by Quevedo, a Spanish writer whose works had been published in English at Edinburgh in 1798.. -x *April* 2.—... J. B. writes gloomily about *Woodstock,* but commends the conclusion. I think he is right. Besides, my manner is nearly caught, and, like Captain Bobadil, I have taught nearly a hundred gentlemen to fence very nearly, if not altogether, as well as myself. I will strike out something new. *April* 3.—I have from Ballautyne and Gibson the extraordinary and gratifying news that *Woodstock* is sold for £8228 in all, ready money—a matchless sum for less than three months' work....
There are few novels in the language whose genesis and progress in composition we may thus follow from day to day. Will an examination of the work produced under such singular stress of adversity,—written, if any book was ever written, for pounds and shillings alone,—reveal traces, direct or indirect, of the state of its author's mind during those sorrowful months?
III.
"It is no wonder," says Lockhart *(Life,* VIII., 86), "that the book, which it was known he had been writing during this crisis of distress, should have been expected with solicitude. Shall we find him, asked thousands, to have been master truly of his genius in the moment of this ordeal? Shall we trace anything of his own experiences in the construction of his imaginary personages and events? I know not how others interpreted various passages in 'Woodstock,' but there were not a few that carried deep meaning for such of Scott's own friends as were acquainted with, not his pecuniary misfortune alone, but the drooping health of his wife, and the consolation

afforded him by the dutiful devotion of his daughter Anne, in whose character and demeanour a change had occurred exactly similar to that painted in poor Alice Lee:—' A light, joyous air, with something of a humorous expression, which seemed to be looking for amusement, had vanished before the touch of affliction, and a calm melancholy supplied its place, which seemed on the watch to administer comfort to others. ' In several mottoes and other scraps of verse, the curious reader will find similar traces of the facts and feelings recorded in the author's Diary."

Some of the passages to which Lockhart alludes are pointed out in the footnotes to the present edition. Other Ben Jonson's *Every Man in his Humour,* Act. IV., So. 5.

and more indirect evidence of the mental strain to which Scott was just then subjected is perhaps to be found in the lack of certain qualities present in his very finest novels,— a deficiency, when compared with them, in power, brilliancy, swiftness of action. But it is easy to exaggerate proof of this kind. It is remarkable that Scott could write a novel in that gloomy time, though he said himself, in the letter to Mr. Morrit already referred to, that it was " nothing, however, to writing ' Ivanhoe ' when I had the actual cramp in my stomach; but I have no idea of these things preventing a man from doing what he has a mind." Given a man like this, who exclaims in the darkest hour of his trial, "Indeed, I do not like to have it thought that there is any way in which I can be beaten,"1 and if he can write fiction at all, the result will probably be much like his fiction written in happier hours. He will be able to hold the actual and the ideal worlds apart. On the whole, this is true of " Woodstock." Its faults are those which Scott's other books often exhibit, and result from the nature of the subject chosen, and the limitations of his mind in certain directions, rather than from the immediate circumstances in which the book was composed.

The plot, for instance, as the *Journal* has confessed, was thrown together absolutely at random. Pushing for the pleasantest road towards the end of a story is not the method Scott would recommend to young authors,—nor was it, it may be added, the method followed in "Henry Esmond "or "The Scarlet Letter " or "Adam Bede,"— but Scott himself could not work in any other way. His plots have most unity when they are connected with the movement of some historical event, with which the private fortunes of his personages are intertwined, as in" Waverley" and " Old Mortality." No particular culmination is required by the historical setting of "Woodstock," and the plot is " wound up "—in Scott's phrase—as handsomely as may be, in a conventional though delightful fashion quite familiar to readers of the Waverley novels.

In handling the figures of his story, the success or relative failure is just about what an acquaintance with Scott's previous work would lead one to expect. The art is neither better nor worse than his average. The minor characters, like Tomkins, Joliffe, and the Commissioners make, as so *Journal,* June 17, 1826.

often in Scott, a more sharply denned impression than the. major characters. The reckless cavalier Wildrake is painted *con arnore.* The clergymen, whatever their creed, are worldlings at heart. The characterizing traits of the old knight Sir Henry Lee—his irascibility and his fondness for Shakespeare—are insisted upon with wearisome iteration. The hero, Markham Everard, is one of those irreproachable followers of the middle course, that band of commonplace but "excellent young men, rather strong, able to ride and climb and jump,"1 whom Scott, by some singular fatality, frequently chose to play the role of hero. The heroine is beautiful, like all the rest of them except Jeanie Deans, and quite beyond the reach of analysis on the author's part. Scott worshipped his heroines too much to dissect them; and the fair Alice Lee, who is more real than most of her rivals, nevertheless does not always speak like a human woman, or succeed in making us think she is more than a "fancy portrait" produced by some process long since gone out of date.

When' " Woodstock" touches history, too, its mingled strength and weakness is characteristic. The book is full of little inaccuracies in such matters as dates and minor happenings. Some of these are pointed out in the notes, though such labour always seems ungracious, and is not playing the game of fiction-reading at all as Scott meant it should be played. Inerrancy as to fact was the last thing he troubled himself about in his historical novels, and remembering Ebers, we may be sure Scott knew pretty well what his art required. As for the treatment of known historical characters, it must be confessed that the Charles II. of "Woodstock" is not comparable for brilliancy and force of delineation with many of Scott's royal personages. One page of his grandfather's talk in "The Fortunes of Nigel" bears more of the stamp of Scott's genius than all that is put into the mouth of the cool cynical Stuart of "Woodstock;" though the general bearing of the character, and its place in the story, are admirably conceived. The knowledge of the political and religious parties of the period is thorough, as one need not say. Scott's temperament, however, constantly limits his judgment of the Puritans. His eye for the merely ludicrous or fanatical side of the Puritan character was keen enough, but be. » L. »' Bagehot's essay on Scott neath the odd garb and cant phrases was a spiritual aspiration, a sense of the infinite issues of this finite life, about which Scott did not particularly care. Like most literary men of the eighteenth century, he looked upon all this as "enthusiasm." The result is that he fails to sound the depths of the nature of the greatest historical figure in "Woodstock," Oliver Cromwell. Cromwell cannot be dismissed, as it was the fashion in Scott's day to dismiss him, as a compound of " enthusiast" and hypocrite. All question of fidelity to the truth of history aside, and considering Scott's Cromwell simply from the standpoint of the art of fiction, the character is not a success. It fails in consistency, in adequate adjustment of action to motive, in real personality. Perhaps it is not wholly fair to estimate Scott's failure as a painter of the great Protector by the light of Carlyle's success, but the comparison will inevitably be made, and it will always serve to exhibit Scott's weakness in delineating a soul profoundly wrought upon by spiritual forces.

James Ballantyne, friendliest and frankest of Scott's critics, called the style of " Woodstock " " careless," whereupon the author remarked, with that absolute freedom from posing and literary vanity which was one of his most winning traits, "I do not think I am more careless than usual." He was probably right. Throughout his productive period, Scott spun his impromptu web into a singularly uniform texture. There are no "purple patches," few quotable things. For style as such, Scott cared little; neither the constitution of his mind nor his method of composition allowed him any elaborate effort after verbal felicity. A self-conscious striving for the most delicate possible adjustment of words to thought, like Walter Pater's, for instance, Scott would very likely have despised. The exquisite sensitiveness which makes such striving a sort of religion would have seemed to the robust laird of Abbotsford like effeminacy. Nor did he often write passages,—like Byron and other Englishmen who followed mainly the extempore method,—that haunt us with a sense of their unstudied perfection. We do not turn to Scott, great story-teller as he is, for sentences like this from " Henry Esmond ": "Esmond thought of the courier now galloping on the North road to inform him who was Earl of Arran yesterday that he was Duke of Hamilton to-day, and of a thousand great schemes, hopes, ambitions, that were alive in the gallant heart, beating a few hours since, and now in a little dust quiescent." Not more than twice or thrice in " Woodstock " has Scott attained to such supreme distinction of style. One of these passages, inserted toward the close of Chapter XVI. subsequently to the first edition of the novel, gives a hint of the sombre images which must often have hovered in Scott's mind through his last melancholy years, though he rarely allowed them to darken the cheerful surface of his narrative. "His Harrison's delight, in short, resembled the joy of an eagle, who preys upon a lamb in the evening with not the less relish because she descries in the distant landscape an hundred thousand men about to join battle with daybreak, and to give her an endless feast on the hearts and life-blood of the valiant."

In the style of "Woodstock," therefore, as in the plot and characters, one can trace with difficulty, and usually not at all, the influence of the peculiar circumstances in which the book was written. If its composition had been an unforced delight instead of an iron task, and if the personality of some of the leading characters had not been so foreign to Scott's own, it is easy to believe that the capital theme of the novel and the trained powers of its author would have resulted in a book rivalling "Old Mortality" and "Kenilworth" and "Quentin Durward." "Woodstock" does not belong with these; but it is, nevertheless, a thoroughly representative piece of work.

IV. *It* "Woodstock" may thus be fairly called a representative novel of Scott, a word remains to be said about Sir Walter's place in Action. The tone of critical opinion at the time of the centenary of his birth in 1871 now seems somewhat apologetic. Scott is undoubtedly having his inning again, and the inning promises to be a long one. The "romantic revival" in the last ten years among young English and Scotch novelists has undoubtedly contributed to the new interest in Scott, though considering the patronizing way in which the school of writers just referred to generally mention him, it may be well to remember that, barring Stevenson, Scott's little finger was thicker than all their loins. Worse than being patronized by his Romantic imitators, perhaps, is Scott's frequent fate at the hands of Realist critics, who go out of their way to cast stones at him, quite forgetting that the most enduring elements of Scott's art,—his shrewd observation, his knowledge of the facts, his sympathy with the poor, his fidelity to the primal truths of human nature, his acceptance of life as it is, — are of the very essence of Realism. "He can still amuse young people," admits Mr. Howells, "but they ought to be instructed how false and how mistaken he often is, with his mediaeval ideals, his blind Jacobitism, his intense devotion to aristocracy and royalty; his acquiescence in the division of men into noble and ignoble, patrician and plebeian, sovereign and subject, as if it were the law of God; for all which, indeed, he is not to blame, as he would be if he were one of our contemporaries." The young people who may read this Introduction will, it is hoped, instruct themselves to distinguish the false from the true in Sir Walter's novels, but they must try not to be unduly exalted because they live in 1895, and they must remember that human nature —the stuff a novelist works in—is very much what it was when the Waverley novels were written.

It is easy to call the roll of Scott's faults. His careless plot-building, his inability to deal artistically with certain classes of society and types of mind, and the commonplaceness of much of his style, have already been commented upon in connection with "Woodstock." He was undoubtedly a Jacobite at heart—though that was no very deadly sin—and his fondness for the middle ages made him something too much of a Tory to suit the present generation; yet these characteristics of the man are scarcely flaws in the artist. More serious deficiencies are the unreality of some of his historical costuming, and the worse unrealities of character-sketching into which an overromantic imagination sometimes leads him. Finally, it is true that Scott's philosophy of life was of the comfortable worldly sort; that as he fails in purely intellectual passion, he fails also in spiritual depth.

But after these admissions are frankly made, how much there is left to admire and to love! This is not the place *Criticism, and Fiction,* Chapter IV. to dwell upon Scott's immense significance in the history of English and Continental fiction, nor upon the mass and total excellence of his work. In the last analysis, what we most care about in a work of art is its revelation of the man that is back of it. Scott's novels bring us into touch with a glorious man, kindly, loving, and brave; a man with strong sense and keen sagacity and a wide horizon; healthy to the core; with genuine enthusiasms, boyish spirits, and an honest relish of the good things of the sunshiny world; a man sweet-tempered in trial, stout-hearted in disaster, and with such an infectious good-fellowship about him from first to last that to know Scott's novels means to love Sir Walter himself. It is after all no unfit test of the man's perennial power that in the third generation " he can still amuse young people." Of how many fiction-writers of to-day is that likely to be said, after seventy years?

Bliss Perry.

Princeton, July, 1895.

SUGGESTIONS FOR TEACHERS AND STUDENTS

While the reading of one of Scott's novels as a part of the English preparation of a pupil ought to be made as little like task-work as possible, it has seemed best in the present edition to append to most of the chapters a few questions bearing upon the art of fiction, or designed to illustrate Scott's methods in other tales. Pupils should of course have access to some complete edition of the Waverley novels, and should be encouraged to make comparisons of their own between " Woodstock " and other historical novels, at every feasible point. "The Fortunes of Nigel" and "Peveril of the Peak," in particular, are stories of the seventeenth century that afford interesting parallels to "Woodstock " in many details. The more mature pupils may be asked to read Shorthouse's "John Inglesant" and Thackeray's " Henry Esmond " for the same purpose.

History Of The Period.—The teacher will find it advisable to read in class—or set pupils on the trace of—passages from standard histories of England that illustrate customs or events touched upon in " Woodstock." Some detailed references to Hume and Macaulay will be found in the foot-notes. Clarendon's "History of the Great Rebellion " will not be accessible to many teachers, but G. D. Boyle's " Selections from Clarendon" (Clarendon Press, 1889) contains many passages that throw light upon "Woodstock." J. R. Green's " Short History of the English People" gives a vivid picture of the Puritans, and of Cromwell's campaigns. Frederic Harrison's "Oliver Cromwell" (Twelve English Statesmen, Macmillan, 1888) is an admirable little book, and extracts from Carlyle's "Cromwell's Letters and Speeches " and Masson's " Life of Milton" may be read in the classroom to advantage. S. R. Gardiner's "History of the Commonwealth and Protectorate," Vol. I., 1649-1651 (Longmans, 1894), is likely to prove the standard authority for this period of English history.

Bioqraphies Of Scott.—J. Gr. Lockhart's "Life of Scott" (the references in the foot-notes are to the Household edition, Ticknor and Fields, Boston, 1861, in nine volumes) and "The Journal of Sir Walter Scott" (Harper's, 2 vols., 1890) should by all means be accessible to pupils. R. H. Hutton's "Life of Scott" (English Men of Letters Series, Harper's) is the best of the shorter biographies. C. D. Yonge's (Great Writers Series) contains a valuable bibliography, compiled by John P. Anderson. Consult also Washington Irving's "Abbotsford " and James F. Hunnewell's " Lands of Scott " (Osgood, Boston, 1871).

Criticisms.—-A caustic and extremely able contemporary review of " Woodstock " will be found in the *Westminster Review,* Vol. V., 1826. Carlyle's *Westminster* article on Scott (Vol. XXX., 1838), reprinted in his "Miscellanies," is one of his most brilliant pieces of writing. Scott's relation to the Romantic movement in European literature is well discussed by Julia Wedgwood, in the *Contemporary Review,* October, 1878 (also in *Littell's Living Age,* Vol. 139). Ruskin's "Fiction, Fair and Foul" *Nineteenth Century,* June, 1880) is devoted to Scott, and should be compared with the view of Scott expressed in Books III. and V. of " Modern Painters." Consult also the essays by Walter Bagehot (in "Literary Studies ") and Leslie Stephen (" Hours in a Library "), tne article on the Scott centenary in the *Nation* (August 17, 1871); T. S. Perry's article in the *Atlantic* (Vol. 46, 1880); N. W. Senior's "Essays in Fiction" (London, 1864); David Masson's "British Novelists," Chapter III. (Boston, 1875), and W. D. Howells's "Criticism and Fiction," Chapter IV. (Harper's, 1891). For other critical articles upon Scott see Poole's " Index to Periodical Literature."

De&tcatton TO THE KING'S MOST GEACIOUS MAJESTY

Sire:

The author of this collection of Works of Fiction would not have presumed to solicit for them your Majesty's august patronage, were it not that the perusal has been supposed in some instances to have succeeded in amusing hours of relaxation, or relieving those of languor, pain or anxiety, and therefore must have so far aided the warmest wish of your Majesty's heart, by contributing, in however small a degree, to the happiness of your people.

They are therefore humbly dedicated to your Majesty, agreeably to your gracious permission, by

Your Majesty's Dutiful Subject,

WALTER SCOTT.

Abbotsford, 1st January, 1839.

= From the 1829 edition of Scott's Collected Works. WOODSTOCK CHAPTER THE FIRST

Some were for gospel ministers,
And some for red coat seculars,
As men most fit t' hold forth the word,
And wield the one and th' other sword.

Butler's Hudibras.

Theee is a handsome parish church in the town of Woodstock—I am told so, at least, for I never saw it, having scarce time, when at the place, to view the magnificence of Blenheim, its painted halls, and tapestried bowers, and then return in due season to dine in hall with my learned friend, the provost of;being one of those occasions on which a man wrongs himself extremely, if he lets his curiosity interfere with his punctuality. I had the church accurately described to me, with a view to this work; but, as I have some reason to doubt whether my informant had ever seen the inside of it himself, I shall be content to say that it is now a handsome edifice, most part of which was rebuilt forty or fifty years since, although it still contains some arches of the old chantry, founded, it is said, by King John. It is to this more ancient part of the building that my story refers.

" The scraps of poetry which have been in most cases tacked to the beginning of chapters in these novels, are sometimes quoted either from reading or from memory, but, in the general case, are pure invention. I found it too troublesome to turn to the collection of the British Poets to discover apposite mottoes, and in the situation of the theatrical mechanist, who, when the white paper which represented his shower of snow was exhausted, continued the storm by snowing brown, I drew on my memory as long as I could, and, when that failed, eked it out with invention. I believe that, in some cases, where actual names are affixed to the supposed quotations, it would be to little purpose to seek them in the works of the authors referred to. In some cases, I have been entertained when Dr. Watts and other graver authors have been ransacked in vain for stanzas for which the novelist alone was responsible."—Scott's Introduction to *Chronicles of the Canongate.* See also note to the motto of Chapter V. Woodstock Manor was presented to the first Duke of Marlborough in recognition of his services. Parliament voted him half a million pounds to build a residence. Vanbrugh was the architect, and it was named Blenheim Palace in memory of the Duke's great victory over the French and Bavarians in 1704. The head of one of the colleges at Oxford, eight miles from Woodstock.

On a morning in the end of September, or beginning of October, in the year 1652 1651, being a day appointed for a solemn thanksgiving for the decisive victory at Worcester, a respectable audience was assembled in the old chantry, or chapel of King John. The condition of the church and character of the audience both bore witness to the rage of civil war, and the peculiar spirit of the times. The sacred edifice shewed many marks of dilapidation. The windows, once filled with stained glass, had been dashed to pieces with pikes and muskets, as matters of and pertaining to idolatry. The carving on the readingdesk was damaged, and two fair screens of beautiful sculptured oak had been destroyed, for the same pithy and conclusive reason. The high altar had been removed, and the gilded railing, which was once around it, was broken down and carried off. The effigies of several tombs were mutilated, and now lay scattered about the church,

Torn from their destined niche,—unworthy meed
Of knightly counsel or heroic deed 1

The autumn wind piped through empty aisles, in which the remains of stakes and trevisses of rough-hewn timber, as well as a quantity of scattered hay and trampled straw, seemed to intimate that the hallowed precincts had been, upon some late emergency, made the quarters of a troop of horse.

Little now remains of this ancient church, it being rebuilt in 1785, except on the southern side, where a portion of the old structure, with a Norman doorway, is still preserved. Laing Cromwell defeated the Scotch Royalists under Charles I. at Worcester, Sept. 3, 1651. It was the closing battle of the civil war. Divisions between the stalls in a stable. The audience, like the building, was abated in splendour. None of the ancient and habitual worshippers during peaceful times, were now to be seen in their carved galleries, with hands shadowing their brows, while composing their minds to pray where their fathers had prayed, and after the same mode of worship. The eye of the yeoman and peasant sought in vain the tall form of old Sir Henry Lee of Ditchley, as, wrapped in his laced cloak, and with beard and whiskers duly composed, he moved slowly through the aisles, followed by the faithful mastiff, or bloodhound, which in old time had saved his master by his fidelity, and which regularly followed him to church. Bevis, indeed, fell under the proverb which avers, "He is a good dog which goes to church;" for, bating an occasional temptation to warble along with the accord, he behaved himself as decorously as any of the congregation, and returned as much edified, perhaps, as most of them. The damsels of Woodstock looked as vainly for the laced cloaks, jingling spurs, slashed boots, and tall plumes, of the young cavaliers of this and other high-born houses, moving through the streets and the churchyard with the careless ease, which indicates perhaps rather an overweening degree of self-confidence, yet shews graceful when mingled with good-humour and courtesy. The good old dames, too, in their white hoods and black velvet gowns— their daughters, "the cynosure of neighbouring eyes,"— where were they all now, who, when they entered the church, used to divide men's thoughts between them and Heaven?" But, ah! Alice Lee—so sweet, so gentle, so condescending in thy loveliness—thus proceeds a contemporary annalist, whose manuscript we have deciphered— why is my story to turn upon thy fallen fortunes? and why not rather to the period when, in the very dismounting from your palfrey, you attracted as many eyes as if an angel had descended,—as many blessings as if the benignant being had come fraught with good tidings? No creature wert thou of an idle romancer s imagination—no being fantastically bedizened with inconsistent perfections; — thy merits made me love thee well—and for thy faults —so well did they shew amid thy good qualities, that I think they made me love thee better." Named after Sir Bevis of Hampton, a hero of the Arthurian romances. Chord.

With the house of Lee had disappeared from the chantry of King John others of gentle blood and honoured lineage, —Freemantles, Winklecombes, Drycotts, etc.; for the air that blew over the towers of Oxford was unfavourable to the growth of Puritanism, which was more general in the neighbouring counties. There were among the congregation, however, one or two that, by their habits and demeanour, seemed country gentlemen of consideration, and there were also present some of the notables of the town of Woodstock, cutlers or glovers chiefly, whose skill in steel or leather had raised them to a comfortable livelihood. These dignitaries wore long black cloaks, plaited close at the neck, and, like peaceful citizens, carried their Bibles and memorandum-books at their girdles, instead of knife or sword. This respectable, but least numerous part of the audience, were such decent persons as had adopted the Presbyterian form of faith, renouncing the liturgy and hierarchy of the Church of England, and living under the tuition of the Rev. Nehemiah Holdenough, much famed for the length and strength of his powers of predication. With these grave seniors sat their goodly dames in ruff and gorget, like the portraits which in catalogues of paintings are designed "wife of a burgomaster;" and their pretty daughters, whose study, like that of Chaucer's physician, was not always in the Bible, but who were, on the contrary, when a glance could escape the vigilance of their honoured mothers, inattentive themselves, and the cause of inattention in others.

But, besides these dignified persons, there were in the church a numerous collection of the lower orders, some brought thither by curiosity, but many of them unwashed artificers, bewildered in the theological discussions of the time, and of as many various sects as there are colours in the rainbow. The presumption of these learned Thebans being in exact proportion to their ignorance, the last was total, and the first boundless. Their behaviour in the church was any thing but reverential or edifying. Most of them affected a cynical contempt for all that was only held sacred by human sanction—the church was to these men but a steeple-house, the clergyman, an ordinary person; her ordinances, dry bran, and sapless pottage, unfitted for the spiritualized palates of the saints, and the prayer, an address to Heaven, to which each acceded or not, as in his too critical judgment he conceived fit.

This custom among the Puritans is mentioned often in old plays, and among others in the *Widow of Watting Street.*

Scott. Oxford had been the Royalist stronghold early in the civil war, and was long noted for its zeal toward the High Church party. The symbolism of the names of some of Scott's characters is commented upon at the close of Chapter V. An ornamental covering for the throat. *Prologue* to the *Canterbury Tales,* 1. 438. 6See *King Lear,* Act III., Sc. 4, 1.162.

The elder amongst them sat or lay on the benches, with their high steeple-crowned hats pulled over their severe and knitted brows, waiting for the Presbyterian parson, as mastiffs sit in dumb expectation of the bull that is to be brought to the stake. The younger mixed, some of them, a bolder license of manners with their heresies; they gazed round on the women, yawned, coughed, and whispered, ate apples, and cracked, nuts, as if in the gallery of a theatre ere the piece commences.

Besides all these, the congregation contained a few soldiers, some in corselets and steel caps, some in buff, and others in red coats. These men of war had their bandoliers, with ammunition, slung round them, and rested on their pikes and muskets. They, too, had their peculiar doctrines on the most difficult points of religion, and united the extravagances of enthusiasm with the most determined courage and resolution in the field. The burghers of AVoodstock looked on these military saints with no small degree of awe; for though not often sullied with deeds of plunder or cruelty, they had the power of both absolutely in their hands, and the peaceful citizens had no alternative, save submission to whatever the ill-regulated and enthusiastic imaginations of their martial guides might suggest.

After some time spent in waiting for him, Mr. Holdenough began to walk up the aisles of the chapel, not with the slow and dignified carriage with which the old Rector was of yore wont to maintain the dignity of the surplice, See a curious vindication of this indecent simile here for the Common Prayer, in Note A. Scott.

Shoulder belts for cartridges. Here, and generally throughout *Woodstock,* used in the archaic sense of "ecstasy of mind, a belief or conceit of being divinely inspired or commissioned." The word is a favorite one with Hume, whose *History of England* Scott follows in many details. but with a hasty step like one who arrives too late at an appointment, and bustles forward to make the best use of his time. He was a tall thin man, with an adust complexion, and the vivacity of his eye indicated some irascibility of temperament. His dress was brown, not black, and over his other vestments he wore, in honour of Calvin, a Geneva cloak of a blue colour, which fell backwards from his shoulders as he posted on to the pulpit. His grizzled hair was cut as short as shears could perform the feat, and covered with a black silk skull-cap, which stuck so close to his head, that the two ears expanded from under it as if they had been intended as handles by which to lift the whole person. Moreover, the worthy divine wore spectacles, and a long grizzled peaked beard, and he carried in his hand a small pocket-bible with silver clasps. Upon arriving at the pulpit, he paused a moment to take breath, then began to ascend the steps by two at a time.

But his course was arrested by a strong hand, which seized his cloak. It was that of one who had detached himself from the group of soldiery. He was a stout man of middle stature, with a quick eye, and a countenance, which, though plain, had yet an expression that fixed the attention. His dress, though not strictly military, partook of that character. He wore large hose made of calves-leather, and a tuck, as it was then called, or rapier, of tremendous length, balanced on the other side by a dagger. The belt was morocco, garnished with pistols.

The minister, thus intercepted in his duty, faced round upon the party who had seized him, and demanded, in no gentle tone, the meaning of the interruption.

"Friend," quoth the intruder, "is it thy purpose to hold forth to these good people?"

"Ay, marry is it," said the clergyman, "and such is my bounden duty. Woe to me if I preach not the gospel —Prithee, friend, let me not in my labour" Burned. John Calvin (1509-64), the Protestant reformer and theologian. He was a professor of theology at Geneva, which became under his leadership the centre of Protestantism. By English non-conformists, aud particularly by the Presbyterians, Calvin was held in the greatest reverence. Even the dress of the Geneva preachers was imitated in England and Scotland. Breeches. Hinder.

"Nay," said the man of warlike mien, "I am myself minded to hold forth; therefore, do thou desist, or if thou wilt do by mine advice, remain and fructify with those poor goslings, to whom I am presently about to shake forth the crumbs of comfortable doctrine."

"Give place, thou man of Satan," said the priest, waxing wroth, "respect mine order—my cloth."

"I see no more to respect in the cut of thy cloak, or in the cloth of which it is fashioned," said the other, "than thou didst in the Bishop's rochets—they were black and white, thou art blue and brown. Sleeping dogs every one of you, lying down, loving to slumber—shepherds that starve the flock, but will not watch it, each looking to his own gain—hum."

Scenes of this indecent kind were so common at the time, that no one thought of interfering; the congregation looked on in silence, the better class scandalized, and the lower orders, some laughing, and others backing the soldier or minister as their fancy dictated. Meantime, the struggle waxed fiercer; Mr. Holdenough clamoured for assistance.

"Master Mayor of Woodstock," he exclaimed, "wilt thou be among those wicked magistrates who bear the sword in vain?—Citizens, will you not help your pastor?—Worthy Aldermen, will you see me strangled on the pulpit stairs by this man of buff and Belial?—But lo, I will overcome him, and cast his cords from me."

As Holdenough spoke, he struggled to ascend the pulpit stairs, holding hard on the banisters. His tormentor held fast by the skirts of the cloak, which went nigh to the choking of the wearer, until, as he spoke the words last mentioned, in a half-strangled voice, Mr. Holdenough dexterously slipped the string which tied it round his neck, so that the garment suddenly gave way; the soldier fell backwards down the steps, and the liberated divine skipped into the pulpit, and began to give forth a psalm of triumph over his prostrate adversary. But a great hubbub in the church marred his exultation, and although he and his faithful clerk continued to sing the hymn of victory, their notes were only heard by fits, like the whistle of a curlew during a gale of wind.

Be made fruitful. Close-fitting vestments of linen or lawn, worn chiefly by bishops. " Wherever they the Parliamentary officers were quartered, they excluded the minister from his pulpit; and, usurping his place, conveyed their sentiments to the audience, with all the authority which followed their power, their valour, and their military exploits, united to their appearing zeal and fervour."—Hume's *History of England,* Chap. LVIII.

"One of Cromwell's chief difficulties was to restrain his pikemen and dragoons from invading by main force the pulpits of ministers whose discourses, to use the language of that time, were not savory." —Macaulay's *History of England,* Chap. I.

The Hebrew name for a worthless or wicked person; hence, Satan himself.

The cause of the tumult was as follows:—The Mayor was a zealous Presbyterian, and witnessed the intrusion of the soldier with great indignation from the very beginning, though he hesitated to interfere with an armed man while on his legs and capable of resistance. But no sooner did he behold the champion of independency sprawling on his back, with the divine's Geneva cloak fluttering in his hands, than the magistrate rushed forward, exclaiming that such insolence was not to be endured, and ordered his constables to seize the prostrate champion, proclaiming, in the magnanimity of wrath, "I will commit every red-coat of them all—I will commit him were he Noll Cromwell himself!"

The worthy Mayor's indignation had overmastered his reason when he made this mistimed vaunt; for three soldiers, who had hitherto stood motionless like statues, made each a stride in advance, which placed them betwixt the municipal officers and the soldier, who was in the act of rising; then making at once the movement of resting arms according to the manual as then practised, their musketbutts rang on the church pavement, within an inch of the gouty toes of Master Mayor. The energetic magistrate, whose efforts in favour of order were thus checked, cast one glance on his supporters, but that was enough to shew him that force was not on his side. All had shrunk back on hearing that ominous clatter of stone and iron. He was obliged to descend to expostulation.

"What do you mean, my masters?" said he; "is it like a decent and God-fearing soldiery, who have wrought such things for the land as have never before been heard of, to brawl and riot in the church, or to aid, abet, and comfort a profane fellow, who hath, upon a solemn thanksgiving, excluded the minister from his own pulpit?" Popular nickname for Oliver.

"We have nought to do with thy chnrch, as thou call'st it," said he who, by a small feather in front of his morion, appeared to be the corporal of the party;—"we see not why men of gifts should not be heard within these citadels of superstition, as well as the voice of the men of crape of old, and the men of cloak now. Wherefore, we will pluck yon Jack Presbyter out of his wooden sentinel box, and our own watchman shall relieve the guard, and mount thereon, and cry aloud and spare not."

"Nay, gentlemen," said the Mayor, "if such be your purpose, we have not the means to withstand you, being, as you see, peaceful and quiet men—But let me first speak with this worthy minister, Nehemiah Holdenough, to persuade him to yield up his place for the time without farther scandal."

The peace-making Mayor then interrupted the quavering of Holdenough and the clerk, and prayed both to retire, else there would, he said, be certainly strife.

"Strife!" replied the Presbyterian divine, with scorn; "no fear of strife, among men that dare not testify against this open profanation of the church, and daring display of heresy. Would your neighbours of Banbury have brooked such an insult?"

"Come, come, Master Holdenough," said the Mayor, "put us not to mutiny and cry Clubs. I tell you once more, we are not men of war or blood."

"Not more than may be drawn by the point of a needle," said the preacher, scornfully,—" Ye tailors of Woodstock! —for what is a glover but a tailor working on kidskin?—I forsake you, in scorn of your faint hearts and feeble hands, and will seek me elsewhere a flock which will not fly from their shepherd at the braying of the first wild ass which cometh from out the great desert."

So saying, the aggrieved divine departed from his pulpit, and shaking the dust from his shoes, left the church as hastily as he had entered it, though with a different reason for his speed. The citizens saw his retreat with sorrow, and not without a compunctious feeling, as if conscious that they were not playing the most courageous part in the world. The Mayor himself and several others left the church, to follow and appease him.

A hat-shaped helmet of metal. A reference to the vestments worn by the clergymen of the Church of England.

'Popular nickname for a Presbyterian minister.

A small town fifteen miles distant. The rallying-cry of a mob.

The Independent orator, late prostrate, was now triumphant, and inducting himself into the pulpit without farther ceremony, he pulled a Bible from his pocket, and selected his text from the forty-fifth psalm,—" Gird thy sword upon thy thigh, O most mighty, with thy glory and thy majesty: and in thy majesty ride prosperously."— Upon this theme he commenced one of those wild declamations common at the period, in which men were accustomed to wrest and pervert the language of Scripture, by adapting it to modern events.

The language which, in its literal sense, was applied to King David, and typically referred to the coming of the Messiah, was, in the opinion of the military orator, most properly to be interpreted of Oliver Cromwell, the victorious general of the infant Commonwealth, which was never destined to come of age. "Gird on thy sword!" exclaimed the preacher emphatically; "and was not that a pretty bit of steel as ever dangled from a corselet, or rung against a steel saddle? Ay, ye prick up your ears now, ye cutlers of Woodstock, as if ye should know something of a good fox broadsword —Did you forge it, I trow?—was the steel quenched with water from Rosamond's well, or the blade blessed by the old cuckoldly priest of Godstow? You would have us think, I warrant me, that you wrought it and welded it, grinded and polished it, and all the while it never came on a Woodstock stithy! You were all too busy making whittles 1 for the lazy crape-men of Oxford, bouncing priests, whose eyes were so closed up with fat, that they could not see Destruction till she had them by the throat. But I can tell you where the sword was forged, and tempered, and welded, and grinded, and polished. When you were, as I said before, making whittles for false priests, and daggers for dissolute Gr—d d—n—me cavaliers, to cut the people of England's throat with—it was forged at Long Marston Moor, where blows went faster than ever rung hammer on anvil—and it was tempered at Naseby, in the best blood of the cavaliers—and it was welded in Ireland against the walls of Drogheda—and it was grinded on Scottish lives at Dunbar—and now of late it was polished in Worcester, till it shines as bright as the sun in the middle heaven, and there is no light in England that shall come nigh unto it." Note A. Vindication of the Book of Common Prayer against the contumelious slanders of the Fanatic Party terming it Porridge. Scott.

The Independents, who had heen increasing in numbers and influence since the time of Elizabeth (see note on Brownists in Chapter II.), maintained that the local church should be free from external control. At the opening of the Long Parliament they asserted themselves vigorously, became leaders in the army, which was gradually remodelled (the "New Model") through their instrumentality, and were the strongest weapon in the hand of Cromwell. Their jealousy of the Presbyterians, with whose general religious views they had so much in common, was constant. At the Restoration the Act of Uniformity drove both Independents and Presbyterians out of the National Church.

'A slang term for sword, of uncertain origin.

See "A Short Survey of Woodstock," Appendix. Fair Rosamond is said to have been educated at Godstow nunnery, and buried beneath the high altar there. See Chapter XXVI.; also, Scott's *Talisman* and Tennyson's *Becket*.

Here the military part of the congregation raised a hum of approbation, which being a sound like the "hear, hear," of the British House of Commons, was calculated to heighten the enthusiasm of the orator, by intimating the sympathy of the audience. "And then," resumed the preacher, rising in energy as he found that his audience partook in these feelings, "what sayeth the text?—Ride on prosperously—do not stop—do not call a halt—do not quit the saddle—pursue the scattered fliers—sound the trumpet—not a levant or a flourish, but a point of war —sound, boot and saddle —to horse and away—a charge! —follow after the young Man!—what part have we in him?—Slay, take, destroy, divide the spoil! Blessed art thou, Oliver, on account of thine honour—thy cause is clear, thy call is undoubted—never has defeat come near thy leading staff, nor disaster attended thy banner. Ride on, flower of England's soldiers! ride on, chosen leader of God's champions! gird up the loins of thy resolution, and be steadfast to the mark of thy high calling!" Large knives.

'For an account of the battles of Marston Moor, Naseby, Drogheda, Dunbar, and Worcester, see Frederic Harrison's *Cromwell,* Carlyle's *Cromwell's Letters and Speeches,* and

J. R. Green's *Short History of the English People.* A trumpet signal, such as is blown at sunrise or the time of changing guard.

Signal for attack. Compare Browning's Cavalier Song: "Boot, saddle, to horse, and away!" A name given by the Roundheads to Charles II., suggested perhaps by the scripture story of Absalom.

Another deep and stern hum, echoed by the ancient embow'd arches of the old chantry, gave him an opportunity of an instant's repose; when the people of Woodstock heard him, and not without anxiety, turn the stream of his oratory into another channel.

"But wherefore, ye people of Woodstock, do I say these things to you, who claim no portion in our David, no interest in England's son of Jesse? —You, who were fighting as well as your might could (and it was not very formidable) for the late Man, under that old bloodthirsty papist Sir Jacob Aston —are you not now plotting, or ready to plot, for the restoring, as ye call it, of the young Man, the unclean son of the slaughtered tyrant—the fugitive after whom the true hearts of England are now following, that they may take and slay him?—' Why should your rider turn his bridle our way?' say you in your hearts; 'we will none of him; if we may help ourselves, we will rather turn us to wallow in the mire of monarchy, with the sow that was washed but newly.' Come, men of Woodstock, I will ask, and do you answer me. Hunger ye still after the flesh-pots of the monks of Godstow? and ye will say, Nay;—but wherefore, except that the pots are cracked and broken, and the fire is extinguished wherewith thy oven used to boil? And again, I ask, drink ye still of the well of the fornications of the fair Rosamond? —ye will say, Nay;—but wherefore?"—

Here the orator, ere he could answer the question in his own way, was surprised by the following reply, very pithily pronounced by one of the congregation:—" Because you, and the like of you, have left us no brandy to mix with it."

All eyes turned to the audacious speaker, who stood be The staff or baton of a field-marshal. *'I.e.,* Cromwell.
" More probably It should be Sir Arthur Aston, the only general officer of the Catholic religion in the Royalist army. "—D. *Exodus* xvi. 3. side one of the thick sturdy Saxon pillars, which he himself somewhat resembled, being short of stature, but very strongly made, a squat broad Little John sort of figure, leaning on a quarterstaff, and wearing a jerkin, which, though now sorely stained and discoloured, had once been of the Lincoln green, and shewed remnants of having been laced. There was an air of careless good-humoured audacity about the fellow; and, though under military restraint, there were some of the citizens who could not help crying out,—" Well said, Joceline Joliffe!" "Jolly Joceline, call ye him?" proceeded the preacher, without shewing either confusion or displeasure at the interruption,—" I will make him Joceline of the jail, if he interrupts me again. One of your park-keepers, I warrant, that can never forget they have borne 0. R. upon their badges and bugle-horns, even as a dog bears his owner's name on his collar—a pretty emblem for Christian men! But the brute beast hath the better of him,—the brute weareth his own coat, and the caitiff thrall wears his master's. I have seen such a wag make a rope's end wag ere now.—Where was I?—Oh, rebuking you for your backslidings, men of Woodstock.—Yes, then ye will say ye have renounced Popery, and ye have renounced Prelacy, and then ye wipe your mouth like Pharisees as ye are; and who but you for purity of religion! But I tell you, ye are but like Jehu the son of Nimshi, who broke down the house of Baal, yet departed not from the sons of Jeroboam. Even so ye eat not fish on Friday with the blinded Papists, nor minced-pies on the twenty-fifth day of December, like the slothful Prelatists; but ye will gorge on sackposset each night in the year with your blind Presbyterian guide, and ye will speak evil of dignities, and revile the Commonwealth; and ye will glorify yourselves in your park of Woodstock, and say, 'Was it not walled in first of any other in England, and that by Henry, son of William called the Conqueror?' And ye have a princely Lodge therein, and call the same a Eoyal Lodge; and ye have an oak which ye call the King's Oak; and ye steal and eat the venison of the park; and ye say, 'This is the king's venison, we will wash it down with a cup to the king's health —better we eat it than those roundhead ed commonwealth knaves.' But listen unto me, and take warning. For these things come we to controversy with you. Ad our name shall be a cannon-shot, before which your Lodge, in the pleasantness whereof ye take pastime, shall be blown into ruins; and we will be as a wedge to split asunder the King's Oak into billets to heat a brown baker's oven; and we will dispark your park, and slay your deer, and eat them ourselves, neither shall you have any portion thereof, whether in neck or haunch. Ye shall not haft a tenpenny knife with the horns thereof, neither shall ye cut a pair of breeches out of the hide, for all ye be cutlers and glovers; and ye shall have no comfort or support neither from the sequestered traitor Henry Lee, who called himself Ranger of Woodstock, nor from any on his behalf; for they are coming hither who shall be called Maher-shalal-hash-baz, because he maketh haste to the spoil." The pillars in Saxon architecture, a rude variety of Romanesque, were very thick in proportion to their height.

"One of the chief followers of Robin Hood, the outlaw of Sherwood Forest, in the time of Richard the Lion-Heart. See Percy's *Seliques,* and Scott's *Ivanhoe* and *Talisman*. Lincoln at one time dyed the best green in all England, and Coventry the best blue. See "Coventry blue," Chapter XVIII.

Uarolus Rex (King Charles). The system of church government by prelates, which had been championed by Archbishop Laud. A King of Israel, who destroyed Baal-worship, yet returned to idolatry. 1 *Kings* xix.; 2 *Kings* ix., x. 1 *Kings* xii.

"A drink of hot milk curdled by sack,—a strong, light-colored Southern wine.

Here ended this wild effusion, the latter part of which fell heavy on the souls of the poor citizens of Woodstock, as tending to confirm a report of an unpleasing nature which had been lately circulated. The communication with London was indeed slow, and the news which it transmitted were uncertain: no less uncertain were the times themselves, and the rumours which were circulated, exaggerated by the hopes and fears of so many various factions. But the general stream of report, so far as Woodstock was concerned, had of late run uniformly in one direction. Day after day they had been informed, that the fatal fiat of Parliament had gone out, for selling the park of Woodstock, destroying its lodge, disparking its forest, and erasing, as far as they could be erased, all traces of its ancient fame. Many of the citizens were likely to be sufferers on this occasion, as several of them enjoyed, either by sufferance or right, various convenient privileges of pasturage, cutting firewood, and the like, in the royal chase; and all the inhabitants of the little burgh were hifrt to think, that the scenery of the place was to be destroyed, its edifices ruined, and its honours rent away. This is a patriotic sensation often found in such places, which ancient distinctions and long-cherished recollections of former days, rendered so different from towns of recent date. The natives of Woodstock felt it in the fullest force. They had trembled at the anticipated calamity; but now, when it was announced by the appearance of those dark, stern, and at the same time omnipotent soldiers—now that they heard it proclaimed by the mouth of one of their military preachers—they considered their fate as inevitable. The causes of disagreement among themselves were for the time forgotten, as the congregation, dismissed without psalmody or benediction, went slowly and mournfully homeward, each to his own place of abode.

The famous "King's Oak " in which Charles II. hid himself after his flight from Worcester, was at Bosoobel, on the border of Staffordshire. An epithet applied to the Puritans on account of their practice of cropping the hair. Long curls were the badge of a Cavalier. For sequestrated, *i.e.,* one whose lands have been confiscated to the State... The officer of a forest, whose duty it was to prevent trespassing. *Isaiah* viii. 1-4. SUGGESTIONS TO STUDENTS.

The function of. the opening chapter of a novel is ordinarily to give a picture of the place or time in which the story is to move, or to introduce some of the minor—sometimes the leading—characters, or to strike the key-note of the dramatic action. If it is prevailingly narrative, rather than descriptive, it usually deals with an event from which the subsequent events of the book distinctly take their origin, or an event or scene which must be explained before the reader can advance into the story, or one to the explanation of which the entire book is to be devoted. Which of these various purposes does the first chapter of *Woodstock* seem to yon to fulfil? Compare it, for effectiveness, with the opening chapter of Scott's earliest novels, such as *Waverley* and *Ouy Mannering;* with some of his later novels, such as *Kenttimrth* and *Quentin Durward.* Compare the religious exhortations with those found in *Old Mortality* and *Hob Hoy.* CHAPTER THE SECOND

Come forth, old man—Thy daughters side Is now the fitting place for thee:
When Time hath quelled the oak's hold pride,
The youthful tendril yet may hide
The ruins of the parent tree.

When' the sermon was ended, the military orator wiped his brow; for, notwithstanding the coolness of the weather, he was heated with the vehemence of his speech and action. He then descended from the pulpit, and spoke a word or two to the corporal who commanded the party of soldiers, who, replying by a sober nod of intelligence, drew his men together, and marched them in order to their quarters in the town.

The preacher himself, as if nothing extraordinary had happened, left the church and sauntered through the streets of Woodstock, with the air of a stranger who was viewing the town, without seeming to observe that he was himself in his turn anxiously surveyed by the citizens, whose furtive yet frequent glances seemed to regard him as something alike suspected and dreadful, yet on no account to be provoked. He heeded them not, but stalked on in the manner affected by the distinguished fanatics of the day; a stiff solemn pace, a severe and at the same time a contemplative look, like that of a man discomposed at the interruptions which earthly objects forced upon him, obliging him by their intrusion to withdraw his thoughts for an instant from celestial things. Innocent pleasures of what kind soever they held in suspicion and contempt, and innocent mirth they abominated. It was, however, a cast of mind that formed men for great and manly actions, as it adopted principle, and that of an unselfish character, for the ruling motive, instead of the gratification of passion. Some of these men were indeed hypocrites, using the cloak of religion only as a covering for their ambition; but many really possessed the devotional character, and the severe republican virtue, which others only affected. By far the greater number hovered between these extremes, felt to a certain extent the power of religion, and complied with the times in affecting a great deal.

"This is probably one of the passages in which Scott, as Lockhart says, refers to the noble behaviour of his daughter Anne in the time of his misfortunes. See also motto to Chapter IV."—Andrew Lang.— See Editor's Introduction.

The individual, whose pretensions to sanctity, written as they were upon his brow and gait, have given rise to the above digression, reached at length the extremity of the principal street, which terminates upon the park of Woodstock. A battlemented portal of Gothic appearance defended the entrance to the avenue. It was of mixed architecture, but on the whole, though composed of the styles of the different ages when it had received additions, had a striking and imposing effect. An immense gate, composed of rails of hammered iron, with many a flourish and scroll, displaying as its uppermost ornament the illfated cipher of C. R., was now decayed, being partly wasted with rust, partly by violence.

The stranger paused, as if uncertain whether he should demand or assay entrance. He looked through the grating down an avenue skirted by majestic oaks, which led onward with a gentle curve, as if into the depths of some ample and ancient forest. The wicket of the large iron gate being left unwittingly open, the soldier was tempted to enter, yet with some hesitation, as he that intrudes upon ground which he conjectures may be prohibited—indeed his manner shewed more reverence for the scene than could have been expected from his condition and character. He slackened his stately and consequential pace, and at length stood still, and looked around him.

Not far from the gate, he saw rising from the trees one or two ancient and venerable turrets, bearing each its own vane of rare device glittering in the autumn sun. These indicated the ancient hunting seat, or Lodge, as it was called, which had, since the time of Henry II. , been occasionally the residence of the English monarchs, when it pleased them to visit the woods of An inexact epithet for the Pointed type of mediaeval architecture. 'Edward the Black Prince was horn at Woodstock, and the PrinOxford, which then so abounded with game, that, according to old Fuller, huntsmen and falconers were nowhere better pleased. The situation which the Lodge occupied was a piece of flat ground, now planted with sycamores, not far from the entrance to that magnificent spot, where the spectator first stops to gaze upon Blenheim, to think of Marlborough's victories, and to applaud or criticise the cumbrous magnificence of Vanbrugh's style.

There, too, paused our military preacher, but with other thoughts, and for other purpose, than to admire the scene around him. It was not long afterwards when he beheld two persons, a male and a female, approaching slowly, and so deeply engaged in their own conversation that they did not raise their eyes to observe that there stood a stranger in the path before them. The soldier took advantage of their state of abstraction, and desirous at once to watch their motions and avoid their observation, he glided beneath one of the huge trees which skirted the path, and whose boughs, sweeping the ground on every side, ensured him against discovery, unless in case of an actual search.

In the meantime, the gentleman and lady continued to advance, directing their course to a rustic seat, which still enjoyed the sunbeams, and was placed adjacent to the tree where the stranger was concealed.

The man was elderly, yet seemed bent more by sorrow and infirmity, than by the weight of years. He wore a mourning cloak, over a dress of the same melancholy colour, cut in that picturesque form which Vandyck has rendered immortal. But although the dress was handsome, it was put on and worn with a carelessness which shewed the mind of the wearer ill at ease. His aged, yet still handsome countenance, had the same air of consequence which distinguished his dress and his gait. A striking part of his appearance was a long white beard, which descended far over the breast of his slashed doublet, andlooked singular from its contrast in colour with his habit.

cess Elizabeth was confined there for some time by her sister, Queen Mary. See Tennyson's *Queen Mary*. Thomas Fuller (1008-1661), the well-known divine, author of the *History of the Worthies of England* and other works. Sir Anthony Vandyck (1599-1641), the famous Flemish painter. He was knighted and made court painter to Charles I. in 1632. His portraits of the king and the royal family are among his best-known Works.

The young lady, by whom this venerable gentleman seemed to be in some degree supported as they walked arm in arm, was a slight and sylph-form, with a person so delicately made, and so beautiful in countenance, that it seemed the earth on which she walked was too grossly massive a support for a creature so aerial. But mortal beauty must share human sorrows. The eyes of the beautiful being shewed tokens of tears; her colour was heightened as she listened to her aged companion; and it was plain, from his melancholy yet displeased look, that the conversation was as distressing to himself as to her. When they sat down on the bench we have mentioned, the gentleman's discourse could be distinctly overheard by the eavesdropping soldier, but the answers of the young lady reached his ear rather less distinctly.

"It is not to be endured!" said the old man, passionately; "it would stir up a paralytic wretch to start up a soldier. My people have been thinned, I grant you, or have fallen off from me in these times—I owe them no grudge for it, poor knaves; what should they do waiting on me when the pantry has no bread and the buttery no ale? But we have still about us some rugged foresters of the old Woodstock breed—old as myself most of them— what of that? old wood seldom warps in the wetting;— I will hold out the old house, and it will not be the first time that I have held it against ten times the strength that we hear of now."

"Alas! my dear father!"—said the young lady, in a tone which seemed to intimate his proposal of defence to be altogether desperate.

"And why, alas?" said the gentleman, angrily; "is it because I shut my door against a score or two of these bloodthirsty hypocrites?"

"But their masters can as easily send a regiment or an army, if they will," replied the lady; "and what good would your present defence do, excepting to exasperate them to your utter destruction?"

"Be it so, Alice," replied her father; "I have lived my time, and beyond it. I have outlived the kindest and 1A waistcoat with slashes or narrow openings to show the lining.

most princelike of masters. What do I do on the earth since the dismal thirtieth of January F The parricide of that day was a signal to all true servants of Charles Stuart to avenge his death, or die as soon after as they could find a worthy opportunity."

"Do not speak thus, sir," said Alice Lee; "it does not become your gravity and your worth to throw away that life which may yet be of service to your king and country, —it will not and cannot always be thus. England will not long endure the rulers which these bad times have assigned her. In the meanwhile—here a few words escaped the listener's ears—and beware of that impatience, which makes bad worse.

"Worse?" exclaimed the impatient old man. "*What* can be worse? Is it not at the worst already? Will not these people expel us from the only shelter we have left—dilapidate what remains of royal property under my charge—make the palace of princes into a den of thieves, and then wipe their mouths and thank God, as if they had done an almsdeed?"

"Still," said his daughter, "there is hope behind, and I trust the King is ere this out of their reach—We have reason to think well of my brother Albert's safety."

"Ay, Albert! there again," said the old man, in a tone of reproach; "had it not been for thy entreaties I had gone to Worcester myself; but I must needs lie here like a worthless hound when the hunt is up, when who knows what service I might have shewn? An old man's head is sometimes useful when his arm is but little worth. But you and Albert were so desirous that he should go alone— and now, who can say what has become of him?"

"Nay, nay, father," said Alice, "we have good hope that Albert escaped from that fatal day; young Abney saw him a mile from the field." 1 Charles I. was executed on Jan. 30, 1649.
"The truth is. no modern reader can conceive the then atrocity, ferocity, unspeakability of this fact execution of the King. First, after long reading in the old dead pamphlets does one see the magnitude of it. To be equalled, nay to be preferred, think some, in point of horror, to 'the Crucifixion of Christ.' Alas, in these irreverent times of ours, if all the Kings of Europe were cut in pieces at one swoop, and flung in heaps in St. Margaret's Church-yard on the same day, the emotion would, in strict arithmetical truth, be small in comparison I "— Carlyle's *Cromwell's Letters, etc.,* end of Part IV.

"Young Abney lied, I believe," said the father, in the same humour of contradiction—" Young Abney's tongue seems quicker than his hands, but far slower than his horse's heels when he leaves the roundheads behind him. I would rather Albert's dead body were laid between Charles and Cromwell, than hear he fled as early as young Abney."

"My dearest father," said the young lady, weeping as she spoke, "what can I say to comfort you?"

"Comfort me, sayest thou, girl? I am sick of comfort —an honourable death, with the ruins of Woodstock for my monument, were the only comfort to old Henry Lee. Yes, by the memory of my fathers! I will make good the Lodge against these rebellious robbers."

"Yet be ruled, dearest father," said the maiden, "and submit to that which we cannot gainsay. My uncle Everard"

Here the old man caught at her unfinished words. "Thy uncle Everard, wench!—Well, get on.—What of thy precious and loving uncle Everard?"

"Nothing, sir," she said, "if the subject displeases you."

"Displeases me?" he replied, "why should it displease me? or if it did, why shouldst thou, or any one affect to care about it? What is it that hath happened of late years—what is it can be thought to happen that astrologer can guess at, which can give pleasure to us?"

"Fate," she replied, "may have in store the joyful restoration of our banished Prince."

"Too late for my time, Alice," said the knight; "if there be such a white page in the heavenly book, it will not be turned until long after my day.—But I see thou wouldst escape me In a word, what of thy uncle Everard?"

"Nay, sir," said Alice, "God knows I would rather be silent forever, than speak what might, as you would take it, add to your present distemperature."

"Distemperature!" said her father; "Oh, thou art a sweet-lipped physician, and would st, I warrant me, drop nought but sweet balm, and honey, and oil, on my distemperature—if that is the phrase for an old man's ailment, when he is well-nigh heart-broken.—Once more what of thy uncle Everard?"

His last words were uttered in a high and peevish tone of voice; and Alice Lee answered her father in a trembling and submissive tone.

"I only meant to say, sir, that I am well assured that my uncle Everard, when we quit this place"

"That is to say, when we are kicked out of it by cropeared canting villains like himself.—But on with thy bountiful uncle—what will he do?—will he give us the remains of his worshipful and economical housekeeping, the fragments of a thrice-sacked capon twice a week, and a plentiful fast on the other five days?—Will he give us beds beside his half-starved nags, and put them under a short allowance of straw, that his sister's husband—that I should have called my deceased angel by such a name!— and his sister's daughter, may not sleep on the stones? Or will he send us a noble each, with a warning to make it last, for he had never known the ready penny so hard to come by? Or what else will your uncle Everard do for us? Get us a furlough to beg? Why I can do that without him."

"You misconstrue him much," answered Alice, with more spirit than she had hitherto displayed; "and would you but question your own heart, you would acknowledge —I speak with reverence—that your tongue utters what your better judgment would disown. My uncle Everard is neither a miser nor a hypocrite,—neither so fond of the goods of this world that he would not supply our distresses amply, nor so wedded to fanatical opinions as to exclude charity for other sects beside his own."

"Ay, ay, the Church of England is a *sect* with him, I doubt not, and perhaps with thee too, Alice," said the knight. "What is a Muggletonian, or a Banter, or a Brownist, but a sectary? and thy phrase places them all, with Jack Presbyter himself, on the same footing with our learned prelates and religious clergy! Such is the cant of the day thou livest in, and why shouldst thou not talk like one of the wise virgins and psalm-singing sisters, since, though thou hast a profane old cavalier for a father, thou art own niece to pious uncle Everard?"

Contemptuous term for Puritans. Cropping of the ears was a form of punishment then in vogue. See reference to Prynne in Chapter XIV.

'A fowl whose bones have been thrice picked.

A coin worth 6s. 8d. A member of a sect founded by Ludovic Muggleton, "a mad tailor who wandered from pot house to pot-house, tippling ale, and denouncing eternal torments against those who refused to believe, on his testi. mony, that the Supreme Being was only six feet high, and that the sun was just four miles from the earth."—Macaulay's *History of England,* Chap. II. A member of an Antinomian sect of the Commonwealth period, associated with the Familists, who are characterized by Scott in Chapter XXIX.

"If you speak thus, my dear father," said Alice, "what can I answer you? Hear me but one patient word, and I shall have discharged my uncle Everard's commission."

"Oh, it is a commission then? Surely, I suspected so much from the beginning—nay, have some sharp guess touching the ambassador also.—Come madam, the mediator, do your errand, and you shall have no reason to complain of my patience."

"Then, sir," replied his daughter, "my uncle Everard desires you would be courteous to the commissioners, who come here to sequestrate the parks and the property; or, at least, needfully to abstain from giving them obstacle or opposition: it can, he says, do no good, even on your own principles, and it will give a pretext for proceeding against you as one in the worst degree of malignity, which he thinks may otherwise be prevented. Nay, he has good hope, that if you follow his counsel, the committee may, through the interest he possesses, be inclined to remove the sequestration of your estate on a moderate fine. Thus says my uncle; and having communicated his advice, I have no occasion to urge your patience with farther argument."

"It is well thou dost not, Alice," answered Sir Henry Lee, in a tone of suppressed anger; "for, by the blessed Rood, thou hast well-nigh led me into the heresy of thinking thee no daughter of mine.—Ah! my beloved companion, who art now far from the sorrows and cares of this weary world, couldst thou have thought that the daughter thou didst clasp to thy bosom, would, like the wicked wife of Job, become a temptress to her father in the hour of affliction, and recommend to him to make his conscience truckle to his interest, and to beg back at the bloody hands of his master's and perhaps his son's murderers, a wretched remnant of the royal property he has been robbed of!— Why, wench, if I must beg, think'st thou I would sue to those who have made me a mendicant? No. I will never shew my gray beard, worn in sorrow for my sovereign's death, to move the compassion of some proud sequestrator, who perhaps was one of the parricides. No. If Henry Lee must sue for food, it shall be of some sound loyalist like himself, who, having but half a loaf remaining, will not nevertheless refuse to share it with him. For his daughter, she may wander her own way, which leads her to a refuge with her wealthy roundhead kinsfolk; but let her no more call him father, whose honest indigence she has refused to share!" A follower of Robert Brown, a clergyman of Queen Elizabeth's time. The Brownists objected alike to Episcopacy and to the Presbyterian form of church government, and favored a purely congregational system, without convocation or synod. Many of them emigrated to Holland, and thence to America. They were the founders of modern Congregationalism.

Royalists, and particularly those who had borne arms for the King, were known by the Puritans as Malignauts. Cross.

"You do me injustice, sir," answered the young lady, with a voice animated yet faltering, "cruel injustice. God knows, your way is my way, though it lead to ruin and beggary; and while you tread it, my arm shall support you while you will accept an aid so feeble."

"Thou word'st me, girl," answered the old cavalier, "thou word'st me, as Will Shakspeare says—thou speakest of lending me thy arm; but thy secret thought is thyself to hang upon Markham Everard's."

"My father, my father," answered Alice in a tone of deep grief, "what can thus have altered your clear judgment and kindly heart?—Accursed be these civil commotions! not only do they destroy men's bodies, but they pervert their souls; and the brave, the noble, the generous, become suspicious, harsh, and mean! Why upbraid me with Markham Everard? Have I seen or spoken to him since you forbid him my company, with terms less kind— I will speak it truly—than was due even to the relationship betwixt you? Why think I would sacrifice to that young man my duty to you? Know, that were I capable of such criminal weakness, Markham Everard were the first to despise me for it."

She put her handkerchief to her eyes, but she could not *Job* ii. 9.

'*Antony and Cleopatra,* Act V., Sc. 2, l. 191.

hide her sobs, nor conceal the distress they intimated. The old man was moved.

"I cannot tell," he said, "what to think of it. Thou seem'st sincere, and wert ever a good and kindly daughter —how thou hast let that rebel youth creep into thy heart I wot not; perhaps it is a punishment on me, who thought the loyalty of my house was like undefiled ermine. Yet here is a damned spot, and on the fairest gem of all—my own dear Alice. But do not weep—we have enough to vex us. Where is it that Shakspeare hath it:—

Gentle daughter,
Give even way unto my rough affairs;
Put you not on the temper of the times,
Nor be, like them, to Percy troublesome." 1

"I am glad," answered the young lady, "to hear you quote your favourite again, sir. Our little jars are ever well-nigh ended when Shakspeare comes in play."

"His book was the closet companion of my blessed master," said Sir Henry Lee; "after the Bible (with reverence for naming them together), he felt more comfort in it than in any other; and as I have shared his disease, why, it is natural I should take his medicine. Albeit, I pretend not to my master's art in explaining the dark passages; for I am but a rude man, and rustically brought up to arms and hunting."

"You have seen Shakspeare yourself, sir?" said the young lady.

"Silly wench," replied the knight, " he died when I was a mere child—thou hast heard me say so twenty times; but thou wouldst lead the old man away from the tender subject. Well, though I am not blind, I can shut my eyes and follow. Ben Jonson I knew, and could tell thee many a tale of our meetings at the Mermaid, where, if there was much wine, there was much wit also. We did not sit blowing tobacco in each other's faces, and turning up the whites of our eyes as we turned up the bottom of the wine-pot. Old Ben adopted me as one of his sons in the muses. I have shewn you, have I not, the verses, 'To my much beloved son, the worshipful Sir Henry Lee of Ditchley, Knight and Baronet?'"

1 *Henry IV.*, Act II., Sc. 3, 11. 1-1.
This is one of the anachronisms in *Woodstock* to which attention has frequently been drawn. Shakespeare died in 1616, but thirtyfive years before the time of the story. Ben Jonson (1574-1637), the dramatist, was a member of the celebrated club which met at the Mermaid Tavern, and which was founded by Sir Walter Raleigh, it is said, in 1603. Beaumont, Fletcher, Selden, and probably Shakespeare were also members. Fuller has described the wit combats there between Shakespeare and Ben Jonson, "which he beheld," though he was but eight years old when Shakespeare died.

"I do not remember them at present, sir," replied Alice.

"I fear ye lie, wench," said her father; "but no mattor—thou canst not get any more fooling out of me just now. The Evil Spirit hath left Saul for the present. We are now to think what is to be done about leaving Woodstock—or defending it?"

"My dearest father," said Alice, "can you still nourish a moment's hope of making good the place?"

"I know not, wench," replied Sir Henry; "I would fain have a parting blow with them, 'tis certain—and who knows where a blessing may alight? But then, my poor knaves that must take part with me in so hopeless a quarrel—that thought hampers me, I confess."

"Oh, let it do so, sir," replied Alice, "there are soldiers in the town, and there are three regiments at Oxford!"

"Ah, poor Oxford!" exclaimed Sir Henry, whose vacillating state of mind was turned by a word to any new subject that was suggested,—"Seat of learning and loyalty! these rude soldiers are unfit inmates for thy learned halls and poetical bowers; but thy pure and brilliant lamp shall defy the foul breath of a thousand churls, were they to blow at it like Boreas. The burning bush shall not be consumed, even by the heat of this persecution."

"True, sir," said Alice, "and it may not be useless to recollect, that any stirring of the royalists at this unpropitious moment will make them deal yet more harshly with the University, which they consider as being at the bottom of everything which moves for the King in these parts." This honor was claimed by several younger poets whom Jonson befriended, and who called themselves "of the tribe of Ben." 1 *Samuel* xvi. 14-23. Browning's fine poem "Saul" is based upon the incident referred to.
The personification of the north wind, in Greek mythology. *Exodus* iii. 2.
"It is true, wench," replied the knight; "and small cause would make the villains sequestrate the poor remains which the civil wars have left to the colleges. That, and the risk of my poor fellows—Well! thou hast disarmed me, girl. I will be as patient and calm as a martyr."

"Pray God you keep your word, sir!" replied his daughter; "but you are ever so much moved at the sight of any of these men, that"

"Would you make a child of me, Alice?" said Sir Henry. "Why, know you not that I can look upon a viper, or a toad, or a bunch of engendering adders, without any worse feeling than a little disgust? and though a roundhead, and especially a red-coat, are in my opinion more poisonous than vipers, more loathsome than toads, more hateful than knotted adders, yet can I overcome my nature so far, that should one of them appear at this moment, thyself should see how civilly I would entreat him."

As he spoke, the military preacher abandoned his leafy screen, and stalking forward, stood unexpectedly before the old cavalier, who stared at him as if he had thought his expressions had actually raised a devil.

"Who art thou?" at length said Sir Henry, in a raised and angry voice, while his daughter clung to his arm in terror, little confident that her father's pacific resolutions would abide the shock of this unwelcome apparition.

"I am one," replied the soldier, "who neither fear nor shame to call myself a poor day-labourer in the great work of England—umph!—Ay, a simple and sincere upholder of the good old cause."

"And what the devil do you seek here?" said the old knight, fiercely.

"The welcome due to the steward of the Lords Commissioners," answered the soldier.

"Welcome art thou as salt would be to sore eyes," said the cavalier; "but who be your Commissioners, man?"

The soldier with little courtesy held out a scroll, which Sir Henry took from him betwixt his finger and thumb, as if it were a letter from a pest-house; and held it at as much distance from his eyes, as his purpose of reading it would permit. He then read aloud, and as he named the parties one by one, he added a short commentary on each name, addressed indeed to Alice, but in such a tone that shewed he cared not for its being heard by the soldier.

"*Desborough*—the ploughman Desborough—as grovelling a clown as is in England—a fellow that would be best at home, like an ancient Scythian, under the tilt of a waggon — d—n him. *Har-*

rison, a bloody-minded, ranting enthusiast, who read the Bible to such purpose that he never lacked a text to justify a murder—d—n him too. *Bletson* — a true-blue Commonwealth's man, one of Harrison's (Harrington's Rota Club, with his noddle full of newangled notions about government, the clearest object of which is to establish the tail upon the head; a fellow who leaves you the statutes and law of old England, to prate of Rome and Greece—sees the Areopagus in WestminsterHall, and takes old Noll for a Roman consul—Adad, he is like to prove a dictator amongst them instead. Never mind—d—n Bletson too."

"Friend," said the soldier, "I would willingly be civil, but it consists not with my duty to hear these godly men, in whose service I am, spoken of after this irreverent and unbecoming fashion. And albeit I know that you malignants think you have a right to make free with that damnation, which you seem to use as your own portion, yet it is superfluous to invoke it against others, who have better hopes in their thoughts and better words in their mouths."

"Thou art but a canting varlet," replied the knight; "and yet thou art right in some sense—for it is superfluous to curse men who already are damned as black as the smoke of hell itself."

"I prithee forbear," continued the soldier, "for manners' sake, if not for conscience—grisly oaths suit ill with gray beards."

"Nay, that is truth, if the devil spoke it," said the knight; "and I thank Heaven I can follow good counsel, though old Nick gives it. And so, friend, touching these same Commissioners, bear them this message; that Sir Henry Lee is keeper of Woodstock Park, with right of waif and stray, vert and venison, as complete as any of them have to their estate—that is, if they possess any estate but what they have gained by plundering honest men. Nevertheless, he will give place to those who have made their might their right, and will not expose the lives of good and true men, where the odds are so much against them. And he protests that he makes this surrender, neither as acknowledging of these so termed Commissioners, nor as for his own individual part fearing their force, but purely to avoid the loss of English blood, of which so much hath been spilt in these late times." For notes upon Desborough and Harrison, consult Chapter XL, where Scott characterizes them in detail.

Bletson is probably an imaginary character. No such name appears in the list of members of the Long Parliament. D. James Harrington (1611-1677), a political writer and author of *The Commonwealth of Oemna* (1656), a sketch of an ideal republic, founded, though not until 1659, a debating club called the Rota, for diffusing Republican opinions. See Pepys's *Diary* for Jan. 10, 1659. An Athenian court of justice.

"The "great hall of William Rufus," a structure adjoining the houses of Parliament on the west, and forming a part of the ancient palace of Westminster. Some of the first English Parliaments sat here, and it witnessed the condemnation of Charles I.

"It is well spoken," said the steward of the Commissioners; "and therefore, I pray you, let us walk together into the house, that thou may'st deliver up unto me the vessels, and gold and silver ornaments, belonging unto the Egyptian Pharaoh who committed them to thy keeping."

"What vessels?" exclaimed the fiery old knight; "and belonging to whom? Unbaptized dog, speak civil of the Martyr in my presence, or I will do a deed misbecoming of me on that caitiff corpse of thine!"—And shaking his daughter from his right arm, the old man laid his hand on his rapier.

His antagonist, on the contrary, kept his temper completely, and waving his hand to add impression to his speech, he said, with a calmness which aggravated Sir Henry's wrath, "Nay, good friend, I prithee be still, and brawl not—it becomes not gray hairs and feeble arms to rail and rant like drunkards. Put me not to use the carnal weapon in mine own defence, but listen to the voice of reason. See'st thou not that the Lord hath decided this great controversy in favour of us and ours, against thee and thine? Wherefore, render up thy stewardship peaceably, and deliver up to me the chattels of the Man, Charles Stuart."

"Patience is a good nag, but she will bolt," said the Right over property on animals without an owner, over the forest trees, and game among them.

A reference to Charles I., perhaps with an allusion to "spoiling the Egyptians," *Exodus* iii. 22. knight, unable longer to rein in his wrath. He plucked his sheathed rapier from his side, struck the soldier a severe blow with it, and instantly drawing it, and throwing the scabbard over the trees, placed himself in a posture of defence, with his sword's point within half a yard of the steward's body. The latter stepped back with activity, threw his long cloak from his shoulders, and drawing his long tuck, stood upon his guard. The swords clashed smartly together, while Alice, in her terror, screamed wildly for assistance. But the combat was of short duration. The old cavalier had attacked a man as cunning of fence as he himself, or a little more so, and possessing all the strength and activity of which time had deprived Sir Henry, and the calmness which the other had lost in his passion. They had scarce exchanged three passes ere the sword of the knight flew up in the air, as if it had gone in search of the scabbard; and burning with shame and anger, Sir Henry stood disarmed, at the mercy of his antagonist. The republican shewed no purpose of abusing his victory; nor did he, either during the combat, or after the victory was won, in any respect alter the sour and grave composure which reigned upon his countenance—a combat of life and death seemed to him a thing as familiar, and as little to be feared, as an ordinary bout with foils.

"Thou art delivered into my hands," he said, "and by the law of arms I might smite thee under the fifth rib, even as Asahel was struck dead by Abner, the son of Ner, as he followed the chase on the hill of Ammah, that lieth before Giah, in the way of the wilderness of Gibeon; but far be it from me to spill thy remaining drops of blood. True it is, thou art the captive of my sword and of my spear; nevertheless, seeing that there may be a turning from thine evil ways, and a returning to those which are good, if the Lord enlarge thy date for repentance and amendment, wherefore should it be shortened by a poor sinful mortal, who is, speaking truly, but thy fellowworm?"

Sir Henry Lee remained still confused, and unable to answer, when there arrived a fourth person, whom the cries of Alice had summoned to the spot. This was Joceline Joliffe, one of the underkeepers of the walk, who, seeing how matters stood, brandished his quarterstaff, a 2 *Samud* ii. 18-24.

weapon from which he never parted, and having made it describe the figure of eight in a flourish through the air, would have brought it down with a vengeance upon the head of the steward, had not Sir Henry interposed.

"We must trail bats now, Joceline—our time of shouldering them is past. It skills not striving against the stream—the devil rules the roast, and makes our slaves our tutors."

At this moment another auxiliary rushed out of the thicket to the knight's assistance. It was a large wolf-dog, in strength a mastiff, in form and almost in fleetness a greyhound. Bevis was the noblest of the kind which ever pulled down a stag, tawny-coloured like a lion, with a black muzzle and black feet, just edged with a line of white round the toes. He was as tractable as he was strong and bold. Just as he was about to rush upon the soldier, the words, "Peace, Bevis " from Sir Henry, converted the lion into a lamb, and, instead of pulling the soldier down, he walked round and round, and snuffed, as if using all his sagacity to discover who the stranger could be, towards whom, though of so questionable an appearance, he was enjoined forbearance. Apparently he was satisfied, for he laid aside his doubtful and threatening demonstrations, lowered his ears, smoothed down his bristles, and wagged his tail.

Sir Henry, who had great respect for the sagacity of his favourite, said in a low voice to Alice, '' Bevis is of thy opinion, and counsels submission. There is the finger of Heaven in this to punish the pride, ever the fault of our house.—Friend," he continued, addressing the soldier, "thou hast given the finishing touch to a lesson, which ten years of constant misfortune have been unable fully to teach me. Thou hast distinctly shewn me the folly of thinking that a good cause can strengthen a weak arm. God forgive me for the thought, but I could almost turn infidel, and believe that Heaven's blessing goes ever with the longest sword; but it will not be always thus. God knows his time.—Reach me my Toledo, Joceline, yonder it lies; and the scabbard, see where it hangs on the tree. —Do not pull at my cloak, Alice, and look so miserably frightened; I shall be in no hurry to betake me to bright steel again, I promise thee.—For thee, good fellow, I thank thee, and will make way for thy masters without farther dispute or ceremony. Joceline Joliffe is nearer thy degree than I am, and will make surrender to thee of the Lodge and household stuff. Withhold nothing, Joliffe—let them have all. For me, I will never cross the threshold again— but where to rest for a night? I would trouble no one in Woodstock—hum—ay—it shall be so. Alice and I, Joceline, will go down to thy hut by Rosamond's well; we will borrow the shelter of thy roof for one night at least; thou wilt give us welcome, wilt thou not?—How now—a clouded brow?" The quarterstaff was a stout pole about six and one half feet long. It was grasped by one hand in the middle, and by the other between the middle and the end. In the attack the latter hand shifted from one quarter of the staff to the other, giving the weapon a rapid circular motion, which brought the ends on the adversary at unexpected points.

Has chief authority. See Scott's note upon Bevis, at the close of the final chapter. Compare the description of other dogs which Scott has introduced in *The Lady of the Lake, Ivan/we, The Antiquary,* etc.

Joceline certainly looked embarrassed, directed first a glance to Alice, then looked to heaven, then to earth, and last to the four quarters of the horizon, and then murmured out, "Certainly—without question—might he but run down to put the house in order."

"Order enough—order enough—for those that may soon be glad of clean straw in a barn," said the knight; "but if thou hast an ill will to harbour any obnoxious or malignant persons, as the phrase goes, never shame to speak it out, man. 'Tis true, I took thee up when thou wert but a ragged Robin, made a keeper of thee, and so forth. What of that? Sailors think no longer of the wind than when it forwards them on the voyage—thy betters turn with the tide, why should not such a poor knave as thou?"

"God pardon your honour for your harsh judgment," said Joliffe. "The hut is yours, such as it is, and should be were it a king's palace, as I wish it were even for your honour's sake, and Mistress Alice's—only I could wish your honour would condescend to let me step down before, in case any neighbour be there—or—or—just to put matters something into order for Mistress Alice and your honour—just to make things something seemly and shapely. " The keeper's followers in the New Forest are called in popular language ragged Robins. Scott.

A general name for a sword, from Toledo, in Spain, where excellent swords were made.

"Not a whit necessary," said the knight, while Alice had much trouble in concealing her agitation. "If thy matters are unseemly, they are fitted for a defeated knight—if they are unshapely, why, the liker to the rest of a world which is all unshaped. Go thou with that man. —What is thy name, friend *t*" "Joseph Tomkins is my name in the flesh," said the steward. "Men call me Honest Joe, and Trusty Tomkins."

"If thou hast deserved such names, considering what trade thou hast driven, thou art a jewel indeed," said the knight; "yet if thou hast not, never blush for the matter, Joseph, for if thou art not in truth honest, thou hast all the better chance to keep the fame of it—the title and the thing itself have long walked separate ways. Farewell to thee,—and farewell to fair Woodstock!"

So saying, the old knight turned round, and pulling his daughter's arm through his own, they walked onward into the forest, in the same manner in which they were introduced to the reader.

Compare Sir Henry Lee with similar characters already delineated hy Scott, such as Sir Geoffrey in *lleveril of the Peak,* Baron Bradwardine in *Waverley,* and Lady Margaret Bellenden in *Old Mortality.* What traits possessed by Alice Lee fit her to be the heroine of the story? Is she like Scott's other heroines of gentle birth, such as Miss Wardour *(Antiquary),* Edith Bellenden *(Old Mortality),* Lucy Bertram and Julia Mannering *(Guy Mannering)*? Notice carefully whether the main characters develop as the story progresses, or are left stationary as regards mental and moral growth, as is usual with minor characters in fiction. What does the conversation about Albert Lee and Markham Everard in this chapter suggest to you about the future plot of the story? Does the name Trusty Tomkins betray anything as to the function of this character? Do you think it an advantage or a disadvantage to have the " villain " of the book introduced as such, as in *KenUworth* and frequently in Dickens?

CHAPTER THE THIRD

Now, ye wild blades, that make loose inns your stage,
To vapour forth the acts of this sad age,
Stout Edgehill fight, the Newberries and the West,
And northern clashes, where you still fought best;
Your strange escapes, your dangers void of fear,
When bullets flew between the head and ear,
Whether you fought by Damme or the Spirit,
Of you I speak.
　　　Legend Of Captain Jones.

Joseph Tomkins and Joliffe the keeper remained for some time in silence, as they stood together looking along the path in which the figures of the Knight of Ditchley and pretty Mistress Alice had disappeared behind the trees. Then they gazed on each other in doubt, as men who scarce knew whether they stood on hostile or on friendly terms together, and were at a loss how to open a conversation. They heard the knight's whistle summon Bevis; but though the good hound turned his head and pricked his ears at the sound, yet he did not obey the call, but continued to snuff around Joseph Tomkins's cloak.

"Thou art a rare one, I fear me," said the keeper, looking to his new acquaintance. "I have heard of men who have charms to steal both dogs and deer."

"Trouble not thyself about my qualities, friend," said Joseph Tomkins, " but bethink thee of doing thy master's bidding."

Joceline did not immediately answer, but at length, as if in sign of truce, stuck the end of his quarterstaff upright in the ground, and leant upon it as he said gruffly,—" So, my tough old knight and you were at drawn bilbo, by way of afternoon service, sir preacher—Well for you I came not up till the blades were done jingling, or I had rung evensong upon your pate." A term for a sword taken from Bilbao, Spain, famous, like Toledo, for its swords. A service appointed to be said or sung at evening; *i.e.,* a death stroke. Compare the slang phrase, "It would have been all day with you."

The independent smiled grimly as he replied, "Nay, friend, it is well for thyself, for never should sexton have been better paid for the knell he tolled. Nevertheless, why should there be war betwixt us, or my hand be against thine? Thou art but a poor knave, doing thy master's order, nor have I any desire that my own blood or thine should be shed touching this matter.—Thou art, I understand, to give me peaceful possession of the Palace of Woodstock, so called—though there is now no palace in England, no, nor shall be in the days that come after, until we shall enter the palace of the New Jerusalem, and the reign of the Saints shall commence on earth."

"Pretty well begun already, friend Tomkins," said the keeper; "you are little short of being kings already upon the matter as it now stands; and for your Jerusalem I wot not, but Woodstock is a pretty nest-egg to begin with.— Well, will you shog—will you on—will you take sasine and livery?—You heard my orders."

"Umph—I know not," said Tomkins. "I must beware of ambuscades, and I am alone here. Moreover, it is the High Thanksgiving appointed by Parliament, and owned to by the army—also the old man and the young woman may want to recover some of their clothes and personal property, and I would not that they were balked on my account. Wherefore, if thou wilt deliver me possession to-morrow morning, it shall be done in personal presence of my own followers, and of the Presbyterian man the Mayor, so that the transfer may be made before witnesses; whereas, were there none with us but thou to deliver, and I to take possession, the men of Belial might say, Go to, Trusty Tomkins hath been an Edomite—Honest Joe hath been as an Ishmaelite, rising up early and dividing the spoil with them that served the Man—yea, they that wore beards and green jerkins, as in remembrance of the Man and of his government." *Revelation* xxi.

See note on Fifth Monarchy men, Chapter XI. Move on.

'In English law, "livery with seisin," an old form of conveying land.

A descendant of Esau,—an outlaw.

A son of Ishmael, "whose hand was against every man."

Joceline fixed his keen dark eyes upon the soldier as he spoke, as if in design to discover whether there was fair play in his mind or not. He then applied his five fingers to scratch a large shock head of hair, as if that operation was necessary to enable him to come to a conclusion. "This is all fair sounding, brother," said he; "but I tell you plainly, there are some silver mugs, and platters, and flagons, and so forth, in yonder house, which have survived the general sweep that sent all our plate to the smeltingpot, to put our knight's troop on horseback. Now, if thou takest not these off my hand, I may come to trouble, since it may be thought I have minished their numbers.— Whereas, I being as honest a fellow"

"As ever stole venison," said Tomkins—"nay, I do owe thee an interruption."

"Go to, then," replied the keeper; "if a stag may have come to mischance in my walk, it was no way in the course of dishonesty, but merely to keep my old dame's pan from rusting; but for silver porringers, tankards, and such like, I would have as soon drunk the melted silver as stolen the vessel made out of it. So that I would not wish blame or suspicion fell on me in this matter. And therefore, if you will have the things rendered even now,—why so—and if not, hold me blameless."

"Ay, truly?" said Tomkins; "and who is to hold me blameless, if they should see cause to think anything minished? Not the right worshipful Commissioners, to whom the property of the estate is as their own; therefore, as thou say'st, we must walk warily in the matter. To lock up the house and leave it, were but the work of simple ones. What say'st thou to spend the night there, and then nothing can be touched without the knowledge of us both?"

"Why, concerning that," answered the keeper, "I should be at my hut to make matters somewhat conformable for the old knight and Mistress Alice, for my old dame Joan is something dunny, and will scarce know how to manage—and yet, to speak the truth, by the mass I would rather not see Sir Henry to-night, since what has happened to-day hath roused his spleen, and it is a peradventure he may have met something at the hut which will scarce tend to cool it."

"It is a pity," said Tomkins, "that being a gentleman Deaf; dull of apprehension.

of such grave and goodly presence, he should be such a malignant cavalier, and that he should, like the rest of that generation of vipers, have clothed himself with curses as with a garment.''

"Which is as much as to say, the tough old knight hath a habit of swearing," said the keeper, grinning at a pun,

which has been repeated since his time; "but who can help it? it comes of use and wont. Were you now, in your bodily self, to light suddenly on a Maypole, with all the blithe morris-dancers prancing around it to the merry pipe and tabor, with bells jingling, ribands fluttering, lads frisking and laughing, lasses leaping till you might see where the scarlet garter fastened the light-blue hose, I think some feeling, resembling either natural sociality, or old use and wont would get the better, friend, even of thy gravity, and thou wouldst fling thy cuckoldy steeple-hat one way, and that blood-thirsty long sword another, and trip, like the noodles of Hogs-Norton, when the pigs play on the organ."

The independent turned fiercely round on the keeper, and replied, "How now, Mr. Green Jerkin? what language is this to one whose hand is at the plough? I advise thee to put curb on thy tongue, lest thy ribs pay the forfeit."

"Nay, do not take the high tone with me, brother," answered Joceline; "remember thou hast not the old knight of sixty-five to deal with, but a fellow as bitter and prompt as thyself—it may be a little more so—younger at all events—and prithee, why shouldst thou take such umbrage at a Maypole? I would thou hadst known one Phil Hazeldine of these parts—He was the best morris-dancer betwixt Oxford and Burford."

"The more shame to him," answered the Independent; "and I trust he has seen the error of his ways, and made himself (as, if a man of action, he easily might), fit for better company than wood-hunters, deer-stealers, Maid Marions, swash-bucklers, deboshed revellers, bloody brawlers, maskers, and mummers, lewd men and light women, fools and fiddlers, and carnal self-pleasers of every description." The May-day ceremonies were the object of special antipathy to the Puritans. "One ordinance directed that all the Maypoles in England should forthwith be hewn down."—Macaulay's *History*, Chapter II. Dancers, according to the Moorish fashion, who appeared in fantastic costumes.

'" An old English proverb, pointing to boorishness or stupidity."—D.
1 A market town seventeen miles from Oxford.

"Well," replied the keeper, "you are out of breath in time; for here we stand before the famous Maypole of Woodstock."

They paused in an open space of meadow-land, beautifully skirted by large oaks and sycamores, one of which, as king of the forest, stood a little detached from the rest, as if scorning the vicinity of any rival. It was scathed and gnarled in the branches, but the immense trunk still shewed to what gigantic size the monarch of the forest can attain in the groves of merry England.

"That is called the King's oak," said Joceline, "the oldest men of Woodstock know not how old it is; they say Henry used to sit under it with fair Rosamond, and see the lasses dance, and the lads of the village run races, and wrestle for belts or bonnets."

"I nothing doubt it, friend," said Tomkins; "a tyrant and a harlot were fitting patron and patroness for such vanities."

"Thou mayst say thy say, friend," replied the keeper, "so thou lettest me say mine. There stands the Maypole, as thou seest, half a flight-shot from the King's oak, in the midst of the meadow. The King gave ten shillings from the customs of Woodstock to make a new one yearly, besides a tree fitted for the purpose out of the forest. Now it is warped, and withered, and twisted, like a wasted brierrod. The green, too, used to be close-shaved, and rolled till it was smooth as a velvet mantle—now it is rough and overgrown."

"Well, well, friend Joceline," said the Independent, "but where was the edification of all this?—what use of doctrine could be derived from a pipe and tabor? or was there ever aught like wisdom in a bagpipe?"

"You may ask better scholars that," said Joceline, " but methinks men cannot be always grave, and with the hat over their brow. A young maiden will laugh as a tender flower will blow—ay, and a lad will like her the better for it; just as the same blithe Spring that makes the young birds whistle, bids the blithe fawns skip. There have come worse days since the jolly old times have gone by:— I tell thee, that in the holidays which you, Mr. Longsword, have put down, I have seen this greensward alive with merry maidens and manly fellows. The good old rector himself thought it was no sin to come for a while and look on, and his goodly cassock and scarf kept us all in good order, and taught us to limit our mirth within the bounds of discretion. We might, it may be, crack a broad jest, or pledge a friendly cup a turn too often, but it was in mirth and good neighbourhood—Ay, and if there was a bout at singlestick, or a bellyful of boxing, it was all for love and kindness; and better a few dry blows in drink, than the bloody doings we have had in sober earnest, since the presbyter's cap got above the bishop's mitre, and we exchanged our goodly rectors and learned doctors, whose sermons were all bolstered up with as much Greek and Latin as might have confounded the devil himself, for weavers and cobblers, and such other pulpit volunteers as—as we heard this morning—It will out." Robin Hood's sweetheart, an earl's daughter, who disguised herself as a page, and followed her lover to the merry greenwood. (See Tennyson's *Foresters.)* In the May-day morris-dance, a boy dressed in girl's clothes was introduced to represent her.

Debauched. Masked buffoons. An arrow's flight.

"Well, friend," said the Independent, with patience scarcely to have been expected, "I quarrel not with thee for nauseating my doctrine. If thine ear is so much tickled with tabor tunes and morris tripping, truly it is not likely thou shouldst find pleasant savour in more wholesome and sober food. But let us to the Lodge, that we may go about our business there before the sun sets."

"Troth, and that may be advisable for more reasons than one," said the keeper; "for there have been tales about the Lodge which have made men afeard to harbour there after nightfall."

"Were not yon old knight, and yonder damsel, his daughter, wont to dwell there?" said the Independent. "My information said so."

"Ay, truly did they," said Joceline; "and while they kept a jolly household, all went well enough; for nothing banishes fear like good ale. But after the best of our men A cudgel for use with one hand. A oout at single-stick or rather at veast, a game very closely allied to it, is well described in *Tom Brawn at Rugby,* Chapter II.

went to the wars, and were slain at Naseby fight, they who were left found the lodge more lonesome, and the old knight has been much deserted of his servants:—marry, it might be, that he has lacked silver of late to pay groom and lackey."

"A potential reason for the diminution of a household," said the soldier.

'' Eight, sir, even so," replied the keeper. "They spoke of steps in the great gallery, heard by dead of the night, and voices that whispered at noon in the matted chambers; and the servants pretended that these things scared them away; but in my poor judgment, when Martinmas and Whitsuntide came round without a penny-fee, the old blue-bottles of serving men began to think of creeping elsewhere before the frost chilled them—No devil so frightful as that which dances in the pocket where there is no cross to keep him out."

"You were reduced, then, to a petty household?" said the Independent.

"Ay, marry were we," said Joceline; "but we kept some half score together, what with blue-bottles in the Lodge, what with green caterpillars of the chase, like him who is yours to command; we stuck together till we found a call to take a morning's ride somewhere or other."

"To the town of Worcester," said the soldier, "where you were crushed like vermin and palmer worms, as you are."

"You may say your pleasure," replied the keeper; "I'll never contradict a man who has got my head under his belt. Our backs are at the wall or you would not be here."

"Nay, friend," said the Independent, "thou riskest nothing by thy freedom and trust in me. I can be *ion camarado* to a good soldier, although I have striven with him even to the going down of the sun.—But here we are in front of the Lodge."

They stood accordingly in front of the old Gothic building, irregularly constructed, and at different times, as the humour of the English monarchs led them to taste the pleasures of Woodstock Chase, and to make such improvements for their own accommodation as the increasing luxury of each age required. The oldest part of the structure had been named by tradition Fair Rosamond's Tower; it was a small turret of great height, with narrow windows, and walls of massive thickness. The tower had no opening to the ground, or means of descending, a great part of the lower portion being solid mason-work. It was traditionally said to have been accessible only by a sort of small drawbridge, which might be dropped at pleasure from a little portal near the summit of the turret, to the battlements of another tower of the same construction, but twenty feet lower, and containing only a winding staircase, called in Woodstock Love's Ladder; because, it is said, that by ascending this staircase to the top of the tower, and then making use of the drawbridge, Henry obtained access to the chamber of his paramour.

St. Martin's Day, November 11th. In Scotland, servants are then hired for the next half year, which terminates at Whitsuntide, or Pentecost Day. An allusion to the blue coats worn by house servants. A silver coin bearing a cross on its reverse. They were coined from William I. to James I. *I.e.,* the green-coated foresters. *Joel* i. 4. A nondescript foreign phrase for good comrade.

This tradition had been keenly impugned by Dr. Rochecliffe, the former rector of Woodstock, who insisted, that what was called Rosamond's Tower, was merely an interior keep, or citadel, to which the lord or warden of the castle might retreat, when other points of safety failed him; and either protract his defence, or, at the worst, stipulate for reasonable terms of surrender. The people of Woodstock, jealous of their ancient traditions, did not relish this new mode of explaining them away; and it is even said, that the Mayor, whom we have already introduced, became Presbyterian, in revenge of the doubts cast by the rector upon this important subject, rather choosing to give up the Liturgy than his fixed belief in Rosamond's Tower, and Love's Ladder.

The rest of the Lodge was of considerable extent, and of different ages; comprehending a nest of little courts, surrounded by buildings which corresponded with each other, sometimes within doors, sometimes by crossing the courts, and frequently in both ways. The different heights of the buildings announced that they could only be connected by the usual variety of staircases, which exercised the limbs of our ancestors in the sixteenth and earlier centuries, and seem sometimes to have been contrived for no other purpose.

The varied and multiplied fronts of this irregular building were, as Dr. Rochecliffe was wont to say, an absolute banquet to the architectural antiquary, as they certainly contained specimens of every style which existed, from the

Eure Norman1 of Henry of Anjou, down to the composite, alf Gothic half classical architecture of Elizabeth and her successor. Accordingly, the rector was himself as much enamoured of Woodstock as ever was Henry of Fair Rosamond; and as his intimacy with Sir Henry Lee permitted him entrance at all times to the Royal Lodge, he used to spend whole days in wandering about the antique apartments, examining, measuring, studying, and finding out excellent reasons for architectural peculiarities, which probably only owed their existence to the freakish fancy of a Gothic artist. But the old antiquary had been expelled from his living by the intolerance and troubles of the times, and his successor, Nehemiah Holdenough, would have considered an elaborate investigation of the profane sculpture and architecture of blinded and bloodthirsty Papists, together with the history of the dissolute amours of old Norman monarchs, as little better than a bowing down before the calves of Bethel, and a drinking of the cup of abominations.— We return to the course of our story.

"There is," said the Independent Tomkins, after he had carefully perused the front of the building, "many a rare monument of olden wickedness about this miscalled Royal Lodge; verily, I shall rejoice much to see the same destroyed, yea, burned to ashes, and the ashes thrown into the brook Kedron, or any other brook, that the land may be cleansed from the memory thereof, neither remember the iniquity with which their fathers have sinned." The keeper heard him with secret indignation, and began to consider with himself, whether, as they stood but one to one, and without chance of speedy interference, he was not called upon, by his official duty, to castigate the rebel who used language so defamatory. But he fortunately recollected, that the strife must be a doubtful one— that the advantage of arms was against him—and that, in especial, even if he should succeed in the combat, it would be at the risk of severe retaliation. It must be owned, too, that there was something about the Independent so dark and mysterious, so grim and grave, that the more open spirit of the keeper felt oppressed, and, if not overawed, at least kept in doubt concerning him; and he thought it wisest, as well as safest, for his master and himself, to avoid all subjects of dispute, and know better with whom he was dealing, before he made either friend or enemy of him.

A round-arched style of architecture, a variety of the Romanesque, introduced into Great Britain from Normandy before the Norman Conquest, and prevailing until the end of the twelfth century. Henry II. (reigned 1154-1189) was the son of Geoffrey V., Count of Anjou, and became the first Angevin king of England. Richard II. (1377-1309) was the last. A mingling of the pointed arches required by the Gothic style with the round arches and straight lintels of the Romanesque. A term for idolatry, frequently used in *Woodstock*. See 1 *Kingt* xii. 38-33. *Bev.* xvii. 4. 1 *Kings* xv. 13; 2 *Chronicles* xxx. 14.

The great gate of the Lodge was strongly bolted, but the wicket opened on Joceline's raising the latch. There was a short passage of ten feet, which had been formerly closed by a portcullis at the inner end, while three loopholes opened on either side, through which any daring intruder might be annoyed, who, having surprised the first gate, must be thus exposed to a severe fire before he could force the second. But the machinery of the portcullis was damaged, and it now remained a fixture, brandishing its jaw, well furnished with iron fangs, but incapable of dropping it across the path of invasion.

The way, therefore, lay open to the great hall or outer vestibule of the Lodge. One end of this long and dusky apartment was entirely occupied by a gallery, which had in ancient times served to accommodate the musicians and minstrels. There was a clumsy staircase at either side of it, composed of entire logs of a foot square; and in each angle of the ascent was placed, by way of sentinel, the figure of a Norman foot-soldier, having an open casque on his head, which displayed features as stern as the painter's genius could devise. Their arms were buff-jackets, or shirts of mail, round bucklers, with spikes in the centre, and buskins which adorned and defended the feet and ankles, but left the knees bare. These wooden warders held great swords, or maces, in their hands, like military guards on duty. Many an empty hook and brace, along the walls of the gloomy apartment, marked the spots from which arms, long preserved as trophies, had been, in the pressure of the wars, once more taken down to do service in the field, like veterans whom extremity of danger recalls to battle. On other rusty fastenings were still displayed the hunting trophies of the monarchs to whom the Lodge belonged, and of the silvan knights to whose care it had been from time to time confided.

At the nether end of the hall, a huge, heavy, stonewrought chimney-piece projected itself ten feet from the wall, adorned with many a cipher, and many

a scutcheon of the Royal House of England. In its present state, it yawned like the arched mouth of a funeral vault, or perhaps might be compared to the crater of an extinguished volcano. But the sable complexion of the massive stonework, and all around it, shewed that the time had been when it sent its huge fires blazing up the huge chimney, besides puffing many a volume of smoke over the heads of the jovial guests, whose royalty or nobility did not render them sensitive enough to quarrel with such slight inconvenience. On these occasions, it was the tradition of the house, that two cart-loads of wood was the regular allowance for the fire between noon and curfew, and the andirons, or dogs, as they were termed, constructed for retaining the blazing firewood on the hearth, were wrought in the shape of lions of such gigantic size, as might well warrant the legend. There were long seats of stone within the chimney, where, in despite of the tremendous heat, monarchs were sometimes said to have taken their station, and amused themselves with broiling the *umbles,* or *dotosets,* of the deer, upon the glowing embers, with their own royal hands, when happy the courtier who was invited to taste the royal cookery. Tradition was here also ready with her record, to shew what merry jibes, such as might be exchanged between prince and peer, had flown about at the jolly banquet which followed the Michaelmas hunt. She could tell too, exactly, where King Stephen sat when he darned his own princely hose, and knew most of the odd tricks he had put upon little Winkin, the tailor of Woodstock. Monogram. Entrails or similar choice morsels. 'September 29th, named in honor of the Archangel Michael.
Stephen of Blois (reigned 1135-1154), grandson of the Conqueror.
His traditional stinginess is referred to in an old ballad quoted in
Othello, II.; 3, 92:
"King Stephen was a worthy peere;
I trowe his hose cost but a crowne;
He held them sixpence all too deere,
With that he called the tailor clowne."

Most of this rude revelry belonged to the Plantagenet times. When the house of Tudor acceded to the throne, they were more chary of their royal presence, and feasted in halls and chambers far within, abandoning the outmost hall to the yeomen of the guard, who mounted their watch there and passed away the night with wassail and mirth, exchanged sometimes for frightful tales of apparitions and sorceries, which made some of those grow pale, in whose ears the trumpet of a French foeman would have sounded as jollily as a summons to the woodland chase.

Joceline pointed out the peculiarities of the place to his gloomy companion more briefly than we have detailed them to the reader. The Independent seemed to listen with some interest at first, but, flinging it suddenly aside, he said, in a solemn tone, "Perish, Babylon, as thy master Nebuchadnezzar hath perished! He is a wanderer, and thou shalt be a waste place—yea, and a wilderness—yea, a desert of salt, in which there shall be thirst and famine"

"There is like to be enough of both tonight," said Joceline, "unless the good knight's larder be somewhat fuller than it is wont."

"We must care for the creature-comforts," said the Independent, "but in due season, when our duties are done. — Whither lead these entrances?"

"That to the right," replied the keeper, "leads to what are called the state apartments, not used since the year sixteen hundred and thirty-nine, when his blessed Majesty" Probably a pure creation of Scott's fancy, on the hint afforded by the ballad just quoted.
"Name by which the Kings of the House of Anjou are generally known, taken from *planta genista,* the broom-plant.
The English sovereigns from Henry VII. (1485-1509) to Elizabeth (1558-1603) belonged to the house of Tudor, which was of Welsh origin. The great Babylonian King (see *Daniel iv.).* The allusion is probably both to Charles I., who had perished on the scaffold, and to Charles II., who was then a fugitive. Charles I. marched northward in this year to make terms with his reoellious Scotch subjects. As for his occupying the state apartments at Woodstock, compare Lady Margaret Bellenden's stock remark about entertaining her sovereign, in *Old Mortality.* "How, sir!" interrupted the Independent, in a voice of thunder, "dost thou speak of Charles Stuart as blessing, or blessed?—beware the proclamation to that effect."

"I meant no harm," answered the keeper, suppressing his disposition to make a harsher reply. "My business is with bolts and bucks, not with titles and state affairs. But yet, whatever may have happened since, that poor King was followed with blessings enough from Woodstock; for he left a glove full of broad pieces1 for the poor of the place"

"Peace, friend," said the Independent; "I will think thee else one of those besotted and blinded Papists, who hold, that bestowing of alms is an atonement and washing away of the wrongs and oppressions which have been wrought by the almsgiver. Thou sayest, then, these were the apartments of Charles Stuart?"

"And of his father, James, before him, and Elizabeth, before *him,* and bluff King Henry, who builded that wing, before them all."

"And there, I suppose, the knight and his daughter dwelt?"

"*No,"* replied Joceline; "Sir Henry Lee had too much reverence for—for things which are now thought worth no reverence at all—Besides, the state-rooms are unaired, and in indifferent order, since of late years. The Knight Ranger's apartment lies by that passage to the left."

"And whither goes yonder stair, which seems both to lead upwards and downwards?"

"Upwards," replied the keeper, "it leads to many apartments, used for various purposes, of sleeping, and other accommodation. Downwards, to the kitchen, offices and vaults of the castle, which, at this time of the evening, you cannot see without lights."

"We will to the apartments of your knight, then," said the Independent. "Is there fitting accommodation there?"

"Such as has served a person of condition, whose lodging is now worse appointed," answered the honest keeper, his bile rising so fast that he added, in a muttering and inaudible tone, "so it may well serve a crop-eared knave like thee." 1 A twenty-shilling gold coin, of the reign of James II. Scott never troubled himself about minor anachronisms of this kind. 'Henry VIII., "bluff King Hal." Apartments where the domestics perform their labours, etc

He acted as the usher however, and led on towards the ranger's apartments.

This suite opened by a short passage from the hall, secured at time of need by two oaken doors, which could be fastened by large bars of the same, that were drawn out of the wall, and entered into square holes, contrived for their reception on the other side of the portal. At the end of this passage a small anteroom received them, into which opened the sitting apartment of the good knight—which in the style of the times, might have been termed a fair summer parlour—lighted by two oriel windows, so placed as to command each of them a separate avenue, leading distant and deep into the forest. The principal ornament of the apartment, besides two or three family portraits of less interest, was a tall full-length picture, that hung above the chimney-piece, which, like that in the hall, was of heavy stonework, ornamented with carved scutcheons, emblazoned with various devices. The portrait was that of a man about fifty years of age, in complete plate armour, and painted in the harsh and dry manner of Holbein 1— probably, indeed, the work of that artist, as the dates corresponded. The formal and marked angles, points, and projections of the armour, were a good subject for the harsh pencil of that early school. The face of the knight was, from the fading of the colours, pale and dim, like that of some being from the other world, yet the lines expressed forcibly pride and exultation.

He pointed with his leading-staff, or truncheon, to the background, where, in such perspective as the artist possessed, were depicted the remains of a burning church, or monastery, and four or five soldiers, in red cassocks, bearing away in triumph what seemed a brazen font or laver. Above their heads might be traced in scroll, "*Lee Victor sic voluit.*" Right opposite to the picture, hung in a niche in the wall, a complete set of tilting armour, the black and gold colours, and ornaments of which, exactly corresponded with those exhibited in the portrait.

Hans Holbein the Younger (1497-1543), one of the most distinguished portrait painters who ever lived. His home was in London from 1532 till his death, and his pictures of Henry VIII. and the members of his court are among Holbein's most masterly works. "Harsh and dry," repeated a few lines below, is a curiously unsympathetic judgment on Scott's part. Victor Lee willed thus.

The picture was one of those which, from something marked in the features and expression, attract the observation even of those who are ignorant of art. The Independent looked at it until a smile passed transiently over his clouded brow. Whether he smiled to see the grim old cavalier employed in desecrating a religious house—(an occupation much conforming to the practice of his own sect) —whether he smiled in contempt of the old painter's harsh and dry mode of working—or whether the sight of this remarkable portrait revived some other ideas, the underkeeper could not decide.

The smile passed away in an instant, as the soldier looked to the oriel windows. The recesses within them were raised a step or two from the wall. In one was placed a walnut-tree reading-desk, and a huge stuffed arm-chair, covered with Spanish leather. A little cabinet stood beside, with some of its shuttles and drawers open, displaying hawks-bells, dog-whistles, instruments for trimming falcons' feathers, bridle-bits of various constructions, and other trifles connected with sylvan sport.

The other little recess was differently furnished. There lay some articles of needle-work on a small table, besides a lute, with a book having some airs written down in it, and a frame for working embroidery. Some tapestry was displayed around the recess, with more attention to ornament than was visible in the rest of the apartment; the arrangement of a few bow-pots, with such flowers as the fading season afforded, shewed also the superintendence of female taste.

Tomkins cast an eye of careless regard upon these subjects of female occupation, then stepped into the farther window, and began to turn the leaves of a folio, which lay open on the reading-desk, apparently with some interest. Joceline, who had determined to watch his motions without interfering with them, was standing at some distance in dejected silence, when a door behind the tapestry suddenly opened, and a pretty village maid tripped out with a napkin in her hand, as if she had been about some household duty.

Armour used in the tournament. The bolts of a door. Bough-pots, vases for holding boughs or flowers for ornament.

"How now, Sir Impudence?" she said to Joceline, in a smart tone; "what do you here prowling about the apartments when the master is not at home?"

But instead of the answer which perhaps she expected, Joceline Joliffe cast a mournful glance towards the soldier in the oriel window, as if to make what he said fully intelligible, and replied with a dejected appearance and voice, "Alack, my pretty Phoebe, there come those here that have more right or might than any of us, and will use little ceremony in coming when they will, and staying while they please."

He darted another glance at Tomkins, who still seemed busy with the book before him, then sidled close to the astonished girl, who had continued looking alternately at the keeper and at the stranger, as if she had been unable to understand the words of the first, or to comprehend the meaning of the second being present.

"Go," whispered Joliffe, approaching his mouth so near her cheek, that his breath waved the curls of her hair; "go, my dearest Phoebe, trip it as fast as a fawn down to my lodge—I will soon be there, and"

"Your lodge, indeed!" said Phoebe; "you are very bold, for a poor killbuck that never frightened any thing before save a dun deer—*Your* lodge, indeed!—I am like to go there, I think."

"Hush, hush! Phoebe—here is no time for jesting. Down to my hut, I say, like a deer, for the knight and Mrs. Alice are both there, and I fear will not return hither again.—All's naught, girl—and our evil days are come at last with a vengeance—we are fairly at bay and fairly hunted down."

"Can this be, Joceline ?" said the poor girl, turning to the keeper with an expression of fright in her countenance, which she had hitherto averted in rural coquetry.

"As sure, my dearest Phœbe, as"

The rest of the asseveration was lost in Phoebe's ear, so closely did the keeper's lips approach it; and if they approached so very near as to touch her cheek, grief, like impatience, hath its privileges, and poor Phoebe had enough of serious alarm to prevent her from demurring upon such a trifle.

But no trifle was the approach of Joceline's lips to Phoebe's pretty though sunburnt cheek, in the estimation of the Independent, who, a little before the object of Joceline's vigilance, had been more lately in his turn the observer of the keeper's demeanour, so soon as the interview betwixt Phoebe and him had become so interesting. And when he remarked the closeness of Joceline's argument, he raised his voice to a pitch of harshness, that would have rivalled that of an ungreased and rusty saw, and which at once made Joceline and Phoebe spring six feet apart, each in contrary directions, and if Cupid was of the party, must have sent him out at the window like a wild duck flying from a culverin. Instantly throwing himself into the attitude of a preacher and a reprover of vice, "How now!" he exclaimed, "shameless and impudent as you are!— What—chambering and wantoning in our very presence!— How—would you play your pranks before the steward of the Commissioners of the High Court of Parliament, as ye would in a booth at the fulsome fair, or amidst the trappings and tracings of a profane dancing-school, where the scoundrel minstrels make their ungodly weapons to squeak, 'Kiss and be kind, the fiddler's blind?'—But here," he said, dealing a perilous thump upon the volume—" Here is the King and high priest of those vices and follies!— Here is he, whom men of folly profanely call nature's miracle!—Here is he, whom princes chose for their cabinetkeeper, and whom maids of honour take for their bed-fellow!—Here is the prime teacher of fine words, foppery and folly—Here!"—(dealing another thump upon the volume—and oh! revered of the Roxburghe, it was the first folio—beloved of the Bannatyne, it was Hemmings and Condel—it was the *editio princeps*)—" On thee," he continued—" on thee, William Shakspeare, I charge whate'er of such lawless idleness and immodest folly hath defiled the land since thy day!" The largest gun used in the sixteenth century, sometimes of extraordinary length.

A book club, instituted in London in 1812, at the time of the sale of the library of John, Duke of Roxburghe, for printing a limited number of old and rare books. An Edinburgh club, named after George Bannatyne, the collector of Scotch poetry. It was founded in 1823, by Sir Walter and others, for printing rare works illustrating Scottish history, literature, etc. It was dissolved in 1861. John Hemminge, or Heming, and Henry Condell were fellowactors with Shakespeare, and published in 1623 the first folio edition of his collected plays. First edition.

"By the mass, a heavy accusation," said Joceline, the bold recklessness of whose temper could not be long overawed; "Odds pitlikins, is our master's old favourite, Will of Stratford, to answer for every buss that has been snatched since James's time?—a perilous reckoning truly—but I wonder who is sponsible for what lads and lasses did before his day?"

"Scoff not," said the soldier, "lest I, being called thereto by the voice within me, do deal with thee as a scorner. Verily I say, that since the devil fell from Heaven, he never lacked agents on earth; yet nowhere hath he met with a wizard having such infinite power over men's souls as this pestilent fellow Shakspeare. Seeks a wife a foul example for adultery, here she shall find it— Would a man know how to train his fellow to be a murderer, here shall he find tutoring—Would a lady marry a heathen negro, she shall have chronicled example for it—Would any one scorn at his Maker, he shall be furnished with a jest in this book—Would he defy his brother in the flesh, he shall be accommodated with a challenge—Would you be drunk, Shakspeare will cheer you with a cup—Would you plunge in sensual pleasures, he will soothe you to indulgence, as with the lascivious sounds of a lute. This, I say, this book is the wellhead and source of all those evils which have overrun the land like a torrent, making men scoffers, doubters, deniers, murderers, makebates, and lovers of the wine-pot, haunting unclean places, and sitting long at the evening-wine. Away with him, away with him, men of England! to Tophet with his wicked book, and to the Vale of Hinnom with his accursed bones! Verily but that our march was hasty when we passed Stratford, in the year 1643, with Sir William Waller; but that our march was hasty" Exciters of quarrels.

'Literally, "a place to be spit upon," situated at the extremity of Gehenna or the Valley of Hinnom, to the south of Jerusalem. There the idolatrous Jews had worshipped the fire-gods, and a perpetual fire was kept for burning carcasses. It became the symbol for the place of torment in the future life.

An English general, at one time second in command of the Parliamentary forces. "Because Prince Rupert 1 was after you with his cavaliers," muttered the incorrigible Joceline.

"I say," continued the zealous trooper, raising his voice and extending his arm—" but that our march was by command hasty, and that we turned not aside in our riding, closing our ranks each one upon the other as becomes men of war, I had torn on that day the bones of that preceptor of vice and debauchery from the grave, and given them to the next dunghill. I would have made his memory a scoff and a hissing!"

"That is the bitterest thing he has said yet," observed the keeper. "Poor Will would have liked the hissing worse than all the rest."

"Will the gentleman say any more?" inquired Phoebe in a whisper. "Lack-a-day, he talks brave words, if one knew but what they meant. But it is a mercy our good knight did not see him ruffle the book at that rate—Mercy on us, there would certainly have been bloodshed.—But oh, the father—see how he is twisting his face about!— Is he ill of the colic, think'st thou, Joceline? Or, may I offer him a glass of strong waters?"

"Hark thee hither, wench!" said the keeper, "he is but loading his blunderbuss for another volley; and while he turns up his eyes, and twists about his face, and clenches his fist, and shuffles and tramples with his feet in that fashion, he is bound to take no notice of anything. I would be sworn to cut his purse, if he had one, from his side, without his feeling it."

"La! Joceline," said Phoebe, "and if he abides here in this turn of times, I dare say the gentleman will be easily served."

"Care not thou about that," said Joliffe; "but tell me softly and hastily, what is in thelpantry?"

"Small housekeeping enough," said Phoebe; "a cold capon and some comfits, and the great standing venison pasty, with plenty of spice—a manchet1 or two besides, and that is all." Prince Rupert of the Palatinate (1619-1683), grandson of James I. of England. He served in the thirty years' war against the Imperialists, and at the outbreak of the English civil war his uncle, Charles I., made him the commander-in-chief of the Royalist cavalry. He was famous for his dashing qualities, hut was beaten by Cromwell at Marston Moor and Naseby. After the Restoration he was a privy councillor and admiral of the fleet.
Having been an actor. An expletive.
"Well, it will serve for a pinch—wrap thy cloak round thy comely body—get a basket and a brace of trenchers and towels, they are heinously impoverished down yonder— carry down the capon and the manchets—the pasty must abide with this same soldier and me, and the pie-crust will serve us for bread."

"Rarely," said Phoebe; "I made the paste myself—it is as thick as the walls of Fair Rosamond's Tower."

"Which two pairs of jaws would be long in gnawing through, work hard as they might," said the keeper. "But what liquor is there?

"Only a bottle of Alicant, and one of sack, with the stone jug of strong waters," answered Phoebe.

"Put the wine-flasks into thy basket," said Joceline, "the knight must not lack his evening draught—and down with thee to the hut like a lapwing. There is enough for supper, and to-morrow is a new day.—Ha! by heaven I thought yonder man's eye watched us—No—he only rolled it round him in a brown study—Deep enough doubtless, as they all are.—But d—n him, he must be bottomless if I cannot sound him before the night's out.—Hie thee away Phoebe."

But Phoebe was a rural coquette, and, aware that Joceline's situation gave him no advantage of avenging the challenge in a fitting way, she whispered in his ear, "Do you think our knight's friend, Shakspeare, really found out all these naughty devices the gentleman spoke of?"

Off she darted while she spoke, while Joliffe menaced future vengeance with his finger, as he muttered, "Go thy way, Phoebe Mayflower, the lightest-footed and lightest-hearted wench that ever tripped the sod in Woodstockpark!—After her, Bevis, and bring her safe to our master at the hut."

The large greyhound arose like a human servitor who had received an order, and followed Phoebe through the hall, first licking her hand to make her sensible of his presence, and then putting himself to a slow trot, so as best to accommodate himself to the light pace of her whom he convoyed, whom Joceline had not extolled for her ac A loaf of fine white bread.
A strong dark wine brought from Alicante in Spain. tivity without due reason. While Phoebe and her guardian thread the forest glades, we return to the Lodge.

The Independent now seemed to start as if from a reverie. "Is the young woman gone?" said he.

"Ay, marry is she," said the keeper, "and if your worship hath farther commands, you must rest contented with male attendance."

"Commands—umph—I think the damsel might have tarried for another exhortation," said the soldier—" truly I profess my mind was much inclined toward her for her edification."

"Oh, sir," replied Joliffe, "she will be at church next Sunday, and if your military reverence is pleased again to hold forth amongst us, she will have use of the doctrine with the rest. But young maidens of these parts hear no private homilies.—And what is now your pleasure? Will you look at the other rooms, and at the few plate articles which have been left?"

"Umph—no," said the Independent—" it wears late, and gets dark—thou hast the means of giving us beds, friend?"

"Better you never slept in," replied the keeper.

"And wood for a fire, and a light, and some small pittance of creature-comforts for refreshment of the outward man?" continued the soldier.

"Without doubt," replied the keeper, displaying a prudent anxiety to gratify this important personage.

In a few minutes a great standing candlestick was placed on an oaken table. The mighty venison pasty, adorned with parsley, was placed on the board on a clean napkin; the stone-bottle of strong waters, with a black-jack full of ale, formed comfortable appendages; and to this meal sat down in social manner the soldier, occupying a great elbow-chair, and the keeper, at his invitation, using the more lowly accommodation of a stool, at the opposite side of the table. Thus agreeably employed, our history leaves them for the present.
A rude drinking vessel, commonly of leather.

Study the conversation of Joliffe and Tomkins as affording an example of character-contrast. Compare Joliffe and Phoebe with other serving-men and serving-women of Scott *Old Mortality, Mob Boy,* etc.). Compare the description of the palace at Woodstock with those of similar buildings in *Kenilwortli, Quentin Durward, Ivanhoe,* and elsewhere.

CHAPTER THE FOURTH Yon path of greensward
Winds round by sparry grot and gay pavilion;
There is no flint to gall thy tender foot,
There's ready shelter from each breeze, or shower.—
But Duty guides not that way—see her stand,
With wand entwined with amaranth, near yon cliffs.
Oft where she leads thy blood must mark thy footsteps,
Oft where Rhe leads thy head must bear the storm,
And thy shrunk form endure heat, cold, and hunger;
But she will guide thee up to noble heights,
Which he who gains seems native of the sky,
While earthly things lie stretched beneath his feet,
Diminished, shrunk, and valueless
   Anonymous.

The reader cannot have forgotten that after his scuffle with the commonwealth soldier, Sir Henry Lee, with his daughter Alice, had departed to take refuge in the hut of the stout keeper Jooeline Joliffe. They walked slow, as before, for the old knight was at once oppressed by perceiving these last vestiges of royalty fall into the hands of republicans, and by the recollection of his recent defeat. At times he paused, and, with his arms folded on his bosom, recalled all the circumstances attending his expulsion from a house so long his home. It seemed to him that, like the champions of romance of whom he had sometimes read, he himself was retiring from the post which it was his duty to guard, defeated by a Paynim knight, for whom the adventure had been reserved by fate.

Alice had her own painful subjects of recollection, nor had the tenor of her last conversation with her father been so pleasant as to make her anxious to renew it until his temper should be more composed; for with an excellent disposition, and much love to his daughter, age and misfortunes, which of late came thicker and thicker, had given to the good knight's passions a wayward irritability unknown to his See note on the motto of Chapter II.
better days. His daughter, and one or two attached servants, who still followed his decayed fortunes, soothed his frailty as much as possible, and pitied him even while they suffered under its effects.

It was a long time ere he spoke, and then he referred to an incident already noticed. "It is strange," he said, "that Bevis should have followed Joceline and that fellow rather than me."

"Assure yourself, sir," replied Alice, "that his sagacity saw in this man a stranger, whom he thought himself obliged to watch circumspectly, and therefore he remained with Joceline."

"Not so, Alice," answered Sir Henry; "he leaves me because my fortunes have fled from me. There is a feeling in nature, affecting even the instinct, as it is called, of dumb animals, which teaches them to fly from misfortune. The very deer there will butt a sick or wounded buck from the herd; hurt a dog, and the whole kennel will fall on him and worry him; fishes devour their own kind when they are wounded with a spear; cut a crow's wing, or break its leg, the others will buffet it to death."

"That may be true of the more irrational kinds of animals among each other," said Alice, "for their whole life is well-nigh a warfare; but the dog leaves his own race to attach himself to ours; forsakes, for his master, the company, food, and pleasure of his own kind; and surely the fidelity of such a devoted and voluntary servant as Bevis hath been in particular, ought not to be lightly suspected."

"I am not angry with the dog, Alice; I am only sorry," replied her father. "I have read, in faithful chronicles, that when Richard II. and Henry of Bolingbroke were at Berkeley Castle, a dog of the same kind deserted the King, whom he had always attended upon, and attached himself to Henry, whom he then saw for the first time. Richard foretold, from the desertion of his favourite, his approaching deposition. The dog was afterwards kept at Woodstock, and Bevis is said to be of his breed, which was heedfully kept up. What I might foretell of mischief from his desertion, I cannot guess, but my mind assures me it bodes no good."

The story occurs, I think, in Froissart's Chronicles. Scott. Vol. IV., chap. 132, of Johnes's translation.—D. Bolingbroke was the cousin of Richard, but conquered him in 1399 and was crowned as Henry IV. See Shakespeare's *Richard II.* and *Henry IV.*
There was a distant rustling among the withered leaves, a bouncing or galloping sound on the path, and the favourite dog instantly joined his master.

"Come into court, old knave," said Alice cheerfully, "and defend thy character, which is well-nigh endangered by this absence." But the dog only paid her courtesy by gamboling around them, and instantly plunged back again, as fast as he could scamper.

"How now, knave? said the knight; "thou art too well trained, surely, to take up the chase without orders." A minute more shewed them Phoebe Mayflower approaching, her light pace so little impeded by the burden which she bore, that she joined her master and young mistress just as they arrived at the keeper's hut, which was the boundary of their journey. Bevis, who had shot ahead to pay his compliments to Sir Henry his master, had returned again to his immediate duty, the escorting Phoebe and her cargo of provisions. The whole party stood presently assembled before the door of the keeper's hut.

In better times, a substantial stone habitation, fit for the yeoman-keeper of a royal walk, had adorned this place. A fair spring gushed out near the spot, and once traversed yards and courts, attached to well-built and convenient kennels and mews. But in some of the skirmishes which were common during the civil wars, this little silvan dwelling had been attacked and defended, stormed and burnt. A neighbouring squire, of the Parliament side of the question, took advantage of Sir Henry Lee's absence, who was then in Charles's camp, and of the decay of the royal cause, and had, without scruple, carried off the hewn stones, and such building materials as the fire left unconsumed, and repaired his own manor-house with them. The yeomankeeper, therefore, our friend Joceline, had constructed, for his own accommodation, and that of the old woman he called his dame, a wattled hut, such as his own labour, with that of a neighbour or two, had erected in the course of a few days. The walls were plastered with clay, whitewashed, and covered with vines and other creeping plants; Where falcons were kept. The term is now applied to the royal stables. the roof was neatly thatched, and the whole, though merely a hut, had, by the neat-handed Joliffe, been so arranged as not to disgrace the condition of the dweller.

The knight advanced to the entrance; but the ingenuity of the architect, for want of a better lock to the door, which itself was but of wattles curiously twisted, had contrived a mode of securing the latch on the inside with a pin, which prevented it from rising; and in this manner it was at present fastened. Conceiving that this was some precaution of Joliffe's old housekeeper, of whose deafness they were all aware, Sir Henry raised his voice to demand admittance, but in vain. Irritated at this delay, he pressed the door at once with foot and hand, in a way which the frail barrier was unable to resist; it gave way accordingly, and the knight thus forcibly entered the kitchen, or outward apartment, of his servant. In the midst of the floor, and with a posture which indicated embarrassment, stood a youthful stranger, in a riding-suit.

"This may be my last act of authority here," said the knight, seizing the stranger by the collar, "but I am still Hanger of Woodstock for this night at least—Who, or what art thou?"

The stranger dropped the riding-mantle in which his face was muffled, and at the same time fell on one knee.

"Your poor kinsman, Markham Everard," he said, ' who came hither for your sake, although he fears you will scarce make him welcome for his own.

Sir Henry started back, but recovered himself in an instant, as one who recollected that he had a part of dignity to perform. He stood erect, therefore, and replied, with considerable assumption of stately ceremony:

"Fair kinsman, it pleases me that you are come to Woodstock upon the very first night that, for many years which have past, is likely to promise you a worthy or a welcome reception."

"Now God grant it be so, that I rightly hear and duly understand you," said the young man; while Alice, though she was silent, kept her looks fixed on her father's face, as if desirous to know whether his meaning was kind towards his nephew, which her knowledge of his character inclined her greatly to doubt.

The knight meanwhile darted a sardonic look, first on his nephew, then on his daughter, and proceeded—"I need not, I presume, inform Mr. Markham Everard, that it cannot be our purpose to entertain him, or even to offer him a seat in this poor hut."

"I will attend you most willingly to the Lodge," said the young gentleman. "I had, indeed, judged you were already there for the evening, and feared to intrude upon you. But if you would permit me, my dearest uncle, to escort my kinswoman and you back to the Lodge, believe me, amongst all which you have so often done of good and kind, you never conferred benefit that will be so dearly prized."

"You mistake me greatly, Mr. Markham Everard," replied the knight. "It is not our purpose to return to the Lodge to-night, nor, by Our Lady, to-morrow neither. I meant but to intimate to you in all courtesy, that at Woodstock Lodge you will find those for whom you are fitting society, and who, doubtless, will afford you a willing welcome, which I, sir, in this my present retreat, do not presume to offer to a person of your consequence."

"For heaven's sake," said the young man, turning to Alice, "tell me how I am to understand language so mysterious."

Alice, to prevent his increasing the restrained anger of her father, compelled herself to answer, though it was with difficulty, "We are expelled from the Lodge by soldiers."

"Expelled—by soldiers!" exclaimed Everard, in surprise—" there is no legal warrant for this."

"None at all," answered the knight, in the same tone of cutting irony which he had all along used, "and yet as lawful a warrant, as for aught that has been wrought in England this twelvemonth and more. You are, I think, or were, an Inns-of-Court-man—marry, sir, your enjoyment of your profession is like that lease which a prodigal wishes to have of a wealthy widow. You have already survived the law which you studied, and its expiry doubtless has not been without a legacy—some decent pickings, some merciful increases, as the phrase goes. You have deserved it two ways—you wore buff and bandolier, as well as wielded pen and ink—I have not heard if you held forth too." The Virgin Mary. A lawyer. The Inns of Court are the legal societies in London which have the exclusive privilege of calling candidates to the bar. The term is also used of the premises occupied by the societies. There are four Inns of Court: the Inner Temple, Middle Temple, Lincoln's Inn, and Gray's Inn. The first two originally belonged to the Knights Templars, whence the name.

"Think of me and speak of me as harshly as you will, sir," said Everard, submissively. "I have but, in this evil time, guided myself by my conscience, and my father's commands."

"0, an you talk of conscience," said the old knight, *"I must have mine eye upon you, as Hamlet says. Never yet did Puritan cheat so grossly as when'he was appealing to his conscience; and as for thy *father*"

He was about to proceed in a tone of the same invective, when the young man interrupted him, by saying, in a firm tone, "Sir Henry Lee, you have ever been thought noble—Say of me what you will, but, speak not of my father what the ear of a son should not endure, and which yet his arm cannot resent. To do me such wrong is to insult an unarmed man, or to beat a captive."

Sir Henry paused, as if struck by the remark. "Thou hast spoken truth in that, Mark, wert thou the blackest Puritan whom hell ever vomited, to distract an unhappy country."

"Be that as you will to think it," replied Everard; "but let me not leave you to the shelter of this wretched hovel. The night is drawing to storm—let me but conduct you to the Lodge, and expel those intruders, who can, as yet at least, have no warrant for what they do. I will not linger a moment behind them, save just to deliver my father's message.—Grant me but this much, for the love you once bore me!"

"Yes, Mark," answered his uncle, firmly, but sorrowfully, "thou speakest truth—I did love thee once. The bright-haired boy whom I taught to ride, to shoot, to hunt— whose hours of happiness were spent with me, wherever those of graver labours were employed—I did love that boy —ay, and I am weak enough to love even the memory of what he was.—But he is gone, Mark—he is gone; and in his room I only behold an avowed and determined rebel to his religion and to his king—a rebel more detestable on account of his success, the more infamous through the plundered wealth with which he hopes to gild his villany *Hamlet,* IL, 2, 301.

But I am poor, thou think'st, and should hold my peace, lest men say, 'Speak, sirrah, when you should.'—Know, however, that, indigent and plundered as I am, I feel myself dishonoured in holding even but this much talk with the tool of usurping rebels.—Go to the Lodge, if thou wilt —yonder lies the way—but think not that, to regain my dwelling there, or all the wealth I ever possessed in my wealthiest days, I would willingly accompany thee three steps on the greensward. If I must be thy companion, it shall be only when thy red-coats have tied my hands behind me, and bound my legs beneath my horse's belly. Thou mayst be my fellow traveller then, I grant thee, if thou wilt, but not sooner."

Alice, who suffered cruelly during this dialogue, and was well aware that farther argument would only kindle the knight's resentment still more highly, ventured at last, in her anxiety, to make a sign to her cousin to break off the interview, and to retire, since her father commanded his absence in a manner so peremptory. Unhappily she was observed by Sir Henry, who, concluding that what he saw was evidence of a private understanding betwixt the cousins, his wrath acquired new fuel, and it required the utmost exertion of self-command, and recollection of all that was due to his own dignity, to enable him to veil his real fury under the same ironical manner which he had adopted at the beginning of this angry interview.

"If thou art afraid," he said, "to trace our forest glades by night, respected stranger, to whom I am perhaps bound to do honour as my successor in the charge of these walks, here seems to be a modest damsel, who will be most willing to wait on thee, and be thy bow-bearer.—Only, for her mother's sake, let there pass some slight form of marriage between you—Ye need no license or priest in these happy days, but may be buckled like beggars in a ditch, with a hedge for a church-roof, and a tinker for a priest. I crave pardon of you for making such an officious and simple request—peryou are a Ranter—or one of the family of Love, or 1 *Henry VI.,* 111,1,62.
" Familists," a division of the Anabaptists, or adherents to the doctrine of adult baptism, who were notorious in England during the times of Queen Elizabeth and James I. See Scott's note in Chapter UIX. hold marriage rites as unnecessary, as Knipperdoling, or Jack of Leyden *?"*

"For mercy's sake, forbear such dreadful jesting, my father! and do you, Markham, begone, in God's name, and leave us to our fate—Your presence makes my father rave."

"Jesting!" said Sir Henry, "I was never more serious —Raving!—I was never more composed—I could never brook that falsehood should approach me—I would no more bear by my side a dishonoured daughter than a dishonoured sword; and this unhappy day hath shewn that both can fail."

"Sir Henry," said young Everard, "load not your soul with a heavy crime, which be assured you do, in treating your daughter thus unjustly. It is long now since you denied her to me, when we were poor and you were powerful. I acquiesced in your prohibition of all suit and intercourse. God knoweth what I suffered—but I acquiesced. Neither is it to renew my suit that I now come hither, and have, I do acknowledge, sought speech of her—not for her own sake only, but for yours also. Destruction hovers over you, ready to close her pinions to stoop, and her talons to clutch—Yes, sir, look contemptuous as you will, such is the case; and it is to protect both you and her that I am here."

"You refuse then my free gift," said Sir Henry Lee; "or perhaps you think it loaded with too hard conditions?"

"Shame, shame on you, Sir Henry!" said Everard, waxing warm in his turn; "have your political prejudices so utterly warped every feeling of a father, that you can speak with bitter mockery and scorn of what concerns your dwn daughter's honour?—Hold up your head, fair Alice, and tell your father he has forgotten nature in his fantastic spirit of loyalty.—Know, Sir Henry, that though I would prefer your daughter's hand to every blessing which Heaven could bestow on me, I would not accept it—my conscience would not permit me to do so— when I knew it must withdraw her from her duty to you." An Anabaptist leader at Mtinster in Westphalia in 1534-35.
Johann Bockhold, who was crowned " King of the new Zion " that the Anabaptists established at Minister. They indulged in the wildest excesses. Their leader, who was finally taken prisoner and tortured, is the hero of Meyerbeer's opera, *The Prupliet.*

"Your conscience is over scrupulous, young man;— carry it to some dissenting rabbi, and he who takes all that comes to net, will teach thee it is sinning against our mercies to refuse any good thing that is freely offered to us."

"When it is freely offered, and kindly offered—not when the offer is made in irony and insult—Fare thee well, Alice—if aught could make me desire to profit by thy father's wild wish to cast thee from him in a moment of unworthy suspicion, it would be that while indulging in such sentiments, Sir Henry Lee is tyrannically oppressing the creature, who of all others is most dependent on his kindness—who of all others will most feel his severity, and whom, of all others, he is most bound to cherish and support."

"Do not fear for me, Mr. Everard," exclaimed Alice, aroused from her timidity by a dread of the consequences not unlikely to ensue, where civil war sets relations, as well as fellow-citizens, in opposition to each other.—" Oh, begone, I conjure you, begone. Nothing stands betwixt me and my father's kindness, but these unhappy family divisions—but your ill-timed presence here—For Heaven s sake, leave us!"

"Soh, mistress!" answered the hot old cavalier, "you play lady paramount already; and who but you!—you would dictate to our train, I warrant, like Goneril and Regan! But I tell thee no man shall leave my house— and, humble as it is, *this* is now my house—while he has aught to say to me that is to be spoken, as this young man now speaks, with a bent brow and a lofty tone.—Speak out, sir, and say your worst!"

"Fear not my temper, Mrs. Alice," said Everard, with equal firmness and placidity of manner; "and you, Sir Henry, do not think that if I speak firmly, I mean therefore to speak in anger, or officiously. You have taxed me with much, and, were I guided by the wild spirit of romantic chivalry, much which, even from so near a relative, I ought not, as being by birth, and in the world's estimation, a gentleman, to pass over without reply. Is it your pleasure to give me patient hearing?" Some clergyman among the Dissenters from the Church of England.

The daughters of King Lear, who diminished the numbers of his retinue; *Lear* I., 4, 27U. Shakespeare's delineation of King Lear and his faithful daughter Cordelia has unmistakably influenced Scott's characterization of Sir Henry Lee and his daughter Alice. The relation of Scott's own daughter to him at the time of his misfortunes has already been commented upon, but should be kept in mind throughout many of the scenes between Alice and Sir Henry.

"If you stand on your defence," answered the stout old knight, "God forbid that you should not challenge a patient hearing—aye, though your pleading were two parts disloyalty and one blasphemy—Only, be brief—this has already lasted but too long."

"I will, Sir Henry," replied the young man; "yet it is hard to crowd into a few sentences, the defence of a life which, though short, has been a busy one—too busy, your indignant gesture would assert. But I deny it; I have drawn my sword neither hastily, nor without due consideration, for a people whose rights have been trampled on, and whose consciences have been oppressed—Frown not, sir—such is not your view of the contest, but such is mine. For my religious principles, at which you have scoffed, believe me, that though they depend not on set forms, they are no less sincere than your own, and thus far purer—excuse the word—that they are unmingled with the bloodthirsty dictates of a barbarous age, which you and others have called the code of chivalrous honour. Not my own natural disposition, but the better doctrine which my creed has taught, enables me to bear your harsh revilings without answering in a similar tone of wrath and reproach. You may carry insult to extremity against me at your pleasure—not on account of your relationship alone, but because I am bound in charity to endure it. This, Sir Henry, is much from one of our house. But, with forbearance far more than this requires, I can refuse at your hands the gift, which, most of all things under Heaven, I should desire to obtain, because duty calls upon her to sustain and comfort you, and because it were sin to permit you, in your blindness, to spurn your comforter from your side.—Farewell, sir—not in anger but in pity—We may meet in a better time, when your heart and your principles shall master the unhappy prejudices by which they are now overclouded.—Farewell—farewell, Alice!"

The last words were repeated twice, and in a tone of feeling and passionate grief, which differed utterly from the steady and almost severe tone in which he had addressed Sir Henry Lee. He turned and left the hut so soon as he had uttered these last words; and, as if ashamed of the tenderness which had mingled with his accents, the young common weal th's-man turned and walked sternly and resolvedly forth into the moonlight, which now was spreading its broad light and autumnal shadows over the woodland.

Note, however, that in a later chapter Everard's action is not quite consistent with this speech.

So soon as he departed, Alice, who had been during the whole scene in the utmost terror that her father might have been hurried, by his natural heat of temper, from violence of language into violence of action, sunk down upon a settle twisted out of willow-boughs, like most of Joceline's few movables, and endeavoured to conceal the tears which accompanied the thanks she rendered in broken accents to Heaven, that, notwithstanding the near alliance and relationship of the parties, some fatal deed had not closed an interview so perilous and so angry. Phoebe Mayflower blubbered heartily for company, though she understood but little of what had passed; just, indeed, enough to enable her afterwards to report to some half-dozen particular friends, that her old master, Sir Henry, had been perilous angry, and almost fought with young Master Everard, because he had wellnigh carried away her young mistress.—" And what could he have done better?" said Phoebe, "seeing the old man had nothing left either for Mrs. Alice or himself; and as for Mr. Mark Everard, and our young lady, oh! they had spoken such loving things to each other, as are not to be found in the history of Argalus and Parthenia, who, as the story-book tells, were the truest pair of lovers in all Arcadia, and Oxfordshire to boot."

Old Goody Jellycot had popped her scarlet hood into the kitchen more than once while the scene was proceeding; but as the worthy dame was parcel blind, and more than parcel deaf, knowledge was excluded by two principal entrances; and though she comprehended, by a sort of general instinct, that the gentlefolk were at high words, yet why they chose Joceline's hut for the scene of their dispute, was as great a mystery as the subject of the quarrel.

But what was the state of the old cavalier's mood, thus contradicted, as his most darling principles had been, by the last words of his departing nephew? The truth is, that he was less thoroughly moved than his daughter expected; and in all probability his nephew's bold defence of his religious and political opinions rather pacified than aggravated his displeasure. Although sufficiently impatient of contradiction, still evasion and subterfuge were more alien to the blunt old Ranger's nature than manly vindication and direct opposition; and he was wont to say, that he ever loved the buck best who stood boldest at bay. He graced his nephew's departure, however, with a quotation from Shakspeare, whom, as many others do, he was wont to quote from a sort of habit and respect, as a favourite of his unfortunate master, without having either much real taste for his works, or great skill in applying the passages which he retained on his memory.

The Most Pleasant and Delightful History of Argalus and Parthenia was a chapbook very popular in the seventeenth century. Laing. The plot is drawn from Sidney's *Arcadia*. Pepys notes in his *Diary* (31 Dec, 1660) the first performance of Glapthorne's tragedy, of the same title; "the house was exceeding full." -Partially.

"Mark," he said, "mark this, Alice—the devil can quote Scripture for his purpose. Why, this young fanatic cousin of thine, with no more beard than I have seen on a clown playing Maid Marion on May-day, when the village barber had shaved him in too great a hurry, shall match any bearded Presbyterian or Independent of them all, in laying down his doctrines and his uses, and bethumping us with his texts and his homilies. I would worthy and learned Doctor Rochecliffe had been here, with his battery ready-mounted from the Vulgate, and the Septuagint, and what not—he would have battered the Presbyterian spirit out of him with a wanion. However, I am glad the young man is no sneaker; for, were a man of the devil's opinion in religion, and of old Noll's in politics, ho were better open on it full cry, than deceive you by hunting counter, or running a false scent. Come—wipe thino eyes—the fray is over, and not like to be stirred again soon, I trust."

Encouraged by these words, Alice rose, and, bewildered as she was, endeavoured to superintend the arrangements for their meal and their repose in their new habitation. But her tears fell so fast, they marred her counterfeited diligence; and it was well for her that Phoebe, though too ignorant and too simple to comprehend the extent of her distress, could afford her material assistance, in lack of mere sympathy.

Merchant of Venice, I., 3. 99. St. Jerome's Latin version of the Bible, made in the fourth century, and now used, with some modifications, as the authorized version of the Roman Catholic Church. The Greek version of the Old Testament, made between 280 and 130 B.C. According to tradition, the translation was made at Alexandria by seventy or seventy-two learned Jews from Jerusalem, who were called the Seventy. Hence the name of the version, from the Latin word for seventy, *septuaginta*. With a vengeance.

With great readiness and address, the damsel set about every thing that was requisite for preparing the supper and the beds; now screaming into Dame Jellycot's ear, now whispering into her mistress's, and artfully managing, as if she was merely the agent under Alice's orders. When the cold viands were set forth, Sir Henry Lee kindly pressed his daughter to take refreshment, as if to make up, indirectly, for his previous harshness towards her; while he himself, like an experienced campaigner, shewed, that neither the mortifications nor brawls of the day, nor the thoughts of what was to come to-morrow, could diminish his appetite for supper which was his favourite meal. He ate up two-thirds of the capon, and, devoting the first bumper to the happy restoration of Charles, second of the name, he finished a quart of wine; for he belonged to a school accustomed to feed the flame of their loyalty with copious brimmers. He even sang a verse of " The King shall enjoy his own again,"1 in which Phoebe, half-sobbing, and Dame Jellycot screaming against time and tune, were contented to lend their aid to cover Mistress Alice's silence.

At length the jovial knight betook himself to his rest on the keeper's straw pallet, in a recess adjoining to the kitchen, and, unaffected by his change of dwelling, slept fast and deep. Alice had less quiet rest in old Goody Jellycot's wicker couch, in the inner apartment; while the dame and PliGebe slept on a mattress, stuffed with dry leaves, in the same chamber, soundly as those whose daily toil gains their daily bread, and whom morning calls up only to renew the toils of yesterday.

See Chapter XXXVIII.

Note that this ohapt jr introduces the hero, and poses the problem of his relations to the heroine. The negative character and dramatically neutral position of most of Scott's heroes is commented upon in the Introduction. See also Leslie Stephen's essay on Scott *(Hours in a Library)* and Walter Bagehot's in *Literary Studies.*

CHAPTER THE FIFTH

My tongue pads slowly under this new language,
And starts and stumbles at these uncouth phrases.
They may be great in worth and weight, but hang
Upon the native glibness of my language
Like Saul's plate-armour on the shepherd boy,
Encumbering and not arming him.

J.B.

As Markbam Everard pursued his way towards the Lodge, through one of the long sweeping glades which traversed the forest, varying in breadth, till the trees were now so close that the boughs made darkness over his head, then receding farther to let in glimpses of the moon, and anon opening yet wider into little meadows, or savannahs, on which the moonbeams lay in silvery silence; as he thus proceeded on his lonely course, the various effects produced by that delicious light on the oaks, whose dark leaves, gnarled branches, and massive trunks it gilded, more or less partially, might have drawn the attention of a poet or a painter.

But if Everard thought of any thing saving the painful scene in which he had just played his part, and of which the result seemed the destruction of all his hopes, it was of the necessary guard to be observed in his night-walk. The times were dangerous and unsettled; the roads full of disbanded soldiers, and especially of royalists, who made their political opinions a pretext for disturbing the country with marauding parties and robberies. Deer-stealers also, who are ever a desperate banditti, had of late infested Woodstock Chase. In short, the dangers of the place and period were such, that Markham Everard wore his loaded pistols at his belt, and carried his drawn sword under his arm, that he might be prepared for whatever peril should cross his path.

1"James Ballantyne, the printer. 'Where is this f rom?' asked Ballantyne on the proof-sheet. 'The Devil,' wrote Scott; but crossing that out, he substituted J. B. "—D.

"It may be worth noting, that it was in correcting the proof-sheets of this novel *The Antiquary* that Scott first took to equipping his chapters with mottoes of his own fabrication. On one occasion he happened to ask John Ballantyne, who was sitting by him, to hunt for a particular passage in Beaumont and Fletcher. John did as he was bid. but did not succeed in discovering the lines. 'Hang it, Johnnie,' cried Scott. 'I believe I can make a motto sooner than you will find one.' He did so accordingly, and from that hour, whenever memory failed to suggest an appropriate epitaph, he had recourse to the inexhaustible mines of '*old play*' or '*old ballad,*' to which we owe some of the most exquisite verses that ever flowed from his pen "— Lockhart's *Life of Scott,* Vol. IV., 292; for Scott's own comment upon this practice, see Vol. IX., 212.

Scott's use of landscape is commented upon at the close of this chapter.

He heard the bells of Woodstock Church ring curfew, just as he was crossing one of the little meadows we have described, and they ceased as he entered an overshadowed and twilight part of the path beyond. It was there that he heard some one whistling; and, as the sound became clearer, it was plain the person was advancing towards him. This could hardly be a friend; for the party to which he belonged rejected, generally speaking, all music, unless psalmody. "If a man is merry, let him sing psalms," 1 was a text which they were pleased to interpret as literally and to as little purpose as they did some others; yet it was too continued a sound to be a signal amongst night-walkers, and too light and cheerful to argue any purpose of concealment on the part of the traveller, who presently exchanged his whistling for singing, and trolled forth the following stanza to a jolly tune, with which the old cavaliers were wont to wake the night owl:

Hey for cavaliers I Ho for cavaliers I
Pray for cavaliers I
Rub a dub—rub a dub!
Have at old Beelzebub—
Oliver smokes for fear.

"I should know that voice," said Everard, uncocking the pistol which he had drawn from his belt, but continuing to hold it in his hand. Then came another fragment:

Hash them—slash them—
All to pieces dash them.
James v. 13. Fumes.

"So ho!" cried Markham, "who goes there, and for whom?"

"For Church and King," answered a voice, which presently added, "No, d—n me—I mean *against* Church and King, and for the people that are uppermost—I forget which they are."

"Roger Wildrake, as I guess?" said Everard.

"The same—Gentleman; of Squattle-sea-mere, in the moist county of Lincoln."

"Wildrake!" said Markham—"Wildgoose you should be called. You have been moistening your own throat to some purpose, and using it to gabble tunes very suitable to the times, to be sure!"

"Faith, the tune's a pretty tune enough, Mark, only out of fashion a little—the more's the pity."

"What could I expect," said Everard, "but to meet some ranting, drunken cavalier, as desperate and dangerous as night and sack usually make them. What if I had rewarded your melody by a ball in the gullet?"

"Why, there would have been a piper paid—that's all," said Wildrake. "But wherefore come you this way now? I was about to seek you at the hut."

"I have been obliged to leave it—I will tell you the cause hereafter," replied Markham.

"What! the old play-hunting cavalier was cross, or Chloe was unkind?"

"Jest not, Wildrake — it is all over with me," said Everard.

"The devil it is," exclaimed Wildrake, "and you take it thus quietly!—Zounds! let us back together—I'll plead your cause for you—I know how to tickle up an old knight and a pretty maiden—Let me alone for putting you *rectus in curia,* you canting rogue—D—n me, Sir Henry Lee, says I, your nephew is a piece of a Puritan—it won't deny— but I'll uphold him a gentleman and a pretty fellow, for all that.—Madam, says I, you may think your cousin looks like a psalm-singing weaver, in that bare felt, and with that rascally brown cloak; that band, which looks like a baby's clout, and those loose boots, which have a whole calf-skin in each of them—but let him wear on the one side of his head a castor, with a plume befitting his quality; give him a good Toledo by his side, with a broidered belt and an inlaid hilt, instead of the ton of iron contained in that basket-hilted black Andrew Ferrara; put a few smart words in his mouth—and, blood and wounds! madam, says I"

', 'Note the symbolical character of these names. See Suggestions to Students at the close of this chapter.
A country maiden in love with Daphnis, in the Greek romance of the third or fourth century entitled " Daphnis and Chloe;" hence a poetic name for any shepherdess or country girl. "When Chloe is unkind " is a current phrase in seventeenth-century poetry. Of good character before the court.

"Prithee, truce with this nonsense, Wildrake," said Everard, "and tell me if you are sober enough to hear a few words of sober reason?"

"Pshaw! man, I did but crack a brace of quarts with yonder puritanic, round-headed soldiers, up yonder at the town; and rat me, but I passed myself for the best man of the party; twanged my nose, and turned up my eyes, as I took my can—Pah! the very wine tasted of hypocrisy. I think the rogne corporal smoked something at last—as for the common fellows, never stir, but *they* asked me to say grace over another quart!"

"This is just what I wished to speak with you about, Wildrake," said Markham—"You hold me, I am sure, for your friend?"

"True as steel.—Chums at College and at Lincoln's Inn —we have been Nisus and Euryalus, Theseus and Pirithous,? Orestes and Pylades; and, to sum up the whole, with a puritanic touch, David and Jonathan, all in one breath. Not even politics, the wedge that rends families and friendships asunder, as iron rives oak, have been able to split us."

"True," answered Markham; "and when you followed the King to Nottingham, and I enrolled under Essex, we swore, at our parting, that whichever side was victorious, he of us who adhered to it, should protect his less fortunate comrade." A wide collar or ruff. Swaddling-cloth. A beaver hat. General name for a large sword, of the kind first made by Andrea of Ferrara, a famous Italian smith. Suspected. '*JEneid,* Book IX.. 11. 176-502. Pirithous was one of the Lapitha3, who accompanied his friend Theseus, the hero, to the lower world.

"Pylades was the companion of Orestes, when the latter was pursued by the Furies for the murder of his mother Clytemnestra.
1 *Samuel* xviii., 1-4. *"*Surely, man, surely; and have you not protected me accordingly? Did you not save me from hanging? and am I not indebted to you for the bread I eat?"

"I have but done that which, had the times been otherwise, you, my dear Wildrake, would, I am sure, have done for me. But, as I said, that is just what I wished to speak to you about. Why render the task of protecting you more difficult than it must necessarily be at any rate? Why thrust thyself into the company of soldiers, or such like, where thou art sure to be warmed into betraying thyself? Why come hollowing and whooping out cavalier ditties, like a drunken trooper of Prince Rupert, or one of Wilmot's swaggering body-guards?" *"*Because I may have been both one and t'other in my day, for aught that you know," replied Wildrake. "But, oddsfish! is it necessary I should always be reminding you, that our obligation of mutual protection, our league of offensive and defensive, as I may call it, was to be carried into effect without reference to the politics or religion of the party protected, or the least obligation on him to conform to those of his friend*?" "*True," said Everard; "but with this most necessary qualification, that the party should submit to such outward conformity to the times as should make it more easy and safe for his friend to be of service to him. Now, you are perpetually breaking forth, to the hazard of your own safety and my credit." 1The raising of the Royal standard at Nottingham, August 23, 1642, marked the outbreak of the civil war. The commander of the army raised by Parliament in 1642, and "the darling of the swordmen." As a general, however, he often showed irresolution, and he laid down his commission at the time of the Self-Denying Ordinance in 1645.

The student should note carefully whether a conversation like this, intended to inform us of the past history of the characters, is well disguised; *i. e.*, whether it seems to arise naturally from the present circumstances, or betrays itself as purposely introduced to give the reader information. See Hennequin's *Art of Play-writing,* "Exposition by Implication," p. 104. 1 Henry Wilmot, Earl of Rochester, father of John, second Earl of Rochester. The latter was the companion of Charles the Second's flight from Worcester (see Chapter XXIV.) and a noted wit after the Restoration.

"I tell you, Mark, and I would tell your namesake the apostle, that you are hard on me. You have practised sobriety and hypocrisy from your hanging sleeves till your Geneva cassock—from the cradle to this day,—and it is a thing of nature to you; and you are surprised that a rough, rattling, honest fellow, accustomed to speak truth all his life, and especially when he found it at the bottom of a flask, cannot be so perfect a prig as thyself—Zooks! there is no equality betwixt us—A trained diver might as well, because he can retain his breath for ten minutes without inconvenience, upbraid a poor devil for being like to burst in twenty seconds, at the bottom of ten fathoms' water—And, after all, considering the guise is so new to me, I think I bear myself indifferently well—try me!"

"Are there any more news from Worcester fight*?"* asked Everard, in a tone so serious that it imposed on his companion, who replied in his genuine character—

"Worse!—d—n me, worse an hundred times than reported—totally broken—Noll hath certainly sold himself to the devil, and his lease will have an end one day—that is all our present comfort. "

"What! and would this be your answer to the first redcoat who asked the question?" said Everard. "Methinks you would find a speedy passport to the next corps de garde."

"Nay, nay," answered Wildrake, "I thought you asked me in your own person.—Lack-a-day! a great mercy—a glorifying mercy—a crowning mercy—a vouchsafing—an uplifting—I profess the malignants are scattered from Dan to Beersheba—smitten, hip and thigh, even until the going down of the sun!*"*Hear you aught of Colonel Thornhaugh's wounds?"

"He is dead," answered Wildrake, "that's one comfort —the roundheaded rascal!—Nay, hold! it was but a trip of the tongue—I meant, the sweet godly youth." The loose sleeves of a baby's gown.
The long close fitting vestments worn by the clergy, used here to twit Markham with his Calvinism. Detachment of soldiers, or sentinels on guard. 'From one end of the kingdom to the other.

"And hear you aught of the young man, King of Scotland, as they call him?" said Everard.

"Nothing, but that he is hunted like a partridge on the mountains. May God deliver him, and confound his enemies!—Zoons, Mark Everard, I can fool it no longer. Do you not remember, that at the Lincoln's-Inn gambols — though you did not mingle much in them, I think—I used always to play as well as any of them, when it came to the action, but they could never get me to rehearse conformably. It's the same at this day. I hear your voice, and I answer to it in the true tone of my heart; bat when I am in the company of your snuffling friends, you have seen me act my part indifferent well."

"But indifferent, indeed/'replied Everard; "however, there is little call on you to do aught, save to be modest and silent. Speak little, and lay aside, if you can, your big oaths and swaggering looks—set your hat even on your brows."

"Ay, that is the curse! I have been always noted for the jaunty manner in which I wear my castor—hard when a man's merits become his enemies!"

"You must remember you are my clerk."

"Secretary," answered Wildrake; "let it be secretary, if you love me."

"It must be clerk, and nothing else—plain clerk— and remember to be civil and obedient," replied Everard.

"But you should not lay on your commands with so much ostentatious superiority, Master Markham Everard. Remember I am your senior of three years' standing. Confound me, if I know how to take it!"

"Was ever such a fantastic wronghead!—For my sake, if not for thine own, bend thy freakish folly to listen to reason. Think that I have incurred both risk and shame on thy account."

"Nay, thou art a right good fellow, Mark," replied the cavalier, "and for thy sake I will do much—but remember to cough, and cry hem! when thou seest me like to break bounds. And now tell me whither we are bound for the night?" The Scotch Presbyterians proclaimed Charles II. King at Edinburgh in February, 1649. He was then upon the Continent.
'l *Samuel* xxvi. 20. Students at the Inns of Court used frequently to present masks, revels, and other histrionic performances.
"To Woodstock Lodge, to look after my uncle's property," answered Markham Everard; "lam informed that soldiers have taken possession—Yet how could that be, if thou foundest the party drinking in Woodstock!"

"There was a kind of commissary or steward, or some such rogue, had gone down to the Lodge," replied Wildrake; "I had a peep at him."

"Indeed!" replied Everard.

"Ay, verily," said Wildrake, "to speak your own language. Why, as I passed through the park in quest of you, scarce half an hour since, I saw a light in the Lodge —Step this way, you will see it yourself."

"In the north-west angle ?" returned Everard. "It is from a window in what they call Victor Lee's apartment."

"Well," resumed Wildrake, "I had been long one of Lundsford's lads, and well used to patrolling duty—So, rat me, says I, if I leave a light in my rear, without knowing what it means. Besides, Mark, thou hadst said so much to me of thy pretty cousin, I thought I might as well have a peep, if I could."

"Thoughtless, incorrigible man! to what dangers do you expose yourself and your friends, in mere wantonness!—But go on."

"By this fair moonshine, I believe thou art jealous, Mark Everard!" replied his gay companion; "there is no occasion; for, in any case, I, who was to see the lady, was steeled by honour against the charms of my friend's Chloe —Then the lady was not to see me, so could make no comparisons to thy disadvantage, thou knowest—Lastly, as it fell out, neither of us saw the other at all."

"Of that I am well aware. Mrs. Alice left the Lodge long before sunset, and never returned. What didst thou see to introduce with such preface?"

"Nay, no great matter," replied Wildrake; "only getting upon a sort of buttress (for I can climb like any cat that ever mewed in any gutter), and holding on by the vines and creepers which grew around, I obtained a station where I could see into the inside of that same parlour thou spokest of just now."

"And what saw'st thou there?" once more demanded Everard.
1 Sir Thomas Lunsford, a Royalist captain of cavalry. See Scott's note on " Cannibalism imputed to the Cavaliers," Chapter XX. *"*Nay, no great matter, as I said before," replied the cavalier; "for in these times it is no new thing to see churls carousing in royal or noble chambers. I saw two rascallions engaged in emptying a solemn stoup of strong waters, and despatching a huge venison pasty, which greasy mess, for their convenience, they had placed on a lady's work-table—One of them was trying an air on a lute."

"The profane villains!" exclaimed Everard, "it was Alice's."

"Well said, comrade—I am glad your phlegm can be moved. I did but throw in these incidents of the lute and the table, to try if it was possible to get a spark of human spirit out of you, be-sanctified as you are."

"What like were the men?" said young Everard.

"The one a slouch-hatted, long-cloaked, sour-faced fanatic, like the rest of you, whom I took to be the steward or commissary I heard spoken of in the town; the other was a short sturdy fellow, with a wood-knife at his girdle, and a long quarterstaff lying beside him— a black-haired knave, with white teeth and a merry countenance—one of the under-rangers or bow-bearers of these walks, I fancy."

"They must have been Desborough's favourite, trusty Tomkins," said Everard, "and Joceline Joliffe, the keeper. Tomkins is Desborough's right hand— an Independent, and hath pourings forth, as he calls them. Some think that his gifts have the better of his grace. I have heard of his abusing opportunities."

"They were improving them when I saw them," replied Wildrake, "and made the bottle smoke1 for it—when, as the devil would have it, a stone, which had been dislodged from the crumbling buttress, gave way under my weight. A clumsy fellow like thee would have been so long thinking what was to be done, that he must needs have followed it before he could make up his mind; but I, Mark, I hopped like a squirrel to an ivy twig, and stood fast—was well-nigh shot, though, for the noise alarmed them both. They looked to the oriel, and saw me on the outside; the fanatic fellow took out a pistol—as they have always such texts in readiness hanging beside the little clasped Bible, thou know'st — the keeper seized his hunting-pole — I treated them both to a roar and a grin—thou must know I can grimace like a baboon—I learned the trick from a French player, who could twist his jaws into a pair of nutcrackers—and therewithal I dropped myself sweetly on the grass, and ran off so trippingly, keeping the dark side of the wall as long as I could, that I am well-nigh persuaded they thought I was their kinsman, the devil, come among them uncalled. They were abominably startled." i Suffer.

"Thou art most fearfully rash, Wildrake," said his companion; "we are now bound for the house—what if they should remember thee?"

"Why, it is no treason is it? No one has paid for peeping since Tom of Coventry's1 days; and if he came in for a reckoning, belike it was for a better treat than mine. But trust me, they will no more know me, than a man who had only seen your friend Noll at a conventicle of saints, would know the same Oliver on horseback, and charging with his lobster-tailed squadron; or.the same Noll cracking a jest and a bottle with wicked Waller the poet."

"Hush! not a word of Oliver, as thou dost value thyself and me. It is ill jesting with the rock you may split on.—But here is the gate—we will disturb these honest gentlemen's recreations."

As he spoke, he applied the large and ponderous knocker to the hall-door.

"Rat-tat-tat-too!" said Wildrake; "there is a fine alarm to you cuckolds and roundheads." He then halfmimicked, half-sung the march so called:—

Cuckolds, come dig, cuckolds, come dig;
Bound about cuckolds, come dance to my jig!

"By Heaven! this passes Midsummer frenzy," said Everard, turning angrily to him.
For the legend of Peeping Tom of Coventry read Tennyson's *Oodinn*. A religious meeting of dissenters, particularly among the Scotch Covenanters. Conventicles are described in *Old Mortality* and *Peveril of the Peak*. 'So named from the armour they wore, which consisted of plates slipping over one another, like those of a lobster's shell (French *erevisse*).
'Edmund Waller, a leader in the Long Parliament, exiled in 1643, returning under Cromwell, and a court favourite after the Restoration. The political complexion of his poems ranged from a lament for Cron wells death to a hymn of congratulation on Charles's return from exile. As a matter of fact, he was a most obstinate water-drinker. See Boswell s *Johnson,* G. B. Hill s edition, III., 372.

"Not a bit, not a bit," replied Wildrake; "it is but a slight expectoration, just like what one makes before beginning a long speech. I will be grave for an hour together, now I have got that point of war out of my head."

As he spoke, steps were heard in the hall, and the wicket of the great door was partly opened, but secured with a chain in case of accidents. The visage of Tomkins, and that of Joceline beneath it, appeared at the chink, illuminated by the lamp which the latter held in his hand, and Tomkins demanded the meaning of this alarm.

"I demand instant admittance!" said Everard. "Joliffe, you know me well*?"*
"I do, sir," replied Joceline, "and could admit you with all my heart; but, alas! sir, you see I am not keykeeper—Here is the gentleman whose warrant I must walk by—The Lord help me, seeing times are such as they be!"

"And when that gentleman, who I think may be Master Desborough's valet"

"His honour's unworthy secretary, an it please you," interposed Tomkins; while Wildrake whispered in Everard's ear, "I will be no longer secretary. Mark, thou wert quite right—the clerk must be the more gentlemanly calling."

"And if you are Master Desborough's secretary, I presume you know me and my condition well enough," said Everard, addressing the Independent, "not to hesitate to admit me and my attendant to a night's quarters in the Lodge?"

"Surely not, surely not," said the Independent—"that is, if your worship thinks you would be better accommodated here than up at the house of entertainment in the town, which men unprofitably 1 call Saint George's Inn. There is but confined accommodation here, your honour —and we have been frayed out of our lives already by the visitation of Satan—albeit his fiery dart is now quenched."

"This may be all well in its place, Sir Secretary," said Everard; "and you may find a corner for it when you are next tempted to play the preacher. But I will take it for no apology for keeping me here in the cold harvest wind; and if not presently received, and suitably too, I will report you to your master for insolence in your office." The Puritans disliked anything which tended to perpetuate the old Catholic traditions, like that of St. George (the patron saint of England) and the Dragon.

The secretary of Desborough did not dare offer farther opposition; for it is well known that Desborough himself only held his consequence as a kinsman of Cromwell; and the Lord General, who was well-nigh paramount already, was known to be strongly favourable both to the elder and younger Everard. It is true, they were Presbyterians and he an Independent; and that those sharing those feelings of correct morality and more devoted religious feeling, by which, with few exceptions, the Parliamentary party were distinguished, the Everards were not disposed to carry these attributes to the extreme of enthusiasm, practised by so many others at the time. Yet it was well known that whatever might be Cromwell's own religious creed, he was not uniformly bounded by it in the choice of his favourites, but extended his countenance to those who could serve him, even although, according to the phrase of the time, they came out of the darkness of Egypt. The character of the elder Everard stood very high for wisdom and sagacity; besides, being of a good family and competent fortune, his adherence would lend a dignity to any side he might espouse. Then his son had been a distinguished and successful soldier, remarkable for the discipline he maintained among his men, the bravery which he shewed in the time of action, and the humanity with which he was always ready to qualify the consequences of victory. Such men were not to be neglected, when many signs combined to shew that the parties in the state, who had successfully accomplished the deposition and death of the king, were speedily to quarrel among themselves about the division of the spoils. The two Everards were therefore much courted by Cromwell, and their influence with him was supposed to be so great, that trusty Master Secretary Tomkins cared not to expose himself to risk, by contending with Colonel Everard for such a trifle as a night's lodging.

Joceline was active on his side—more lights were obtained—more wood thrown on the fire—and the two newly-arrived strangers were introduced into Victor Lee's parlour, as it was called from the picture over the chimneypiece, which we have already described. It was several minutes ere Colonel Everard could recover his general stoicism of deportment, so strongly was he impressed by finding himself in the apartment, under whose roof he had passed so many of the happiest hours of his life. There was the cabinet, which he had seen opened with such feelings of delight when Sir Henry Lee deigned to give him instructions in fishing, and to exhibit hooks and lines, together with all the materials for making the artificial fly, then little known. There hung the ancient family picture, which, from some odd mysterious expressions of his uncle relating to it, had become to his boyhood, nay, his early youth, a subject of curiosity and of fear. He remembered how, when left alone in the apartment, the searching eye of the old warrior seemed always bent upon his, in whatever part of the room he placed himself, and how his childish imagination was perturbed at a phenomenon, for which he could not account.

With these came a thousand dearer and warmer recollections of his early attachment to his pretty cousin Alice, when he assisted her at her lessons, brought water for her flowers, or accompanied her while she sung; and he remembered that while her father looked at them with a good-humoured and careless smile, he had once heard him mutter, "And if it should turn out so—why it might be best for both," and the theories of happiness he had reared on these words. All these visions had been dispelled by the trumpet of war, which called Sir Henry Lee and himself to opposite sides; and the transactions of this very day had shewn, that even Everard's success as a soldier and a statesman seemed absolutely to prohibit the chance of their being revived.

He was waked out of this unpleasing reverie by the approach of Joceline, who, being possibly a seasoned toper, had made the additional arrangements with more expedition and accuracy, than could have been expected from a person engaged as he had been since night-fall.

He now wished to know the Colonel's directions for the night.

"Would he eat anything?"

"No." "This is hardly correct. Thomas Barker's 'Art of Angling' had already been published; and indeed Dame Juliana Berners, or whoever wrote the work attributed to her. shows that fly-fishing was familiar perhaps two centuries before the date of *Woodstock.*"—Andrew Lang.

"Did his honour choose to accept Sir Henry Lee's bed, which was ready prepared?"

"Yes."

"That of Mistress Alice Lee should be prepared for the Secretary."

"On pain of thine ears—No," replied Everard.

"Where, then, was the worthy Secretary to be quartered?" "In the dog-kennel, if you list," replied Colonel Everard; "but," added he, stepping to the sleeping apartment of Alice, which opened from the parlour, locking it, and taking out the key, "no one shall profane this chamber."

"Had his honour any other commands for the night?" "None, save to clear the apartment of yonder man.— My clerk will remain with me—I have orders which must be written out.—Yet stay—Thou gavest my letter this morning to Mistress Alice?"

"I did."

"Tell me, good Joceline, what she said when she received it?"

"She seemed much concerned, sir; and indeed I think that she wept a little—but indeed she seemed very much distressed."

"And what message did she send to me?"

"None, may it please your honour—She began to say, 'Tell my cousin Everard that I will communicate my uncle's kind purpose to my father, if I can get fitting opportunity—but that I greatly fear'—and there checked herself, as it were, and said, 'I will write to my cousin; and as it may be late ere I have an opportunity of speaking with my father, do thou come for my answer after service.' —So I went to church myself, to while away the time; but when I returned to the Chase, I found this man had summoned my master to surrender, and, right or wrong, I must put him in possession of the Lodge. I would fain have given your honour a hint that the old knight and my young mistress were like to take you on the form, but I could not mend the matter."

"Thou hast done well, good fellow, and I will remember thee.—And now, my masters," he said, advancing to the brace of clerks or secretaries, who had in the meanwhile sat quietly down beside the stone bottle, and made up acquaintance over a glass of its contents—" Let me remind you that the night wears late." 'There is something cries tinkle, tinkle, in the bottle yet," said Wildrake, in reply.

"Hem! hem! hem!" coughed the Colonel of the Parliament service; and if his lips did not curse his companion's imprudence, I will not answer for what arose in his heart.—" Well!" he said, observing that Wildrake had filled his own glass and Tomkins's, "take that parting glass and begone."

"Would you not be pleased to hear first," said Wildrake, "how this honest gentleman saw the devil to-night look through a pane in yonder window, and how he thinks he had a mighty strong resemblance to your worship's humble slave and varlet scribbler? Would you but hear this, sir, and just sip a glass of this very recommendable strong waters?"

"I will drink none, sir," said Colonel Everard, sternly; "and I have to tell *you*, that you have drunken a glass too much already.—Mr. Tomkins, sir, I wish you good night."

"A word in season at parting," said Tomkins, standing up behind the long leathern back of a chair, hemming and snuffing as if preparing for an exhortation.

"Excuse me, sir," replied Markham Everard, sternly; "you are not now sufficiently yourself to guide the devotion of others."

"Woe be to them that reject!" said the Secretary of the Commissioners, stalking out of the room—the rest was lost in shutting the door, or suppressed for fear of offence.

"And now, fool Wildrake, begone to thy bed—yonder it lies," pointing to the knight's apartment.

"What, thou hast secured the lady's for thyself? I saw thee put the key in thy pocket."

"I would not—indeed I could not sleep in that apartment—I can sleep nowhere—but I will watch in this armchair.—I have made him place wood for repairing the fire. —Good now, go to bed thyself, and sleep off thy liquor."

"Liquor!—I laugh thee to scorn, Mark—thou art a milksop, and the son of a milksop, and know'st not what a good fellow can do in the way of crushing an honest cup."

"The whole vices of his faction are in this poor fellow individually," said the Colonel to himself, eyeing his pro *Borneo and Juliet,* I., 2, 80.

tege askance, as the other retreated into the bedroom, with no very steady pace—" He is reckless, intemperate, dissolute; and if I cannot get him safely shipped for France, he will certainly be both his own ruin and mine Yet, withal, he is kind, brave, and generous, and would have kept the faith with me which he now expects from me; and in what consists the merit of our truth, if we observe not our plighted word when we have promised, to our hurt? I will take the liberty, however, to secure myself against farther interruption on his part."

So saying, he locked the door of communication betwixt the sleeping-room, to which the cavalier had retreated, and the parlour;—and then, after pacing the floor thoughtfully, returned to his seat, trimmed the lamp, and drew out a number of letters.—" I will read these over once more," he said, "that, if possible, the thought of public affairs may expel this keen sense of personal sorrow. Gracious Providence, where is this to end! We have sacrificed the peace of our families, the warmest wishes of our young hearts, to right the country in which we were born, and to free her from oppression; yet it appears, that every step we have made towards liberty, has but brought us in view of new and more terrific perils, as he who travels in a mountainous region, is, by every step which elevates him higher, placed in a situation of more imminent hazard. "

He read long and attentively, various tedious and embarrassed letters, in which the writers, placing before him the glory of God, and the freedom and liberties of England, as their supreme ends, could not, by all the ambagitory1 expressions they made use of, prevent the shrewd eye of Markham Everard from seeing, that self-interest and views of ambition were the principal moving-springs at the bottom of their plots. Roundabout.

Landscape is commonly introduced«in fiction either for its purely picturesque effect in itself, or serving as a background, harmonious or contrasting, for the characters, or as positively influencing the moods or actions of the characters. Find illustrations of these various functions, in Scott's novels. Compare his prose fiction with his poetry, in this regard. Do you find his use of landscape more or less significant than its use by Dickens, George Eliot. Hawthorne V

Note the symbolism by which Wildrake's name is made to suit his character. Study the usage, in this respect, of the old Morality Plays (with personages named Good Fame, Virtuous Living, Tom Tosspot, Cuthbert Cutpurse); of the Elizabethan drama; of Banyan's *Pilgrim's Progress.* Note Scott's own distinction between names of minor characters like Peter Poundtext, Habukknk Mucklewrath, etc., and the purely colorless names of Henry Morton, Edward Waverley. Find names in other novelists that seem to you felicitous for their symbolical character.

Compare the character of Wildrake, as it is brought before us chapter by chapter, with that of soldiers of fortune in Scott's other novels, as Bothwell in *Old Mortality*, Dalgetty in *A Legend of Montrose,* etc. What was there in Scott himself that accounts for his fondness for a character like Wildrake?

CHAPTER THE SIXTH

Sleep steals on us even like his brother Death—
We know not when it comes—we know it must come—
We may affect to scorn and to contemn it,
For 'tis the highest pride of human misery
To say it knows not of an opiate.
Yet the reft parent, the despairing lover,
Even the poor wretch who waits for execution,
Feels this oblivion, against which he thought
His woes had armed his senses, steal upon him,
And through the fenceless citadel—the body,—
Surprise that haughty garrison—the mind.
Herbert.

Colonel Everard experienced the truth contained in the verses of the quaint old bard whom we have quoted above. Amid private grief, and anxiety for a country long a prey to civil war, and not likely to fall soon under any fixed or well-established form of government, Everard and his father had, like many others, turned their eyes to General Cromwell, as the person whose valour had made him the darling of the army, whose strong sagacity had hitherto predominated over the high talents by which he had been assailed in Parliament, as well as over his enemies in the field, and who was alone in the situation to *settle the nation,* as the phrase then went; or, in other words, to dictate the mode of government. The father and son were both reputed to stand high in the General's favour. But Markham Everard was conscious of some particulars, which induced him to doubt whether Cromwell actually, and at heart, bore either to his father or to himself that good-will which was generally believed. He knew him for a profound politician, who could veil for any length of time his real sentiments of men and things, until they could be displayed without prejudice to his interest. And he moreover knew that the General was not likely to forget the opposition which the Presbyterian party had offered to For this view of Cromwell, see Editor's Introduction.
what Oliver called the Great Matter—the trial, namely, and execution of the King. In this opposition, his father and he had anxiously concurred, nor had the arguments, nor even the half expressed threats of Cromwell, induced them to flinch from that course, far less to permit their names to be introduced into the commission nominated to sit in judgment on that memorable occasion.

This hesitation had occasioned some temporary coldness between the General and the Everards, father and son. But as the latter remained in the army, and bore arms under Cromwell both in Scotland, and finally at Worcester, his services very frequently called forth the approbation of his commander. After the fight at Worcester, in particular, he was among the number of those officers on whom Oliver, rather considering the actual and practical extent of his own power, than the name under which he exercised it, was with difficulty withheld from imposing the dignity of Knights-Bannerets1 at his own will and pleasure. It therefore seemed, that all recollection of former disagreement was obliterated, and that the Everards had regained their former stronghold in the General's affections. There were, indeed, several who doubted this, and who endeavoured to bring over this distinguished young officer to some other of the parties which divided the infant Commonwealth. But to these proposals he turned a deaf ear. Enough of blood, he said, had been spilled—it was time that the nation should have repose under a firmly-established government, of strength sufficient to protect property, and of lenity enough to encourage the return of tranquillity. This, he thought, could only be accomplished by means of Cromwell, and the greater part of England was of the same opinion. It is true, that, in thus submitting to the domination of a successful soldier, those who did so, forgot the principles upon which they had drawn the sword against the late King. But in revolutions, stern and high principles are often obliged to give way to the current of existing circumstances; and in many a case, where wars have been waged for points of metaphysical right, they have been at last gladly terminated, upon the mere hope of obtaining general tranquillity, as, after many a long siege, a garrison is often glad to submit on mere security for life and limb.

i A knight made in the field, for his prowess in battle, was termed a " knight-banneret" because the ceremony consisted in tearing off the pointed ends of his banner, leaving it square.

Colonel Everard, therefore, felt that the support which he afforded Cromwell, was only under the idea, that, amid a choice of evils, the least was likely to ensue from a man of the General's wisdom and valour being placed at the head of the state; and he was sensible, that Oliver himself was likely to consider his attachment as lukewarm and imperfect, and measure his gratitude for it upon the same limited scale.

In the meanwhile, however, circumstances compelled him to make trial of the General's friendship. The sequestration of Woodstock, and the warrant to the commissioners to dispose of it as national property, had been long granted, but the interest of the elder Everard had for weeks and months deferred its execution. The hour was now approaching when the blow could be no longer parried, especially as Sir Henry Lee, on his side, resisted every proposal of submitting himself to the existing government, and was therefore, now that his hour of grace was passed, enrolled in the list of stubborn and irreclaimable malignants, with whom the Council of State was determined no longer to keep terms. The only mode of protecting the old knight and his daughter, was to interest, if possible, the General himself in the matter; and revolving all the circumstances connected with their intercourse, Colonel Everard felt that a request, which would so immediately interfere with the interests of Desborough, the brother-inlaw of Cromwell, and one of the present Commissioners, was putting to a very severe trial the friendship of the latter. Yet no alternative remained.

With this view, and agreeably to a request from Cromwell, who at parting had been very urgent to have his written opinion upon public affairs, Colonel Everard passed the earlier part of the night in arranging his ideas upon the state of the Commonwealth, in a plan which he thought likely to be acceptable to Cromwell, as it exhorted him, under the aid of Providence, to become the saviour of the state, by convoking a free Parliament, and by their aid placing himself at the head of some form of liberal and established Government, which might supersede the state of anarchy, in which the nation was otherwise likely to be merged. Taking a general view of the totally broken condition of the Royalists, and of the various factions which now convulsed the state, he shewed how this might be done without bloodshed or violence. From this topic he descended to the propriety of keeping up the becoming state of the executive Government, in whose hands soever it should be lodged, and thus shewed Cromwell, as the future Stadtholder, or Consul, or Lieutenant-General of Great Britain and Ireland, a prospect of demesne and residences becoming his dignity. Then he naturally passed to the disparking and destroying of the royal residences of England, made a woful picture of the demolition which impended over Woodstock, and interceded for the preservation of that beautiful seat, as a matter of personal favour, in which he found himself deeply interested.

This was the name given to the Assembly elected on Feb. 14, 1649, immediately after Charles the First's death. It had more than royal executive powers. - Not overawed by the monarchy.

Colonel Bverard, when he had finished his letter, did not find himself greatly risen in his own opinion. In the course of his political conduct, he had till this hour avoided mixing up personal motives with his public grounds of action, and yet he now felt himself making such a composition. But he comforted himself, or at least silenced this unpleasing recollection, with the consideration, that the weal of Britain, studied under the aspect of the times, absolutely required that Cromwell should be at the head of the government; and that the interest of Sir Henry Lee, or rather his safety and his existence, no less emphatically demanded the preservation of Woodstock, and his residence there. Was it a fault of his, that the same road should lead to both these ends, or that his private interest, and that of the country, should happen to mix in the same letter? He hardened himself, therefore, to the act, made up and addressed his packet to the Lord General, and then sealed it with his seal of arms. This done, he lay back in the chair; and, in spite of his expectations to the contrary, fell asleep in the course of his reflections, anxious and harassing as they were, and did not awaken until the cold gray light of dawn was peeping through the eastern oriel.

Title of the chief magistrate of the Netherlands. Compare the action of Morton in *Old Mortality,* and Edward Waverley in *Waveiley.*

He started at first, rousing himself with the sensation of one who awakes in a place unknown to him; but the localities instantly forced themselves on his recollection. The lamp burning dimly in the socket, the wood fire almost extinguished in its own white embers, the gloomy picture over the chimney-piece, the sealed packet on the table—all reminded him of the events of yesterday, and his deliberations of the succeeding night.

"There is no help for it," he said; "it must be Cromwell or anarchy. And probably the sense that his title, as head of the executive Government, is derived merely from popular consent, may check the too natural proneness of power to render itself arbitrary. If he govern by Parliaments, and with regard to the privileges of the subject, wherefore not Oliver as well as Charles? But I must take measures for having this conveyed safely to the hands of this future sovereign prince. It will be well to take the first word of influence with him, since there must be many who will not hesitate to recommend counsels more violent and precipitate."

He determined to intrust the important packet to the charge of Wildrake, whose rashness was never so distinguished, as when by any chance he was left idle and unemployed; besides, even if his faith had not been otherwise unimpeachable, the obligations which he owed to his friend Everard must have rendered it such.

These conclusions passed through Colonel Everard's mind, as, collecting the remains of wood in the chimney, he gathered them into a hearty blaze, to remove the uncomfortable feeling of chillness which pervaded his limbs; and by the time he was a little more warm, again sunk into a slumber, which was only dispelled by the beams of morning peeping into his apartment.

He arose, roused himself, walked up and down the room, and looked from the large oriel window on the nearest objects, which were the untrimmed hedges and neglected walks of a certain wilderness, as it is called in ancient treatises on gardening, which, kept of yore well ordered, and in all the pride of the topiary art, presented a succession of yew-trees cut into fantastic forms, of close alleys, and of open walks, filling about two or three acres of ground on that side of the Lodge, and forming a boundary between its The art of landscape-gardening.

immediate precincts and the open Park. Its enclosure was now broken down in many places, and the hinds with their fawns fed free and unstartled up to the very windows of the silvan palace.

This had been a favourite scene of Markham's sports when a boy. He could still distinguish, though now grown out of shape, the verdant battlements of a Gothic castle, all created by the gardener's shears, at which he was accustomed to shoot his arrows; or, stalking before it like the Knight-errants of whom he read, was wont to blow his horn, and bid defiance to the supposed giant or Paynim knight, by whom it was garrisoned. He remembered how he used to train his cousin, though several years younger than himself, to bear a part in these revels of his boyish fancy, and to play the character of an elfin page, or a fairy, or an enchanted princess. He remembered, too, many particulars of their later acquaintance, from which he had been almost necessarily led to the conclusion, that from an early period their parents had entertained some idea, that there might be a well-fitted match betwixt his fair cousin and himself. A thousand visions, formed in so bright a prospect, had vanished along with it, but now returned like shadows, to remind him of all he had lost— and for what?—" For the sake of England, " his proud consciousness replied,—" Of England, in danger of becoming the prey at once of bigotry and tyranny." And he strengthened himself with the recollection, "If I have sacrificed my private happiness, it is that my country may enjoy liberty of conscience, and personal freedom; which, under a weak prince and usurping statesman, she was but too likely to have lost. "

But the busy fiend in his breast would not be repulsed by the bold answer. "Has thy resistance," it demanded, "availed thy country, Markham Everard? Lies not England, after so much bloodshed, and so much misery, as low beneath the sword of a fortunate soldier, as formerly under the sceptre of an encroaching prince? Are Parliament, or what remains of them, fitted to contend with a leader, master of his soldiers' hearts, as bold and subtle as lie is impenetrable in his designs? This General, who holds the army, and by that the fate of the nation in his hand, will he lay down his power because philosophy would pronounce it his duty to become a subject?"

He dared not answer that his knowledge of Cromwell authorized him to expect any such act of self-denial. Yet still he considered that in times of such infinite difficulty, that must be the best government, however little desirable in itself, which should most speedily restore peace to the land, and stop the wounds which the contending parties were daily inflicting on each other. He imagined that Cromwell was the only authority under which a steady government could be formed, and therefore had attached himself to his fortune, though not without considerable and recurring doubts, how far serving the views of this impenetrable and mysterious General was consistent with the principles under which he had assumed arms.

While these things passed in his mind, Everard looked upon the packet which lay on the table addressed to the Lord General, and which he had made up before sleep. He hesitated several times, when he remembered its purport, and in what degree he must stand committed with that personage, and bound to support his plans of aggrandizement, when once that communication was in Oliver Cromwell's possession.

"Yet it must be so," he said at last, with a deep sigh. "Among the contending parties, he is the strongest—the wisest and most moderate—and ambitious though he be, perhaps not the most dangerous. Some one must be trusted with power to preserve and enforce general order, and who can possess or wield such power like him that is head of the victorious armies of England? Come what will in future, peace and the restoration of law ought to be our first and most pressing object. This remnant of a parliament cannot keep their ground against the army, by mere appeal to the sanction of opinion. If they design to reduce the soldiery, it must be by actual warfare, and the land has been too long steeped in blood. But Cromwell may, and I trust will, make a moderate accommodation with them, on grounds by which peace may be preserved; and it is to this which we must look and trust for a settlement of the kingdom, alas! and for the chance of protecting my obstinate kinsman from the consequences of his honest though absurd pertinacity."

Silencing some internal feelings of doubt and reluctance by such reasoning as this, Markham Everard continued in his resolution to unite himself with Cromwell in the struggle which was evidently approaching betwixt the civil and military authorities; not as the course which, if at perfect liberty, he would have preferred adopting, but as the best choice between two dangerous extremities to which the times had reduced him. He could not help trembling, however, when he recollected that his father, though hitherto the admirer of Cromwell, as the implement by whom so many marvels had been wrought in England, might not be disposed to unite with his interest against that of the Long Parliament, of which he had been, till partly laid aside by continued indisposition, an active and leading member. This doubt also he was obliged to swallow, or strangle, as he might; but consoled himself with the ready argument, that it was impossible his father could see matters in another light than that in which they occurred to himself.

As far as you know the history of this period, was Everard's attitude toward Cromwell the one that a sensible man would have been bound to take? Is the sensible middle course in politics the most interesting one for the hero of a historical novel to follow? Compare Shorthouse's *John Inglesant* and Thackeray's *Henry Esmond*. CHAPTER THE SEVENTH

Determined at length to despatch his packet to the General without delay, Colonel Everard approached the door of the apartment, in which, as was evident from the heavy breathing within, the prisoner Wildrake enjoyed a deep slumber, under the influence of liquor at once and of fatigue. In turning the key, the bolt, which was rather rusty, made a resistance so noisy, as partly to attract the sleeper's attention, though not to awake him. Everard stood by his bedside, as he heard him mutter, "Is it morning already, jailor?—Why, you dog, an you had but a cast of humanity in you, you would qualify your vile news with a cup of sack; hanging is sorry work, my masters—and sorrow's dry."

"Up, Wildrake—up thou ill-omened dreamer," said his friend, shaking him by the collar.

"Hands off!" answered the sleeper.—" I can climb a ladder without help, I trow."—He then sat up in the bed, and opening his eyes, stared around him, and exclaimed, "Zounds! Mark, is it only thou? I thought it was all over with me—fetters were struck from my legs—rope drawn round my gullet—irons knocked off my hands— hempen cravat tucked on—all ready for a dance in the open element upon slight footing."

"Truce with thy folly, Wildrake; sure the devil of drink, to whom thou hast, I think, sold thyself"

"For a hogshead of sack," interrupted Wildrake; "the bargain was made in a cellar in the Vintry."1

"I am as mad as thou art, to trust anything to thee," said Markham; "I scarce believe thou hast thy senses yet."

"What should ail me *?"* said Wildrake—" I trust I have not tasted liquor in my sleep, saving that I dreamed of drinking small-beer with Old Noll, of his own brewing. But do not look so glum, man—I am the same Roger Wildrake that I ever was; as wild as a mallard, but as true as a game-cock. I am thine own chum, man—bound to thee by thy kind deeds—*devinctus beneficio*—there is Latin for it; and where is the thing thou wilt charge me with, that I will not, or dare not execute, were it to pick the devil's teeth with my rapier, after he had breakfasted upon roundheads?" 1The vintners' or wine-merchants' quarter in London. "In this neighbourhood was the great house called the *Vintrie,* with vast winevaults underneath."—Pennant's *London,* II., 466.

"You will drive me mad," said Everard.—" When I am about to intrust all I have most valuable on earth to your management, your conduct and language are those of a mere Bedlamite. Last night I made allowance for thy drunken fury; but who can endure thy morning madness? —it is unsafe for thyself and me, Wildrake—it is unkind— I might say ungrateful."

"Nay, do not say *that,* my friend," said the cavalier, with some show of feeling; "and do not judge of me with a severity that cannot apply to such as I am. We who have lost our all in these sad jars, who are compelled to shift for our living, not from day to day, but from meal to meal—we whose only hiding-place is the jail, whose prospect of final repose is the gallows,—what canst thou expect from us, but to bear such a lot with a light heart, since we should break down under it with a heavy one?"

This was spoken in a tone of feeling which found a responding string in Everard's bosom. He took his friend's hand, and pressed it kindly.

"Nay, if I seemed harsh to thee, Wildrake, I profess it was for thine own sake more than mine. I know thou hast at the bottom of thy levity, as deep a principle of honour and feeling as ever governed a human heart. But thou art thoughtless—thou art rash—and I protest to thee, that wert thou to betray thyself in this matter in which I trust thee, the evil consequences to myself would not afflict me more than the thought of putting thee into such danger."

"Nay, if you take it on that tone, Mark," said the cavalier, making an effort to laugh, evidently that he might conceal a tendency to a different emotion, "thou wilt make children of us both—babes and sucklings, by the hilt of this bilbo.—Come, trust me; I can be cautious when time requires it—no man ever saw me drink when an alert1 was expected—and not one poor pint of wine will I taste until I have managed this matter for thee. Well, I am thy secretary — clerk — I had forgot — and carry thy despatches to Cromwell, taking good heed not to be surprised or choused out of my lump of loyalty striking his finger on the packet, and I am to deliver it to the most loyal hands to which it is most humbly addressed—Adzooks, Mark, think of it a moment longer—Surely thou wilt not carry thy perverseness so far, as to strike in with this bloody-minded rebel?—Bid me give him three inches of my dudgeon-dagger, and I will do it much more willingly than present him with thy packet." Bound by a benefit.

A crazy person. The term ig a corruption from Bethlehem, the hospital of St. Mary of Bethlehem, in London, having been long used as a lunatic asylum.

"Go to," replied Everard, "this is beyond our bargain. If you will help me it is well; if not, let me lose no time in debating with thee, since I think every moment an age till the packet is in the General's possession. It is the only way left me to obtain some protection, and a place of refuge for my uncle and his daughter."

"That being the case," said the cavalier, "I will not Bpare the spur. My nag up yonder at the town will be ready for the road in a trice, and thou mayst reckon on my being with Old Noll—thy General, I mean—in as short time as man and horse may consume betwixt Woodstock and Windsor, where I think I shall for the present find thy friend keeping possession where he has slain."

"Hush, not a word of that. Since we parted last night, I have shaped thee a path which will suit thee better than to assume the decency of language, and of outward manner, of which thou hast so little. I have acquainted the General that thou hast been by bad example and bad education"

"Which is to be interpreted by contraries, I hope," said Wildrake; "for sure I have been as well born and bred up as any lad of Leicestershire Lincolnshire might desire."

"Now, I prithee, hush—thou hast, I say, by bad example become at one time a malignant, and mixed in the party of the late King. But seeing what things were wrought in the nation by the General, thou hast come to a clearness touching his calling to be a great implement in the settlement of these distracted kingdoms. This account of thee will not only lead him to pass over some of thy eccentricities, should they break out in spite of thee, but will also give thee an interest with him as being more especially attached to his own person." An alarm-signal. Cheated.

"A dagger with an ornamental hilt of wood; worn by a civilian in distinction from a soldier. The distance is about fifty miles. D.

"Doubtless," said Wildrake, "as every fisher loves best the trouts that are of his own tickling."

"It is likely, I think, he will send thee

hither with letters to me," said the Colonel, "enabling me to put a stop to the proceedings of these sequestrators, and to give poor old Sir Henry Lee permission to linger out his days among the oaks he loves to look upon. I have made this my request to General Cromwell, and I think my father's friendship and my own may stretch so far on his regard without risk of cracking, especially standing matters as they now do—thou dost understand?"

"Entirely well," said the cavalier; "stretch, quotha! —I would rather stretch a rope than hold commerce with the old King-killing ruffian. But I have said I will be guided by thee, Markham, and rat me but I will."

"Be cautious then," said Everard, "mark well what he does and says—more especially what he does; for Oliver is one of those whose mind is better-known by his actions than by his words; and stay—I warrant thee thou wert setting off without a cross in thy purse?"

"Too true, Mark," said Wildrake, "the last noble melted last night among yonder blackguard troopers of yours."

"Well, Roger," replied the Colonel, "that is easily mended." So saying, he slipped his purse into his friend's hand. "But art thou not an inconsiderate weatherbrained fellow, to set forth as thou wert about to do, without anything to bear thy charges—what couldst thou have done?"

"Faith, I never thought of that; I must have cried *Stand,* I suppose, to the first pursy townsman, or greasy grazier, that I met o' the heath—it is many a good fellow's shift in these bad times."

"Go to," said Everard; "be cautious—use none of your loose acquaintance—rule your tongue—beware of the winepot—for there is little danger if thou couldst only but keep thyself sober—Be moderate in speech, and forbear oaths or vaunting."

"In short, metamorphose myself into such a prig as thou art, Mark.—Well," said Wildrake, "so far as outside will go, I think I can make a *Hope-on-high Bomby* as well as thou canst. Ah! those were merry days when we saw Mills present Bomby at the Fortune playhouse, Mark, ere I had lost my laced cloak and the jewel in my ear, or thou hadst gotten the wrinkle on thy brow, and the puritanic twist of thy mustache!"

"They were like most worldly pleasures, Wildrake," replied Everard, "sweet in the mouth and bitter in digestion. —But away with thee; and when thou bring'st back my answer, thou wilt find me either here or at Saint George's Inn, at the little borough.—Good luck to thee—Be but cautious how thou bearest thyself."

The Colonel remained in deep meditation.—" I think," he said, "I have not pledged myself too far to the General. A breach between him and the Parliament seems inevitable, and would throw England back into civil war, of which all men are wearied. He may dislike my messenger—yet that I do not greatly fear. He knows I would choose such as I can myself depend on, and hath dealt enough with the stricter sort to be aware that there are among them, as well as elsewhere, men who can hide two faces under one hood." A puritanic character in one of Beaumont and Fletcher's plays. Scott. The play was *Women Pleased.* The Fortune theatre was built in 1599 for Henslowe, the moneylender, and Alleyn, the actor. It was a rival of the Globe and the Blackfriars.

CHAPTER THE EIGHTH

For there in lofty air was seen to stand
The stern Protector of the conquered land;
Drawn in that look with which he wept and swore,
Turned out the members, and made fast the door,
Bidding the house of every knave and drone,
Forced—though it grieved his soul—to rule alone.
    The Frank Cqurtship.—Crabbe.

Leaving Colonel Everard to his meditations, we. follow the jolly cavalier, his companion, who, before mounting at the George, did not fail to treat himself to his morningdraught of eggs and muscadine, to enable him to face the harvest wind.

Although he had suffered himself to be sunk in the extravagant license which was practised by the cavaliers, as if to oppose their conduct in every point to the preciseness of their enemies, yet Wildrake, well-born and welleducated, and endowed with good natural parts, and a heart which even debauchery, and the wild life of a roaring cavalier, had not been able entirely to corrupt, moved on his present embassy with a strange mixture of feelings, such as perhaps he had never in his life before experienced.

His feelings as a loyalist led him to detest Cromwell, whom in other circumstances he would scarce have wished to see, except in a field of battle, where he could have had the pleasure to exchange pistol-shots with him. But with this hatred there was mixed a certain degree of fear. Always victorious wherever he fought, the remarkable person whom Wildrake was now approaching had acquired that influence over the minds of his enemies, which constant success is so apt to inspire—they dreaded while they hated him—and joined to these feelings, was a restless meddling curiosity, which made a particular feature in Wildrake's character, who, having long had little business of his own, and caring nothing about that which he had, A wine made from Muscat grapes. was easily attracted by the desire of seeing whatever was curious or interesting around him.

"I should like to see the old rascal after all," he said, "were it but to say that I *had* seen him."

He reached Windsor in the afternoon, and felt on his arrival the strongest inclination to take up his residence at some of his old haunts, when he had occasionally frequented that fair town in gayer days. But resisting all temptations of this kind, he went courageously to the principal inn, from which its ancient emblem, the Garter, had long disappeared. The master, too, whom Wildrake, experienced in his knowledge of landlords and hostelries, had remembered a dashing Mine Host of Queen Bess's school, had now sobered down to the temper of the times, shook his head when he spoke of the Parliament, wielded his spigot with the gravity of a priest conducting a sacrifice, wished England a happy issue out of all her afflictions, and greatly lauded his Excellency the Lord General. Wildrake also remarked, that his wine was better than it was wont to be, the Puritans having an excellent gift at detecting every fallacy in that matter; and that his measures were less and his charges larger—circumstances which he was induced to attend to, by mine host talking a good deal about his conscience.

He was told by this important personage, that the Lord General received frankly all sorts of persons; and that he might obtain access to him next morning, at eight o'clock, for the trouble of presenting himself at the Castle gate, and announcing himself as the bearer of despatches to his Excellency.

To the Castle the disguised cavalier repaired at the hour appointed. Admittance was freely permitted to him by the red-coated soldier, who, with austere looks, and his musket on his shoulder, mounted guard at the external gate of that noble building. Wildrake passed through the underward or court, gazing as he passed upon the beautiful Chapel, which had but lately received, in darkness and silence, the unhonored remains of the slaughtered King of England. Rough as Wildrake was, the recollection of this circumstance affected him so strongly, that he had nearly turned back in a sort of horror, rather than face the dark and daring man, to whom, amongst all the actors in that melancholy affair, its tragic conclusion was chiefly to be imputed. But he felt the necessity of subduing all sentiments of this nature, and compelled himself to proceed in a negotiation intrusted to his conduct by one to whom he was so much obliged as Colonel Everard. At the ascent, which passed by the Round Tower, he looked to the ensign-staff, from which the banner of England was wont to float. It was gone, with all its rich emblazonry, its gorgeous quarterings, and splendid embroidery; and in its room waved that of the Commonwealth, the cross of Saint George, in its colours of blue and red, not yet intersected by the diagonal cross of Scotland, which was soon after assumed, as if in evidence of England's conquest over her ancient enemy. This change of ensigns increased the train of his gloomy reflections, in which, although contrary to his wont, he became so deeply wrapped, that the first thing which recalled him to himself, was the challenge from the sentinel, accompanied with a stroke of the butt of his musket on the pavement, with an emphasis which made Wildrake start.

So named in honour of the Order of the Garter, the highest decoration given in England, founded by Edward III. Windsor Castle has been one of the principal residences of the English sovereigns from William the Conqueror to Queen Victoria. It is, perhaps, the finest royal castle in the world. The body of Charles I. was buried in St. George's Chapel at night, February 8, 1649.

"Whither away, and who are you?"

"The bearer of a packet," answered Wildrake, "to the worshipful the Lord General."

"Stand till I call the officer of the guard."

The corporal made his appearance, distinguished above those of his command by a double quantity of band round his neck, a double height of steeple-crowned hat, a larger allowance of cloak, and a treble proportion of sour gravity of aspect. It might be read on his countenance, that he was one of those resolute enthusiasts to whom Oliver owed his conquests, whose religious zeal made them even more than a match for the high-spirited and high-born cavaliers, that exhausted their valour in vain defence of their sovereign's person and crown. He looked with grave solemnity at Wildrake, as if he was making in his own mind an inventory of his features and dress; and having fully perused them, he required "to know his business." In the Round Tower, built by Edward III., David Bruce and James I., Kings of Scotland, were once confined. By quartering is meant the grouping of two or more coats of arms in the quarters of a shield or escutcheon. Colored plates of the Royal Standard and Union Flag of Great Britain, referred to in this passage, may be found in the *Standard Dictionary.*

"My business," said Wildrake, as firmly as he could— for the close investigation of this man had given him some unpleasant nervous sensations—" my business is with your General."

"With his Excellency the Lord General, thou wouldst say?" replied the corporal. "Thy speech, my friend, savours too little of the reverence due to his Excellency."

"D—n his Excellency!" was at the lips of the cavalier; but prudence kept guard, and permitted not the offensive words to escape the barrier. He only bowed, and was silent.

"Follow me," said the starched figure whom he addressed; and Wildrake followed him accordingly, into the guardhouse, which exhibited an interior characteristic of the times, and very different from what such military stations present at the present day.

By the fire sat two or three musketeers, listening to one who was expounding some religious mystery to them. He began half beneath his breath, but in tones of great volubility, which tones, as he approached the conclusion, became sharp and eager, as challenging either instant answer or silent acquiescence. The audience seemed to listen to the speaker with immovable features, only answering him with clouds of tobacco-smoke, which they rolled from under their thick mustaches. On a bench lay a soldier on his face; whether asleep, or in a fit of contemplation, it was impossible to decide. In the midst of the floor stood an officer, as he seemed by his embroidered shoulder-belt and scarf round his waist, otherwise very plainly attired, who was engaged in drilling a stout bumpkin, lately enlisted, to the manual, as it was then used. The motions and words of command were twenty at the very least; and until they were regularly brought to an end, the corporal did not permit Wildrake either to sit down or move forward beyond the threshold of the guard-house. So he had to listen in succession to—Poise your musket—Rest your musket—Oock your musket—Handle your primers —

and many other forgotten words of discipline, until at length the words, "Order your musket," ended the drill for the time.

Utensil for holding a small amount of powder and introducing it into the priming pan of a gun. in the days of flint lock muskets.

"Thy name, friend?" said the officer to the recruit, when the lesson was over.

"Ephraim," answered the fellow, with an affected twang through the nose.

"And what besides Ephraim?" "Ephraim Cobb, from the godly city of Glo'cester, where I have dwelt for seven years, serving apprentice to a praise-worthy cordwainer."

"It is a goodly craft," answered the officer; "but casting in thy lot with ours, doubt not that thou shalt be set beyond thine awl, and thy last to boot."

A grim smile of the speaker accompanied this poor attempt at a pun; and then turning round to the corporal, who stood two paces off, with the face of one who seemed desirous of speaking, said, "How now, corporal, what tidings?" "Here is one with a packet, an it please your Excellency," said the corporal—" Surely my spirit doth not rejoice in him, seeing I esteem him as a wolf in sheep's clothing."

By these words, Wildrake learned that he was in the actual presence of the remarkable person to whom he was commissioned; and he paused to consider in what manner he ought to address him.

The figure of Oliver Cromwell was, as is generally known, in no way prepossessing. He was of middle stature, strong and coarsely made, with harsh and severe features, indicative, however, of much natural sagacity and depth of thought. His eyes were grey and piercing; his nose too large in proportion to his other features, and of a reddish hue.

His manner of speaking, when he had the purpose to make himself distinctly understood, was energetic and forcible, though neither graceful nor eloquent. No man could on such occasion put his meaning into fewer and more decisive words. But when, as it often happened, he had a mind to play the orator, for the benefit of people's ears, without enlightening their understanding, Cromwell was wont to invest his meaning, or that which seemed to be his meaning, in such a mist of words, surrounding it with so many exclusions and exceptions, and fortifying it with such a labyrinth of parentheses, that though one of the most shrewd men in England, he was, perhaps, the most unintelligible speaker that ever perplexed an audience. It has been long since said by the historian, that a collection of the Protector's speeches would make, with a few exceptions, the most nonsensical book in the world; 1 but he ought to have added, that nothing could be more nervous, concise, and intelligible, than what he really intended should be understood.

1 Ground arms. s Shoemaker; so called from a certain kind of leather once manufactured at Cordova, in Spain. D.

It was also remarked of Cromwell, that though born of a good family, both by father and mother, and although he had the usual opportunities of education and breeding connected with such an advantage, the fanatic democratic ruler could never acquire, or else disdained to practise, the courtesies usually exercised among the higher classes in their intercourse with each other. His demeanour was so blunt as sometimes might be termed clownish, yet there was in his language and manner a force and energy corresponding to his character, which impressed awe, if it did not impose respect; and there were even times when that dark and subtle spirit expanded itself, so as almost to conciliate affection. The turn for humour, which displayed itself by fits, was broad, and of a low, and sometimes practical character. Something there was in his disposition congenial to that of his countrymen; a contempt of folly, a hatred of affectation, and a dislike of ceremony, which, joined to the strong intrinsic qualities of sense and courage, made him in many respects not an unfit representative of the democracy of England.

It is uncertain to whom Scott refers here; Clarendon and Hume express themselves to the same general effect. Whoever originated the saying could scarcely have anticipated how completely Carlyle's *Cromwell's Letters and Speeches* would reveal the shallowness of it. He attended the Grammar School at Huntingdon, and was admitted to Sidney Sussex College. Cambridge, on April 23, 1616, the day of Shakespeare's death. How long he remained there is not known. He smeared Henry Marten's face with ink, at the siguing of the death-warrant of Charles I.

'Scott's own political sympathies were far from being with the "democracy," but this passage shows his essential sanity and tolerance of view.

His religion must always be a subject of much doubt, and probably of doubt which he himself could hardly have cleared up. Unquestionably there was a time in his life when he was sincerely enthusiastic, and when his natural temper, slightly subject to hypochondria, was strongly agitated by the same fanaticism which influenced so many persons of the time. On the other hand, there were periods during his political career, when we certainly do him no injustice in charging him with a hypocritical affectation. We shall probably judge him, and others of the same age, most truly, if we suppose that their religious professions were partly influential in their own breast, partly assumed in compliance with their own interest. And so ingenious is the human heart in deceiving itself as well as others, that it is probable neither Cromwell himself, nor those making similar pretensions to distinguished piety, could exactly have fixed the point at which their enthusiasm terminated and their hypocrisy commenced; or rather, it was a point not fixed in itself, but fluctuating with the state of health, of good or bad fortune, of high or low spirits, affecting the individual at the period.

Such was the celebrated person, who, turning round on Wildrake, and scanning his countenance closely, seemed so little satisfied with what he beheld, that he instinctively hitched forward his belt, so as to bring the handle of his tuck-sword within his reach. But yet, folding his arms in his cloak, as if upon second thoughts laying aside suspicion, or thinking precaution beneath him, he asked the cavalier what he was, and whence he came?

"A poor gentleman, sir,—that is, my lord,"—answered Wildrake; "last from Woodstock."

"And what may your tidings be, sir *gentleman?*" said Cromwell, with an emphasis. "Truly I have seen those most willing to take upon them that title, bear themselves somewhat short of wise men, and good men, and true men, with all their gentility; yet gentleman was a good title in old England, when men remembered what it was construed to mean." Frederic Harrison admits the truth of this. '' And doubtless the taste for improving the occasion became at last a snare to Cromwell, ending even with him, as it ended with others, in no little unction, mannerism.—even self-deception. A certain profusion of tears of hyperbolic asseverations and calling God to witness, an excessive expression of each passing emotion which grew with the habit of spiritual stimulants — these are things too well attested and too consonant with the tone of his generation to suffer us to doubt that Cromwell's nature was more than touched by the disease. It was touched, but not poisoned."—F. Harrison's *Cromwell,* p. 104.

"You say truly, sir," replied Wildrake, suppressing, with difficulty, some of his usual wild expletives; "formerly gentlemen were found in gentlemen's places, but now the world is so changed, that you shall find the broidered belt has changed place with the under spur-leather." *"*Say'st thou me?" said the General; "I profess thou art a bold companion, that can bandy words so wantonly; —thou ring'st somewhat too loud to be good metal, methinks. And, once again, what are thy tidings with me?"

"This packet," said Wildrake, "commended to your hands by Colonel Markham Everard."

"Alas, I must have mistaken thee," answered Cromwell, mollified at the mention of a man's name whom he had great desire to make his own; "forgive us, good friend, for such, we doubt not, thou art. Sit thee down, and commune with thyself as thou may'st, until we have examined the contents of thy packet. Let him be looked to, and have what he lacks." So saying, the General left the guard-house, where Wildrake took his seat in the corner, and awaited with patience the issue of his mission.

The soldiers now thought themselves obliged to treat him with more consideration, and offered him a pipe of Trinidado, and a black jack filled with October. But the look of Cromwell, and the dangerous situation in which he might be placed by the least chance of detection, induced Wildrake to decline these hospitable offers, and stretching back in his chair, and affecting slumber, he escaped notice or conversation, until a sort of aide-de-camp, or military officer in attendance, came to summon him to Cromwell's presence.

By this person he was guided to a postern-gate, through which he entered the body of the Castle, and penetrating through many private passages and staircases, he at length was introduced into a small cabinet, or parlour, in which was much rich furniture, some bearing the royal cipher The strap *by* which a spur is secured to the foot. Trinidad tobacco. Ale of the October brewing. displayed, but all confused and disarranged, together with several paintings in massive frames, having their faces turned towards the wall, as if they had been taken down for the purpose of being removed.

In this scene of disorder, the victorious General of the Commonwealth was seated in a large easy chair, covered with damask, and deeply embroidered, the splendour of which made a strong contrast with the plain, and even homely character of his apparel; although in look and action he seemed like one who felt that the seat which might have in former days held a prince, was not too much distinguished for his own fortunes and ambition. Wildrake stood before him, nor did he ask him to sit down.

"Pearson," said Cromwell, addressing himself to the officer in attendance, "wait in the gallery, but be within call." Pearson bowed, and was retiring. "Who are in the gallery besides?"

"Worthy Mr. Gordon, the chaplain, was holding forth but now to Colonel Overton, and four captains of your Excellency's regiment."

"We would have it so," said the General; "we would not there were any corner in our dwelling where the hungry soul might not meet with manna. Was the good man carried onward in his discourse?"

"Mightily borne through," said Pearson; "and he was touching the rightful claims which the army, and especially your Excellency, hath acquired, by becoming the instruments in the great work;—not instruments to be' broken asunder and cast away when the day of their service is over, but to be preserved, and held precious and prized for their honourable, and faithful labours, for which they have fought and marched, and fasted, and prayed, and suffered cold and sorrow; while others, who would now gladly see them disbanded, and broken, and cashiered, eat of the fat, and drink of the-strong." The heaven sent food of the children of Israel in the wilderness; here used in the sense of spiritual food Deprived of their commissions or reduced to the ranks.

The language of Cromwell and his soldiers is so saturated with Scriptural expressions that it is needless in most cases to call attention to the specific quotations. "Never were the thought and the expression of any people more powerfully transformed than were the thought and language of England by the translation of the Bible.... The years of Cromwell's life exactly kept pace with the growth, oulmination aud waning of this first intense influence.... After a few generations the Biblical terms ceased to sound as the very words in which God had spoken, but grew to be mere customary phrases; they became the dialect of an order of men; they grew to be a fashion; they were imitated; and soon withered up into a *cant."*—F. Harrison's *Cromwell,* pp. 26-30. See also Macaulay's passage on the Puritans in his essay on Milton, and an eloquent passage in J. R. Green's *Short History of the English People,* Chapter on "Puritan England."

"Ah, good man!" said Cromwell, "and did he touch upon this so feelingly! I could say something—but not now. Begone, Pearson, to the gallery. Let not our friends lay aside their swords, but watch as well as pray."

Pearson retired; and the General, holding the letter of Everard in his hand, looked again for a long while fixedly at Wildrake, as if considering in what strain he should address him.

When he did speak, it was at first in one of those ambiguous discourses which we have already described, and by which it was very difficult for any one to understand his meaning, if indeed he knew it himself. We shall be as concise in our statement as our desire to give the very words of a man so extraordinary will permit.

"This letter," he said, "you have brought us from your master, or patron, Markham Everard; truly an excellent and honourable gentleman as ever bore a sword upon his thigh, and one who hath ever distinguished himself in the great work of delivering these three poor and unhappy nations. Answer me not: I know what thou wouldst say.— And this letter he hath sent to me by thee, his clerk, or secretary, in whom he hath confidence, and in whom he prays me to have trust, that there may be a careful messenger between us. And lastly, he hath sent thee to me— Do not answer—I know what thou wouldst say,— to me, who, albeit I am of that small consideration, that it would be too much honour, for me even to bear a halberd in this great and victorious army of England, am nevertheless exalted to the rank of holding the guidance and the leadingstaff thereof.—Nay, do not answer, my friend—I know what thou wouldst say. Now, when communing thus together, our discourse taketh, in respect to what I have said, a threefold argument, or division: Eirst, as it concerneth thy master; secondly, as it concerneth us and our office; thirdly and lastly, as it toucheth thyself.—Now, as concerning this good and worthy gentleman, Colonel Markham Everard, truly hath he played the man from the beginning of these unhappy buffetings, not turning to the right or to the left, but holding ever in his eye the mark at which he aimed. Ay, truly, a faithful, honourable gentleman, and one who may well call me friend; and truly I am pleased to think that he doth so. Nevertheless, in this vale of tears, we must be governed less by our private respects and partialities, than by those higher principles and points of duty, whereupon the good Colonel Markham Everard hath ever framed his purposes, as, truly, I have endeavoured to form mine, that we may all act as becometh good Englishmen and worthy patriots. Then, as for Woodstock, it is a great thing which the good Colonel asks, that it should be taken from the spoil of the godly, and left in keeping of the men of Moab, and especially of the malignant, Henry Lee, whose hand hath been ever against us when he might find room to raise it; I say he hath asked a great thing, both in respect of himself and me. For we of this poor but godly army of England, are holden, by those of the Parliament, as men who should render in spoil for them, but be no sharer of it ourselves; even as the buck, which the hounds pull to earth, furnisheth no part of their own food, but they are lashed off from the carcass with whips, like those which require punishment for their forwardness, not reward for their services. Yet I speak not this so much in respect of this grant of Woodstock, in regard that, perhaps, their Lordships of the Council, and also the Committee-men of this Parliament, may graciously think they have given me a portion in the matter, in relation that my kinsman Desborough hath an interest allowed him therein; which interest, as he hath well deserved it for his true and faithful service to these unhappy and devoted countries, so it would ill become me to diminish the same to his prejudice, unless it were upon great and public respects. Thus thou seest how it stands with me, my honest friend, and in what mind I stand touching thy master's request to me; which yet I do not say that I can altogether, or unconditionally, grant or refuse, but only tell my simple thoughts with regard thereto. Thou understandeth me, I doubt not?" Now, Roger Wildrake, with all the attention he had 1 Enemies of the children of Israel, *i.e.,* Royalists.
been able to pay to the Lord General's speech, had got so much confused among the various clauses of the harangue, that his brain was bewildered, like that of a country clown, when he chances to get himself involved among a crowd of carriages, and cannot stir a step to get out of the way of one of them, without being in danger of being ridden over by the others.

The General saw his look of perplexity, and began a new oration, to the same purpose as before; spoke of his love for his kind friend the Colonel,—his regard for his pious and godly kinsman, Master Desborough,—the great importance of the Palace and Park of Woodstock,— the determination of the Parliament that it should be confiscated, and the produce brought into the coffers of the state,—his own deep veneration for the authority of Parliament, and his no less deep sense of the injustice done to the army,— how it was his wish and will that all matters should be settled in an amicable and friendly manner, without self-seeking, debate, or strife, betwixt those who had been the hands acting, and such as had been the heads governing, in that great national cause,—how he was willing, truly willing, to contribute to this work, by laying down, not his commission only, but his life also, if it were requested of him, or could be granted with safety to the" poor soldiers, to whom, silly poor men, he was bound to be as a father, seeing that they had followed him with the duty and affection of children.

And here he arrived at another dead pause, leaving Wildrake as uncertain as before, whether it was or was not his purpose to grant Colonel Everard the powers he had asked for the protection of Woodstock against the Parliamentary commissioners. Internally he began to entertain hopes that the justice of Heaven, or the effects of remorse had confounded the regicide's understanding. But no—he could see nothing but sagacity in that steady stern eye, which, while the tongue poured forth its periphrastic language in such profusion, seemed to watch with severe accuracy the effect which his oratory produced on the listener.

Those who sat in the High Court of Justice which condemned Charles I. were termed Regicides by the Royalists. Several of them were executed after the Restoration. Others fled to America. The romantic story of Whalley, one of these latter, is told in Scott's *Pevetil of Hie Peak* and Hawthorne's *The Gray Champion*. "Egad," thought the cavalier to himself, becoming a little familiar with the situation in which he was placed, and rather impatient of a conversation which led to no visible conclusion or termination. "If Noll were the devil himself, as he is the devil's darling, I will not be thus nose-led by him. Ill e'en brusque it a little, if he goes on at this rate, and try if I can bring him to a more intelligible mode of speaking."

Entertaining this bold purpose, but half afraid to execute it, Wildrake lay by for an opportunity of making the attempt, while Cromwell was apparently unable to express his own meaning. He was already beginning a third panegyric upon Colonel Everard, with sundry varied expressions of his own wish to oblige him, when Wildrake took the opportunity to strike in, on the General making one of his oratorical pauses.

"So please you," he said, bluntly, "your worship has already spoken on two topics of your discourse, your own worthiness, and that of my master, Colonel Everard. But, to enable me to do mine errand, it would be necessary to bestow a few words on the third head."

"The third!" said Cromwell.

"Ay," said Wildrake, "which, in your honour's subdivision of "your discourse, touched on my unworthy self. What am I to do—what portion am I to have in this matter?"

Oliver started at once from the tone of voice he had hitherto used, and which somewhat resembled the purring of a domestic cat, into the growl of the tiger when about to spring. "*Thy* portion, jail-bird!" he exclaimed, "the gallows—thou shalt hang as high as Hainan, if thou betray counsel!—But," he added, softening his voice, "keep it like a true man, and my favour will be the making of thee. Come hither—thou art bold, I see, though somewhat saucy. Thou hast been a malignant—so writes my worthy friend, Colonel Everard; but thou hast now given up that fallen cause. I tell thee, friend, not all that the Parliament or the army could do would have pulled down the Stuarts out of their high places, saving that Heaven had a controversy with them. Well, it is a sweet and comely thing to buckle on one's armour in behalf of Heaven's cause; otherwise truly, for mine own part, these *Esther* iii.-viii.

men might have remained upon the throne even unto this day. Neither do I blame any for aiding them, until these successive great judgments have overwhelmed them and their house. I am not a bloody man, having in me the feeling of human frailty; but, friend, whosoever putteth his hand to the plough, in the great actings which are now on foot in these nations, had best beware that he do not look back; for, rely upon my simple word that if you fail me, I will not spare on you one foot's length of the gallows of Haman. Let me therefore know, at a word, if the leaven of thy malignancy is altogether drubbed out of thee?"

"Your honourable lordship," said the cavalier, shrugging up his shoulders, "has done that for most of us, so far as cudgelling to some tune can perform it."

"Sayst thou?" said the General, with a grim smile on his lip, which seemed to intimate that he was not quite inaccessible to flattery; "yea, truly, thou dost not lie in that—we have been an instrument. Neither are we, as I have already hinted, so severely bent against those who have striven against us as malignants, as others may be. The parliament-men best know their own interest and their own pleasure; but, to my poor thinking, it is full time to close these jars, and to allow men of all kinds the means of doing service to their country; and we think it will be thy fault if thou art not employed to good purpose for the state and thyself, on condition thou puttest away the old man entirely from thee, and givest thy earnest attention to what I have to tell thee."

"Your lordship need not doubt my attention," said the cavalier.

And the republican General, after another pause, as one who gave his confidence not without hesitation, proceeded to explain his views with a distinctness which he seldom used, yet not without his being a little biassed now and then, by his long habits of circumlocution, which indeed he never laid entirely aside, save in the field of battle.

"Thou seest," he said, "my friend, how things stand with me. The Parliament, I care not who knows it, love me not—still less do the Council of State, by whom they manage the executive government of the kingdom. I cannot tell why they nourish suspicion against me, unless it is because I will not deliver this poor innocent army, which has followed me in so many military actions, to be now pulled asunder, broken piecemeal and reduced, so that they who have protected the state at the expense of their blood, will not have, perchance, the means of feeding themselves by their labour; which, methinks, were hard measure, since it is taking from Esau his birthright, even without giving him a poor mess of pottage."

"Esau is likely to help himself, I think," replied Wildrake.

"Truly, thou sayst wisely," replied the General; "it is ill starving an armed man, if there is food to be had for taking—nevertheless, far be it from me to encourage rebellion, or want of due subordination to these our rulers. I would only petition in a due and becoming, a sweet and harmonious manner, that they would listen to our conditions, and consider our necessities. But, sir, looking on me, and estimating me so little as they do, you must think that it would be a provocation in me towards the Council of State, as well as the Parliament, if, simply to gratify your worthy master, I were to act contrary to their purposes, or deny currency to the commission under their authority, which is as yet the highest in the State—and long may it be so for me!—to carry on the sequestration which they intend. And would it not also be said, that I was lending myself to the malignant interest, affording this den of the bloodthirsty and lascivious tyrants of yore, to be in this our day a place of refuge to that old and inveterate Amalekite, Sir Henry Lee, to keep possession of the place in which he hath so long glorified himself? Truly it would be a perilous matter."

"Am I then to report," said Wildrake, "an it please you, that you cannot stead Colonel Everard in this matter?"

"Unconditionally, ay—but, taken conditionally, the answer may be otherwise,"—answered Cromwell. "I see thou art not able to fathom my purpose, and therefore I will partly unfold it to thee.— But take notice, that, should thy tongue betray my counsel, save in so far as carrying it to thy master, by all the blood which has been shed in these wild times, thou shalt die a thousand deaths

"Do not fear me, sir," said Wildrake, whose natural boldness and carelessness of character was for the present time borne down and quelled, like that of falcons in the presence of the eagle.

"Hear me, then," said Cromwell, "and let no syllable escape thee. Knowest thou not the young Lee whom they call Albert, a malignant like his father, and one who went up with the young man to that last ruffle which we had with him at Worcester—May we be grateful for the victory!"

"I know there is such a young gentleman as Albert Lee," said Wildrake.

"And knowest thou not—I speak not by way of prying into the good Colonel's secrets, but only as it behooves me to know something of the matter, that I may best judge how I am to serve him—Knowest thou not that thy master, Markham Everard, is a suitor after the sister of this same malignant, a daughter of the old Keeper, called Sir Henry Lee?"

"All this I have heard," said Wildrake, "nor can I deny that I believe in it."

"Well, then, go to.—When the young man Charles Stuart fled from the field of Worcester, and was by sharp chase and pursuit compelled to separate himself from his followers, I know by sure intelligence that this Albert Lee was one of the last who remained with him, if not indeed the very last." "It was devilish like him," said the cavalier, without sufficiently weighing his expressions, considering in what presence they were to be uttered—"And I'll uphold him with my rapier, to be a. true chip of the old block!"

"Ha, swearest thou?" said the General. "Is this thy reformation?"

"I never swear, so please you," replied Wildrake, recollecting himself, "except there is some mention of malignants and cavaliers in my hearing; and then the old habit returns, and I swear like one of Goring's troopers." 1Young John Wilmot, second Earl of Rochester, was really the last to leave the King. Pepys's *Diary* for May *23,* 1060, gives the King's own narrative of his escape from Worcester. The fullest account is in Clarendon's *Ilis'ory of the Rebellion,* a passage from which is quoted in the Editor's Introduction.

Lord George Goring's troopers were notorious for their dissoluteness. "Out upon thee," said the General; "what can it avail thee to practise a profanity so horrible to the ears of others, and which brings no emolument to him who uses it?"

"There are, doubtless, more profitable sins in the world than the barren and unprofitable vice of swearing," was the answer which rose to the lips of the cavalier; but that was exchanged for a profession of regret for having given offence. The truth was, the discourse began to take a turn which rendered it more interesting than ever to Wildrake, who therefore determined not to lose the opportunity for obtaining possession of the secret that seemed to be suspended on Cromwell's lips; and that could only be through means of keeping guard upon his own.

"What sort of a house is Woodstock?" said the General abruptly.

"An old mansion," said Wildrake, in reply; "and, so far as I could judge by a single night's lodgings, having abundance of backstairs, also subterranean passages, and all the communications under ground, which are common in old raven-nests of the sort."

"And places for concealing priests, unquestionably," said Cromwell. "It is seldom that such ancient houses lack secret stalls wherein to mew up these calves of Bethel."

"Your Honour's Excellency," said Wildrake, "may swear to that." "I swear not at all," replied the General drily.—" But what think'st thou, good fellow?— I will ask thee a blunt question—Where will those two Worcester fugitives that thou wottest of be more likely to take shelter—and that they must be sheltered somewhere-, I well know—than in this same old palace, with all the corners and concealments whereof young Albert hath been acquainted ever since his earliest infancy?"

"Truly," said Wildrake, making an effort to answer the question with seeming indifference, while the possibility of such an event, and its consequences, flashed fearfully upon his mind,—" Truly, I should be of your honour's opinion, but that I think the company, who, by the commission of Parliament, have occupied Woodstock, are likely to fright them thence, as a cat scares doves from a pigeon-house. The neighbourhood, with reverence, of Generals Des To hide away these idols.

borough and Harrison, will suit ill with fugitives from Worcester field."

"I thought as much, and so, indeed, would I have it," answered the General. Long may it be ere our names shall be aught but a terror to our enemies. But in this matter, if thou art an active plotter for thy master's interest, thou might'st, I should think, work out something favourable to his present object."

"My brain is too poor to reach the depth of your honourable purpose," said Wildrake.

"Listen then, and let it be to profit," answered Cromwell. "Assuredly the conquest at Worcester was a great and crowning mercy; yet might we seem to be but small in our thankfulness for the same, did we not do what in us lies towards the ultimate improvement and final conclusion of the great work which has been thus prosperous in our hands, professing in pure humility and singleness of heart, that we do not, in any way, deserve our instrumentality to be remembered, nay, would rather pray and intreat, that our name and fortunes were forgotten, than that the great work were in itself incomplete. Nevertheless, truly, placed as we now are, it concerns us more nearly than others,— that is, if so poor creatures should at all speak of themselves as concerned, whether more or less, with these changes which have been wrought around, not, I say, by ourselves, or our own power, but by the destiny to which we were called, fulfilling the same with all meekness and humility,—I say it concerns us nearly that all things should be done in conformity with the great work which hath been wrought, and is yet working, in these lands. Such is my plain and simple meaning. Nevertheless, it is much to be desired that this young man, this King of Scots, as he called himself—this Charles Stuart—should not escape forth from the nation, where his arrival has wrought so much disturbance and bloodshed."

"I have no doubt," said the cavalier, looking down, "that your lordship's wisdom hath directed all things as they may best lead towards such a consummation; and I pray your pains may be paid as they deserve."

"I thank thee, friend," said Cromwell, with much humility; "doubtless we shall meet our reward, being in the hands of a good paymaster, who never passeth Saturday night. But understand me, friend—I desire no more than my own share in the good work. I would heartily do what poor kindness I can to your worthy master, and even to you in your degree—for such as I do not converse with ordinary men, that our presence may be forgotten like an every-day's occurrence. We speak to men like thee for their reward or their punishment; and I trust it will be the former which thou in thine office wilt merit at my hand."

"Your honour," said Wildrake, "speaks like one accustomed to command."

"True; men's minds are likened to those of my degree by fear and reverence," said the General; "but enough of that, desiring, as I do, no other dependency on my special person than is alike to us all upon that which is above us. But I would desire to cast this golden ball into your master's lap. He hath served against this Charles Stuart and his father. But he is a kinsman near to the old knight, Lee, and stands well affected towards his daughter. *Thou* also wilt keep a watch, my friend—that ruffling look of thine will procure thee the confidence of every malignant, and the prey cannot approach this cover, as though to shelter, like a coney in the rocks, but thou wilt be sensible of his presence."

"I make a shift to comprehend your Excellency," said the cavalier; "and I thank you heartily for the good opinion you have put upon me, and which, I pray I may have some handsome opportunity of deserving, that I may shew my gratitude by the event. But still, with reverence, your Excellency's scheme seems unlikely, while Woodstock remains in possession of the sequestrators. Both the old knight and his son, and far more such a fugitive as your honour hinted at, will take special care not to approach it till they are removed."

"It is for that I have been dealing with thee thus long," said the General.—" I told thee that I was something unwilling, upon slight occasion, to dispossess the sequestrators by my own proper warrant, although having, perhaps, sufficient authority in the state both to do so, and to despise the murmurs of those who blame me. In brief, I would be loath to tamper with my privileges, and make experiments between their strength, and the powers of the commission granted by others, without pressing need, *Proverbs* xxx. 26.
or at least great prospect of advantage. So, if thy Colonel will undertake, for his love of the Republic, to find the means of preventing its worst and nearest danger, which must needs occur from the escape of this young man, and will do his endeavour to stay him, in case his flight should lead him to Woodstock, which I hold very likely, I will give thee an order to these sequestrators, to evacuate the palace instantly; and to the next troop of my regiment, which lies at Oxford, to turn them out by the shoulders, if they make any scruples—Ay, even for example's sake, if they drag Desborough out foremost, though he be wedded to my sister."

"So please you, sir," said Wildrake, "and with your most powerful warrant, I trust I might expel the commissioners, even without the aid of your most warlike and devout troopers."

"That is what I am least anxious about," replied the General; "I should like to see the best of them sit after I had nodded to them to begone—always excepting the worshipful House, in whose name our commissions run; but who, as some think, will be done with politics ere it be time to renew them. Therefore, what chiefly concerns me to know, is, whether thy master will embrace a traffic which hath such a fair promise of profit with it. I am well convinced that, with a scout like thee, who hast been in the cavalier's quarters, and canst, I should guess, resume thy drinking, ruffianly, health-quaffing manners whenever thou hast a mind, he must discover where this Stuart hath ensconced himself. Either the young Lee will visit the old one in person, or he will write to him, or hold communication with him by letter. At all events, Markham Everard and thou must have an eye in every hair of your head." While he spoke, a flush passed over his brow, he rose from his chair, and paced the apartment in agitation. "Woe to you, if you suffer the young adventurer to escape me!—you had better be in the deepest dungeon in Europe, than breathe the air of England, should you but dream of playing me false. I have spoken freely to thee, fellow—more freely than is my wont—the time required it. But, to share my confidence is like keeping a watch over a powder-magazine, the least and most insignificant spark Cromwell himself broke up the Long Parliament by force on April 20, 1653.

blows thee to ashes. Tell your master what I said—but not how I said it—Fie, that I should have been betrayed into this distemperature of passion!—begone, sirrah. Pearson shall bring thee sealed orders—Yet, stay—thou hast something to ask."

"I would know," said Wildrake, to whom the risible anxiety of the General gave some confidence, "what is the figure of this young gallant, in case I should find him?" "A tall, rawboned, swarthy lad, they say he has shot up into. Here is his picture by a good hand, some time since." He turned round one of the portraits which stood with its face against the wall; but it proved not to be that of Charles the Second, but of his unhappy father.

The first motion of Cromwell indicated a purpose of hastily replacing the picture, and it seemed as if an effort was necessary to repress his disinclination to look upon it. But he did repress it, and, placing the picture against the wall, withdrew slowly and sternly, as if, in defiance of his own feelings, he was determined to gain a place from which to see it to advantage. It was well for Wildrake that his dangerous companion had not turned an eye on him, for *his* blood also kindled when he saw the portrait of his master in the hands of the chief author of his death. Being a fierce and desperate man, he commanded his passion with great difficulty; and if, on its first violence, he had been provided with a suitable weapon, it is possible Cromwell would never have ascended higher in his bold ascent towards supreme power.

But this natural and sudden flush of indignation, which rushed through the veins of an ordinary man like Wildrake, was presently subdued, when confronted with the strong yet stifled emotion displayed by so powerful a character as Cromwell. As the cavalier looked on his dark and bold countenance, agitated by inward and indescribable feelings, he found his own violence of spirit die away and lose itself in fear and wonder. So true it is, that as greater lights swallow up and extinguish the display of those which are less, so men of great, capacious, and overruling minds, bear aside and subdue, in their climax of passion, the more feeble wills and passions of others; as, when a river joins a brook, the fiercer torrent shoulders aside the smaller stream.

Wildrake stood a silent, inactive, and almost a terrified spectator, while Cromwell, assuming a firm sternness of eye and manner, as one who compels himself to look on what some strong internal feeling renders painful and disgustful to him, proceeded, in brief and interrupted expressions, but yet with a firm voice, to comment on the portrait of the late King. His words seemed less addressed to Wildrake, than to be the spontaneous unburdening of his own bosom, swelling under recollection of the past and anticipation of the future.

"That Flemish painter," he said—" that Antonio Vandyke—what a power he has! Steel may mutilate, warriors may waste and destroy—still the King stands uninjured by time; and our grandchildren, while they read his history, may look on his image, and compare the melancholy features with the woful tale.—It was a stern necessity—it was an awful deed! The calm pride of that eye might have ruled worlds of crouching Frenchmen, or supple Italians, or formal Spaniards; but its glances only roused the native courage of the stern Englishman.—Lay not on poor sinful man, whose breath is in his nostrils, the blame that he falls, when Heaven never gave him strength of nerves to stand! The weak rider is thrown by his unruly horse, and trampled to death—the strongest man, the best cavalier, springs to the empty saddle, and uses bit and spur till the fiery steed knows its master. Who blames him, who, mounted aloft, rides triumphantly amongst the people, for having succeeded, where the unskilful and feeble fell and died? Verily, he hath his reward: Then, what is that piece of painted canvas to me more than others? No; let him shew to others the reproaches of that cold, calm face, that proud yet complaining eye: Those who have acted on higher respects have no cause to start at painted shadows. Not wealth nor power brought me from my obscurity. The oppressed consciences, the injured liberties of England, were the banner that I followed."

He raised his voice so high, as if pleading in his own defence before some tribunal, that Pearson, the officer in attendance, looked into the apartment; and observing his master, with his eyes kindling, his arm extended, his foot advanced, and his voice raised, like a general in the act of commanding the advance of his army, he instantly withdrew.

"It was other than selfish regards that drew me forth to action," continued Cromwell, "and I dare the world—ay, living or dead I challenge—to assert that I armed for a private cause, or as a means of enlarging my fortunes. Neither was there a trooper in the regiment who came there with less of personal evil will to yonder unhappy"

At this moment the door of the apartment opened and a gentlewoman entered, who, from her resemblance to the general, although her features were soft and feminine, might be immediately recognised as his daughter. She walked up to Cromwell, gently but firmly passed her arm through his, and said to him in a persuasive tone, " Father, this is not well—you have promised me this should not happen."

The General hung down his head, like one who was either ashamed of the passion to which he had given way, or of the influence which was exercised over him. He yielded, however, to the affectionate impulse, and left the apartment, without again turning his head towards the portrait which had so much affected him, or looking towards Wildrake, who remained fixed in astonishment.

i Cromwell's favourite daughter, Mrs. Claypole. Her influence over him is commented upon by most of his biographers. Clarendon notes that shortly before Cromwell's death " that which chiefly broke his peace was the death of his daughter Claypole; who had always been his greatest joy. and who, in her sickness, which was of a nature the physicians knew not how to deal with,

had several conferences with him which exceedingly perplexed him. Though nobody was near enough to hear the particulars, yet her often mentioning, in the pains she endured, the blood her father had spilt, made people conclude that she had presented his worst actions to his consideration. And though he never made the least show of remorse for any of those actions, it is very certain, that either what she said, or her death affected him wonderfully."—*History of t/te Rebellion,* Book XV. fin the delineation of a well-known historical character like Cromwell, how far do you think the novelist is forced to follow the popular conception of his hero? (Compare Scott's figure of Queen Mary in *T/te Abbot.)* Does Cromwell impress you in this chapter as a great man? Does Scott paint him as powerfully as he does the Regent Murray in *The Abbot,* the Duke of Burgundy and Louis XI. in *Quentin Dnrward?* Do you think Cromwell's talk is skilfully managed? If it is self-consistent, is there any reason why it should imitate the actual style of Cromwell, as preserved in his letters and speeches? Is Cromwell's self revelation—at the close of the chapter—melodramatic, that is, is a situation secured at the expense of naturalness and consistency in the character? After the hints given in this chapter would you not expect a struggle on Everard's part over surrendering Charles I., should the opportunity offer; as for instance, a conflict between his duty toward the Commonwealth and his pity for Charles, or between his love for Alice and the possibility of advancement through yielding to Cromwell's wishes? Note whether Scott works out these hints, or abandons them. CHAPTER THE NINTH *Doctor.*—Go to, go to—You have known what yon should not.
Macbeth.

Wildeake was left in the cabinet, as we have said, astonished and alone. It was often noised about, that Cromwell, the deep and sagacious statesman, the calm and intrepid commander, he who had overcome such difficulties, and ascended to such heights, that he seemed already to bestride the land which he had conquered, had, like many other men of great genius, a constitutional taint of melancholy, which sometimes displayed itself both in words and actions, and had been first observed in that sudden and striking change, when, abandoning entirely the dissolute freaks1 of his youth, he embraced a very strict course of religious observances, which, upon some occasions, he seemed to consider as bringing him into more near and close contact with the spiritual world. This extraordinary man is said sometimes, during that period of his life, to have given way to spiritual delusions, or, as he himself conceived them, prophetic inspirations of approaching grandeur, and of strange, deep, and mysterious agencies, in which he was in future to be engaged, in the same manner as his younger years had been marked by fits of exuberant and excessive frolic and debaucheries. Something of this kind seemed to explain the ebullition of passion which he had now manifested.

With wonder at what he had witnessed, Wildrake felt some anxiety on his own account. Though not the most reflecting of mortals, he had sense enough to know, that it is dangerous to be a witness of the infirmities of men high in power; and he was left so long by himself, as induced him to entertain some secret doubts, whether the General might not be tempted to take means of confining or removing a witness, who had seen him lowered, as it seemed, by the suggestions of his own conscience, beneath that lofty flight, which, in general, he affected to sustain above the rest of the sublunary world.
1There is no evidence in support of this charge, which Scott apparently borrows from Hume. "The charge of early debauchery may safely be dismissed."—*Dictionary of National Biography.*
In this, however, he wronged Cromwell, who was free either from an extreme degree of jealous suspicion, or from anything which approached towards bloodthirstiness. Pearson appeared, after a lapse of about an hour, and, intimating to Wildrake that he was to follow, conducted him into a distant apartment, in which he found the General seated on a low couch His daughter was in the apartment, but remained at some distance, apparently busied with some female needle-work, and scarce turned her head as Pearson and Wildrake entered.

At a sign from the Lord General, Wildrake approached him as before. "Comrade," he said, "your old friends the cavaliers look on me as their enemy, and conduct themselves towards me as if they desired to make me such. I profess they are labouring to their own prejudice; for I regard, and have ever regarded them, as honest and honourable fools, who were silly enough to run their necks into nooses, and their heads against stone-walls, that a man called Stuart, and no other, should be king over them. Fools! are there no words made of letters that would sound as well as Charles Stuart, with that magic title beside them? Why, the word King is like a lighted lamp, that throws the same bright gilding upon any combination of the alphabet, and yet you must shed your blood for a name! But thou, for thy part, shalt have no wrong from me. Here is an order, well warranted, to clear the Lodge at Woodstock, and abandon it to thy master's keeping, or those whom he shall appoint. He will have his uncle and pretty cousin with him, doubtless. Fare thee well—think on what I told thee. They say beauty is a loadstone to yonder long lad, thou dost wot of; but I reckon he has other stars at present to direct his course than bright eyes and fair hair. Be it as it may, thou knowest my purpose—peer out, peer out; keep a constant and careful look-out on every ragged patch that wanders by hedgerow or lane—these are days when a beggar's cloak may cover a king's ransom. There are some broad Portugal pieces for thee—something strange to thy pouch, I ween.—Once more, think on what thou hast heard, and," he added, in a lower and more impressive tone of voice, "forget what thou hast seen. My service to thy master; —and, yet once again, *remember*—and *forget."—* Wild rake made his obeisance, and, returning to his inn, left Windsor with all possible speed.

Cromwell's innate blood-thirstiness is proved, in the opinion of many people, by the massacres at Drogheda and Wexford in Ireland, which were in accordance with his orders. Scott probably viewed them as military necessities, however. Carlyle praises them. F. Harrison's view is commendably impartial. The refusal of the Irish members of Parliament to vote an appropriation for a statue of Cromwell helped to precipitate the fall of the Liberal Government in June, 1895.

It was afternoon in the same day when the cavalier rejoined his roundhead friend, who was anxiously expecting him at the inn in Woodstock appointed for their rendezvous.

"Where hast thou been?—what hast thou seen?—what strange uncertainty is in thy looks?—and why dost thou not answer me?"

"Because," said Wildrake, laying aside his riding cloak and rapier, "you ask so many questions at once. A man has but one tongue to answer with, and mine is well-nigh glued to the roof of my mouth."

"Will drink unloosen it?" said the Colonel; "though I dare say thou hast tried that spell at every ale-house on the road. Call for what thou wouldst have, man, only be quick."

"Colonel Bverard," answered Wildrake, "I have not tasted so much as a cup of cold water this day."

"Then thou art out of humour for that reason," said the Colonel; "salve thy sore with brandy, if thou wilt, but leave being so fantastic and unlike to thyself, as thou she west in this silent mood."

"Colonel Everard," replied the cavalier, very gravely, "I am an altered man."

"I think thou dost alter," said Bverard, "every day in the year, and every hour of the day. Come, good now, tell me, hast thou seen the General, and got his warrant for clearing out the sequestrators from Woodstock?"

"I have seen the devil," said Wildrake, "and have, as thou say est, got a warrant from him."

"Give it me hastily," said Everard, catching at the packet.

"Forgive me, Mark," said Wildrake; "if thou knewest the purpose with which this deed is granted—if thou knewest—what it is not my purpose to tell thee—what manner of hopes are founded on thy accepting it, I have that opinion of thee, Mark Everard, that thou wouldst as soon take a red-hot horseshoe from the anvil with thy bare hand, as receive into it this slip of paper."

"Come, come," said Everard, "this comes of some of your exalted ideas of loyalty, which, excellent within certain bounds, drive us mad when encouraged up to some heights. Do not think, since I must needs speak plainly with thee, that I see without sorrow the downfall of our ancient monarchy, and the substitution of another form of government in its stead; but ought my regret for the past to prevent my acquiescing and aiding in such measures as are likely to settle the future? The royal cause is ruined, hadst thou and every cavalier in England sworn the contrary; ruined, not to rise again,—for many a day at least. The Parliament, so often draughted and drained of those who were courageous enough to maintain their own freedom of opinion, is now reduced to a handful of statesmen, who have lost the respect of the people, from the length of time during which they have held the supreme management of affairs. They cannot stand long unless they were to reduce the army; and the army, late servants, are now masters, and will refuse to be reduced. They know their strength, and that they may be an army subsisting on pay and free quarters throughout England as long as they will. I tell thee, Wildrake, unless we look to the only man who can rule and manage them, we may expect military law throughout the land; and I, for mine own part, look for any preservation of our privileges that may be vouchsafed to us, only through the wisdom and forbearance of Cromwell. Now you have my secret. You are aware that I am not doing the best I would, but the best I can. I wish—not so ardently as thou, perhaps—yet I *do* wish that the King could have been restored on good terms of composition, safe for us and for himself. And now, good Wildrake, rebel as thou thinkest me, make me no worse a rebel than an unwilling one. God knows, I never laid aside love and reverence to the King, even in drawing my sword against his ill advisers."

"Ah, plague on you," said Wildrake, "that is the very cant of it—that's what you all say. All of you fought against the King in pure love and loyalty, and not otherwise. However, I see your drift, and I own that I like it better than I expected. The army is your bear now, and old Noll is your bearward; and you are like a country constable, who makes interest with the bearward that he may prevent him from letting bruin loose. Well, there may come a day when the sun will shine on our side of the fence, and thereon shall you, and all the good fair-weather folks who love the stronger party, come and make common cause with us."

Without much attending to what his friend said, Colonel Everard carefully studied the warrant of Cromwell. "It is bolder and more peremptory than I expected," he said. "The General must feel himself strong, when he opposes his own authority so directly to that of the Council of State and the Parliament."

"You will not hesitate to act upon it?" said Wildrake.

"That I certainly will not," answered Everard; "but I must wait till I have the assistance of the Mayor, who, I think, will gladly see these fellows ejected from the Lodge. I must not go altogether upon military authority, if possible." Then stepping to the door of the apartment, he despatched a servant of the house in quest of the Chief Magistrate, desiring he should be made acquainted that Colonel Everard desired to see him with as little loss of time as possible.

"You are sure he will come like a dog at a whistle," said Wildrake. "The word captain, or colonel, makes the fat citizen trot in these days, when one sword is worth fifty corporation charters. But there are dragoons yonder, as well as the grim-faced knave whom I frightened the other evening when I shewed my face in at the window. Think'st thou the knaves will shew no rough play?" 'The General's warrant will weigh more with them than a dozen acts of Parliament," said Everard.—" But it is time thou eatest, if thou hast in truth ridden from Windsor hither without baiting."

"I care not about it," said Wildrake: "I tell thee, your

General gave me a breakfast, which, I think, will serve me one while, if I am ever able to digest it. By the mass, it lay so heavy on my conscience, that I carried it to church to see if I could digest it there with my other sins. But not a whit. " Bear-keeper.

"To church!—to the door of the church, thou meanest," said Everard. "I know thy way—thou art ever wont to pull thy hat off reverently at the threshold, but for crossing it, that day seldom comes."

"Well," replied Wildrake, "and if I do pull off my castor and kneel, is it not seemly to shew the same respects in a church which we offer in a palace? It is a dainty matter, is it not, to see your Anabaptists, and Brownists, and the rest of you, gather to a sermon with as little ceremony as hogs to a trough! But here comes food, and now for a grace, if I can remember one."

Everard was too much interested about the fate of his uncle and his fair cousin, and the prospect of restoring them to their quiet home, under the protection of that formidable truncheon which was already regarded as the leading-staff of England, to remark, that certainly a great alteration had taken place in the manners and outward behaviour at least of his companion. His demeanour frequently evinced a sort of struggle betwixt old habits of indulgence, and some newly formed resolutions of abstinence; and it was almost ludicrous to see how often the hand of the neophyte directed itself naturally to a large black leathern jack, which contained two double flagons of strong ale, and how often, diverted from its purpose by the better reflections of the reformed toper, it seized, instead, upon a large ewer of salubrious and pure water.

It was not difficult to see that the task of sobriety was not yet become easy, and that, if it had the recommendation of the intellectual portion of the party who had resolved upon it, the outward man yielded a reluctant and restive compliance. But honest Wildrake had been dreadfully frightened at the course proposed to him by Cromwell, and, with a feeling not peculiar to the Catholic religion, had formed a solemn resolution within his own mind, that, if he came off safe and with honour from this dangerous interview, he would shew his sense of Heaven's favour, by renouncing some of the sins which most easily beset him, and especially that of intemperance, to which, like many of his wild compeers, he was too much addicted.

This resolution, or vow, was partly prudential as well as religious; for it occurred to him as very possible, that some matters of a difficult and delicate nature might be thrown into his hands at the present emergency, during the conduct of which it would be fitting for him to act by some better oracle than that of the Bottle, celebrated by Rabelais. In full compliance with this prudent determination, he touched neither the ale nor the brandy which were placed before him, and declined peremptorily the sack with which his friend would have garnished the board. Nevertheless, just as the boy removed the trenchers and napkins, together with the large blackjack which we have already mentioned, and was one or two steps on his way to the door, the sinewy arm of the cavalier, which seemed to elongate itself on purpose (as it extended far beyond the folds of the threadbare jacket), arrested the progress of the retiring Ganymede, and seizing on the blackjack, conveyed it to the lips, which were gently breathing forth the aspiration, " D—n—I mean, Heaven forgive me —we are poor creatures of clay—one modest sip must be permitted to our frailty."

So murmuring, he glued the huge flagon to his lips, and as the head was slowly and gradually inclined backwards, in proportion as the right hand elevated the bottom of the pitcher, Everard had great doubts whether the drinker and the cup were likely to part until the whole contents of the latter had been transferred to the person of the former. Roger Wildrake stinted, however, when, by a moderate computation, he had swallowed at one draught about a quart and a half.

He then replaced it on the salver, fetched a long breath to refresh his lungs, bade the boy get him gone with the rest of the liquors, in a tone which inferred some dread of his constancy, and then, turning to his friend Everard, he expatiated in praise of moderation, observing, that the mouthful which he had just taken had been of more service to him than if he had remained quaffing healths at table for four hours together.

His friend made no reply, but could not help being privately of opinion that Wildrake's temperance had done as much execution on the tankard in his single draught, as some more moderate topers might have effected if they had sat sipping for an evening. But the subject was changed by the entrance of the landlord, who came to announce to his honour, Colonel Everard, that the worshipful Mayor of Woodstock, with the Rev. Master Holdenough, were come to wait upon him.

1The French satirist (1495-1553). He narrates in *Pantagrud,* Books IV. and V. . the search for the oracular bottle that was to give an answer to the question, ''Shall Panurge marry?" The only answer was ''Drink." In Greek mythology, oupbearer to the gods. CHAPTER THE TENTH -Here we have one head

Upon two bodies—your two-headed bullock

Is but an ass to such a prodigy.

These two have but one meaning, thought, and counsel;

And, when the single noddle has spoke out,

The four legs scrape assent to it.

Old Play.

In the goodly form of the honest Mayor, there was a bustling mixture of importance and embarrassment, like the deportment of a man who was conscious that he had an important part to act, if he could but exactly discover what that part was. But both were mingled with much pleasure at seeing Everard, and he frequently repeated his welcomes and all-hails before he could be brought to attend to what that gentleman said in reply.

"Good, worthy Colonel, you are indeed a desirable sight to Woodstock at all times, being, as I may say, almost our townsman, as you have dwelt so much and so long at the palace. Truly, the matter begins almost to pass my wit, though I have transacted the affairs of this borough for many a long day; and you are come to my assistance like, like"

"*Tanquam Deus ex machina,* as the Ethnic poet hath it," said Master Holdenough, "although T do not often quote from such books,—Indeed, Master Markham Everard,—or worthy Colonel, as I ought rather to say,—you are simply the most welcome man who has come to Woodstock since the days of old King Harry."

"I had some business with you, my good friend," said the Colonel, addressing the Mayor; "I shall be glad if it should so happen at the same time, that I may find occasion to pleasure you or your worthy pastor." " Like a god from a machine." *i.e.,* the personal intervention of a deity, in the tragic drama, to get the hero out of a difficulty from which the poet can contrive no natural means to extricate him. It is a proverbial phrase of dramatic criticism. Horace, the " Ethnic" or pagan Roman poet, refers to it in line 191 of his *Art Poetica.*

"No question you can do so, good sir;" interposed Master Holdenough; "you have the heart, sir, and you have the hand; and we are much in want of good counsel, and that from a man of action. I am aware, worthy Colonel, that you and your worthy father have ever borne yourselves in these turmoils like men of a truly Christian and moderate spirit, striving to pour oil into the wounds of the land, which some would rub with vitriol and pepper; and we know you are faithful children of that church which we have reformed from its papistical and prelatical tenets."

"My good and reverend friend," said Everard, "I respect the piety and learning of many of your teachers; but I am also for liberty of conscience to all men. I neither side with sectaries, nor do I desire to see them the object of suppression by violence."

"Sir, sir," said the Presbyterian, hastily, "all this hath a fair sound; but I would you should think what a fine country and church we are like to have of it, amidst the errors, blasphemies, and schisms, which are daily introduced into the church and kingdom of England, so that worthy Master Edwards, in his Gangrena, declareth, that our native country is about to become the very sink and cess-pool of all schisms, heresies, blasphemies, and confusions, as the army of Hannibal was said to be the refuse of all nations—*Colluvies omnium gentium?*—Believe me, worthy Colonel, that they of the Honourable House view all this over lightly, and with the winking connivance of old Eli. These instructors, the schismatics, shoulder the orthodox ministers out of their pulpits, thrust themselves into families, and break up the peace thereof, stealing away men's hearts from the established faith."

" My good Master Holdenough," replied the Colonel, interrupting the zealous preacher, "there is ground of sorrow for all these unhappy discords; and I hold with you, that the fiery spirits of the present time have raised men's minds at once above sober-minded and sincere religion, and above decorum and common sense. But there is no help save patience. Enthusiasm is a stream that may foam off in its own time, whereas it is sure to bear down every barrier which is directly opposed to it. —But what are these schismatical proceedings to our present purpose?" i Thomas Edwards (1599-1647), a fanatical Puritan divine, author of *Qangrmna, or a Catalogue of Many of the Errors, Blasphemies and Pernicious Practices of the Sectaries of this Time.* Offscourings of all nations.
The Hebrew high priest, who connived at the wickedness of his sous. 1 *Samuel* iii. 13.

"Why, partly this, sir," said Holdenough, "although perhaps you may make less of it than I should have thought before we met.—I was myself—I, Nehemiah Holdenough he added consequentially, was forcibly expelled from my own pulpit, even as a man should have been thrust out of his own house, by an alien, and an intruder, a wolf, who was not at the trouble even to put on sheep's clothing, but came in his native wolfish attire of buff and bandolier, and held forth in my stead to the people, who were to me as a flock to the lawful shepherd. It is too true, sir—Master Mayor saw it, and strove to take such order to prevent it as man might, though," turning to the Mayor, " I think still you might have striven a little more."

"Good now, good Master Holdenough, do not let us go back on that question," said the Mayor. "Guy of Warwick, or Bevis of Hampton, might do something with this generation; but truly, they are too many, and too strong for the Mayor of Woodstock."

"I think Master Mayor speaks very good sense," said the Colonel; "if the Independents are not allowed to preach, I fear me they will not fight;—and then if you were to have another rising of cavaliers?"

"There are worse folks may rise than cavaliers," said Holdenough.

"How, sir?" replied Colonel Everard. "Let me remind you, Master Holdenough, that is no safe language in the present state of the nation."

"I say," said the Presbyterian, "there are worse folk may rise than cavaliers; and I will prove what I say. The devil is worse than the worst cavalier that ever drank a health or swore an oath—and the devil has arisen at Woodstock Lodge!"

"Ay, truly hath he," said the Mayor, "bodily and visibly in figure and form— An awful time we live in!"

"Gentlemen, I really know not how I am to understand you," said Everard. A hero of the early English romances, like Sir Bevis of Hampton.

"Why, it was even about the devil we came to speak with you," said the Mayor; "but the worthy minister is always so hot upon the sectaries"

"Which are the devil's brats, and

nearly akin to him," said Master Holdenough. "But true it is, that the growth of these sects has brought up the Evil One even upon the face of the earth, to look after his own interest, where he finds it most thriving."

"Master Holdenough," said the Colonel, "if you speak figuratively, I have already told you that I have neither the means nor the skill sufficient to temper these religious heats. But if you design to say that there has been an actual apparition of the devil, I presume to think that you, with your doctrine and your learning, would be a fitter match for him than a soldier like me."

"True, sir; and I have that confidence in the commission which I hold, that I would take the field against the foul fiend without a moment's delay," said Holdenough; "but the place in which he hath of late appeared, being Woodstock, is filled with those dangerous and impious persons, of whom I have been but now complaining; and though, confident in my own resources, I dare venture in disputation with their Great Master himself, yet without your protection, most worthy Colonel, I see not that I may with prudence trust myself with the tossing and goring ox Desborough, or the bloody and devouring bear Harrison, or the cold and poisonous snake Bletson—all of whom are now at the Lodge, doing license and taking spoil as they think meet; and, as all men say, the devil has come to make a fourth with them."

"In good truth, worthy and noble sir," said the Mayor, "it is even as Master Holdenough says—our privileges are declared void, our cattle seized in the very pastures. They talk of cutting down and disparking the fair Chase, which has been so long the pleasure of so many kings, and making Woodstock of as little note as any paltry village. I assure you we heard of your arrival with joy, and wondered at your keeping yourself so close in your lodgings. We know no one save your father or you, that are like to stand the poor burgesses' friend in this extremity, since almost all the gentry around are malignants, and under sequestration. We trust, therefore, you will make strong intercession in our behalf." Note how admirably these epithets are sustained in the subsequent depiction of the three men.

"Certainly, Master Mayor," said the Colonel, who saw himself with pleasure anticipated; "it was my very purpose to have interfered in this matter; and I did but keep myself alone until I should be furnished with some authority from the Lord General."

"Powers from the Lord General!" said the Mayor, thrusting the clergyman with his elbow—" Dost thou hear that?—What cock will fight that cock? We shall carry it now over their necks, and Woodstock shall be brave Woodstock still!"

"Keep thine elbow from my side, friend," said Holdenough, annoyed by the action which the Mayor had suited to his words; "and may the Lord send that Cromwell prove not as sharp to the people of England as thy bones against my person! Yet I approve that we should use his authority to stop the course of these men's proceedings."

"Let us set out, then," said Colonel Everard; "and I trust we shall find the gentlemen reasonable and obedient."

The functionaries, laic and clerical, assented with much joy; and the Colonel required and received Wildrake's assistance in putting on his cloak and rapier, as if he had been the dependent whose part he acted. The cavalier contrived, however, while doing him these menial offices, to give his friend a shrewd pinch, in order to maintain the footing of secret equality betwixt them.

The Colonel was saluted, as they passed through the streets, by many of the anxious inhabitants, who seemed to consider his intervention as affording the only chance of saving their fine Park, and the rights of the corporation, as well as of individuals, from ruin and confiscation.

As they entered the Park, the Colonel asked his companions, "What is this you say of apparitions being seen amongst them?"

"Why, Colonel," said the clergyman, "you know yourself that Woodstock was always haunted?"

"I have lived therein many a day," said the Colonel; "and I know that I never saw the least sign of it, although idle people spoke of the house as they do of all old mansions, and gave the apartments ghosts and spectres to fill up the places of as many of the deceased great, as had ever dwelt there."

"Nay, but, good Colonel," said the clergyman, "I trust you have not reached the prevailing sin of the times, and become indifferent to the testimony in favour of apparitions, which appears so conclusive to all but atheists and advocates for witches?"

"I would not absolutely disbelieve what is so generally affirmed," said the Colonel; "but my reason leads me to doubt most of the stories which I have heard of this sort, and my own experience never went to confirm any of them."

"Ay, but trust me," said Holdenough, "there was always a demon of one or the other species about this Woodstock. Not a man or woman in the town but has heard stories of apparitions in the forest, or about the old castle. Sometimes it is a pack of hounds that sweep along, and the whoops and hollows of the huntsmen, and the winding of horns and the galloping of horse, which is heard as if first more distant, and then close around you—and then anon it is a solitary huntsman, who asks if you can tell him which way the stag has gone. He is always dressed in green; but the fashion of his clothes is some five hundred years old. This is what we call Demon Meridianum—the noonday spectre."

"My worthy and reverend sir," said the Colonel, "I have lived at Woodstock many seasons, and have traversed the Chase at all hours. Trust me, what you hear from the villagers, is the growth of their idle folly and superstition."

"Colonel," replied Holdenough, "a negative proves nothing. What signifies, craving your pardon, that you have not seen anything, be it earthly, or be it of the other world, to detract from the evidence of a score of people who have?—And, besides, there is the Demon Nocturnum —the being that walketh by night; he has been among these Independents and schismatics last night.—Ay, Colonel, you may stare; but it is even so—they may try whether he will mend their gifts, as they profanely call them, of exposition and prayer. No, sir, I trow, to master the foul fiend there goeth some competent knowledge of theology, and an acquaintance of the humane letters, ay, and a regular clerical education, and clerical calling."

"I do not in the least doubt," said the Colonel, "the efficacy of your qualifications to lay the devil; but still I think some odd mistake has occasioned this confusion amongst them, if there has any such in reality existed. Desborough is a blockhead, to be sure; and Harrison is fanatic enough to believe anything. But there is Bletson, on the other hand, who believes nothing.—What do you know of this matter, good Master Mayor?" "In sooth, and it was Master Bletson who gave the first alarm," replied the magistrate, "or, at least, the first distinct one. You see, sir, I was in bed with my wife, and no one else; and I was as fast asleep as a man can desire to be at two hours after midnight, when, behold you, they came knocking at my bedroom door, to tell me there was an alarm in Woodstock, and that the bell of the Lodge was ringing at that dead hour of the night, as hard as ever it rung when it called the court to dinner."

"Well, but the cause of this alarm?" said the Colonel.

"You shall hear, worthy Colonel, you shall hear," answered the Mayor, waving his hand with dignity; for he was one of those persons who will not be hurried out of their own pace. "So Mrs. Mayor would have persuaded me, in her love and affection, poor wretch, that to rise at such an hour out my own warm bed, was like to bring on my old complaint the lumbago, and that I should send the people to Alderman Dutton.—Alderman Devil, Mrs. Mayor, said I;—I beg your reverence's pardon for using such a phrase—Do you think I am going to lie a-bed when the town is on fire, and the cavaliers up, and the devil to pay?—I beg pardon again, parson But here we are before the gate of the Palace; will it not please you to enter?"

"I would first hear the end of your story," said the Colonel; "that is, Master Mayor, if it happens to have an end."

"Everything hath an end," said the Mayor, "and that which we call a pudding hath two.—Your worship will forgive me for being facetious. Where was I?—O, I jumped out of bed, and put on my red plush breeches, with the blue nether stocks, for I always make a point of being dressed suitably to my dignity, night and day, summer or winter, Colonel Everard; and I took the Constable along with me, in case the alarm should be raised by nightwalkers or thieves, and called up worthy Master Holdenough out of his bed, in case it should turn out to be the devil. And so I thought I was provided for the worst—and so away we came; and, by and by, the soldiers who came to the town with Master Tomkins, who had been called to arms, came marching down to Woodstock as fast as their feet would carry them; so I gave our people the sign to let them pass us, and outmarch us, as it were, and this for a twofold reason."

"I will be satisfied/' interrupted the Colonel, "with one good reason. You desired the red-coats should have *the first* of the fray?"

"True, sir, very true;—and also that they should have the *last* of it, in respect that-fighting is their especial business. However, we came on at a slow pace, as men who are determined to do their duty without fear or favour, when suddenly we saw something white haste away up the avenue towards the town, when six of our constables and assistants fled at once, as conceiving it to be an apparition called the White Woman of Woodstock."

"Look you there, Colonel," said Master Holdenough, "I told you there were demons of more kinds than one, which haunt the ancient scenes of royal debauchery and cruelty."

"I hope you stood your own ground, Master Mayor?" said the Colonel.

"I—yes—most assuredly—that is, I did not, strictly speaking, keep my ground; but the town-clerk and I retreated— retreated, Colonel, and without confusion or dishonour, and took post behind worthy Master Holdenough, who, with the spirit of a lion, threw himself in the way of the supposed spectre, and attacked it with such a siserary1 of Latin as might have scared the devil himself, and thereby plainly discovered that it was no devil at all, nor white woman, neither woman of any colour, but worshipful Master Bletson, a member of the House of Commons, and one of the commissioners sent hither upon this unhappy sequestration of the Wood, Chase, and Lodge of Woodstock/'

"And this was all you saw of the demon?" said the Colonel.

"Truly, yes," answered the Mayor; "and I had no wish to see more. However, we conveyed Master Bletson, as in duty bound, back to the Lodge, and he was ever maundering by the way how that he met a party of scarlet devils incarnate marching down to the Lodge; but, to my poor thinking, it must have been the Independent dragoons who had just passed us." Corruption of the legal term "a writ of certiorari;" meaning here an effective, a telling blow.

See the legend of the White Lady of Avenel, in Scott's *Monastery.*

"And more incarnate devils I would never wish to see," said Wildrake, who could remain silent no longer. His voice, so suddenly heard, shewed how much the Mayor's nerves were still alarmed, for he started and jumped aside with an alacrity of which no one would at first sight suppose a man of his portly dignity to have been capable. Everard imposed silence on his intrusive attendant; and, desirous to hear the conclusion of this strange story, requested the Mayor to tell him how the matter ended, and whether they stopped the supposed spectre.

"Truly, worthy sir," said the Mayor, " Master Holdenough was quite venturous upon confronting, as it were, the devil, and compelling him to appear under the real form of Master Joshua Bletson, member of Parliament for the borough of Littlefaith."

"In sooth, Master Mayor," said the divine, "I were strangely ignorant of my own commission and its immunities, if I were to value opposing myself to Satan, or any Independent in his likeness, all of whom, in the name of Him I serve, I do defy, spit at, and trample under my feet; and because Master Mayor is something tedious, I will briefly inform your honour that we saw little of the Enemy that night, save what Master Bletson said in the first feeling of his terrors, and save what we might collect from the disordered appearance of the Honourable Colonel Desborough and Major-General Harrison."

"And what plight were they in, I pray you?" demanded the Colonel.

"Why, worthy sir, every one might see with half an eye that they had been engaged in a fight wherein they had not been honoured with perfect victory; seeing that General Harrison was stalking up and down the parlour, with his drawn sword in his hand, talking to himself, his doublet unbuttoned, his points untrussed, his garters loose, and like to throw him down as he now and then trode on them, and gaping and grinning like a mad player. And yonder sat Desborough with a dry pottle of sack before him, which he had just emptied, and which, though the element in which he trusted, had not restored him sense enough to speak, or courage enough to look over his shoulder. He had a Bible in his hand, forsooth, as if it would of itself make battle against the Evil One; but I peered over his shoulder, and, alas! the good gentleman held the bottom of the page uppermost. It was as if one of your musketeers, noble and valued sir, were to present the butt of his piece at the enemy instead of the muzzle—ha, ha, ha! it was a sight to judge of schismatics by; both in point of head, and in point of heart, in point of skill, and in point of courage.—Oh! Colonel, then was the time to see the true character of an authorized pastor of souls over those unhappy men, who leap into the fold without due and legal authority, and will, forsooth, preach, teach, and exhort, and blasphemously term the doctrine of the church saltless porridge and dry chips!" A tag-lace used In place of buttons for holding together certain parts of the dress. Untied.

"I have no doubt you were ready to meet the danger, reverend sir; but I would fain know of what nature it was, and from whence it was to be apprehended?"

"Was it for me to make such inquiry?" said the clergyman, triumphantly. "Is it for a brave soldier to number his enemies, or inquire from what quarter they are to come? No, sir, I was there with match lighted, bullet in my mouth, and my harquebuss shouldered, to encounter as many devils as hell could pour in, were they countless as motes in the sunbeam, and although they came from all points of the compass. The Papists talk of the temptation of St. Anthony—pshaw! let them double all the myriads which the brain of a crazy Dutch painter hath invented, and you will find a poor Presbyterian divine—I will answer for one at least,—who, not in his own strength, but his Master's, will receive the assault in such sort, that far from returning against him as against yonder poor hound, day after day, and night after night, he will at once pack them off as with a vengeance to the uttermost parts of Assyria!" Drinking vessel, tankard.

A hand fire-arm, commonly used with, a forked rest, to give steadier aim. , ' An Egyptian abbot, founder of asceticism. He was sorely tempted in his solitude, as he believed, by the devil, who appeared to him under manifold forms. This "temptation of St. Anthony" was a favorite subject of medieval painters. Perhaps the Dutchman referred to is Peter Brueghel, whose " St. Anthony " hangs in the Dresden gallery,

"Still," said the Colonel, "I pray to know whether you saw anything upon which to exercise your pious learning?"

"Saw?" answered the divine; "no, truly, I saw nothing, nor did I look for anything. Thieves will not attack well-armed travellers, nor will devils or evil spirits come against one who bears in his bosom the word of truth, in the very language in which it was first dictated. No, sir, they shun a divine who can understand the holy text, as a crow is said to keep wide of a gun loaded with hail-shot." 1

They had walked, a little way back upon their road, to give time for this conversation; and the Colonel, perceiving it was about to lead to no satisfactory explanation of the real cause of alarm on the preceding night, turned round, and observing it was time they should go to the Lodge, began to move in that direction with his three companions.

It had now become dark, and the towers of Woodstock arose high above the umbrageous shroud which the forest spread around the ancient and venerable mansion. From one of the highest turrets, which could still be distinguished as it rose against the clear blue sky, there gleamed a light like that of a candle within the building. The Mayor stopt short, and catching fast hold of the divine, and then of Colonel Everard, exclaimed, in a trembling and hasty, but suppressed tone,

"Do you see yonder light?"

"Ay, marry do I," said Colonel Everard; "and what does that matter?—a light in a garret-room of such an old mansion as Woodstock is no subject for wonder, I trow."

"But a light from Rosamond's Tower is surely so," said the Mayor.

"True," said the Colonel, something surprised, when, after a careful examination, he satisfied himself that the worthy magistrate's conjecture was right. "That is indeed Rosamond's Tower; and as the drawbridge by which it was accessible has been destroyed for centuries, it is hard to say what chance could have lighted a lamp in such an inaccessible place." Small shot.

"That light burns with no earthly fuel," said the Mayor; "neither from whale nor olive oil, nor bees-wax, nor mutton-suet either. I dealt in these commodities, Colonel, before I went into my present line; and I can assure you I could distinguish the sort of light they give, one from another, at a greater distance than yonder turret— Look you, that is no earthly flame.—See you not something blue and reddish upon the edges?—that bodes full well where it comes from.— Colonel, in my opinion we had better go back to sup at the town, and leave the Devil and the red-coats to settle their matters together for to-night; and then when we come back the next morning, we will have a pull with the party that chances to keep a-field."

"You will do as you please, Master Mayor, said Everard, "but my duty requires me that I should see the Commissioners to-night."

"And mine requires me to see the foul Fiend," said Master Holdenough, "if he dare make himself visible to me. I wonder not that, knowing who is approaching, he betakes himself to the very citadel, the inner and the last defences of this ancient and haunted mansion. He is dainty, I warrant you, and must dwell where is a relish of luxury and murder about the walls of his chamber. In yonder turret sinned Rosamond, and in yonder turret she suffered; and there she sits, or more likely, the enemy in her shape, as I have heard true men of Woodstock tell. I wait on you, good Colonel—Master Mayor will do as he Sleases. The strong man hath fortified himself in his welling-house, but, lo, there cometh another stronger than he."

"For me," said the Mayor, "who am as unlearned as I am unwarlike, I will not engage either with the Powers of the Earth, or the Prince of the Powers of the Air, and I would we were again at Woodstock;—and hark ye, good fellow," slapping Wildrake on the shoulder, "I will bestow on thee a shilling wet and a shilling dry if thou wilt go back with me."

"Gadzookers, Master Mayor," said Wildrake, neither flattered by the magistrate's familiarity of address, nor captivated by his munificence—"I wonder who the devil made you and me fellows? and, besides, do you think I would go back to Woodstock with your worshipful cod'shead, when, by good management, I may get a peep of fair Rosamond, and see whether she was that choice and incomparable piece of ware, which the world has been told of by rhymers and ballad-makers?"

'"Powers" were considered angels of the sixth order in the celestial hierarchy. See *Epliesians* i. 21. Satan. » A shilling's worth of drink and a shilling in cash.

"Speak less lightly and wantonly, friend," said the divine; "we are to resist the Devil that he may flee from us, and not to tamper with him, or enter into his counsels, or traffic with the merchandise of his great Vanity Fair."

"Mind what the good man says, Wildrake," said the Colonel; "and take heed another time how thou dost suffer thy wit to outrun discretion."

"I am beholden to the reverend gentleman for his advice," answered Wildrake, upon whose tongue it was difficult to impose any curb whatever, even when his own safety rendered it most desirable. "But, gadzookers, let him have had what experience he will in fighting with the Devil, he never saw one so black as I had a tussle with— not a hundred years ago."

"How, friend," said the clergyman, who understood everything literally when apparitions were mentioned, "have you had so late a visitation of Satan? Believe me, then, that I wonder why thou darest to entertain his name so often and so lightly, as I see thou dost use it in thy ordinary discourse. But when and where didst thou see the Evil One?"

Everard hastily interposed, lest by something yet more strongly, alluding to Cromwell, his imprudent squire should, in mere wantonness, betray his interview with the General. "The young man raves," he said, "of a dream which he had the other night, when he and I slept together in Victor Lee's chamber, belonging to the ranger's apartments at the Lodge."

"Thanks for help at a pinch, good patron," said Wildrake, whispering into Everard's ear, who in vain endeavoured to shake him off,—" a fib never failed a fanatic." Symbol of stupidity.
The world, with its follies and vanities. Scott takes the phrase from Bunyan's *Pilgrim's Progress,* which was not published, however, until 1678. It is the title of Thackeray's best-known novel.
"Yon, also, spoke something too lightly of these matters, considering the work which we have in hand, worthy Colonel," said the Presbyterian divine.

"Believe me, the young man, thy servant, was more likely to see visions than to dream merely idle dreams in that apartment; for I have always heard, that, next to Rosamond's Tower, in which, as I said, she played the wanton, and was afterwards poisoned by Queen Eleanor, Victor Lee's chamber was the place in the Lodge of Woodstock more peculiarly the haunt of evil spirits.—I pray you, young man, tell me this dream or vision of yours."

"With all my heart, sir," said Wildrake—then addressing his patron, who began to interfere, he said, "Tush, sir, you have had the discourse for an hour, and why should not I hold forth in my turn? By this darkness, if you keep me silent any longer, I will turn Independent preacher, and stand up in your despite for the freedom of private judgment.—And so, reverend sir, I was dreaming of a carnal divertisement called a bull-baiting;1 and methought they were venturing dogs at head, as merrily as e'er I saw them at Tutbury bull-running; and methought I heard some one say, there was the Devil come to have a sight of the bull-ring. Well, I thought that, gadswoons, I would have a peep at his Infernal Majesty. So I looked, and there was a butcher in greasy woollen, with his steel by his side; but he was none of the Devil. And there was a drunken cavalier, with his mouth full of oaths, and his stomach full of emptiness, and a gold-laced waistcoat in a very dilapidated condition, and a ragged hat, with a piece of a feather in it; and he was none of the Devil neither. And here was a miller, his hands dusty with meal, and every atom of it stolen; and there was a vintner, his green apron stained with wine, and every drop of it sophisticated; but neither was the old gentleman I looked for to be detected among these artizans of iniquity. At length, sir, I saw a grave person with cropped hair, a pair of longish and projecting ears, a band as broad as a slobbering bib under his chin, a brown coat, surmounted by a Geneva cloak, and I had old Nicholas at once in his genuine paraphernalia, by" The old English sport of attacking bulls with dogs. It is described in Lecky's *History of the Eighteenth Century,* Vol. I., Chap. 4.

" Under a charter granted by John of Gaunt in 1381, the minstrels in the honour of Tutbury, Staffordshire, held a court there every Kith August, and were allowed to chase a maddened bull, which, if tliey caught it before sunset, they were permitled to keep."—D. Adulterated.

"Shame, shame! said Colonel Everard. "What! behave thus to an old gentleman and a divine!"—

"Nay, let him proceed," said the minister, with perfect equanimity, "if thy friend, or secretary, is gibing, I must have less patience than becomes my profession, if I could not bear an idle jest, and forgive him who makes it. Or if, on the other hand, the Enemy has really presented himself to the young man in such a guise as he intimates, wherefore should we be surprised that he, who can take upon him the form of an angel of light, should be able to assume that of a frail and peccable mortal, whose spiritual calling and profession ought, indeed, to induce him to make his life an example to others; but whose conduct, nevertheless, such is the imperfection of our unassisted nature, sometimes rather presents us with a warning of what we should shun*?"* "Now, by the mass, honest Dominie—I mean reverend sir—I crave you a thousand pardons/' said Wildrake, penetrated by the quietness and patience of the presbyter's rebuke. "By St. George, if quiet patience will do it, thou art fit to play a game at foils with the Devil himself, and I would be contented to hold stakes. "

As he concluded an apology, which was certainly not uncalled for, and seemed to be received in perfectly good Eart, they approached so close to the exterior door of the lodge, that they were challenged with the emphatic *Stand,* by a sentinel who mounted guard there. Colonel Everard replied, *A friend;* and the sentinel repeating his command, "Stand, friend," proceeded to call the corporal of the guard. The corporal came forth, and at the same time turned out his guard. Colonel Everard gave his name and designation, as well as those of his companions, on which the corporal said, "he doubted not there would be orders for his instant admission; but, in the first place, Master Tomkins must be consulted, that he might learn their honours' mind."

"How, sir!" said the Colonel, " do you, knowing who I am, presume to keep me on the outside of your post?" Title of a minister in the Dutch Reformed Church, but given to clergymen of other sects as well.

"Not if your honour pleases to enter," said the corporal, "and undertakes to be my warranty; but such are the orders of my post."

"Nay, then, do your duty," said the Colonel; "but are the cavaliers up, or what is the matter, that you keep so close and strict a watch?"

The fellow gave no distinct answer, but muttered between his mustaches something about the Enemy, and the roaring Lion who goeth about seeking whom he may devour. Presently afterwards Tomkins appeared, followed by two servants, bearing lights in great standing brass candlesticks. They marched before Colonel Everard and his party, keeping as close to each other as two cloves of the same orange, and starting from time to time; and shouldering as they passed through sundry intricate passages, they led up a large and ample wooden staircase, the bannisters, rail, and lining of which were executed in black oak, and finally into a long saloon, or parlour, where there was a prodigious fire, and about twelve candles of the largest size distributed in sconces against the wall. There were seated the Commissioners, who now held in their power the ancient mansion and royal domain of Woodstock.
Satan. Oranges stuck full of cloves were formerly carried in the hand or at the belt, for perfume and as a preventive of disease. *See Love's Labour Lost,* V., 2, 654.
Compare Holdenough with other clerical characters in Scott. Do these characters, the fanatics aside, impress you as being men of real religious nature? What is gained here by testing the effect of the apparitions upon the minor characters, before the main characters are confronted by them? Compare *Hamlet.*

CHAPTER THE ELEVENTH

The bloody bear, an independent beast,
Unlicked to forms, in groans his hate expressed—
Next him the buffoon ape, as atheists use,
Mimicked all sects, and had his own to choose.
Hind And Pantheb.

The strong light in the parlour which we have described, served to enable Everard easily to recognise his acquaintances, Desborough, Harrison, and Bletson, who had assembled round an oak table of large dimensions, placed near the blazing chimney, on which were arranged wine, and ale, and materials for smoking, then the general indulgence of the time.-There was a species of movable cupboard set betwixt the table and the door, calculated originally for a display of plate upon grand occasions, but at present only used as a screen; which purpose it served so effectually, that, ere he had coasted around it, Everard heard the following fragment of what Desborough was saying in his strong coarse voice: "Sent him to share with us, I'se warrant ye—It was always his Excellency my brother-in-law's way—if he made a treat for five friends, he would invite more than the table could hold—I have known him ask three men to eat two eggs."

"Hush, hush,"said Bletson; and the servants making their appearance from behind the tall cupboard, announced Colonel Everard. It may not be uninteresting to the reader to have a description of the party into which he now entered.

Desborough was a stout, bull-necked man, of middle size, with heavy vulgar features, grizzled bushy eyebrows, and walleyes. The flourish of his powerful relative's fortunes had burst forth in the finery of his dress, which was much more ornamented than was usual among the roundheads. There was embroidery on his cloak, and lace upon his band; his hat displayed a feather with a golden clasp, and all his habiliments were those of a cavalier, or follower of the court, rather than the plain dress of a parliamentarian officer. But, Heaven knows, there was little of courtlike grace or dignity in the person or demeanour of the individual, who became his fine suit as the hog on the sign-post docs his gilded armour. It was not that he was positively deformed, or misshaped, for, taken in detail, the figure was well enough. But his limbs seemed to act upon different and contradictory principles. They were not as the play says, in concatenation accordingly; — the right hand moved as if it were upon bad terms with the left, and the legs shewed an inclination to foot it in different and opposite directions. In short, to use an extravagant comparison, the members of Colonel Desborough seemed rather to resemble the disputatious representatives of a federative congress, than the well-ordered union of the orders of the state, in a firm and well-compacted monarchy, where each holds his own place, and all obey the dictates of a common head.

A satirical poem by Dryden, published in 1687, in defence of Roman Catholicism. The hind typified the Church of Rome; the panther, the Church of England. John Desborough (1008-1660), was bred an attorney, but paid more attention to farming. He married the sixth daughter of Robert Cromwell of Huntingdon, sister of the future Lord Protector. He was a brave soldier in the civil war, and fought at Worcester as a majorgeneral. His patriotism, however, was tempered by a strict regard for his own interests, and his rustic origin, person, and manners are constantly ridiculed in the "Rump " songs and other effusions of cavalier hate. He figures in *Hudibras*.—Condensed from the *Dictionary of National Biography.*

General Harrison, the second of the commissioners, was a tall, thin, middle-aged man, who had risen into his high situation in the army, and his intimacy with Cromwell, by his dauntless courage in the field, and the popularity he had acquired by his exalted enthusiasm amongst the military saints, sectaries, and Independents, who composed the strength of the existing army. Harrison was of mean extraction, and bred up to his father's employment of a butcher. Nevertheless, his appearance, though coarse, was not vulgar, like that of Desborough, who had so much the advantage of him in birth and education. He had a masculine height and strength of figure, was well made, and in his manner announced a rough military character, which might be feared, but could not easily become the object of contempt or ridicule. His aquiline nose and dark black eyes set off to some advantage a countenance otherwise irregular, and the wild enthusiasm that sometimes sparkled in them as he dilated on his opinions to others, and often seemed to slumber under his long dark eyelashes as he mused upon them himself, gave something strikingly wild, and even noble, to his aspect. He was one of the chief leaders of those who were called Fifth-monarchy men, who, going even beyond the general fanaticism of the age, presumptuously interpreted the Book of the Revelations after their own fancies, considered that the second Advent of the Messiah, and the Millennium, or reign of the Saints upon earth, was close at hand, and that they themselves, illuminated as they believed, with the power of foreseeing these approaching events, were the chosen instruments for the establishment of the New Reign, or Fifth Monarchy, as it was called, and were fated also to win its honours, whether celestial or terrestrial.

General Thomas Harrison (1606-1660), was the son of a butcher or grazier of Staffordshire. "The son of a butcher, and the most furious enthusiast in the army," says Hume. He fought throughout the civil war (for the story of his shooting down an actor see note in Chapter XIV.), was zealous in bringing the King to trial, and signed the death-warrant. Roger Williams describes him as "the second in the nation of late,... . a very gallant, most deserving, heavenly man, but most high-flown for the Kingdom of the Saints, and the Fifth Monarchy, now risen, and their sun never to set again." During the Protectorate he took part in Anabaptist plots against the government. After the Restoration he was condemned as a regicide and executed at Charing Cross. "Where is your good old cause now?" said a scoffer in the crowd. Harrison, with a smile, clapped his hand on his breast and said, " Here it is, and I am going to seal it with my blood." —See *Dictionary of National Biography.* " I went out to- Charing Cross to see Major-General Harrison hanged, drawn, and quartered; which was done then, he looking as cheerful as any man could do in that condition. He was presently cut down, and his head and heart shown to the people, at which there was great shouts of joy. It is said, that he said that he was sure to come shortly at the right hand of Christ to judge them that now had judged him; and that his wife do expect his coming again. Thus it was my chance to see the King beheaded at White Hall, and to see the first blood shed in revenge for the King at Charing Cross."—Pepys's *Diary* for September 13, 1660 They differed from other Second Adventists in believing not only in a literal second coming of Christ, but also that it was their duty to inaugurate this Kingdom by force. The four preceding monarchies were those of Assyria, Persia, Greece, and Rome. There were unsuccessful risings of this sect against the government in 1657 and 1661.

When this spirit of enthusiasm, which operated like a partial insanity, was not immediately affecting Harrison's mind, he was a shrewd worldly man, and a good soldier; one who missed no opportunity of mending his fortune, and who, in expecting the exaltation of the Fifth Monarchy, was, in the meanwhile, a ready instrument for the establishment of the Lord General's supremacy. Whether it was owing to his early occupation, and habits of indifference to pain or bloodshed acquired in the shambles, to natural disposition and want of feeling, or, finally, to the awakened character of his enthusiasm, which made him look upon those who opposed him, as opposing the Divine will, and therefore meriting no favour or mercy, is not easy to say; but all agreed, that after a victory, or the successful storm of a town, Harrison was one of the most cruel and pitiless men in Cromwell's army; always urging some misapplied text to authorize the continued execution of the fugitives, and sometimes even putting to death those who had surrendered themselves prisoners. It was said, that at times the recollection of some of these cruelties troubled his conscience, and disturbed the dreams of beatification in which his imagination indulged.

When Everard entered the apartment, this true representative of the fanatical soldiers of the day, who filled those ranks and regiments which Cromwell had politically kept on foot, while he procured the reduction of those in which the Presbyterian interest predominated, was seated a little apart from the others, his legs crossed, and stretched out at length towards the fire, his head resting on his elbow, and turned upwards, as if studying, with the most profound gravity, the half-seen carving of the Gothic roof.

Bletson remains to be mentioned, who, in person and figure, was diametrically different from the other two. There was neither foppery nor slovenliness in his exterior, nor had he any marks of military service or rank about his person. A small walking rapier seemed merely worn as a badge of his rank as a gentleman, without his hand having the least purpose of becoming acquainted with the hilt, or his eye with the blade. His countenance was thin and acute, marked with lines which thought father than age had traced upon it; and a habitual sneer on his countenance, even when he least wished to express contempt on his features, seemed to assure the individual addressed, that in Bletson he conversed with a person of intellect far superior to his own. This was a triumph of intellect only, however; for on all occasions of difference respecting speculative opinions, and indeed on all controversies whatsoever, Bletson avoided the ultimate *ratio* of blows and knocks.

Yet this peaceful gentleman had found himself obliged to serve personally in the Parliamentary army at the commencement of the Civil War, till happening unluckily to come in contact with the fiery Prince Rupert, his retreat was judged so precipitate, that it required all the shelter his friends could afford, to keep him free of an impeachment or a court-martial. But as Bletson spoke well, and with great effect in the House of Commons, which was his natural sphere, and was on that account high in the estimation of his party, his behaviour at Edgehill was passed over, and he continued to take an active share in all the political events of that bustling period, though he faced not again the actual front of war.

Bletson's theoretical politics had long inclined him to espouse the opinions of Harrington and others, who adopted the visionary idea of establishing a pure democratical republic in so extensive a country as Britain. This was a rash theory, where there is such an infinite difference betwixt ranks, habits, education, and morals—where there is such an immense disproportion betwixt the wealth of individuals—and where a large portion of the inhabitants consist of the inferior classes of the large towns and manufacturing districts—men unfitted to bear that share in the direction of a state, which must be exercised by the members of a republic in the proper sense of the word. Accordingly, as soon as the experiment was made, it became obvious that no such form of government could be adopted with the smallest chance of stability; and the question came only to be, whether the remnant, or, as it was vulgarly called, the Rump of the Long Parliament, now reduced by the seclusion of so many of the members to a few scores of persons, should continue, in spite of their unpopularity, to rule the affairs of Britain? Whether they should cast all loose by dissolving themselves, and issuing writs to convoke a new Parliament, the composition of which no one could answer for, any more than for the measures they might take when assembled? Or lastly, whether Cromwell, as actually happened, was not to throw the sword into the balance, and boldly possess himself of that power which the remnant of the Parliament were unable to hold, and yet afraid to resign?

Argument. The first battleof the civil war. It was indecisive. It should be borne in mind that Sir Walter was a stout opponent of the Reform Bill, passed in the year of his death.

Such being the state of parties, the Council of State, in distributing the good things in their gift, endeavoured to soothe and gratify the army, as a beggar flings crusts to a growling mastiff. In this view Desborough had been created a Commissioner in the Woodstock matter to gratify Cromwell, Harrison to soothe the fierce Fifth-Monarchy men, and Bletson as a sincere republican, and one of their own leaven.

But if they supposed Bletson had the least intention of becoming a martyr to his republicanism, or submitting to any serious loss on account of it, they much mistook the man. He entertained their principles sincerely, and not the less that they were found impracticable; for the miscarriage of his experiment no more converts the political speculator, than the explosion of a retort undeceives an alchymist. But Bletson was quite prepared to submit to Cromwell, or any one else who might be possessed of the actual authority. He was a ready subject in practice to the powers existing, and made little difference betwixt various kinds of government, holding in theory all to be nearly equal in imperfection, so soon as they diverged from the model of Harrington's Oceana. Cromwell had already been tampering with him, like wax between his finger and thumb, and which he was ready shortly to seal with, smiling at the same time to himself when he beheld the Council of State giving rewards to Bletson as their faithful adherent, while he himself was secure of his allegiance, how soon soever the expected change of government should take place.

But Bletson was still more attached to his metaphysical ian his political creed, and carried his doctrines of the It has been noted already that the *Oceana* was not published until 1656.
perfectibility of mankind as far as he did those respecting the conceivable perfec-

tion of a model of government; and as in the one case he declared against all power which did not emanate from the people themselves, so, in his moral speculations, he was unwilling to refer any of the phenomena of nature to a final cause. When pushed, indeed, very hard, Bletson was compelled to mutter some inarticulate and unintelligible doctrines concerning an *Animus Mundi*, or Creative Power in the works of Nature, by which she originally called into existence, and still continues to preserve, her works. To this power, he said, some of the purest metaphysicians rendered a certain degree of homage; nor was he himself inclined absolutely to censure those, who, by the institution of holidays, choral dances, songs, and harmless feasts and libations, might be disposed to celebrate the great goddess Nature; at least dancing, singing, feasting, and sporting, being comfortable things to both young and old, they might as well sport, dance, and feast, in honour of such appointed holidays, as under any other pretext. But then this moderate show of religion was to be practised under such exceptions as are admitted by the Highgate oath; and no one was to be compelled to dance, drink, sing, or feast, whose taste did not happen to incline them to such divertisements; nor was any one to be obliged to worship the creative power, whether under the name of the *Animus Mundi*, or any other whatsoever. The interference of the Deity in the affairs of mankind he entirely disowned, having proved to his own satisfaction that the idea originated entirely in priestcraft. In short, with the shadowy metaphysical exception aforesaid, Mr. Joshua Bletson of Darlington, member for Littlefaith, came as near the predicament of an atheist, as it is perhaps possible for a man to do. But we say this with the necessary salvo; for we have known many like Bletson, whose curtains have been shrewdly shaken by superstition, though their fears were unsanctioned by any religious faith. The devils, we are assured, believe and tremble; but on earth there are many, who, in worse plight than even the natural children of perdition, tremble without believing, and fear even while they blaspheme. Soul of the world. The oath said to have been formerly exacted from travellers passing over Highgate Hill, on the north side of London, that they would never eat brown bread when they could get white, etc.. but with the proviso, "unless they preferred it."—D. Reservation.

It follows, of course, that nothing could be treated with more scorn by Mr. Bletson, than the debates about Prelacy and Presbytery, about Presbytery and Independency, about Quakers and Anabaptists, Muggletonians and Brownists, and all the various sects with which the Civil War had commenced, and by which its dissensions were still continued. "It was," he said, "as if beasts of burden should quarrel amongst themselves about the fashion of their halters and pack-saddles instead of embracing a favourable opportunity of throwing them aside." Other witty and pithy remarks he used to make when time and place suited; for instance, at the club called the Rota, frequented by St. John, and established by Harrington, for the free discussion of political and religious subjects.

But when Bletson was out of this academy, or stronghold of philosophy, he was very cautious how he carried his contempt of the general prejudice in favour of religion and Christianity further than an implied objection or a sneer. If he had an opportunity of talking in private with an ingenuous and intelligent youth, he sometimes attempted to make a proselyte, and shewed much address in bribing the vanity of inexperience, by suggesting that a mind like his ought to spurn the prejudices impressed upon it in childhood; and when assuming the *latus clavus* of reason, assuring him that such as he, laying aside the *bulla* of juvenile incapacity, as Bletson called it, should proceed to examine and decide for himself. It frequently happened, that the youth was induced to adopt the doctrines in whole, or in part, of the sage who had seen his natural genius, and who had urged him to exert it in examining, detecting, and declaring for himself; and thus flattery gave proselytes to infidelity, which could not have been gained by all the powerful eloquence, or artful sophistry, of the infidel.

Oliver St. John (1598-1673), a politician and lawyer, the defender of Hampden in the "ship-money" trial—at this time a member of the Council of State. See note on the Rota Club in Chapter II. The broad stripe placed on a young Roman noble's tunic when he became a Senator. An ornament worn by Roman youths around the neck, but laid aside on attaining manhood.

These attempts to extend the influence of what was called free-thinking and philosophy, were carried on, as we have hinted, with a caution dictated by the timidity of the philosopher's disposition. He was conscious his doctrines were suspected, and his proceedings watched, by the two principal sects of Prelatists and Presbyterians, who, however inimical to each other, were still more hostile to one who was an opponent, not only to a church establishment of any kind, but to every denomination of Christianity. He found it more easy to shroud himself among the Independents, whose demands were for a general liberty of conscience, or an unlimited toleration, and whose faith, differing in all respects and particulars, was by some pushed into such wild errors, as to get totally beyond the bounds of every species of Christianity, and approach very near to infidelity itself, as extremes of each kind are said to approach each other. Bletson mixed a good deal among those sectaries; and such was his confidence in his own logic and address, that he is supposed to have entertained hopes of bringing to his opinions in time the enthusiastic Vane, as well as the no less enthusiastic Harrison, provided he could but get them to resign their visions of a Fifth Monarchy, and induce them to be contented with a reign of Philosophers in England for the natural period of their lives, instead of the reign of the Saints during the Millenium.

Such was the singular group into which Everard was now introduced; shewing, in their various opinions, upon how many devious coasts human nature may make shipwreck, when she has once let go her hold on the anchor which religion has given her to lean upon; the acute self-conceit and worldly learning of Bletson—the rash and ignorant conclusions of the fierce and underbred Harrison, leading them into the opposite extremes of enthusiasm and infidelity, while Desborough, constitutionally stupid, thought nothing about religion at all; and while the others were active in making sail on different but equally erroneous courses, he might be said to perish like a vessel, which springs a leak and founders in the roadstead. It was wonderful to behold what a strange variety of mistakes and errors, on the part of the King and his Ministers, on the part of the Parliament and their leaders, on the part of the allied kingdoms of Scotland and England towards each other, had combined to rear up men of such dangerous opinions and interested characters among the arbiters of the destiny of Britain.

Sir Harry Vane the younger (1612-1662), one of the foremost figures of the time. He was governor of the Massachusetts Bay Colony from 1636 to 1637, was prominent throughout the Parliamentary struggle, lost sympathy with Cromwell toward the last (" The Lord deliver me from Sir Harry Vane! "), and was executed after the Restoration, like Harrison, on the charge of treason.

Those who argue for party's sake, will see all the faults on the one side, without deigning to look at those on the other; those who study history for instruction, will perceive that nothing but the want of concession on either side, and the deadly height to which the animosity of the King's and Parliament's parties had arisen, could have so totally overthrown the well-poised balance of the English constitution. But we hasten to quit political reflections, the rather that ours, we believe, will please neither Whig nor Tory.

Note the admirable ease and precision of the character-drawing here. This chapter is Scott's main justification in his claim that the whole apparition machinery was not introduced for its own sake (compare Horace Walpole s *Castle of Otranto* or Mrs. Radcliffe's *Mysteries of Udolplu),* but designed to show the effect of certain phenomena upon certain types of character.—Compare Harrison with Major Bridgenorth in *Peveril of the Peak* and Balfour of Burley in *Old Mortality.* CHAPTER THE TWELFTH

Three form a College—an you give us four,
Let him bring his share with him.
Beaumont And Fletchbk.

Mr. Bletson arose, and paid his respects to Colonel Everard, with the ease and courtesy of a gentleman of the time; though on every account grieved at his intrusion as a religious man who held his free-thinking principles in detestation, and would effectually prevent his conversion of Harrison, and even of Desborough, if anything could be moulded out of such a clod, to the worship of the *Animus Mundi.* Moreover, Bletson knew Everard to be a man of steady probity, and by no means disposed to close with a scheme on which he had successfully sounded the other two, and which was calculated to assure the Commissioners of some little private indemnification for the trouble they were to give themselves in the public business. The philosopher was yet less pleased, when he saw the magistrate and the pastor who had met him in his flight of the preceding evening, when he had been seen, *parma non bene relicia,* with cloak and doublet left behind him.

The presence of Colonel Everard was as unpleasing to Desborough as to Bletson; but the former having no philosophy in him, nor an idea that it was possible for any man to resist helping himself out of untold money, was chiefly embarrassed by the thought, that the plunder which they might be able to achieve out of their trust, might, by this unwelcome addition to their number, be divided into four parts instead of three; and this reflection added to the natural awkwardness with which he grumbled forth a sort of welcome, addressed to Everard.

As for Harrison, he remained like one on higher thoughts intent; his posture unmoved, his eyes fixed on the ceiling as before, and in no way indicating the least consciousness that the company had been more than doubled around him.

"His shield being ingloriously left behind." The phrase, which is not quite correctly quoted, is found in Horace, *Odes,* Book II., 1. 7, where he is describing his own flight from the battle of Philippi.

Meantime, Everard took his place at the table, as a man who assumed his own right, and pointed to his companions to sit down nearer the foot of the board. Wildrake so far misunderstood his signals, as to sit down above the Mayor; but rallying his recollection at a look from his patron, he rose and took his place lower, whistling, however, as he went, a sound at which the company stared, as at a freedom highly unbecoming. To complete his indecorum, he seized upon a pipe, and filling it from a large tobacco-box, was soon immersed in a cloud of his own raising; from which a hand shortly after emerged, seized on the blackjack of ale, withdrew it within the vapoury sanctuary, and, after a potential draught, replaced it upon the table, its owner beginning to renew the cloud which his intermitted exercise of the tube had almost allowed to subside.

Nobody made any observation on his conduct, out of respect, probably, to Colonel Everard, who bit his lip, but continued silent; aware that censure might extract some escapade more unequivocally characteristic of a cavalier, from his refractory companion. As silence seemed awkward, and the others made no advances to break it, beyond the ordinary salutation, Colonel Everard at length said, "I presume, gentlemen, that you are somewhat surprised at my arrival here, and thus intruding myself into your meeting?"

"Why the dickens should we be surprised, Colonel?" said Desborough: "we know his Excellency, my brotherin-law Noll's—I mean my Lord Cromwell's way, of overquartering his men in the towns he marches through. Thou hast obtained a share in our commission?'

"And in that," said Bletson, smiling and bowing, "the Lord-General has given us the most acceptable colleague that could have been added to our number. No doubt your authority for joining with us must be under warrant of the Council of State?

"Of that, gentlemen," said the Colonel, "I will presently advise you. "—He took out his warrant accordingly, and was about to communicate the contents; but observing that there were three or four half-empty flasks upon the table, that Desborough looked more stupid than usual, and that the philosopher's eyes were reeling in his head, notwithstanding the temperance of Bletson's usual habits, he concluded that they had been fortifying themselves against the horrors of the haunted mansion, by laying in a store of what is called Dutch courage, and therefore prudently resolved to postpone his more important business with them till the cooler hour of morning. He, therefore, instead of presenting the General's warrant superseding their commission, contented himself with replying,—" My business has, of course, some reference to your proceedings here. But here is— excuse my curiosity—a reverend gentleman," pointing to Holdenough, "who has told me that you are so strangely embarrassed here, as to require both the civil and spiritual authority to enable you to keep possession of Woodstock."

"Before we go into that matter," said Bletson, blushing up to the eyes at the recollection of his own fears, so manifestly displayed, yet so inconsistent with his principles, "I should like to know who this other stranger is, who has come with the worthy magistrate, and the no less worthy Presbyterian?"

"Meaning me?" said Wildrake, laying his pipe aside; "Gadzooks, the time hath been that I could have answered the question with a better title; but at present I am only his honour's poor clerk, or secretary, whichever is the current phrase."

"'Fore George, my lively blade, thou art a frank fellow of thy tattle," said Desborough. "There is my secretary Tomkins, whom men sillily enough call Fibbet, and the honourable Lieutenant-General Harrison's secretary Bibbet, who are now at supper below stairs, that durst not for their ears speak a phrase above their breath in the presence of their betters, unless to answer a question."

"Yes, Colonel Everard," said the philosopher with his quiet smile, glad, apparently, to divert the conversation from the topic of last night's alarm, and recollections which humbled his self-love and self-satisfaction,—"yes; and when Master Fibbet and Master Bibbet *do* speak, their affirmations are as much in a common mould of mutual attestation, as their names would accord in the verses of a poet. If Master Fibbet happens to tell a fiction, Master Bibbet swears it as truth. If Master Bibbet chances to have gotten drunk in the fear of the Lord, Master Fibbet swears he is sober. I have called my own secretary Gibbet, though his name chances to be only Gibeon, a worthy Israelite at your service, but as pure a youth as ever picked a lamb-bone as Paschal. But I call him Gibbet, merely to make up the holy trefoil with another rhyme. This squire of thine, Colonel Everard, looks as if he might be worthy to be coupled with the rest of the fraternity." Inspired by liquor. The phrase came into use at a slightly later time than this.
-Tomkins is spoken of later as Harrison's secretary.

"Not I, truly," said the cavalier; "I'll be coupled with no Jew that was ever whelped, and no Jewess, neither."

"Scorn not for that, young man," said the philosopher; "the Jews are, in point of Religion, the elder brethren, you know."

"The Jews older than the Christians?" said Desborough; "'fore George, they will have thee before the General Assembly, Bletson, if thou venturest to say so."

Wildrake laughed without ceremony at the gross ignorance of Desborough, and was joined by a sniggling response from behind the cupboard, which, when inquired into, proved to be produced by the serving-men. These worthies, timorous as their betters, when they were supposed to have left the room, had only withdrawn to their present place of concealment.

"How now, ye rogues," said Bletson, angrily; "do you not know your duty better?"

"We beg your worthy honour's pardon," said one of the men, "but we dared not go down stairs without a light."

"A light, ye cowardly poltroons?" said the philosopher; "what—to shew which of you looks palest when a rat squeaks?—but take a candlestick and begone, you cowardly villains! the devils you are so much afraid of must be but paltry kites, if they hawk at such bats as you are."

The servants, without replying, took up one of the candlesticks, and prepared to retreat, Trusty Tomkins at the head of the troop, when suddenly, as they arrived at the door of the parlour, which had been left half open, it was shut violently. The three terrified domestics tumbled back into the middle of the room, as if a shot had been discharged in their face, and all who were at the table started to their feet.
Among the Jews, a lamb was slain and eaten at the time of the Passov«r.
'A trinity like that of the three-leaved clover.
The highest ecclesiastical tribunal of churches of the Presbyterian order.
Colonel Everard was incapable of a moment's fear, even if anything frightful had been seen; but he remained stationary, to see what his companions would do, and to get at the bottom, if possible, of the cause of their alarm upon an occasion so trifling. The philosopher seemed to think that *he* was the person chiefly concerned to shew manhood on the occasion.

He walked to the door accordingly, murmuring at the cowardice of the servants; but at such a snail's pace, that it seemed he would most willingly have been anticipated by any one whom his reproaches had roused to exertion. "Cowardly blockheads!" he said at last, seizing hold of the handle of the door, but without turning it effectually round—" dare you not open a door?"—(still fumbling with the lock)—"dare you not go down a staircase without a light? Here, bring me the candle, you cowardly villains!—By Heavens, something sighs on the outside!"

As he spoke, he let go the handle of the parlour door, and stepped back a pace or two into the apartment, with cheeks as pale as the band he wore.

"*Deus adjutor mens!*" said the Presbyterian clergyman, rising from his seat. "Give place, sir," addressing Bletson; "it would seem I know more of this matter than thou, and I bless Heaven I am armed for the conflict."

Bold as a grenadier about to mount a breach, yet with the same belief in the existence of a great danger to be encountered, as well as the same reliance in the goodness of his cause, the worthy man stepped before the philosophical Bletson, and taking a light from a sconce in one hand, quietly opened the door with the other, and standing in the threshold, said, " Here is nothing!"

"And who expected to see anything," said Bletson, "excepting those terrified oafs, who take fright at every puff of wind that whistles through the passages of this old dungeon!" " God *my* helper 1"

"Mark you, Master Tomkins," said one of the waitingmen in a whisper to the steward,—" See how boldly the minister pressed forward before all of them. Ah! Master Tomkins, our parson is the real commissioned officer of the church—your lay-preachers are no better than a parcel of club-men and volunteers."

"Follow me those who list," said Master Holdenough, "or go before me those who choose, I will walk through the habitable places of this house before I leave it, and satisfy myself whether Satan hath really mingled himself among these dreary dens of ancient wickedness, or whether, like the wicked of whom holy David speaketh, we are afraid, and flee when no one pursueth."

Harrison, who had heard these words, sprung from his seat, and drawing his sword, exclaimed,—" Were there as many fiends in the house as they are hairs on my head, upon this cause I will charge them up to their very trenches!"

So saying, he brandished his weapon, and pressed to the head of the column, where he moved side by side with the minister. The Mayor of Woodstock next joined the body, thinking himself safer perhaps in the company of his pastor; and the whole train moved forward in close order, accompanied by the servants bearing lights, to search the Lodge for some cause of that panic with which they seemed to be suddenly seized.

"Nay, take me with you, my friends," said Colonel Everard, who had looked on in surprise, and was now about to follow the party, when Bletson laid hold on his cloak, and begged him to remain.

"You see, my good Colonel," he said, affecting a courage which his shaking voice belied, "here are only you and I, and honest Desborough, left behind in garrison, while all the others are absent on a sally. We must not hazard the whole troops in one sortie—that were unmilitary—Ha, ha, ha!"

"In the name of Heaven, what means all this?" said Everard. "I heard a foolish tale about apparitions as I came this way, and now I find you all half mad with fear, and cannot get a word of sense among so many of you. Fie, Colonel Desborough—fie, Master Bletson—try to compose yourselves, and let me know, in Heaven's name, the cause of all this disturbance. One would be apt to think your brains were turned." Members of the " clubs," or loose political organizations formed In certain districts during the civil war, to defend property, etc.

"And so mine well may," said Desborough, " ay, and overturned too, since my bed last night was turned upside down, and I was placed for ten minutes heels uppermost, and head downmost, like a bullock going to be shod."

"What means this nonsense, Master Bletson?—Desborough must have had the nightmare."

"No, faith, Colonel; the goblins, or whatever else they were, had been favourable to honest Desborough, for they reposed the whole of his person on that part of his body which—Hark, did you not hear something?—is the central point of gravity, namely, his head."

"Did you see anything to alarm you?" said the Colonel.

"Nothing," said Bletson; "but we heard hellish noises, as all our people did; and I, believing little of ghosts and apparitions, concluded the cavaliers were taking us at advantage; so, remembering Rainsborough's1 fate, I e'en jumped the window, and ran to Woodstock, to call the soldiers to the rescue of Harrison and Desborough."

"And did you not first go to see what the danger was?"

"Ah, my good friend, you forget that I laid down my commission at the time of the self-denying ordinance. It would have been quite inconsistent with my duty as a Parliament-man, to be brawling amidst a set of ruffians, without any military authority. No—when the Parliament commanded me to sheath my sword. Colonel, I have too much veneration for their authority, to be found again with it drawn in my hand."

"But the Parliament," said Desborough, hastily, "did not command you to use your heels when your hands could have saved a man from choking. Ods dickens! you might have stopped when you saw my bed canted heels uppermost, and me half stifled in the bedclothes—you might, I say, have stopped and lent a hand to put it to rights, instead of jumping out of the window, like a new-shorn sheep, so soon as you had run across my room." " Rainsborough was a Parliamentary leader. In 1648, he had his headquarters at Doncaster. Some of the Royalist garrison of Pontefract Castle determined to seize him as a hostage for their captured general, Sir Marmaduke Langdale. A small party, pretending to carry a message from Cromwell, were admitted to Rainsborough's rooms, seized, bound him, and carried him into the street. There he struggled and called for a rescue, so they conceived it best to slay him and make their escape. So rapid and well contrived was this adventure that the Parliamentarians thought the Devil had been there (Clarendon, vi., 122, edition of 1836).''—Andrew Lang.

An ordinance passed by Parliament in 1645, requiring members of either House, holding military or civil office, to vacate such positions. Cromwell was made an exception.

"Nay, worshipful Master Desborough," said Bletson winking on Everard, to shew that he was playing on his thick-skulled colleague, "how could I tell your particular mode of reposing?—there are many tastes—I have known men who slept by choice on a slope or angle of forty-five."

"Yes, but did ever a man sleep standing on his head, except by miracle?" said Desborough.

"Now, as to miracles"—said the philosopher, confident in the presence of Everard, besides that an opportunity of scoffing at religion really in some degree diverted his fear—" I leave these out of the question, seeing that the evidence on such subjects seems as little qualified to carry conviction, as a horse-hair to land a leviathan."

A loud clap of thunder, or a noise as formidable, rang through the Lodge as the scoffer had ended, which struck him pale and motionless, and made Desborough throw himself on his knees, and repeat exclamations and prayers in much admired confusion.

"There must be contrivance here," exclaimed Everard; and snatching one of the candles from a sconce, he rushed out of the apartment, little heeding the entreaties of the philosopher, who, in the extremity of his distress, conjured him by the *Animus Mundi* to remain to the assistance of a distressed philosopher endangered by witches, and a Parliament-man assaulted by ruffians. As for Desborough, he only gaped like a clown in a pantomine; and, doubtful whether to follow or stop, his natural indolence prevailed, and he sat still.

When on the landing-place of the stairs, Everard paused a moment to consider which was the best course to take. lie heard the voices of men talking fast and loud, like people who wish to drown their fears, in the lower storey; and aware that nothing could be discovered by those whose inquiries were conducted in a manner so noisy, he resolved to proceed in a different direction, and examine the second floor, which he had now gained.

Deception.

He had known every corner, both of the inhabited and uninhabited part of the mansion, and availed himself of the candle to traverse two or three intricate passages, which he was afraid he might not remember with sufficient accuracy. This movement conveyed him to a sort of *mil-debmuf,* an octagon vestibule, or small hall, from which various rooms opened. Amongst these doors, Everard selected that which led to a very long, narrow, and dilapidated gallery, built in the time of Henry VIII., and which, running along the whole south-west side of the building, communicated at different points with the rest of the mansion. This he thought was likely to be the post occupied by those who proposed to act the sprites upon the occasion; especially as its length and shape gave him some idea that it was a spot where the bold thunder might in many ways be imitated.

Determined to ascertain the truth if possible, he placed his light on a table in the vestibule, and applied himself to open the door into the gallery. At this point he found himself strongly opposed either by a bolt drawn, or, as he rather conceived, by somebody from within resisting his attempt. He was induced to believe the latter, because the resistance slackened and was renewed, like that of human strength, instead of presenting the permanent opposition of an inanimate obstacle. Though Everard was a strong and active young man, he exhausted his strength in the vain attempt to open the door; and having paused to take breath, was about to renew his efforts with foot and shoulder, and to call at the same time for assistance, when to his surprise, on again attempting the door more gently, in order to ascertain if possible where the strength of the opposing obstacle was situated, he found it give way to a very slight impulse, some impediment fell broken to the ground, and the door flew wide open. The gust of wind, occasioned by the sudden opening of the door, blew out the candle, and Everard was left in darkness, save where the moonshine which the long side-row of lattice windows dimmed, could imperfectly force its way into the gallery, which lay in ghostly length before him.

Bull's eye; a term given to the oral windows common in the seventeenth century, then to the apartments containing them. It was the name of Louis the Fourteenth's chamber at Versailles. Here it means simply an octagonal hall. The melancholy and doubtful twilight was increased by a quantity of creeping plants on the outside, which, since all had been neglected in these ancient halls, now completely overgrown, had in some instances greatly diminished, and in others almost quite choked up, the space of the lattices, extending between the heavy stone shaftwork which divided the windows, both lengthways and across. On the other side there were no windows at all, and the gallery had been once hung round with paintings, chiefly portraits, by which that side of the apartment had been adorned. Most of the pictures had been removed, yet the empty frames of some, and the tattered remnants of others, were still visible along the extent of the waste gallery; the look of which was so desolate, and it appeared so well adapted for mischief, supposing there were enemies near him, that Everard could not help pausing at the entrance, and recommending himself to God, ere, drawing his sword, he advanced into the apartment, treading as lightly as possible, and keeping in the shadow as much as he could.

Markham Everard was by no means superstitious, but he had the usual credulity of the times; and though he did not yield easily to tales of supernatural visitations, yet he could not help thinking he was in the very situation, where, if such things were ever permitted, they might be expected to take place, while his own stealthy and ill-assured pace, his drawn weapon, and extended arms, being the very attitude and action of doubt and suspicion, tended to increase in his mind the gloomy feelings of which they are the usual indications, and with which they are constantly associated. Under such unpleasant impressions, and conscious of the neighbourhood of something unfriendly, Colonel Everard had already advanced about half along the gallery, when he heard some one sigh very near him, and a low soft voice pronounce his name.

"Here I am," he replied, while his heart beat thick and short. "Who calls on Markham Everard?"

Another sigh was the only answer.

"Speak," said the Colonel, "whoever or whatsoever you are, and tell with what intent and purpose you are lurking in these apartments?"

"With a better intent than yours," returned the soft voice.

"Than mine!" answered Everard in great surprise. "Who are you that dare judge of my intents?" "What, or who are you, Markham Everard, who wander by moonlight through these deserted halls of royalty, where none should be but those who mourn their downfall, or are sworn to avenge it?"

"It is—and yet it cannot be," said Everard; "yet it is, and must be. Alice Lee, the devil or you speaks. Answer me, I conjure you!—speak openly—on what dangerous scheme are you engaged? where is your father? why are you here?—wherefore do you run so deadly a venture? —Speak, I conjure you, Alice Lee!"

"She whom you call on is at the distance of miles from this spot. What if her Genius speaks when she is absent? —what if the soul of an ancestress of hers and yours were now addressing you?—what if"

"Nay," answered Everard, "but what if the dearest of human beings has caught a touch of her father's enthusiasm?—what if she is exposing her person to danger, her reputation to scandal, by traversing in disguise and darkness a house filled with armed men? Speak to me, my fair cousin, in your own person. I am furnished with powers to protect my uncle, Sir Henry—to protect you too, dearest Alice, even against the consequences of this visionary and wild attempt. Speak—I see where you are, and, with all my respect, I cannot submit to be thus practised upon. Trust me—trust your cousin Markham with your hand, and believe that he will die or place you in honourable safety."

As he spoke, he exercised his eyes as keenly as possible to detect where the speaker stood; and it seemed to him, that about three yards from him there was a shadowy form, of which he could not discern even the outline, placed as it was within the deep and prolonged shadow thrown by a space of wall intervening betwixt two windows, upon that side of the room from which the light was admitted. He endeavoured to calculate, as well as he could, the distance betwixt himself and the object which he watched, under the impression, that if, by even using a slight degree of compulsion, he could detach his beloved Alice from the confederacy into which he supposed her father's zeal for the cause of royalty had engaged her, he would be rendering them both the most essential favour. He could not indeed but conclude, that however successfully the plot which he conceived to be in agitation had proceeded against the timid Bletson, the stupid Desborough, and the crazy Harrison, there was little doubt that at length their artifices must necessarily bring shame and danger on those engaged in it.

It must also be remembered, that Everard's affection to his cousin, although of the most respectful and devoted character, partook less of the distant veneration which a lover of those days entertained for the lady whom he worshipped with humble diffidence, than of the fond and familiar feelings which a brother entertains towards a younger sister, whom he thinks himself entitled to guide, advise, and even in some degree to control. So kindly and intimate had been their intercourse, that he had little more hesitation in endeavouring to arrest her progress in the dangerous course in which she seemed to be engaged, even at the risk of giving her momentary offence, than he would have had in snatching her from a torrent or conflagration, at the chance of hurting her by the violence of his grasp. All this passed through his mind in the course of a single minute; and he resolved at all events to detain her on the spot, and compel, if possible, an explanation from her.

With this purpose, Everard again conjured his cousin, in the name of Heaven, to give up this idle and dangerous mummery; and lending an accurate ear to her answer, endeavoured from the sound to calculate as nearly as possible the distance between them.

"I am not she for whom you take me," said the voice; "and dearer regards than aught connected with her life or death, bid me warn you to keep aloof, and leave this place."

"Not till I have convinced you of your childish folly," said the Colonel, springing forward, and endeavouring to catch hold of her who spoke to him. But no female form was within his grasp. On the contrary, he was met by a shock which could come from no woman's arm, and which was rude enough to stretch him on his back on the floor. At the same time he felt the point of a sword at his throat, and his hands so completely mastered, that not the slightest defence remained to him.

"A cry for assistance," said a voice near him, but not that which he had hitherto heard, "will be stifled in your blood!—No harm is meant you—be wise, and be silent."

The fear of death, which Everard had often braved in the field of battle, became more intense as he felt himself in the hands of unknown assassins, and totally devoid of all means of defence. The sharp point of the sword pricked his bare throat, and the foot of him who held it was upon his breast. He felt as if a single thrust would put an end to life, and all the feverish joys and sorrows which agitate us so strangely, and from which we are yet 'so reluctant to part. Large drops of perspiration stood upon his forehead—his heart throbbed, as if it would burst from its confinement in the bosom—he experienced the agony which fear imposes on the brave man, acute in proportion to that which pain inflicts when it subdues the robust and healthy.

"Cousin Alice," — he attempted to speak, and the sword's point pressed his throat yet more closely,—" Cousin, let me not be murdered in a manner so fearful?"

"I tell you," replied the voice, "that you speak to one who is not here; but your life is not aimed at, provided you swear on your faith as a Christian, and your honour as a gentleman, that you will conceal what has happened, whether from the people below, or from any other person. On this condition you may rise; and if you seek her, you will find Alice Lee at Joceline's cottage, in the forest."

"Since I may not help myself otherwise," said Everard, "I swear, as I have a sense of religion and honour, I will say nothing of this violence, nor make any search after those who are concerned in it."

"For that we care nothing," said the voice. "Thou hast an example how well thou may'st catch mischief on thy own part; but we are in case to defy thee. Rise, and begone!

The foot, the sword's-point, were withdrawn, and Everard was about to start up hastily, when the voice, in the same softness of tone which distinguished it at first, said, "No haste—cold and bare steel is yet around thee. Now—now—now—the words dying away as at a distance— thou art free. Be secret and be safe."

Markham Everard arose, and, in rising, embarrassed his feet with his own sword, which he had dropped when springing forward, as he supposed, to lay hold of his fair cousin. He snatched it up in haste, and as his hand clasped the hilt, his courage, which had given way under the apprehension of instant death, began to return; he considered, with almost his usual composure, what was to be done next. Deeply affronted at the disgrace which he had sustained, he questioned for an instant whether he ought to keep his extorted promise, or should not rather summon assistance, and make haste to discover and seize those who had been recently engaged in such violence on his person. But these persons, be they who they would, had had his life in their power—he had pledged his word in ransom of it—and

what was more, he could not divest himself of the idea that his beloved Alice was a confidant, at least, if not an actor, in the confederacy which had thus baffled him. This prepossession determined his conduct; for, though angry at supposing she must have been accessory to his personal ill-treatment, he could not in any event think of an instant search through the mansion, which might have compromised her safety, or that of his uncle. "But I will to the hut," he said—" I will instantly to the hut, ascertain her share in this wild and dangerous confederacy, and snatch her from ruin, if it be possible."

As, under the influence of this resolution which he had formed, Bverard groped his way through the gallery, and regained the vestibule, he heard his name called by the well-known voice of Wildrake. "What—ho!—holla!—Colonel Everard—Mark Everard—it is dark as the devil's mouth—speak—where are you?—The witches are keeping their hellish sabbath here, as I think—Where are you?"

"Here, here!" answered,Everard. "Cease your bawling. Turn to the left, and you will meet me."

Guided by his voice, Wildrake soon appeared, with a light in one hand, and his drawn sword in the other. "Where have you been?" he said—" what has detained you?—Here are Bletson and the brute Desborough terrified out of their lives, and Harrison raving mad, because the devil will not be civil enough to rise to fight him in single *duello*." "Saw or heard you nothing as you came along?" said Everard.

"Nothing," said his friend, "excepting that when I first entered this cursed ruinous labyrinth, the light was struck out of my hand, as if by a switch, which obliged me to return for another." Their stated midnight revel.

"I must come by a horse instantly, Wildrake, and another for thyself, if it be possible."

"We can take two of those belonging to the troopers," answered Wildrake. "But for what purpose should we run away, like rats, at this time in the evening?—Is the house falling?"

"I cannot answer you," said the Colonel, pushing forward into a room where there were some remains of furniture.

Here the cavalier took a more strict view of his person, and exclaimed in wonder, "What the devil have you been fighting with, Markham, that has bedizened you after this sorry fashion?"

"Fighting!" exclaimed Everard.

"Yes," replied his trusty attendant, "I say fighting. Look at yourself in the mirror."

He did, and saw he was covered with dust and blood. The latter proceeded from a scratch which he had received in the throat, as he struggled to extricate himself. With unaffected alarm, Wildrake undid his friend's collar, and with eager haste, proceeded to examine the wound, his hands trembling, and his eyes glistening with apprehension for his benefactor's life. When, in spite of Everard's opposition, he had examined the hurt, and found it trifling, he resumed the natural wildness of his character, perhaps the more readily that he had felt shame in departing from it, into one which expressed more of feeling than he would be thought to possess.

"If that be the devil's work, Mark," said he, "the foul fiend's claws are not nigh so formidable as they are represented; but no one shall say that your blood has been shed unrevenged, while Roger Wildrake was by your side. Where left you this same imp? I will back to the field of fight, confront him with my rapier, and were his nails ten-penny nails, and his teeth as long as those of a harrow, he shall render me reason for the injury he has done you."

"Madness—madness!" exclaimed Everard; "I had this trifling hurt by a fall—a basin and towel will wipe it away. Meanwhile, if you will ever do me kindness, get the troop horses—command them for the service of the public, in the name of his Excellency the General. I will but wash and join you in an instant before the gate."

"Well, I will serve you, Everard, as a mute serves the

Grand Signior, without knowing why or wherefore. But will you go without seeing these people below?"

"Without seeing any one," said Bverard; "lose no time for God's sake."

He found out the non-commissioned officer, and demanded the horses in a tone of authority, to which the corporal yielded undisputed obedience, as one well aware of Colonel Ererard's military rank and consequence. So all was in a minute or two ready for the expedition.

Formerly the popular European name for the Sultan of Turkey.

For a parallel to the hero's behaviour here, see Lovel's conduct in the haunted chamber in *The Antiquary.* From what you know of Scott, do you think he personally shared any of the superstitious weakness which he often attributes to his characters? Note the exalted language used by the apparitions, and see if it is satisfactorily accounted for when the mystery is explained.

CHAPTER THE THIRTEENTH

She kneeled, and saintlike

Cast her eyes to heaven, and prayed devoutly.

King Henky VIII.

Colonel Everard's departure at the late hour, for so it was then thought, of seven in the evening, excited much speculation. There was a gathering of menials and dependents in the outer chamber, or hall, for no one doubted that his sudden departure was owing to his having, as they expressed it, "seen something," and all desired to know how a man of such acknowledged courage as Everard, looked under the awe of a recent apparition. But he gave them no time to make comments; for, striding through the hall wrapt in his riding suit, he threw himself on horseback, and rode furiously through the Chase, towards the hut of the keeper Joliffe.

It was the disposition of Markham Everard to be hot, keen, earnest, impatient, and decisive to a degree of precipitation. The acquired habits which education had taught, and which the strong moral and religious discipline of his sect had greatly strengthened, were such as to enable him to conceal, as well as to check, this constitutional violence, and to place him upon His guard against indulging it. Hut when in the high tide of violent excitation, the natural impetuosity of the young soldier's temper was sometimes apt to overcome these artificial obstacles, and then, like a torrent foaming over a wear, it became more furious, as if in revenge for the constrained calm which it had been for some time obliged to assume. In these instances he was accustomed to see only that point to which his thoughts were bent, and to move straight towards it, whether a moral object, or the storming of a breach, without either calculating, or even appearing to see, the difficulties which were before him.

At present, his ruling and impelling motive was to detach his beloved cousin, if possible, from the dangerous and discreditable machinations in which he suspected her to have engaged, or, on the other hand, to discover that she really had no concern with these stratagems. He should know how to judge of that in some measure, he thought, by finding her present or absent at the hut, towards which he was now galloping. He had read, indeed, in some ballad or minstrel's tale, of a singular deception practised on a jealous old man, by means of a subterranean communication between his house and that of a neighbour, which the lady in question made use of to present herself in the two places alternately, with such speed, and so much address, that, after repeated experiments, the dotard was deceived into the opinion, that his wife, and the lady who was so very like her, and to whom his neighbour paid so much attention, were two different persons. But in the present case there was no room for such a deception; the distance was too great, and as he took by much the nearest way from the castle, and rode full speed, it would be im

Eossible, he knew, for his cousin, who was a timorous orsewoman even by daylight, to have got home before him.

Her father might indeed be displeased at his interference; but what title had he to be so?—Was not Alice Lee the near relation of his blood, the dearest object of his heart, and would he now abstain from an effort to save her from the consequences of a silly and wild conspiracy, because the old knight's spleen might be awakened by Everard's making his appearance at their present dwelling contrary to his commands? No. He would endure the old man's harsh language, as he endured the blast of the autumn wind, which was howling around him, and swinging the crashing branches of the trees under which he passed, but could not oppose, or even retard, his journey. If he found not Alice, as he had reason to believe she would be absent, to Sir Henry Lee himself he would explain what he had witnessed. However she might have become accessory to the juggling tricks performed at Woodstock, he could not but think it was without her father's knowledge, so severe a judge was the old knight of female propriety, and so strict an assertor of female decorum. He would take the same opportunity, he thought, of stating to him the well-grounded hopes he entertained, that his dwelling at the Lodge might be prolonged, and the sequestrators removed from the royal mansion and domains by other means than those of the absurd species of intimidation which seemed to be resorted to, to scare them from thence.

All this seemed to be so much within the line of his duty as a relative, that it was not until he halted at the door of the ranger's hut, and threw his bridle into Wildrake's hand, that Everard recollected the fiery, high, and unbending character of Sir Henry Lee, and felt, even when his fingers were on the latch, a reluctance to intrude himself upon the presence of the irritable old knight.

But there was no time for hesitation. Bevis, who had already bayed more than once from within the Lodge hut , was growing impatient, and Everard had but just time to bid Wildrake hold the horses until he should send Joceline to his assistance, when old Joan unpinned the door, to demand who was without at that time of the night. To have attempted anything like an explanation with poor dame Joan, would have been quite hopeless; the Colonel, therefore, put her gently aside, and shaking himself loose from the hold she had laid on his cloak, entered the kitchen of Joceline's dwelling. Bevis, who had advanced to support Joan in her opposition, humbled his lion-port, with that wonderful instinct which makes his race remember so long those with whom they have been familiar, and acknowledged his master's relative, by doing homage in his fashion, with his head and tail.

Colonel Everard, more uncertain in his purpose every moment as the necessity of its execution drew near, stole over the floor like one who treads in a sick chamber, and opening the door of the interior apartment with a slow and trembling hand, as he would have withdrawn the curtains of a dying friend, he saw, within, the scene which we are about to describe.

Sir Henry Lee satin a wicker armchair by the fire. He was wrapped in a cloak, and his limbs extended on a stool, as if he were suffering from gout or indisposition. His long white beard flowing over the dark-coloured garment, gave him more the appearance of a hermit than of an aged soldier or man of quality; and that character was increased by the deep and devout attention with which he listened to a respectable old man, whose dilapidated dress shewed still something of the clerical habit, and who, with a low, but full and deep voice, was reading the Evening Service according to the Church of England. Alice Lee kneeled at the feet of her father, and made the responses with a voice that might have suited the choir of angels; and a modest and serions devotion, which suited the melody of her tone. The face of the officiating clergyman would have been goodlooking, had it not been disfigured with a black patch which covered the left eye and a part of his face, and had not the features which were visible been marked with the traces of care and suffering.

When Colonel Everard entered, the clergyman raised his finger, as cautioning him to forbear disturbing the divine service of the evening, and pointed to a seat; to which, struck deeply with the scene he had witnessed, the intruder stole with as light a step as possible, and knelt devoutly down as one of the little congregation.

Everard had been bred by his father what was called a Puritan; a member of a sect who, in the primitive sense of the word, were persons that did not except against the doctrines of the Church of England, or even in all respects against its hierarchy, but chiefly dissented from it on the subject of certain ceremonies, habits, and forms of ritual, which were insisted upon by the celebrated and unfortunate Laud, with ill-timed tenacity. But even if, from the habits of his father's house, Everard's opinions had been diametrically opposed to the doctrines of the English Church, he must have been reconciled to them by the regularity with which the service was performed in his uncle's family at Woodstock, who, during the blossom of his fortunes, generally had a chaplain residing in the Lodge for that special purpose.

Yet deep as was the habitual veneration with which he heard the impressive service of the Church, Everard's eyes could not help straying towards Alice, and his thoughts wandering to the purpose of his presence there. She seemed to have recognised him at once, for there was a deeper glow than usual upon her cheek, her fingers trembled as they turned the leaves of her prayerbook, and her voice, lately as firm as it was melodious, faltered when she repeated the responses. It appeared to Everard, as far as he could collect by the stolen glances which he directed towards her, that the character of her beauty, as well as of her outward appearance, had changed with her fortunes.

1William Laud (1573-1645), archbishop of Canterbury, and one of the foremost supporters of Charles I. He was impeached by the Long Parliament, and executed on Tower Hill.

The beautiful and high-born young lady had now approached as nearly as possible to the brown-stuff dress of an ordinary village maiden; but what she had lost in gaiety of appearance, she had gained as it seemed in dignity. Her beautiful light-brown tresses, now folded around her head, and only curled where nature had so arranged them, gave her an air of simplicity, which did not exist when her head-dress shewed the skill of a curious tirewoman. A light joyous air, with something of a humorous expression, which seemed to be looking for amusement, had vanished before the touch of affliction, and a calm melancholy supplied its place, which seemed on the watch to administer comfort to others. Perhaps the former arch though innocent expression of countenance, was uppermost in her lover's recollection, when he concluded that Alice had acted a part in the disturbances which had taken place at the Lodge. It is certain, that when he now looked upon her, it was with shame for having nourished such a suspicion, and the resolution to believe rather that the devil had imitated her voice, than that a creature, who seemed so much above the feelings of this world, and so nearly allied to the purity of the next, should have had the indelicacy to mingle in such manoeuvres as he himself and others had been subjected to.

These thoughts shot through his mind, in spite of the impropriety of indulging them at such a moment. The service now approached the close; and a good deal to Colonel Everard's surprise as well as confusion, the officiating priest, in firm and audible tone, and with every attribute of dignity, prayed to the Almighty to bless and preserve " Our Sovereign Lord, King Charles, the lawful and undoubted King of these realms." The petition (in those days most dangerous) was pronounced with a full, raised, and distinct articulation, as if the priest challenged all who heard him to dissent if they dared. If the republican officer did not assent to the petition, he thought at least it was no time to protest against it.

This is another of the passages in which Scott is supposed to have had his daughter Anne in mind.

The service was concluded in the usual manner, and the little congregation arose. It now included Wildrake, who had entered during the latter prayer, and was the first of the party to speak, running up to the priest, and shaking him by the hand most heartily, swearing at the same time, that he truly rejoiced to see him. The good clergyman returned the pressure with a smile, observing he should have believed his asseveration without an oath. In the meanwhile, Colonel Everard, approaching his uncle's seat, made a deep inclination of respect, first to Sir Henry Lee, and then to Alice, whose colour now spread from her cheek to her brow and bosom.

"I have to crave your excuse," said the Colonel with hesitation, "for having chosen for my visit, which I dare not hope would be very agreeable at any time, a season most peculiarly unsuitable."

"So far from it, nephew," answered Sir Henry, with much more mildness of manner than Everard had dared to expect, "that your visits at other times would be much more welcome, had we the fortune to see you often at our hours of worship."

"I hope the time will soon come, sir, when Englishmen of all sects and denominations," replied Everard, "will be free in conscience to worship in common the great Father, whom they all after their manner call by that affectionate name."

"I hope so, too, nephew," said the old man in the same unaltered tone; "and we will not at present dispute, whether you would have the Church of England coalesce with the Conventicle, or the Conventicle conform to the Church. It was, I ween, not to settle jarring creeds, that you have honoured our poor dwelling, where, to say the truth, we dared scarce have expected to see you again, so coarse was our last welcome."

"I should be happy to believe," said Colonel Everard, hesitating, "that—that—in short my presence was not now so unwelcome here as on that occasion."

"Nephew," said Sir Henry, "I will be frank with you. When you were last here, I thought you had stolen from me a precious pearl, which at one time it would have been my pride and happiness to have bestowed on you; but which, being such as you have been of late, I would bury in the depths of the earth rather than give to your keeping. This somewhat chafed, as honest Will says, ' the rash humour which my mother gave me." I thought I was robbed, and I thought I saw the robber before me. I am mistaken —I am not robbed; and the attempt without the deed I can pardon."

"I would not willingly seek offence in your words, sir," said Colonel Everard, "when their general purport sounds kind; but I can protest before Heaven, that my views and wishes towards you and your family are as void of selfish hopes and selfish ends, as they are fraught with love to you and to yours."

"Let us hear them, man; we are not much accustomed to good wishes now-a-days; and their very rarity will make them welcome."

"I would willingly, Sir Henry, since you might not choose me to give you a more affectionate name, convert those wishes into something effectual for your comfort. Your faith, as the world now stands, is bad, and, I fear, like to be worse."

"Worse than I expect it cannot be. Nephew, I do not shrink before my changes of fortunes. I shall wear coarser clothes,—I shall feed on more ordinary food,—men will not doff their cap to me as they were wont, when I was the great and the wealthy. What of that? Old Harry Lee loved his honour better than his title, his faith better than his land and lordship. Have I not seen the 30th of January? I am neither Philomath nor astrologer; but old Will teaches me, that when green leaves fall winter is at hand, and that darkness will come when the sun sets."

"Bethink you, sir," said Colonel Everard, "if without any submission asked, any oath taken, any engagement imposed, express or tacit, excepting that you are not to excite disturbances in the public peace, you can be restored to your residence in the Lodge, and your usual fortunes and perquisites there—I have great reason to hope this may be permitted, if not expressly, at least on sufferance."

"Yes, I understand you. I am to be treated like the royal coin, marked with the ensign of the Rump to make it pass current, although I am too old to have the royal *Julius Cassar,* IV., 3, 120. 'One who loves learning. *Richard III.,* XL, 3, 33. insignia grinded off from me. Kinsman, I will have none of this. I have lived at the Lodge too long; and let me tell you, I had left it in scorn long since but for the orders of one whom I may yet live to do service to. I will take nothing from the usurpers, be their name Rump or Cromwell—be they one devil or legion—I will not take from them an old cap to cover my grey hairs—a cast cloak to protect my frail limbs from the cold. They shall not say they have, by their unwilling bounty, made Abraham rich—I will live, as I will die, the Loyal Lee."

"May I hope you will think of it, sir; and that you will, perhaps, considering what slight submission is asked, give me a better answer?"

"Sir, if I retract my opinion, which is not my wont, you shall hear of it.—And now, cousin, have you more to say? We keep that worthy clergyman in the outer room."

"Something I had to say—something touching my cousin Alice," said Everard, with embarrassment; "but I fear that the prejudices of both are so strong against me"

"Sir, I dare turn my daughter loose to you—I will go join the good doctor in dame Joan's apartment. I am not unwilling that you should know that the girl hath, in all reasonable sort, the exercise of her free will."

He withdrew, and left the cousins together.

Colonel Everard advanced to Alice, and was about to take her hand. She drew back, took the seat which her father had occupied, and pointed out to him one at some distance.

"Are we then so much estranged, my dearest Alice?" he said.

"We will speak of that presently," she replied. "In the first place, let me ask the cause of your visit here at so late at hour."

"You heard," said Everard, "what I stated to your father?" "I did; but that seems to have been only part of your errand—something there seemed to be which applied particularly to me."

"It was a fancy—a strange mistake," answered Everard. "May I ask if you have been abroad this evening?"

"Certainly not," she replied. "I have small temptation *Genesis* xiv. 23. to wander from my present home, poor as it is; and whilst here, I have important duties to discharge. But why does Colonel Everard ask so strange a question?"

"Tell me in turn, why your cousin Markham has lost the name of friendship and kindred, and even of some nearer feeling, and then I will answer you, Alice."

"It is soon answered," she said. "When you drew your sword against my father's cause—almost against his person —I studied, more than I should have done, to find excuse for you. I knew, that is, I thought I knew, your high feelings of public duty—I knew the opinions in which you had been bred up; and I said I will not, even for this, cast him off—he opposes his King because he is loyal to his country. You endeavoured to avert the great and concluding tragedy of the 30th of January; and it confirmed me in my opinion, that Markham Everard might be misled, but could not be base or selfish."

"And what has changed your opinion, Alice? or who dare," said Everard, reddening, "attach such epithets to the name of Markham Everard?"

"I am no subject," she said, " for exercising your valour, Colonel Everard, nor do I mean to offend. But you will find enough of others who will avow, that Colonel Everard is truckling to the usurper Cromwell, and that all his fair pretexts of forwarding his country's liberties, are but a screen for driving a bargain with the successful encroacher, and obtaining the best terms he can for himself and his family."

"For myself—Never!"

"But for your family you have—Yes, I am well assured that you have pointed out to the military tyrant, the way in which he and his satraps may master the government. Do you think my father or I would accept an asylum purchased at the price of England's liberty, and your honour?"

"Gracious Heaven, Alice, what is this? You accuse me of pursuing the very course which so lately had your approbation!"

"When you spoke with authority of your father, and recommended our submission to the existing government, such as it was, I own I thought—that my father's grey head might, without dishonour, have remained under the roof where it had so long been sheltered. But did your father sanction your becoming the adviser of yonder ambitious soldier to a new course of innovation, and his abettor in the establishment of a new species of tyranny?—It is one thing to submit to oppression, another to be the agent of tyrants—And 0, Markham—their bloodhound!"

"How! bloodhound?—what mean you?—I own it is true I could see with content the wounds of this bleeding country stanched, even at the expense of beholding Cromwell, after his matchless rise, take a yet farther step to power—but to be his bloodhound! What is your meaning?"

"It is false, then?—I thought I could swear it had been false."

"What, in the name of God, is it you ask?" "It is false that you are engaged to betray the young King of Scotland?"

"Betray him! / betray him, or any fugitive? Never! I would he were well out of England—I would lend him my aid to escape, were he in the house at this instant; and think in acting so I did his enemies good service, by preventing their soiling themselves with his blood—but betray him, never!"

"I knew it—I was sure it was impossible. Oh, be yet more honest; disengage yourself from yonder gloomy and ambitious soldier! Shun him and his schemes, which are formed in injustice, and can only be realized in yet more blood!"

"Believe me," replied Bverard, "that I choose the line of policy best befitting the times."

"Choose that," she said, "which best befits duty, Markham—which best befits truth and honour. Do your duty, and let providence decide the rest. Farewell! we tempt my father's patience too far—you know his temper—farewell, Markham."

She extended her hand, which he pressed to his lips, and left the apartment. A silent bow to his uncle, and a sign to Wildralce, whom he found in the kitchen of the cabin, where the only tokens of recognition exhibited, and leaving the hut, he was soon mounted, and, with his companion, advanced on his return to the Lodge.

Note that this chapter re-establishes the mutual confidence of the hero and heroine, by clearing her from complicity in the plot at the Lodge, and by clearing him, in her eyes, from any suspicion of baseness toward Charles I.

CHAPTER THE FOTTKTEENTH Deeds are done on earth,
Which have their punishment ere the earth closes
Upon the perpetrators. Be it the working
Of the remorse-stirred fancy, or the vision,
Distinct and real, of unearthly being.
All ages witness, that beside the couch
Of the fell homicide oft stalks the ghost
Of him he slew, and shows the shadowy wound.
Old Play.

Everard had come to Joceline's hut as fast as horse could bear him, and with the same impetuosity of purpose as of speed. He saw no choice in the course to be pursued, and felt in his own imagination the strongest right to direct, and even reprove, his cousin, beloved as she was, on account of the dangerous machinations with which she appeared to have connected herself. He returned slowly, and in a very different mood.

Not only had Alice, prudent as beautiful, appeared completely free from the weakness of conduct which seemed to give him some authority over her, but her views of policy, if less practicable, were so much more direct and noble than his own, as led him to question whether he had not compromised himself too rashly with Cromwell, even although the state of the country was so greatly divided and torn by faction, that the promotion of the General to the possession of the executive government seemed the only chance of escaping a renewal of the Civil War. The more exalted and purer sentiments of Alice lowered him in his own eyes; and though unshaken in his opinion, that it were better the vessel should be steered by a pilot having no good title to the office, than that she should run upon the breakers, he felt that he was not espousing the most direct, manly, and disinterested side of the question.

As he rode on, immersed in these unpleasant contemplations, and considerably lessened in his own esteem by what had happened, Wildrake, who rode by his side, and was no friend to long silence, began to enter into conversation. "I have been thinking, Mark," said he, "that if you and I had been called to the bar—as, by the by, has been in danger of happening to me in more senses than one—I say, had we become barristers, I would have had the better oiled tongue of the two—the fairer art of persuasion."

"Perhaps so," replied Everard, "though I never heard thee use any, save to induce an usurer to lend thee money, or a taverner to abate a reckoning."

"And yet this day, or rather night, I could have, as I think, made a conquest which baffled you."

"Indeed?" said the Colonel, becoming attentive.

"Why, look you," said Wildrake, "it was a main object with you to induce Mistress Alice Lee—By Heaven, she is an exquisite creature—I approve of your taste, Mark—I say you desire to persuade her, and the stout old Trojan her father, to consent to return to the Lodge, and live there quietly, and under connivance, like gentlefolk, instead of lodging in a hut hardly fit to harbour a Tom of Bedlam."

"Thou art right; such, indeed, was a great part of my object in this visit," answered Everard.

"But, perhaps, you also expected to visit there yourself, and so keep watch over pretty Mistress Lee—eh?"

"I never entertained so selfish a thought," said Everard; "and if this nocturnal disturbance at the mansion were explained and ended, I would instantly take my departure."

"Your friend Noll would expect something more from you," said Wildrake—"he would expect, in case the knight's reputation for loyalty should draw any of our poor exiles and wanderers about the Lodge, that you should be on the watch, and ready to snap them. In a word—as far as I can understand his long-winded speeches —he would have Woodstock a trap, your uncle and his pretty daughter the bait of toasted cheese—craving your Chloe's pardon for the comparison—you the spring-fall which should bar their escape, his Lordship himself being the great grimalkin to whom they are to be given over to be devoured." A stout-hearted fellow, like the men of ancient Troy.
King Lear, I., 2, 148, and III., so. 4 throughout.
'Spring-door.
"Dared Cromwell mention this to thee in express terms?" said Everard, pulling up his horse, and stopping in the midst of the road.

"Nay, not in express terms, which I do not believe he ever used in his life; you might as well expect a drunken man to go straight forward; but he insinuated as much to me, and indicated that you might deserve well of him— Gadzo— the damnable proposal sticks in my throat—by betraying our noble and rightful King here he pulled off his hat, whom God grant in health and wealth long to reign, as the worthy clergyman says, though I fear just now his Majesty is both sick and sorry, and never a penny in his pouch to boot."

"This tallies with what Alice hinted," said Everard; "but how could she know it? didst thou give her any hint of such a thing?"

"I?" replied the cavalier, "I, who never saw Mistress Alice in my life till to-night, and then only for an instant — zooks, man, how is that possible?"

"True," replied Everard, and seemed lost in thought. At length he spoke—" I should call Cromwell to account for his bad opinion of me; for, even though not seriously expressed, but, as I am convinced it was, with the sole view of proving you, and perhaps myself, it was, nevertheless, a misconstruction to be resented."

"I'll carry a cartel for you, with all my heart and soul," said Wildrake; "and turn out with his godliness's second, with as good will as I ever drank a glass of sack."

"Pshaw," replied Everard, "those in his high place fight no single combats. But tell me, Roger Wildrake, didst thou thyself think me capable of the falsehood and treachery implied in such a message?"

"I!" exclaimed Wildrake. "Markham Everard, you have been my early friend, my constant benefactor. When Colchester was reduced, you saved me from the gallows, and since that thou hast twenty times saved me from starving. But, by Heaven, if I thought you capable of such villany as your General recommended—by yonder blue sky and all the works of creation which it bends over, I would stab you with my own hand!" Written challenge to a duel.
Colchester was captured by the Royalists under Goring in 1648,, but Fairfax reduced it after a siege of eleven weeks.
"Death," replied Everard, "I should indeed deserve, but not from you, perhaps;—but fortunately, I cannot, if I would, be guilty of the treachery you would punish. Know that I had this day secret notice, and from Cromwell himself, that the young man has escaped by sea from Bristol."

"Now, God Almighty be blessed, who protected him through so many dangers!" exclaimed Wildrake.—" Huzza!—Up hearts, cavaliers!—Hey for cavaliers!—God bless King Charles!—Moon and stars, catch my hat!"—and he threw it up as high as he could into the air. The celestial bodies which he invoked did not receive the present despatched to them; but, as in the case of Sir Henry Lee's scabbard, an old gnarled oak became a second time the receptacle of a waif and stray of loyal enthusiasm. Wildrake looked rather foolish at the circumstance, and his friend took the opportunity of admonishing him.

"Art thou not ashamed to bear thee so like a schoolboy?"

"Why," said Wildrake, "I have but sent a Puritan's hat upon a loyal errand. I laugh to think how many of the schoolboys thou talk'st of will be cheated into climbing the pollard next year, expecting to find the nest of some unknown bird in yonder unmeasured margin of felt."

"Hush now, for God's sake, and let us speak calmly," said Everard. ' Charles has escaped, and I am glad of it. I would willingly have seen him on his father's tlfrone by composition, but not by the force of the Scottish army, and the incensed and vengeful royalists"

"Master Markham Everard," began the cavalier interrupting him

"Nay, hush, dear Wildrake," said Everard; "let us not dispute a point on which we cannot agree, and give me leave to go on.—I say, since the young man has escaped, Cromwell's offensive and injurious stipulation falls to the ground; and I see not why my uncle and his family should not again enter their own house, under the same terms of connivance as many other royalists. What may be incumbent on me is different, nor can I determine my course until I have an interview with the General, which, as I think, will end in his confessing that he threw in this As the result of a compromise.

offensive proposal to sound us both. It is much in his manner; for he is blunt, and never sees or feels the punctilious honour which the gallants of the day stretch to such delicacy."

"I'll acquit him of having any punctilio about him," said Wilddrake, "either touching honour or honesty.— Now, to come back to where we started. Supposing you were not to reside in person at the Lodge, and to forbear even visiting there, unless on invitation, when such a thing can be brought about, I tell you frankly, I think your uncle and his daughter might be induced to come back to the Lodge, and reside there as usual. At least the clergyman, that worthy old cock, gave me to hope as much."

"

"He had been hasty in bestowing his confidence," said Everard.

"True," replied Wildrake; "he confided in me at once; for he instantly saw my regard for the church. I thank Heaven I never passed a clergyman in his canonicals without pulling my hat off— (and thou knowest, the most desperate duel I ever fought was with young Grayless of the Inner Temple, for taking the wall 1 of the Reverend Dr. Bunce)—Ah, I can gain a chaplain's ear instantly. Gadzooks, they know whom they have to trust to in such a one as I."

"Dost thou think, then," said Colonel Everard, "or rather does this clergyman think, that if they were secure of intrusion from me, the family would return to the Lodge, supposing the intruding Commissioners gone, and this nocturnal disturbance explained and ended?"

"The old Knight," answered Wildrake, "may be wrought upon by the Doctor to return, if he is secure against intrusion. As for disturbances, the stout old boy, so far as I can learn in two minutes' conversation, laughs at all this turmoil as the work of mere imagination, the consequence of the remorse of their own evil consciences; and says that goblin or devil was never heard of at Woodstock, until it became the residence of such men as they, who have now usurped the possession."

"There is more than imagination in it," said Everard. "I have personal reason to know there is some conspiracy carrying on, to render the house untenable by the Com *Borneo and Juliet,* I., 1, 15.

missioners. I acquit my uncle of accession to such a silly trick; but I must see it ended ere I can agree to his and my cousin's residing where such a confederacy exists; for they are likely to be considered as the contrivers of such pranks, be the actual agent who he may. "

"With reference to your better acquaintance with the gentleman, Everard, I should rather suspect the old father of Puritans (I beg your pardon again) has something to do with the business; and if so, Lucifer will never look near the true old Knight's beard, nor abide a glance of yonder maiden's innocent blue eyes. I will uphold them as safe as pure gold in a miser's chest."

"Sawest thou aught thyself, which makes thee think thus?"

"Not a quill of the devil's pinion saw I," replied Wildrake. "He supposes himself too secure of an old cavalier, who must steal, hang, or drown, in the long run, so he gives himself no trouble to look after the assured booty. But I heard the serving-fellows prate of what they had seen and heard; and though their tales were confused enough, yet if there was any truth among them at all, I should say the devil must have been in the dance.—But, holla! here comes some one upon us.—Stand, friend— who art thou?"

"A poor day-labourer in the great work of England—Joseph Tomkins by name—Secretary to a godly and wellendowed leader in this poor Christian army of England, called General Harrison." 1

"What news, Master Tomkins *?"* said Everard; "and why are you on the road at this late hour?"

"I speak to the worthy Colonel Everard, as I judge?" said Tomkins; "and truly I am glad of meeting your honour. Heaven knows, I need such assistance as yours. —Oh, worthy Master Everard!—Here has been a sounding of trumpets, and a breaking of vials, and a pouring forth, and"

"Prithee, tell me in brief, what is the matter—where is thy master—and, in a word, what has happened?"

"My master is close by, parading it in the little meadow, beside the hugeous oak, which is called by the name of the late Man; ride but two steps forward, and you may see 1 Tomkins was introduced in Chapter XII. as the secretary of Desborough.

him walking swiftly to and fro, advancing all the while the naked weapon."

Upon proceeding as directed, but with as little noise as possible, they descried a man, whom of course they concluded must be Harrison, walking to and fro beneath the King's Oak, as a sentinel under arms, but with more wildness of demeanour. The tramp of the horses did not escape his ear; and they heard him call out, as if at the head of the brigade—"Lower pikes against cavalry!—Here comes Prince Rupert—Stand fast, and you shall turn them aside, as a bull would toss a cur-dog.—Lower your pikes still, my hearts, the end secured against your foot—down on your right knee, front rank—spare not for the spoiling of your blue aprons.—Ha—Zerobabel—ay, that is the word!"

"In the name of Heaven, about whom or what is he talking?" said Everard; "wherefore does he go about with his weapon drawn?"

"Truly, sir, when aught disturbs my master, General Harrison, he is something rapt in the spirit, and conceives that he is commanding a reserve of pikes at the great battle of Armageddon—and for his weapon, alack, worthy sir, wherefore should he keep Sheffield steel in calves' leather, when there are fiends to be combated—incarnate fiends on earth, and raging infernal fiends under the earth?"

"This is intolerable," said Everard. "Listen to me, Tomkins. Thou art not now in the pulpit, and I desire none of thy preaching language. I know thou canst speak intelligibly when thou art so minded. Remember, I may serve or harm thee; and as you hope or fear anything on my part, answer straight-forward—What has happened to drive out thy master to the wild wood at this time of night?"

"Forsooth, worthy and honoured sir, I will speak with the precision I may. True it is, and of verity, that the breath of man, which is in his nostrils, goeth forth and returneth"

"Hark you, sir," said Colonel Everard, " take care where you ramble in your correspondence with me. You have heard how at the great battle of Dunbar in Scotland, the General himself held a pistol to the head of Lieutenant Hewcreed, threatening to shoot him through the brain if he did not give up holding forth, and put his squadron in line to the front. Take care, sir." The front part of the pikeman's dress.

Leader of the Hebrews on their return from the Babylonian captivity. *Rev.* xvi. 14-16. September 3, 1650. The student should read, if possible, Carlyle's description of this battle in *Cromwell's Letters and Speeches.*

"Verily, the lieutenant then charged with an even and unbroken order," said Tomkins, "and bore a thousand plaids and bonnets over the beach before him into the sea. Neither shall I pretermit or postpone your honour's commands, but speedily obey them, and that without delay."

"Go to, fellow; thou knowest what I would have," said Everard; "speak at once—I know thou canst if thou wilt. Trusty Tomkins is better known than he thinks for."

"Worthy sir," said Tomkins, in a much less periphrastic style, "I will obey your worship as far as the spirit will permit. Truly, it was not an hour since, when my worshipful master being at table with Master Bibbet and myself, not to mention the worshipful Master Bletson and Colonel Desborough, and behold there was a violent knocking at the gate, as of one in haste. Now, of a certainty, so much had our household been harassed with witches and spirits, and other objects of sound and sight, that the sentinels could not be brought to abide upon their posts without doors, and it was only by a provision of beef and strong liquors that we were able to maintain a guard of three men in the hall, who nevertheless ventured not to open the door, lest they should be surprised with some of the goblins, wherewith their imaginations were overwhelmed. And they heard the knocking, which increased until it seemed that the door was well-nigh about to be beaten down. Worthy Master Bibbet was a little overcome with liquor (as is his fashion, good man, about this time of the evening), not that he is in the least given to ebriety, but simply, that since the Scottish campaign, he hath had a perpetual ague, which obliges him so to nourish his frame against the damps of the night; wherefore, as it is wellknown to your honour that I discharge the office of a faithful servant, as well to Ma-

jor-General Harrison, and the other Commissioners, as to my just and lawful master, Colonel Desborough"

"I know all that.—And now that thou art trusted by both, I pray to Heaven thou mayst merit the trust," said Colonel Everard.

The Royalist army was composed mainly of Scots under Alexander Leslie. "They were made by the Lord of Hosts as stubble to our swords," wrote Cromwell in his official despatch after the battle.

"And devoutly do I pray," said Tomkins, "that your worshipful prayers may be answered with favour; for certainly to be, and to be called and entitled, Honest Joe, and Trusty Tomkins, is to me more than ever would be an Earl's title, were such things to be granted anew in this regenerated government."

"Well, go on—go on—or if thou dalliest much longer, I will make bold to dispute the article of your honesty. I like short tales, sir, and doubt what is told with a long unnecessary train of words. "

"Well, good sir, be not hasty. As I said before, the doors rattled till you would have thought the knocking was reiterated in every room of the Palace. The bell rung out for company, though we could not find that any one tolled the clapper, and the guards let off their firelocks, merely because they knew not what better to do. So, Master Bibbet being, as I said, unsusceptible of his duty, I went down with my poor rapier to the door, and demanded who was there; and I was answered in a voice, which, I must say, was much like another voice, that it was one wanting Major-General Harrison. So as it was then late, I answered mildly, that General Harrison was betaking himself to his rest, and that any one who wished to speak to him must return on the morrow morning, for that after nightfall the door of the Palace, being in the room of a garrison, would be opened to no one. So the voice replied, and bid me open directly, without which he would blow the folding leaves of the door into the middle of the hall. And therewithal the noise recommenced, that we thought the house would have fallen; and I was in some measure constrained to open the door, even like a besieged garrison which can hold out no longer."

"By my honour, and it was stoutly done of you, I must say," said Wildrake, who had been listening with much interest. "I am a bold dare-devil enough, yet when I had two inches of oak plank between the actual fiend and me, hang him that would demolish the barrier between us, say I —I would as soon, when aboard, bore a hole in the ship, and let in the waves; for you know we always compare the devil to the deep sea."

"Prithee, peace, Wildrake," said Everard, " and let him go on with his history.—Well, and what saw'st thou when the door was opened?—the great devil with his horns and claws thou wilt say, no doubt."

"No sir, I will say nothing but what is true. When I undid the door, one man stood there, and he, to seeming, a man of no extraordinary appearance. He was wrapped in a taffeta cloak, of a scarlet colour, and with a red lining. He seemed as if he might have been in his time a very handsome man, but there was something of paleness and sorrow in his face—a long love-lock' and long hair he wore, even after the abomination of the cavaliers, and the unloveliness, as learned Master Prynne well termed it, of love-locks—a jewel in his ear—a blue scarf over his shoulder, like a military commander for the King, and a hat with a white plume, bearing a peculiar hat-band."

"Some unhappy officer of cavaliers, of whom so many are in hiding, and seeking shelter through the country, briefly replied Everard.

"True, worthy sir—right as a judicious exposition. But there was something about this man (if he was a man) whom I, for one, could not look upon without trembling; nor the musketeers who were in the hall, without betraying much alarm, and swallowing, as they themselves will aver, the very bullets which they had in their mouths for loading their carabines and muskets. Nay, the wolf and deer-dogs, that are the fiercest of their kind, fled from this visiter, and crept into holes and corners, moaning and wailing in a low and broken tone. He came into the middle of the hall, and still he seemed no more than an ordinary man, only somewhat fantastically dressed, in a doublet of black velvet pinked upon scarlet satin under his cloak, a jewel in his ear, with large roses in his shoes, and a kerchief in his hand, which he sometimes pressed against his left side." A fine silk.

A long flowing lock curled or tied with a ribbon, and allowed to hang down over the neck and in front of the shoulder. It was the mark of a man of careful and elegant dress in the first part of the seventeenth century. William Prynne (1600-69), a bitter Puritan pamphleteer. In 1633 he published *Histi'io Mastix,* a satire on the stage, in which he criticised Charles I. and Laud. For this he was set in the pillory, and lost both his ears. The reference in the text is to an attack upon the Cavaliers published in 1627, entitled *The Unloveliness of Love-Lockes.* Rosettes. "Gracious Heaven!" said Wildrake, coming close up to Everard, and whispering in his ear, with accents which terror rendered tremulous (a mood of mind most unusual to the daring man, who seemed now overcome by it)—" it must have been poor Dick Robison 1 the player, in the very dress in which I have seen him play Philaster—ay, and drunk a jolly bottle with him after it at the Mermaid! I remember how many frolics we had together, and all his little fantastic fashions. He served for his old master, Charles, in Mohun's troop, and was murdered by this butcher's dog, as I have heard, after surrender, at the battle of Naseby-field."

"Hush! I have heard of the deed," said Everard; "for God's sake hear the man to an end.—Did this visitor speak to thee, my friend?"

"Yes, sir, in a pleasing tone of voice, but somewhat fanciful in the articulation, and like one who is speaking to an audience as from a bar or a pulpit, more than in the voice of ordinary men on ordinary matters. He desired to see Major-General Harrison."

"He did!—and you," said Everard, infected by the spirit of the time, which, as is well known, leaned to credulity upon all matters of supernatural agency,—" what did you do?"

"I went up to the parlour, and related that such a person inquired for him. He started when I told him, and eagerly desired to know the man's dress; but no sooner did I mention his dress, and the jewel in his ear, than he said, 'Begone! tell him I will not admit him to speech of me. Say that I defy him, and will make my defiance good at the great battle in the valley of Armageddon, when the voice of the angel shall call all fowls which fly under the face of heaven to feed on the flesh of the captain and the soldier, the war-horse and his rider. Say to the Evil One, I have power to appeal our conflict even till that day, and that in the front of that fearful day he will again meet with Harrison.' I went back with this answer to the stranger, and his face was writhed into such a deadly frown as a mere human brow hath seldom worn. 'Return to him,' he said, 'and say it is My Houb; and that if he come not instantly down to speak with me, I will mount the stairs to him. Say that I Command him to descend, by the token that, on the field of Naseby, *he did not the work negligently.'"* 1, " At the storming of Basing a fortress which had held out against Parliament for four years and was finally carried by a brilliant assault led by Cromwell in person in 1645 Harrison ' slew one Robinson, son to the door-keeper of Blackfriars playhouse, and the Marquis's of Winchester Major, with his own hands, as they were getting over the works.' A story afterward circulated among the Royalists that Harrison had shot Robinson with a pistol after he had laid, down his arms, saying, 'Cursed is he that doeth the work of the Lord negligently.' "—*Diet. Nat. Biog.* A character in a play by that title, written by Beaumont and Fletcher.

Miohael Mohun, a captain in the Royalist army, was also an actor. Pepys, after the Restoration, speaks of him as "the best actor in the world." "I have heard," whispered Wildrake—who felt more and more strongly the contagion of superstition—" that these words were blasphemously used by Harrison when he shot my poor friend Dick."

"What happened next?" said Everard. "See that thou speakest the truth."

"As gospel unexpounded by a steeple-man," said the Independent; "yet truly it is but little I have to say. I saw my master come down, with a blank, yet resolved air; and when he entered the hall and saw the stranger, he made a pause. The other waved on him as if to follow, and walked out at the portal. My worthy patron seemed as if he were about to follow, yet again paused, when this visitant, be he man or fiend, re-entered, and said, Obey thy doom.

'By pathless march, by greenwood tree,
It is thy weird to follow me—
To follow me through the ghastly moonlight—
To follow me through the shadows of night—
To follow me, comrade, still art thou bound:
I conjure thee by the unstanched wound—
I conjure thee by the last words I spoke,
When the body slept and the spirit awoke,
In the very last pangs of the deadly stroke.'

So saying, he stalked out, and my master followed him into the wood.— I followed also at a distance. But when I came up, my master was alone, and bearing himself as you now behold him."

"Thou hast had a wonderful memory, friend," said the Colonel, coldly, "to remember these rhymes in a single recitation — there seems something of practice in all this."

"A single recitation, my honoured sir?" exclaimed the Independent,— "alack, the rhyme is seldom out of my poor master's mouth, when, as sometimes haps, he is less triumphant in his wrestles with Satan. But it was the first time I ever heard it uttered by another; and, to say truth, he ever seems to repeat it unwillingly, as a child after his pedagogue, and as it was not indited by his own head, as the Psalmist saith."

"It is singular," said Everard;—" I have heard and read that the spirits of the slaughtered have strange power over the slayer; but I am astonished to have it insisted upon that there may be truth in such tales. Roger Wildrake—what art thou afraid of, man?—why dost thou shift thy place thus?"

"Fear? it is not fear—it is hate, deadly hate.—I see the murderer of poor Dick before me, and—see, he throws himself into a posture of fence—Sa—sa—say'st thou, brood of a butcher's mastiff? thou shalt not want an antagonist."

Ere any one could stop him, Wildrake threw aside his cloak, drew his sword, and almost with a single bound cleared the distance betwixt him and Harrison, and crossed swords with the latter, as he stood brandishing his weapon, as if in immediate expectation of an assailant. Accordingly, the Republican General was not for an instant taken at unawares, but the moment the swords clashed, he shouted, "Ha! I feel thee now, thou hast come in body at last.— Welcome! welcome!—the sword of the Lord and of Gideon!"

"Part them, part them," cried Everard, as he and Tomkins, at first astonished at the suddenness of the affray, hastened to interfere. Everard, seizing on the cavalier, drew him forcibly backwards, and Tomkins contrived, with risk and difficulty, to master Harrison's sword, while the General exclaimed, "Ha, two to one—two to one!— thus fight demons." Wildrake, on his side, swore a dreadful oath, and added, "Markham, you have cancelled every obligation I owed you—they are all out of sight—gone, d—n me!"

"You have indeed acquitted these obligations rarely," Artifice, deceit. *Judges* vii. 20. said Everard. "Who knows how this affair shall be explained and answered?"

"I will answer it with my life," said Wildrake.

"Good now, be silent," said Tomkins, "and let me manage. It shall be so ordered that the good General shall never know that he hath encountered with a mortal man; only let that man of Moab put his sword into the scabbard's rest, and be still."

""Wildrake, let me entreat thee to sheathe thy sword," said Everard, "else, on my life, thou must turn against me."

"No, 'fore George, not so mad as that neither, but I'll have another day with him."

"Thou, another day!" exclaimed Harrison, whose eye had still remained fixed on the spot where he found such palpable resistance. "Yes, I know thee well; day by day, week by week, thou makest the same idle request, for thou knowest that my heart quivers at thy voice. But my hand trembles not when opposed to thine—the spirit is willing to the combat, if the flesh be weak when opposed to that which is not of the flesh."

"Now, peace all, for Heaven's sake,"—said the steward Tomkins; then added, addressing his master, "there is no one here, if it please your Excellence, but Tomkins and the worthy Colonel Everard."

General Harrison, as sometimes happens in cases of partial insanity (that is, supposing his to have been a case of mental delusion), though firmly and entirely persuaded of the truth of his own visions, yet was not willing to speak on the subject to those who, he knew, would regard them as imaginary. Upon this occasion, he assumed the appearance of perfect ease and composure, after the violent agitation he had just manifested, in a manner which shewed how anxious he was to disguise his real feelings from Everard, whom he considered as unlikely to participate them.

He saluted the Colonel with profound ceremony, and talked of the fineness of the evening, which had summoned him forth of the Lodge, to take a turn in the Park, and enjoy the favourable weather. He then took Everard by the arm, and walked back with him towards the Lodge, Wildrake and Tomkins following close behind and leading the horses. Everard, desirous to gain some light on these mysterious incidents, endeavoured to come on the subject more than once, by a mode of interrogation, which Harrison (for madmen are very often unwilling to enter on the subject of their mental delusion) parried with some skill, or addressed himself for aid to his steward Tomkins, who was in the habit of being voucher for his master upon all occasions, which led to Desborough's ingenious nickname of Fibbet.

"And wherefore had you your sword drawn, my worthy General," said Everard, "when you were only on an evening walk of pleasure?"

"Truly, excellent Colonel, these are times when men must watch with their loins girded, and their lights burning, and their weapons drawn. The day draweth nigh, believe me or not as you will, that men must watch lest they be found naked and unarmed, when the seven trumpets shall sound, Boot and saddle; and the pipes of Jezerl shall strike up, Horse and away."

"True, good General; but methought I saw you making passes even now as if you were fighting?" said Everard.

"I am of a strange fantasy, friend Everard," answered Harrison; "and when I walk alone, and happen, as but now, to have my weapon drawn, I sometimes, for exercise' sake, will practise a thrust against such a tree as that. It is a silly pride men have in the use of weapons. I have been accounted a master of fence, and have fought prizes when I was unregenerated, and before I was called to do my part in the great work, entering as a trooper into onr victorious General's first regiment of horse."

"But methought," said Everard, "I heard a weapon clash with yours?"

"How? a weapon clash with my sword?—How could that be, Tomkins?"

"Truly, sir," said Tomkins, "it must have been a bough of the tree; they have them of all kinds here, and your honour may have pushed against one of them, which the Brazilians call iron-wood, a block of which, being struck with a hammer, saith Purchas in his Pilgrimage, ringeth like an anvil." A Hebrew, of the family of Naphtali.

Rev. Samuel Purchas, author of *Purchas, his Pilgrimage; or Relations of the World and the Religions Observed in all Ages* (1613).

"Truly, it may be so," said Harrison; "for those rulers who are gone, assembled in this their abode of pleasure many strange trees and plants, though they gathered not of the fruit of that tree which beareth twelve manner of fruits, or of those leaves which are for the healing of the nations."

Everard pursued his investigation; for he was struck with the manner in which Harrison evaded his questions, and the dexterity with which he threw his transcendental and fanatical notions, like a sort of veil, over the darker visions excited by remorse and conscious guilt.

"But," said he, "if I may trust my eyes and ears, I cannot but still think that you had a real antagonist—Nay, I am sure I saw a fellow, in a dark-coloured jerkin, retreat through the wood."

"Did you?" said Harrison, with a tone of surprise, while his voice faltered in spite of him—"Who could he be?—Tomkins, did you see the fellow Colonel Everard talks of with the napkin in his hand—the bloody napkin which he always pressed to his side?"

This last expression, in which Harrison gave a mark different from that which Everard had assigned, but corresponding to Tomkins's original description of the supposed spectre, had more effect on Everard in confirming the steward's story, than anything he had witnessed or heard. The voucher answered the draft upon him as promptly as usual, that he had seen such a fellow glide past them into the thicket—that he dared to say he was some deer-stealer, for he had heard they were become very audacious.

"Look ye there now, Master Everard," said Harrison, hurrying from the subject—" Is it not time now that we should lay aside our controversies, and join hand in hand to repairing the breaches of our Zion? Happy and contented were I, my excellent friend, to be a treader of mortar, or a bearer of a hod, upon this occasion, under our great leader, with whom Providence has gone forth in this great national controversy; and truly, so devoutly do I hold by our excellent and victorious General Oliver, whom Heaven long preserve—that were he to command me, I should not scruple to pluck forth of his high place the man whom they call Speaker, even as I lent a poor hand to pluck down the man whom they called King. Wherefore, *Revelation* xxii. 2.

as I know your judgment holdeth with mine on this matter, let me urge unto you lovingly, that we may act as brethren, and build up the breaches, and re-establish the bulwarks of our English Zion, whereby we shall be doubtless chosen as pillars and buttresses, under our excellent Lord General, for supporting and sustaining the same, and endowed with proper revenues and incomes, both spiritual and temporal, to serve as a pedestal, on which we may stand, seeing that otherwise our foundation will be on the loose sand.—Nevertheless," continued he, his mind again diverging from his views of temporal ambition into his visions of the Fifth Monarchy, "these things are but vanity in respect of the opening of the book which is sealed; for all things approach speedily towards lightning and thundering, and unloosing of the great dragon from the bottomless pit, wherein he is chained."1

With this mingled strain of earthly politics, and fanatical prediction, Harrison so overpowered Colonel Everard, as to leave him no time to urge him farther on the particular circumstances of his nocturnal skirmish, concerning which it is plain he had no desire to be interrogated. They now reached the Lodge of Woodstock.

Revelation v. and *xx*.

After the temporary lull of Chapter XIII. , observe how the fine scene with Harrison heightens the mystery which surrounds the occupants of the Lodge, and prepares the way for Chapter XV.

CHAPTER THE FIFTEENTH

Now the wasted brands do glow,
While the screech-owl, sounding loud,
   Puts the wretch that lies in wo,
In remembrance of a shroud.
   Now it is the time of night That the graves, all gaping wide,
Every one lets out his sprite,
   In the church-way paths to glide.
   Midsummer Night's Dream.

Before the gate of the palace the guards were now doubled. Everard demanded the reason of this from the corporal, whom he found in the hall with his soldiers, sitting or sleeping around a great fire, maintained at the expense of the carved chairs and benches with fragments of which it was furnished.

"Why, verily," answered the man, "the *corps-de-garde,* as your worship says, will be harassed to pieces by such duty; nevertheless, fear hath gone abroad among us, and no man will mount guard alone. We have drawn in, however, one or two of our outposts from Banbury and elsewhere, and we are to have a relief from Oxford to-morrow."

Everard continued minute inquiries concerning the sentinels that were posted within as well as without the Lodge; and found that, as they had been stationed under the eye of Harrison himself, the rules of prudent discipline had been exactly observed in the distribution of the posts. There remained nothing therefore for Colonel Everard to do, but, remembering his own adventure of the evening, to recommend that an additional sentinel should be placed, with a companion, if judged indispensable, in that vestibule, or anteroom, from which the long gallery where he had met with the rencontre, and other suites of apartments, diverged. The corporal respectfully promised all obedience to his orders. The serving-men being called, appeared also in double force. Everard demanded to know whether the Commissioners had gone to bed, or whether he could get speech with them?

"They are in their bedroom, forsooth," replied one of the fellows, "but I think they be not yet undressed."

"What!" said Everard, "are Colonel Desborough and Master Bletson both in the same sleeping apartment?"

"Their honours have so chosen it," said the man; "and their honours' secretaries remain upon guard all night."

"It is the fashion to double guards all over the house," said Wildrake. "Had I a glimpse of a tolerably goodlooking housemaid now, I should know how to fall into the fashion."

"Peace, fool!" said Everard—"and where are the Mayor and Master Holdenough?"

"The Mayor is returned to the borough on horseback, behind the trooper, who goes to Oxford for the reinforcement; and the man of the steeple-house hath quartered himself in the chamber which Colonel Desborough had last night, being that in which he is most likely to meet the your honour understands. The Lord pity us, we are a harassed family!"

"And where be General Harrison's knaves," said Tomkins, "that they do not marshal him to his apartment?"

"Here—here—here, Master Tomkins," said three fellows, pressing forward, with the same consternation on their faces which seemed to pervade the whole inhabitants of Woodstock.

"Away with you, then," said Tomkins;—" speak not to his worship—you see he is not in the humour."

"Indeed," observed Colonel Everard, "he looks singularly wan—his features seem writhen1 as by a palsy stroke; and though he was talking so fast while we came along, he hath not opened his mouth since we came to the light."

"It is his manner after such visitations," said Tomkins. —" Give his honour your arms, Zedekiah and Jonathan, to lead him off—I will follow instantly-You, Nicodemus, tarry to wait upon me—it is not well walking alone in this mansion."

"Master Tomkins," said Everard, "I have heard of you often as a sharp, intelligent man—tell me fairly, are you Distorted.

in earnest afraid of anything supernatural haunting this house?"

"I would be loath to run the chance, sir," said Tomkins very gravely; "by looking on my worshipful master, you may form a guess how the living look after they have spoken with the dead. " He bowed low, and took his leave. Everard proceeded to the chamber which the two remaining Commissioners had, for comfort's sake, chosen to inhabit in company. They were preparing for bed as he went into their apartment. Both started as the door opened—both rejoiced when they saw it was only Everard who entered.

"Hark ye hither," said Bletson, pulling him aside. "Sawest thou ever ass equal to Desborough?—the fellow is as big as an ox, and as timorous as a sheep. He has insisted on my sleeping here to protect him. Shall we have a merry night on't, ha? We will, if thou wilt take the third bed, which was prepared for Harrison; but he is gone out, like a mooncalf, to look for the valley of Armageddon in the park of Woodstock."

"General Harrison has returned with me but now," said Everard.

"Nay but, as I shall live, he comes not into our apartment," said Desborough, overhearing his answer. "No man that has been supping, for aught I know, with the Devil, has a right to sleep among Christian folk."

"He does not propose so," said Everard; "he sleeps, as I understand, apart—and alone."

"Not quite alone, I dare say," said Desborough, "for Harrison hath a sort of attraction for goblins—they fly round him like moths about a candle. But, I prithee, good Everard, do thou stay with us. I know not how it is, but although thou hast not thy religion always in thy mouth, nor speakest many hard words about it, like Harrison— nor makest long preachments, like a certain most honourable relation of mine who shall be nameless, yet somehow I feel myself safer in thy company than with any of them. As for this Bletson, he is such a mere blasphemer, that I fear the Devil will carry him away ere morning."

"Did you ever hear such a paltry coward!" said Bletson apart to Everard. "Do tarry, however, mine honoured Colonel—I know your zeal to assist the distressed, and you see Desborough is in that predicament that he will require near him more than one good example to prevent him thinking of ghosts and fiends."

"I am sorry I cannot oblige you, gentlemen," said Everard; "but I have settled my mind to sleep in Victor Lee's apartment, so I wish you good night; and if you would repose without disturbance, I would advise that you com-mend yourselves, during the watches of the night, to Him unto whom night is even as mid-day. I had intended to have spoken with you this evening on the subject of my being here; but I will defer the conference till to-morrow, when, I think, I will be able to shew you excellent reasons for leaving Woodstock."

"We have seen plenty such already," said Desborough; "for one, I came here to serve the estate, with some moderate advantage doubtless to myself for my trouble; but if I am set upon my head again to-night, as I was the night before, I would not stay longer to gain a king's crown; for I am sure my neck would be unfitted to bear the weight of it."

"Good night," exclaimed Everard; and was about to o, when Bletson again pressed close, and whispered to im, "Hark thee, Colonel—you know my friendship for thee—I do implore thee to leave the door of thy apartment open, that if thou meetest with any disturbance, I may hear thee call, and be with thee upon the very instant. I)o this, dear Everard, my fears for thee will keep me awake else; for I know that, notwithstanding your excellent sense, you entertain some of those superstitious ideas which we suck in with our mother's milk, and which constitute the ground of our fears in situations like the present; therefore leave thy door open, if you love me, that you may have ready assistance from me in case of need.

"My master," said Wildrake, "trusts, first, in his Bible, sir, and then in his good sword. He has no idea that the Devil can be baffled by the charm of two men lying in one room, still less that the foul fiend can be argued out of existence by the Nullifidians1 of the Rota."

Everard seized his imprudent friend by the collar, and dragged him off as he was speaking, keeping fast hold of him till they were both in the chamber of Victor Lee, where they had slept on a former occasion. Even then he continued to hold Wildrake, until the servant had arranged the lights, and was dismissed from the room; then letting him go, addressed him with the upbraiding question, '' Art thou not a prudent and sagacious person, who in times like these seek'st every opportunity to argue yourself into a broil, or embroil yourself in an argument? Out on you!" Believers in nothing. Many members of the Rota Club were free-thinkers.

"Ay, out on me, indeed," said the cavalier; "out on me for a poor tame-spirited creature, that submits to be bandied about in this manner, by a man who is neither better born nor better bred than myself. I tell thee, Mark, you make an unfair use of your advantages over me. Why will you not let me go from you, and live and die after my own fashion?"

"Because, before we had been a week separate, I should hear of your dying after the fashion of a dog. Come, my good friend, what madness was it in thee to fall foul on Harrison, and then to enter into useless argument with Bletson?"

"Why, we are in the Devil's house, I think, and I would willingly give the landlord his due wherever I travel. To have sent him Harrison, or Bletson now, just as a lunch to stop his appetite, till Crom"

"Hush! stone walls have ears," said Everard, looking around him. "Here stands thy night-drink. Look to thy arms, for we must be as careful as if the Avenger of Blood were behind us. Yonder is thy bed—and I, as thou seest, have one prepared in the parlour. The door only divides us."

"Which I will leave open, in case thou shouldst holla for assistance, as yonder Nullifidian hath it. — But how hast thou got all this so well put in order, good patron?"

"I gave the steward Tomkins notice of my purpose to sleep here."

"A strange fellow that," said Wildrake, "and, as I judge, has taken measure of every one's foot—all seems to pass through his hands."

"He is, I have understood," replied Everard, "one of the men formed by the times—has a ready gift of preaching and expounding, which keeps him in high terms with the Independents; and recommends himself to the more moderate people by his intelligence and activity." *Joshua* xx. 1-6.

"Has his sincerity ever been doubted?" said Wildrake.

"Never, that I heard of," said the Colonel; "on the contrary, he has been familiarly called Honest Joe, and Trusty Tomkins. For my part, I believe his sincerity has always kept pace with his interest.—But come, finish thy cup, and to bed.—What, all emptied at one draught!"

"Adzookers, yes—my vow forbids me to make two on't; but, never fear—the nightcap will only warm my brain, not clog it. So, man or devil, give me notice if you are disturbed, and rely on me in a twinkling." So saying, the cavalier retreated into his separate apartment, and Colonel Everard, taking off the most cumbrous part of his dress, lay down in his hose and doublet, and composed himself to rest.

He was awakened from sleep by a slow and solemn strain of music, which died away as at a distance. He started up, and felt for his arms, which he found close beside him. His temporary bed being without curtains, he could look around him without difficulty; but as there remained in the chimney only a few red embers of the fire, which he had arranged before he went to sleep, it was impossible he could discern anything. He felt, therefore, in spite of his natural courage, that undefined and thrilling species of tremour which attends a sense that danger is near, and an uncertainty concerning its cause and character. Reluctant as he was to yield belief to supernatural occurrences, we have already said he was not absolutely incredulous; as perhaps, even in this more sceptical age, there are many fewer complete and absolute infidels on this particular than give themselves out for such. Uncertain whether he had not dreamed of these sounds which seemed yet in his ears, he was unwilling to risk the raillery of his friend by summoning him to his assistance. He sat up, therefore, in his bed, not without experiencing that nervous agitation to which brave men as well as cowards are subject; with this difference, that the one sinks under it, like the vine under the hail-storm, and the other collects his energies to shake it off, as the cedar of

Lebanon is said to elevate its boughs to disperse the snow which accumulates upon them.

The story of Harrison, in his own absolute despite, and notwithstanding a secret suspicion which he had of trick or connivance, returned on his mind at this dead and solitary hour. Harrison, he remembered, had described the vision by a circumstance of its appearance different from that which his own remark had been calculated to suggest to the mind of the visionary;—that bloody napkin, always pressed to the side, was then a circumstance present either to his bodily eye, or to that of his agitated imagination. Did, then, the murdered revisit the living haunts of those who had forced them from the stage with all their sins unaccounted for? And if they did, might not the same permission authorize other visitations of a similar nature, to warn—to instruct—to punish? Rash are they, was his conclusion, and credulous, who receive as truth every tale of the kind; but no less rash may it be, to limit the power of the Creator over the works which he has made, and to suppose that, by the permission of the Author of Nature, the laws of Nature may not, in peculiar cases, and for high purposes, be temporarily suspended.

While these thoughts passed through Everard's mind, feelings unknown to him, even when he stood first on the rough and perilous edge of battle, gained ground upon him. He feared he knew not what; and where an open and discernible peril would have drawn out his courage, the absolute uncertainty of his situation increased his sense of the danger. He felt an almost irresistible desire to spring from his bed and heap fuel on the dying embers, expecting by the blaze to see some strange sight in his chamber. He was also strongly tempted to awaken Wildrake; but shame, stronger than fear itself, checked these impulses. What! should it be thought that Markham Everard, held one of the best soldiers who had drawn sword in this sad war—Markham Everard, who had obtained such distinguished rank in the army of the Parliament, though so young in years, was afraid of remaining by himself in a twilight-room at midnight? It never should be said.

This was, however, no charm for his unpleasant current of thought. There rushed on his mind the various traditions of Victor Lee's chamber, which, though he had often despised them as vague, unauthenticated, and inconsistent rumours, engendered by ancient superstition, and transmitted from generation to generation by loquacious credulity, had yet something in them, which did not tend to allay the present unpleasant state of his nerves. Then, when he recollected the events of that very afternoon, the weapon pressed against his throat, and the strong arm which threw him backward on the floor—if the remembrance served to contradict the idea of flitting phantoms, and unreal daggers, it certainly induced him to believe, that there was in some part of this extensive mansion a party of cavaliers, or malignants, harboured, who might arise in the night, overpower the guards, and execute upon them all, but on Harrison in particular, as one of the regicide judges, that vengeance, which was so eagerly thirsted for by the attached followers of the slaughtered monarch.

He endeavoured to console himself on this subject, by the number and position of the guards, yet still was dissatisfied with himself for not having taken yet more exact precautions, and for keeping an extorted promise of silence, which might consign so many of his party to the danger of assassination. These thoughts, connected with his military duties, awakened another train of reflections. He bethought himself, that all he could now do, was to visit the sentries, and ascertain that they were awake, alert, on the watch, and so situated, that in time of need they might be ready to support each other.—"This better befits me," he thought, "than to be here like a child, frightening myself with the old woman's legend, which I have laughed at when a boy. What although old Victor Lee was a sacrilegious man, as common report goes, and brewed ale in the font which he brought from the ancient palace of Holyrood, while church and building were in flames? And what although his eldest son was when a child scalded to death in the same vessel? How many churches have been demolished since his time? How many fonts desecrated? So many indeed, that were the vengeance of Heaven to visit such aggressions in a supernatural manner, no corner in England, no, not the most petty parish church, but would have its apparition.—Tush, these are idle fancies, unworthy, especially, to be entertained by those educated to believe that sanctity resides in the intention and the act, not in the buildings, or fonts, or the form of worship."

As thus he called together the articles of his Calvinistic creed, the bell of the great clock (a token seldom silent in such narratives) tolled three, and was immediately followed by the hoarse call of the sentinels through vault and gallery, up stairs and beneath, challenging and answering each other with the usual watch-word, All's well. Their voices mingled with the deep boom of the bell, yet ceased before that was silent, and when they had died away, the tingling echo of the prolonged knell was scarcely audible. Ere yet that last distant tingling had finally subsided into silence, it seemed as if it again was awakened; and Everard could hardly judge at first whether a new echo had taken up the falling cadence, or whether some other and separate sound was disturbing anew the silence to which the deep knell had, as its voice ceased, consigned the ancient mansion and the woods around it.

The Royal Palace of Scotland at Edinburgh, originally an abbey of the Holy Rood, or cross. It was several times burned in its early history. It was the residence of Mary Queen of Scots, and reference to it is frequent in Scott's novels.

But the doubt was soon cleared up. The musical tones, which had mingled with the dying echoes of the knell, seemed at first to prolong, and afterwards to survive them. A wild strain of melody, beginning at a distance, and growing louder as it advanced, seemed to pass from room to room, from cabinet to gallery, from hall to bower, through the deserted and dishonoured ruins of the ancient residence of so many sovereigns; and, as it approached, no soldier gave alarm, nor did any of the numerous guests of various degrees, who spent an unpleasant and terrified night in that ancient mansion, seem to dare to announce to each other the inexplicable cause of apprehension.

Everard's excited state of mind did not permit him to be so passive. The sounds approached so nigh, that it seemed they were performing, in the very next apartment, a solemn service for the dead, when he gave the alarm, by calling loudly to his trusty attendant and friend Wildrake, who slumbered in the next chamber with only a door betwixt them, and even that ajar.

"Wildrake—Wildrake!—Up—up! Dost thou not hear the alarm?"

There was no answer from Wildrake, though the musical sounds, which now rung through the apartment, as if the performers had actually been within its precincts, would have been sufficient to awaken a sleeping person, even without the shout of his comrade and patron.

"Alarm! — Roger Wildrake— alarm!" again called Everard, getting out of bed and grasping his weapons — " Get a light, and cry alarm *I*"

There was no answer. His voice died away as the sound of the music seemed also to die; and the same soft sweet voice, which still to his thinking resembled that of Alice Lee, was heard in his apartment, and, as he thought, at no distance from him.

"Your comrade will not answer," said the low soft voice. "Those only hear the alarm whose consciences feel the call."

"Again this mummery!" said Everard. "I am better armed than I was of late; and but for the sound of that voice, the speaker had bought his trifling dear. "

It was singular, we may observe in passing, that the instant the distinct sounds of the human voice were heard by Everard, all idea of supernatural interference was at an end, and the charm by which he had been formerly fettered appeared to be broken; so much is the influence of imaginary or superstitious terror dependent (so far as respects strong judgments at least) upon what is vague or ambiguous; and so readily do distinct tones, and express ideas, bring such judgments back to the current of ordinary life. The voice returned answer, as addressing his thoughts as well as his words.

"We laugh at the weapons thou thinkest should terrify us—Over the guardians of Woodstock they have no power. Fire, if thou wilt, and try the effect of thy weapons. But know, it is not our purpose to harm thee—thou art of a falcon breed, and noble in thy disposition, though, unreclaimed and ill nurtured, thou hauntest with kites and carrion crows. Wing thy flight from hence on the morrow, for if thou tarriest with the bats, owls, vultures, and ravens, which have thought to nestle here, thou wilt inevitably share their fate. Away then, that these halls may be swept and garnished for the reception of those who have a better right to inhabit them."

Everard answered in a raised voice. —" Once more I warn you, think not to defy me in vain. I am no child to be frightened by goblins' tales; and no coward, armed as I am, to be alarmed at the threats of banditti. If I give you a moment's indulgence, it is for the sake of dear and misguided friends, who may be concerned with this dangerous gambol. Know, I can bring a troop of soldiers round the castle, who will search its most inward recesses for the author of this audacious frolic; and if that search should fail, it will cost but a few barrels of gunpowder to make the mansion a heap of ruins, and bury under them the authors of such an ill-judged pastime."

"You speak proudly, Sir Colonel," said another voice, similar to that harsher and stronger tone by which he had been addressed in the gallery; "try your courage in this direction."

"You should not dare me twice," said Colonel Everard, "had I a glimpse of light to take aim by."

As he spoke, a sudden gleam of light was thrown with a brilliancy which almost dazzled the speaker, shewing distinctly a form somewhat resembling that of Victor Lee, as represented in his picture, holding in one hand a lady completely veiled, and in the other his leading-staff, or truncheon. Both figures were animated, and, as it appeared, standing within six feet of him.

"Were it not for the woman," said Everard, "I would not be thus mortally dared."

"Spare not for the female form,but do your worst,"replied the same voice. "I defy you."

"Repeat your defiance when I have counted thrice," said Everard, "and take the punishment of your insolence. Once—I have cocked my pistol— Twice—I never missed my aim—By all that is sacred, I fire if you do not withdraw. When I pronounce the next number, I will shoot you dead where you stand. I am yet unwilling to shed blood—I give you another chance of flight—once—twice—Thrice!"

Everard aimed at the bosom, and discharged his pistol. The figure waved its arm in an attitude of scorn; and a loud laugh arose, during which the light, as gradually growing weaker, danced and glimmered upon the apparition of the aged knight, and then disappeared. Everard's life-blood ran cold to his heart—" Had he been of human mould," he thought, "the bullet must have pierced him—but I have neither will nor power to fight with supernatural beings. "

The feeling of oppression was now so strong as to be actually sickening. He groped his way, however, to the fireside, and flung on the embers which were yet gleaming, a handful of dry fuel. It presently blazed, and afforded him light to see the room in every direction. He looked cautiously, almost timidly, arpund, and half expected some horrible phantom to become visible. But he saw nothing save the old furniture, the reading-desk, and other articles, which had been left in the same state as when Sir Henry Lee departed. He felt an uncontrollable desire, mingled with much repugnance, to look at the portrait of the ancient knight, which the form he had seen so strongly resembled. He hesitated betwixt the opposing feelings, but at length snatched, with desperate resolution, the taper which he had extinguished, and relighted it, ere the blaze of the fuel had again died away. He held it up to the ancient portrait of Victor Lee, and gazed on it with eager curiosity, not unmingled with fear. Almost the childish terrors of his earlier days returned, and he thought the severe pale eye of the ancient warrior followed his, and menaced him with its displeasure. And although he quickly argued himself out of such an absurd belief, yet the mixed feelings of his mind were expressed in words that seemed half addressed to the ancient portrait.

"Soul of my mother's ancestor," he said, "be it for weal or for woe, by designing men, or by supernatural beings, that these ancient halls are disturbed, I am resolved to leave them on the morrow."

"I rejoice to hear it, with all my soul," said a voice behind him.

He turned, saw a tall figure in white, with a sort of turban upon its head, and dropping the candle in the exertion, instantly grappled with it.

"*Thou* at least are palpable," he said.

"Palpable?" answered he whom he grasped so strongly —" 'Sdeath, methinks you might know that without the risk of choking me; and if you loose me not, I'll shew you that two can play at the game of wrestling."

"Roger Wildrake!" said Everard, letting the cavalier loose, and stepping back.

"Roger Wildrake? ay, truly. Did you take me for Roger Bacon, come to help you to raise the devil?—for the place smells of sulphur consumedly."

"It is the pistol I fired—Did you not hear it?"

"Why, yes, it was the first thing waked me—for that nightcap which I pulled on, made me sleep like a dormouse —Pshaw, I feel my brains giddy with it yet."

"And wherefore came you not on the instant?—I never needed help more." The celebrated English philosopher (1214-1294), who for many centuries was reputed to be a sorcerer.

"I came as fast as I could," answered Wildrake; "but it was some time ere I got my senses collected, for I was dreaming of that cursed field at Naseby—and then the door of my room was shut, and hard to open, till I played the locksmith "with my foot."

"How! it was open when I went to bed," said Everard.

"It was locked when I came out of bed, though," said Wildrake; "and I marvel you heard me not when I forced it open."

"My mind was occupied otherwise," said Everard.

"Well," said Wildrake, "but what has happened?— Here am I bolt upright, and ready to fight, if this yawning fit will give me leave—Mother Redcap's mightiest is weaker than I drank last night, by a bushel to a barleycorn—I have quaffed the very elixir of malt— Ha—yaw."

"And some opiate besides, I should think," said Everard.

"Very like—very like—less than the pistol-shot would not waken me; even me, who with but an ordinary gracecup sleep as lightly as a maiden on the first of May, when she watches for the earliest beam to go to gather dew. But what are you about to do next?"

"Nothing," answered Everard.

"Nothing *?*" said Wildrake, in surprise.

"I speak it," said Colonel Everard, "less for your information, than for that of others who may hear me, that I will leave the Lodge this morning, and if it is possible, remove the Commissioners."

"Hark," said Wildrake, "do you not hear some noise, like the distant sound of the applause of a theatre? The goblins of the place rejoice in your departure."

"I shall leave Woodstock," said Everard, "to the occupation of my uncle Sir Henry Lee, and his family, if they choose to resume it; not that I am frightened into this as a concession to the series of artifices which have been played off on this occasion, but solely because such was my intention from the beginning. But let me warn" (he added raising his voice),—"let me warn the parties concerned in this combination, that though it may pass off successfully on a fool like Desborough, a visionary like Harrison, a coward like Bletson" General name for a hostess, or old woman. See *Fortunes of Nigel*. The last draught. This was one of the old Mayday customs in England. Many of them are referred to in Herriok's *Hesperides.*

Here a voice distinctly spoke, as standing near them— "Or a wise, moderate, and resolute person like Colonel Everard."

"By Heaven, the voice came from the picture," said Wildrake, drawing his sword; "I will pink his plated armour for him."

"Offer no violence," said Everard, startled at the interruption, but resuming with firmness what he was saying,— "Let those engaged be aware, that however this string of artifices may be immediately successful, it must, when closely looked into, be attended with the punishment of all concerned—the total demolition of Woodstock, and the irremediable downfall of the family of Lee. Let all concerned think of this, and desist in time."

He paused, and almost expected a reply, but none such came.

"It is a very odd thing," said Wildrake; "but—yawha—my brain cannot compass it just now; it whirls round like a toast in a bowl of muscadine. I must sit down—hawyaw—and discuss it at leisure—Gramercy, good elbowchair."

So saying, he threw himself, or rather sank gradually down, on a large easy-chair, which had been often pressed by the weight of stout Sir Henry Lee, and in an instant was sound asleep. Everard was far from feeling the same inclination for slumber, yet his mind was relieved of the apprehension of any farther visitation that night; for he considered his treaty to evacuate Woodstock, as made known to, and accepted in all probability by, those whom the intrusion of the Commissioners had induced to take such singular measures for expelling them. His opinion, which had for a time bent towards a belief in something supernatural in the disturbances, had now returned to the more rational mode of accounting for them, by dexterous combination, for which such a mansion as Woodstock afforded so many facilities.

He heaped the hearth with fuel, lighted the candle, and examining poor Wildrake's situation, adjusted him as easily in the chair as he could, the cavalier stirring his limbs no more than an infant. His situation went far, in his patron's opinion, to infer trick and confederacy, for ghosts have no occasion to drug men's possets. He threw himself on the bed, and while he thought these strange circumstances over, a sweet and low strain of music stole through the chamber, the words "Good night—good night—good night," thrice repeated, each time in a softer and more distant tone, seeming to assure him that the goblins and he were at truce, if not at peace, and that he had no more disturbance to expect that night. He had scarcely the courage to call out a "good night;" for, after all his conviction of the existence of a trick, it was so well performed as to bring with it a feeling of fear just like what an audience experience during the performance of a tragic scene, which they know to be unreal, and which yet affects their passions by its near approach to nature. Sleep overtook him at last, and left him not till broad daylight on the ensuing morning. Prick through.

This final challenge of the apparitions by Everard marks the highest point of the "mystery interest" in the plot. Compare Scott's handling of these apparently supernatural appearances with that of any other novelists you know who have attempted the same thing.

CHAPTER THE SIXTEENTH

And yonder shines Aurora's harbinger,
  At whose approach ghosts, wandering here and there,
  Troop home to churchyard
  Midsummer Night's Dream.

With the fresh air, and the rising of morning, every feeling of the preceding night had passed away from Colonel Everard's mind, excepting wonder how the effects which he had witnessed could be produced. He examined the whole room, sounding bolt, floor, and wainscot, with his knuckles and cane, but was unable to discern any secret passages; while the door, secured by a strong cross bolt, and the lock besides, remained as firm as when he had fastened it on the preceding evening. The apparition resembling Victor Lee next called his attention. Ridiculous stories had been often circulated, of this figure, or one exactly resembling it, having been met with by night among the waste apartments and corridors of the old palace; and Markham Everard had often heard such in his childhood. He was angry to recollect his own deficiency of courage, and the thrill which he felt on the preceding night, when by confederacy, doubtless, such an object was placed before his eyes.

"Surely," he said, "this fit of childish folly could not make me miss my aim—rmore likely that the bullet had been withdrawn clandestinely from my pistol."

He examined that which was undischarged—he found the bullet in it. He investigated the apartment opposite to the point at which he had fired, and, at five feet from the floor in a direct line, between the bedside and the place where the appearances had been seen, a pistol-ball had recently buried itself in the wainscot. He had little doubt, therefore, that he had fired in a just direction; and indeed to have arrived at the place where it was lodged, the bullet must have passed through the appearance at which he aimed, and proceeded point blank to the wall beyond. This was mysterious, and induced him to doubt whether the art of witchcraft or conjuration had not been called in to assist the machinations of those daring conspirators, who, being themselves mortal, might, nevertheless, according to the universal creed of the times, have invoked and obtained assistance from the inhabitants of another world.

His next investigation respected the picture of Victor Lee itself. He examined it minutely as he stood on the floor before it, and compared its pale, shadowy, faintlytraced outlines, its faded colours, the stern repose of the eye, and deathlike pallidness of the countenance, with its different aspect on the preceding night, when illuminated by the artificial light which fell full upon it, while it left every other part of the room in comparative darkness. The features seemed then to have an unnatural glow, while the rising and falling of the flame in the chimney gave the head and limbs something which resembled the appearance of actual motion. Now, seen by day, it was a mere picture of the hard and ancient school of Holbein; last night, it seemed for the moment something more. Determined to get to the bottom of this contrivance if possible, Everard, by the assistance of a table and chair, examined the portrait still more closely, and endeavoured to ascertain the existence of any private spring, by which it might be slipt aside,—a contrivance not unfrequent in ancient buildings, which usually abounded with means of access and escape, communicated to none but the lords of the castle, or their immediate confidants. But the panel on which Victor Lee was painted was firmly fixed in the wainscoting of the apartment, of which it made a part, and the Colonel satisfied himself that it could not have been used for the purpose which he had suspected.

He next aroused his faithful squire Wildrake, who, notwithstanding his deep share of the "blessedness of sleep," had scarce even yet got rid of the effects of the grace-cup of the preceding evening. "It was the reward," according to his own view of the matter, "of his temperance; one single draught having made him sleep more late and more sound than a matter of half-a-dozen, or from thence to a dozen pulls, would have done, when he was guilty of the enormity of rere-suppers, and of drinking deep after them."

"Had your temperate draught," said Everard, "been but a thought more strongly seasoned, Wildrake, thou hadst slept so sound that the last trump only could have waked thee."

"And then," answered Wildrake, "I should have waked with a headache, Mark; for I see my modest sip has not exempted me from that epilogue.—But let us go forth, and see how the night, which we have passed so strangely, has been spent by the rest of them. I suspect they are all right willing to evacuate Woodstock, unless they have either rested better than we, or at least been more lucky in lodgings."

"In that case, I will despatch thee down to Joceline's hut, to negotiate the re-entrance of Sir Henry Lee and his family into their old apartments, where, my interest with the General being joined with the indifferent repute of the place itself, I think they have little chance of being disturbed either by the present, or by any new Commissioners."

"But how are they to defend themselves against the fiends, my gallant Colonel?" said Wildrake. "Methinks had I an interest in yonder pretty girl, such as thou dost boast, I should be loath to expose her to the terrors of a residence at Woodstock, where these devils—I beg their pardon, for I suppose they hear every word we say— these merry goblins—make such gay work from twilight till morning."

"My dear Wildrake," said the Colonel, "I, as well as you, believe it possible that our speech may be overheard; but I care not, and will speak my mind plainly. I trust Sir Henry and Alice are not engaged in this silly plot; I cannot reconcile it with the pride of the one, the modesty of the other, or the good sense of both, that any motive could engage them in so strange a conjunction. But the fiends are all of your own political persuasion, Wildrake, all true-blue cavaliers; and I am convinced, that Sir Henry and Alice Lee, though they be unconnected with them, have not the slightest cause to be apprehensive of their goblin machinations. Besides, Sir Henry and Joceline must know every corner about the place: it will be far more difficult to play off any ghostly machinery upon him than upon strangers. But let us to our toilet, and when water and brush have done their work, we will inquire what is next to be done." Rere suppers *quasi arri&rc)* belonged to a species of luxury introduced in the jolly days of King James's extravagance, and continued through the subsequent reign. The supper took place at an early hour, six or seven o'clock at latest —the rere-supper was a postliminary banquet, a *hors d'amvre,* which made its appearance at ten or eleven, and served as an apology for prolonging the entertainment till midnight. Scott.

"Nay, that wretched puritan's garb of mine is hardly worth brushing," said Wildrake; "and but for this hundredweight of rusty iron, with which thou hast bedizened me, I look more like a bankrupt Quaker than anything else. But I'll make *you* as spruce as ever was a canting rogue of your party."

So saying, and humming at the same time the cavalier tune,—

"Though for a time we see Whitehall
With cobwebs hung around the wall,
Yet Heaven shall make amends for all,
When the King shall enjoy his own again"

"Thou forgettest who are without," said Colonel Everard.

"No—I remember who are within," replied his friend. "I only sing to my merry goblins, who will like me all the better for it. Tush, man, the devils are my *bonos socios,* and when I see them, I will warrant they prove such roaring boys as I knew when I served under Lumford and Goring, fellows with long nails that nothing escaped, bottomless stomachs, that nothing filled,—mad for pillaging, ranting, drinking, and fighting,—sleeping rough on the trenches, and dying stubbornly in their boots. Ah! those merry days are gone. Well, it is the fashion to make a grave face on't among cavaliers, and specially the parsons that have lost their tithe-pigs; but I was fitted for the element of the time, and never did or can desire merrier days than I had during that same barbarous, bloody, and unnatural rebellion."

"Thou wert ever a wild sea-bird, Roger, even according to your name; liking the gale better than the calm, the boisterous ocean better than the smooth lake, and yonr rough, wild struggle against the wind, than daily food, ease, and quiet." Boon companions.
The pigs given in payment of the tithes to which clergymen were entitled from their parishioners.—*liomeo and Juliet,* I., 4, 79.

"Pshaw! a fig for your smooth lake, and your old woman to feed me with brewer's grains, and the poor drake obliged to come swattering 1 whenever she whistles! Everard, I like to feel the wind rustle against my pinions, —now diving, now on the crest of the wave, now in ocean, now in sky—that is the wilddrake's joy, my grave one! And in the Civil War so it went with us—down in one county, up in another, beaten to-day, victorious to-morrow—now starving in some barren leaguer—now revelling in a Presbyterian's pantry—his cellars, his plate-chest, his old judicial thumb-ring, his pretty serving-wench, all at command!"

"Hush, friend," said Everard; "remember I hold that persuasion."

"More the pity, Mark, more the pity," said Wildrake; "but, as you say, it is needless talking of it. Let us e'en go and see how your Presbyterian pastor, Mr. Holdenough, has fared, and whether he has proved more able to foil the foul Fiend than have you his disciple and auditor."

They left the apartment accordingly, and were overwhelmed with the various incoherent accounts of sentinels and others, all of whom had seen or heard something extraordinary in the course of the night. It is needless to describe particularly the various rumours which each contributed to the common stock, with the greater alacrity that in such cases there seems always to be a sort of disgrace in not having seen or suffered as much as others.

The most moderate of the narrators only talked of sounds like the mewing of a cat, or the growling of a dog, especially the squeaking of a pig. They heard also as if it had been nails driven and saws used, and the clashing of fetters, and the rustling of silk gowns, and the notes of music, and in short all sorts of sounds which have nothing to do with each other. Others swore they had smelt savours of various kinds, chiefly bituminous, indicating a Satanic derivation; others did not indeed swear, but protested, to visions of men in armour, horses without heads, asses with horn and cows with six legs, not to mention black figures, whose cloven hoofs gave plain information what realm they belonged to.

Spluttering through the water. Sealring.

But these strongly-attested cases of nocturnal disturbances among the sentinels had been so general, as to prevent alarm and succour on any particular point, so that those who were on duty called in vain on the *corps-degarde,* who were trembling on their own post; and an alert enemy might have done complete execution on the whole garrison. But amid this general *alerted* no violence appeared to be meant, and annoyance, not injury, seemed to have been the goblin's object, excepting in the case of one

Eoor fellow, a trooper, who had followed Harrison in half is battles, and now was sentinel in that very vestibule upon which Everard had recommended them to mount a guard. He had presented his carabine at something which came suddenly upon him, when it was wrested out of his hands, and he himself knocked down with the but-end of it. His broken head, and the drenched bedding of Desborough, upon whom a tub of ditch water had been emptied during his sleep, were the only pieces of real evidence to attest the disturbances of the night.

The reports from Harrison's apartment were, as delivered by the grave Master Tomkins, that truly the General had passed the night undisturbed, though there was still upon him a deep sleep, and a folding of the hands to slumber; from which Everard argued that the machinators had esteemed Harrison's part of the reckoning sufficiently paid off on the preceding evening.

He then proceeded to the apartment doubly garrisoned by the worshipful Desborough, and the philosophical Bletson. They were both up and dressing themselves, the former open-mouthed in his feeling of fear and suffering. Indeed, no sooner had Everard entered, than the ducked and dismayed Colonel made a dismal complaint of the way he had spent the night, and murmured not a little against his worshipful kinsman, for imposing a task upon him which inferred so much annoyance.

"Could not his Excellency, my kinsman, Noll," he said, "have given his poor relative and brother-in-law a sop somewhere else, than out of this Woodstock, which seems to be the devil's own porridge-pot? I cannot sup broth with the devil; I have no long spoon—not I. Could he not have quartered me in some quiet corner, and given this haunted place to some of his preachers and prayers, who Signal of alarm.

know the Bible as well as the muster-roll? whereas I know the four hoofs of a clean-going nag, or the points of a team of oxen, better than all the books of Moses. But I will give it over, at once and for ever; hopes of earthly gain shall never make me run the risk of being carried, away bodily by the devil, besides being set upon my head one whole night, and soused with ditch water the next— No, no; I am too wise for that."

Master Bletson had a different part to act. He complained of no personal annoyances; on the contrary, he declared he should have slept as well as ever he did in his life, but for the abominable disturbances around him, of men calling to arms every half hour, when so much as a cat trotted by one of their posts— He would rather, he said, "have slept among a whole sabaoth1 of witches, if such creatures could be found."

"Then you think there are no such things as apparitions, Master Bletson?" said Everard. "fused to be sceptical on the subject; but on my life, to-night has been a strange one."

"Dreams, dreams, dreams, my simple Colonel," said Bletson, though his pale face, and shaking limbs, belied the assumed courage with which he spoke. "Old Chaucer, sir, hath told us the real moral on't—He was an old frequenter of the forest of Woodstock, here"

"Chaser?" said Desborough; "some huntsman belike, by his name—Does he walk, like Hearne at Windsor *?"*

"Chaucer," said Bletson, "my dear Desborough, is one of those wonderful fellows, as Colonel Everard knows, who live many a hundred years after they are buried, and whose words haunt our ears after their bones are long mouldered in the dust."

"Ay, ay! well," answered Desborough, to whom this description of the old poet was unintelligible—" I for one desire his room rather than his company—one of your conjurors, I warrant him. But what says he to the matter?" A Hebrew word meaning host; here used in confusion with sabbath.

See Longfellow's sonnet on Chaucer at Woodstock Park. The tradition of his residence there, however, lacks historical support. "There is no evidence that he ever dwelt a day in Woodstock."—T. R. Lounsbury, *Studies in Chaucer,* Vol. I., pp. 103, 175. *Merry Wives of Windsor,* Act IV., Sc. 4, and thereafter.

"Only a slight spell, which I will take the freedom to repeat to Colonel Everard," said Bletson; "but which would be as bad as Greek to thee, Desborough.— Old Geoffrey lays the whole blame of our nocturnal disturbance on superfluity of humours,

Which causen folke to dred in their dreams

Of arrowes, and of fire with red gleams, Right as the humour of Melancholy Causeth many a man in sleep to cry For fear of great bulls and bears black, ADd others that black devils will them take.

While he was thus declaiming, Everard observed a book sticking out from beneath the pillow of the bed lately occupied by the honourable member.

"Is that Chaucer?" he said, making to the volume— "I would like to look at the passage"

'Chaucer"?—said Bletson, hastening to interfere; "no—that is Lucretius, my darling Lucretius. I cannot let you see it—I have some private marks."

But by this time Everard had the book in his hand. "Lucretius?" he said; "no, Master Bletson—this is not Lucretius, but a fitter comforter in dread or in danger— Why should you be ashamed of it?—Only, Bletson, instead of resting your head, if you can but anchor your heart upon this volume, it may serve you in better stead than Lucretius or

Chaucer either."

"Why, what book is it ?" said Bletson, his pale cheek colouring with the shame of detection.—" Oh! the Bible!" throwing it down contemptuously—" some book of my fellow Gibeon's— these Jews have been always superstitious —ever since Juvenal's time, thou knowest—

Qualiacunque voles Judsei somnia vendunt.

He left me the old book for a spell, I warrant you, for 'tis a well-meaning fool." 1 Chaucer's *Nortme Preenten Tale,* 11. 109-115.
The Roman poet (96-55 B.C.), a professed disbeliever in religious influences. His great work is the *De Rrum Natura.* See Tennyson's poem. *Lucretius. "]* The Roman satirist (about 60-140 A r). The quotation. "The Jews will sell you whatever dreams you wish for," is from his *Satires,* Book VI., 547.
"He would scarce have left the New Testament, as well as the Old," said Everard. "Come, my dear Bletson, do not be ashamed of the wisest thing you ever did in your life, supposing you took your Bible in an hour of apprehension, with a view to profit by the contents."

Bletson's vanity was so much galled, that it overcame his constitutional cowardice. His little thin fingers quivered for eagerness, his neck and cheeks were as red as scarlet, and his articulation was as thick and vehement as—in short, as if he had been no philosopher.

"Master Everard," he said, "you are a man of the sword, sir; and, sir, you seem to suppose yourself entitled to say whatever comes into your mind with respect to civilians, sir. But I would have you remember, sir, that there are bounds beyond which human patience may be urged, sir,—and jests which no man of honour will endure, sir,— and therefore, I expect an apology for your present language, Colonel Everard, and this unmannerly jesting, sir —or you may chance to hear from me in a way that will not please you."

Everard could not help smiling at this explosion of valour, engendered by irritated self-love.

"Look you, Master Bletson," he said, "I have been a soldier, that is true, but I was never a bloody-minded one; and as a Christian, I am unwilling to enlarge the kingdom of darkness by sending a new vassal thither before his time. If Heaven gives you time to repent, I see no reason why my hand should deprive you of it, which, were we to have a rencontre,1 would be your fate in the thrust of a sword, or the pulling of a trigger— I therefore prefer to apologize; and I call Desborough, if he has recovered his wits, to bear evidence that I *do* apologize for having suspected you, who are completely the slave of your own vanity, of any tendency, however slight, towards grace or good sense. And I farther apologize for the time that I have wasted in endeavouring to wash an Ethiopian white, or in recommending rational inquiry to a self-willed atheist."

Bletson, overjoyed at the turn the matter had taken— for the defiance was scarce out of his month ere he began to tremble for the consequences—answered with great eagerness and servility of manner,—" Nay, dearest Colonel, say no more of it—an apology is all that is necessary among Encounter.
men of honour—it neither leaves dishonour with him who asks it, nor infers degradation on him who makes it."

"Not such an apology as I have made, I trust," said the Colonel.

"No, no—not in the least," answered Bletson,—" one apology serves me just as well as another, and Desborough will bear witness you have made one, and that is all there can be said on the subject."

"Master Desborough and you," rejoined the Colonel, "will take care how the matter is reported, I daresay, and I only recommend to both, that, if mentioned at all, it may be told correctly."

"Nay, nay, we will not mention it at all," said Bletson, "we will forget it from this moment. Only, never suppose me capable of superstitious weakness. Had I been afraid of an apparent and real danger—why such fear is natural to man—and I will not deny that the mood of mind may have happened to me as well as to others. But to be thought capable of resorting to spells, and sleeping with books under my pillow to secure myself against ghosts,—on my word, it was enough to provoke one to quarrel, for the moment, with his very best friend.—And now, Colonel, what is to be done, and how is our duty to be executed at this accursed place? If I should get such a wetting as Desborough's, why I should die of catarrh, though you see it hurts him no more than a bucket of water thrown over a posthorse. You are, I presume, a brother in our commission,—how are you of opinion we should proceed?"

"Why, in good time here comes Harrison," said Everard, "and I will lay my commission from the Lord General before you all; which, as you see, Colonel Desborough, commands you to desist from acting on your present authority, and intimates his pleasure accordingly, that you withdraw from this place."

Desborough took the paper and examined the signature. —" It is Noll's signature sure enough," said he, dropping his under jaw; "only, every time of late he has made the *Oliver* as large as a giant, while the *Cromwell* creeps after like a dwarf, as if the surname were like to disappear one of these days altogether. But is his Excellency, our kinsman, Noll Cromwell (since he has the surname yet) so unreasonable as to think his relations and friends are to be set upon their heads till they have the crick in their neck —drenched as if they had been plunged in a horsepond— frightened, day and night, by all sorts of devils, witches, and fairies, and get not a penny of smart-money?1 Adzooks (forgive me for swearing), if that's the case I had better home to my farm, and mind team and herd, than dangle after such a thankless person though I *have* wived his sister. She was poor enough when I took her, for as high as Noll holds his head now."

"It is not my purpose," said Bletson, " to stir debate in this honourable meeting; and no one will doubt the veneration and attachment which I bear to our noble General, whom the current of events, and his own matchless qualities of courage and constancy, have raised so high in these deplorable days.—If I were to term him a direct and immediate emanation of the *Animus Mundi* itself—something which Nature had produced in her proudest hour, while exerting herself, as is her law, for the preservation of the creatures to whom she has given existence—I should scarce exhaust the ideas which I entertain of him. Always protesting, that I am by no means to be held as admitting, but merely as granting for the sake of argument, the possible existence of that species of emanation, or exhalation, from the *Animus Mundi,* of which I have made mention. I appeal to you, Colonel Desborough, who are his excellency's relation—to you, Colonel Everard, who hold the dearer title of his friend, whether I have overrated my zeal in his behalf?"

Everard bowed at this pause, but Desborough gave a more complete authentication. "Nay, I can bear witness to that. I have seen when you were willing to tie his points or brush his cloak, or the like—and to be treated thus ungratefully—and gndgeoned of the opportunities which had been given you"

"It is not for that," said Bletson, waving his hand gracefully. "You do me wrong, Master Desborough— you do indeed, kind sir—although I know you meant it not—No, sir—no partial consideration of private interest prevailed on me to undertake this charge. It was conferred on me by the Parliament of England, in whose name this war commenced, and by the Council of State, who are the conservators of England's liberty. And the Compensation.

chance and serene hope of serving the country, the confidence that I—and you Master Desborough—and you worthy General Harrison—superior, as I am, to all selfish considerations—to which I am sure you also, good Colonel Everard, would be superior, had you been named in this Commission, as I would to Heaven you had—I say, the hope of serving the country, with the aid of such respectable associates, one and all of them—as well as you Colonel Everard, supposing you to have been of the number, induced me to accept of this opportunity, whereby I might, gratuitously, with your assistance, render so much advantage to our dear mother the Commonwealth of England.— Such was my hope—my trust—my confidence. And now comes my Lord General's warrant to dissolve the authority by which we are entitled to act. Gentleman, I ask this honourable meeting (with all respect to his Excellency), whether his Commission be paramount to that from which he himself directly holds *his* commission? No one will say so. I ask whether he has climbed into the seat from which the late Man descended, or hath a great seal, or means to proceed by prerogative in such a case? I cannot see reason to believe it, and therefore I must resist such doctrine. I am in your judgment, my brave and honourable colleagues; but, touching my own poor opinion, I feel myself under the unhappy necessity of proceeding in our commission, as if the interruption had not taken place; with this addition, that the Board of Sequestrators should sit, by day, at this same Lodge of Woodstock, but that, to reconcile the minds of weak brethren, who may be afflicted by superstitious rumours, as well as to avoid any practice on our persons by the malignants, who, I am convinced, are busy in this neighbourhood, we should remove our sittings after sunset to the George Inn, in the neighbouring borough."

"Good Master Bletson," replied Colonel Everard, "it is not for me to reply to you; but you may know in what characters this army of England and their General write their authority. I fear me the annotation on this precept of the General, will be expressed by the march of a troop of horse from Oxford to see it executed. I believe there are orders out for that effect; and you know by late ex The seal of state, of which the Lord Chancellor is the official custodian. "I will defer to you.

perience, that the soldier will obey his General equally against King and Parliament."

"That obedience is conditional," said Harrison, starting fiercely up. "Know'st thou not, Markham Everard, that I have followed the man Cromwell as close as the bull-dog follows his master?—and so I will yet;—but I am no spaniel, either to be beaten, or to have the food I have earned snatched from me, as if I were a vile cur, whose wages are a whipping, and free leave to wear my own skin. I looked, amongst the three of us, that we might honestly, and piously, and with advantage to the Commonwealth, have gained out of this commission three, or it maybe five thousand pounds. And does Cromwell imagine I will part with it for a rough word? No man goeth a warfare on his own charges. He that serves the altar must live by the altar— and the saints must have means to provide them with good harness and fresh horses against the unsealing and the pouring forth. Does Cromwell think I am so much of a tame tiger as to permit him to rend from me at pleasure the miserable dole he hath thrown me? Of a surety I will resist; and the men who are here, being chiefly of my own regiment—men who wait, and who expect, with lamps burning and loins girded, and each one his weapon bound upon his thigh, will aid me to make this house good against every assault—ay, even against Cromwell himself, until the latter coming—Selah! Selah!"

"And *I,"* said Desborough, "will levy troops and protect your out-quarters, not choosing at present to close myself up in garrison"

"And I," said Bletson, "will do my part, and hie me to town and lay the matter before Parliament, arising in my place for that effect."

Everard was little moved by all these threats. The only formidable one, indeed, was that of Harrison, whose enthusiasm, joined with his courage, and obstinacy, and character among the fanatics of his own principles, made him a dangerous enemy. Before trying any arguments with the refractory Major-General, Everard endeavoured to moderate his feelings, and threw something in about the late disturbances.

"Talk not to me of supernatural disturbances young man—talk not to me of enemies in the body or out of the body. Am I not the champion chosen and commissioned to encounter and to conquer the great Dragon, and the Beast which cometh out of the sea? Am I not to command the left wing, and two regiments of the centre, when the Saints shall encounter with the countless legions of Gog and Magog? I tell thee that my name is written on the sea of glass mingled with fire, and that I will keep this place of Woodstock against all mortal men, and against all devils, whether in field or chamber, in the forest or in the meadow, even till the Saints reign in the fulness of their glory." In preparation for the coming millennium.

A Hebrew musical term, occurring in the *Psalms* to mark a pause.

Everard saw it was then time to produce two or three lines under Cromwell's hand, which he had received from the General, subsequently to the communication through Wildrake. The information they contained was calculated to allay the disappointment of the Commissioners. This document assigned as the reason of superseding the Woodstock Commission, that he should probably propose to the Parliament to require the assistance of General Harrison, Colonel Desborough, and Master Bletson, the honourable member for Littlefaith, in a much greater matter, namely, the disposing of the royal property, and disparking of the King's forest at Windsor. So soon as this idea was started, all parties pricked up their ears; and their drooping, and gloomy, and vindictive looks began to give place to courteous smiles, and to a cheerfulness, which laughed in their eyes, and turned their mustaches upwards.

Colonel Desborough acquitted his right honourable and excellent cousin and kinsman of all species of unkindness; Master Bletson discovered, that the interest of the state was trebly concerned in the good administration of Windsor more than in that of Woodstock. As for Harrison, he exclaimed, without disguise or hesitation, that the gleaning of the grapes of Windsor was better than the vintage of Woodstock. Thus speaking, the glance of his dark eye expressed as much triumph in the proposed earthly advantage, as if it had not been, according to his vain persuasion, to be shortly exchanged for his share in the general reign of the Millennium. His delight, in short, resembled the joy of an eagle, who preys upon a lamb in the evening with not the less relish, because she descries in the distant land *Revelation,* xii. and xiii. *Revelation* xx. 7-10.

scape a hundred thousand men about to join battle with daybreak, and to give her an endless feast on the hearts and life-blood of the valiant.

Yet though all agreed that they would be obedient to the General's pleasure in this matter, Bletson proposed, as a precautionary measure, in which all agreed, that they should take up their abode for some time in the town of Woodstock, to wait for their new commissions respecting Windsor; and this upon the prudential consideration, that it was best not to slip one knot until another was first tied.

Each commissioner, therefore, wrote to Oliver individually, stating in his own way, the depth and height, length and breadth, of his attachment to him. Each expressed himself resolved to obey the General's injunctions to the uttermost; but with the same scrupulous devotion to the Parliament, each found himself at a loss how to lay down the commission intrusted to them by that body, and therefore felt bound in conscience to take up his residence at the borough of Woodstock, that he might not seem to abandon the charge committed to them, until they should be called to administer the weightier matter of Windsor, to which they expressed their willingness instantly to devote themselves, according to his Excellency's pleasure.

This was the general style of their letters, varied by the characteristic flourishes of their writers. Desborough, for example, said something about the religious duty of providing for one's own household, only he blundered the text. Bletson wrote long and big words about the political obligation incumbent on every member of the community, on every person, to sacrifice his time and talents to the service of his country; while Harrison talked of the littleness of present affairs, in comparison of the approaching tremendous change of all things beneath the sun. But although the garnishing of the various epistles was different, the result came to the same, that they were determined at least to keep sight of Woodstock, until they were well assured of some better and more profitable commission.

Everard also wrote a letter in the most grateful terms to Cromwell, which would probably have been less warm had he known more distinctly than his follower chose to tell him, the expectation under which the wily General had granted his request. He acquainted his Excellency with his purpose of continuing at Woodstock, partly to assure himself of the motions of the three commissioners, and to watch whether they did not again enter upon the execution of the trust, which they had for the present renounced,— and partly to see that some extraordinary circumstances, which had taken place in the Lodge, and which would doubtless transpire, were not followed by any explosion to the disturbance of the public peace. He knew (as he expressed himself) that his Excellency was so much the friend of order, that he would rather disturbances or insurrections were prevented than punished; and he conjured the General to repose confidence in his exertions for the public service by every mode within his power; not aware, it will be observed, in what peculiar sense his general pledge might be interpreted.

These letters being made up into a packet, were forwarded to Windsor by a trooper, detached on that errand.

CHAPTER THE SEVENTEENTH
We do that in our zeal,

Our calmer moments are afraid to answer.

Anonymous.

While the Commissioners were preparing to remove themselves from the Lodge to the inn at the borough of Woodstock, with all that state and bustle which attend the movements of great persons, and especially of such to whom greatness is not entirely familiar, Everard held some colloquy with the Presbyterian clergyman, Master Holdenough, who had issued from the apartment which he had occupied, as it were in defiance of the spirits by whom the mansion was supposed to be disturbed, and whose pale cheek and pensive brow gave token that he had not passed the night more comfortably than the other inmates of the Lodge of Woodstock. Colonel Everard having offered to procure the reverend gentleman some refreshment, received this reply:—" This day shall I not taste food, saving that which we are assured of as sufficient for our sustenance, where it is promised that our bread shall be given us, and our water shall be sure. Not that I fast, in the papistical opinion that it adds to those merits, which are but an accumulation of filthy rags; but because I hold it needful that no grosser sustenance should this day cloud my understanding, or render less pure and vivid the thanks I owe to Heaven for a most wonderful preservation."

"Master Holdenough," said Everard, "you are, I know, both a good man and a bold one, and I saw you last night courageously go upon your sacred duty, when soldiers, and tried ones, seemed considerably alarmed."

"Too courageous—too venturous," was Master Holdenough's reply, the boldness of whose aspect seemed completely to have died away. "We are frail creatures, Master Everard, and frailest when we think ourselves strongest. Oh, Colonel Everard," he added, after a pause, and as if the confidence was partly involuntary, "I have seen that which I shall never survive!"

"You surprise me, reverend sir," said Everard;— "may I request you will speak more plainly? I have heard some stories of this wild night, nay, have witnessed strange things myself; but, methinks, I would be much interested in knowing the nature of your disturbance."

"Sir," said the clergyman, "you are a discreet gentleman; and though I would not willingly that these heretics, schismatics, Brownists, Muggletonians, Anabaptists, and so forth, had such an opportunity of triumph, as my defeat in this matter would have afforded them, yet with you, who have been ever a faithful follower of our church, and are pledged to the good cause by the great National League and Covenant, surely I would be more open. Sit we down, therefore, and let me call for a glass of pure water, for as yet I feel some bodily faltering; though, I thank Heaven, I am in mind resolute and composed as a merely mortal man may after such a vision.—They say, worthy Colonel, that looking on such things, foretells, or causes, speedy death—I know not if it be true; but if so, I only depart like the tired sentinel when his officer releases him from his post; and glad shall I be to close these wearied eyes against the sight, and shut these harassed ears against the croaking, as of frogs, of Antinomians, and Pelagians, and Socinians, and Arminians, and Arians, and Nullifidians, which have come up into our England, like those filthy reptiles into the house of Pharaoh." Pledging uniformity of religion in England, Scotland, and Ireland. The Parliament subscribed to it in September, 1643, in order to win the support of the Scotch Presbyterians, and the latter had forced Charles II to subscribe to it also, at the time of his coronation at Scone in 1650. One who denies that Christians are bound by the moral law as set forth in the Old Testament. At this time the doctrine was held by an extreme Calvinistic sect in England. Followers of Pelagius, a British monk (about 400 A.D.) who denied the doctrine of our original sin through Adam's transgression, and held to the freedom of the will. Followers of Laelius and Faustus Socinus, Italian theologians of the sixteenth century, who denied the doctrine of the Trinity, and held that Christ was a man divinely endowed, but not entitled to divine worship. Followers of Arminius (1560-1609), a Dutch divine who objected to the Calvinistic doctrine of predestination.

"Adherents to the doctrine of Arius, a presbyter of Alexandria in the fourth century, who held that Christ was not coeternal nor of one substance with the Father, but was created by and consequently subordinate to him.

Here one of the servants who had been summoned, entered with a cup of water, gazing at the same time in the face of the clergyman, as if his stupid gray eyes were endeavouring to read what tragic tale was written on his brow; and shaking his empty skull as he left the room, with the air of one who was proud of having discovered that all was not exactly right, though he could not so well guess what was wrong.

Colonel Everard invited the good man to take some refreshment more genial than the pure element, but he declined: "I am in some sort a champion," he said; "and though I have been foiled in the late controversy with the Enemy, still I have my trumpet to give the alarm, and my sharp sword to smite withal; therefore, like the Nazarites of old, I will eat nothing that cometh of the vine, neither drink wine nor strong drink, until these my days of combat shall have passed away."

Kindly and respectfully the Colonel anew pressed Master Holdenough to communicate the events that had befallen him on the preceding night; and the good clergyman proceeded as follows, with that little characteristic touch of vanity in his narrative, which naturally arose out of the

Eart he had played in the world, and the influence which e had exercised over the minds of others. "I was a young man at the University of Cambridge," he said, "when I was particularly bound in friendship to a fellowstudent, perhaps because we were esteemed (though it is vain to mention it) the most hopeful scholars at our college; and so equally advanced, that it was difficult, perhaps, to say which was the greater proficient in his studies. Only our tutor, Master Purefoy, used to say, that if my comrade had the advantage of me in gifts, I had the better of him in grace; for he was attached to the profane learning of the classics, always unprofitable, often impious and impure; and I had light enough to turn my studies into" the sacred tongues. Also we differed in our opinions touching the Church of England, for he held Arminian opinions, with Laud, and those who would connect our ecclesiastical establishment with the civil, and make the Church dependent on the breath of an earthly man. In *Exodus* viii. 1-14. *Judges* xvi. 17. fine, he favoured Prelacy both in essentials and ceremonial; and although we parted with tears and embraces, it was to follow very different courses. He obtained a living, and became a great controversial writer in behalf of the Bishops and of the Court. I also, as is well known to you, to the best of my poor abilities, sharpened my pen in the ca" of the poor oppressed people, whose tend"-consciences rejected the ritoa and ceremonies more befitting a papistical than a reformed Church, and which, according to the blinded policy of the Court, were enforced by pains and penalties. Then came the Civil War, and I—called thereunto by my conscience, and nothing fearing or suspecting what miserable consequences have chanced, through the rise of these Independents—consented to lend my countenance and labour to the great work, by becoming chaplain to Colonel Harrison's regiment. Not that I mingled with carnal weapons in the field—which Heaven forbid that a minister of the altar should—but I preached, exhorted, and, in time of need, was a surgeon, as well to the wounds of the body as of the soul. Now, it fell, towards the end-of the war, that a party of malignants had seized on a strong house in the shire of Shrewsbury, situated on a small island, advanced into a lake, and accessible only by a small and narrow causeway. From thence they made excursions, and vexed the country; and high time it was to suppress them, so that a part of our regiment went to reduce them; and I was requested to go, for they were few in number to take in so strong a place, and the Colonel judged that my exhortations would make them do valiantly. And so, contrary to my wont, I went forth with them, even to the field, where there was valiant fighting on both sides. Nevertheless, the malignants shooting their wall-pieces at us, had so much the advantage, that, after bursting their gates with a salvo of our cannon, Colonel Harrison ordered his men to advance on the causeway, and try to carry the place by storm. Natheless, although our men did valiantly, advancing in good order, yet being galled on every side by the fire, they at length fell into disorder, and were retreating with much loss, Harrison himself valiantly bringing up the rear, and defending them as he could against the enemy, who sallied forth in pursuit of them, to smite them hip and thigh. Now, Colonel Bverard, I A parish. am a man of a quick and vehement temper by nature, though better teaching than the old law hath made me mild and patient as you now see me. I could not bear to see our Israelites flying before the Philistines, so I rushed upon the causeway, with the Bible in one hand, and a halberd, which I had caught up, in the other, and turned back tko foremost fugitives, by threatening to strike them down, pointing out to them at the same time a priest in his cassock, as they call it, who was among the malignants, and asking them whether they would not do as much for a true servant of Heaven, as the uncircumcised would for a priest of Baal. My words and strokes prevailed; they turned at once, and shouting out, Down with Baal and his worshippers! they charged the malignants so unexpectedly home, that they not only drove them back into their house of garrison, but entered it with them, as the phrase is, pell mell. I also was there, partly hurried on by the crowd, partly to prevail on our enraged soldiers to give quarter; for it grieved my heart to see Christians and Englishmen hasked down with swords and gunstocks, like curs in the street when there is an alarm of mad-dogs. In this way, the soldiers fighting and slaughtering, and I calling to them to stay their hand, we gained the very roof of the building, which was in part leaded, and to which, as a last tower of refuge, those of the cavaliers, who yet escaped, had retired. I was myself, I may say, forced up the narrow winding staircase, by our soldiers, who rushed on like dogs of chase upon their prey; and when extricated from the passage, I found myself in the midst of a horrid scene. The scattered defenders were, some resisting with the fury of despair; some on their knees, imploring for compassion in words and tones to break a man's heart when he thinks on them; some were calling on God for mercy; and it was time, for man had none. They were stricken down, thrust through, flung from the battlements into the lake; and the wild cries of the victors, mingled with the groans, shrieks, and clamours, of the vanquished, made a sound so horrible, that only death can erase it from my memory. And the men who butchered their fellow creatures thus, were neither Pagans from distant savage lands, nor ruffians, the refuse and offscourings of our own people. They were in calm blood reasonable, nay, religious men, maintaining a fair repute both heavenward and earthward. Oh, Master Everard, your trade of war should be feared and avoided, since it converts such men into wolves towards their fellow-creatures!"

"It is a stern necessity," said Everard, looking down, "and as such alone is justifiable. But proceed, reverend sir; I see not how this storm, an incident but e'en too frequent on both sides during the late war, connects with the affair of last night."

"You shall hear anon," said Mr. Holdenough; then paused as one who makes an effort to compose himself before continuing a relation, the tenor of which agitated him with much violence. —"In this infernal tumult," he resumed—" for surely nothing on earth could so much resemble hell, as when men go thus loose in mortal malice on their fellow-creatures,—I saw the same priest whom I had distinguished on the causeway, with one or two other malignants, pressed into a corner by the assailants, and defending themselves to the last, as those who had no hope.— I saw him—I knew him—Oh, Colonel Everard!"

He grasped Everard's hand with his own left hand, and pressed the palm of his right to his face and forehead, sobbing aloud.

"It was your college companion?" said Everard, antic ipating the catastrophe.

"Mine ancient—mine only friend—with whom I had spent the happy days of youth!—I rushed forward—I struggled—I entreated.—But my eagerness left me neither voice nor language—all was drowned in the wretched cry which I had myself raised—Down with the priest of Baal —Slay Mattan—slay him were he between the altars!— Forced over the battlements, but struggling for life, I could see him cling to one of those projections which were formed to carry the water from the leads—but they hacked at his arms and hands.—I heard the heavy fall into the bottomless abyss below.—Excuse me—I cannot go on."

"He may have escaped."

"Oh! no, no, no—the tower was four storeys in height. Even those who threw themselves into the lake from the lower windows, to escape by swimming, had no safety; for mounted troopers on the shore caught the same bloodthirsty humour which had seized the storming party, gal 2 *Kings* xi. 18.
loped around the margin of the lake, and shot those who were struggling for life in the water, or cut them down as they strove to get to land. They were all cut off and destroyed.—Oh! may the blood shed on that day remain silent!—Oh! that the earth may receive it in her recesses!—Oh! that it may be mingled for ever with the dark waters of that lake, so that it may never cry for vengeance against those whose anger was fierce, and who slaughtered in their wrath!—And, oh! may the erring man be forgiven who came into their assembly, and lent his voice to encourage their cruelty!—Oh! Albany, my brother, my brother—I have lamented for thee even as David for Jonathan!"

The good man sobbed aloud, and so much did Colonel Everard sympathize with his emotions, that he forbore to press him upon the subject of his own curiosity until the full tide of remorseful passion had for the time abated. It was, however, fierce and agitating, the more so, perhaps, that indulgence in strong mental feeling of any kind was foreign to the severe and ascetic character of the man, and was therefore the more overpowering when it had at once surmounted all restraints. Large tears flowed down the trembling features of his thin, and usually stern, or at least austere countenance; he eagerly returned the compression of Everard's hand, as if thankful for the sympathy which the caress implied.

Presently after, Master Holdenough wiped his eyes, withdrew his hand gently from that of Everard, shaking it kindly as they parted, and proceeded with more composure: "Forgive me this burst of passionate feeling, worthy Colonel. I am conscious it little becomes a man of my cloth, who should be the bearer of consolation to others, to give way in mine own person to an extremity of grief, weak at least, if indeed it is not sinful; for what are we, that we should weep and murmur touching that which is permitted? But Albany was to me as a brother. The happiest days of my life, ere my call to mingle myself in the strife of the land had awakened me to my duties, were spent in his company. I—but I will make the rest of my story short."—Here he drew his chair close to that of Everard, and spoke in a solemn and mysterious tone of voice, almost lowered to a whisper—" I saw him last night." Note B. Dr. Michael Hudson. Scott.

"Saw *him*—saw whom?" said Everard. "Can you mean the person whom"

"Whom I saw so ruthlessly slaughtered," said the clergyman—" My ancient college-friend—Joseph Albany."

"Master Holdenough, your cloth and your character alike must prevent your jesting on such a subject as this."

"Jesting!" answered Holdenough; "I would as soon jest on my death-bed—as soon jest upon the Bible."

"But you must have been deceived," answered Everard, hastily; "this tragical story necessarily often returns to your mind, and in moments when the imagination overcomes the evidence of the outward senses, your fancy must have presented to you an unreal appearance. Nothing more likely, when the mind Is on the stretch after something supernatural, than that the imagination should supply the place with a chimera, while the over-excited feelings render it difficult to dispel the delusion."

"Colonel Everard," replied Holdenough, with austerity, "in discharge of my duty I must not fear the face of man; and, therefore, I tell you plainly, as I have done before with more observance, that when you bring your carnal learning and judgment, as it is but too much your nature to do, to investigate the hidden things of another world, you might as well measure with the palm of your hand the waters of thelsis. Indeed, good sir, you err in this, and give men too much pretence to confound your honourable name with witch-advocates, free-thinkers, and atheists, even with such as this man Bletson, who, if the discipline of the church had its hands strengthened, as it was in the beginning of the great conflict, would have been long ere now cast out of the pale, and delivered over to the punishment of the flesh, that his spirit might, if possible, be yet saved."

"You mistake, Master Holdenough," said Colonel Everard; "I do not deny the existence of such preternatural visitations, because I cannot, and dare not, raise the voice of my own opinion against the testimony of ages, supported by such learned men as yourself. Nevertheless, though I grant the possibility of such things, I have scarce yet heard of an instance in my days so well fortified by evidence, that I could at once and distinctly say, This must have happened by supernatural agency, and not otherwise." The stream on which Oxford is situated. Out of the boundaries of the Church.

"Hear, then, what I have to tell," said the divine, "on the faith of a man, a Christian, and, what is more, a servant of our Holy Church; and therefore, though unworthy, an elder and a teacher among Christians. I had taken my post yester evening in the half furnished apartment, wherein hangs a huge mirror, which might have served Goliath of Gath to have admired himself in, when clothed from head to foot in his brazen armour. I the rather chose this place, because they informed me it was the nearest habitable room to the gallery in which they say you had been yourself assailed that evening by the Evil One.—Was it so, I pray you?"

"By some one with no good intentions I was assailed in that apartment. So far," said Colonel Everard, "you were correctly informed."

"Well, I chose my post as well as I might, even as a resolved general approaches his camp, and casts up his mound as nearly as he can to the besieged city. And, of a truth, Colonel Everard, if I felt some sensation of bodily fear,— for even Elias, and the prophets, who commanded the elements, had a portion in our frail nature, much more such a poor sinful being as myself—yet was my hope and my courage high; and I thought of the texts which I might use, not in the wicked sense of periapts, or spells, as the blinded Papists employ them, together with the sign of the cross, and other fruitless forms, but as nourishing and supporting that true trust and confidence in the blessed promises, being the true shield of faith wherewith the fiery darts of Satan may be withstood and quenched. And thus armed and prepared, I sat me down to read, at the same time to write, that I might compel my mind to attend to those subjects which became the situation in which I was placed as preventing any unlicensed excursions of the fancy, and leaving no room for my imagination to brood over idle fears. So I methodized, and wrote down what I thought meet for the time, and peradventure some hungry souls may yet profit by the food which I then prepared."

"It was wisely and worthily done, good and reverend sir," replied Colonel Everard: "I pray you to proceed."

"While I was thus employed, sir, and had been upon the Put in order. matter for about three hours, not yielding to weariness, a strange thrilling came over my senses,—and the large and old-fashioned apartment seemed to wax larger, more gloomy, and more cavernous, while the air of the night grew more cold and chill; I know not if it was that the fire began to decay, or whether there cometh before such things as were then about to happen, a breath and atmosphere, as it were, of terror, as Job saith in a well-known passage, 'Fear came upon me, and trembling, which made my bones to shake; and there was a tingling noise in my ears, and a dizziness in my brain, so that I felt like those who call for aid when there is no danger, and was even prompted to flee, when I saw no one to pursue. It was then that something seemed to pass behind me, casting a reflection on the great mirror before which I had placed my writing-table, and which I saw by assistance of the large standing light which was then in front of the glass. And I looked up, and I saw in the glass distinctly the appearance of a man—as sure as these words issue from my mouth, it was no other than the same Joseph Albany—the companion of my youth —he whom I had seen precipitated down the battlements of Clidesthrough Castle into the deep lake below!"

"What did you do?"

"It suddenly rushed on my mind," said the divine, "that the stoical philosopher Athenodorus had eluded the horrors of such a vision by patiently pursuing his studies; and it shot at the same time across my mind, that I, a Christian divine, and a Steward of the Mysteries, had less reason to fear evil, and better matter on which to employ my thoughts, than was possessed by a Heathen, who was blinded even by his own wisdom. So, instead of betraying any alarm, or even turning my head around, I pursued my writing, but with a beating heart, I admit, and with a throbbing hand."

"If you could write at all," said the Colonel, "with such an impression on your mind, you may take the head of the English army for dauntless resolution."

"Our courage is not our own, Colonel," said the divine, "and not as ours should it be vaunted of. And again, when you speak of this strange vision as an impression on my fancy, and not a reality obvious to my senses, let me tell you once more, your worldly wisdom is but foolishness touching the things that are not worldly." *Job* iv. 14.

A Stoic philosopher, native of Tarsus, who possessed some influence with the Emperor Augustus.

"Did you not look again upon the mirror?" said the Colonel.

"I did, when I had copied out the comfortable text, 'Thou shalt tread down Satan under thy feet.'"[1]

"And what did you then see?"

"The reflection of the same Joseph Albany," said Holdenough, "passing slowly as from behind my chair, the same in member and lineament that I had known him in his youth, excepting that his cheek had the marks of the more advanced age at which he died, and was very pale."

"What did you then?"

"I turned from the glass, and plainly saw the figure which had made the reflection in the mirror retreating towards the door, not fast, nor slow, but with a gliding, steady pace. It turned again when near the door, and again shewed me its pale, ghastly countenance, before it disappeared. But how it left the room, whether by the door, or otherwise, my spirits were too much hurried to remark exactly; nor have I been able, by any effort of recollection, distinctly to remember."

"This is a strange, and, as coming from you, a most excellently well-attested apparition," answered Everard. "And yet, Master Holdenough, if the other world has been actually displayed, as you apprehend, and I will not dispute the possibility, assure yourself there are also wicked men concerned in these machinations. I myself have undergone some rencontres with visitants who possessed bodily strength, and wore, I am sure, earthly weapons."

"Oh! doubtless, doubtless," replied Master Holdenough; "Beelzebub loves to charge with horse and foot mingled, as was the fashion of the old Scottish general, Davie Leslie. He has his devils in the body as well as his devils disembodied, and uses the one to support and back the other." *Romans* xvi. 20.' Leslie was a colonel of horse under Gustavns Adolphus. He supported the Covenanters at the outbreak of the civil war, and commanded with Cromwell at Marston Moor (1644). Later he followed his countrymen into the Royalist service, and was in Alexander Leslie's army, which Cromwell defeated at Dunbar.

"It may be as you say, reverend sir," answered the Colonel.—"But what do you advise in this case?"

"For that I must consult with my brethren," said the divine; "and if there be but left in our borders five ministers of the true kirk, we will charge Satan in full body, and you shall see whether we have not power over him to resist till he shall flee from us. But failing that ghostly armament against these strange and unearthly enemies, truly I would recommend, that as a house of witchcraft and abomination, this polluted den of ancient tyranny and prostitution should be totally consumed by fire, lest Satan, establishing his headquarters so much to his mind, should find a garrison and a fastness from which he might sally forth to infest the whole neighbourhood. Certain it is, that I would recommend to no Christian soul to inhabit the mansion; and, if deserted, it would become a place for wizards to play their pranks, and witches to establish their Sabbath, and those who, like Demas, go about after the wealth of this world, seeking for gold and silver to practise spells and charms to the prejudice of the souls of the covetous. Trust me, therefore, it were better that it were spoiled and broken down, not leaving one stone upon another."

"I say nay to that, my good friend," said the Colonel; "for the Lord General hath permitted, by his license, my mother's brother, Sir Henry Lee, and his family, to return into the house of his fathers, being indeed the only roof under which he hath any chance of obtaining shelter for his gray hairs."

"And was this done by your advice, Markham Everard?" said the divine, austerely.

"Certainly it was," returned the Colonel. — " And wherefore should I not exert mine influence to obtain a place of refuge for the brother of my mother?"

"Now, as sure as thy soul liveth," answered the presbyter, "I had believed this from no tongue but thine own. Tell me, was it not this very Sir Henry Lee, who, by the force of his buffcoats and his green-jerkins, enforced the Papist Laud's order to remove the altar to the eastern end of the church at Woodstock?—and did he not swear by his beard, that he would hang in the very street of Woodstock whoever should deny to drink the King's health?— and is not his hand red with the blood of the saints? and hath there been a ruffler1 in the field for prelacy and high prerogative more unmitigable or fiercer?" 1 2 *Timothy* iv. 10.

'In obedience to the uniform practice in Romanist churches. Laud was constantly irritating the English Puritans by requirements of this sort.

"All this may have been as you say, good Master Holdenough," answered the Colonel; "but my uncle is now old and feeble, and hath scarce a single follower remaining, and his daughter is a being whom to look upon would make the sternest weep for pity; a being who"

"Who is dearer to Everard," said Holdenough, "than his good name, his faith to his friends, his duty to his religion;—this is no time to speak with sugared lips. The paths in which you tread are dangerous. You are striving to raise the papistical candlestick which Heaven in its justice removed out of its place—to bring back to this hall of sorceries those very sinners who are bewitched with them. I will not permit the land to be abused by their witchcrafts.—They shall not come hither."

He spoke this with vehemence, and striking his stick against the ground; and the Colonel very much dissatisfied, began to express himself haughtily in return. "You had better consider your power to accomplish your threats, Master Holdenough," he said, "before you urge them so peremptorily."

"And have I not the power to bind and to loose?" said the clergyman.

"It is a power little available, save over those of your own church," said Everard, with a tone something contemptuous.

"Take heed—take heed," said the divine, who, though an excellent, was, as we have elsewhere seen, an irritable man.—"Do not insult me; but think honourably of the messenger, for the sake of Him whose commission he carries l)o not, I say, defy me—I am bound to discharge my duty, were it to the displeasing of my twin brother." A boastful combatant.

A legal exercise of the royal prerogative. Under the Tudor despotism, however, this was strained until the King had an extraordinary power as extensive as the whole province of government. This " high prerogative " was effaced by the action of the Long Parliament. *Itevelation* ii. 5. *"I* can see nought your office has to do in the matter," said Colonel Everald; "and I, on my side, give you warning not to attempt to meddle beyond your commission."

"Right—you hold me already to be as submissive as one of your grenadiers," replied the clergyman, his acute features trembling with a sense of indignity, so as even to agitate his gray hair; "but beware, sir, I am not so powerless as you suppose. I will invoke every true Christian in Woodstock to gird up his loins, and resist the restoration of prelacy, oppression, and malignancy within our borders. I will stir up the wrath of the righteous against the oppressor—the Ishmaelite—the Edomite —and against his race, and against those who support him and encourage him to rear up his horn. I will call aloud, and spare not, and arouse the many whose love hath waxed cold, and the multitude who care for none of these things. There shall be a remnant to listen to me; and I will take the stick of Joseph, which was in the hand of Ephraim, and go down to cleanse this place of witches and sorcerers, and of enchantments, and will cry and exhort, saying—Will yon plead for Baal?—will you serve him? Nay, take the prophets of Baal—let not a man escape!"

"Master Holdenough, Master Holdenough," said Colonel Everard, with much impatience, "by the tale yourself told me, you have exhorted upon that text once too often already."

The old man struck his palm forcibly against his forehead, and fell back into a chair as these words were uttered, as

suddenly, and as much without power of resistance, as if the Colonel had fired a pistol through his head. Instantly regretting the reproach which he had suffered to escape him in his impatience, Everard hastened to apologize, and to offer every conciliatory excuse, however inconsistent, which occurred to him on the moment. But the old man was too deeply affected—he rejected his hand, lent no ear to what he said, and finally started up, saying sternly, "You have abused my confidence, sir—abused it vilely, to turn it into my own.reproach: had I been a man of the sword, you dared not—But enjoy your triumph, sir, Biblical symbol of strength and honour. *Ezekiel* xxxvii. 19.
1 *Kings* xviii. 40.
over an old man, and your father's friend—strike at the wound his imprudent confidence shewed you."

"Nay, my worthy and excellent friend," said the Colonel

"Friend!" answered the old man, starting up—" We are foes, sir—foes now and for ever!"

So saying, and starting from the seat into which he had rather fallen than thrown himself, he ran out of the room with a precipitation of step which he was apt to use upon occasions of irritable feeling, and which was certainly more eager than dignified, especially as he muttered while he ran, and seemed as if he were keeping up his own passion, by recounting over and over the offence which he had received.

"Soh!" said Colonel Everard, "and there was not strife enough between mine uncle and the people of Woodstock already, but I must needs increase it, by chafing this irritable and quick-tempered old man, eager as I knew him to be on his ideas of church-government, and stiff in his prejudices respecting all who dissent from him! The mob of Woodstock will rise; for though he would not get a score of them to stand by him in any honest or intelligible purpose, yet let him cry havoc and destruction, and I will warrant he has followers enow. And my uncle is equally wild and unpersuadable. For the value of all the estate he ever had, he would not allow a score of troopers to be quartered in the house for defence; and if he be alone, or has but Joceline to stand by him, he will be as sure to fire upon those who come to attack the Lodge, as if he had a hundred men in garrison; and then what can chance but danger and bloodshed?"

This progress of melancholy anticipation was interrupted by the return of Master Holdenough, who, hurrying into the room, with the same precipitate pace at which he had left it, ran straight up to the Colonel, and said, "Take my hand, Markham—take my hand hastily; for the old Adam is whispering at my heart, that it is a disgrace to hold it extended so long."

"Most heartily do I receive your hand, my venerable friend," said Everard, "and I trust in sign of renewed amity."

"Surely, surely" — said the divine, shaking his hand kindly; "thou hast, it is true, spoken bitterly, but thou hast spoken truth in good time; and I think—though your words were severe — with a good and kindly purpose. Verily, and of a truth, it were sinful in me again to be hasty in provoking violence, remembering that which you have upbraided me with"

"Forgive me, good Master Holdenough," said Colonel Everard, "it was a hasty word; I meant not in serious earnest to *upbraid." "*Peace, 1 pray you, peace," said the divine; "I say, the allusion to that which you have *most justly* upbraided me with—though the charge aroused the gall of the old man within me, the inward tempter being ever on the watch to bring us to his lure—ought, instead of being resented, to have been acknowledged by me as a favour, for so are the wounds of a friend termed faithful. And surely I, who have by one unhappy exhortation to battle and strife sent the living to the dead—and I fear brought back even the dead among the living—should now study peace and good will, and reconciliation of difference, leaving punishment to the Great Being whose laws are broken, and vengeance to Him who hath said, I will repay it."

The old man's mortified features lighted up with a humble confidence as he made this acknowledgment; and Colonel Everard, who knew the constitutional infirmities, and the early prejudices of professional consequence and exclusive party opinion, which he must have subdued ere arriving at such a tone of candour, hastened to express his admiration of his Christian charity, mingled with reproaches on himself for having so deeply injured his feelings.

"Think not of it—think not of it, excellent young man," said Holdenough; "we have both erred—I in suffering my zeal to outrun my charity, you, perhaps, in pressing hard on an old and peevish man, who had so lately poured out his sufferings into your friendly bosom. Be it all forgotten. Let your friends—if they are not deterred by what has happened at this manor of Woodstock—resume their habitation as soon as they will. If they can protect themselves against the powers of the air, believe me, that if I can prevent it by aught in my power, they shall have no annoyance from earthly neighbours; and assure yourself, good sir, that my voice is still worth something with the worthy Mayor, and the good Aldermen, and the better sort of housekeepers up yonder in the town, although the lower classes are blown about with every wind of doctrine. And yet farther be assured, Colonel, that should your mother's brother, or any of his family, learn that they have taken up a rash bargain in returning to this unhappy and unhallowed house, or should they find any qualms in their own hearts and consciences which require a ghostly1 comforter, Nehemiah Holdenough will be as much at their command by night or day, as if they had been bred up within the holy pale of the church in which he is an unworthy minister; and neither the awe of what is fearful to be seen within these walls, nor his knowledge of their blinded and carnal state, as bred up under a prelatic dispensation, shall prevent him doing what lies in his poor abilities for their protection and edification."

"I feel all the force of your kindness, reverend sir," said Colonel Everard, "but I do not think it likely that my uncle will give you trouble on either score. He is a man much accustomed to be his own protector in temporal danger, and in spiritual doubts to trust to his own prayers and those of his Church."

"I trust I have not been superfluous in offering mine assistance," said the old man, something jealous that his proffered spiritual aid had been held rather intrusive. "I ask pardon if that is the case—I humbly ask pardon—I would not willingly be superfluous." . The Colonel hastened to appease this new alarm of the watchful jealousy of his consequence, which, joined with a natural heat of temper which he could not always subdue, were the good man's only faults.

They had regained their former friendly footing, when Eoger Wildrake returned from the hut of Joceline, and whispered his master that his embassy had been successful. The Colonel then addressed the divine, and informed him, that as the Commissioners had already given up Woodstock, and as his uncle, Sir Henry Lee, proposed to return to the Lodge about noon, he would, if his reverence pleased, attend him up to the borough.

"Will you not tarry," said the reverend man, with something like inquisitive apprehension in his voice, "to welcome your relatives upon their return to this their house?" Spiritual.

"No, my good friend," said Colonel Everard; "the part which I have taken in these unhappy broils—perhaps also the mode of worship in which I have been educated— have so prejudiced me in mine uncle's opinion, that I must be for some time a stranger to his house and family."

"Indeed! I rejoice to hear it, with all my heart and soul," said the divine. "Excuse my frankness—I do indeed rejoice; I had thought—no matter what I had thought; I would not again give offence. But truly though the maiden hath a pleasant feature, and he, as all men say, is in human things unexceptionable, yet—but I give you pain—in sooth, I will say no more unless you ask my sincere and unprejudiced advice, which you shall command, but which I will not press on you superfluously. Wend we to the borough together—the pleasant solitude of the forest may dispose us to open our hearts to each other."

They did walk up to the little town in company, and, somewhat to Master Holdenough's surprise, the Colonel, though they talked on various subjects, did not request of him any ghostly advice on the subject of his love to his fair cousin, while, greatly beyond the expectation of the soldier, the clergyman kept his word, and, in his own phrase, was not so superfluous as to offer upon so delicate a point his unasked counsel.

Does Holdenough's experience strike you as an anticlimax, coming after the narration of the hero's experience? Would it have been introduced with better effect before Chapter XV.? Note the device at the end of the chapter for keeping the love-affair still before us.

CHAPTER THE EIGHTEENTH

Then are the harpies gone—Yet ere we perch
Where such foul birds have roosted, let us cleanse
The foul obscenity they've left behind them.
    Agamemnon.

The embassy of Wildrake had been successful, chieflythrough the mediation of the Episcopal divine, whom we formerly found acting in the character of a chaplain to the family, and whose voice had great influence on many accounts with its master.

A little before high noon, Sir Henry Lee, with his small household, were again in unchallenged possession of their old apartments at the Lodge of Woodstock; and the combined exertions of Joceline Joliffe, of Phoebe, and of old Joan, were employed in putting to rights what the late intruders had left in great disorder.

Sir Henry Lee had, like all persons of quality of that period, a love of order amounting to precision, and felt, like a fine lady whose dress has been disordered in a crowd, insulted and humiliated by the rude confusion into which his household goods had been thrown, and impatient till his mansion was purified from all marks of intrusion. In his anger he uttered more orders than the limited number of his domestics were likely to find time or hands to execute. "The villains have left such sulphureous steams behind them, too," said the old knight, "as if old Davie Leslie and the whole Scottish army had quartered among them."

"It may be near as bad," said Joceline, "for men say, for certain, it was the devil came down bodily among them, and made them troop off."

"Then," said the knight, "is the Prince of Darkness a gentleman, as old Will Shakspeare says. He never interferes with those of his own coat, for the Lees have been here, father and son, these five hundred years, without dis *King Lear; III.,* 4, 148.
quiet; and no sooner came these misbegotten churls, than he plays his own part among them."

"Well, one thing he and they have left us," said Joliffe, "which we may thank them for; and that is, such a wellfilled larder and buttery as has been seldom seen in Woodstock Lodge this many a day: carcasses of mutton, large rounds of beef, barrels of confectioners' ware, pipes and runlets1 of sack, muscadine, ale, and what not. We shall have a royal time on't through half the winter; and Joan must get to salting and pickling presently."

"Out, villain!" said the knight; "are we to feed on the fragments of such scum of the earth as these? Cast them forth instantly! Nay," checking himself, "that were a sin; but give them to the poor, or see them sent to the owners. And, hark ye, I will none of their strong liquors. I would rather drink like a hermit all my life, than seem to pledge such scoundrels as these in their leavings, like a miserable drawer, who drains off the ends of the bottles after the guests have paid their reckoning and gone off. And, hark ye, I will taste no water from the cistern out of which these slaves have been serving themselves—fetch me down a pitcher from Rosamond's spring."

Alice heard this injunction, and well guessing there was enough for the other members of the family to do, she quietly took a small pitcher, and flinging a cloak around her, walked out in person to procure Sir Henry the water which he desired. Meantime, Joceline said, with some hesitation, "that a man still remained, belonging to the party of these strangers, who was directing about the removal of some trunks and mails which belonged to the Commissioners, and who could receive his honour's commands about the provisions."

"Let him come hither." (The dialogue was held in the hall.) "Why do you hesitate and drumble in that manner?"

"Only, sir," said Joceline, "only perhaps your honour might not wish to see him, being the same who, not long since"

He paused.

"Sent my rapier a-hawking through the firmament, thou wouldst say? Why, when did I take spleen at a man for standing his ground against me? Roundhead as he is, Small barrels. Baggage. Mumble.

man, I like him the better of that, not the worse. I hunger and thirst to have another turn with him. I have thought on his passado1 ever since, and I believe, were it to try again, I know a feat would control it. Fetch him directly."

Trusty Tomkins was presently ushered in, bearing himself with an iron gravity, which neither the terrors of the preceding night, nor the dignified demeanour of the highborn personage before whom he stood, were able for an instant to overcome.

"How now, good fellow?" said Sir Henry; "I would fain see something more of thy fence, which baffled me the other evening; but truly, I think the light was somewhat too faint for my old eyes. Take a foil, man—I walk here in the hall, as Hamlet says; and 'tis the breathingtime of day with me—Take a foil, then, in thy hand."

"Since it is your worship's desire," said the steward, letting fall his long cloak, and taking the foil in his hand.

"Now," said the knight, "if your fitness speaks, mine is ready. Methinks the very stepping on this same old pavement hath charmed away the gout which threatened me. Sa—sa—I tread as firm as a gamecock."

They began the play with great spirit; and whether the old knight really fought more coolly with the blunt than with the sharp weapon, or whether the steward gave him some grains of advantage in this merely sportive encounter, it is certain Sir Henry had the better in the assault. His success put him into excellent humour.

"There," said he, "I found your trick,—nay, you cheat me not twice the same way. There was a very palpable hit. Why, had I had but light enough the other night— But it skills not speaking of it—Here we leave off. I must not fight, as we unwise cavaliers did with you roundhead rascals, beating you so often that we taught you to beat us at last. And good now, tell me why you are leaving your larder so full here? Do you think I or my family can use broken victuals? What, have you no better employment for your rounds of sequestrated beef than to leave them behind you when you shift your quarters?"

"So please your honour," said Tomkins, "it may be that you desire not the flesh of beeves, of rams, or of goats. Nevertheless, when you know that the provisions were provided and paid for out of your own rents and stock at Ditchley, sequestrated to the use of the state more than a year since, it may be you will have less scruple to use them for your own behoof." A forward thrust in fencing. a *Hamlet,* V. 2, 181.

'For *Ca-ca,* a fencing term. *Samlet,* V. 2, 292.

"Rest assured that I shall," said Sir Henry; "and glad you have helped me to share of mine own. Certainly I was an ass to suspect your masters of subsisting, save at honest men's expense."

"And as for the rumps of beeves," continued Tomkins, with the same solemnity, "there is a rump at Westminster, which will stand us of the army much hacking and hewing yet, ere it is discussed to our mind."

Sir Henry paused, as if to consider what was the meaning of this innuendo; for he was not a person of very quick apprehension. But having at length caught the meaning of it, he burst into an explosion of louder laughter than Joceline had seen him indulge in for a good while.

"Right, knave," he said, "I taste thy jest—It is the very moral of the puppet-show. Faustus raised the devil, as the Parliament raised the army—and then, as the devil flies away with Faustus, so will the army flyaway with the Parliament—or the rump, as thou call'st it, or sitting part of the so-called Parliament. And then, look you, friend, the very devil of all hath my willing consent to fly away with the army in its turn, from the highest general down to the lowest drum-boy. Nay, never look fierce for the matter; remember there is daylight enough now for a game at sharps."

Trusty Tomkins appeared to think it best to suppress his displeasure; and observing that the wains were ready to transport the Commissioners' property to the borough, took a grave leave of Sir Henry Lee.

Meantime the old man continued to pace his recovered hall, rubbing his hands, and evincing greater signs of glee than he had shewn since the fatal 30th of January.

"Here we are again in the old frank, Joliffe; well victualled too. How the knave solved my point of conscience!—the dullest of them is a special casuist where the question concerns profit. Look out if there are not some of our own ragged regiment lurking about, to whom a bellyful would be a God-send, Joceline. Then his fence, Joceline, though the fellow foins 1 well, very sufficient well. But thou saw'st how I dealt with him when I had fitting light, Joceline." The German scholar of mediveval legend, who in old age sold his soul to the devil in return for twenty-four years of youth and pleasure, during which the devil was always to stand ready to do his bidding. See Marlowe s *Dr. Faustus,* and Goethe's *Faust.* For sword-play. Freehold.

"Ay, and so your honour did," said Joceline. "You taught him to know the Duke of Norfolk from Saunders Gardner. I'll warrant him he will not wish to come under your honour's thumb again.

"Why, I am waxing old," said Sir Henry; "but skill will not rust through age, though sinews must stiffen. But my age is like a lusty winter, as old Will says, frosty but kindly; and what if, old as we are, we live to see better days yet! I promise thee, Joceline, I love this jarring betwixt the rogues of the board and the rogues of the sword. When thieves quarrel, true men have a chance of coming by their own."

Thus triumphed the old cavalier, in the treble glory of having recovered his dwelling—regained, as he thought, his character as a man of fence, and finally, discovered some prospect of a change of times, in which he was not without hopes that something might turn up for the royal interest.

Meanwhile, Alice, with a prouder and a lighter heart than had danced in her bosom for several days, went forth with a gaiety to which she of late had been a stranger, to contribute her assistance to the regulation and supply of the household, by bringing the fresh water wanted from fair Rosamond's well.

Perhaps she remembered, that when she was but a girl, her cousin Markham used, among others, to make her perform that duty, as presenting the character of some captive Trojan princess, condemned by her situation to draw the waters from some Grecian spring, for the use of the proud victor. At any rate, she certainly joyed to see her father reinstated in his ancient habitation; and the joy was not the less sincere, that she knew their return to Woodstock had been procured by means of her cousin, and that even in her father's prejudiced eyes, Everard had been in some degree exculpated of the accusations the old knight had brought against him; and that, if a reconciliation had not yet taken place, the preliminaries had been established on which such a desirable conclusion might easily be founded. It was like the commencement of a bridge; when the foundation is securely laid, and the piers raised above the influence of the torrent, the throwing of the arches may be accomplished in a subsequent season.

Thrusts.'" A proverbial expression. 'I believe the genuine reading is to teach a man to know the Lord his God from Tom Frazer.' Scott's marginal note on proof-sheet."—D.—Andrew Lang, however, explains "Duke of Norfolk " and " Saunders Gardner " as fencing terms. *As You Like It,* II., 2, 53 Rosamond's well, a shallow spring shaded by magnificent elms, is Btill (1895) shown to visitors at Woodstock.

The doubtful fate of her only brother might have clouded even this momentary gleam of sunshine; but Alice had been bred up during the close and frequent contests of civil war, and had acquired the habit of hoping in behalf of those dear to her, until hope was lost. In the present case, all reports seemed to assure her of her brother's safety.

Besides these causes for gaiety, Alice Lee had the pleasing feeling that she was restored to the habitation and the haunts of her childhood, from which she had not departed without much pain, the more felt, perhaps, because suppressed, in order to avoid irritating her father's sense of his misfortune. Finally, she enjoyed for the instant the gleam of self-satisfaction by which we see the young and welldisposed so often animated, when they can be, in common phrase, helpful to those whom they love, and perform at the moment of need some of those little domestic tasks, which age receives with so much pleasure from the dutiful hands of youth. So that, altogether, as she hasted through the remains and vestiges of a wilderness already mentioned, and from thence about a bow-shot into the Park, to bring a pitcher of water from Rosamond's spring, Alice Lee, her features enlivened and her complexion a little raised by the exercise, had, for the moment, regained the gay and brilliant vivacity of expression which had been the characteristic of her beauty in her earlier and happier days.

This fountain of old memory had been once adorned with architectural ornaments in the style of the sixteenth century, chiefly relating to ancient mythology. All these were now wasted and overthrown, and existed only as moss-covered ruins, while the living spring continued to furnish its daily treasures, unrivalled in purity, though the quantity was small, gushing out amid disjointed stones, and bubbling through fragments of ancient sculpture.

With a light step and laughing brow the young Lady of Lee was approaching the fountain usually so solitary, when she paused on beholding some one seated beside it. She proceeded, however, with confidence, though with a step something less gay, when she observed that the person was a female; some menial perhaps from the town, whom a fanciful mistress occasionally despatched for the water of a spring, supposed to be peculiarly pure, or some aged woman, who made a little trade by carrying it to the better sort of families, and selling it for a trifle. There was no cause, therefore, for apprehension.

Yet the terrors of the times were so great, that Alice did not see a stranger even of her own sex without some apprehension. Denaturalized women had as usual followed the camps of both armies during the Civil War; who, on the one side with open profligacy and profanity, on the other with the fraudful tone of fanaticism or hypocrisy, exercised nearly in like degree their talents for murder or plunder. But it was broad daylight, the distance from the Lodge was but trifling, and though a little alarmed at seeing a stranger where she expected deep solitude, the daughter of the haughty old Knight had too much of the lion about her, to fear without some determined and decided cause.

Alice walked, therefore, gravely on toward the fount, and composed her looks as she took a hasty glance of the female who was seated there, and addressed herself to her task of filling her pitcher.

The woman, whose presence had surprised and somewhat startled Alice Lee, was a person of the lower rank, whose red cloak, russet kirtle, handkerchief trimmed with Coventry blue, and a coarse steeple hat, could not indicate at best anything higher than the wife of a small farmer, or, perhaps, the helpmate of a bailiff or hind. It was well if she proved nothing worse. Her clothes, indeed, were of good materials; but, what the female eye discerns with half a glance, they were indifferently adjusted and put on. This looked as if they did not belong to the person by whom they were worn, but were articles of which she had become the mistress by some accident, if not by some successful robbery. Her size, too, as did not escape Alice, even in the short perusal she afforded the stranger, was unusual; her features swarthy and singularly harsh, and her manner altogether unpropitious. The young lady almost wished, as she stooped to fill her pitcher, that she had rather turned back, and sent Joceline on the errand; but repentance was too late now, and she had only to disguise as well as she could her unpleasant feelings.

"The blessings of this bright day to one as bright as it is," said the stranger, with no unfriendly, though a harsh voice.

"I thank you," said Alice in reply; and continued to fill her pitcher busily, by assistance of an iron bowl which remained still chained to one of the stones beside the fountain.

"Perhaps, my pretty maiden, if you would accept my help, your work would be sooner done," said the stranger.

"I thank you," said Alice; "but had I needed assistance, I could have brought those with me who had rendered it."

"I do not doubt of that, my pretty maiden," answered the female; "their are too many lads in Woodstock with eyes in their heads—No doubt you could have brought with you any one of them who looked on you, if you had listed?"

Alice replied not a syllable, for she did not like the freedom used by the speaker, and was desirous to break off the conversation.

"Are you offended, my pretty mistress?" said the stranger; "that was far from my purpose.—I will put my question otherwise—Are the good dames of Woodstock so careless of their pretty daughters as to let the flower of them all wander about the wild chase without a mother, or a somebody to prevent the fox from running away with the lamb?—that carelessness, methinks, shews small kindness."

"Content yourself, good woman, I am not far from protection and assistance," said Alice, who liked less and less the effrontry of her new acquaintance.

"Alas! my pretty maiden," said the stranger, patting with her large and hard hand the head which Alice had kept bended down towards the water which she was laving, "it would be difficult to hear such a pipe as yours at the town of Woodstock, scream as loud as you would."

Alice shook the woman's hand angrily off, took up her pitcher, though not above half full, and as she saw the stranger rise at the same time, said, not without fear doubtless, but with a natural feeling of resentment and dignity, "I have no reason to make my cries heard as far as Woodstock; were there occasion for my crying for help at all, it is nearer at hand."

She spoke not without a warrant; for at the moment, broke through the bushes, and stood by her side, the noble hound Bevis; fixing on the stranger his eyes that glanced fire, raising every hair on his gallant mane as upright as the bristles of a wild boar when hard pressed, grinning till a case of teeth, which would have matched those of any wolf in Russia, were displayed in full array, and, without either barking or springing, seeming, by his low determined growl, to await but the signal for dashing at the female, whom he plainly considered as a suspicious person.

But the stranger was undaunted. "My pretty maiden," she said, "you have indeed a formidable guardian there, where cockneys or bumpkins are concerned; but we who have been at the wars know spells for taming such furious dragons; and therefore let not your four-footed protector go loose on me, for he is a noble animal, and nothing but self-defence would induce me to do him injury." So saying, she drew a pistol from her bosom, and cocked itpointing it towards the dog, as if apprehensive that he would spring upon her.

"Hold, woman, hold!" said Alice Lee; "the dog will not do you harm.—Down, Bevis, couch down—And ere you attempt to hurt him, know he is the favourite hound of Sir Henry Lee of Ditchley, the keeper of Woodstock Park, who would severely revenge any injury offered to him."

"And you, pretty one, are the old knight's housekeeper, doubtless? I have often heard the Lees have good taste."

"I am his daughter, good woman."

"His daughter!—I was blind—but yet it is true, nothing less perfect could answer the description which all the world has given of Mistress Alice Lee. I trust that my folly has given my young mistress no offence, and that she will allow me, in token of reconciliation, to fill her pitcher, and carry it as far as she will permit."

"As you will, good mother; but I am about to return instantly to the Lodge, to which, in these times, I cannot admit strangers. You can follow me no farther than the verge of the wilderness, and I am already too long from home: I will send some one to meet and relieve you of the pitcher." So saying, she turned her back, with a feeling of terror which she could hardly account for, and began to walk quickly towards the Lodge, thinking thus to get rid of her troublesome acquaintance.

But she reckoned without her host; for in a moment her new companion was by her side, not running, indeed, but walking with prodigious long unwomanly strides, which soon brought her up with the hurried and timid steps of the frightened maiden. But her manner was more respectful than formerly, though her voice sounded remarkably harsh and disagreeable, and her whole appearance suggested an undefined, yet irresistible feeling of apprehension.

"Pardon a stranger, lovely Mistress Alice," said her persecutor, "that was not capable of distinguishing between a lady of your high quality and a peasant wench, and who spoke to you with a degree of freedom, ill-befitting your rank, certainly, and condition, and which, I fear, has given you offence."

"No offence whatever," replied Alice; "but, good woman, I am near home, and can excuse your farther company.—You are unknown to me."

"But it follows not," said the stranger, "that *your* fortunes may not be known to *me,* fair Mistress Alice. Look on my swarthy brow—England breeds none such—and in the lands from which I come, the sun which blackens our complexion, pours, to make amends, rays of knowledge into our brains, which are denied to those of your lukewarm climate. Let me look upon your pretty hand—attempting to possess herself of it — and I promise you, you shall hear what will please you."

"I hear what does *not* please me," said Alice, with dignity; "you must carry your tricks of fortune-telling and palmistry to the women of the village—We of the gentry hold them to be either imposture or unlawful knowledge." " All the description of Charles in disguise, and especially of his awkwardness in crossing brooks, is derived from the Highland adventures of Charles Edward,"—Andrew Lang.

"Yet you would fain hear of a certain Colonel, I warrant you, whom certain unhappy circumstances have separated from his family; you would give better than silver if I could assure you that you would see him in a day or two—ay, perhaps, sooner."

"I know nothing of what you speak, good woman; if you want alms, there is a piece of silver—it is all I have in my purse."

"It were pity that I should take it," said the female; "and yet give it me—for the princess in the fairy tale must ever deserve, by her generosity, the bounty of the benevolent fairy, before she is rewarded by her protection."

"Take it—take it—give me my pitcher," said Alice, "and begone,—yonder comes one of my father's servants.—What, ho!—Joceline—Joceline!"

The old fortune-teller hastily dropped something into the pitcher as she restored it to Alice Lee, and, plying her long limbs, disappeared speedily under cover of the wood.

Bevis turned, and backed, and shewed some inclination to harass the retreat of this suspicious person, yet, as if uncertain, ran towards Joliffe, and fawned on him, as to demand his advice and encouragement. Joceline pacified the animal, and, coming up to his young lady, asked her, with surprise, what was the matter, and whether she had been frightened. Alice made light of her alarm, for which, indeed, she could not have assigned any very competent reason, for the manners of the woman, though bold and intrusive, were not menacing. She only said she had met a fortune-teller by Rosamond's Well, and had had some difficulty in shaking her off.

"Ah, the gipsy thief," said Joceline, "how well she scented there was food in the pantry!—they have noses like ravens, these strollers. Look you, Mistress Alice, you shall not see a raven, or a carrion crow, in all the blue sky for a mile round you; but let a sheep drop suddenly down on the greensward, and before the poor creature's dead you shall see a dozen of such guests croaking, as if inviting each other to the banquet.—Just so it is with these sturdy beggars. You will see few enough of them when there's nothing to give, but when hough's in the pot, they will have share on't."

"You are so proud of your fresh supply of provender," Hock joint; *i.e.,* when there is food to be had. said Alice, "that you suspect all of a design on't. I do not think this woman will venture near your kitchen, Joceline."

"It will be best for her health," said Joceline, "lest I give her a ducking for digestion.—But give me the pitcher, Mistress Alice—meeter I bear it than you.—How now? what jingles at the bottom? have you lifted the pebbles as well as the water?"

"I think the woman dropped something into the pitcher," said Alice.

"Nay, we must look to that, for it is like to be a charm, and we have enough of the devil's ware about Woodstock already—we will not spare for the water—I can run back and fill the pitcher." He poured out the water upon the grass, and at the bottom of the pitcher was found a gold ring, in which was set a ruby, apparently of some value.

"Nay, if this be not enchantment, I know not what is," said Joceline. "Truly, Mistress Alice, I think you had better throw away this gimcrack. Such gifts from such hands are a kind of press-money which the devil uses for enlisting his regiment of witches; and if they take but so much as a bean from him, they become his bond-slaves for life—Ay, you look at the gew-gaw, but to-morrow you will find a lead ring and a common pebble in its stead."

"Nay, Joceline, I think it will be better to find out that dark-complexioned woman, and return to her what seems of some value. So, cause inquiry to be made, and be sure you return her ring. It seems too valuable to be destroyed."

"Umph! that is always the way with women," murmured Joceline. "You will never get the best of them, but she is willing to save a bit of finery.—Well, Mistress Alice, I trust that yon are too young and too pretty to be enlisted in a regiment of witches."

"I shall not be afraid of it till you turn conjurer," said Alice; "so hasten to the well, where you are like still to find the woman, and let her know that Alice Lee desires none of her gifts, any more than she did of her society."

So saying, the young lady pursued her way to the Lodge, while Joceline went down to Rosamond's Well to execute her commission. But the fortune-teller, or whoever she might be, was nowhere to be found; neither, finding that to be the case, did Joceline give himself much trouble in tracking her farther.

Money given to soldiers at the time of enlistment, to make the contract binding.

"If this ring, which I dare say the jade stole somewhere," said the underkeeper to himself, "be worth a few nobles, it is better in honest hands than in that of vagabonds. My master has a right to all waifs and strays, and certainly such a ring, in possession of a gipsy, must be a waif. So I shall confiscate it without scruple, and apply the produce to the support of Sir Henry's household, which is like to be poor enough. Thank heaven, my military experience has taught me how to carry hooks at my finger-ends—that is trooper's law. Yet, hang it, after all, I had best take it to Mark Everard and ask his advice—I hold him now to be your learned counsellor in law where Mistress Alice's affairs are concerned, and my learned Doctor, who shall be nameless, for such as concern Church and State and Sir Henry Lee—and I'll give them leave to give mine umbles to the kites and ravens if they find me conferring my confidence where it is not safe."

Sir Henry Lee's recovery of the Lodge marks the close of the first part of the plot. Henceforth Scott silently discards the " ghost business," as if having amused himself sufficiently with it, and turns our attention to a new set of interests.

CHAPTER THE NINETEENTH

Being skilless in these parts, which, to a stranger,
Unguided and unfriended, often prove
Rough and inhospitable.
　Twelfth Night.

There was a little attempt at preparation, now that the dinner hour was arrived, which shewed that, in the opinion of his few but faithful domestics, the good knight had returned in triumph to his home.

The great tankard, exhibiting in bas-relief the figure of Michael subduing the Arch-enemy, was placed on the table, and Joceline and Phoebe dutifully attended; the one behind the chair of Sir Henry, the other to wait upon her young mistress, and both to make out, by formal and regular observance, the want of a more numerous train.

"A health to King Charles!" said the old knight, handing the massive tankard to his daughter; "drink it, my love, though it be rebel ale which they have left us. I will pledge thee; for the toast will excuse the liquor, had Noll himself brewed it."

The young lady touched the goblet with her lip, and returned it to her father, who took a copious draught.

"I will not say blessing on their hearts," said he; "though I must own they drank good ale."

"No wonder, sir; they come lightly by the malt, and need not spare it," said Joceline.

"Say'st thou?" said the knight; "thou shalt finish the tankard thyself for that very jest's sake."

Nor was his follower slow in doing reason to the royal pledge. He bowed, and replaced the tankard, saying, after a triumphant glance at the sculpture, " I had a gibe with that same red-coat about the Saint Michael just now."

"Red-coat—ha! what red-coat?" said the hasty old man. "Do any of these knaves still lurk about Woodstock?—Quoit1 him down stairs instantly, Joceline.— Know we not Galloway nags?" The chief of the archangels, who was said to have overthrown Satan in single combat *(Juile* 9).

"So please you, he is in some charge here, and will speedily be gone.—It is he—he who had a rencontre with your honour in the wood."

"Ay, but I paid him off for it in the hall, as you yourself saw.—I was never in better fence in my life, Joceline. That same steward fellow is not so utterly black-hearted a rogue as the most of them, Joceline. He fences well—excellent well. I will have thee try a bout in the hall with him to-morrow, though I think he will be too hard for thee. I know thy strength to an inch."

He might say this with some truth; for it was Joceline's fashion when called on, as sometimes happened, to fence with his patron, just to put forth as much of his strength and skill as obliged the knight to contend hard for the victory, which, in the long run, he always contrived to yield up to him, like a discreet serving-man.

"And what said this roundheaded steward of our great Saint Michael's standing-cup?"

"Marry, he scoffed at our good saint, and said he was little better than one of the golden calves of Bethel. But I told him he should not talk so, until one of their own roundheaded saints had given the devil as complete a crossbuttock as Saint Michael had given him, as 'tis carved upon the cup there. I trow that made him silent enough. And then he would know whether your honour and Mistress Alice, not to mention old Joan and myself, since it is your honour's pleasure I should take my bed here, were not afraid to sleep in a house that had been so much disturbed. But I told him we feared no fiends or goblins, having the prayers of the Church read every evening."

"Joceline," said Alice, interrupting him, "wert thou mad? You know at what risk to ourselves and the good doctor the performance of that duty takes place."

"Oh, Mistress Alice," said Joceline, a little abashed, "you may be sure I spoke not a word of the doctor—No, no—I did not let him into the secret that we had such a reverend chaplain—I think I know the length of this man's *2 Henry IV.,* IX, 4, 205.
A large ornamental drinking oup, made especially for the decoration of cupboards. A peculiar throw used by wrestlers, particularly in Cornwall. foot. We have had a jollification or so together. He is hand and glove with me, for as great a fanatic as he is."

"Trust him not too far," said the knight. "Nay, I fear thou hast been imprudent already, and that it will be unsafe for the good man to come here after nightfall, as is proposed. These Independents have noses like bloodhounds, and can smell out a loyalist under any disguise."

"If your honour thinks so," said Joceline, "I'll watch for the doctor with good will, and bring him into the Lodge by the old condemned postern, and so up to this apartment; and sure this man Tomkins would never presume to come hither; and the doctor may have a bed in Woodstock Lodge, and he never the wiser; or, if your honour does not think that safe, I can cut his throat for you, and I would not mind it a pin."

"God forbid!" said the knight. "He is under our roof, and a guest, though not an invited one.—Go, Joceline; it shall be thy penance, for having given thy tongue too much license, to watch for the good doctor, and to take care of his safety while he continues with us. An October night or two in the forest would finish the good man."

"He's more like to finish our October

than our October is to finish him," said the keeper; and withdrew under the encouraging smile of his patron.

He whistled Bevis along with him to share in his watch; and having received exact information where the clergyman was most likely to be found, assured his master that he would give the most pointed attention to his safety. When the attendants had withdrawn, having previously removed the remains of the meal, the old knight, leaning back in his chair, encouraged pleasanter visions than had of late passed through his imagination, until by degrees he was surprised by actual slumber; while his daughter, not venturing to move but on tiptoe, took some needlework, and bringing it close by the old man's side, employed her fingers on this task, bending her eyes from time to time on her parent, with the affectionate zeal, if not the effective power, of a guardian angel. At length, as the light faded away, and night came on, she was about to order candles to be brought. But, remembering how indifferent a couch Joceline's cottage had afforded, she could Our October ale.
not think of interrupting the first sound and refreshing sleep which her father had enjoyed, in all probability, for the last two nights and days.

She herself had no other amusement, as she sat facing one of the great oriel windows, the same by which Wildrake had on a former occasion looked in upon Tomkins and Joceline while at their compotations, than watching the clouds, which a lazy wind sometimes chased from the broad disk of the harvest-moon, sometimes permitted to accumulate, and exclude her brightness. There is, I know not.why, something peculiarly pleasing to the imagination, in contemplating the Queen of Night, when she is *loading,* as the expression is, among the vapours which she has not power to dispel, and which on their side are unable entirely to quench her lustre. It is the striking image of patient virtue, calmly pursuing her path through good report and bad report, having that excellence in herself which ought to command all admiration, but bedimmed in the eyes of the world, by suffering, by misfortune, by calumny.

As some such reflections, perhaps, were passing through Alice's imagination, she became sensible, to her surprise and alarm, that some one had clambered up upon the window, and was looking into the room. The idea of supernatural fear did not in the slightest degree agitate Alice. She was too much accustomed to the place and situation; for folk do not see spectres in the scenes with which they have been familiar from infancy. But danger from marauders in a disturbed country was a more formidable subject of apprehension, and the thought armed Alice, who was naturally high-spirited, with such desperate courage, that she snatched a pistol from the wall, on which some fire-arms hung, and while she screamed to her father to awake, had the presence of mind to present it at the intruder. She did so the more readily, because she imagined she recognised in the visage, which she partially saw, the features of the woman whom she had met with at Rosamond's Avell, and which had appeared to her peculiarly harsh and suspicious. Her father at the same time seized his sword and came forward, while the person at the window, alarmed at these demonstrations, and endeavouring to descend, missed footing, as had Cavaliero Wildrake before, and went down to the earth with no small noise. Potations.

Nor was the reception on the bosom of our common mother either soft or safe; for, by a most terrific bark and growl, they heard that Bevis had come up and seized on the party, ere he or she could gain their feet.

"Hold fast, but worry not," said the old knight.— "Alice, thou art the queen of wenches! Stand fast here till I run down and secure the rascal."

"For God's sake, no, my dearest father!" Alice exclaimed; "Joceline will be up immediately—Hark—I hear him."

There was indeed a bustle below, and more than one light danced to and fro in confusion, while those who bore them called to each other, yet suppressing their voices as they spoke, as men who would only be heard by those they addressed. The individual who had fallen under the power of Bevis was most impatient in his situation, and called with least precaution,—"Here, Lee—Forester—take the dog off, else I must shoot him!"

"If thou dost," said Sir Henry from the window, "I blow thy brains out on the spot—Thieves, Joceline, thieves! come up and secure this ruffian.—Bevis, hold on!"

"Back, Bevis; down, sir," cried Joceline.—"I am coming, I am coming, Sir Henry—Saint Michael, I shall go distracted!"

A terrible thought suddenly occurred to Alice,—could Joceline have become unfaithful, that he was calling Bevis off the villain, instead of encouraging the trusty dog to secure him! Her father, meantime, moved perhaps by some suspicion of the same kind, hastily stepped aside out of the moonlight, and pulled Alice close to him, so as to be invisible from without, yet so placed as to hear what should pass. The scuffle between Bevis and his prisoner seemed to be ended by Joceline's interference, and there was close whispering for an instant, as of people in consultation.

"All is quiet now," said one voice; "I will up and prepare the way for you. "—And immediately a form presented itself on the outside of the window, pushed open the lattice, and sprung into the parlour. But almost ere his step was upon the floor, certainly before he had obtained any secure footing, the old knight, who stood ready with his rapier drawn, made a desperate pass, which bore the intruder to the ground. Joceline, who clambered up next with a dark lantern in his hand, uttered a dreadful exclamation, when he saw what had happened, crying out, "Lord in heaven, he has slain his own son!"

"No, no—I tell you no," said the fallen young man, who was indeed young Albert Lee, the only son of the old knight—"I am not hurt.—No noise on your lives—get lights instantly." At the same time, he started from the floor as quickly as he could, under the embarrassment of a cloak and doublet skewered as it were together by the rapier of the old knight, whose pass, most fortunately, had been diverted from the body of Albert by the interruption of his cloak, the blade passing right across his back, piercing the clothes, while the hilt coming against his side with the whole force of the longe, had borne him to the ground.

Joceline all the while enjoined silence to every one, under the strictest conjurations. "Silence as you would long live on earth—silence, as you would have a place in Heaven,—be but silent for a few minutes—all our lives depend on it."

Meantime he procured lights with inexpressible despatch, and they then beheld that Sir Henry, on hearing the fatal words, had sunk back on one of the large chairs, without either motion, colour, or sign of life.

"Oh, brother, how could you come in this manner?" said Alice.

"Ask no questions—Good God! for what am I reserved!" He gazed on his father as he spoke, who, with clay-cold features rigidly fixed, and his arms extended in the most absolute helplessness, looked rather the image of death upon a monument, than a being in whom existence was only suspended. "Was my life spared," said Albert, raising his hands with a wild gesture to Heaven, "only to witness such a sight as this!"

"We suffer what Heaven permits, young man—we endure our lives while Heaven continues them. Let me approach." The same clergyman who had read the prayers at Joceline's hut now came forward. "Get water," he said, "instantly." And the helpful hand and light foot of Alice, with the ready-witted tenderness which never stagnates in vain lamentations while there is any room for hope, provided with incredible celerity all that the clergyman called for.

"It is but a swoon," he said, on feeling Sir Henry's palm,—"a. swoon produced from the instant and unexpected shock. Rouse thee up, Albert; I promise thee it will be nothing save a syncope—A cup, my dearest Alice, and a ribbon, or a bandage—I must take some blood—some aromatics, too, if they can be had, my good Alice."

But while Alice procured the cup and bandage, stripped her father's sleeve, and seemed by intuition even to anticipate every direction of the reverend doctor, her brother, hearing no word, and seeing no sign of comfort, stood with both hands clasped and elevated into the air, a monument of speechless despair. Every feature in his face seemed to express the thought, "Here lies my father's corpse, and it is I whose rashness has slain him!"

But when a few drops of blood began to follow the lancet—at first falling singly, and then trickling in a freer stream—when, in consequence of the application of cold water to the temples, and aromatics to the nostrils, the old man sighed feebly, and made an effort to move his limbs, Albert Lee changed his posture, at once to throw himself at the feet of the clergyman, and kiss, if he would have permitted him, his shoes and the hem of his raiment.

"Rise, foolish youth," said the good man, with a reproving tone; "must it be always thus with you? Kneel to Heaven, not to the feeblest of its agents. You have been saved once again from great danger—would you deserve Heaven's bounty, remember you have been preserved for other purposes than you now think on. Begone you and Joceline, you have a duty to discharge; and be assured it will go better with your father's recovery that he see you not for a few minutes. Down—down to the wilderness, and bring in your attendant."

"Thanks, thanks, a thousand thanks," answered Albert Lee; and, springing through the lattice, he disappeared as unexpectedly as he had entered. At the same time Joceline followed him, and by the same road.

Alice, whose fears for her father were now something abated, upon this new movement among the persons of the scene, could not resist appealing to her venerable assistant. "Good doctor, answer me but one question. Was my brother Albert here just now, or have I dreamed all that has happened for these ten minutes past? Methinks, but for your presence, I could suppose the whole had passed in my sleep—that horrible thrust—that death-like, corpse-like old man—that soldier in mute despair—I must indeed have dreamed."

"If you have dreamed, my sweet Alice," said the doctor, "I wish every sick-nurse had your property, since you have been attending to our patient better during your sleep, than most of these old dormice can do when they are most awake. But your dream came through the gate of horn, my pretty darling, which you must remind me to explain to you at leisure. Albert has really been here, and will be here again."

"Albert!" repeated Sir Henry, " who names my son?"

"It is I, my kind patron," said the doctor; "permit me to bind up your arm."

"My wound?—with all my heart, doctor," said Sir Henry, raising himself, and gathering his recollection by degrees. "I knew of old thou wert body-curer as well as soul-curer, and served my regiment for surgeon as well as chaplain.—But where is the rascal I killed?—I never made a fairer *stramaQon* in my life. The shell of my rapier struck against his ribs. So dead he must be, or my right hand has forgot its cunning."

"Nobody was slain," said the doctor; "we must thank God for that, since there were none but friends to slay. Here is a good cloak and doublet, though, wounded in a fashion which will require some skill in tailor-craft to cure. But I was your last antagonist, and took a little blood from you, merely to prepare you for the pleasure and surprise of seeing your son, who, though hunted pretty close, as you may believe, hath made his way from Worcester hither, where, with Joceline's assistance, we will care well enough for his safety. It was even for this reason that I pressed you to accept of your nephew's proposal to return to the old Lodge, where a hundred men might be concealed, though a thousand were making search to discover them. Never such a place for hide-and-seek, as I shall make good when I can find means to publish my Wonders of Woodstock." According to the ancients, dreams come to us through two gates;

one of ivory, and these are illusory,—the-other of horn, and these come true—*JEnsid* VI., 893-896.
A downright stroke. "I made a kind of stramazoun, ran him up to the hilts through the doublet, through the shirt, and yet missed the skin."—Ben Jonson, *Every Man. Out of his Humour,* IV., 4.
Guard.

"But, my son—my dear son," said the knight, "shall I not then instantly see him! and wherefore did you not forewarn me of this joyful event?"

"Because I was uncertain of his motions," said the doctor, "and rather thought he was bound for the seaside, and that it would be best to tell you of his fate when he was safe on board, and in full sail for France. We had appointed to let you know all when I came hither to-night to join you. But there is a red-coat in the house whom we care not to trust farther than we could not help. We dared not, therefore, venture in by the hall; and so, prowling round the building, Albert informed us, that an old prank of his when a boy consisted of entering by this window. A lad who was with us would needs make the experiment, as there seemed to be no light in the chamber, and the moonlight without made us liable to be detected. His foot slipped, and our friend Bevis came upon us."

"In good truth, you acted simply," said Sir Henry, "to attack a garrison without a summons. But all this is nothing to my son Albert—where is he?—Let me see him."

"But, Sir Henry, wait," said the doctor, "till your restored strength"

"A plague of my restored strength, man!" answered the knight, as his old spirit began to awaken within him. — "Dost not remember, that I lay on Edgehill-field all night, bleeding like a bullock from five several wounds, and wore my armour within six weeks? and you talk to me of the few drops of blood that follow such a scratch as a cat's claw might have made!"

"Nay, if you feel so courageous," said the doctor, "I will fetch your son—he is not far distant."

So saying, he left the apartment, making a sign to Alice to remain, in case any symptoms of her father's weakness should return.

It was fortunate, perhaps, that Sir Henry never seemed to recollect the precise nature of the alarm, which had at once, and effectually-as the shock of the thunderbolt, for the moment suspended his faculties. Something he said more than once of being certain he had done mischief with that *stramafon,* as he called it; but his mind did not recur to that danger, as having been incurred by his son. Alice, glad to see that her father appeared to have forgotten a circumstance so fearful (as men often forget the blow, or other sudden cause, which has thrown them into a swoon), readily excused herself from throwing much light on the matter, by pleading the general confusion. And in a few minutes, Albert cut off all farther inquiry, by entering the room, followed by the doctor, and throwing himself alternately into the arms of his father and of his sister.

Note that with the entrance of Albert Lee, Kerneguy, and Dr. Rochecliffe, all the elements for working out the story are now at hand. Find other instances of successful disguises iu Scott's novels *(Ivanhoe, The Abbot,* etc.).

CHAPTER THE TWENTIETH
The boy is—hark ye, sirrah—what's your name?—
Oh, Jacob!—ay, I recollect—the same.
Cbabbb.

The affectionate relatives were united as those who, meeting under great adversity, feel still the happiness of sharing it in common. They embraced again and again, and gave way to those expansions of the heart, which at once express and relieve the pressure of mental agitation. At length the tide of emotion began to subside; and Sir Henry, still holding his recovered son by the hand, resumed the command of his feelings which he usually practised.

"So you have seen the last of our battles, Albert," he said, "and the King's colours have fallen for ever before the rebels?"

"It is but even so," said the young man—" the last cast of the die was thrown, and, alas! lost, at Worcester; and Cromwell's fortune carried it there, as it has wherever he has shewn himself."

"Well—it can but be for a time—it can but be for a time," answered his father; "the devil is potent, they say, in raising and gratifying favourites, but he can grant but short leases.—And the King—the King, Albert—the King—in my ear—close, close!"

"Our last news were confident that he had escaped from Bristol."

"Thank God for that—thank God for that!" said the knight. "Where didst thou leave him?"

"Our men were almost all cut to pieces at the bridge,"1 Albert replied; "but I followed his Majesty, with about five hundred other officers and gentlemen, who were resolved to die around him, until, as our numbers and ap For a detailed account of this, see Carlyle's *Cromwell's Letters and Speeches,* or F. Harrison's *Cromwell.* pearance drew the whole pursuit after us, it pleased his Majesty to dismiss us, with many thanks and words of comfort to us in general, and some kind expressions to most of us in especial. He sent his royal greeting to you, sir, in particular, and said more than becomes me to repeat."

"Nay, I will hear it every word, boy," said Sir Henry; "is not the certainty that thou hast discharged thy duty, and that King Charles owns it, enough to console me for all we have lost and suffered, and wouldst thou stint me of it from a false shamefacedness?—I will have it out of thee, were it drawn from thee with cords!"

"It shall need no such compulsion," said the young man—" It was his Majesty's pleasure to bid me tell Sir Henry Lee, in his name, that if his son could not go before his father in the race of loyalty, he was at least following him closely, and would soon move side by side."

"Said he so?" answered the knight—" Old Victor Lee will look down with pride on thee, Albert!—But I forget — you must be weary and hungry."

"Even so, sir," said Albert; "but these are things which of late I have been in the habit of enduring for safety's sake."

"Joceline!—what ho, Joceline!"

The underkeeper entered, and received orders to get supper prepared directly.

"My son and Dr. Rochecliffe are half starving," said the knight.

"And there is a lad, too, below," said Joceline; "a page, he says, of Colonel Albert's, whose belly rings cupboard too, and that to no common tune; for I think he could eat a horse, as the Yorkshireman says, behind the saddle. He had better eat at the sideboard; for he has devoured a whole loaf of bread and butter, as fast as Phoebe could cut it, and it has not stayed his stomach for a minute—and truly I think you had better keep him under your own eyes, for the steward beneath might ask him troublesome questions if he went below—And then he is impatient, as all your gentlemen pages are, and is saucy among the women."

"Whom is it he talks of?—what page hast thou got, Albert, that bears himself so ill?" said Sir Henry.

"The son of a dear friend, a noble lord of Scotland, who followed the great Montrose's banner—afterwards joined the King in Scotland, and came with him as far as Worcester. He was wounded the day before the battle, and conjured me to take this youth under my charge, which I did, something unwillingly; but I could not refuse a father, perhaps on his death-bed, pleading for the safety of an only son."

"Thou hadst deserved an halter, hadst thou hesitated," said Sir Henry; "the smallest tree can always give some shelter,—and it pleases me to think the old stock of Lee is not so totally prostrate, but it may yet be a refuge for the distressed. Fetch the youth in;—he is of noble blood, and these are no times of ceremony—he shall sit with us at the same table, page though he be; and if you have not schooled him handsomely in his manners, he may not be the worse of some lessons from me."

"You will excuse his national drawling accent, sir?" said Albert, "though I know you like it not."

"I have small cause, Albert," answered the knight— "small cause. — Who stirred up these disunions?—the Scots. Who strengthened the hands of Parliament, when their cause was well-nigh ruined? — the Scots again. Who delivered up the King, their countryman, who had flung himself upon their protection?—the Scots again. But this lad's father, you say, has fought on the part of the noble Montrose; and such a man as the great Marquis may make amends for the degeneracy of a whole nation."

"Nay, father," said Albert, "and I must add, that though this lad is uncouth and wayward, and, as you will see, something wilful, yet the King has not a more zealous friend in England; and, when occasion offered, he fought stoutly, too, in his defence—I marvel he comes not." James Graham (1612-1650), fifth Earl and first Marquis of Montrose. He served in the Presbyterian army at the beginning of the civil war, but afterward joined the King, by whom he was made lieutenant-general of Scotland in 1644. He won many battles against the Covenanters, but was defeated by David Leslie at Philiphaugh in 1645, and expelled from Scotland. In 1650 he led an ineffectual Royalist rising, was captured and executed. See the fine poem by W. E. Aytoun; also Scott's *Legend of Montrose*. The reference is to the rising of the Scotch Presbyterians in 1639.

The English Parliament took the Solemn League and Covenant, the Presbyterian charter, in September, 1643, as the condition of obtaining an army from Scotland. Charles I. surrendered to the army of the Scots before Newark in 1646. and by them he was delivered for a ransom, in the form of indemnity for war expenses, to their English allies.

"He hath taken the bath,"said Joceline, "and nothing less would serve than that he should have it immediately —the supper, he said, might be got ready in the meantime; and he commands all about him as if he were in his father's old castle, where he might have called long enough, I warrant, without any one to hear him."

"Indeed?" said Sir Henry, "this must be a forward chick of the game, to crow so early.—What is his name?"

"His name?—it escapes me every hour, it is so hard a one," said Albert— "Kerneguy in his name—Louis Kerneguy; his father was Lord Killstewers, of Kincardineshire."

"Kerneguy, and Killstewers, and Kin—what d'ye call it?—Truly," said the knight, "these northern men's names and titles smack of their origin—they sound like a north-west wind, rumbling and roaring among heather and rocks."

"It is but the ausperities of the Celtic and Saxon dialects," said Dr. Rochecliffe, "which, according to Verstegan, still linger in those northern parts of the island. — But peace — here comes supper, and Master Louis Kerneguy."

Supper entered accordingly, borne in by Joceline and Phoebe, and after it, leaning on a huge knotty stick, and having his nose in the air like a questing hound—for his attention was apparently more fixed on the good provisions that went before him than anything else—came Master Kerneguy, and seated himself, without much ceremony, at the lower end of the table.

He was a tall, rawboned lad, with a shock head of hair, fiery red, like many of his country, while the harshness of his national features was increased by the contrast of his complexion, turned almost black by the exposure to all sorts of weather, which, in that skulking and rambling mode of life, the fugitive royalists had been obliged to encounter. His address was by no means prepossessing, being a mixture of awkwardness and forwardness, and shewing, in a remarkable degree, how a want of easy address may be consistent with an admirable stock of assurance. His face intimated having received some recent scratches, and the care of Dr. Rochecliffe had decorated it with a number of patches, which even enhanced its natural plainness. Yet the eyes were brilliant and expressive, and, amid his ugliness—for it amounted to that degree of irregularity—the face was not deficient in some lines which expressed both sagacity and resolution. One of the north-eastern connties of

Scotland. Richard Verstegan, an English antiquary, whose chief work, *The Restitution of Decayed Antiquities,* appeared in 1605.

The dress of Albert himself was far beneath his quality, as the son of Sir Henry Lee and commander of a regiment in the royal service; but that of his page was still more dilapidated. A disastrous green jerkin, which had been changed to a hundred hues by sun and rain, so that the original could scarce be discovered, huge clouterly shoes, leathern breeches—such as were worn by hedgers—coarse gray worsted stockings, were the attire of the honourable youth, whose limping gait, while it added to the ungainliness of his manner, shewed, at the same time, the extent of his sufferings. His appearance bordered so much upon what is vulgarly called the queer, that even with Alice it would have excited some sense of ridicule, had not compassion been predominant.

The grace was said; and the young squire of Ditchley, as well as Dr. Rochecliffe, made an excellent figure at a meal, the like of which, in quality and abundance, did not seem to have lately fallen to their share. But their feasts were child's play to those of the Scottish youth. Far from betraying any symptoms of the bread and butter with which he had attempted to close the orifice of his stomach, his appetite appeared to have been sharpened by a ninedays' fast; and the knight was disposed to think that the very genius of famine himself, come forth from his native regions of the north, was in the act of honouring him with a visit, while, as if afraid of losing a moment's exertion, Master Kerneguy never looked either to right or left, or spoke a single word to any at table.

"I am glad to see that you have brought a good appetite for our country fare, young gentleman, said Sir Henry.

"Bread of gude! sir," said the page, "an ye'll find flesh, I'se find appetite conforming ony day o' the year. But the truth is, sir, that the appeteezement has been God. 1 will.

coming on for three days or four, and the meat in this southland of yours has been scarce, and hard to come by, so, sir, I'm making up for lost time, as the piper of Sligo said, when he eat a hail side o' mutton."

"You have been country-bred, young man," said the knight, who, like others of his time, held the reins of discipline rather tight over the rising generation; "at least, to judge from the youths of Scotland whom I have seen at his late Majesty's court, in former days;—they had less appetite, and more—more"—As he sought the qualifying phrase, which might supply the place of "good manners," his guest closed the sentence in his own way—" And more meat, it may be—the better luck theirs."

Sir Henry stared and was silent. His son seemed to think it time to interpose—"My dear father," he said, "think how many years have run since the Thirty-eight, when the Scottish troubles first began, and I am sure that you will not wonder that, while the Barons of Scotland have been, for one cause or other, perpetually in the field, the education of their children at home must have been much neglected, and that young men of my friend's age know better how to use a broad-sword, or to toss a pike, than the decent ceremonials of society."

"The reason is a sufficient one," said the knight, "and since thou sayest thy follower Kernigo can fight, we'll not let him lack victuals, a God's name.—See, he looks angrily still at yonder cold loin of mutton—for God's sake put it all on his plate!"

"I can bide the bit and the buffet," said the honourable Master Kerneguy—" a hungry tike ne'er minds a blaud with a rough bane."

"Now, God ha'e mercy, Albert, but if this be the son of a Scots peer," said Sir Henry to his son, in a low tone of voice, "I would not be the English ploughman who would change manners with him for his ancient blood, and his nobility, and his estate to boot, an he has one.—He has eaten, as I am a Christian, near four pounds of solid butcher's meat, and with the grace of a wolf tugging at the carcass of a dead horse.—Oh he is about to drink at last—Soh!—he wipes his mouth, though,—and dips his fingers in the ewer—and dries them, I profess, with the napkin!—there is some grace in him after all." A county in Ireland. Whole.

Andrew Lang thinks "the exaggerated Caledonian rusticity of Kerneguy " is admirable. 1 can endure a good meal as well as a blow. A hungry dog doesn't mind a blow with a rough bone.

"Here is wussing1 all your vera gude healths!" said the youth of quality, and took a draught in proportion to the solids which he had sent before; he then flung his knife and fork awkwardly on the trencher, which he pushed back towards the centre of the table, extended his feet beneath it till they rested on their heels, folded his arms on his well-replenished stomach, and lolling back in his chair, looked much as if he was about to whistle himself asleep.

"Soh!" said the knight—"the honourable Master Kernigo hath laid down his arms.—Withdraw these things, and give us our glasses—Fill them around, Joceline; and if the devil or the whole Parliament were within hearing, let them hear Henry Lee of Ditchley drink a health to King Charles and confusion to his enemies!"

"Amen!" said a voice from behind the door.

All the company looked at each other in astonishment, at a response so little expected. It was followed by a solemn and peculiar tap, such as a kind of freemasonry had introduced among royalists, and by which they were accustomed to make themselves and their principles known to each other, when they met by accident.

"There is no danger," said Albert, knowing the sign— "it is a friend;—yet I wish he had been at a greater distance just now."

"And why, my son, should you wish the absence of one true man, who may, perhaps, wish to share our abundance, on one of those rare occasions when we have superfluity at our disposal?—Go, Joceline, see who knocks—and, and if a safe man, admit him."

"And if otherwise," said Joceline, "methinks I shall be able to prevent his troubling the good company!"

"No violence, Joceline, on your life," said Albert Lee; and Alice echoed, "For God's sake no violence!"

"No unnecessary violence at least," said the good knight; "for if the time demands it, I will have it seen that I am master of my own house." Joceline Joliffe nodded assent to all parties, and went on tiptoe to exchange one or two other mysterious symbols and knocks, ere he opened the door. It may be here remarked, that this species of secret association, with its signals of union, existed among the more dissolute and desperate class of cavaliers, men habituated to the dissipated life which they had been accustomed to in an ill-disciplined army, where every thing like order and regularity was too apt to be accounted a badge of puritanism. These were the "roaring boys" who met in hedge ale-houses, and when they had by any chance obtained a little money, or a little credit, determined to create a counter-revolution by declaring their sittings permanent, and proclaimed, in the words of one of their choicest ditties,— Wishing. A tacit understanding, like that among Freemasons.

We'll drink till we bring
In triumph back the king.

The leaders and gentry, of a higher description and more regular morals, did not indeed partake such excesses, but they still kept their eye upon a class of persons, who, from courage and desperation, were capable of serving on an advantageous occasion the fallen cause of royalty; and recorded the lodges and blind taverns at which they met, as wholesale merchants know the houses of call of the mechanics whom they may have occasion to employ, and can tell where they may find them when need requires. It is scarce necessary to add, that among the lower class, and sometimes even among the higher, there were men found capable of betraying the projects and conspiracies of their associates, whether well or indifferently combined, to the governors of the state. Cromwell, in particular, had gained some correspondents of this kind of the highest rank, and of the most undoubted character, among the royalists, who, if they made scruple of impeaching or betraying individuals who confided in them, had no hesitation in giving the government such general information as served to enable him to disappoint the purposes of any plot or conspiracy.

To return to our story. In much shorter time than we have spent in reminding the reader of these historical particulars, Joliffe had made his mystic communication; and being duly answered as by one of the initiated, he undid the door, and there entered our old friend Roger Wildrake, roundhead in dress, as his safety and his dependence on Colonel Everard compelled him to be, but that dress worn in a most cavalier-like manner, and forming a stronger contrast than usual with the demeanour and language of the wearer, to which it was never very congenial.

A tavern not known by the general public to be such. A house where journeymen connected with a particular trade assemble, especially when out of work, and where the unemployed can be hired by those in search of hands.

His puritanic hat, the emblem of that of Ralpho in the prints to Hudibras, or, as he called it, his felt umbrella, was set most knowingly on one side of the head, as if it had been a Spanish hat and feather; his straight squarecaped sad-coloured cloak was flung gaily upon one shoulder, as if it had been of three-piled taffeta, lined with crimson silk; and he paraded his huge calf-skin boots, as if they had been silken hose and Spanish leather shoes, with roses on the instep. In short, the airs which he gave himself, of a most thorough-paced wild gallant and cavalier, joined to a glistening of self-satisfaction in his eye, and an inimitable swagger in his gait, which completely announced his thoughtless, conceited, and reckless character, formed a most ridiculous contrast to his gravity of attire.

It could not, on the other hand, be denied, that in spite of the touch of ridicule which attached to his character, and the loose morality which he had learned in the dissipation of town pleasures, and afterwards in the disorderly life of a soldier, Wildrake had points about him both to make him feared and respected. He was handsome, even in spite of his air of debauched effrontery; a man of the most decided courage, though his vaunting rendered it sometimes doubtful; and entertained a sincere sense of his political principles, such as they were, though he was often so imprudent in asserting and boasting of them as, joined with his dependence on Colonel Everard, induced prudent men to doubt his sincerity.

Such as he was, however, he entered the parlour of Victor Lee, where his presence was anything but desirable to the parties present, with a jaunty step, and a consciousness of deserving the best possible reception. This assurance was greatly aided by circumstances which rendered it obvious, that if the jocund cavalier had limited himself to one draught of liquor that evening, in terms of his vow of temperance, it must have been a very deep and long one.

1, Ralpho was an Independent clerk who acted as squire to Sir Hudibras, the Presbyterian justice in Samuel Butler's *lludttras,* a satire upon the Puritans, something in the style of *Don Quixote,* published in 1663.

"Save ye, gentlemen, save ye.—Save you, good Sir Henry Lee, though I have scarce the honour to be known to you.—Save you, worthy doctor, and a speedy resurrection to the fallen Church of England."

"You are welcome, sir," said Sir Henry Lee, whose feelings of hospitality, and of the fraternal reception due to a royalist sufferer, induced him to tolerate this intrusion more than he might have done otherwise. "If you have fought or suffered for the King, sir, it is an excuse for joining us, and commanding our services in anything in our power—although at present we are a family-party

But I think I saw you in waiting upon Master Markham Everard, who calls himself Colonel Everard.—If your message is from him, you may wish to see me in private?"

"Not at all, Sir Henry, not at all.—It is true, as my ill hap will have it, that being on the stormy side of the hedge —

like all honest men — you understand me, Sir Henry,—I am glad, as it were, to gain something from my old friend and comrade's countenance—not by truckling or disowning my principles, sir—I defy such practices;— but, in short, by doing him any kindness in my power when he is pleased to call on me. So I came down here with a message from him to the old roundheaded son of a (I beg the young lady's pardon, from the crown of her head down to the very toes of her slipper)—And so, sir, chancing as I was stumbling out in the dark, I heard you give a toast, sir, which warmed my heart, sir, and ever will, sir, till death chills it;—and so I made bold to let you know there was an honest man within hearing."

Such was the self-introduction of Master Wildrake, to which the knight replied, by asking him to sit down, and take a glass of sack to his Majesty's glorious restoration. Wildrake, at this hint, squeezed in without ceremony beside the young Scotsman, and not only pledged his landlord's toast, but seconded its import, by volunteering a verse or two of his favourite loyal ditty,—" The King shall enjoy his own again." The heartiness which he threw into his song opened still farther the heart of the old knight, though Albert and Alice looked at each other with looks resentful of the intrusion, and desirous to put an end to it. The honourable Master Kerneguy either possessed that happy indifference of temper which does not deign to notice such circumstances, or he was able to assume the appearance of it to perfection, as he sat sipping sack, and cracking walnuts, without testifying the least sense that an addition had been made to the party. Wildrake, who liked the liquor and the company, shewed no unwillingness to repay his landlord, by being at the expense of the conversation.

"You talk of fighting and suffering, Sir Henry Lee— Lord help us, we have all had our share. All the world knows what Sir Henry Lee has done from Edge hill field downwards, wherever a loyal sword was drawn, or a loyal flag fluttered. Ah, God help us! I have done something too.—My name is Roger Wildrake of Squattlesea-mere, Lincoln—not that you are ever like to have heard it before, but I was captain in Lunsford's light-horse, and afterwards with Goring. I was a child-eater, sir—a babe-bolter."

"I have heard of your regiment's exploits, sir; and perhaps you may find I have seen some of them, if we should spend ten minutes together—And I think I have heard of your name too. —I beg to drink your health, Captain Wildrake of Squattlesea-mere, Lincolnshire."

"Sir Henry, I drink yours in this pint bumper, and upon my knee; and I would do as much for that young gentleman "—(looking at Albert)—-" and the squire of the green cassock too, holding it for green, as the colours are not to my eyes altogether clear and distinguishable."

It was a remarkable part of what is called by theatrical folk the by-play of this scene, that Albert was conversing apart with Dr. Rochecliffe in whispers, even more than the divine seemed desirous of encouraging; yet to whatever their private conversation referred, it did not deprive the young Colonel of the power of listening to what was going forward in the party at large, and interfering from time to time, like a watch-dog, who can distinguish the slightest alarm, even when employed in the engrossing process of taking his food.

"Captain Wildrake," said Albert, " we have no objection —I mean my friend and I—to be communicative on proper occasions; but you, sir, who are so old a sufferer, must needs know, that at such casual meetings as this, men do not D. See Scott's note a few paragraphs later. mention their names unless they are specially wanted. It is a point of conscience, sir, to be able to say, if your principal, Captain Everard or Colonel Everard, if he be a Colonel, should examine you upon oath, I did not know who the persons were whom I heard drink such and such toasts."

"Faith, I have a better way of it, worthy sir," answered Wildrake; "I never can, for the life of me, remember that there were any such and such toasts drunk at all. It's a strange gift of forgetfulness I have."

"Well, sir," replied the younger Lee; "but we, who have unhappily more tenacious memories, would willingly abide by the more general rule."

"Oh, sir," answered Wildrake, " with all my heart. I intrude on no man's confidence, d—n me—and I only spoke for civility's sake, having the purpose of drinking your health in a good fashion. —(Then he broke forth into melody)—

"Then let the health go round, a-round, around, a-round,
Then let the health go round;
For though your stocking he of silk,
Your knee shall kiss the ground, a ground, a-ground, aground,
Your knee shall kiss the ground."

"Urge it no farther," said Sir Henry, addressing his son; "Master Wildrake is one of the old school—one of the tantivy boys; and we must bear a little, for if they drink hard they fought well. I will never forget how a party came up and rescued us clerks of Oxford, as they-called the regiment I belonged to, out of a cursed embroglio during the attack on Brentford. I tell you we were enclosed with the cockneys' pikes both front and rear, and we should have come off but ill, had not Lunsford's light horse, the babe-eaters as they called them, charged up to the pike's point and brought us off."

"I am glad you thought on that, Sir Henry," said Wildrake; "and do you remember what the officer of Lunsford's said?"

"I think I do," said Sir Henry smiling. A rattling, headlong Royalist. The term was in frequent use in the time of James II., to denote a High Church Tory. Brentford, near London, was carried by assault under Prince Rupert in 1043, but was promptly retaken by the Parliamentary troops.

"Well, then, did not he call out, when the women were coming down, howling like sirens as they were—' Have none of you a plump child that you could give us, to break our fast upon?'" "Truth itself!" said the knight; "and a great fat woman stepped forward with a baby, and offered it to the supposed cannibal.

"

All at the table, Master Kerneguy excepted, who seemed to think that good food of any kind required no apology, held up their hands in token of amazement.

"Ay," said Wildrake, "the ahem!—I crave the lady's pardon again, from tip of top-knot to hem of farthingale —but the cursed creature proved to be a parish nurse, who had been paid for the child half a year in advance. Gad, I took the baby out of the bitch-wolf's hand; and I have contrived, though God knows I have lived in a skeldering sort of way myself, to breed up. bold Breakfast, as I call him, ever since.—It was paying dear for a jest, though."

"Sir, I honour you for your humanity," said the old knight—" Sir, I thank you for your courage—Sir, I am glad to see you here," said the good knight, his eyes watering almost to overflowing. "So you were the wild officer who cut us out of the toils; Oh, sir, had you but stopped when I called on you, and allowed us to clear the streets of Brentford with our musketeers, we would have been at London stone that day! But your good will was the same."

"Ay, truly was it," said Wildrake, who now sat triumphant and glorious in his easy chair; "and here is to all the brave hearts, sir, that fought and fell in that same storm of Brentford. We drove all before us like chaff, till the shops, where they sold strong waters and other temptations, brought us up. Gad, sir, we, the babe-eaters, had too many acquaintances in Brentford, and our stout Prince Rupert was ever better at making way than drawing off. Gad, sir, for my own poor share, I did but go into the house of a poor widow lady, who maintained a charge of daughters, and whom I had known of old, to get my horse fed, a morsel of meat, and so forth, when these cockney pikes of the artillery ground, as you yery well call them, rallied, and came in with their armed heads, as boldly as so many Cotswold rams. I sprang down stairs, got to my horse—but, egad, I fancy all my troop had widows and orphan maidens to comfort as well as I, for only five of us got together. We cut our way through successfully—and Gad, gentlemen, I carried my little Breakfast on the pommel before me; and there was such a hollowing and screeching, as if the whole town thought I was to kill, roast, and eat the poor child, so soon as I got to quarters. But devil a cockney charged up to my bonny bay, poor lass, to rescue little cake-bread; they only cried haro, and out upon me." Petticoat. Vagrant.

A stone now in the wall of St. Swithin's Church, London, which is said to have been the point from which all the Roman milestones in Britain took their departure. Some think it is even older than the Roman occupation of Britain.

"Alas, alas!" said the knight, "we made ourselves seem worse than we were; and we were too bad to deserve God's blessing even in a good cause. But it is needless to look back—we did not deserve victories when God gave them, for we never improved them like good soldiers, or like Christian men; and so we gave these canting scoundrels the advantage of us, for they assumed, out of mere hypocrisy, the discipline and orderly behaviour which we who drew our swords in a better cause, ought to have practised out of true principle. But here is my hand, Captain. I have often wished to see the honest fellow who charged up so smartly in our behalf, and I reverence you for the care you took of the poor child. I am glad this dilapidated place has still some hospitality to offer you, although we cannot treat you to roasted babes or stewed sucklings— eh, Captain?"

"Troth, Sir Henry, the scandal was sore against us on that score. I remember Lacy, who was an old play-actor, and a lieutenant in ours, made drollery on it in a play which was sometimes acted at Oxford, when our hearts were something up, called I think the Old Troop." A breed raised on the Cotswold Hills in Gloucestershire.

' Chaucer's *Nonne Preestes Tale,* 1. 650. Also Tennyson's *Harold,* Act V., Sc. I.

John Lacy, acomic actor, who died in 1681. His "Old Troop " was not produced until about 1665 *(Century Cyclopedia).* Scott's own confession of his frequent inaccuracy in dates is frankly made. "In truth, often as I have been complimented on the strength of my memory, I have through life been entitled to adopt old Beattie of Meikledale's answer to his parish minister when eulogizing him with respect to the same faculty. 'No, Doctor,' said the honest borderlaird, 'I have no command of my memory; it only retains what happens to hit my fancy, and like enough, sir, if you were to preach to me for a couple of hours on end, I might be unable at the close of the discourse to remember one word of it.' Perhaps there are few men whose memory serves them with equal fidelity as to many different classes of subjects; but.I am sorry to say, that while mine has rarely failed me as to any snatch of verse or trait of character that had once interested my fancy, it has generally been a frail support, not only as to names, and dates, and other minute technicalities of history, but as to many more important things."—Introduction to *Anne of Oeierstein.*

So saying, and feeling more familiar as his merits were known, he hitched his chair up against that of the Scottish lad, who was seated next him, and who in shifting his place, was awkward enough to disturb, in his turn, Alice Lee, who sate opposite, and, a little offended, or at least embarrassed, drew her chair away from the table.

"I crave pardon," said the honourable Master Kerneguy; "but, sir," to Master Wildrake, "ye hae e'en garr'd 1 me hurt the young lady's shank."

"I crave your pardon, sir, and much more that of the fair lady, as is reasonable; though, rat me, sir, if it was I set your chair a-trundling in that way. Zooks, sir, I have brought with me no plague, nor pestilence, nor other infectious disorder, that ye should have started away as if I had been a leper, and discomposed the lady, which I would have prevented with my life, sir. Sir, if ye be northern born, as your tongue bespeaks, egad, it was I ran the risk in drawing near you; so there was small reason for you to bolt."

"Master Wildrake," said Albert, interfering, "this young gentleman is a stranger as well as you, under protection of Sir Henry's hospitality, and it cannot be agreeable for my father to see disputes arise among his guests. You may mistake the young gentleman's quality from his present appearance—this is the Honourable Master Louis Kerneguy, sir, son of my Lord Kilstewers of Kincardineshire, one who has fought for the King, young as he is."

"No dispute shall rise through me, sir—none through me," said Wildrake; "your exposition sufficeth, sir.— Master Louis Girnigo, son of my Lord Kilsteer, in Gringardenshire, I am your humble slave, sir, and drink your health, in token that I honour you, and all true Scots who draw their Andrew Ferraras on the right side, sir." Note C. Cannibalism imputed to the Cavaliers. Scott. Made.

"Fse beholden to you, and thank you, sir," said the young man, with some haughtiness of manner, which hardly corresponded with his rusticity; "and I wuss your health in a ceevil way."

Most judicious persons would have here dropped the conversation; but it was one of Wildrake's marked peculiarities, that he could never let matters stand when they were well. He continued to plague the shy, proud, and. awkward lad with his observations. "You speak your national dialect pretty strongly, Master Girnigo," said he, "but I think not quite the language of the gallants that I have known among the Scottish cavaliers—I knew, for example, some of the Gordons, and others of good repute, who always put an *f* for the *wh*, as *faat* for *what, fan* for *when,* and the like."

Albert Lee here interposed, and said that the provinces of Scotland, like those of England, had their different modes of pronunciation.

"You are very right, sir," said Wildrake. "I reckon myself, now, a pretty good speaker of their cursed jargon — no offence, young gentleman; and yet, when I took a turn with some of Montrose's folk in the South Hielands, as they call their beastly wildernesses (no offence again), I chanced to be by myself, and to lose my way, when I said to a shepherd-fellow, making my mouth as wide, and my voice as broad as I could, *whore am I ganging till?*—confound me if the fellow could answer me, unless, indeed, he was sulky, as the bumpkins will be now and then to the gentlemen of the sword."

This was familiarly spoken, and though partly addressed to Albert, was still more directed to his immediate neighbour, the young Scotsman, who seemed, from bashfulness, or some other reason, rather shy of his intimacy. To one or two personal touches from Wildrake's elbow, administered during his last speech, by way of a practical appeal to him in particular, he only answered, "Misunderstandings were to be expected when men converse in national deealects." Where am I going to?

Wildrake, now considerably drunker than he ought to have been in civil company, caught up the phrase, and repeated it;—"Misunderstanding, sir—Misunderstanding, sir?—I do not know how I am to construe that, sir; but to judge from the information of these scratches on your honourable visnomy, I should augur that you had been of late at misunderstanding with the cat, sir."

"You are mistaken, then, friend, for it was with the dowg," answered the Scotsman, dryly, and cast a look towards Albert.

"We had some trouble with the watch-dogs in entering so late in the evening," said Albert, in explanation, "and this youth had a fall among some rubbish, by which he came by these scratches."—

"And now, dear Sir Henry," said Dr. Rochecliffe, "allow us to remind you of your gout, and our long journey. I do it the rather that my good friend your son has been, during the whole time of supper, putting questions to me aside, which had much better be reserved till to-morrow— May we therefore ask permission to retire to our night's rest?"

"These private committees in a merry meeting," said Wildrake, "are a solecism in breeding. They always put me in mind of the cursed committees at Westminster.— But shall we to roost before we rouse the night-owl with a catch?"

"Aha, canst thou quote Shakspeare?" said Sir Henry, pleased at discovering a new good quality in his acquaintance, whose military services were otherwise but just able to counterbalance the intrusive freedom of his conversation. "In the name of merry Will," he continued,—" whom I never saw, though I have seen many of his comrades, as Alleyn, Hemmings, and so on,—we will have a single catch,and one rouse about, and then to bed."

After the usual discussion about the choice of the song, and the parts which each was to bear, they united their voices in trolling a loyal glee, which was popular among the party at the time, and in fact believed to be composed by no less a person than Doctor Rochecliffe himself. Physiognomy. "*Twelfth Night,* II., 3, 60.

The celebrated actor. Edward Alleyn (1566-1626), one of the builders of the Fortune Theatre, and the founder of Dulwich College. One of the editors of the First Folio Shakespeare, already referred to. A round, or part song. Bumper. *Othello,* II., 3, 66. GLEE FOR KING CHARLES.

Bring the bowl which you boast, Fill it up to the brim;
'Tis to him we love most,
And to all who love him.
Brave gallants, stand up,
And avaunt, ye base carles I
Were there death in the cup,
   Here's a health to King Charles!
   Though he wanders through dangers,
Unaided, unknown.
Dependent on strangers,
Estranged from his own;
Though 'tis under our breath
Amidst forfeits and perils,
Here's to honour and faith,
   And a health to King Charles!
   Let such honours abound As the time can afford,
The knee on the ground,
And the hand on the sword;
But the time shall come round,
When, mid Lords, Dukes, and Earls,
The loud trumpets shall sound
   Here's a health to King Charles!

After this display of loyalty, and a final libation, the party took leave of each other for the night. Sir Henry offered his old acquaintance Wildrake a bed for the evening, who weighed the matter somewhat in this fashion: "Why, to speak truth, my patron will expect me at the borough—but then he is used to my staying out of doors a-nights. Then there's the Devil, that they say haunts Woodstock; but with the blessing of this reverend doctor, I defy him and all his works—I saw him not when I slept here twice before, and I am sure if he was absent then, he has not come back with Sir Henry Lee and his family. So I accept your courtesy, Sir Henry, and I thank you, as a cavalier of Lunsford should thank one of the fighting clerks of Oxon. God bless the King! I care not who hears it, and confusion The glee is of Scott's own composition, as may be imagined,

a Churls.

to Noll and his red nose!" Off he went accordingly with a bottle-swagger, guided by Joceline, to whom Albert, in the meantime, had whispered, to be sure to quarter him far enough from the rest of the family.

Young Lee then saluted his sister, and, with the formality of those times, asked and received his father's blessing with an affectionate embrace. His page seemed desirous to imitate one part of his example, but was repelled by Alice, who only replied to his offered salute with a courtesy. He next bowed his head in an awkward fashion to her father, who wished him a good night. "I am glad to see, young man," he said, "that you have at least learned the reverence due to age. It should always be paid, sir; because in doing so you render that honour to others which you will expect yourself to receive when you approach the close of your life. More will I speak with you at leisure, on your duties as a page, which office in former days used to be the very school of chivalry; whereas of late, by the disorderly times, it has become little better than a school of wild and disordered license; which made rare Ben Jonson exclaim"

"Nay, father," said Albert, interposing, "you must consider this day's fatigue, and the poor lad is almost asleep on his legs—to-morrow he will listen with more profit to your kind admonitions.—And you, Louis, remember at least one part of your duty—take the candles and light us—here Joceline comes to shew us the way. Once more, good night, good Doctor Rochecliffe—good night, all."

Distinguish carefully chapters like the preceding, designed to give a picture of characters in a certain mood, from chapters containing situations or events that directly advance the plot.

CHAPTER THE TWENTY-FIRST *Oroom.* Hail, noble prince!

King Richard. Thanks, noble peer!
The cheapest of us is a groat too dear.
Richard II.

Albert and his page were ushered by Joceline to what was called the Spanish chamber, a huge old scrambling bed-room, rather in a dilapidated condition, but furnished with a large standing-bed for the master, and a truckle-bed for the domestic, as was common at a much later period in old English houses, where the gentleman often required the assistance of a groom of the chambers to help him to bed, if the hospitality had been exuberant. The walls were covered with hangings of cordovan leather, stamped with gold, and representing fights between the Spaniards and Moriscoes, bull-feasts, and other sports peculiar to the Peninsula, from which it took its name of the Spanish chamber. These hangings were in some places entirely torn down, in others defaced and hanging in tatters. But Albert stopped not to make observations, anxious, it seemed, to get Joceline out of the room; which he achieved by hastily answering his offers of fresh fuel, and more liquor, in the negative, and returning, with equal conciseness, the under-keeper's good wishes for the evening. He at length retired, somewhat unwillingly, and as if he thought that his young master might have bestowed a few more words upon a faithful old retainer after so long absence.

Joliffe was no sooner gone, than, before a single word was spoken between Albert Lee and his page, the former hastened to the door, examined lock, latch, and bolt, and made them fast, with the most scrupulous attention. He super-added to these precautions that of a long screw bolt, which he brought out of his pocket, and which he screwed on to the staple in such a manner as to render it impossible to withdraw it, or open the door unless by breaking it down. The page held a light to him during the operation, which his master went through with much exactness and dexterity. But when Albert arose from his knee, on which he had rested during the accomplishment of this task, the manner of the companions was on the sudden entirely changed towards each other. The honourable Master Kerneguy, from a cubbish lout of a raw Scotsman, seemed to have acquired at once all the grace and ease of motion and manner, which could be given by an acquaintance of the earliest and most familiar kind with the best company of the time.

Moors.

He gave the light he held to Albert, with the easy indifference of a superior, who rather graces than troubles his dependent by giving him some slight service to perform. Albert, with the greatest appearance of deference, assumed in his turn the character of torch-bearer, and lighted his page across the chamber, without turning his back upon him as he did so. He then set the light on the table by the bedside, and approaching the young man with deep reverence, received from him the soiled green jacket, with the same profound respect as if he had been a first lord of the bedchamber, or other officer of the household of the highest distinction, disrobing his Sovereign of the Mantle 1 of the Garter. The person to whom this ceremony was addressed endured it for a minute or two with profound gravity, and then bursting out a-laughing, exclaimed to Albert, "What a devil means all this formality?—thou complimentest with these miserable rags as if they were silks and sables, and with poor Louis Kerneguy as if he were the King of Great Britain?"

"And if your Majesty's commands, and the circumstances of the time, have made me for a moment seem to forget that you are my sovereign, surely I may be permitted to render my homage as such while you are in your own royal palace of Woodstock?"

"Truly," replied the disguised Monarch, " the sovereign and the palace are not ill matched; these tattered hangings and my ragged jerkin suit each other admirably.— *This* Woodstock!—*this* the bower where the royal Norman revelled with the fair Bosamond Clifford!—Why it is a place of assignation for owls!" Then, suddenly recollecting himself, with his natural courtesy, he added, as if fearing he might have hurt Albert's feelings—" But the more obscure and retired, it is the fitter for our purpose, Lee; and if it does seem to be a roost for owls, as there is no denying, why we know it has nevertheless brought up eagles." Mantle belonging to the order of the Garter, already commented upon.

He threw himself as he spoke upon a chair, and indolently, but gracefully, received the kind offices of Albert, who undid the coarse buttonings of the leathern gamashes which defended his legs, and spoke to him the whilst:— "What a fine specimen of the olden time is your father, Sir Henry! It is strange I should not have seen him before;—but I heard my father often speak of him as being among the flower of our real old English gentry. By the mode in which he began to school me, I can guess you had a tight taskmaster of him, Albert—I warrant you never wore hat in his presence, eh?"

"I never cocked it at least in his presence, please your Majesty, as I have seen some youngsters do," answered Albert; "Indeed if I had, it must have been a stout beaver to have saved me from a broken head."

"Oh, I doubt it not," replied the king; "a fine old gentleman—but with that, methinks in his countenance, that assures you he would not hate the child in sparing the rod.—Hark ye, Albert— Suppose the same glorious Restoration come round,—which, if drinking to its arrival can hasten it, should not be far distant,—for in that particular our adherents never neglect their duty,—suppose it come, therefore, and that thy father, as must be of course, becomes an Earl and one of the Privy Council, oddsfish, man, I shall be as much afraid of him as ever was my grandfather Henri Quatre of old Sully.—Imagine there were such a trinket now about the Court as the fair Rosamond, or La Belle Gabrielle, what a work there would be of pages, and grooms of the chamber, to get the pretty rogue clandestinely shuffled out by the backstairs, like a prohibited commodity, when the step of the Earl of Woodstock was heard in the antechamber f" Riding-boots.

The principal body of advisers of the English sovereign. There are at present something over two hundred members. Henry of Navarre (reigned 1589-1610), one of the most popular of French Kings. His youngest daughter, Henrietta Maria, married Charles I. of England. The Duke of Sully (1560-1041), chief minister of Henry IV., and a man of surly and imperious temper Gabrielle d'Estrees (1571-1599), mistress of Henry IV.

"I am glad to see your Majesty so merry after your fatiguing journey."

"The fatigue was nothing, man," said Charles; "a kind welcome and a good meal made amends for all that. But they must have suspected thee of bringing a wolf from the braes of Badenoch along with you, instead of a twolegged being, with no more than the usual allowance of mortal stowage for provisions. I was really ashamed of my appetite; but thou knowest I had eat nothing for twenty-four hours, save the raw egg you stole for me from the old woman's henroost—I tell thee I blushed to shew myself so ravenous before that high-bred and respectable old gentleman your father, and the very pretty girl your sister—or cousin, is she?"

"She is my sister," said Albert Lee, dryly, and added, in the same breath, "Your Majesty's appetite suited well enough with the character of a raw northern lad.—Would your Majesty now please to retire to rest*?"*

"Not for a minute or two," said the King, retaining his seat. "Why, man, I have scarce had my tongue unchained to-day; and to talk with that northern twang, and besides, the fatigue of being obliged to speak every word in character,—Gad, it's like walking as the galley slaves do on the Continent, with a twenty-four pound shot chained to their legs—they may drag it along, but they cannot move with comfort. And, by the way, thou art slack in paying me my well-deserved tribute of compliments on my counterfeiting.—Did I not play Louis Kerneguy as round as a ring?"

"If your Majesty asks my serious opinion, perhaps I may be forgiven if I say your dialect was somewhat too coarse for a Scottish youth of high birth, and your behaviour perhaps a little too churlish. I thought too— though I pretend not to be skilful—that some of your Scottish sounded as if it were not genuine."

"Not genuine?—there is no pleasing thee, Albert.— Why, who should speak genuine Scottish but myself?— Was I not their King for a matter of ten months? and if I did not get knowledge of their language, I wonder what else I got by it. Did not east country, and south country, and west country, and Highlands, caw, croak, and shriek about me, as the deep guttural, the broad drawl, and the high sharp yelp predominated by turns?—Odds-fish, man, have I not been speeched at by their orators, addressed by their senators, rebuked by their kirkmen? Have I not sate on the cutty-stool, mon again resuming the northern dialect, and thought it grace of worthy Mas John Gillespie, that I was permitted to do penance in mine own privy chamber, instead of the face of the congregation? and wilt thou tell me, after all, that I cannot speak Scotch enough to baffle an Oxon Knight and his family?" A wild district in eastern Scotland.

The Scotch dialect in Scott's novels is often open to this same charge, in the opinion of careful students of dialect.

"May it please your Majesty,—I began by saying I was no judge of the Scottish language."

"Pshaw—it is mere envy; just so you said at Norton's that I was too courteous and civil for a young page—now you think me too rude."

"And there is a medium, if one could find it," said Albert, defending his opinion in the same tone in which the King attacked him; "so this morning, when you were in the woman's dress, you raised your petticoats rather unbecomingly high, as you waded through the first little stream; and when I told you of it, to mend the matter, you draggled through the next without raising them at all."

"0, the devil take the woman's dress!" said Charles; "I hope I shall never be driven to that disguise again. Why, my ugly face was enough to put gowns, caps, and kirtles, out of fashion for ever—the very dogs fled from me— Had I passed any hamlet that had but five huts in it, I could not have escaped the cucking stool. I was a libel on womanhood. These leathern conveniences are none of the gayest, but they are *propria qum maribus;* and right glad am I to be repossessed of them. I can tell you, too, my friend, I shall resume all my masculine privileges with my proper habiliments; and as you say I have been too coarse to-night, I will behave myself like a courtier to Mistress Alice to-morrow. I made a sort of acquaintance with her already, when I seemed to be of the same sex with herself, and found out there are other Colonels in the wind besides you, Colonel Albert Lee." The seat in old Scottish churches, where offenders were placed on Sunday, to be publicly rebuked by the minister.
Gillespie was one of the Remonstrants, or extreme party in Scotland. The young King was obliged to listen to long sermons,—once, it is said, to five in succession without a break,—upon the sins of the Stuart family. "The Duke of Buckingham was the only English courtier allowed to attend him; and by his ingenious talent for ridicule he had rendered himself extremely agreeable to his master. While so many objects of derision surrounded them, it was difficult to be altogether insensible to the temptation, and wholly to suppress the laugh. Obliged to attend from morning to night at prayers and sermons, they betrayed evident symptoms of weariness or contempt The clergy never could esteem the King sufficiently regenerated: and by continual exhortations, remonstrances, and reprimands, they still endeavoured to bring him to a juster sense of his spiritual duty."— Hume's *History of England,* Chapter LX.

"May it please your Majesty," said Albert—and then stopped short, from the difficulty of finding words to express the unpleasant nature of his feelings. They could not escape Charles; but he proceeded without scruple. *"I* pique myself on seeing as far into the hearts of young ladies as most folk, though God knows they are sometimes too deep for the wisest of us. But I mentioned to your sister in my character of fortuneteller,—thinking, poor simple man, that a country girl must have no one but her brother to dream about,—that she was anxious about a certain Colonel. I had hit the theme, but not the person; for I alluded to you, Albert; and I presume the blush was too deep ever to be given to a brother. So up she got, and away she flew from me like a lapwing. I can excuse her—for, looking at myself in the well, I think if I had met such a creature as I seemed, I should have called fire and fagot against it.—Now, what think you, Albert—who can this Colonel be, that more than rivals you in your sister's affection?"

Albert, who well knew that the King's mode of thinking, where the fair sex was concerned, was far more gay than delicate, endeavoured to put a stop to the present topic, by a grave answer.

"His sister," he said, "had been in some measure educated with the son of her maternal uncle, Markham Everard; but as his father and he himself had adopted the cause of the roundheads, the families had in consequence been at variance; and any projects which might have been formerly entertained, were of course long since dismissed on all sides. " A chair in which according to old English custom a common scold was placed, to be dipped into a pool of water.
The right thing for men. Raised the alarm; a phrase taken from the mob-cries in the days of public burning for heresy or other causes.
"You are wrong, Albert, you are wrong," said the King, pitilessly pursuing his jest. "You Colonels, whether you wear blue or orange sashes, are too pretty fellows to be dismissed so easily, when once you have acquired an interest. But Mistress Alice, so pretty, and who wishes the restoration of the King with such a look and accent, as if she were an angel whose prayers must needs bring it down, must not be allowed to retain any thoughts of a canting roundhead—What say you—will you give me leave to take her to task about it?—After all, I am the party most concerned in maintaining true allegiance among my subjects; and if I gain the pretty maiden's good-will, that of the sweetheart's will soon follow. This was jolly King Edward's way—Edward the Fourth, you know. The king-making Earl of Warwick—the Cromwell of his day —dethroned him more than once; but he had the hearts of the merry dames of London, and the purses and veins of the cockneys bled freely, till they brought him home again. How say you?—shall I shake off my northern slough, and speak with Alice in my own character, showing what education and manners have done for me, to make the best amends they can for an ugly face?"

"May it please your Majesty," said Albert, in an altered and embarrassed tone, "I did not expect"

Here he stopped, not able to find words adequate at the same time to express his sentiments, and respectful enough to the King, while in his father's house, and under his own protection.

"And what is it that Master Lee does not expect?" said Charles, with marked gravity on his part.

Again Albert attempted a reply, but advanced no farther than, "I would hope, if it please your Majesty "—when he again stopped short, his deep and hereditary respect for his sovereign, and his sense of the hospitality due to his misfortunes, preventing his giving utterance to his irritated feelings.
Blue was the color adopted by the

Covenanters (whence the phrase "true blue "); orange was the color of the Royalists. Edward IV. (reigned 1461-1483) was personally popular, largely on account of his pleasure-loving ways, but was utterly unprincipled.

'Richard Neville, Earl of Warwick (1428-1471), called the "KingMaker" from his political and military authority during the Wars of the Roses. He fought now on one side and now on the other, and was finally killed by Edward IV. at the battle of Barnet.

"And what does Colonel Albert Lee hope?" said Charles, in the same dry and cold manner in which he had before spoken.—" No answer?—Now, *I hope* that Colonel Lee does not see in a silly jest anything offensive to the honour of his family, since methinks that were an indifferent compliment to his sister, his father, and himself, not to mention Charles Stuart, whom he calls his King; and *I expect,* that I shall not be so hardly construed, as to be supposed capable of forgetting that Mistress Alice Lee is the daughter of my faithful subject and host, and the sister of my guide and preserver.—Come, come, Albert," he added, changing at once to his naturally frank and unceremonious manner, "you forget how long I have been abroad, where men, women, and children talk gallantry morning, noon, and night, with no more serious thought than just to pass away the time; and I forget, too, that you are of the old-fashioned English school, a son after Sir Henry's own heart, and don't understand raillery upon such subjects.— But I ask your pardon, Albert, sincerely, if I have really hurt you."

So saying, he extended his hand to Colonel Lee, who, feeling he had been rather too hasty in construing the King's jest in an unpleasant sense, kissed it with reverence, and attempted an apology.

"Not a word—not a word," said the good-natured Prince, raising his penitent adherent as he attempted to kneel; "we understand each other. You are somewhat afraid of the gay reputation which I acquired in Scotland; but I assure you, I will be as stupid as you, or your cousin Colonel could desire, in presence of Mrs. Alice Lee, and only bestow my gallantry, should I have any to throw away, upon the pretty little waiting-maid who attended at supper—unless you should have monopolized her ear for your own benefit, Colonel Albert?"

"It is monopolized, sure enough, though not by me, if it please your Majesty, but by Joceline Joliffe, the underkeeper, whom we must not disoblige, as we have trusted him so far already, and may have occasion to repose even entire confidence in him. I half think he suspects who Louis Kerneguy may in reality be."

"You are an engrossing set, you wooers of Woodstock," said the King, laughing. "Now, if I had a fancy, as a Frenchman would not fail to have in such a case, to make pretty speeches to the deaf old woman I saw in the kitchen, as *npisaller,* I dare say I should be told that *her* ear was engrossed for Dr. Rochecliffe's sole use?"

"I marvel at your Majesty's good spirits," said Albert, "that, after a day of danger, fatigue, and accidents, you should feel the power of amusing yourself thus."

"That is to say, the groom of the chambers wishes his Majesty would go to sleep?—Well, one word or two on more serious business, and I have done. —I have been completely directed by you and Rochecliffe—I have changed my disguise from female to male upon the instant, and altered my destination from Hampshire to take shelter here— Do you still hold it the wiser course?"

"I have great confidence in Dr. Rochecliffe," replied Albert, "whose acquaintance with the scattered royalists enables him to gain the most accurate intelligence. His pride in the extent of his correspondence, and the complication of his plots and schemes for your Majesty's service, is indeed the very food he lives upon; but his sagacity is equal to his vanity. I repose, besides, the utmost faith in Joliffe. Of my father and sister I would say nothing; yet I would not, without reason, extend the knowledge of your Majesty's person farther than it is indispensably necessary."

"Is it handsome in me," said Charles, pausing, "to withhold my full confidence from Sir Henry Lee?"

"Your Majesty heard of his almost death-swoon of last night—what would agitate him most deeply must not be hastily communicated."

"True; but are we safe from a visit of the red-coats— they have them in Woodstock as well as in Oxford?" said Charles.

"Dr. Rochecliffe says, not unwisely," answered Lee, "that it is best sitting near the fire when the chimney smokes; and that Woodstock, so lately in possession of the sequestrators, and still in the vicinity of the soldiers, will be less suspected, and more carelessly searched, than more Last resource.
distant corners, which might seem to promise more safety. Besides," he added, "Rochecliffe is in possession of curious and important news concerning the state of matters at Woodstock, highly favourable to your Majesty's being concealed in the palace for two or three days, till shipping is Erovided. The Parliament, or usurping Council of State, ad sent down sequestrators, whom their own evil conscience, assisted, perhaps, by the tricks of some daring cavaliers, had frightened out of the Lodge, without much desire to come back again. Then the more formidable usurper, Cromwell, had granted a warrant of possession to Colonel Everard, who had only used it for the purpose of repossessing his uncle in the Lodge, and who kept watch in person at the little borough, to see that Sir Henry was not disturbed."

"What! Mistress Alice's Colonel?" said the King— "that sounds alarming;—for grant that he keeps the other fellows at bay, think you not, Master Albert, he will have an hundred errands a-day to bring him here in person?"

"Dr. Rochecliffe says," answered Lee, "the treaty between Sir Henry and his nephew binds the latter not to approach the Lodge, unless invited;—indeed, it was not without great difficulty, and strongly arguing the good consequences it might produce to your

Majesty's cause, that my father could be prevailed on to occupy Woodstock at all: but be assured he will be in no hurry to send an invitation to the Colonel."

"And be you assured that the Colonel will come without waiting for one," said Charles. "Folk cannot judge rightly where sisters are concerned—they are too familiar with the magnet to judge of its powers of attraction.— Everard will be here, as if drawn by cart-ropes—fetters, not to talk of promises, will not hold him—and then, methinks, we are in some danger."

"I hope not," said Albert. "In the first place, I know Markham is a slave to his word; besides, were any chance to bring him here, I think I could pass your Majesty upon him without difficulty, as Louis Kerneguy. Then, although my cousin and I have not been on good terms for these some years, I believe him incapable of betraying your Majesty; and lastly, if I saw the least danger of it, I would, were he ten times the son of my mother's sister brother, rnn my sword through his body, ere he had time to execute his purpose."

"There is but another question," said Charles, "and I will release you, Albert:—You seem to think yourself secure from search. It may be so; but, in any other country, this tale of goblins which is flying about would bring down priests and ministers of justice to examine the reality of the story, and mobs of idle people to satisfy their curiosity."

"Respecting the first, sir, we hope and understand that Colonel Everard's influence will prevent any immediate inquiry, for the sake of preserving undisturbed the peace of his uncle's family; and as for any one coming without some sort of authority, the whole neighbours have so much love and fear of my father, and are, besides, so horribly alarmed about the goblins of Woodstock, that fear will silence curiosity."

"On the whole, then," said Charles, "the chances of safety seem to be in favour of the plan we have adopted, which is all I can hope for in a condition where absolute safety is out of the question. The Bishop recommended Dr. Rochecliffe as one of the most inge-nious, boldest, and most loyal sons of the Church of England; you, Albert Lee, have marked your fidelity by a hundred proofs. To you and your local knowledge I submit myself.—And now, prepare our arms—alive I will not be taken; yet I will not believe that a son of the King of England, and heir of her throne, could be destined to danger in his own palace, and under the guard of the loyal Lees."

Albert Lee laid pistols and swords in readiness by the King's bed and his own; and Charles, after some slight apology, took his place in the larger and better bed, with a sigh of pleasure, as from one who had not lately enjoyed such an indulgence. He bid good night to his faithful attendant, who deposited himself on his truckle; and both monarch and subject were soon fast asleep.
1D.
Compare Scott's delineation of the characteristic traits of Charles II. with his previous portraits of the Stuarts (Queen Mary in *The Abbot,* James I. in *The Fortunes of Nigel,* Charles II. in *Peveril of the Peak,* the Chevalier Charles Edward in *Waiierley).* Make as close a comparison as you can between this chapter and the corresponding scene between James Edward Stuart and Henry Esmond in Thackeray's *Esmond.I* CHAPTER THE TWENTY-SECOND

Give Sir Nicholas Threlkeld praise;
Hear it, good man, old in days,
Thou tree of succour and of rest
To this young hird that was distressed
Beneath thy branches he did stay;
And he was free to sport and play,
When falcons were abroad for prey.
Wordsworth.

The fugitive Prince slept, in spite of danger, with the profound repose which youth and fatigue inspire. But the young cavalier, his guide and guard, spent a more restless night, starting from time to time, and listening; anxious, notwithstanding Doctor Rochecliffe's assurances, to procure yet more particular knowledge concerning the state of things around them, than he had been yet able to collect.

He rose early after daybreak; but although he moved with as little noise as was possible, the slumbers of the hunted Prince were easily disturbed. He started up in his bed, and asked if there was any alarm.

"None, please your Majesty," replied Lee; "only, thinking on the questions your Majesty was asking last night, and the various chances there are of your Majesty's safety being endangered from unforeseen accidents, I thought of going thus early, both to communicate with Doctor Rochecliife, and to keep such a look-out as befits the place, where are lodged for the time the Fortunes of England. I fear I must request of your Majesty, for your own gracious security, that you have the goodness to condescend to secure the door with your own hand after I go out."

"Oh, talk not to Majesty, for Heaven's sake, dear Albert?" answered the poor King, endeavouring in vain to put on a part of his clothes in order to traverse the room. —" When a king's doublet and hose are so ragged that he can no more find his way into them than he could have travelled through the forest of Deane without a guide, good faith, there should be an end of Majesty, until it chances to be better accommodated. Besides, there is the chance of these big words bolting out at unawares, when there are ears to hear them whom we might think dangerous."

"Your commands shall be obeyed," said Lee, who had now succeeded in opening the door; from which he took his departure, leaving the King, who had hustled along the floor for that purpose, with his dress wofully ill arranged, to make it fast again behind him, and begging him in no case to open to any one, unless he or Rochecliffe were of the party who summoned him.

Albert then set out in quest of Dr. Rochecliffe's apartment, which was only known to himself and the faithful Joliffe, and had at different times accommodated that steady churchman with a place of concealment, when, from his bold and busy temper, which led him into the most extensive and hazardous machinations on the King's behalf, he had been strictly sought after by the opposite party. Of late, the inquest after him had died entirely away, as he had prudently withdrawn himself from the scene of his intrigues. Since the loss of the battle of Worcester, he had been afloat again, and more active than ever; and had, by friends and correspondents, and especially the Bishop of, been the means of directing the

King's flight towards Woodstock, although it was not until the very day of his arrival that he could promise him a safe reception at that ancient mansion.

Albert Lee, though he revered both the undaunted spirit and ready resources of the bustling and intriguing churchman, felt he had not been enabled by him to answer some of Charles's questions yesternight, in a way so distinct as one trusted with the King's safety ought to have done; and it was now his object to make himself personally acquainted, if possible, with the various bearings of so weighty a matter, as became a man on whom so much of the responsibility was likely to descend.

Even his local knowledge was scarce adequate to find the Doctor's secret apartment, had he not traced his way after a genial flavour of roasted game through divers blind A great forest, mainly of oaks and beeches, in Gloucestershire.

passages, and up and down certain very useless stairs, through cupboards and hatchways, and so forth, to a species of sanctum sanctorum, where Joceline Joliffe was ministering to the good doctor a solemn breakfast of wildfowl, with a cup of small beer stirred with a sprig of rosemary, which Doctor Rochecliffe preferred to all strong potations. Beside him sat Bevis on his tail, slobbering and looking amiable, moved by the rare smell of the breakfast, which had quite overcome his native dignity of disposition.

The chamber in which the doctor had established.himself was a little octangular room, with walls of great thickness, within which were fabricated various issues leading in different directions, and communicating with different parts of the building. Around him were packages with arms, and near him one small barrel, as it seemed, of gunpowder; many papers in different parcels, and several keys for correspondence in cipher; two or three scrolls covered with hieroglyphics were also beside him, which Albert took for plans of nativity; and various models of machinery, in which Doctor Rochecliffe was an adept. There were also tools of various kinds, masks, cloaks, and a dark lantern, and a number of other indescribable trinkets belonging to the trade of a daring plotter in dangerous times. Last there was a casket with gold and silver coin of different countries, which was left carelessly open as if it were the least of Doctor Rochecliffe's concern, although his habits in general announced narrow circumstances, if not actual poverty. Close by the divine's plate lay a Bible and Prayerbook, with some proof-sheets, as they are technically called, seemingly fresh from the press. There were also within the reach of his hand a dirk, or Scottish poniard, a powder-horn, and a musketoon, or blunderbuss, with a pair of handsome pocket-pistols. In the midst of this miscellaneous collection, the doctor sat eating his breakfast, with great appetite, as little dismayed by the various implements of danger around him, as a workman is when accustomed to the perils of a gunpowder manufactory.

"Soh, young gentleman," he said, getting up and extending his hand, "are you come to breakfast with me in good fellowship, or to spoil my meal this morning, as Holy of holies, *i.e.,* innermost apartment.

you did my supper last night by asking untimely questions?"

"I will pick a bone with you, with all my heart;" said Albert; "and if you please, doctor, I would ask some questions which seem not quite untimely."

So saying, he sat down, and assisted the doctor in giving a very satisfactory account of a brace of wild-ducks and a leash of teal. Bevis, who maintained his place with great patience and insinuation, had his share of a collop, which was also placed on the well-furnished board; for, like most highbred dogs, he declined eating waterfowl.

"Come hither then, Albert Lee," said the doctor, laying down his knife and fork, and plucking the towel from his throat, so soon as Joceline was withdrawn; "thou art still the same lad thou wert when I was thy tutor—never satisfied with having got a grammar rule, but always persecuting me with questions why the rule stood so, and not otherwise—over-curious after information which thou couldst not comprehend, as Bevis slobbered and whined for the duck-wing which he could not eat."

"I hope you will find me more reasonable, doctor," answered Albert; "and at the same time, that you will recollect I am not now *sub ferula,* but am placed in circumstances where I am not at liberty to act upon the *ipse dixit* of any man, unless my own judgment be convinced. I shall deserve richly to be hanged, drawn, and quartered, should any misfortune happen by my misgovernment in this business."

"And it is therefore, Albert, that I would have thee trust the whole to me, without interfering. Thou sayest, forsooth, thou art not *sub ferula;* but recollect that while you have been fighting in the field, I have been plotting in the study—that I know all the combinations of the King's friends, ay, and all the motions of his enemies, as well as a spider knows every mesh of his web. Think of my experience, man. Not a cavalier in the land but has heard of Rochecliffe the Plotter. I have been a main limb in everything that has been attempted since forty-two—penned declarations, conducted correspondence, communicated with chiefs, recruited followers, commissioned arms, levied money, appointed rendezvouses. I was in the Western Rising; and before that, in the City Petition, and in Sir John Owen's stir in Wales; in short, almost in every plot for the King, since Tomkins and Challoner's matter.' A brace and a half, *i.e.,* three. Slice of meat.

Under the rod, *i.e.,* a pupil. He himself has said it; used to typify an arbitrary command.

"But were not all these plots unsuccessful!" said Albert; "and were not Tomkins and Challoner hanged, doctor?"

"Yes, my young friend," answered the doctor, gravely, "as many others have been with whom I have acted; but only because they did not follow my advice implicitly. You never heard that I was hanged myself."

"The time may come, doctor," said Albert; "The pitcher goes oft to the well—The proverb, as my father would say, is somewhat musty. But I, too, have some confidence in my own judgment; and, much as I honour the church, I cannot altogether subscribe to passive obedience. I will tell you in one word what points I must have explanation on; and it will remain with you to give it, or to return a message to the King that you will not explain your plan; in which case, if lie acts by my advice, he will leave Woodstock, and resume his purpose of getting to the coast without delay."

"Well, then," said the doctor, "thou suspicious monster, make thy demands, and, if they be such as I can answer without betraying confidence, I will reply to them."

"In the first place, then, what is all this story about ghosts, and witchcrafts, and apparitions? and do you consider it as safe for his Majesty to stay in a house subject to such visitations, real or pretended?" "In 1645 the Royalists organized the Western Association of Cornwall, Devon, Somerset, and Dorset, as a counterpoise to the Parliamentary Association of the Eastern Counties"—D. It is very possible, however, that Scott refers to the Scotch invasion of England in 1648.

It is not clear to which Petition the text refers. The best known City Petition was Alderman Pennington's in 1641, craving the abolition of Episcopacy, but Dr. Rochecliffe could scarcely have been instrumental in that. Possibly a petition for the King's restoration, brought to Westminster after the King's escape from Hampton Court in 1647, is the one Scott had in mind. Sir John Owen attempted to stir up North Wales, with the object of rescuing Charles I. from prison, in 1648. He was tried for it in 1649. but was pardoned by the intercession of Ireton. In 1643 these gentlemen, with Waller and others, tried to foment trouble in London, with the aim of aiding the King. They were executed by the House of Commons. "You must be satisfied with my answer *in verbo sacerdotis*—the circumstances you allude to will not give the least annoyance to Woodstock during the King's residence. I cannot explain farther; but for this I will be bound, at the risk of my neck."

"Then," said Lee, "we must take Doctor Rochecliffe's bail that the devil will keep the peace towards our Sovereign Lord the King—good. Now there lurked about this house the greater part of yesterday, and perhaps slept here, a fellow called Tomkins—a bitter Independent, and a secretary, or clerk, or something or other, to the regicide dog Desborough. The man is well known—a wild ranter in religious opinions, but in private affairs far-sighted, cunning, and interested even as any rogue of them all."

"Be assured we will avail ourselves of his crazy fanaticism to mislead his wicked cunning;—a child may lead a hog, if it has Wit to fasten a cord to the ring in its nose," replied the doctor.

"You may be deceived," said Albert; "the age has many such as this fellow, whose views of the spiritual and temporal world are so different, that they resemble the eyes of a squinting man; one of which, oblique and distorted, sees nothing but the end of his nose, while the other, instead of partaking the same defect, views strongly, sharply, and acutely, whatever is subjected to its scrutiny."

"But we will put a patch on the better eye," said the doctor, "and he shall only be allowed to speculate with the imperfect optic. You must know, this fellow has always seen the greatest number, and the most hideous apparitions; he has not the courage of a cat in such matters, though stout enough when he hath temporal antagonists before him. I have placed him under the charge of Joceline Joliffe, who, betwixt plying him with sack and ghost-stories, would make him incapable of knowing what was done, if you were to proclaim the King in his presence."

"But why keep such a fellow here at all?"

"Oh, sir, content you;—he lies leaguer, as a sort of ambassador for his worthy masters, and we are secure from any intrusion so long as they get all the news of Woodstock from trusty Tomkins."

"I know Joceline's honesty well," said Albert; "and Upon the word of a priest.

if he can assure me that he will keep a watch over this fellow, I will so far trust in him. He doos not know the depth of the stake, 'tis true, but that my life is concerned will be quite enough to keep him vigilant.—Well, then, I proceed: What if Markham Everard comes down on us?"

"We have his word to the contrary," answered RochecliffEe—" his word of honour, transmitted by his friend:— Do you think it likely he will break it?"

"I hold him incapable of doing so," answered Albert; "and, besides, I think Markham would make no bad use of anything which might come to his knowledge—Yet God forbid we should be under the necessity of trusting any who ever wore the Parliament's colours in a matter of such dear concernment!"

"Amen!" said the doctor.—" Are your doubts silenced

"I still have an objection," said Albert, "to yonder impudent rakehelly fellow, styling himself a cavalier, who pushed himself on our company last night, and gained my father's heart by a story of the storm of Brentford, which I daresay the rogue never saw."

"You mistake him, dear Albert," replied Rochecliffe— "Roger Wildrake, although till of late I only knew him by name, is a gentleman, was bred at the Inns of Court, and spent his estate in the King's service."

"Or rather in the devil's service," said Albert. "It is such fellows as he, who, sunk from the license of their military habits into idle debauched ruffians, infest the land with riots and robberies, brawl in hedge ale-houses and cellars where strong waters are sold at midnight, and, with their deep oaths, their hot loyalty, and their drunken valour, make decent men abominate the very name of cavalier."

"Alas!" said the doctor, "it is but too true; but what can you expect? When the higher and more qualified classes are broken down and mingled undistinguishably with the lower orders, they are apt to lose the most valuable marks of their quality in the general confusion of morals and manners—just as a handful of silver medals will become defaced and discoloured if jumbled about among the vulgar copper coin. Even the prime medal of all, which we royalists would so willingly wear next our very hearts, has not, perhaps, entirely escaped some deterioration—But let other tongues than mine speak on that subject."

Albert Lee paused deeply after having heard these communications on the part of Rochecliffe. "Doctor," he said, "it is generally agreed, even by some who think you may occasionally have been a little over busy in putting men upon dangerous actions"

"May God forgive them who entertain so false an opinion of me!" said the doctor.

"That, nevertheless, you have done and suffered more in the King's behalf than any man of your function."

"They do me but justice there," said Doctor Rochecliffe —" absolute justice."

"I am therefore disposed to abide by your opinion, if, all things considered, you think it safe that we should remain at Woodstock."

"That is not the question," answered the divine.

"And what is the question, then?" replied the young soldier.

"Whether any safer course can be pointed out. I grieve to say, that the question must be comparative, as to the point of option. Absolute safety is—alas the while!—out of the question on all sides. Now, I say Woodstock is, fenced and guarded as at present, by far the most preferable place of concealment.

"Enough," replied Albert, "I give up to you the question, as to a person whose knowledge of such important affairs, not to mention your age and experience, is more intimate and extensive than mine can be."

"You do well," answered Rochecliffe; "and if others had acted with the like distrust of their own knowledge, and confidence in competent persons, it had been better for the age. This makes Understanding bar himself up within his fortalice and Wit betake himself to his high tower." (Here he looked around his cell with an air of self-complacency.) "The wise man foreseeth the tempest, and hideth himself."

"Doctor," said Albert, "let our foresight serve others far more precious than either of us. Let me ask you, if you have well considered whether our precious charge should remain in society with the family, or betake himself to some of the more hidden corners of the house?" Fortress.

"Hum!" said the Doctor, with an air of deep reflection —" I think he will be safest as Louis Kerneguy, keeping himself close beside you"

"I fear it will be necessary," added Albert, "that I scout abroad a little, and shew myself in some distant part of the country, lest, coming here in quest of me, they should find higher game."

"Pray do not interrupt me—Keeping himself close beside you or your father, in or near to Victor Lee's apartment, from which you are aware he can make a ready escape, should danger approach. This occurs to me as best for the present—I hope to hear of the vessel today— to-morrow at farthest."

Albert Lee bid the active but opinionated man good morrow; admiring how this species of intrigue had become a sort of element in which the doctor seemed to enjoy himself, notwithstanding all that the poet has said concerning the horrors which intervene betwixt the conception and execution of a conspiracy.

In returning from Doctor Rochecliffe's sanctuary, he met with Joceline, who was anxiously seeking him. "The young Scotch gentleman," he said, in a mysterious manner, "has arisen from bed, and, hearing me pass, he called me into his apartment."

"Well," replied Albert, "I will see him presently."

"And he asked me for fresh linen and clothes. Now, sir, he is like a man who is quite accustomed to be obeyed, so I gave him a suit which happened to be in a wardrobe in the west tower, and some of your linen to conform; and when he was dressed he commanded me to shew him to the presence of Sir Henry Lee and my young lady.—I would have said something, sir, about waiting till you came back, but he pulled me good-naturedly by the hair (as, indeed, he has a rare humour of his own), and told me he was guest to Master Albert Lee, and not his prisoner; so, sir, though I thought you might be displeased with me for giving him the means of stirring abroad, and perhaps being seen by those who should not see him, what could I say?"

"You are a sensible fellow, Joceline, and comprehend always what is recommended to you.—This youth will not be controlled, I fear, by either of us; but we must look *Julius Ccesar*, II., 1, 62.
the closer after his safety—You keep your watch over that prying fellow the steward*?"*

"Trust him to my care—on that side have no fear.—But ah, sir! I would we had the young Scot in his old clothes again, for the riding-suit of yours which he now wears hath set him off in other-guess fashion."

From the manner in which the faithful dependent expressed himself, Albert saw that he suspected who the Scottish page in reality was; yet he did not think it proper to acknowledge to him a fact of such importance, secure as he was equally of his fidelity, whether explicitly trusted to the full extent, or left to his own conjectures. Full of anxious thought, he went to the apartment of Victor Lee, in which Joliffe told him he would find the party assembled. The sound of laughter, as he laid his hand on the lock of the door, almost made him start, so singularly did it jar with the doubtful and melancholy reflections which engaged his own mind. He entered, and found his father in high good humour, laughing and conversing freely with his young charge, whose appearance was, indeed, so much changed to the better in externals, that it seemed scarce possible a night's rest, a toilet, and a suit of decent clothes could have done so much in his favour in so short a time. It could not, however, be imputed to the mere alteration of dress, although that, no doubt, had its effect. There was nothing splendid in that which Louis Kerneguy (we continue to call him by his assumed name) now wore. It was merely a riding-suit of gray cloth, with some silver lace, in the fashion of a country gentleman of the time. But it happened to fit him very well, and to become his very dark complexion, especially as he now held up his head, and used the manners, not only of a well-behaved but of a highly-accomplished gentleman. When he moved, his clumsy and awkward limp was exchanged for a sort of shuffle, which, as it might be the consequence of a wound in those perilous times, had rather an interesting than an ungainly effect. At least it was as genteel an expression that the party had been overhard travelled, as the most polite pedestrian could propose to himself.

The features of the Wanderer were harsh as ever, but his red shock peruke, for such it proved, was laid aside, his sable elf-locks were trained, by a little of Joceline's as Different.
sistance, into curls, and his fine black eyes shone from among the shades of these curls, and corresponded with the animated, though not handsome, character of the whole head. In his conversation, he had laid aside all the coarseness of dialect which he had so strongly affected on the preceding evening; and although he continued to speak a little Scotch, for the support of his character as a young gentleman of that nation, yet it was not in a degree which rendered his speech either uncouth or unintelligible, but merely afforded a certain Doric1 tinge essential to the personage he represented. No person on earth could better understand the society in which he moved; exile had made him acquainted with life in all its shades and varieties—his spirits, if not uniform, were elastic—he had that species of Epicurean philosophy, which, even in the most extreme difficulties and dangers, can in an interval of ease, however brief, avail itself of the enjoyments of the moment—he was, in short, in youth and misfortune, as afterwards in his regal condition, a good-humoured but hard-hearted voluptuary— wise, save where his passions intervened—beneficent, save when prodigality had deprived him of the means, or prejudice of the wish, to confer benefits—his faults such as might often have drawn down hatred, but that they were mingled with so much urbanity, that the injured person felt it impossible to retain the full sense of his wrongs.

Albert Lee found the party, consisting of his father, sister, and the supposed page, seated by the breakfast-table, at which he also took his place. He was a pensive and anxious beholder of what passed, while the page, who had already completely gained the heart of the good old cavalier, by mimicking the manner in which the Scottish divines preached in favour of Ma gude Lord Marquis of Argyle and the Solemn League and Covenant, was now endeavouring to interest the fair Alice by such anecdotes, partly of warlike and perilous adventure, as possessed the same degree of interest for the female ear which they have had ever since Desdemona's days. But it was not only of dangers by land and sea that the disguised page spoke; but much more, and much oftener, on foreign revels, banquets, balls, where the pride of France, of Spain, or of the Low Countries, was exhibited in the eyes of their most eminent beauties. Alice being a very young girl, who, in consequence of the Civil War, had been almost entirely educated in the country, and often in great seclusion, it was certainly no wonder that she should listen with willing ears, and a ready smile, to what the young gentleman, their guest, and her brother's protege, told with so much gaiety, and mingled with such a shade of dangerous adventure, and occasionally of serious reflection, as prevented the discourse from being regarded as merely light and frivolous.

Rustic; so called from the character and speech of the Spartans when contrasted with that of the Athenians.

'So called from Epicurus, the Greek philosopher (342-270 B.C.), who taught that pleasure is the only rational end of action.

Archibald Campbell, eighth earl and first Marquis of Argyle, a leader of the Scotch Covenanters. He was defeated by Montrose in 1645, sided with Charles II. after the death of Charles I. , but submitted later to Cromwell, and consequently after the Restoration was beheaded for treason. The agreement before referred to, made by the Scottish Parliament in 1638, and by the English Parliament in 1643, to uphold the reformed religion.

In a word, Sir Henry Lee laughed, Alice smiled from time to time, and all were satisfied but Albert, who would himself, however, have been scarce able to allege a sufficient reason for his depression of spirits.

The materials of breakfast were at last removed, under the active superintendence of the neat-handed Phoebe, who looked over her shoulder, and lingered more than once, to listen to the fluent discourse of their new guest, whom, on the preceding evening, she had, while in attendance at supper, accounted one of the most stupid inmates to whom the gates of Woodstock had been opened since the times of Fair Rosamond.

Louis Kerneguy then, when they were left only four in the chamber, without the interruption of domestics, and the successive bustle occasioned by the discussion and removal of the morning meal, became apparently sensible, that his friend and ostensible patron Albert ought not altogether to be suffered to drop to leeward in the conversation, while he was himself successfully engaging the attention of those members of his family to whom he had become so recently known. He went behind his chair, therefore, and, leaning on the back, said with a goodhumoured tone, which made his purpose entirely intelligible,—

"Either my good friend, guide, and patron has heard 'Othello, I., 3,128-170. worse news this morning than he cares to tell us, or he must have stumbled over my tattered jerkin and leathern hose, and acquired, by contact, the whole mass of stupidity which I threw off last night with those most dolorous garments. Cheer up, my dear Colonel Albert, if your affectionate page may presume to say so—you are in company with those whose society, dear to strangers, must be doubly so to you. Odds-fish, man, cheer up! I have seen you gay on a biscuit and a mouthful of water-cresses—don't let your heart fail you on Rhenish wine and venison."

"Dear Louis," said Albert, rousing himself into exertion, and somewhat ashamed of his own silence, "I have slept worse, and been astir earlier than you."

"Be it so," said his father; "yet I hold it no good excuse for your sullen silence. Albert, you have met your sister and me, so long separated from you, so anxious on your behalf, almost like mere strangers, and yet you are returned safe to us, and you find us well."

"Returned indeed—but for safety, my dear father, that word must be a stranger to us Worcester folk for some time. However, it is not my own safety about which I am anxious."

"About whose, then, should you be anxious?—All accounts agree that the King is safe out of the dogs' jaws."

"Not without some danger though," muttered Louis, thinking of his encounter with Bevis on the preceding evening.

"No, not without danger, indeed," echoed the knight; "but, as old Will says,—

There's such divinity doth hedge a king,
That treason dares not peep at what it would.1

No, no—thank God, that's cared for; our Hope and Fortune is escaped, so all news affirm, escaped from Bristol—if I thought otherwise, Albert, I should be as sad as you are. For the rest of it, I have lurked a month in this house when discovery would have been death, and that is no longer since than after Lord Holland and the Duke of Buckingham's rising at Kingston; and hang me, if I thought once of twisting my brow into such a tragic fold as yours, but cocked my hat at misfortune as a cavalier should." *Hamlet,* IV., 5, 123, 124.

- This was an unsuccessful Royalist rising in Kent in 1648.

"If I might put in a word," said Louis, "it would be to assure Colonel Albert Lee that I verily believe the King would think his own hap, wherever he may be, much the worse that his best subjects were seized with dejection on his account."

"You answer boldly on the King's part, young man," said Sir Henry.

"Oh, my father was meikle about the King's hand," answered Louis, recollecting his present character.

"No wonder, then," said Sir Henry, "that you have so soon recovered your good spirits and good breeding, when you heard of his Majesty's escape. Why, you are no more like the lad we saw last night, than the best hunter I ever had was like a dray-horse."

"Oh, there is much in rest, and food, and grooming," answered Louis. "You would hardly know the tired jade you dismounted from last night, when she is brought out prancing and neighing the next morning, rested, refreshed, and ready to start again—especially if the brute hath some good blood, for such pick up unco fast."

"Well, then, but since thy father was a courtier, and thou hast learned, I think, something of the trade, tell us a little, Master Kerneguy, of him we love most to hear about—the King; we are all safe and secret, you need not be afraid. He was a hopeful youth; I trust his flourishing blossom now gives promise of fruit?"

As the knight spoke, Louis bent his eyes on the ground, and seemed at first uncertain what to answer. But admirable at extricating himself from such dilemmas, he replied, "That he really could not presume to speak on such a subject in the presence of his patron, Colonel Albert Lee, who must be a much better judge of the character of King Charles than he could pretend to be."

Albert was accordingly next assailed by the knight, seconded by Alice, for some account of his Majesty's character.

"I will speak but according to facts," said Albert; "and then I must be acquitted of partiality. If the King had not possessed enterprise and military skill, he never would have attempted the expedition to Worcester;—had i Much. Very. he not had personal courage, he had not so long disputed the battle that Cromwell almost judged it lost. That he possesses prudence and patience, must be argued from the circumstances attending his flight; and that he has the love of his subjects is evident, since, necessarily known to many, he has been betrayed by none."

"For shame, Albert!" replied his sister; "is that the way a good cavalier doles out the character of his Prince, applying an instance at every concession, like a pedlar measuring linen with his rod?—Out upon you!—no wonder you were beaten, if you fought as coldly for your King as you now talk for him."

"I did my best to trace a likeness from what I have seen and known of the original, sister Alice," replied her brother. —"If you would have a fancy portrait, you must get an artist of more imagination than I have to draw it for you."

"I will be that artist myself," said Alice, "and in *my* portrait, our Monarch shall shew all that he ought to be, having such high pretensions—all that he must be, being so loftily descended—all that I am sure he is, and that every loyal heart in the kingdom ought to believe him."

"Well said, Alice," quoth the old knight.—"Look thou upon this picture, and on this!—Here is our young friend shall judge. I wager my best nag—that is, I would wager him had I one left—that Alice proves the better painter of the two.—My son's brain is still misty, I think, since his defeat—he has not got the smoke of Worcester out of it. Plague on thee!—a young man, and cast down for one beating! Had you been banged twenty times like me, it had been time to look grave.—But come, Alice, forward; the colours are mixed on your pallet—

forward with something that shall shew like one of Vandyke's living portraits, placed beside the dull dry presentation there of our ancestor Victor Lee."

Alice, it must be observed, had been educated by her father in the notions of high, and even exaggerated loyalty which characterised the cavaliers, and she was really an enthusiast in the royal cause. But besides, she was in good spirits at her brother's happy return, and wished to prolong the gay humour, in which her father had of late scarcely ever indulged.

"Well then," she said, "though I am no Apelles, I will A famous Greek painter of the time of Philip and Alexander.

try to paint an Alexander, such as I hope, and am determined to believe, exists in the person of our exiled sovereign, soon I trust to be restored. And I will not go farther than his own family. He shall have all the chivalrous courage, all the warlike skill, of Henry of France, his grandfather, in order to place him on the throne; all his benevolence, love of his people, patience even of unpleasing advice, sacrifice of his own wishes and pleasures to the commonweal, that, seated there, he may be blessed while living, and so long remembered when dead, that for ages after it shall be thought sacrilege to breathe an aspersion against the throne which he has occupied! Long after he is dead, while there remains an old man who has seen him, were the condition of that survivor no higher than a groom or a menial, his age shall be provided for at the public charge, and his gray hairs regarded with more distinction than an earl's coronet, because he remembers the Second Charles, the monarch of every heart in England!"

While Alice spoke, she was hardly conscious of the presence of any one save her father and brother; for the page withdrew himself somewhat from the circle.

And there was nothing to remind her of him. She gave the reins, therefore, to her enthusiasm, and as the tears glittered in her eye, and her beautiful features became animated, she seemed like a descended cherub proclaiming the virtues of a patriot monarch. The person chiefly interested in her description held himself back, as we have said, and concealed his own features, yet so as to preserve a full view of the beautiful speaker.

Albert Lee, conscious in whose presence this eulogium was pronounced, was much embarrassed; but his father, all whose feelings were flattered by the panegyric, was in rapture.

"So much for the *King,* Alice," he said, "and now for the *Man.*" "For the man," replied Alice, in the same tone, "need I wish him more than the paternal virtues of his unhappy father, of whom his worst enemies have recorded, that if moral virtues and religious faith were to be selected as the qualities which merited a crown, no man could plead the possession of them in a higher or more indisputable degree. Temperate, wise, and frugal, yet munificent in rewarding merit—a friend to letters and the muses, but a severe discourager of the misuse of such gifts—a worthy gentleman — a kind master—the best friend, the best father, the best

Christian "Her voice began to falter, and her father's handkerchief was already at his eyes.

"He was, girl—he was!" exclaimed Sir Henry; "but no more on't, I charge ye—no more on't—enough; let his son but possess his virtues, with better advisers, and better fortunes, and he will be all that England, in her warmest wishes, could desire."

There was a pause after this; for Alice felt as if she had spoken too frankly and too zealously, for her sex and youth. Sir Henry was occupied in melancholy recollections on the fate of his late sovereign, while Kerneguy and his supposed patron felt embarrassed, perhaps from a consciousness that the real Charles fell far short of his ideal character, as designed in such glowing colours. In some cases, exaggerated or unappropriate praise becomes the most severe satire.

But such reflections were not of a nature to be long willingly cherished by the person, to whom they might have been of great advantage. He assumed a tone of raillery, which is, perhaps, the readiest mode of escaping from the feelings of self-reproof. "Every cavalier," he said, "should bend his knee to thank Mistress Alice Lee for having made such a flattering portrait of the King their master, by laying under contribution for his benefit the virtues of all his ancestors; only there was one point he would not have expected a female painter to have passed over in silence. When she made him, in right of his grandfather and father, a muster of royal and individual excellences, why could she not have endowed him at the same time with his mother's personal charms? Why should not the son of Henrietta Maria, the finest woman of her day, add the recommendations of a handsome face and figure to his internal qualities? he had the same hereditary title to good looks as to mental qualifications; and the picture, with such an addition, would be perfect in its way— and God send it might be a resemblance!"

"I understand you, Master Kerneguy," said Alice, "but I am no fairy, to bestow, as those do in the nursery tales, gifts which Providence has denied. I am woman enough to have made inquiries on the subject, and I know the general report is, that the King, to have been the son of such handsome parents, is unusually hard-favoured." "Good God, sister!" said Albert, starting impatiently from his seat.

"Why, you yourself told me so," said Alice, surprised at the emotion he testified; "and you said"

"This is intolerable," muttered Albert; "I must out to speak with Joceline without delay—Louis" (with an imploring look to Kerneguy), "you will surely come with me?"

"I would with all my heart," said Kerneguy, smiling maliciously; "but you see how I suffer still from lameness.—Nay, nay, Albert," he whispered, resisting young Lee's attempt to prevail on him to leave the room, "can you suppose I am fool enough to be hurt by this?—on the contrary, I have a desire of profiting by it."

"May God grant it!" said Lee to himself, as he left the room—" it will be the first lecture you ever profited by; and the devil confound the plots and plotters who made me bring you to this place!" So saying, he carried his discontent forth into the Park.

Contrast the character sketch of Dr. Rochecliffe with that of other political intriguers in Scott (as Sir Frederick Vernon in *Bob Sop);* also with Father Holt in *Eimcmd,* and the Jesuit in *John Inglesant.* Notice that this chapter prepares the way for Charles the Second's designs upon the heroine.

CHAPTER THE TWENTY-THIRD

For there, they say, he daily doth frequent
   With unrestrained loose companions;
   While he, young, wanton, and effeminate boy,
Takes on the point of honour, to support
   So dissolute a crew. _ _ _
   Richard II.

The conversation which Albert had in vain endeavoured to interrupt flowed on in the same course after he had left the room. It entertained Louis Kerneguy; for personal vanity, or an over sensitiveness to deserved reproof, were not among the faults of his character, and were indeed incompatible with an understanding which, combined with more strength of principle, steadiness of exertion, and self-denial, might have placed Charles high on the list of English monarchs. On the other hand, Sir Henry listened with natural delight to the noble sentiments uttered by a being so beloved as his daughter. His own parts were rather steady than brilliant; and he had that species of imagination which is not easily excited without the action of another, as the electrical globe only scintillates when rubbed against its cushion. He was well pleased, therefore, when Kerneguy pursued the conversation, by observing that Mistress Alice Lee had not explained how the same good fairy that conferred moral qualities, could not also remove corporeal blemishes.

"You mistake, sir," said Alice. "I confer nothing. I do but attempt to paint our King such as I *hope* he is— such as I am sure he *may* be, should he himself desire to be so. The same general report which speaks of his countenance as unprepossessing, describes his talents as being of the first order. He has, therefore, the means of arriving at excellence, should he cultivate them sedulously and employ them usefully—should he rule his passions and be guided by his understanding. Every good man cannot be wise; but it is in the power of every wise man, if he pleases, to be as eminent for virtue as for talent."

Young Kerneguy rose briskly, and took a turn through the room; and ere the knight could make any observation on the singular vivacity in which he had indulged, he threw himself again into his chair, and said, in rather an altered tone of voice—" It seems, then, Mistress Alice Lee, that the good friends who have described this poor King to you, have been as unfavourable in their account of his morals as of his person?"

"The truth must be better known to you, sir," said Alice, "than it can be to me. Some rumours there have been which accuse him of a license, which, whatever allowance flatterers make for it, does not, to say the least, become the son of the Martyr—I shall be happy to have these contradicted on good authority."

"I am surprised at your folly, said Sir Henry Lee, "in hinting at such things, Alice; a pack of scandal, invented by the rascals who have usurped the government —a thing devised by the enemy."

"Nay, sir," said Kerneguy, laughing, "we must not let our zeal charge the enemy with more scandal than they actually deserve. Mistress Alice has put the question to me. I can only answer, that no one can be more devotedly attached to the King than I myself,—that I am very partial to his merits and blind to his defects;—and that, in short, I would be the last man in the world to give up his cause where it was tenable. Nevertheless, I must confess, that if all his grandfather of Navarre's morals have not descended to him, this poor King has somehow inherited a share of the specks that were thought to dim the lustre of that great Prince—that Charles is a little soft-hearted, or so, where beauty is concerned Do not blame him too severely, pretty Mistress Alice; when a man's hard fate has driven him among thorns, it were surely hard to prevent him from trifling with the few roses he may find among them?"

Alice, who probably thought the conversation had gone far enough, rose while Master Kerneguy was speaking, and was leaving the room before he had finished, without apparently hearing the interrogation with which he concluded. Her father approved of her departure, not thinking the turn which Kerneguy had given to the discourse altogether fit for her presence; and, desirous civilly to break off the conversation, "I see," he said, "this is about the time, when, as Will says, the household affairs will call my daughter hence; I will therefore challenge you, young gentleman, to stretch your limbs in a little exercise with me, either at single rapier, or rapier and poniard, back-sword, spadroon, or your national weapons of broadsword and target; for all, or any of which, I think we will find implements in the hall."

It would be too high a distinction, Master Kerneguy said, for a poor page to be permitted to try a passage of arms with a knight so renowned as Sir Henry Lee, and he hoped to enjoy so great an honour before he left Woodstock; but at the present moment his lameness continued to give him so much pain, that he should shame himself in the attempt.

Sir Henry then offered to read him a play of Shakspeare, and for this purpose turned up King Richard II. But hardly had he connected with

Old John of Gaunt, time-honoured Lancaster,' when the young gentleman was seized with such an incontrollable fit of the cramp as could only be relieved by immediate exercise. He therefore begged permission to be allowed to saunter abroad for a little while, if Sir Henry Lee considered he might venture without danger.

"I can answer for the two or three of our people that are still left about the place," said Sir Henry; "and I know my son has disposed them so as to be constantly on the watch. If you hear the bell toll at the Lodge, I advise you to come straight home by the way of the King's Oak, which you see in yonder glade towering above the rest of the trees. We will have some one stationed there to introduce you secretly into the house."

The page listened to these cautions with the impatience of a schoolboy, who, desirous of enjoying his holiday, hears without marking the advice of tutor or parent, about taking care not to catch cold and so forth.

The absence of Alice Lee had removed all which had rendered the interior of the Lodge agreeable, and the mercurial young page fled with precipitation from the exercise and amusement which Sir Henry had proposed. He girded on his rapier, and threw his cloak, or rather that which belonged to his borrowed suit, about him, bringing up the lower part so as to muffle the face, and shew only the eyes over it, which was a common way of wearing them in those days, both in streets, in the country, and in public places, when men had a mind to be private, and to avoid interruption from salutations and greetings in the market-place. He hurried across the open space which divided the front of the Lodge from the wood, with the haste of a bird escaped from the cage, which, though joyful at its liberation, is at the same time sensible of its need of protection and shelter. The wood seemed to afford these to the human fugitive, as it might have done to the bird in question. A sword with one sharp edge used either for thrusting or cutting. A long and heavy sword, usually wielded by both hands. *Richard II.,* I., 1, 1.

When under the shadow of the branches, and within the verge of the forest, covered from observation, yet with the power of surveying the front of the Lodge, and all the open ground before it, the supposed Louis Kerneguy meditated on his escape.

"What an infliction—to fence with a gouty old man, who knows not, I daresay, a trick of the sword, which was not familiar in the days of old Vincent Saviolo! or, as a change of misery, to hear him read one of those wildernesses of scenes which the English call a play, from prologue to epilogue—from Enter the first to the final *Exeunt omnes*—an unparalleled horror—a penance which would have made a dungeon darker, and added dulness even to Woodstock!"

Here he stopped and looked around, then continued his meditations—" So then, it was here that the gay old Norman secluded his pretty mistress — I warrant, without having seen her, that Rosamond Clifford was never half so handsome as that lovely Alice Lee. And what a soul there is in the girl's eye!—with what abandonment of all respects, save that expressing the interest of the moment, she poured forth her tide of enthusiasm! Were I to be long here, in spite of prudence, and half-a-dozen very venerable obstacles beside, I should be tempted to try to reconcile her to the indifferent visage of this same hard-favoured Prince.—Hard-favoured?—it is a kind of treason for one who pretends to so much loyalty, to say so of the King's features, and in my mind deserves punishment. Ah, pretty Mistress Alice! many a Mistress Alice before you has made dreadful exclamations on the irregularities of mankind, and the wickedness of the age, and ended by being glad to look out for apologies for their own share in them. But then her father—the stout old cavalier—my father's old friend—should such a thing befall, it would break his heart.—Break a pudding's-end—he has more sense. If I give his grandson a title to quarter1 the arms of England, what matter if a bar sinister is drawn across them?—Pshaw! far from an abatement, it is a point of addition—the heralds in their next visitation will place him higher in the roll for it. Then, if he did wince a little at first, does not the old traitor deserve it;—first for his disloyal intention of punching mine anointed body black and blue with his vile foils — and secondly, his atrocious complot with Will Shakspeare, a fellow as much out of date as himself, to read me to death with five acts of a historical play, or chronicle, being the piteous Life and Death of Bichard the Second?' Odds-fish, my own life is piteous enough, as I think; and my death may match it, for ought I see coming yet. Ah, but then the brother—my friend—my guide—my guard—So far as this little proposed intrigue concerns him, such practising would be thought not quite fair. But your bouncing, swaggering revengeful brothers exist only on the theatre. Your dire revenge, with which a brother persecuted a poor fellow who had seduced his sister, or been seduced by her, as the case might be, as relentlessly as if he had trodden on his toes without making an apology, is entirely out of fashion, since Dorset killed the Lord Bruce many a long year since. Pshaw! when a King is the offender, the bravest man sacrifices nothing by pocketing a little wrong which he cannot personally resent. And in France, there is not a noble house, where each individual would not cock his hat an inch higher, if they could boast of such a lefthanded alliance with the Grand Monarque." An Italian fencing-master, author of a book upon the subject of his craft, entitled *V. Savolio, his Practice* (1595). The Latin stage direction, "All go out." This melancholy story may be found in the *Guardian*. An intrigue of Lord Sackville, afterwards Earl of Dorset, was the cause of the fatal duel. Scott.

In heraldry, to divide the compartments of a shield in such a way as to indicate, through the different coats of arms, family alliances. The heraldic mark of illegitimate birth. In heraldry, a mark annexed to coat-armor, to indicate a dishonorable act or dishonorable birth.

The reputation of Shakespeare was perhaps at its lowest point during the reign of Charles II.

Such were the thoughts which rushed through the mind of Charles, at his first quitting the Lodge of Woodstock, and plunging into the forest that surrounded it. His profligate logic, however, was not the result of his natural disposition, nor received without scruple by his sound understanding. It was a train of reasoning which he had been led to adopt from his too close intimacy with the witty and profligate youth of quality by whom he had been surrounded. It arose from the evil communication with Villiers, Wilmot, Sedley, and others, whose genius was destined to corrupt that age, and the Monarch on whom its character afterwards came so much to depend. Such men, bred amidst the license of civil war, and without experiencing that curb which in ordinary times the authority of parents and relations imposes upon the headlong passions of youth, were practised in every species of vice, and could recommend it as well by precept as by example, turning into pitiless ridicule all those nobler feelings which withhold men from gratifying lawless passion. The events of the King's life had also favoured his reception of this Epicurean doctrine. He saw himself, with the highest claims to sympathy and assistance, coldly treated by the Courts which he visited, rather as a permitted suppliant, than an exiled Monarch. He beheld his own rights and claims treated with scorn and indifference; and, in the same proportion, he was reconciled to the hardhearted and selfish course of dissipation, which promised him immediate indulgence. If this was obtained at the expense of the happiness of others, should he of all men be scrupulous upon the subject, since he treated others only as the world treated him?

Louis XIV. of France, the "Grand Monarque," was at this time, however, but thirteen years old. George Villiers, the second Duke of Buckingham (1627-1688), the companion of Charles II. during his exile and at Edinburgh (see the quotation from Hume in Chapter XXI), and his favourite courtier after the Restoration. His brilliant, versatile character is depicted at length in Scott's *Peveril of the Peak*. See note in Chapter V. Sir Charles Sedley (1639-1701) the wit, poet and dramatist. His life was scandalous enough to justify Scott's placing him with this group, but he was only twelve years old in 1651.

But although the foundations of this unhappy system had been laid, the Prince was not at this early period so fully devoted to it as he was found to have become, when a door was unexpectedly opened for his restoration. On the contrary, though the train of gay reasoning which we have above stated, as if it had found vent in uttered language, did certainly arise in his mind, as that which would have been suggested by his favourite counsellors on such occasions, he recollected that what might be passed over as a peccadillo in France or the Netherlands, or turned into a diverting novel or pasquinade by the wits of his own wandering Court, was likely to have the aspect of horrid ingratitude and infamous treachery among the English gentry, and would inflict a deep, perhaps an incurable wound upon his interest, among the more aged and respectable part of his adherents. Then it occurred to him—for his own interest did not escape him, even in this mode of considering the subject — that he was in the power of the Lees, father and son, who were always understood to be at least sufficiently punctilious on the score of honour; and if they should suspect such an affront as his imagination had conceived, they could be at no loss to find means of the most ample revenge, either by their own hands, or by those of the ruling faction.

"The risk of reopening the fatal window at Whitehall, and renewing the tragedy of the Man in the Mask, were a worse penalty," was his final reflection, "than the old stool of the Scottish penance; and pretty though Alice Lee is, I cannot afford to intrigue at such a hazard. So, farewell,

Eretty maiden! unless, as sometimes has happened, thou ast a humour to throw thyself at thy King's feet, and then I am too magnanimous to refuse thee my protection. Yet, when I think of the pale clay-cold figure of the old man, as he lay last night extended before me, and imagine the fury of Albert Lee raging with impatience, his hand on a sword which only his loyalty prevents him from plunging into his sovereign's heart,—nay, the picture is too horrible! Charles must forever change his name to Joseph, even if he were strongly tempted; which may Fortune in mercy prohibit!" 1 A petty offence. A lampoon.

Charles I. was executed upon a scaffold erected before one of the windows of the banqueting room of Whitehall palace. The executioner, who was masked. According to Scott's narrative in Chapters XIX. and XX., however, Kerneguy had not seen Sir Henry Lee until after the latter's complete recovery from the shock he had suffered.

To speak the truth of a Prince, more unfortunate in his early companions, and the callousness which he acquired by his juvenile adventures and irregular mode of life, than in his natural disposition, Charles came the more readily to this wise conclusion, because he was by no means subject to those violent and engrossing passions, to gratify which, the world has been thought well lost. His amours, like many of the present day, were rather matters of habit and fashion, than of passion and affection; and, in com faring himself in this respect to his grandfather Henry V., he did neither his ancestor nor himself perfect justice. He was, to parody the words of a bard, himself actuated by the stormy passions which an intriguer often only simulates,—

None of those who loved so kindly,
None of those who loved so blindly.

An amour was with him a matter of amusement, a regular consequence, as it seemed to him, of the ordinary course of things in society. He was not at the trouble to practise seductive arts, because he had seldom found occasion to make use of them; his high rank, and the profligacy of part of the female society with which he had mingled, rendering them unnecessary. Added to this, he had, for the same reason, seldom been crossed by the obstinate interference of relations, or even of husbands, who had generally seemed not unwilling to suffer such matters to take their course.

So that, notwithstanding his total looseness of principle, and systematic disbelief in the virtue of women and the honour of men, as connected with the character of their female relatives, Charles was not a person to have studiously introduced disgrace into a family, where a conquest might have been violently disputed, attained with difficulty, and accompanied with general distress, not to mention the excitation of all fiercer passions against the author of the scandal.

Tho lines are quoted incorrectly from " Ae Fond Kiss," by Robert Burns.

But the danger of the King's society consisted in his being much of an unbeliever in the existence of such cases as were likely to be embittered by remorse on the part of the principal victim, or rendered perilous by the violent resentment of her connexions or relatives. He had even already found such things treated on the continent as matters of ordinary occurrence, subject, in all cases where a man of high influence was concerned, to an easy arrangement; and he was really, generally speaking, sceptical on the subject of severe virtue in either sex, and apt to consider it as a veil assumed by prudery in women, and hypocrisy in men, to extort a higher reward for their compliance.

While we are discussing the character of his disposition to gallantry, the Wanderer was conducted by the walk he had chosen, through several whimsical turns, until at last it brought him under the windows of Victor Lee's apartment, where he descried Alice watering and arranging some flowers placed on the Oriel window, which was easily accessible by daylight, although at night he had found it a dangerous attempt to scale it. But not Alice only, her father also shewed himself near the window and beckoned him up. The family party seemed now more promising than before, and the fugitive Prince was weary of playing battledore and shuttlecock with his conscience, and much disposed to let matters go as chance should determine.

He climbed lightly up the broken ascent, and was readily welcomed by the old knight who held activity in high honour. Alice also seemed glad to see the lively and interesting young man; and by her presence, and the unaffected mirth with which she enjoyed his sallies, he was animated to display those qualities of wit and humour, which nobody possessed in a higher degree.

His satire delighted the old gentleman, who laughed till his eyes ran over as he heard the youth, whose claims to his respect he little dreamed of, amusing him with successive imitations of the Scottish Presbyterian clergyman, of the proud and poor Hidalgo of the North, of the fierce and overweening pride and Celtic1 dialect of the mountain chief, of the slow and more pedantic Lowlander, with all of which his residence in Scotland had made him familiar. Alice also laughed and applauded, amused herself, and delighted to see that her father was so; and the whole party were in the highest glee, when Albert Lee entered, eager to find Louis Kerneguy, and to lead him away to a private colloquy with Doctor Rochecliffe, whose zeal, assiduity, and wonderful possession of information had constituted him their master-pilot in those difficult times.

1 In Spain, anyone having the rank of a gentleman; here used to indicate the "poor and proud " character of the Scotch.

It is unnecessary to introduce the reader to the minute particulars of their conference. The information obtained was so far favourable, that the enemy seemed to have had no intelligence of the King's route towards the south, and remained persuaded that he had made his escape from Bristol, as had been reported, and as had indeed been proposed; but the master of the vessel prepared for the King's passage had taken the alarm, and sailed without his royal freight. His departure, however, and the suspicion of the service in which he was engaged, served to make the belief general, that the King had gone off along with him.

But though this was cheering, the Doctor had more unpleasant tidings from the sea-coast, alleging great difficulties in securing a vessel, to which it might be fit to commit a charge so precious; and, above all, requesting his Majesty might on no account venture to approach the shore, until he should receive advice that all the previous arrangements had been completely settled.

No one was able to suggest a safer place of residence than that which he at present occupied. Colonel Everard was deemed certainly not personally unfriendly to the King; and Cromwell, as was supposed, reposed in Everard an unbounded confidence. The interior presented numberless hiding places, and secret modes of exit, known to no one but the ancient residents of the Lodge—nay, far better to Rochecliffe than to any of them; as, when Rector at the neighbouring town, his prying disposition as an antiquary had induced him to make very many researches among the old ruins—the results of which he was believed, in some instances, to have kept to himself.

1, The Highlands of Scotland were then and are still inhabited by a race in which Celtic blood predominates; the Lowlanders are of Saxon and Danish descent, like the North of England men.

To balance these conveniences, it was no doubt true, that the Parliamentary Commissioners were still at no great distance, and would be ready to resume their authority upon the first opportunity. But no one supposed such an opportunity was likely to occur; and all believed, as the influence of Cromwell and the army grew more and more predominant, that the disappointed Commissioners would attempt nothing in contradiction to his pleasure, but wait with patience an indemnification in some other quarter for their vacated commissions. Report, through the voice of Master Joseph Tomkins, stated, that they had determined, in the first place, to retire to Oxford, and were making preparations accordingly. This promised still farther to insure the security of Woodstock. It was therefore settled, that the King, under the character of Louis Kerneguy, should remain an inmate of the Lodge, until a vessel should be procured for his escape, at the port which might be esteemed the safest and most convenient.

Compare this method of soliloquy—combined with character analysis on the author's part—with passages in Shakespeare where the villain outlines his scheme in pure soliloquy, as in *Michard III., Othello,* etc. Which method do you

think more effective in prose fiction f
CHAPTER THE TWENTY-FOURTH

> The deadliest snakes are those which, twined 'mongst flowers,
> Blend their bright colouring with the varied blossoms,
> Their fierce eyes glittering like the spangled dewdrop;
> In all so like what nature has most harmless,
> That sportive innocence, which dreads no danger,
> Is poisoned unawares.
> Old Plat.

Charles (we must now give him his own name) was easily reconciled to the circumstances which rendered his residence at Woodstock advisable. No doubt he would much rather have secured his safety by making an immediate escape out of England; but he had been condemned already to many uncomfortable lurking-places, and more disagreeable disguises, as well as to long and difficult journeys, during which, between pragmatical officers of justice belonging to the prevailing party, and parties of soldiers whose officers usually took on them to act on their own warrant, risk of discovery had more than once become very imminent. He was glad, therefore, of comparative repose, and of comparative safety.

Then it must be considered, that Charles had been entirely reconciled to the society at Woodstock since he had become better acquainted with it. He had seen, that, to interest the beautiful Alice, and procure a great deal of her company, nothing more was necessary than to submit to the humours, and cultivate the intimacy, of the old cavalier her father. A few bouts at fencing, in which Charles took care not to put out his more perfect skill, and full youthful strength and activity—the endurance of a few scenes from Shakspeare, which the knight read with more zeal than taste—a little skill in music, in which the old man had been a proficient—the deference paid to a few oldfashioned opinions, at which Charles laughed in his sleeve— were all-sufficient to gain for the disguised Prince an interest in Sir Henry Lee, and to conciliate in an equal degree the good-will of his lovely daughter.

Never were there two young persons who could be said to commence this species of intimacy with such unequal advantages. Charles was a libertine, who, if he did not in cold blood resolve upon prosecuting his passion for Alice to a dishonourable conclusion, was at every moment liable to be provoked to attempt the strength of a virtue, in which he was no believer. Then Alice, on her part, hardly knew even what was implied by the word libertine or seducer. Her mother had died early in the commencement of the civil war, and she had been bred up chiefly with her brother and cousin; so that she had an unfearing and unsuspicious frankness of manner, upon which Charles was not unwilling or unlikely to put a construction favourable to his own views. Even Alice's love for her cousin— the first sensation which awakens the most innocent and simple mind to feelings of shyness and restraint towards the male sex in general—had failed to excite such an alarm in *her* bosom. They were nearly related; and Everard, though young, was several years her elder, and had, from her infancy, been an object of her respect as well as of her affection. When this early and childish intimacy ripened into youthful love, confessed and returned, still it differed in some shades from the passion existing between lovers originally strangers to each other, until their affections have been united in the ordinary course of courtship. Their love was fonder, more familiar, more perfectly confidential; purer too, perhaps, and more free from starts of passionate violence, or apprehensive jealousy.

The possibility that any one could have attempted to rival Everard in her affection was a circumstance which never occurred to Alice; and that this singular Scottish lad, whom she laughed with on account of his humour, and laughed at for his peculiarities, should be an object of danger or of caution, never once entered her imagination. The sort of intimacy to which she admitted Kerneguy was the same to which she would have received a companion of her own sex, whose manners she did not always approve, but whose society she found always amusing.

It was natural that the freedom of Alice Lee's conduct, which arose from the most perfect indifference, should pass for something approaching to encouragement in the royal gallant's apprehension, and that any resolutions he had formed against being tempted to violate the hospitality of AVoodstock, should begin to totter, as opportunities for doing so became more frequent.

These opportunities were favoured by Albert's departure from Woodstock the very day after his arrival. It had been agreed in full council with Charles and Rochecliffe, that he should go to visit his uncle Everard in the county of Kent, and, by shewing himself there, obviate any cause of suspicion which might arise from his residence at Woodstock, and remove any pretext for disturbing his father's family on account of their harbouring one who had been so lately in arms. He had also undertaken, at his own great personal risk, to visit different points on the sea-coast, and ascertain the security of different places for providing shipping for the King's leaving England.

These circumstances were alike calculated to procure the King's safety, and facilitate his escape. But Alice was thereby deprived of the presence of her brother, who would have been her most watchful guardian, but who had set down the King's light talk upon a former occasion to the gaiety of his humour, and would have thought he had done his sovereign great injustice, had he seriously suspected him of such a breach of hospitality as a dishonourable pursuit of Alice would have implied.

There were, however, two of the household at Woodstock, who appeared not so entirely reconciled with Louis Kerneguy or his purposes. The one was Bevis, who seemed, from their first unfriendly rencontre, to have kept up a pique against their new guest, which no advances on the part of Charles were able to soften. If the page was by chance left alone with his young mistress, Bevis chose always to be of the party; came close by Alice's chair, and growled audibly when the gallant drew near her. "It is a pity," said the disguised prince, "that your Bevis is not a bulldog, that we might dub him a roundhead at once— He is too handsome, too noble, too aristocratic, to nourish those inhospitable prejudices against a poor houseless cavalier. I am convinced the spirit of Pym 1 or Hampden has transmigrated into the rogue, and continues to demonstrate his hatred against royalty and all its adherents." John Pym (1584-1643). the Parliamentary leader, prominent in the impeachment of Buckingham, Strafford and Land. He was one of the " five members" whose attempted arrest by Charles I. in January. 104?, hastened the outbreak of civil war.

John Hampden (1594-1643), a statesman of great ability, and tlie noblest character. He was prominent in Parliament from 1621 onward, was one of the "five members," and was mortally wounded in the skirmish at Chalgrove Field. His fame rests chiefly upon his resistance, in 1637-38, of the collection of the obsolete tax of shipmoney, which Charles I. attempted to revive without the authority of Parliament.

Alice would then reply, that Bevis was loyal in word and deed, and only partook her father's prejudices against the Scots, which, she could not but acknowledge, were tolerably strong.

"Nay, then," said the supposed Louis, "I must find some other reason, for I cannot allow Sir Bevis's resentment to rest upon national antipathy. So we will suppose that some gallant cavalier, who wended to the wars and never returned, has adopted his shape to look back upon the haunts he left so unwillingly, and is jealous at seeing even poor Louis Kerneguy drawing near to the lady of his lost affections."—He approached her chair as he spoke, and Bevis gave one of his deep growls.

"In that case, you had best keep your distance," said Alice, laughing, "for the bite of a dog possessed by the ghost of a jealous lover cannot be very safe.

" And the King carried on the dialogue in the same strain—which, while it led Alice to apprehend nothing more serious than the apish gallantry of a fantastic boy, certainly induced the supposed Louis Kerneguy to think that he had made one of those conquests which often and easily fall to the share of sovereigns. Notwithstanding the acuteness of his apprehension, he was not sufficiently aware that the Royal Road to female favour is only open to monarchs when they travel in grand costume, and that when they woo incognito, their path of courtship is liable to the same windings and obstacles which obstruct the course of private individuals.

There was, besides Bevis, another member of the family, who kept a lookout upon Louis Kerneguy, and with no friendly eye. Phoebe Mayflower, though her experience extended not beyond the sphere of the village, yet knew the world much better than her mistress, and besides she was five years older. More knowing, she was more suspicious. She thought that odd-looking Scotch boy made more up to her young mistress than was proper for his condition of life; and, moreover, that Alice gave him a little more encouragement than Parthenia would have afforded to any such Jack-a-dandy, in the absence of Argalus—for the volume treating of the loves of these celebrated Arcadians was then the favourite study of swains and damsels throughout merry England. Entertaining such suspicions, Phoebe was at a loss how to conduct herself on the occasion, and yet resolved she would not see the slightest chance of the course of Colonel Everard's true love being obstructed, without attempting a remedy. She had a peculiar favour for Markham himself; and, moreover, he was, according to her phrase, as handsome and personable a young man as was in Oxfordshire; and this Scottish scarecrow was no more to be compared to him than chalk was to cheese. And yet she allowed that Master Girnigy had a wonderfully well-oiled tongue, and that such gallants were not to be despised. What was to be done r—she had no facts to offer, only vague suspicion; and was afraid to speak to her mistress, whose kindness, great as it was, did not, nevertheless, encourage familiarity.

She sounded Joceline; but he was, she knew not why, so deeply interested about this unlucky lad, and held his importance so high, that she could make no impression on him. To speak to the old knight, would have been to raise a general tempest. The worthy chaplain, who was, at Woodstock, grand referee on all disputed matters, would have been the damsel's most natural resource, for he was peaceful as well as moral by profession, and politic by practice. But it happened he had given Phoebe unintentional offence by speaking of her under the classical epithet of *Rustica Fidele,* the which epithet, as she understood it not, she held herself bound to resent as contumelious, and declaring she was not fonder of *& fiddle* than other folk, had ever since shunned all intercourse with Doctor Rochecliffe which she could easily avoid.

Master Tomkins was always coming and going about the house under various pretexts; but he was a roundhead, and she was too true to the cavaliers to introduce any of the enemy as parties to their internal discords; besides, he had talked to Phoebe herself in a manner which induced her to decline everything in the shape of familiarity with him. Lastly, Oavaliero Wildrake might have been consulted; but Phoebe had her own reasons for saying, as she did with some emphasis, that Cavaliero Wildrake was an impudent London rake. At length she resolved to communicate her suspicions to the party having most interest in verifying or confuting them.

Rustica Phidyle, to whom Horace addressed the twenty-third Ode of the third book of his *Odes.*—A similar play upon the words " faithful rustic" occurs in *Peveril of the Peak.*

"I'll let Master Markham Everard know that there is a wasp buzzing about his honey-comb," said Phoebe; "and, moreover, that I know that this young Scotch Scapegrace shifted himself out of a woman's into a man's dress at Goody Green's, and gave Goody Green's Dolly a gold-piece to say nothing about it; and no more she did to any one but me, and she knows best herself whether she gave change for the gold or not—but Master Louis is a saucy jackanapes, and like enough to ask it."

Three or four days elapsed while matters continued in this condition—the disguised Prince sometimes thinking on the intrigue which Fortune seemed to have thrown in his way for his amusement, and taking advantage of such opportunities as occurred to increase his intimacy with Alice Lee; but much oftener harassing Doctor Rochecliffe with questions about the possibility of escape, which the good man finding himself unable to answer, secured his leisure against royal importunity, by retreating into the various unexplored recesses of the Lodge, known perhaps only to himself, who had been for nearly a score of years employed in writing the Wonders of Woodstock.

It chanced on the fourth day, that some trifling circumstance had called the knight abroad; and he had left the young Scotsman, now familiar in the family, along with Alice, in the parlour of Victor Lee. Thus situated, he thought the time not unpropitious for entering upon a strain of gallantry, of a kind which might be called experimental, such as is practised by the Croats in skirmishing, when they keep bridle in hand, ready to attack the enemy, or canter off without coming to close quarters, as circumstances may recommend. After using for nearly ten minutes a sort of metaphysical jargon, which might, according to Alice's pleasure, have been interpreted either into gallantry, or the language of serious pretension, and when he supposed her engaged in fathoming his meaning, he had the mortification to find, by a single and brief Light cavalry in the Imperialist army during the Thirty Years' War, recruited from Croatia, a Slavic country southwest of Hungary.

Question, that he had been totally unattended to, and that dice was thinking on anything at the moment rather than the sense of what he had been saying. She asked him if he could tell what it was o'clock, and this with an air of real curiosity concerning the lapse of time, which put coquetry wholly out of the question.

"I will go look at the sundial, Mistress Alice," said the gallant, rising and colouring, through a sense of the contempt with which he thought himself treated.

"You will do me pleasure, Master Kerneguy," said Alice, without the least consciousness of the indignation she had excited.

Master Louis Kerneguy left the room accordingly, not, however, to procure the information required, but to vent his anger and mortification, and to swear, with more serious purpose than he had dared to do before, that Alice should rue her insolence. Good-natured as he was, he was still a prince, unaccustomed to contradiction, far less to contempt, and his self-pride felt, for the moment, wounded to the quick. With a hasty step he plunged into the Chase, only remembering his own safety so far as to choose the deeper and sequestered avenues, where, walking on with the speedy and active step, which his recovery from fatigue now permitted him to exercise according to his wont, he solaced his angry purposes by devising schemes of revenge on the insolent country coquette, from which no consideration of hospitality was in future to have weight enough to save her.

The irritated gallant passed

The dial-stone, aged and green, without deigning to ask it a single question; nor could it have satisfied his curiosity if he had, for no sun happened to shine at the moment. He then hastened forward, muffling himself in his cloak, and assuming a stooping and slouching gait, which diminished his apparent height. He was soon involved in the deep and dim alleys of the wood, into which he had insensibly plunged himself, and was traversing it at a great rate, without having any distinct idea in what direction he was going, when suddenly his course was arrested, first by a loud hollo, and then by a summons to stand, accompanied by what seemed still more startling and extraordinary, the touch of a cane upon his shoulder, imposed in a good-humoured but somewhat imperious manner.

There were few symptoms of recognition which would have been welcomed at this moment; but the appearance of the person who had thus arrested his course was least of all that he could have anticipated as timely or agreeable. When he turned, on receiving the signal, he beheld himself close to a young man, nearly six feet in height, well made in joint and limb, but the gravity of whose apparel, although handsome and gentlemanlike, and a sort of precision in his habit, from the cleanness and stiffness of his band to the unsullied purity of his Spanish-leather shoes, bespoke a love of order which was foreign to the impoverished and vanquished cavaliers, and proper to the habits of those of the victorious party, who could afford to dress themselves handsomely; and whose rule—that is, such as regarded the higher and more respectable classes— enjoined decency and sobriety of garb and deportment. There was yet another weight against the Prince in the scale, and one still more characteristic of the inequality in the comparison under which he seemed to labour. There was strength in the muscular form of the stranger who had brought him to this involuntary parley, authority and determination in his brow, a long rapier on the left, and a poniard or-dagger on the right side of his belt, and a pair of pistols stuck into it, which would have been sufficient to give the unknown the advantage (Louis Kerneguy having no weapon but his sword), even had his personal strength approached nearer than it did to that of the person by whom he was thus suddenly stopped.

Bitterly regretting the thoughtless fit of passion that brought him into his present situation, but especially the want of the pistols he had left behind, and which do so much to place bodily strength and weakness upon an equal footing, Charles yet availed himself of the courage and

Eresence of mind, in which few of his unfortunate family ad for centuries been deficient. He stood firm and without motion, his cloak still wrapped round the lower part of his face, to give time for explanation, in case he was mistaken for some other person.

This coolness produced its effect; for the other party said, with doubt and surprise on his part, "Joceline Joliffe, is it not?—if I know not Joceline Joliffe, I should at least know my own cloak."

"I am not Joceline Joliffe, as you may see, sir," said Kerneguy, calmly, drawing himself erect to shew the difference of size, and dropping the cloak from his face and person.

"Indeed!" replied the stranger, in surprise; "then, Sir Unknown, I have to express my regret at having used my cane in intimating that I wished you to stop. From that dress, which I certainly recognise for my own, I concluded you must be Joceline, in whose custody I had left my habit at the Lodge."

"If it had been Joceline, sir," replied the supposed Kerneguy, with perfect composure, "methinks you should not have struck so hard."

The other party was obviously confused by the steady calmness with which he was encountered. The sense of politeness dictated, in the first place, an apology for a mistake, when he thought he had been tolerably certain of the person. Master Kerneguy was not in a situation to be punctilious; he bowed gravely as indicating his acceptance of the excuse offered, then turned, and walked, as he conceived, towards the Lodge; though he had traversed the woods, which were cut with various alleys in different directions, too hastily to be certain of the real course which he wished to pursue.

He was much embarrassed to find that this did not get him rid of the companion whom he had thus involuntarily acquired. Walked he slow, walked he fast, his friend in the genteel but puritanic habit, strong in person, and well armed, as we have described him, seemed determined to keep him company, and, without attempting to join, or enter into conversation, never suffered him to outstrip his surveillance for more than two or three yards. The Wanderer mended his pace; but, although he was then, in his youth, as afterwards in his riper age, one of the best walkers in Britain, the stranger, without advancing his pace to a run, kept fully equal to him, and his persecution became so close and constant, and inevitable, that the pride and fear of Charles were both alarmed, and he began to think "His favourite bodily exercise was walking."—*Diet. Nat. Biog.* that, whatever the danger might be of a single-handed rencontre, he would nevertheless have a better bargain of this tall satellite if they settled the debate betwixt them in the forest, than if they drew near any place of habitation, where the man in authority was likely to find friends and concurrents.

Betwixt anxiety, therefore, vexation, and anger, Charles faced suddenly round on his pursuer, as they reached a small narrow glade, which led to the little meadow over which presided the King's Oak, the ragged and scathed branches and gigantic trunk of which formed a vista to the little wild avenue.

"Sir," said he to his pursuer, "you have already been guilty of one piece of impertinence towards me. You nave apologized; and knowing no reason why you should distinguish me as an object of incivility, I have accepted your excuse without scruple. Is there anything remains to be settled betwixt us, which causes you to follow me in this manner? If so, I shall be glad to make it a subject of explanation or satisfaction, as the case may admit of. I think you can owe me no malice; for I never saw you before to my knowledge. If you can give any good reason for asking it, I am willing to render you personal satisfaction. If your purpose is merely impertinent curiosity, I let you know that I will not suffer myself to be dogged in my private walks by any one."

"When I recognise my own cloak on another man's shoulders," replied the stranger dryly, "methinks I have a natural right to follow, and see what becomes of it; for know, sir, though I have been mistaken as to the wearer, yet I am confident I had as good a right to stretch my cane across the cloak you are muffled in, as ever had any one to brush his own garments. If, therefore, we are to be friends, I must ask, for instance, how you came by that cloak, and where you are going with it? I shall otherwise make bold to stop you, as one who has sufficient commission to do so."

"Oh, unhappy cloak," thought the Wanderer, "ay, and thrice unhappy the idle fancy that sent me here with it wrapped around my nose, to pick quarrels and attract observation, when quiet and secrecy were peculiarly essential to my safety!

Associates. "If you will allow me to guess, sir," continued the stranger, who was no other than Markham Everard, "I will convince you, that you are better known than you think for."

"Now, Heaven forbid!" prayed the party addressed, in silence, but with as much devotion as ever he applied to a prayer in his life. Yet even in this moment of extreme urgency, his courage and composure did not fail; and he recollected it was of the utmost importance not to seem startled, and to answer so as, if possible, to lead the dangerous companion with whom he had met, to confess the extent of his actual knowledge or suspicions concerning him.

"If you know me, sir," he said, "and are a gentleman, as your appearance promises, you cannot be at a loss to discover to what accident you must attribute my wearing these clothes, which you say are yours."

"Oh, sir," replied Colonel Everard, his wrath in no sort turned away by the mildness of the stranger's answer, "we have learned our Ovid's Metamorphoses, and we know for what purposes young men of quality travel in disguise—we know that even female attire is resorted to on certain occasions—We have heard of Vertumnus and Pomona."

The Monarch, as he weighed these words, again uttered a devout prayer, that this ill-looking affair might have no deeper root than the jealousy of some admirer of Alice Lee, promising to himself, that, devotee as he was to the fair sex, he would make no scruple of renouncing the fairest of Eve's daughters in order to get out of the present dilemma.

"Sir," he said, "you seem to be a gentleman. I have no objection to tell you as such, that I also am of that class."

"Or somewhat higher perhaps?" said Everard.

"A gentleman," replied Charles, "is a term which comprehends all ranks entitled to armorial bearings —A duke, a lord, a prince, is no more than a gentleman; and if in misfortune, as I am, he may be glad if that general term of courtesy is allowed him." One of the chief works of Publius Ovidius Naso (43 B.C. -17 or 18 A.D.), the Roman poet. Vertumnus was an Etruscan and Roman divinity who assumed various disguises in order to win the love of Pomona, goddess of fruittrees. Coat of arms: the whole heraldic display to which a person is entitled.

"Sir," replied Everard, " I have no purpose to entrap you to any acknowledgment fatal to your own safety,—nor do I hold it my business to be active in the arrest of private individuals, whose perverted sense of national duty may have led them into errors, rather to be pitied than punished by candid men. But if those who have brought civil war and disturbance into their native country, proceed to carry dishonour and disgrace into the bosom of families — if they attempt to carry on their private debaucheries to the injury of the hospitable roofs which afford them refuge from the consequences of their public crimes, do you think, my lord, that we shall bear it with patience?"

"If it is your purpose to quarrel with me," said the Prince, "speak it out at once like a gentleman. You have the advantage, no doubt, of arms, but it is not that odds which will induce me to fly from a single man. If, on the other hand, you are disposed to hear reason, I tell you in calm words, that I neither suspect the offence to which you allude, nor comprehend why you give me the title of my lord."

"You deny, then, being the Lord Wilmot?" said Bverard.

"I may do so most safely," said the Prince.

"Perhaps you rather style yourself Earl of Rochester? We heard that the issuing of some such patent by the King of Scots was a step which your ambition proposed."

"Neither lord nor earl am I, as sure as I have a Christian soul to be saved. My name is" "Do not degrade yourself by unnecessary falsehood, my lord; and that to a single man, who, I promise you, will not invoke public justice to assist his own good sword should he see cause to use it. Can you look at that ring, and deny that you are Lord Wilmot?"

He handed to the disguised Prince a ring which he took from his purse, and his opponent instantly knew it for the same he had dropped into Alice's pitcher at the fountain, obeying only, though imprudently, the gallantry of the moment, in giving a pretty gem to a handsome girl, whom he had accidentally frightened.

"I know the ring," he said; "it has been in my possession. How it should prove me to be Lord Wilmot, I cannot conceive; and beg to say, it bears false witness against me." A privilege or patent of nobility, granted by a royal document known as " letters patent."

"You shall seethe evidence," answered Everard; and resuming the ring, he pressed a spring ingeniously contrived in the collet1 of the setting, on which the stone flew back, and shewed within it the cipher of Lord Wilmot beautifully engraved in miniature, with a coronet— "What say you now, sir?"

"That probabilities are no proofs," said the Prince; "there is nothing here save what can be easily accounted for. I am the son of a Scottish nobleman, who was mortally wounded and made prisoner at Worcester fight. When he took leave, and bid me fly, he gave me the few valuables he possessed, and that among others. I have heard him talk of having changed rings with Lord Wilmot, on some occasion in Scotland, but I never knew the trick of the gem which you have shewn me."

In this it may be necessary to say, Charles spoke very truly; nor would he have parted with it in the way he did, had he suspected it would be easily recognised. He proceeded after a minute's pause:—" Once more, sir,—I have told you much that concerns my safety—if you are generous, you will let me pass, and I may do you on some future day as good service. If you mean to arrest me, you must do so here, and at your own peril, for I will neither walk farther your way, nor permit you to dog me on mine. If you let me pass, I will thank you—if not, take to your weapon. "

"Young gentleman," said Colonel Everard, "whether you be actually the gay young nobleman for whom I took you, you have made me uncertain; but, intimate as you say your family has been with him, I have little doubt that you are proficient in the school of debauchery, of which Wilmot and Villiers are professors, and their hopeful Master a graduated student. Your conduct at Woodstock, where you have rewarded the hospitality of the family by meditating the most deadly wound to their honour, has proved you too apt a scholar in such an academy. I intended only to warn you on this subject—it will be your own fault if I add chastisement to admonition." That part of the ring which holds the seal, or jewel.

The form of the coronet indicated the degree of rank of its bearer. That of an earl, for instance, showed eight pearls raised on golden spires between eight small golden leaves.

"Warn me, sir?" said the Prince, indignantly, "and chastisement! This is presuming more on my patience than is consistent with your own safety—Draw, sir."—So saying, he laid his hand on his sword.

"My religion," said Everard, "forbids me to be rash in shedding blood—Go home, sir—be wise—consult the dictates of honour as well as prudence. Respect the honour of the House of Lee, and know there is one nearly allied to it, by whom your motions will be called to severe account."

"Aha!" said the Prince, with a bitter laugh, "I see the whole matter now—we have our roundheaded Colonel, our puritan cousin, before us—the man of texts and morals, whom Alice Lee laughs at so heartily. If your religion, sir, prevents you from giving satisfaction, it should prevent you from offering insult to a person of honour."

The passions of both were now fully up—they drew mutually, and began to fight, the Colonel relinquishing the advantage he could have obtained by the use of his fire-arms. A thrust of the arm, or a slip of the foot, might, at the moment, have changed the destinies of Britain, when the arrival of a third party broke off the combat.

Upon what ground is Everard's conduct in this chapter reconcilable with his previously expressed sentiments about duelling? Find instances of duels similarly interrupted in Scott's other novels, as in *Waverley, Kenilioorth, Bob Boy,* etc.

CHAPTER THE TWENTY-FIFTH

Stay—for the King has thrown his warder down.
   Richard II.

The combatants whom we left engaged at the end of the last chapter made mutual passes at each other with apparently equal skill and courage. Charles had been too often in action, and too long a party as well as a victim to civil war, to find anything new or surprising in being obliged to defend himself with his own hands; and Everard had been distinguished, as well for his personal bravery, as for the other properties of a commander. But the arrival of a third party prevented the tragic conclusion of a combat, in which the success of either party must have given him much cause for regretting his victory.

It was the old knight himself, who arrived, mounted upon a forest pony, for the war and sequestration had left him no steed of a more dignified description. He thrust himself between the combatants, and commanded them on their lives to hold. So soon as a glance from one to the other had ascertained to him whom he had to deal with, he demanded, "Whether the devils of Woodstock whom folk talked about had got possession of them both, that they were tilting at each other within the verge of the royal liberties?1—Let me tell both of you," he said, "that while old Henry Lee is at Woodstock, the immunities of the Park shall be maintained as much as if the King were still on the throne. None shall fight duellos here, excepting the stags in their season. Put up, both of you, or I shall lug out as thirdsman, and prove perhaps the worst devil of the three!—As Will says—

I'll so maul you and your toasting-irons,
That you shall think the devil has come from hell." In the immediate neighbourhood of a royal residence certain immunities and privileges were allowed, and duelling was forbidden. «Draw the sword. *King John,* IV., 3, 99, 100.

The combatants desisted from their encounter, but stood looking at each other sullenly, as men do in such a situation, each unwilling to seem to desire peace more than the other, and averse therefore to be the first to sheathe his sword.

"Return your weapons, gentlemen, upon the spot,"said the knight yet more peremptorily, "one and both of you, or you will have something to do with me, I promise you. You may be thankful times are changed. I have known them such, that your insolence might have cost each of you your right hand, if not redeemed with a round sum of money. Nephew, if you do not mean to alienate me for ever, I command you to put up Master Kerneguy, you are my guest. I request of you not to do me the insult of remaining with your sword drawn, where it is my duty to see peace observed."

"I obey you, Sir Henry," said the King, sheathing his rapier—" I hardly indeed know wherefore I was assaulted by this gentleman. I assure you, none respects the King's person or privileges more than myself—though the devotion is somewhat out of fashion."

"We may find a place to meet, sir," replied Everard, "where neither the royal person nor privileges can be offended."

"Faith, very hardly, sir," said Charles, unable to suppress the rising jest—" I mean, the King has so few followers, that the loss of the least of them might be some small damage to him; but, risking all that, I will meet you wherever there is fair field for a poor cavalier to get off in safety, if he has the luck in fight."

Sir Henry Lee's first idea had been fixed upon the insult offered to the royal demesne; he now began to turn them towards the safety of his kinsman, and of the young royalist, as he deemed him. "Gentlemen," he said, "I must insist on this business being put to a final end. Nephew Markham, is this your return for my condescension in coming back to Woodstock on your warrant, that you should take an opportunity to cut the throat of my guest?"

"If you knew his purpose as well as I do,"—said Markham, and then paused, conscious that he might only incense his uncle without convincing him, as anything he might say of Kerneguy's addresses to Alice was likely to be imputed to his own jealous suspicions—he looked on the ground, therefore, and was silent.

"And you, Master Kerneguy," said Sir Henry, "can you give me any reason why you seek to take the life of this young man, in whom, though unhappily forgetful of his loyalty and duty, I must yet take some interest, as my nephew by affinity?"

"I was not aware the gentleman enjoyed that honour, which certainly would have protected him from my sword," answered Kerneguy. "But the quarrel is his; nor can I tell any reason why he fixed it upon me, unless it were the difference of our political opinions."

"You know the contrary," said Everard; "you know that I told you you were safe from me as a fugitive royalist — and your last words shewed you were at no loss to guess my connection with Sir Henry. That, indeed, is of little consequence. I should debase myself did I use the relationship as a means of protection from you, or any one."

As they thus disputed, neither choosing to approach the real cause of quarrel, Sir Henry looked from the one to the other, with a peace-making countenance, exclaiming—

'' Why, what an intricate impeach is this?
I think you both have drunk of Circe's oup.

Come, my young masters, allow an old man to mediate between you. I am not short-sighted in such matters—The mother of mischief is no bigger than a gnat's wing; and I have known fifty instances in my own day, when, as Will says—

Gallants have been confronted hardily,

In single opposition, hand to hand, in which, after the field was fought, no one could remember the cause of quarrel Tush! a small thing will do it—the taking of the wall—or the gentle rub of the shoulder in passing each other, or a hasty word, or a misconceived gesture—Come, forget your cause of quarrel, be what it will—you have had your breathing, and though you put up your rapiers unbloodied, that was no default of yours, but by command of your elder, and one who had right to use authority. In Malta, where the duello is punctiliously well understood, the persons engaged in a single combat are bound to halt on the command of a knight, or priest, or lady, and the quarrel so interrupted is held as honourably terminated, and may not be revived. —Nephew, it is, I think, impossible that you can nourish spleen against this young gentleman for having fought for his King. Hear my honest proposal, Markham—You know I bear no malice, though I have some reason to be offended with you—Give the young man your hand in friendship, and we will back to the Lodge, all three together, and drink a cup of sack in token of reconciliation." The enchantress of Greek mythology, who transformed men into beasts through her magic draughts. Ulysses came in his wanderings to her island, and remained a year. *Comedy of Errors,* V., 1, 269, 270. The second line is from Shakespeare's 1 *Henry IV.,* I., 3, 99.

Markham Everard found himself unable to resist this approach towards kindness on his uncle's part. He suspected, indeed, what was partly the truth, that it was not entirely from reviving good will, but also, that his uncle thought, by such attention, to secure his neutrality at least, if not his assistance, for the safety of the fugitive royalist. He was sensible that he was placed in an awkward predicament; and that he might incur the suspicions of his own party, for holding intercourse even with a near relation, who harboured such guests. But, on the other hand, he thought his services to the Commonwealth had been of sufficient importance to outweigh whatever envy might urge on that topic. Indeed, although the Civil War had divided families much, and in many various ways, yet when it seemed ended by the triumph of the republicans, the rage of political hatred began to relent, and the ancient ties of kindred and friendship regained at least a part of their former influence. Many reunions were formed; and those who, like Everard, adhered to the conquering party, often exerted themselves for the protection of their deserted relatives.

As these things rushed through his mind, accompanied with the prospect of a renewed intercourse with Alice Lee, by means of which he might be at hand to protect her against every chance, either of injury or insult, he held out his hand to the supposed Scottish page, saying at the same time, "That, for his part, he was very ready to forget the cause of quarrel, or rather, to consider it as arising out of Malta was held by the Knights of St. John from 1530 to 1798, when it was taken by Napoleon. A strict code of military honour prevailed there. a misapprehension, and to offer Master Kerneguy such friendship as might exist between honourable men, who had embraced different sides in politics."

Unable to overcome the feeling of personal dignity, which prudence recommended to him to forget, Louis Kerneguy in return bowed low, but without accepting Everard's proffered hand.

"He had no occasion," he said, "to make any exertions to forget the cause of quarrel, for he had never been able to comprehend it; but as he had not shunned the gentleman's resentment, so he was now willing to embrace and return any degree of his favour, with which he might be pleased to honour him."

Everard withdrew his hand with a smile, and bowed in return to the salutation of the page, whose stiff reception of his advances he imputed to the proud pettish disposition of a Scotch boy, trained up in extravagant ideas of family consequence and personal importance, which his acquaintance with the world had not yet been sufficient to dispel.

Sir Henry Lee, delighted with the termination of the quarrel, which he supposed to be in deep deference to his own authority, and not displeased with the opportunity of renewing some acquaintance with his nephew, who had, notwithstanding his political demerits, a warmer interest in his affections than he was, perhaps, himself aware of, said, in a tone of consolation, "Never be mortified, young gentlemen. I protest it went to my heart to part you, when I saw you stretching yourselves so handsomely, and in fair love of honour, without any malicious or blood-thirsty thoughts. I promise you, had it not been for my duty as Ranger here, and sworn to the office, I would rather have been your umpire than your hindrance.—But a finished quarrel is a forgotten quarrel; and your tilting should have no further consequence excepting the appetite it may have given you."

So saying, he urged forward his pony, and moved in triumph towards the Lodge by the nearest alley. His feet almost touching the ground, the ball of his toe just resting in the stirrup,—the forepart of the thigh brought round to the saddle,—the heels turned outwards, and sunk as much as possible,—his body precisely erect,—the reins properly and systematically divided in his left hand, his right holding a riding-rod diagonally pointed towards the horse's left ear, —he seemed a champion of the *manige,* fit to have reined Bucephalus himself. His youthful companions, who attended on either hand like equerries, could scarcely suppress a smile at the completely adjusted and systematic posture of the rider, contrasted with the wild and diminutive appearance of the pony, with its shaggy coat, and long tail and main, and its keen eyes sparkling like red coals from amongst the mass of hair which fell over its small countenance. If the reader has the Duke of Newcastle's book on horsemanship *(splendida moles /)* he may have some idea of the figure of the good knight, if he can conceive such a figure as one of the cavaliers there represented, seated in all the graces of his art, on a Welsh or Exmoor pony, in its native savage state, without grooming or discipline of any kind; the ridicule being greatly enhanced by the disproportion of size betwixt the animal and its rider.

Perhaps the knight saw their wonder, for the first words he said after they left the ground were, "Pixie, though small, is mettlesome, gentlemen " (here he contrived that Pixie should himself corroborate the assertion by executing a gambade),—" he is diminutive, but full of spirit;—indeed, save that I am somewhat too large for an elfin horseman" (the knight was upwards of six feet high), "I should remind myself, when I mount him, of the Fairy King, as described by Mike Drayton:—

Himself he on an earwig set,
Yet scarce upon his back could get,
So oft and high he did curvet, Ere he himself did settle.
He made him stop, and turn, and bound,
To gallop, and to trot the round,
He scarce could stand on any ground,
He was so full of mettle." The art of horsemanship.
The favourite horse of Alexander the Great, which no one else could manage. Officers in charge of the horses in the establishment of a prince or a nobleman. William Cavendish (1592-1676), Earl and Duke of Newcastle, an ardent Royalist. His book. *La UHhode et Invention Nounelle de dresser les (Jhevuux* (Antwerp, 1657), was adorned with very fine engravings. It was not among Scott's own books at Abbotsford. The great moor in Devonshire. See Blackmore's *Lorna Doone.* A leap or caper.
'Michael Drayton (1563-1631), the poet, author among other works of *PolyoHrion,* a poetical-geographical description of Great Britain, and a fanciful poem, *Nymphidia,* from which the quotation in the text is made.
"My old friend, Pixie," said Everard, stroking the pony's neck, "I am glad that he has survived all these bustling days—Pixie must be above twenty years old, Sir Henry?"
"Above twenty years, certainly. Yes, nephew Markham, war is a whirlwind in a plantation, which only spares what is least worth leaving. Old Pixie and his old master have survived many a tall fellow, and many a great horse —neither of them good for much themselves. Yet, as Will says, an old man can do somewhat. So Pixie and I still survive."

So saying, he again contrived that Pixie should shew some remnants of activity.

"Still survive?" said the young Scot, completing the sentence which the good knight had left unfinished—" ay, still survive,

To witch the world with noble horsemanship."

Everard coloured, for he felt the irony; but not so his uncle, whose simple vanity never permitted him to doubt the sincerity of the compliment.

"Are you avised of that?" he said. In King James's time, indeed, I have appeared in the tilt-yard, and there you might have said—

You saw young Harry with his beaver up.

As to seeing *old* Harry, why" Here the knight paused, and looked as a bashful man in labour of a pun—" As to old Harry—why, you might as well see the *devil.* You take me, Master Kerneguy— the devil, you know, is my namesake— ha—ha—ha!—Cousin Everard, I hope your precision is not startled by an innocent jest?"

He was so delighted with the applause of both his companions, that he recited the whole of the celebrated passage referred to, and concluded with defying the present age, bundle all its wits, Donne, Cowley, Waller,' and the rest of them together, to produce a poet of a tenth part of the genius of old Will.
2 *Henry V., TV.,* 3, 82. 1 *Henry IV.,TV. ,1,* 110. Assured. 1 *Henry IV.,* IV., 1, 104. Dr. John Donne (1573-1631), the poet and divine, famous for the frigid conceits in which his verse abounded. Abraham Cowley (1618-1667), a Royalist whose poetry was in high favour during his own lifetime. 'See note in Chapter V.

"Why, we are said to have one of his descendants among us—Sir William D'Avenant," said Louis Kerneguy; "and many think him as clever a fellow."

"What!" exclaimed Sir Henry—"Will D'Avenant, whom I knew in the North, an officer under Newcastle, when the Marquis lay before Hull?—why, he was an honest cavalier, and wrote good doggerel enough; but how came he a-kin to Will Shakspeare, I trow?"

"Why," replied the young Scot, "by the surer side of the house, and after the old fashion, if D'Avenant speaks truth. It seems that his mother was a good-looking, laughing, buxom mistress of an inn between Stratford and London, at which Will Shakspeare often quartered as he went down to his native town; and that out of friendship and gossipred, as we say in Scotland, Will Shakspeare became godfather to Will D'Avenant; and not contented with this spiritual affinity, the younger Will is for establishing some claim to a natural one, alleging that his mother was a great admirer of wit, and there were no bounds to her complaisance for men of genius."

"Out upon the hound!" said Colonel Everard; "would he purchase the reputation of descending from poet, or from prince, at the expense of his mother's good fame?— his nose ought to be slit."

"That would be difficult," answered the disguised Prince, recollecting the peculiarity of the bard's countenance, f

"Will D'Avenant the son of Will Shakspeare!" said the knight, who had not yet recovered his surprise at the enormity of the pretension; "why, it reminds me of a verse in the puppetshow of Phaeton, where the hero complains to his mother— This gossiping tale is to be found in the variorum Shakspeare. D'Avenant did not much mind throwing out hints, in which he sacrificed his mother's character to his desire of being held a descendant from the admirable Shakspeare. Scott.
f D'Avenant actually wanted the nose, the foundation of many a jest of the day Scott Sir William Davenant 1005-1008). poet and dramatist lie was made

poet laureate in 1038, and was much at Court after the Restoration. Spiritual affinity.
Besides, by all the village boys I am shamed;
You the Sun's son, you rascal, you be d—d!

I never heard such unblushing assurance in my life!— Will D'Avenant the son of the brightest and best poet that ever was, is, or will be?—But I crave your pardon, nephew —You, I believe, love no stage plays."

"Nay, I am not altogether so precise as you would make me, uncle. I have loved them perhaps too well in my time, and now I condemn them not altogether, or in gross, though I approve not their excesses and extravagances. — I cannot, even in Shakspeare, but see many things both scandalous to decency and prejudicial to good manners, many things which tend to ridicule virtue, or to recommend vice,—at least to mitigate the hideousness of its features. I cannot think these fine poems are a useful study, and especially for the youth of either sex, in which bloodshed is pointed out as the chief occupation of the men, and intrigue as the sole employment of the women."

In making these observations, Everard was simple enough to think that he was only giving his uncle an opportunity of defending a favourite opinion, without offending him by a contradiction, which was so limited and mitigated. But here, as on other occasions, he forgot how obstinate his uncle was in his views, whether of religion, policy, or taste, and that it would be as easy to convert him to the Presbyterian form of government, or engage him to take the abjuration oath, as to shake his belief in Shakspeare. There was another peculiarity in the good knight's mode of arguing, which Everard, being himself of a plain and downright character, and one whose religions tenets were in some degree unfavourable to the suppressions and simulations often used in society, could never perfectly understand. Sir Henry, sensible of his natural heat of temper, was wont scrupulously to guard against it, and would for some time, when in fact much offended, conduct a debate with all the external appearance of composure, till the violence of his feelings would rise so high as to overcome and bear away the artificial barriers opposed to it, and rush down upon the adversary with accumulating wrath. It thus frequently happened, that, like a wily old general, he retreated in the face of his disputant in good order and by degrees, with so moderate a degree of resistance, as to draw on his antagonist's pursuit to the spot, where, at length, making a sudden and unexpected attack, with horse, foot, and artillery at once, he seldom failed to confound the enemy, though he might not overthrow him.

We observe this couplet in Fielding's farce of *Tumbledown-Dick,* founded on the same classical story. As it was current in the time of the Commonwealth, it must have reached the author of *Tom Jones* by tradition—for no one will suspect the present author of making the anachronism. Scott. A dramatic exhibition in which puppets represent the actors, like a Punch and Judy show. In Greek mythology, the son of Phoebus the sun-god. He obtained permission from his father to drive the latter's chariot (the sun) across the heavens, but could not check the horses. The pledge of renunciation of the exiled Stuart family. It first appears in 1690.—Low and Pulling's *Diet, of Eng. Hist*.

It was on this principle, therefore, that, hearing Everard's last observation, he disguised his angry feelings, and answered, with a tone where politeness was called in to keep guard upon passion, "That undoubtedly the Presbyterian gentry had given, through the whole of these unhappy times, such proofs of an humble, unaspiring, and unambitious desire of the public good, as entitled them to general credit for the sincerity of those very strong scruples which they entertained against works, in which the noblest sentiments of religion and virtue,—sentiments which might convert hardened sinners, and be placed with propriety in the mouths of dying saints and martyrs,—happened, from the rudeness and coarse taste of the times, to be mixed with some broad jests, and similar matter, which lay not much in the way, excepting of those who painfully sought such stuff out, that they might use it in vilifying what was in itself deserving of the highest applause. But what he wished especially to know from his nephew was, whether any of those gifted men, who had expelled the learned scholars and deep divines of the Church of England from the pulpit, and now flourished in their stead, received any inspiration from the muses (if he might use so profane a term without offence to Colonel Everard), or whether they were not as sottishly and brutally averse from elegant letters, as they were from humanity and common sense?"

Colonel Everard might have guessed, by the ironical tone in which this speech was delivered, what storm was mustering within his uncle's bosom—nay, he might have conjectured the state of the old knight's feelings from his emphasis on the word Colonel, by which epithet, as that which most connected his nephew with the party he hated, he never distinguished Everard, unless when his wrath was rising; while, on the contrary, when disposed to be on good terms with him, he usually called him Kinsman, or Nephew Markham. Indeed, it was under a partial sense that this was the case, and in the hope to see his cousin Alice, that the Colonel forebore making any answer to the harangue of his uncle, which had concluded just as the old knight had alighted at the door of the Lodge, and was entering the hall, followed by his two attendants.

Phoebe at the same time made her appearance in the hall, and received orders to bring some " beverage " for the gentlemen. The Hebe of 'Woodstock failed not to recognise and welcome Everard by an almost imperceptible courtesy; but she did not serve her interest, as she designed, when she asked the knight, as a question of course, whether he commanded the attendance of Mistress Alice. A stern *JVo* was the decided reply; and the ill-timed interference seemed to increase his previous irritation against Everard for his depreciation of Shakspeare. "I would insist,"—said Sir Henry, resuming the obnoxious subject, "were it fit for a poor disbanded cavalier to use such a phrase towards a commander of the conquering army—upon knowing whether the convulsion which has sent us saints and prophets without end, has not also afforded us a poet with enough both of gifts and grace to outshine poor old Will, the oracle and idol of us blinded and carnal cavaliers?"

"Surely, sir," replied Colonel Everard, "I know verses written by a friend of the Commonwealth, and those, too, of a dramatic character, which, weighed in an impartial scale, might equal even the poetry of Shakspeare, and which are free from the fustian and indelicacy with which that great bard was sometimes content to feed the coarse appetites of his barbarous audience."

"Indeed!" said the knight, keeping down his wrath with difficulty. "I should like to be acquainted with this master-piece of poetry!—May we ask the name of this distinguished person?"

"It must be Vicars, or Withers at least," said the feigned page.

"No, sir," replied Everard, "nor Drummond of Hawthornden, nor Lord Stirling neither. And yet the verses will vindicate what I say, if you will make allowance for indifferent recitation, for I am better accustomed to speak to a battalion than to those who love the muses. The speaker is a lady benighted, who, having lost her way in a pathless forest, at first expresses herself agitated by the supernatural fears to which her situation gave rise."

"A play, too, and written by a roundhead author!" said Sir Henry, in surprise.

"A dramatic production, at least," replied his nephew; and began to recite simply, but with feeling, the lines now so well known, but which had then obtained no celebrity, the fame of the author resting upon the basis rather of his polemical and political publications, than on the poetry doomed in after days to support the eternal structure of his immortality.

"These thoughts may startle, but will not astound

The virtuous mind, that ever walks attended
By a strong-siding champion, Conscience."

"My own opinion, nephew Markham, my own opinion," said Sir Henry, with a burst of admiration; "better expressed, but just what I said when the scoundrelly roundheads pretended to see ghosts at Woodstock—Go on, I prithee." *1* John Vicars (1582-1652), a Puritan zealot, author of a few poems.

"George Wither, or Withers (1588-1667), a poet and satirist of some note, who served as a Royalist captain of horse, and afterwards as a major in the Parliamentary army.
William Drummond (1585-1649), a Scottish poet living at Hawthornden, near Edinburgh, where he at one time entertained Ben Jonson. 'William Alexander (1567?-1 640). Earl of Stirling, a Scottish poet and dramatist. He held from 1621 to 1630 the grant of New Scotland (Nova Scotia and New Brunswick). Milton s *Comus,* 11. 210-222. The first line is inaccurately quoted. *Comus* was presented as a Masque, a kind of dramatic entertainment, before the Earl of Bridgewater at Ludlow Castle in 1634. It was first printed in 1637. Everard proceeded:

"O welcome, pure eyed Faith, white-handed Hope,
Thou hovering angel, girt with golden wings,
And thou unblemished form of Chastity!
I see ye visibly, and now believe
That he the Supreme Good, to whom all things ill
Are but as slavish officers of vengeance,
Would send a glistering guardian, if need were,
To keep my life and honour unassailed.—
Was I deceived, or did a sable cloud,
Turn forth her silver lining on the night?

"The rest has escaped me, said the reciter; "and I marvel I have been able to remember so much."

Sir Henry Lee, who had expected some effusion very different from those classical and beautiful lines, soon changed the scornful expression of his countenance, relaxed his contorted upper lip, and, stroking down his beard with his left hand, rested the forefinger of the right upon his eyebrow, in sign of profound attention. After Everard had ceased speaking, the old man sighed as at the end of a strain of sweet music. He then spoke in a gentler manner than formerly.

"Cousin Markham," he said, "these verses flow sweetly, and sound in my ears like the well-touched warbling of a lute. But thou knowest I am something slow of apprehending the full meaning of that which I hear for the first time. Repeat me these verses again, slowly and deliberately; for I always love to hear poetry twice, the first time for sound, and the latter time for sense."

Thus encouraged, Everard recited again the lines with more hardihood and better effect; the knight distinctly understanding, and from his looks and motions highly applauding them.

"Yes!" he broke out, when Everard was again silent— "Yes—I *do* call that poetry—though it were even written by a Presbyterian, or an Anabaptist either. Ay, there were good and righteous people to be found even amongst the offending towns which were destroyed by fire. And certainly I have heard, though with little credence (begging your pardon, cousin Everard), that there are men among you, who have seen the error of their ways in rebelling against the best and kindest of masters, and bringing it to that pass that he was murdered by a gang yet fiercer than themselves. Ay, doubtless the gentleness of spirit, and the purity of mind, which dictated those beautiful lines, has long ago taught a man so amiable to say, I have sinned, I have sinned. Yes, I doubt not so sweet a harp has been broken, even in remorse, for the crimes he was witness to; and now he sits drooping for the shame and sorrow of England,—all his noble rhymes, as Will says, Sodom and Gomorrah *(Genesis* xviii. 20-33, xix. 1-29.

Like sweet bells jangled out of tune and harsh.

Dost thou not think so, Master Kerneguy?"

"Not I, Sir Henry," answered the page, somewhat maliciously.

"What, dost not believe the author of these lines must needs be of the better file, and leaning to our persuasion?"

"I think, Sir Henry, that the poetry qualifies the author to write a play on the subject of Dame Potiphar and her recusant lover; and has for his calling—that last metaphor of the cloud in a black coat or cloak, with silver lining, would have dubbed him a tailor with me, only that I happen to know that he is a schoolmaster by profession, and by political opinions qualified to be Poet Laureate to Cromwell; for what Colonel Everard has repeated with such unction is the production of no less celebrated a person than John Milton."

"John Milton!" exclaimed Sir Henry, in astonishment —"What! John Milton, the blasphemous and bloodyminded author of the *Defensio Populi Anglicani!*—the advocate of the infernal High Court of Fiends!—the creature and parasite of that grand impostor, that loathsome hypocrite, that detestable monster, that prodigy of the universe, that disgrace of mankind, that landscape of iniquity, that sink of sin, and that compendium of baseness, Oliver Cromwell!" *Hamlet,* III.. 1, 166. *Genesis* xxxix.

Milton acted for a while as tutor to his nephews, John and Edward Phillips. "'In 1643 he began to receive into his house oiher pupils, 'but only,' says Phillips, (who is solicitous that his uncle should not be thought to have kept a school,) 'the sons of some gentlemen that were his intimate friends.'"—Mark Pattison's *Milton.* A poet laureate means literally one who has been publicly crowned with laurel in recognition of his merits In Great Britain he was an officer of the royal household whose duty it was to furnish odes upon the sovereign's birthday, and upon great national events. Wordsworth accepted the honour, however, with the understanding that even these slight duties were not to be formally required of him, and since the death of Lord Tennyson, no appointment as poet laureate has been made. Milton's *Pro Popvlo Anglicano Defensio,* a tract defending the execution of Charles I., appeared in 1650, as an answer to the *Defentio Hegia pro Oarolo I.* by Claude de Saumaise (Salmasius) of Leyden.

"Even the same John Milton," answered Charles; "schoolmaster to little boys, and tailor to the clouds, which he furnishes with suits of black, lined with silver, at no other expense than that of common sense."

"Markham Bverard," said the old knight, "I will never forgive thee—never, never. Thou hast made me speak words of praise respecting one whose offal should fatten the region-kites. Speak not to me, sir, but begone! Am I, your kinsman and benefactor, a fit person to be juggled out of my commendation and eulogy, and brought to bedaub such a whitened sepulchre as the sophist Milton?"

"I profess," said Everard, "this is hard measure Sir Henry. You pressed me—you defied me, to produce poetry as good as Shakspeare's. I only thought of the verses, not of the politics of Milton."

"Oh yes, sir," replied Sir Henry, "we well know your power of making distinctions; "you could make war against the King's prerogative, without having the least design against his person. Oh Heaven forbid! But Heaven will hear and judge you.—Set down the beverage, Phoebe" (this was added by way of parenthesis to Phoebe, who entered with refreshment)—" Colonel Everard is not thirsty.—You have wiped your mouths, and said you have done no evil. But though you have deceived man, yet God you cannot deceive. And you shall wipe no lips in Woodstock, either after meat or drink, I promise you."

Charged thus at once with the faults imputed to his whole religious sect and political party, Everard felt too late of what imprudence he had been guilty in giving the opening, by disputing his uncle's taste in dramatic poetry. He endeavoured to explain—to apologize.

"I mistook your purpose, honoured sir, and thought you really desired to know something of our literature: and in repeating what you deemed not unworthy your hearing, I profess I thought I was doing you pleasure, instead of stirring your indignation." The Court that tried Charles I.

Samlet, II., 2, 607. "*Proverbs* xxx. 20.

"0 ay!" returned the knight, with unmitigated rigour of resentment—"profess—profess—Ay, that is the new phrase of asseveration, instead of the profane adoration of courtiers and cavaliers—Oh, sir, *profess* less and *practise* more—and so good day to you.—Master Kerneguy, you will find beverage in my apartment. "

While Phoebe stood gaping in admiration at the sudden quarrel which had arisen, Colonel Everard's vexation and resentment was not a little increased by the nonchalance of the young Scotsman, who, with his hands thrust into his pockets (with a courtly affectation of the time), had thrown himself into one of the antique chairs, and, though habitually too polite to laugh aloud, and possessing that art of internal laughter by which men of the world learn to indulge their mirth without incurring quarrels, or giving direct offence, was at no particular trouble to conceal that he was exceedingly amused by the result of the Colonel's visit to Woodstock. Colonel Everard's patience, however, had reached bounds which it was very likely to surpass; for, though differing widely in politics, there was a resemblance betwixt the temper of the uncle and nephew.

"Damnation *I"* exclaimed the Colonel, in a tone which became a puritan as little as did the exclamation itself.

"Amen!" said Louis Kerneguy, but in a tone so soft and gentle, that the ejaculation seemed rather to escape him than to be designedly uttered.

"Sir!" said Everard, striding towards him in that sort of humour, when a man, full of resentment, would not unwillingly find an object on which to discharge it.

"*Plait il?*" said the page, in the most equable tone, looking up in his face with the most unconscious innocence.

"I wish to know, sir," retorted Everard, "the meaning of that which you said just now?"

"Only a pouring out of the spirit, worthy sir," returned Kerneguy—"a small skiff despatched to "Heaven on my own account, to keep company with your holy petition just now expressed." What is your pleasure?

"Sir, I have known a merry gentleman's bones broke for such a smile as you wear just now," replied Everard.

"There, look you now!" answered the malicious page, who could not weigh even the thoughts of his safety against the enjoyment of his jest—" If you had stuck to your *professions,* worthy sir, you must have choked by this time; but your round execration bolted like a cork from a bottle of cider and now allows your wrath to come foaming out after it, in the honest unbaptized language of common ruffians."

"For Heaven's sake, Master Girnegy," said Phoebe, "forbear giving the Colonel these bitter words! And do you, good Colonel Markham, scorn to take offence at his hands—he is but a boy."

"If the Colonel or you choose, Mistress Phoebe, you shall find me a man—I think the gentleman can say something to the purpose already.— Probably he may recommend to you the part of the Lady in Comus; and I only hope his own admiration of John Milton will not induce him to undertake the part of Samson Agonistes, and blow up this old house with execrations, or pull it down in wrath about our ears."

"Young man," said the Colonel, still in towering passion, "if you respect my principles for nothing else, be grateful to the protection which, but for them, you would not easily attain."

"Nay, then," said the attendant, "I must fetch those who have more influence with you than I have," and away tripped Phoebe; while Kerneguy answered Everard in the same provoking tone of calm indifference,—

"Before you menace me with a thing so formidable as your resentment, you ought to be certain whether I may not be compelled by circumstances to deny you the opportunity you seem to point at."

At this moment Alice, summoned no doubt by her attendant, entered the hall hastily.

"Master Kerneguy," she said, "my father requests to see you in Victor Lee's apartment."

Kerneguy arose and bowed, but seemed determined to remain till Everard's departure, so as to prevent any explanation betwixt the cousins.

" Samson Contending," the title of one of Milton's poems (published just twenty years later than the time of *Woodstock),* describing the captivity of the blind Samson among the Philistines *(Judges* xiv.xvi.).

"Markham," said Alice, hurriedly—" Cousin Everard— I have but a moment to remain here—for God's sake, do you instantly begone!—be cautious and patient—but do not tarry here—my father is fearfully incensed."

"I have had my uncle's word for that, madam," replied Everard, "as well as his injunction to depart, which I will obey without delay. I was not aware that you would have seconded so harsh an order quite so willingly; but I go, madam, sensible I leave those behind whose company is more agreeable."

"Unjust—ungenerous—ungrateful!" said Alice; but fearful her words might reach ears for which they were not designed, she spoke them in a voice so feeble, that her cousin, for whom they were intended, lost the consolation they were calculated to convey.

He bowed coldly to Alice, as taking leave, and said, with an air of that constrained courtesy which sometimes covers, among men of condition, the most deadly hatred, "I believe, Master Kerneguy, that I must make it convenient at present to suppress my own peculiar opinions on the matter which we have hinted at in our conversation, in which case I will send a gentleman, who, I hope, may be able to conquer yours."

The supposed Scotsman made him a stately, and at the same time a condescending bow, said he should expect the honour of his commands, offered his hand to Mistress Alice, to conduct her back to her father's apartment, and took a triumphant leave of his rival.

Everard, on the other hand, stung beyond his patience, and, from the grace and composed assurance of the youth's carriage, still conceiving him to be either Wilmot, or some of his compeers in rank and profligacy, returned to the town of Woodstock, determined not to be outbearded, even though he should seek redress by means which his principles forbade him to consider as justifiable.

This is a most skilful piece of character-exposition, by the familiar device of engaging three different people in conversation upon a theme that forces them to take sides. Why does Charles appear to advantage in this chapter? Why does Everard fail to do so*'!* Do you think this conversation about literature is as good as the corresponding "literary chapters" in *Henry Esmond?* CHAPTER THE TWENTY-SIXTH Boundless intemperance
In nature is a tyranny—it hath been
The untimely emptying of many a throne,
And fall of many kings. Macbeth.

While Colonel Everard retreated in high indignation from the little refection, which Sir Henry Lee had in his goodhumour offered, and withdrawn under the circumstances of provocation which we have detailed, the good old knight, scarce recovered from his fit of passion, partook of it with his daughter and guest, and shortly after, recollecting some silvan task (for, though to little efficient purpose, he still regularly attended to his duties as Ranger), he called Bevis, and went out, leaving the two young people together.

"Now," said the amorous Prince to himself, "that Alice is left without her lion, it remains to see whether she is herself of a tigress breed.—So, Sir Bevis has left his charge," he said aloud; "I thought the knights of old, those stern guardians of which he is so fit a representative, were more rigorous in maintaining a vigilant guard."

"Bevis," said Alice, "knows that his attendance on me is totally needless; and, moreover, he has other duties to perform, which every true knight prefers to dangling the whole morning by a lady's sleeve."

"You speak treason against all true

affection," said the gallant; "a lady's lightest wish should to a true knight be more binding than aught excepting the summons of his sovereign. I wish, Mistress Alice, you would but intimate your slightest desire to me, and you shall see how I have practised obedience."

"You never brought me word what o'clock it was this morning," replied the young lady, "and there I sat questioning of the wings of Time, when I should have remembered that gentlemen's gallantry can be quite as fugitive as Time himself. How do you know what your disobedience may have cost me and others? Pudding and pastry may have been burned to a cinder, for, sir, I practise the old domestic rule of visiting the kitchen; or I may have missed prayers, or I may have been too late for an appointment, simply by the negligence of Master Louis Kerneguy failing to let me know the hour of the day."

"O," replied Kerneguy, "I am one of those lovers who cannot endure absence—I must be eternally at the feet of my fair enemy—such, I think, is the title with which romances teach us to grace the fair and cruel to whom we devote our hearts and lives.—Speak for me, good lute," he added, taking up the instrument, "and shew whether I know not my duty."

He sung, but with more taste than execution, the air of a French rondelai, to which some of the wits or sonnetteers, in his gay and roving train, had adapted English verses.

An hour with thee!—When earliest day
Dapples with gold the eastern grey,
Oh, what can frame my mind to bear
The toil and turmoil, cark and care,
New griefs, which coming hours unfold,
And sad remembrance of the old?
    One hour with thee!
    One hour with thee! — When burning June
Waves his red flag at pitch of noon;
What shall repay the faithful swain
His labour on the sultry plain;
And more than cave or sheltering bough,
Cool feverish blood, and throbbing brow?—
One hour with thee!
    One hour with thee!—When sun is set,
O, what can teach me to forget
The thankless labours of the day;
The hopes, the wishes, flung away;
The increasing wants, and lessening gains,
The master's pride, who scorns my pains?—
One hour with thee I

"Truly, there is another verse," said the songster; "but I sing it not to you, Mistress Alice, because some of the prudes of the court liked it not." This musical song, in which the technical structure of the French model is not followed carefully, is of course Scott's own.
Composers of sonnets or other minor verse. "I thank yon, Master Louis," answered the young lady, "both for your discretion in singing what has given me pleasure, and in forbearing what might offend me. Though a country girl, I pretend to be so far of the court mode, as to receive nothing which does not pass current among the better class there."

"I would," answered Louis, "that you were so well confirmed in their creed, as to let all pass with you, to which court ladies would give currency.

"And what would be the consequence?" said Alice, with perfect composure.

"In that case," said Louis, embarrassed like a general who finds that his preparations for attack do not seem to strike either fear or confusion into the enemy—" in that case you would forgive me, fair Alice, if I spoke to you in a warmer language than that of mere gallantry—if I told you how much my heart was interested in what you consider as idle jesting—if I seriously owned it was in your power to make me the happiest or the most miserable of human beings."

"Master Kerneguy," said Alice, with the same unshaken nonchalance, "let us understand each other. I am little acquainted with high-bred manners, and I am unwilling, I tell you plainly, to be accounted a silly country girl, who, either from ignorance or conceit, is startled at every word of gallantry addressed to her by a young man, who, for the present, has nothing better to do than coin and circulate such false compliments. But I must not let this fear of seeming rustic and awkwardly timorous carry me too far; and being ignorant of the exact limits, I will take care to stop within them."

"I trust, madam," said Kernegny, "that however severely you may be disposed to judge of me, your justice will not punish me too severely for an offence, of which your charms are alone the occasion?"

"Hear me out, sir, if you please," resumed Alice. "I have listened to you when you spoke *en berger* 1—nay, my complaisance has been so great, as to answer you *en bergere* —for I do not think anything except ridicule can come of dialogues between Lindor and Jeanneton; and the principal fault of the style is its extreme and tiresome silliness and affectation. But when you begin to kneel, offer to take my hand, and speak with a more serious tone, I must remind you of our real characters. I am the daughter of Sir Henry Lee, sir; and you are, or profess to be, Master Louis Kerneguy, my brother's page, and a fugitive for shelter under my father's roof, who incurs danger by the harbour he affords you, and whose household, therefore, ought not to be disturbed by your unpleasing importunities." ' "As a shepherd," "as a shepherdess; " *i.e.,* playing a certain role. The literary type of the love-sick swain in Spanish literature.—D. 'The typical simpleton of the French pastoral romances. —D. Both names became conventionalized, as denoting the shepherd and shepherdess of pastoral poetry.

"I would to Heaven, fair Alice," said the King, "that your objections to the suit which I am urging, not in jest, but most seriously, as that on which my happiness depends, rested only on the low and precarious station of Louis Kerneguy!—Alice, thou hast the soul of thy family, and must needs love honour. I am no more the needy Scottish page, whom I have, for my own purposes, personated, than I am the awkward lout, whose manners I adopted on the first night of our acquaintance. This hand, poor as I seem, can confer a coronet."

"Keep it," said Alice, "for some more ambitious damsel, my lord,—for such I conclude is your title, if this romance be true,—I would not accept your hand, could you confer a duchy.'"

"In one sense, lovely Alice, you have neither overrated my power nor my affection. It is your King—it is Charles Stuart who speaks to you!—he can confer duchies, and if beauty can merit them, it is that of Alice Lee. Nay, nay — rise—do not kneel—it is for your sovereign to kneel to thee, Alice, to whom he is a thousand times more devoted, than the wanderer Louis dared venture to profess himself. My Alice has, I know, been trained up in those principles of love and obedience to her sovereign, that she cannot, in conscience or in mercy, inflict on him such a wound as would be implied in the rejection of his suit."

In spite of all Charles's attempts to prevent her, Alice had persevered in kneeling on one knee, until she had touched with her lip the hand with which he attempted to raise her. But this salutation ended, she stood upright, with her arms folded on her bosom— her looks humble, but composed, keen and watchful, and so possessed of herself, so little flattered by the communication which the King had supposed would have been overpowering, that he scarce knew in what terms next to urge his solicitation.

"Thou art silent—thou art silent," he said, "my pretty Alice. Has the King no more influence with thee than the poor Scottish page?"

"In one sense every influence," said Alice; "for he commands my best thoughts, my best wishes, my earnest prayers, my devoted loyalty, which, as the men of the House of Lee have been ever ready to testify with the sword, so are the women bound to seal, if necessary, with their blood. But beyond the duties of a true and devoted subject, the King is even less to Alice Lee than poor Louis Kerneguy. The page could have tendered an honourable union—the Monarch can but offer a contaminated coronet."

"You mistake, Alice,—you mistake," said the King, eagerly. "Sit down and let me speak to you—sit down— What is't you fear?"

"I fear nothing, my liege," answered Alice. "What *can* I fear from the King of Britain—I, the daughter of his loyal subject, and under my father's roof? But I remember the distance betwixt us, and though I might trifle and jest with mine equal, to my King I must only appear in the dutiful posture of a subject, unless where his safety may seem to require that I do not acknowledge his dignity."

Charles, though young, being no novice in such scenes, was surprised to encounter resistance of a kind which had not been opposed to him in similar pursuits, even in cases where he had been unsuccessful. There was neither anger, nor injured pride, nor disorder, nor disdain, real or affected, in the manners and conduct of Alice. She stood, as it seemed, calmly prepared to argue on the subject, which is generally decided by passion—shewed no inclination to escape from the apartment, but appeared determined to hear with patience the suit of the lover—while her countenance and manner intimated that she had this complaisance, only in deference to the commands of the King.

"She is ambitious," thought Charles; "it is by dazzling her love of glory, not by mere passionate entreaties, that I must hope to be successful.—I pray you to be seated, my fair Alice," he said, "the lover entreats—the King commands you."

"The King," said Alice, "may permit the relaxation of the ceremonies due to royalty, but he cannot abrogate the subject's duty, even by express command. I stand here while it is your Majesty's pleasure to address me—a patient listener, as in duty bound."

"Know then, simple girl," said the King, "that in accepting my proffered affection and protection, you break through no law, either of virtue or morality. Those who are born to royalty are deprived of many of the comforts of private life—chiefly that which is, perhaps, the dearest and most precious, the power of choosing their own mates for life. Their formal weddings are guided upon principles of political expedience only, and those to whom they are wedded are frequently, in temper, person, and disposition, the most unlikely to make them happy. Society has commiseration, therefore, towards us, and binds our unwilling and often unhappy wedlocks with chains of a lighter and more easy character than those which fetter other men, whose marriage ties, as more voluntarily assumed, ought, in proportion, to be more strictly binding. And therefore, ever since the time that old Henry built these walls, priests and prelates, as well as nobles and statesmen, have been accustomed to see a fair Rosamond rule the heart of an affectionate monarch, and console him for the few hours of constraint and state which he must bestow upon some angry and jealous Eleanor. To such a connection the world attaches no blame; they rush to the festival to admire the beauty of the lovely Esther, while the imperious Vashti is left to queen it in solitude; they throng the palace to ask her protection, whose influence is more in the state an hundred times than that of the proud consort; her offspring rank with the nobles of the land, and vindicate by their courage, like the celebrated Longsword, Earl of Salisbury, their descent from royalty and from love. Prom such connections our richest ranks of nobles are recruited; and the mother lives, in the greatness of her posterity, honoured and blessed, as she died lamented and wept in the arms of love and friendship."

"Did Rosamond so die, my lord?" said Alice. "Our records say she was poisoned by the injured Queen— poisoned without time allowed to call to God for the pardon of her many faults. Did her memory so live? I have heard that, when the Bishop purified the church at Godstowe, her monument was broken open by his orders, and her bones thrown out into unconsecrated ground." See the book of *Esther.* The sou of Henry II. and Rosamond.

"Those were rude old days, sweet Alice," answered Charles; "queens are not now so jealous, nor bishops so rigorous. And know, besides, that, in the lands to which I would lead the loveliest of her sex, other laws obtain, which remove from such ties even the slightest show of scandal. There is a mode of matrimony, which, fulfilling all the rites of the church, leaves no stain on the conscience; yet investing the bride with none of the privileges peculiar to her husband's condition, infringes not upon the duties which the King owes to his subjects. So that Alice Lee may, in all respects, become the real and lawful wife of Charles Stuart, except that their private union gives her no title to be Queen of England."

"My ambition," said Alice, "will be sufficiently gratified to see Charles king, without aiming to share either his dignity in public, or his wealth and regal luxury in private."

"I understand thee, Alice," said the King, hurt but not displeased. "You ridicule me, being a fugitive, for speaking like a king. It is a habit, I admit, which I have learned, and of which even misfortune cannot cure me. But my case is not so desperate as you may suppose. My friends are still many in these kingdoms; my allies abroad are bound, by regard to their own interest, to espouse my cause. I have hopes given me from Spain, from France, and from other nations; and I have confidence that my father's blood has not been poured forth in vain, nor is doomed to dry up without due vengeance. My trust is in Him from whom princes derive their title, and, think what thou wilt of my present condition, I have perfect confidence that I shall one day sit on the throne of England."

"May God grant it! said Alice; "and that he *may* grant it, noble Prince, deign to consider whether you now pursue a conduct likely to conciliate his favour. Think of the course you recommend to a motherless maiden, who has no better defence against your sophistry, than what a sense of morality, together with the natural feeling of female dignity inspires. Whether the death of her father, which would be the consequence of her imprudence;—whether the despair of her brother, whose life has been so often in peril to save that of your Majesty;—whether the dishonour of the roof which has sheltered you, will read well in your annals, or are events likely to propitiate God, whose controversy with your House has been but too visible, or recover the affections of the people of England, in whose eyes such actions are an abomination, I leave to your own royal mind to consider."

Charles paused, struck with a turn to the conversation which placed his own interests more in collision with the gratification of his present passion than he had supposed.

"If your Majesty," said Alice, courtesying deeply, "has no farther commands for my attendance, may I be permitted to withdraw?"

"Stay yet a little, strange and impracticable girl," said the King, "and answer me but one question:—Is it the lowness of my present fortunes that makes my suit contemptible?" *"I* have nothing to conceal, my liege," she said, "and my answer shall be as plain and direct as the question you have asked. If I could have been moved to an act of ignominious, insane, and ungrateful folly, it could only arise from my being blinded by that passion, which I believe is pleaded as an excuse for folly and for crime much more often than it has a real existence. I must, in short, have been in love, as it is called—and that might have been with my equal—but surely never with my sovereign, whether such only in title, or in possession of his kingdom."

"Yet loyalty was ever the pride, almost the ruling passion, of your family, Alice," said the King.

"And could I reconcile that loyalty," said Alice, "with indulging my sovereign, by permitting him to prosecute a suit dishonourable to himself as to me? Ought I, as a faithful subject, to join him in a folly, which might throw yet another stumbling-block in the path to his restoration, and could only serve to diminish his security, even if he were seated upon his throne?"

"At this rate," said Charles, discontentedly, "I had better have retained my character of the page, than assumed that of a sovereign, which it seems is still more irreconcilable with my wishes."

"My candour shall go still farther," said Alice. "I could have felt as little for Louis Kerneguy as for the heir of Britain; for such love as I have to bestow (and it is not such as I read of in romance, or hear poured forth in song), has been already conferred on another object. This gives your Majesty pain—I am sorry for it—but the wholesomest medicines are often bitter."

"Yes," answered the King, with some asperity, "and physicians are reasonable enough to expect their patients to swallow them, as if they were honey-comb. It is true, then, that whispered tale of the cousin Colonel; and the daughter of the loyal Lee has set her heart upon a rebellious fanatic?"

"My love was given ere I knew what these words fanatic and rebel meant. I recalled it not, for I am satisfied, that amidst the great distractions which divide the kingdom, the person to whom you allude has chosen his part, erroneously perhaps, but conscientiously — he, therefore, has still the highest place in my affection and esteem. More he cannot have, and will not ask, until some happy turn shall reconcile these public differences, and my father be once more reconciled to him. Devoutly do I pray that such an event may occur by your Majesty's speedy and unanimous restoration!"

"You have found out a reason," said the King pettishly, "to make me detest the thought of such a change—nor have you, Alice, any sincere interest to pray for it. On the contrary, do you not see that your lover, walking side by side with Cromwell, may, or rather must share his power? nay, if Lambert does not anticipate him, he may trip up Oliver's heels, and reign in his stead. And think you not he will find means to overcome the pride of the loyal Lees, and achieve a union, for which things are better prepared than that which Cromwell is said to meditate betwixt one of his brats and the no less loyal heir of Fauconberg?"

"Your Majesty," said Alice, " has found a way at length to avenge yourself—if what I have said deserves vengeance." 1John Lambert (1619-1683), a prominent Parliamentary general, second in command to Cromwell at Worcester. During the Protectorate, he opposed the project of making Cromwell King. After Cromwell's death he was for awhile the principal man in the state, but was forced to yield to General Monk and the Parliament when they declared for Charles II. See Cromwell's depiction of him in Chapter XXXIII.

'1 Cromwell's third daughter, Mary, married Thomas Belasyse, Earl of Fauconberg, in 1657.

"1 could point out a yet shorter road to your union," said Charles, without minding her distress, or perhaps enjoying the pleasure of retaliation. "Suppose that you sent your Colonel word that there was one Charles Stuart here, who had come to disturb the Saints in their peaceful government, which they had acquired by prayer and preaching, pike and gun—and suppose he had the art to bring down a half-score of troopers, quite enough, as times go, to decide the fate of this heir of royalty—think you not the possession of such a prize as this might obtain from the Rumpers, or from Cromwell, such a reward as might overcome your father's objections to a roundhead's alliance, and place the fair Alice and her cousin Colonel in full possession of their wishes?"

"My liege," said Alice, her cheeks glowing, and her eyes sparkling—for she too had her share of the hereditary temperament of her family—" this passes my patience. I have heard without expressing anger, the most ignominious persuasions addressed to myself, and I have vindicated myself for refusing to be the paramour of a fugitive Prince, as if I had been excusing myself from accepting a share of an actual crown. But do you think I can hear all who are dear to me slandered without emotion or reply? I will not, sir, and were you seated with all the terrors of your father's Star-chamber around you, you should hear me defend the absent and the innocent. Of my father I will say nothing, but that if he is now without wealth—without state, almost without a sheltering home and needful food—it is because he spent all in the service of the King. He needed not to commit any act of treachery or villany to obtain wealth— he had an ample competence in his own possessions. For Markham Everard—he knows no such thing as selfishness —he would not, for broad England, had she the treasures of Peru in her bosom, and a paradise on her surface, do a deed that would disgrace his own name, or injure the feelings of another—Kings, my liege, may take a lesson from him. My liege, for the present I take my leave."

"Alice, Alice—stay! exclaimed the King. "She is gone.—This must be virtue — real, disinterested, overawing virtue—or there is no such thing on earth. Yet Wilmot and Villiers will not believe a word of it, but add the tale to the other wonders of Woodstock.— 'Tis a rare wench! and I profess, to use the Colonel's obtestation, that I know not whether to forgive and be friends with her or study a dire revenge. If it were not for that accursed cousin—that puritan Colonel—I could forgive everything else to so noble a wench. But a roundheaded rebel preferred to me — the preference avowed to my face, and justified with the assertion, that a king might take a lesson from him—it is gall and wormwood. If the old man had not come up this morning as he did, the King should have taken or given a lesson, and a severe one. It was a mad rencontre to venture upon with my rank and responsibility—and yet this wench has made me so angry with her, and so envious of him, that if an opportunity offered, I should scarce be able to forbear him.—Ha! Whom have we here?" Members of the Rump, or remnant of the Long Parliament. 'A secret court of civil and criminal jurisdiction at Westminster. It was abolished in 1640.

The interjection at the conclusion of this royal soliloquy was occasioned by the unexpected extrance of another personage of the drama.

Declaration.

The heroine's rejection of Charles's suit marks of course the highest point of the " intrigue interest," which has been dominant since Chapter XXII. Does the language of the heroine seem true to nature 1 CHAPTER THE TWENTY-SEVENTH *Benedict.* Shall I speak a word in your ear?

Claudio. God bless me from a challenge.

Much Ado About Nothing.

As Charles was about to leave the apartment, he was prevented by the appearance of Wildrake, who entered with an unusual degree of swagger in his gait, and of fantastic importance on his brow. "I crave your pardon, fair sir," he said; "but, as they say in my country, when doors are open dogs enter. I have knocked and called in the hall to no purpose; so, knowing the way to this parlour, sir,— for I am a light partisan, and the road I once travel I never forget—I venture to present myself unannounced. "

"Sir Henry Lee is abroad, sir, I believe, in the Chase," said Charles, coldly, for the appearance of this somewhat vulgar debauchee was not agreeable to him at the moment, "and Master Albert Lee has left the Lodge for two or three days."

"I am aware of it, sir," said Wildrake; "but I have no business at present with either."

"And with whom is your business?" said Charles; "that is, if I may be permitted to ask—since I think it cannot in possibility be with me."

"Pardon me in turn, sir," answered the cavalier; "in no possibility can it be imparted to any other but yourself, if you be, as I think you are, though in something better habit, Master Louis Girnigo, the Scottish gentleman who waits upon Master Albert Lee."

"I am all you are like to find for him," answered Charles.

"In truth," said the cavalier, "I do perceive a difference, but rest and better clothing will do much; and I am glad of it, since I would be sorry to have brought a message such as I am charged with, to a tatterdemalion." One engaged in special military service, like scouting, requiring rapid movement.

"Let us get to the business, sir, if you please," said the King—" you have a message for me, you say?"

"True, sir," replied Wildrake; "I am the friend of Colonel Markham Everard, sir, a tall1 man, and a worthy person in the field, although I could wish him a better cause—A message I have to you, it is certain, in a slight note, which I take the liberty of presenting with the usual formalities." So saying, he drew his sword, put the billet he mentioned upon the point, and making a profound bow, presented it to Charles.

The disguised monarch accepted of it, with a grave return of the salute, and said, as he was about to open the letter, "I am not, I presume, to expect friendly contents in an epistle presented in so hostile a manner?"

"A-hem, sir," replied the ambassador, clearing his voice, while he arranged a suitable answer, in which the mild strain of diplomacy might be properly maintained; "not utterly hostile, I suppose, sir, is the invitation, though it be such as must be construed in the commencement rather bellicose and pugnacious. I trust, sir, we shall find that a few thrusts will make a handsome conclusion of the business; and so, as my old master used to say, *Pax nascitur ex hello?* For my own poor share, I am truly glad to have been graced by my friend Markham Everard in this matter—the rather as I feared the puritan principles with which he is imbued (I will confess the truth to you, worthy sir), might have rendered him unwilling, from certain scruples, to have taken the gentlemanlike and honourable mode of righting himself in such a case as the present. And as I render a friend's duty to my friend, so I humbly hope, Master Louis Girnigo, that I do no injustice to you, in preparing the way for the proposed meeting, where, give me leave to say, I trust, that if no fatal accident occur, we shall be all better friends when the skirmish is over than we were before it began."

"I should suppose so, sir, in any case," said Charles, looking at the letter; "worse than mortal enemies we can scarce be, and it is that footing upon which this billet places us."

"You say true, sir," said Wildrake; "it is, sir, a cartel, introducing to a single combat, for the pacific object of restoring a perfect good understanding betwixt the survivors —in case that fortunately that word can be used in the plural after the event of the meeting." Brave. Compare General Webb's challenge to the Duke of Marlborough in Thackeray's *Esmond.* Peace is born from war.

"In short, we only fight, I suppose," replied the King, "that we may come to a perfectly good and amicable understanding?"

"You are right again, sir; and I thank you for the clearness of your apprehension," said Wildrake.—" Ah, sir, it is easy to do with a person of honour and of intellect in such a case as this. And I beseech you, sir, as a personal kindness to myself, that as the morning is like to be frosty, and myself am in some sort rheumatic—as war will leave its scars behind, sir—I say, I will entreat of you to bring with you some gentleman of honour, who will not disdain to take part of what is going forward—a sort of pot-luck, sir—with a poor old soldier like myself—that we may take no harm by standing unoccupied during such cold weather."

"I understand, sir," replied Charles; "if this matter goes forward, be assured I will endeavour to provide you with a suitable opponent."

"I shall remain greatly indebted to you, sir," said Wildrake; "and I am by no means curious about the quality of my antagonist.—It is true I write myself esquire and gentleman, and should account myself especially honoured by crossing my sword with that of Sir Henry or Master Albert Lee; but, should that not be convenient, I will not refuse to present my poor person in opposition to any gentleman who has served the King, which I always hold as a sort of letters of nobility in itself, and, therefore, would on no account decline the duello with such a person."

"The King is much obliged to you, sir," said Charles, "for the honour you do his faithful subjects."

"O, sir, I am scrupulous on that point—very scrupulous.—When there is a roundhead in question, I consult the Herald's books, to see that he is entitled to bear arms, as is Master Markham Everard, without which, I promise you, I had borne none of his cartel. But a cavalier is with me a gentleman, of course—Be his birth ever so low, his loyalty has ennobled his condition." The official register of those who had the right to assume coats of arms.

"*King Henry V.,* IV., 8, 62.

"It is well, sir," said the King. "This paper requests me to meet Master Everard at six to-morrow morning, at the tree called the King's Oak.—I object neither to place nor time. He proffers the sword, at which, he says, we possess some equality—I do not decline the weapon; for company, two gentlemen—I shall endeavour to procure myself an associate, and a suitable partner for you, sir, if you incline to join in the dance."

"I kiss your hand, sir, and rest yours, under a sense of obligation," answered the envoy.

"I thank you, sir," continued the King; "I will therefore be ready at place and time, and suitably furnished; and I will either give your friend such satisfaction with my sword as he requires, or will render him such cause for not doing so as he will be contented with."

"You will excuse me, sir," said Wildrake, "if my mind is too dull, under the circumstances, to conceive any alternative that can remain betwixt two men of honour in such a case, excepting—sa—sa—." He threw himself into a fencing position, and made a pass with his sheathed rapier, but not directed towards the person of the King, whom he addressed.

"Excuse me, sir," said Charles, "if I do not trouble your intellects with the consideration of a case which may not occur.—But, for example, I may plead urgent employment on the part of the public."—This he spoke in a low and mysterious tone of voice, which Wildrake appeared perfectly to comprehend; for he laid his fore-finger on his nose with what he meant for a very intelligent and apprehensive nod.

"Sir," said he, "if you be engaged in any affair for the King, my friend shall have every reasonable degree of patience—Nay, I will fight him myself in your stead, merely to stay his stomach, rather than you should be interrupted. —And, sir, if you can find room in your enterprise for a poor gentleman that has followed Lunsford and Goring, you have but to name day, time, and place of rendezvous; for truly, sir, I am tired of the scald hat, cropped hair, and undertaker's cloak, with which my friend has bedizened me, and would willingly ruffle it out once more in the King's cause, when whether I be banged or hanged, I care not." 1 Bare of nap; or perhaps simply, paltry.

"I shall remember what you say, sir, should an opportunity occur," said the King; "and I wish his Majesty had many such subjects.—I presume our business is now settled?"

"When you shall have been pleased, sir, to give me a trifling scrap of writing, to serve for my credentials—for such, you know, is the custom—your written cartel hath its written answer."

"That, sir, will I presently do," said Charles, "and in good time—here are the materials."

"And, sir," continued the envoy— "Ahi!—ahem!—if you have interest in the household for a cup of sack—I am a man of few words, and am somewhat hoarse with much speaking—moreover, a serious business of this kind always makes one thirsty.—Besides, sir, to part with dry lips, argues malice, which God forbid should exist in such an honourable conjuncture."

"I do not boast much influence in the house, sir," said the King, "but if you would have the condescension to accept of this broad piece 1 towards quenching your thirst at the George"

"Sir," said the cavalier (for the times admitted of this strange species of courtesy, nor was Wildrake a man of such peculiar delicacy as keenly to dispute the matter),—" I am once again beholden to you. But I see not how it consists with my honour to accept of such accommodation, unless you were to accompany and partake?"

"Pardon me, sir," replied Charles, "my safety recommends that I remain rather private at present."

"Enough said," Wildrake observed; "poor cavaliers must not stand on ceremony. I see, sir, you understand cutter's law—when one tall fellow has coin, another must not be thirsty. I wish you, sir, a continuance of health and happiness until to-morrow, at the King's Oak, at six o'clock.'

"Farewell, sir," said the King, and added, as Wildrake went down the stair, whistling, "Hey for cavaliers," to which air his long rapier, jarring against the steps and banisters, bore no unsuitable burden—"Farewell, thou too just emblem of the state, to which war, and defeat, and despair have reduced many a gallant gentleman." A gold coin. Compare the scene between Richard Varny and Lambourne at the beginning of *Keniliorth.* Outlaw's code of honour.

During the rest of the day, there occurred nothing peculiarly deserving of notice. Alice sedulously avoided shewing towards the disguised Prince any degree of estrangement or shyness, which could be discovered by her father, or by any one else. To all appearance, the two young persons continued on the same footing in every respect. Yet she made the gallant himself sensible, that this apparent intimacy was assumed merely to save appearances, and in no way designed as retracting from the severity with which she had rejected his suit. The sense that this was the case, joined to his injured self-love, and his enmity against a successful rival, induced Charles early to withdraw himself to a solitary walk in the wilderness, where, like Hercules in the Emblem of Cebes, divided betwixt the personifications of Virtue and of Pleasure, he listened alternately to the voice of Wisdom and of passionate Folly.

Prudence urged to him the importance of his own life to the future prosecution of the great object in which he had for the present miscarried—the restoration of monarchy in England, the rebuilding of the throne, the regaining the crown of his father, the avenging his death, and restoring to their fortunes and their country the numerous exiles, who were suffering poverty and banishment on account of their attachment to his cause. Pride too, or rather a just and natural sense of dignity, displayed the unworthiness of a Prince descending to actual personal conflict with a subject of any degree, and the ridicule which would be thrown on his memory, should he lose his life for an obscure intrigue by the hand of a private gentleman. What would his sage counsellors, Nicholas and Hyde— what would his kind and wise governor, the Marquis of Hertford, say to such an act of rashness and folly? Would it not be likely to shake the allegiance of the staid and prudent persons of the royalist party, since wherefore should they expose their lives and estates to raise to the government of a kingdom a young man who could not command his own temper? To this was to be added, the consideration that even his success would add double difficulties to his escape, which already seemed sufficiently precarious. If, stopping short of death, he merely bad the better of his antagonist, how did he know that he might not seek revenge by delivering up to government the Malignant Louis Kerneguy, whose real character could not in that case fail to be discovered?

A table exhibiting the dangers and temptations of human life, described in a book by Cebes, a philosopher of Thebes, Boeotia. and friend of Socrates. Its title was *Pmax, i.e.,* the picture, or emblem. Sir Edward Nicholas (1593-1069), secretary of state to Charles I. and Charles II. Sir Edward Hyde (1608-1674), first earl of Clarendon, the chief adviser of Charles I. during the civil war, and of Charles II. during the latter's exile. He was Lord Chancellor from 1660 till 1667, when he was impeached and banished from England. He is the author of the *History of the Rebellion.* William Seymour (1586-1660), Marquis of Hertford, appointed tutor to Prince Charles in 1642.

These considerations strongly recommended to Charles that he should clear himself of the challenge without fighting; and the reservation under which he had accepted it, afforded him some opportunity of doing so.

But Passion also had her arguments, which she addressed to a temper rendered irritable by recent distress and mortification. In the first place, if he was a prince, he was also a gentleman, entitled to resent as such, and obliged to give or claim the satisfaction expected on occasion of differences among gentlemen. With Englishmen, she urged, he could never lose interest by shewing himself ready, instead of sheltering himself under his royal birth and pretensions, to come frankly forward and maintain what he had done or said on his own responsibility. In a free nation, it seemed as if he would rather gain than lose in the public estimation by a conduct which could not but seem gallant and generous. Then a character for courage was far more necessary to support his pretensions, than any other kind of reputation; and the lying under a challenge, without replying to it, might bring his spirit into question. What would Villiers and Wilmot say of an intrigue, in which he had allowed himself to be shamefully baffled by a country girl, and had failed to revenge himself on his rival? The pasquinades which they would compose, the witty sarcasms which they would circulate on the occasion, would be harder to endure than the grave rebukes of Hertford, Hyde, and Nicholas. This reflection, added to the stings of youthful and awakened courage, at length fixed his resolution, and he returned to Woodstock determined to keep his appointment, come of it what might.

Perhaps there mingled with his resolution a secret belief that such a rencontre would not prove fatal. He was in the flower of his youth, active in all his exercises, and no way inferior to Colonel Everard, as far as the morning's experiment had gone, in that of self-defence. At least such recollection might pass through his royal mind, as he hummed to himself a well-known ditty, which he had picked up during his residence in Scotland—

A man may drink and not be drunk;
A man may fight and not be slain;
A man may kiss a bonnie lass,
And yet be welcome back again.

Meanwhile the busy and all-directing Doctor Rochecliffe had contrived to intimate to Alice that she must give him a private audience, and she found him by appointment in what was called the study, once filled with ancient books, which, long since converted into cartridges, had made more noise in the world at their final exit, than during the space which had intervened betwixt that and their first publication. The Doctor seated himself in a high-backed leathern easy-chair, and signed to Alice to fetch a stool and sit down beside him.

"Alice," said the old man, taking her hand affectionately, "thou art a good girl, a wise girl, a virtuous girl, one of those whose price is above rubies—not that *rubies* is the proper translation—but remind me to tell you of that another time—Alice, thou knowest who this Louis Kerneguy is—nay, hesitate not to me—I know everything—I am well aware of the whole matter. Thou knowest this honoured house holds the fortunes of England." Alice was about to answer.—"Nay, speak not, but listen to me, Alice—How does he bear himself towards you?"

Alice coloured with the deepest crimson.—"I am a country-bred girl," she said, "and his manners are too courtlike for me."

"Enough said—I know it all.—Alice, he is exposed to a great danger to-morrow, and you must be the happy means to prevent him."

"I prevent him!—how, and in what manner?" said Alice, in surprise. "It is my duty, as a subject, to do anything—anything that may become my father's daughter" *Proverbs* xxxi. 10.

Here she stopped, considerably embarrassed.

"Yes," continued the Doctor, "tomorrow he hath made an appointment—an appointment with Markham Everard; the hour and place are set—six in the morning, by the King's Oak. If they meet one will probably fall."

"Now, may God forefend they should meet," said Alice, turning as suddenly pale as she had previously reddened.

"But harm cannot come of it—Everard will never lift his sword against the King."'

"For that," said Dr. Rochecliffe, "I would not warrant. But if that unhappy young gentleman shall have still some reserve of the loyalty which his general conduct entirely disavows, it would not serve us here; for he knows not the King, but considers him merely as a cavalier, from whom he has received injury."

"Let him know the truth, Dr. RocheclifEe, let him know it instantly," said Alice; "*he* lift hand against the King, a fugitive and defenceless! He is incapable of it. My life on the issue, he becomes most active in his preservation."

"That is the thought of a maiden, Alice," answered the Doctor; "and, as I fear, of a maiden whose wisdom is misled by her affections. It were worse than treason to admit a rebel officer, the friend of the arch-traitor Cromwell, into so great a secret. I dare not answer for such rashness. Hammond was trusted by his father, and you know what came of it."

"Then let my father know. He will meet Markham, or send to him, representing the indignity done to him by attacking his guest."

"We dare not let your father into the secret who Louis Kerneguy really is. I did but hint the possibility of Charles taking refuge at Woodstock, and the rapture into which Sir Henry broke out, the preparations for accommodation and defence which he began to talk of, plainly shewed that the mere enthusiasm of his loyalty would have led to a risk of discovery. It is you, Alice, who must save the hopes of every true royalist." Colonel Robert Hammond, the governor of Carisbrooke Castle in the Isle of Wight, upon whose protection Charles I. threw himself after his flight from Hampton Court in November, 1647. Hammond, however, treated him, though with deference, as a prisoner, and the Parliamentary Army took possession of the King.

"I!" answered Alice; "it is impossible. —Why cannot my father be induced to interfere, as in behalf of his friend and guest, though he know him as no other than Louis Kerneguy?"

"You have forgot your father's character, my young friend," said the Doctor; "an excellent man, and the best of Christians, till there is a clashing of swords, and then he starts up the complete martialist, as deaf to every pacific reasoning, as if he were a game-cock."

"You forgot, Doctor Rochecliffe," said Alice, "that this very morning, if I understand the thing aright, my father prevented them from fighting."

"Ay," answered the Doctor, "because he deemed himself bound to keep the peace in the Royal Park; but it was done with such regret, Alice, that, should he find them at it again, I am clear to foretell he will only so far postpone the combat as to conduct them to some unprivileged ground, and there bid them tilt and welcome, while he regaled his eyes with a scene so pleasing. No, Alice, it is you, and you only, who can help us in this extremity."

"I see no possibility," said she, again colouring, "how I can be of the least use."

"You must send a note," answered Doctor Rochecliffe, "to the King—a note such as all women know how to write better than any man can teach them—to meet you at the precise hour of the rendezvous. He will not fail you, for I know his unhappy foible."

"Doctor Rochecliffe," said Alice, gravely,—"you have known me from infancy—What have you seen in me to induce you to believe that I should ever follow such unbecoming counsel?"

"And if you have known *me* from infancy," retorted the Doctor, "what have you seen of *me* that you should suspect me of giving counsel to my friend's daughter which it would be misbecoming in her to follow? You cannot be fool enough, I think, to suppose, that I mean you should carry your complaisance farther than to keep him in discourse for an hour or two, till I have all in readiness for his leaving this place, from which I can frighten him by the terrors of an alleged search?—So, C. S. mounts his horse and rides off, and Mistress Alice Lee has the honour of saving him."

"Yes, at the expense of her own reputation," said Alice, "and the risk of an eternal stain on my family. You say you know all. What can the King think of my appointing an assignation with him after what has passed, and how will it be possible to disabuse him respecting the purpose of my doing so?"

"I will disabuse him, Alice; I will explain the whole."

"Doctor Rochecliffe," said Alice, "you propose what is impossible. You can do much by your ready wit and great wisdom; but if new-fallen snow were once sullied, not all your art could wash it white again; and it is altogether the same with a maiden's reputation."

"Alice, my dearest child," said the Doctor, "bethink you that if I recommend this means of saving the life of the King, at least rescuing him from instant peril, it is because I see no other of which to avail myself. If I bid you assume, even for a moment, the semblance of what is wrong, it is but in the last extremity, and under circumstances which cannot return—I will take the surest means to prevent all evil report which can arise from what I recommend."

"Say not so, Doctor," said Alice; "better undertake to turn back the Isis than to stop the course of calumny. The King will make boast to his whole licentious court of the ease with which, but for a sudden alarm, he could have brought off Alice Lee as a paramour— the mouth which confers honour on others will then be the means to deprive me of mine. Take a fitter course, one more becoming your own character and profession. Do not lead him to fail in an engagement of honour, by holding out the prospect of another engagement, equally dishonourable, whether false or true. Go to the King himself, speak to him, as the servants of God have a right to speak, even to earthly sovereigns. Point out to him the folly and the wickedness of the course he is about to pursue— urge upon him, that he fear the sword, since wrath bringeth the punishment of the sword. Tell him, that the friends who died for him in the field at Worcester, on the scaffolds, and on the gibbets, since that bloody day—that the remnant who are in prison, scattered, fled, and ruined on his account, deserve better of him and his father's race, than that he should throw away his life in an idle brawl—Tell him, that it is dishonest to venture that which is not his own, dishonourable to betray the trust which brave men have reposed in his virtue and in his courage."

Doctor Rochecliffe looked on her with a melancholy smile, his eyes glistening as he said, "Alas! Alice, even I could not plead that just cause to him so eloquently or so impressively as thou dost. But alack! Charles would listen to neither. It is not from priests, or women, he would say, that men should receive counsel in affairs of honour."

"Then hear me, Doctor Rochecliffe— I will appear at the place of rendezvous, and I will prevent the combat— do not fear that I can do what I say—at a sacrifice, indeed, but not that of my reputation. My heart may be broken" — she endeavoured to stifle her sobs with difficulty—" for the consequence; but not in the imagination of a man, and far less that man her sovereign, shall a thought of Alice Lee be associated with dishonour." She hid her face in her handkerchief, and burst out into unrestrained tears.

"What means this hysterical passion?" said Doctor Rochecliffe, surprised and somewhat alarmed by the vehemence of her grief—" Maiden, I must have no concealments—I must know."

"Exert your ingenuity, then, and discover it," said Alice—for a moment put out of temper at the Doctor's pertinacious self-importance—" Guess my purpose, as you can guess at everything else. It is enough to have to go through my task, I will not endure the distress of telling it over, and that to one who— forgive me, dear Doctor— might not think my agitation on this occasion fully warranted."

"Nay, then, my young mistress, you must be ruled," said Rochecliffe; "and if I cannot make you explain yourself, I must see whether your father can gain so far on you." So saying, he arose somewhat displeased, and walked towards the door.

"You forget what you yourself told me, Doctor Rochecliffe," said Alice, "of the risk of communicating this great secret to my father."

"It is too true," he said, stopping short and turning round; "and I think, wench, thou art too smart for me, and I have not met many such. But thou art a good girl, and wilt tell me thy device of free will—it concerns my character and influence with the King, that I should be fully acquainted with whatever is *actum atque tractatum,* done and treated of in this matter."

"Trust your character to me, good Doctor," said Alice, attempting to smile; "it is of firmer stuff than those of women, and will be safer in my custody than mine could have been in yours. And thus much I condescend—you shall see the whole scene—you shall go with me yourself, and much will I feel emboldened and heartened by your company."

"That is something," said the Doctor, though not altogether satisfied with this limited confidence. "Thou wert ever a clever wench, and I will trust thee—indeed, trust thee I find I must, whether voluntarily or no."

"Meet me, then," said Alice, "in the wilderness tomorrow. But first tell me, are you well assured of time and place?—a mistake were fatal."

"Assure yourself my information is entirely accurate," said the Doctor, resuming his air of consequence, which had been a little diminished during the latter part of their conference.

"May I ask," said Alice, "through what channel you acquired such important information?"

"You may ask, unquestionably," he answered, now completely restored to his supremacy; "but whether I will answer or not, is a very different question. I conceive neither your reputation nor my own is interested in your remaining in ignorance on that subject. So I have my secrets as well as you, mistress; and some of them, I fancy, are a good deal more worth knowing."

"Be it so," said Alice, quietly; "if you will meet me in the wilderness by the broken dial at half past five exactly, we will go together to-morrow, and watch them as they come to the rendezvous. I will on the way get the better of my present timidity, and explain to you the means I design to employ to prevent mischief. You can perhaps think of making some effort which may render my interference, unbecoming and painful as it must be, altogether unnecessary."

"Nay, my child," said the Doctor, "if you place yourself in my hands, you will be the first that ever had reason to complain of my want of conduct, and you may well judge you are the very last (one excepted) whom I would see suffer for want of counsel.—At half past five, then, at the dial in the wilderness—and God bless our undertaking!"

Here their interview was interrupted by the sonorous voice of Sir Henry Lee, which shouted their names, "Daughter Alice—Doctor Rochecliffe," through passage and gallery.

"What do you here," said he, entering, "sitting like two crows in a mist, when we have such rare sport below? Here is this wild crack-brained boy Louis Kerneguy, now making me laugh till my sides are fit to split, and now playing on his guitar sweetly enough to win a lark from the heavens.—Come away with you, come away. It is hard work to laugh alone."

Distinguish between chapters of this sort, that prepare the way for future action, and chapters significant in themselves alone. Do you find Scott superior or inferior to other novelists of high rank, in the art of calculating his effects, and giving the reader hints of them, a long time in advance? Does what you know of Scott's method of composition throw any light upon this question?

CHAPTER THE TWENTY-EIGHTH
This is the place, the centre of the grove;
Here stands the oak, the monarch of the wood.
John Home.

The sun had risen on the broad boughs of the forest, but without the power of penetrating into its recesses, which hung rich with heavy dewdrops, and were beginning on some of the trees to exhibit the varied tints of autumn; it being the season when Nature, like a prodigal whose race is well-nigh run, seems desirous to make up in profuse gaiety and variety of colours, for the short space which her splendour has then to endure. The birds were silent—and even Robin-red-breast, whose chirruping song was heard among the bushes near the Lodge, emboldened by the largesses with which the good old knight always encouraged his familiarity, did not venture into the recesses of the wood, where he encountered the sparrowhawk, and other enemies of a similar description, preferring the vicinity of the dwellings of man, from whom he, almost solely among the feathered tribes, seems to experience disinterested protection.

The scene was therefore at once lovely and silent, when the good Doctor Rochecliffe, wrapped in a scarlet roquelaure, which had seen service in its day, muffling his face more from habit than necessity, and supporting Alice on his arm (she also defended by a cloak against the cold and damp of the autumn morning), glided through the tangled and long grass of the darkest alleys, almost ankle-deep in dew, towards the place appointed for the intended duel. Both so eagerly maintained the consultation in which they were engaged, that they were alike insensible of the roughness and discomforts of the road, though often obliged to force their way through brushwood and coppice, which poured down on them all the liquid pearls with which they A short cloak worn by both men and women.
were loaded, till the mantles they were wrapped in hung lank by their sides, and clung to their shoulders heavily charged with moisture. They stopped when they had attained a station under the coppice, and shrouded by it, from which they could see all that passed on the little esplanade before the King's Oak, whose broad and scathed form, contorted and shattered limbs, and frowning brows, made it appear like some ancient war-worn champion, well selected to be the

umpire of a field of single combat.

The first person who appeared at the rendezvous was the gay cavalier Roger Wildrake. He also was wrapped in his cloak, but had discarded his puritanic beaver, and wore in its stead a Spanish hat, with a feather and gilt hatband, all of which had encountered bad weather and hard service; but to make amends for the appearance of poverty by the show of pretension, the castor was accurately adjusted after what was rather profanely called the d—me cut, used among the more desperate cavaliers. He advanced hastily, and exclaimed aloud—" First in the field after all, by Jove, though I bilked Everard in order to have my morning draught.—It has done me much good," he added, smacking his lips.—" Well, I suppose I should search the ground ere my principal comes up, whose Presbyterian watch trudges as slow as his Presbyterian step."

He took his rapier from under his cloak, and seemed about to search the thickets around.

"I will prevent him," whispered the Doctor to Alice. "I will keep faith with you—you shall not come on the scene—*nisi dignus vindice nodus*—I'll explain that another time. *Vindex* is feminine as well as masculine, so the quotation is defensible.—Keep you close."

So saying, he stepped forward on the esplanade and bowed to Wildrake.

"Master Louis Kerneguy," said Wildrake, pulling off his hat; but instantly discovering his error, ne added, "But no—-I beg your pardon, sir—Fatter, shorter, older. —Mr. Kerneguy's friend I suppose, with whom I hope to have a turn by and by.—And why not now, sir, before our principals come up? just a snack to stay the orifice of the stomach, till the dinner is served, sir? What say you?" '' Unless the complication call for such a deliverer."—Horace, *Art Poetica,* 1. 191. One who avenges, intervenes, delivers. Open space.

"To open the orifice of the stomach more likely, or to give it a new one," said the doctor.

"True, sir," said Roger, who seemed now in his element; "you say well—that is as thereafter may be.—But come, sir, you wear your face muffled. I grant you, it is honest men's fashion at this unhappy time; the more is the pity. But we do all above board—we have no traitors here. 111 get into my gears first, to encourage you, and shew you that you have to deal with a gentleman, who honours the King, and is a match fit to fight with any who follow him, as doubtless you do, sir, since you are the friend of Master Louis Kerneguy."

All this while, Wildrake was busied undoing the clasps of his square-caped cloak.

"Off—off, ye lendings," he said, "borrowings I should more properly call you—

Via the curtain which shadowed Borgia."

So saying, he threw the cloak from him, and appeared *in cuerpo,* in a most cavalier-like doublet, of greasy crimson satin, pinked and slashed with what had been once white tiffany; breeches of the same; and netherstocks, or, as we now call them, stockings, darned in many places, and which, like those of Poins, had been once peachcoloured. A pair of pumps, ill-calculated for a walk through the dew, and a broad shoulderbelt of tarnished embroidery, completed his equipment.

"Come, sir! he exclaimed; "make haste, off with your slough—Here I stand tight and true—as loyal a lad as ever stuck rapier through a roundhead. —Come, sir, to your tools!" he continued; "we may have half-a-dozen thrusts before they come yet, and shame them for their tardiness.—Pshaw!" he exclaimed, in a most disappointed tone, when the Doctor, unfolding his cloak, shewed his clerical dress; "Tush! it's but the parson after all!"

Wildrake's respect for the Church, however, and his desire to remove one who might possibly interrupt a scene to which he looked forward with peculiar satisfaction, induced him presently to assume another tone.

King Lear, III., 4, 113. Without upper cloak, leaving the body exposed; a Spanish phrase. With small openings and slits to show the lining. A kind of thin silk, or gauze. 2 *Henry IV.,* II., 2, 19.

"I beg pardon," he said, "my dear Doctor—I kiss the hem of your cassock.—I do, by the thundering Jove—I beg your pardon again.—But I am happy I have met with you—They are raving for your presence at the Lodge—to marry, or christen, or bury, or confess, or something very urgent.—For Heaven's sake, make haste!"

"At the Lodge?" said the Doctor; "why, I left the Lodge this instant—I was there later, I am sure, than you could be, who came the Woodstock road."

"Well," replied Wildrake, "it is at Woodstock they want you.—Rat it, did I say the Lodge?—No, no—Woodstock—Mine host cannot be hanged—his daughter married —his bastard christened, or his wife buried—without the assistance of a *real* clergyman—Your Holdenoughs won't do for them. —He's a true man mine host; so, as you value your function, make haste."

"You will pardon me, Master Wildrake," said the Doctor—"I wait for Master Louis Kerneguy."

"The devil you do!" exclaimed Wildrake. "Why, I always knew the Scots could do nothing without their minister; but d—n it, I never thought they put them to this use neither. But I have known jolly customers in orders, who understood to handle the sword as well as their prayerbook. You know the purpose of our meeting, Doctor. Do you come only as a ghostly comforter—or as a surgeon, perhaps—or do you ever take bilboa in hand?— Sa, sa!"

Here he made a fencing demonstration with his sheathed rapier.

"I have done so, sir, on necessary occasion," said Doctor Rochecliffe.

"Good sir, let this stand for a necessary one," said Wildrake. "You know my devotion for the Church. If a divine of your skill would do me the honour to exchange but three passes with me, I should think myself happy for ever."

"Sir," said Rochecliffe, smiling, "were there no other objection to what you propose, I have not the means—I have no weapon."

"What? you want the *de quoi?* that is unlucky indeed. The wherewithal.

But you ave a stout cane in your hand—what hinders our trying a pass (my rapier being sheathed of course) until our principals come up? My pumps are full of this frostdew; and I shall be a toe or two out of pocket, if I am to stand still all the time they are stretching themselves; for, I fancy, Doctor, you are of my opinion, that the matter will not be a fight of cock-sparrows."

"My business here is to make it, if possible, be no fight at all," said the divine.

"Now, rat me, Doctor, but that is too spiteful," said Wildrake; "and were it not for my respect for the Church, I could turn Presbyterian, to be revenged."

"Stand back a little, if you please, sir," said the Doctor; "do not press forward in that direction."—For Wildrake, in the agitation of his movements, induced by his disappointment, approached the spot where Alice remained still concealed.

"And wherefore not, I pray you, Doctor?" said the cavalier.

But on advancing a step, he suddenly stopped short, and muttered to himself, with a round oath of astonishment, "A petticoat in the coppice, by all that is reverend, and at this hour in the morning— *Whew—ew—ew /*"—He gave vent to his surprise in a long low interjectional whistle; then turning to the Doctor, with his finger on the side of his nose, "You're sly, Doctor, d—d sly! But why not give me a hint of your—your commodity there—your contraband goods? Gad, sir, I am not a man to expose the eccentricities of the Church."

"Sir," said Doctor Rochecliffe, "you are impertinent; and if time served, and it were worth my while, I would chastise you."

And the Doctor, who had served long enough in the wars to have added some of the qualities of a captain of horse to those of a divine, actually raised his cane, to the infinite delight of the rake, whose respect for the Church was by no means able to subdue his love of mischief.

"Nay, Doctor," said he, "if you wield your weapon backsword-fashion, in that way, and raise it as high as your head, I shall be through you in a twinkling." So saying he made a pass with his sheathed rapier, not precisely at the Doctor's person, but in that direction; when Rochecliffe, changing the direction of his cane from the broadsword guard to that of the rapier, made the cavalier's sword spring ten yards out of his hand, with all the dexterity of my friend Francalanza. At this moment both the principal parties appeared on the field.

Everard exclaimed angrily to Wildrake, "Is this your friendship? In Heaven's name what make you in that fool's jacket, and playing the pranks of a jack-pudding?" while his worthy second, somewhat crestfallen, held down his head, like a boy caught in roguery, and went to pick up his weapon, stretching his head as he passed, into the coppice, to obtain another glimpse, if possible, of the concealed object of his curiosity.
-Charles, in the meantime, still more surprised at what he beheld, called out on his part—" What! Doctor Rochecliffe become literally one of the church militant, and tilting with my friend cavalier Wildrake? May I use the freedom to ask him to withdraw, as Colonel Everard and I have some private business to settle?"
It was Doctor Rochecliffe's cue, on this important occasion, to have armed himself with the authority of his sacred office, and used a tone of interference which might have overawed even a monarch, and made him feel that his monitor spoke by a warrant higher than his own. But the indiscreet latitude he had just given to his own passion, and the levity in which he had been detected, were very unfavourable to his assuming that superiority, to which so uncontrollable a spirit as that of Charles, wilful as a prince, and capricious as a wit, was at all likely to submit. The Doctor did, however, endeavour to rally his dignity, and replied, with the gravest, and at the same time the most respectful, tone he could assume, that he also had business of the most urgent nature, which prevented him from complying with Master Kerneguy's wishes, and leaving that spot.

"Excuse this untimely interruption," said Charles, taking off his hat, and bowing to Colonel Everard, "which I will immediately put an end to." A fencing-master in Edinburgh,—1826 (Laing). The use of the phrase "my friend" indicates that Scotts disguise, as the author of the *Waverley Novels,* was no longer very carefully sustained. The public announcement of his authorship of them was made by Scott himself at a dinner for the Theatrical Fund at Edinburgh in February, 1827. See Introduction to *Chronicles of the Canongate.* Clown A phrase used to denote the condition of warfare of the Church on earth, as contrasted with the Church triumphant in heaven.

Everard gravely returned his salute, and was silent.

"Are you mad, Doctor Rochecliffe?" said Charles— "or are you deaf?—or have you forgotten your mothertongue? I desired you to leave this place."

"I am not mad," said the divine, rousing up his resolution, and regaining the natural firmness of his voice—" I would prevent others from being so;—I am not deaf—I would pray others to hear the voice of reason and religion; I have not forgotten my mother-tongue—but I have come hither to speak the language of the Master of kings and princes."

"To fence with broomsticks, I should rather suppose," said the King—" Come, Doctor Rochecliffe, this sudden fit of assumed importance befits you as little as your late frolic. You are not, I apprehend, either a Catholic priest or a Scotch Mass-John to claim devoted obedience from your hearers, but a Church-of-England-man, subject to the rules of that Communion—and to its Head." In speaking the last words, the King lowered his voice to a low and impressive whisper. Everard observing this drew back, the natural generosity of his temper directing him to avoid overhearing private discourse, in which the safety of the speakers might be deeply concerned. They continued, however, to observe great caution in their forms of expression.

"Master Kerneguy," said the clergyman, "it is not I who assume authority or control over your wishes—God forbid; I do but tell you what reason, Scripture, religion, and morality, alike prescribe for your rule of conduct."

"And I, Doctor, said the King, smiling, and pointing to the unlucky cane, "will take your example rather than your precept. If a reverend clergyman will himself fight a bout at single-stick, what right can he have to interfere in gentlemen's quarrels?— Come, sir, remove yourself, and do not let your present obstinacy cancel former obligations."

"Bethink yourself," said the divine,—" I can say one word which will prevent all this."

"Do it," replied the King, "and in doing so belie the whole tenor and actions of an honourable life—abandon the principles of your Church, and become a perjured traitor and an apostate, to prevent another person from discharging his duty as a gentleman! This were indeed killing your friend to prevent the risk of his running himself into danger. Let the Passive Obedience, which is so often in your mouth, and no doubt in your head, put your feet for once into motion, and step aside for ten minutes. Within that space your assistance may be needed, either as bodycurer or soulcurer." The sovereign is the head of the Church of England,..

"Nay, then," said Dr. Rochecliffe, "I have but one argument left."

While this conversation was carried on apart, Everard had almost forcibly detained by his own side, his follower, Wildrake, whose greater curiosity, and lesser delicacy, would otherwise have thrust him forward, to get, if possible, into the secret. But when he saw the Doctor turn into the coppice, he whispered eagerly to Everard—" A gold Carolus to a commonwealth farthing, the Doctor has not only come to preach a peace, but has brought the principal conditions along with him!"

Everard made no answer; he had already unsheathed his sword; and Charles hardly saw Rochecliffe's back fairly turned, than he lost no time in following his example. But, ere they had done more than salute each other, with the usual courteous nourish of their weapons, Doctor Rochecliffe again stood between them, leading in his hand Alice Lee, her garments dank with dew, and her long hair heavy with moisture, and totally uncurled. Her face was extremely pale, but it was the paleness of desperate resolution, not of fear. There was a dead pause of astonishment —the combatants rested on their swords—and even the forwardness of Wildrake only vented itself in half-suppressed ejaculations, as, "Well done, Doctor—this beats the ' parson among the pease'— No less than your patron's daughter— And Mistress Alice, whom I thought a very snowdrop, turned out a dog-violet after all — a Lindabrides, by heavens, and altogether one of ourselves!" The doctrine of absolute submission to the royal will, held by the extreme Royalist and Church party.

A twenty-shilling gold piece. A woman of light reputation; the heroine of *The Mirror of Knighthood,* a sixteenth century translation of a Spanish romance of chivalry.

Excepting these unheeded mutterings, Alice was the first to speak.

"Master Everard," she said—" Master Kerneguy, you are surprised to see me here—Yet, why should I not tell the reason at once? Convinced that I am, however guiltlessly, the unhappy cause of your misunderstanding, I am too much interested to prevent fatal consequences to pause upon any step which may end it.—Master Kerneguy, have my wishes, my entreaties, my prayers— have your noble thoughts—the recollections of your own high duties, no weight with you in this matter? Let me entreat you to consult reason, religion, and common sense, and return your weapon."

"I am obedient as an Eastern slave, madam," answered Charles, sheathing his sword; "but I assure you, the matter about which you distress yourself is a mere trifle, which will be much better settled betwixt Colonel Everard and myself in five minutes, than with the assistance of the whole Convocation of the Church, with a female parliament to assist their reverend deliberations.— Mr. Everard, will you oblige me by walking a little farther?—We must change ground, it seems."

"I am ready to attend yon, sir," said Everard, who had sheathed his sword so soon as his antagonist did so.'

"I have then no interest with you, sir," said Alice, continuing to address the King—" Do you not fear I should use the secret in my power to prevent this affair going to extremity? Think you this gentleman, who raises his hand against you, if he knew" "If he knew that I were LordWilmot, madam, you would say?—Accident has given him proof to that effect, with which he is already satisfied, and I think you would find it difficult to induce him to embrace a different opinion."

Alice paused, and looked on the King with great indignation, the following words dropping from her mouth by intervals, as if they burst forth one by one in spite of feelings that would have restrained them—" Cold—selfish— ungrateful—unkind!—Wo to the land which "Here she paused with marked emphasis, then added—" which shall number thee, or such as thee, among her nobles and rulers!" An ecclesiastical body similar to the Synod, meeting at the call of some authority.

"Nay, fair Alice," said Charles, whose good-nature could not but feel the severity of this reproach, though too slightly to make all the desired impression, "You are too unjust to me—too partial to a happier man. Do not call me unkind; I am but here to answer Mr. Everard's summons. I could neither decline attending, nor withdraw now I am here, without loss of honour; and my loss of honour would be a a disgrace which must extend to many—I cannot fly from Mr. Everard—it would be too shameful. If he abides by his message, it must be decided as such affairs usually are. If he retreats or yields it up, I will, for your sake, waive punctilio. I will not even ask an apology for the trouble it has afforded me, but let all pass as if it were the consequence of some unhappy mistake, the grounds of which shall remain on my part uninquired into.—This I will do for your sake, and it is much for a man of honour to condescend so far—You *know* that the condescension from me in particular is great indeed. Then do not call me ungenerous, or ungrateful, or unkind, since I am ready to do all, which, as a man, I can do, and more perhaps, than as a man of honour I ought to do."

"Do you hear this, Markham Everard," exclaimed Alice —" do you hear this?—the dreadful option is left entirely at youT disposal. You were wont to *be* temperate in passion, religious, forgiving—will you, for a mere punctilio, drive on this private and unchristian broil to a murderous extremity? Believe me if you *now,* contrary to all the better principles of your life, give the reins to your passions, the consequences may be such as you will rue for your lifetime, and even, if Heaven have not mercy, rue after your life is finished."

Markham Everard remained for a moment gloomily silent, with his eyes fixed on the ground. At length he looked up, and answered her—" Alice, you are a soldier's daughter—a soldier's sister. All your relations, even including one whom you then entertained some regard for, have been made soldiers by these unhappy discords. Yet you have seen them take the field—in some instances on contrary sides, to do their duty where their principles called them, without manifesting this extreme degree of interest. Answer me—and your answer shall decide my conduct— Is this youth, so short while known, already of more value to you than those dear connections, father, brother, and kinsman, whose departure to battle you saw with comparative indifference?— Say *this,* and it shall be enough—I leave the ground, never to see you or this country again."

"Stay, Markham, stay; and believe me when I say, that if I answer your question in the affirmative, it is because Master Kerneguy's safety comprehends more, much more, than that of any of those you have mentioned."

"Indeed! I did not know a coronet had been so superior in value to the crest of a private gentleman," said Everard; "yet I have heard that many women think so. "

"You apprehend me amiss," said Alice, perplexed between the difficulty of so expressing herself as to prevent immediate mischief, and at the same time anxious to combat the jealousy and disarm the resentment which she saw arising in the bosom of her lover. But she found no words fine enough to draw the distinction, without leading to a discovery of the King's actual character, and perhaps, in consequence, to his destruction. "Markham,' she said, "have compassion on me. Press me not at this moment —believe me, the honour and happiness of my father, of my brother, and of my whole family, are interested in Master Kerneguy's safety—are inextricably concerned in this matter resting where it now does."

"Oh, ay—I doubt not," said Everard; "the House of Lee ever looked up to nobility, and valued in their connections the fantastic loyalty of a courtier beyond the sterling and honest patriotism of a plain country gentleman. For them, the thing is in course. But on your part, you, Alice—Oh! on your part, whom I have loved so dearly— who has suffered me to think that my affection was not unrepaid—Can the attractions of an empty title, the idle court compliments of a mere man of quality, during only a few hours, lead you to prefer a libertine lord to such a heart as mine?"

"No, no—believe me, no," said Alice, in the extremity of distress.

"Put your answer, which seems so painful, in one word, and say for *whose* safety it is you are thus deeply interested?"

"For both—for both," said Alice.

"That answer will not serve, Alice," answered Everard —" here is no room for equality. I must and will know to what I have to trust. I understand not the paltering, which makes a maiden unwilling to decide betwixt two suitors; nor would I willingly impute to *you* the vanity that cannot remain contented with one lover at once." A heraldic device, borne outside of and above the escutcheon, usually supported by a coronet or wreath.

The vehemence of Everard's displeasure, when he supposed his own long and sincere devotion lightly forgotten, amid the addresses of a profligate courtier, awakened the spirit of Alice Lee, who, as we elsewhere said, had a portion in her temper of the lion-humour that was characteristic of her family.

"If I am thus misinterpreted," she said—" If I am not judged worthy of the least confidence or candid construction, hear my declaration, and my assurance, that, strange as my words may seem, they are, when truly interpreted, such as do you no wrong.—I tell you— I tell all present—and I tell this gentleman himself, who well knows the sense in which I speak, that his life and safety are, or ought to be, of more value to me than those of any other man in the kingdom—nay, in the world, be that other who he will."

These words she spoke in a tone so firm and decided, as admitted no farther discussion. Charles bowed low and with gravity, but remained silent. Everard, his features agitated by the emotions which his pride barely enabled him to suppress, advanced to his antagonist, and said, in a tone which he vainly endeavoured to make a firm one, "Sir, you heard the lady's declaration, with such feelings, doubtless, of gratitude as the case eminently demands.— As her poor kinsman, and an unworthy suitor, sir, I presume to yield my interest in her to you; and, as I will never be the means of giving her pain, I trust you will not think I act unworthily in retracting the letter which gave you the trouble of attending this place at this hour.— Alice," he said, turning his head towards her, "Farewell Alice, at once and for ever!"

The poor young lady, whose adventitious spirit had almost deserted her, attempted to repeat the word farewell, but failing in the attempt, only accomplished a broken and imperfect sound, and would have sunk to the ground, but for Doctor Rochecliffe, who caught her as she fell. Roger Wildrake, also, who had twice or thrice put to his eyes what remained of a kerchief, interested by the lady's evident distress, though unable to comprenend the mysterious cause, hastened to assist the divine in supporting so fair a burden.

Meanwhile, the disguised Prince had beheld the whole in silence, but with an agitation to which he was unwonted, and which his swarthy features, and still more his motions, began to betray. His posture was at first absolutely stationary, with his arms folded on his bosom, as one who waits to be guided by the current of events; presently after, he shifted his position, advanced and retired his foot, clenched.and opened his hand, and otherwise shewed symptoms that he was strongly agitated by contending feelings,—was on the point, too, of forming some sudden resolution, and yet still in uncertainty what course he should pursue.

But when he saw Markham Everard, after one look of unspeakable anguish towards Alice, turning his back to depart, he broke out into his familiar ejaculation, "Oddsfish! this must not be." In three strides he overtook the slowly retiring Everard, tapped him smartly on the shoulder, and, as he turned round, said, with an air of command, which he well knew how to adopt at pleasure, "One word with you, sir."

"At your pleasure, sir," replied Everard, and naturally conjecturing the purpose of his antagonist to be hostile, took hold of his rapier with the left hand, and laid the right on the hilt, not displeased at the supposed call; for anger is at least as much akin to disappointment as pity is said to be to love.

"Pshaw!" answered the King, "that cannot be *now*— Colonel Everard, I am Charles Stuabt!"

Everard recoiled in the greatest surprise, and next exclaimed, "Impossible—it cannot be!—The King of Scots has escaped from Bristol.—My Lord Wilmot, your talents for intrigue are well known—but this will not pass upon me."

"The King of Scots, Master Everard," replied Charles —" since you are so pleased to limit his sovereignty—at any rate, the Eldest Son of the late Sovereign of Britain, —is now before you; therefore it is impossible he could have escaped from Bristol. Doctor Bochecliffe shall be my voucher, and will tell you, moreover, that Wilmot is of a fair complexion, and light hair—mine, you may see, is swart as a raven."

Rochecliffe, seeing what was passing, abandoned Alice to the care of Wildrake, whose extreme delicacy in the attempts he made to bring her back to life, formed an amiable contrast to his usual wildness, and occupied him so much, that he remained for the moment ignorant of the disclosure in which he would have been so much interested. As for Doctor Rochecliffe, he came forward, wringing his hands in all the demonstration of extreme anxiety, and with the usual exclamations attending such a state.

"Peace, Doctor Rochecliffe!" said the King, with such complete self-possession as indeed became a prince—" We are in the hands, I am satisfied, of a man of honour. Master Everard must be pleased in finding only a fugitive prince in the person in whom he thought he had discovered a successful rival. He cannot but be aware of the feelings which prevented me from taking advantage of the cover which this young lady's devoted loyalty afforded me, at the risk of her own happiness. He is the party who is to profit by my candour; and certainly I have a right to expect that my condition, already indifferent enough, shall not be rendered worse by his becoming privy to it, under such circumstances. At any rate, the avowal is made; and it is for Colonel Everard to consider how he is to conduct himself."

"Oh, your Majesty! my Liege! my King! my royal Prince!" exclaimed Wildrake, who, at length discovering what was passing, had crawled on his knees, and seizing the King's hand, was kissing it, more like a child mumbling gingerbread, or like a lover devouring the yielded hand of his mistress, than in the manner in which such salutations pass at court—" If my dear friend Mark Everard should prove a dog on this occasion, rely on me I will cut his throat on the spot, were I to do the same for myself the moment afterwards!"

"Hush, hush, my good friend and loyal subject," said the King, "and compose yourself; for though I am obliged to put on the Prince for a moment, we have not privacy or safety to receive our subjects in King Cambyses' In bombastic fashion: an allusion to the supposed ranting speeches of the hero in Thomas Preston's play, *Oamhyaeg, King of Persia* (1561). See Shakespeare's 1 *Henry IV.,* IV., 2. 425. As a matter of fact the anguage of the play is not specially open to this charge.

Everard, who had stood for a time utterly confounded, awoke at length like a man from a dream.

"Sire," he said, bowing low, and with profound deference, "if I do not offer you the homage of a subject with knee and sword, it is because God, by whom kings reign, has denied you for the present the power of ascending your throne without rekindling civil war. For your safety being endangered by me, let not such an imagination for an instant cross your mind. Had I not respected your person—were I not bound to you for the candour with which your noble avowal has prevented the misery of my future life, your misfortunes would have rendered your person as sacred, so far as I can protect it, as it could be esteemed by the most devoted royalist in the kingdom. If your plans are soundly considered, and securely laid, think that all which is now passed is but a dream. If they are in such a state that I can aid them, saving my duty to the Commonwealth, which will permit me to be privy to no schemes of actual violence, your Majesty may command my services."

"It may be I may be troublesome to you, sir," said the King; "for my fortunes are not such as to permit me to reject even the most limited offers of assistance; but if I can, I will dispense with applying to you. I would not willingly put any man's compassion at war with his sense of duty on my account.— Doctor, I think there will be no farther tilting to-day, either with sword or cane; so we may as well return to the Lodge, and leave these"— looking at Alice and

Everard—" who may have more to say in explanation."

"No—no!" exclaimed Alice, who was now perfectly come to herself, and partly by her own observation, and partly from the report of Dr. Rochecliffe, comprehended all that had taken place—" My cousin Everard and I have nothing to explain; he will forgive me for having riddled with him when I dared not speak plainly; and I forgive him for having read my riddle wrong. But my father has my promise—we must not correspond or converse for the present—I return instantly to the Lodge and he to Woodstock, unless you, sire," bowing to the King, "command his duty otherwise.—Instant to the town, Cousin Markham; and if danger should approach, give us warning."

Everard would have delayed her departure, would have excused himself for his unjust suspicion, would have said a thousand things; but she would not listen to him, saying, for all other answer,—" Farewell, Markham, till God send better days!"

"She is an angel of truth and beauty," said Roger Wildrake; "and I, like a blasphemous heretic, called her a Lindabrides!—But has your Majesty—craving your pardon—no commands for poor Hodge Wildrake, who will blow out his own or any other man's brains in England, to do your Grace a pleasure?"

"We entreat our good friend Wildrake to do nothing hastily," said Charles, smiling; "such brains as his are rare, and should not be rashly dispersed, as the like may not be easily collected. We recommend him to be silent and prudent—to tilt no more with loyal clergymen of the Church of England, and to get himself a new jacket with all convenient speed, to which we beg to contribute our royal aid. When fit time comes, we hope to find other service for him."

As he spoke, he slid ten pieces into the hand of poor Wildrake, who, confounded with the excess of his loyal gratitude, blubbered like a child, and would have followed the King, had not Doctor Rochecliffe, in few words, but peremptory, insisted that he should return with his patron, promising him that he should certainly be employed in assisting the King's escape, could an opportunity be found of using his services.

"Be so generous, reverend sir, and you bind me to you for ever," said the cavalier; "and I conjure you not to keep malice against me on account of the foolery you wot

"I have no occasion, Captain Wildrake," said the Doctor,

"for I think I had the best of it."

"Well, then, Doctor, I forgive you on my part; and I pray you, for Christian charity, let me have a finger in this good service; for as I live in hope of it, rely that I shall die of disappointment."

While the Doctor and soldier thus spoke together, Charles took leave of Everard (who remained uncovered while he spoke to him) with his usual grace—"I need not bid you no longer be jealous of me," said the King; "for I presume you will scarce think of a match betwixt Alice Stupid; like a country bumpkin.

and me, which would be too losing a one on her side. For other thoughts, the wildest libertine could not entertain them towards so high-minded a creature; and believe me, that my sense of her merit did not need this last distinguished proof of her truth and loyalty. I saw enough of her from her answers to some idle sallies of gallantry, to know with what a lofty character she is endowed. Mr. Everard, her happiness I see depends on you, and I trust you will be the careful guardian of it. If we can take any obstacle out of the way of your joint happiness, be assured we will use our influence.—Farewell, sir; if we cannot be better friends, do not at least let us entertain harder or worse thoughts of each other than we have now."

There was something in the manner of Charles that was extremely affecting; something, too, in his condition as a fugitive in the kingdom which was his own by inheritance, that made a direct appeal to Everard's bosom—though in contradiction to the dictates of that policy which he judged it his duty to pursue in the distracted circumstances of the country. He remained, as we have said, uncovered; and in his manner testified the highest expression of reverence, up to the point when such might seem a symbol of allegiance. He bowed so low as almost to approach his lips to the hand of Charles—but he did not kiss it. —" I would rescue your person, sir," he said, "with the purchase of my own life. More" He stopped short, and the

King took up his sentence where it broke off—" More you cannot do," said Charles, "to maintain an honourable consistency—but what you have said is enough. You cannot render homage to my proffered hand as that of a sovereign, but you will not prevent my taking yours as a friend, if you allow me to call myself so—I am sure, as a well-wisher at least."

The generous soul of Everard was touched—He took the King's hand, and pressed it to his lips.

"Oh!" he said, "were better times to come"

"Bind yourself to nothing, dear Everard," said the good-natured Prince, partaking his emotion—" We reason ill while our feelings are moved. I will recruit no man to his loss, nor will I have my fallen fortunes involve those of others, because they have humanity enough to pity my present condition. If better times come, why we will meet again, and I hope to our mutual satisfaction. If not, as your future father-in-law would say" (a benevolent smile came over his face, and accorded not unmeetly with his glistening eyes)—"If not, this parting was well made."

Everard turned away with a deep bow, almost choking under contending feelings; the uppermost of which was a sense of the generosity with which Charles, at his own imminent risk, had cleared away the darkness that seemed about to overwhelm his prospects of happiness for life— mixed with a deep sense of the perils by which he was environed. He returned to the little town, followed by his attendant Wildrake, who turned back so often, with weeping eyes, and hands clasped and uplifted as supplicating Heaven, that Everard was obliged to remind him that his gestures might be observed by some one, and occasion suspicion.

The generous conduct of the King during the closing part of this remarkable scene, had not escaped Alice's notice; and, erasing at once from her mind all resentment of Charles's former conduct, and all the suspicions they had deservedly excited, awakened in her bosom a sense of the natural goodness of his disposition, which permitted her to unite regard for his person, with that reverence for his high office in which she had been educated as a portion of her creed. She felt convinced, and delighted with the conviction, that his virtues were his own, his libertinism the fault of education, or rather want of education, and the corrupting advice of sycophants and flatterers. She could not know, or perhaps did not in that moment consider, that in a soil where no care is taken to eradicate tares, they will outgrow and smother the wholesome seed, even if the last is more natural to the soil. For, as Dr. Rochecliffe informed her afterwards for her edification,—promising, as was his custom, to explain the precise words on some future occasion if she would put him in mind— *Virtus rectorem ducemque desiderat; Vitia sine magistro discuntur.*

There was no room for such reflections at present. Conscious of mutual sincerity, by a sort of intellectual communication, through which individuals are led to understand each other better, perhaps, in delicate circumstances, than by words, reserve and simulation appeared to be now banished from the intercourse between the King and Alice. With manly frankness, and, at the same time, with princely condescension, he requested her, exhausted as she was, to accept of his arm on the way homeward, instead of that of Dr. Rochecliffe, and Alice accepted of his support with modest humility, but without a shadow of mistrust or fear.

The quotations of the learned doctor and antiquary were often left uninterpreted, though seldom uncommunicated, owing to his contempt for those who did not understand the learned languages, and his dislike to the labour of translation, for the benefit of ladies and of country gentlemen. That fair readers and country thanes may not on this occasion burst in ignorance, we add the meaning of the passage in the text—" *Virtue requires the aid of a governor and director; vices are learned without a teaelier.*" Scott.

It seemed as if the last half hour had satisfied them perfectly with the character of each other, and that each had full conviction of the purity and sincerity of the other's intentions.

Dr. Rochecliffe, in the meantime, had fallen some four or five paces behind; for, less light and active than Alice (who had, besides, the assistance of the King's support), he was unable, without effort and difficulty, to keep up with the pace of Charles, who then was, as we have elsewhere noticed, one of the best walkers in England, and was sometimes apt to forget (as great men will) that others were inferior to him in activity.

"Dear Alice," said the King, but as if the epithet were entirely fraternal, "I like your Everard much—I would to God he were of our determination—But since that cannot be, I am sure he will prove a generous enemy."

"May it please you, sire," said Alice, modestly, but with some firmness, "my cousin will never be your Majesty's personal enemy—and he is one of the few on whose slightest word you may rely more than on the oath of those who profess more strongly and formally. He is utterly incapable of abusing your Majesty's most generous and voluntary confidence."

"On my honour, I believe so, Alice," replied the King: "But oddsfish! my girl, let Majesty sleep for the presentit concerns my safety, as I told your brother lately—Call me sir, then, which belongs alike to king, peer, knight, and gentleman—or rather let me be wild Louis Kerneguy again."

Alice looked down, and shook her head. "That cannot be, please your Majesty."

"What! Louis was a saucy companion—a naughty presuming boy—and you cannot abide him?—Well, perhaps you are right—But we will wait for Doctor Rochecliffe "— he said, desirous, with good-natured delicacy, to make Alice aware that he had no purpose of engaging her in any discussion which could recall painful ideas. They paused accordingly, and again she felt relieved and grateful.

"I cannot persuade our fair friend, Mistress Alice, Doctor," said the King, "that she must, in prudence, forbear using titles of respect to me, while there are such very slender means of sustaining them."

"It is a reproach to earth and to fortune," answered the divine, as fast as his recovered breath would permit him, "that your most sacred Majesty's present condition should not accord with the rendering of those honours which are your own by birth, and which, with God's blessing on the efforts of your loyal subjects, I hope to see rendered to you as your hereditary right, by the universal voice of the three kingdoms."

"True, Doctor," replied the King; "but, in the meanwhile, can you expound to Mistress Alice Lee two lines of Horace, which I have carried in my thick head several years, till now, they have come pat to my purpose. As my canny subjects of Scotland say, If you keep a thing seven years, you are sure to find a use for it at last—*Telephus*—ay, so it begins— *Telephus*1 *et Peleus cum pauper et exul uterque,*
Prqjicit ampullas et sesquipedalia verba."

"I will explain the passage to Mistress Alice," said the Doctor, "when she reminds me of it—or rather" (he added, recollecting that his ordinary dilatory answer on such occasions ought not to be returned when the order for exposition emanated from his sovereign), "I will repeat a poor couplet from my own translation of the poem—

Heroes and kings, in exile forced to roam,

Leave swelling phrase and seven-leagued words at home."

"A most admirable version, Doctor," said Charles; "I feel all its force, and particularly the beautiful rendering of *sesquipedalia verba* into seven-leagued boots—words I mean—it reminds me, like half the things I meet with in this world, of the *Contes de Commere*

L'Oye." A son of Hercules, wounded by Achilles at the siege of Troy, and forced to wander, incurable, until healed by the rust of the same spear that had wounded him.

"Peleus King of the Myrmidons in Thessaly, having slain his brother Phocus, was long an exile, until purified from his crime.

The quotation is from Horace, *Ars Poetica,* 1. 96, 97.

Thus conversing they reached the Lodge; and as the King went to his chamber to prepare for the breakfast summons, now impending, the idea crossed his mind, "Wilmot, and Villiers, and Killigrew, would laugh at me, did they hear of a campaign in which neither man nor woman had been conquered—But, oddsfish! let them laugh as they will, there is something at my heart which tells me, that for once in my life I have acted well."

That day and the next were spent in tranquillity, the King waiting impatiently for the intelligence, which was to announce to him that a vessel was prepared somewhere on the coast. None such was yet in readiness; but he learned that the indefatigable Albert Lee was, at great personal risk, traversing the seacoast from town to village, and endeavouring to find means of embarkation among the friends of the royal cause, and the correspondents of Doctor Rochecliffe.

Tales of Mother Goose. Scott "The correct title of Perranlt's book (1697) is *Contes de ma Mire L'Oye, Oontes du Temps Passe.* Charles could not have quoted the book, but the name was currently applied to popular tales in France before Perrault's day. (See Scott's *Journal.* II.. 457, and the Editor's note. Appendix V., p. 489.) On Jan. 2. 1832, Scott speaks of intending to edit the *Contes;* probably this was the very last of his literary projects. The phrase ' Mother Goose' is not found in England before the earliest translation of Perrault in 1729, of which no copy is known to exist."—Andrew Lang. '' Words a foot and a half long." Thomas Killigrew (1612-1683), a page of Charles I., and Master of the Revels of Charles II.

Pepys speaks of him as " a merry droll, but a gentleman of great esteem with the King," *Diary,* May 24, 1660. Some of the witticisms in Thackeray's *Esmond* are put into his mouth.

The interruption of this second duel, and the revelation of the King's real personality, naturally puts an end to the "intrigue interest," as a part of the general plot. The "ghost interest" has partly served its turn, in restoring Sir Henry to the Lodge, and has partly disappeared through neglect. Note therefore that our attention must now be concentrated upon the go between, Tomkins, in order that Cromwell should be drawn into the story. Can you find elsewhere in Scott examples of his taking up a sub-plot, or thread of minor interest, keeping it before his readers as long as it amused him to do so, and then dropping it without much regard to the unity of the plot movement as a whole?

CHAPTER THE TWENTY-NINTH

Ruffian, let go that rude uncivil touch!

Two Gentlemen Op Verona.

It is time we should give some account of the other actors in our drama, the interest due to the principal personages having for some time engrossed our attention exclusively.

We are, therefore, to inform the reader, that the lingering longings of the Commissioners, who had been driven forth of their proposed paradise of Woodstock, not by a cherub indeed, but, as they thought, by spirits of another sort, still detained them in the vicinity. They had, indeed, left the little borough under pretence of indifferent accommodation. The more palpable reasons were, that they entertained some resentment against Everard, as the means of their disappointment, and had no mind to reside where their proceedings could be overlooked by him, although they took leave in terms of the utmost respect. They went, however, no farther than Oxford, and remained there, as ravens, who are accustomed to witness the chase, sit upon a tree or crag, at a little distance, and watch the disembowelling of the deer, expecting the relics which fall to their share. Meantime, the University and City, but especially the former, supplied them with some means of employing their various faculties to advantage, until the expected moment, when, as they hoped, they should either be summoned to Windsor, or Woodstock should once more be abandoned to their discretion.

Bletson, to pass the time, vexed the souls of such learned and pious divines and scholars, as he could intrude his hateful presence upon, by sophistry, atheistical discourse, and challenges to them to impugn the most scandalous theses. Desborough, one of the most brutally ignorant men of the period, got himself nominated the head of a college' and lost no time in cutting down trees, and plundering plate. As for Harrison, he preached in full uniform in Saint Mary's Church, wearing his buff-coat, boots, and spurs, as if he were about to take the field for the fight at Armageddon. And it was hard to say, whether that seat of Learning, Religion, and Loyalty, as it is called by Clarendon, was more' vexed by the rapine of Desborough, the cold scepticism of Bletson, or the frantic enthusiasm of the Fifth-Monarchy Champion.

Propositions which one advances and offers to maintain by argument.

Ever and anon, soldiers, under pretence of relieving guard, or otherwise, went and came betwixt Woodstock and Oxford, and maintained, it may be supposed, a correspondence with Trusty Tomkins, who, though he chiefly resided in the town of Woodstock, visited the Lodge occasionally, and to whom, therefore, they doubtless trusted for information concerning the proceedings there.

Indeed, this man Tomkins seemed by some secret means to have gained the confidence in part, if not in whole, of almost every one connected with these intrigues. All closeted him, all conversed with him in private; those who had the means propitiated him with gifts, those who had not were liberal of promises. When he chanced to appear at Woodstock, which always seemed as it were by accident—if he passed through the hall, the knight was sure to ask him to take the foils, and was equally certain to be, after less or more resistance, victorious in the encounter; so, in consideration of so many triumphs, the good Sir Henry almost forgave him the sins of rebellion and puritanism. Then, if his slow and formal step was heard in the passages approaching the gallery, Doctor Rochecliffe, though he never introduced him to his peculiar boudoir, was sure to meet Master Tomkins in some neutral apartment, and to engage him in long conversations, which apparently had great interest for both.

"Those famous commissioners only answered by expelling all those who refused to submit to their jurisdiction, or to take the Covenant; which was, upon the matter, the whole University; scarce one governor or master of college or hall, and an incredible small number of the fellows, or scholars, submitting to either: whereupon that desolation being made, they placed in their rooms the most notorious factious Presbyterians, in the government of the several colleges or halls; and such other of the same leaven in the fellowships, and scholar's places, of those whom they had expelled, without any regard to the statutes of the several Founders, and the incapacities of the persons that were put in."—Clarendon's *History of the Rebellion,* Book X. *"* The University Church at Oxford. John Henry Newman's famous University Sermons were delivered here. Amy Robsart, the heroine of Scott's *Kenilworth,* is buried in the choir. In an eloquent passage in Book X. of the *History,* following immediately after the quotation given above.

Neither was the Independent's reception below stairs less gracious than above. Joceline failed not to welcome him with the most cordial frankness; the pasty and the flagon were put in immediate requisition, and good cheer was the general word. The means for this, it may be observed, had grown more plenty at Woodstock since the arrival of Doctor Rochecliffe, who, in quality of agent for several royalists, had various sums of money at his disposal. By these funds it is likely that Trusty Tomkins also derived his own full advantage.

In his occasional indulgence in what he called a fleshly frailty (and for which he said he had a privilege), which was in truth an attachment to strong liquors, and that in no moderate degree, his language, at other times remarkably decorous and reserved, became wild and animated. He sometimes talked with all the unction of an old debauchee, of former exploits, such as deer-stealing, orchard-robbing, drunken gambols, and desperate affrays in which he had been engaged in the earlier part of his life, sung bacchanalian and amorous ditties, dwelt sometimes upon adventures which drove Phoebe Mayflower from the company, and penetrated even the deaf ears of Dame Jellicot, so as to make the buttery in which he held his carousals no proper place for the poor old woman.

In the middle of these wild rants, Tomkins twice or thrice suddenly ran into religious topics, and spoke mysteriously, but with great animation, and a rich eloquence, on the happy and pre-eminent saints, who were saints, as he termed them, indeed—men who had stormed the inner treasure-house of Heaven, and possessed themselves of its choicest jewels. All other sects he treated with the utmost contempt, as merely quarrelling, as he expressed it, like hogs over a trough about husk and acorns; under which derogatory terms, he included alike the usual rites and ceremonies of public devotion, the ordinances of the established churches of Christianity, and the observances, nay, the forbearances, enjoined by every class of Christians. Scarcely hearing, and not at all understanding him, Joceline, who seemed his most frequent confidant on such occasions, generally led him back into some strain of rude mirth, or old recollection of follies before the Civil Wars, without caring about or endeavouring to analyze the opinion of this saint of an evil fashion, but fully sensible of the protection which his presence afforded at Woodstock, and confident in the honest meaning of so free-spoken a fellow, to whom ale and brandy, when better liquor was not to be come by, seemed to be principal objects of life, and who drank a health to the King, or any one else, whenever required, provided the cup in which he was to perform the libation were but a brimmer.

These peculiar doctrines, which were entertained by a sect sometimes termed the Family of Love, but more commonly Ranters, had made some progress in times when such variety of religious opinions were prevalent, that men pushed the jarring heresies to the verge of absolute and most impious insanity. Secrecy had been enjoined on these frantic believers in a most blasphemous doctrine, by the fear of consequences, should they come to be generally announced; and it was the care of Master Tomkins to conceal the spiritual freedom which he pretended to have acquired, from all whose resentment would have been stirred by his public avowal of it. This was not difficult; for their profession of faith permitted, nay, required, their occasional conformity with the sectaries or professors of any creed which chanced to be uppermost.

Tomkins had accordingly the art to pass himself on Dr. Rochecliffe as still a zealous member of the Church of England, though serving under the enemy's colours as a spy in their camp; and as he had on several times given him true and valuable intelligence, this active intriguer was the more easily induced to believe his professions.

The Familists were originally founded by David George of Delft, an enthusiast, who believed himself the Messiah. They branched off into various sects of Grindletonians, Familists of the Mountains, of the Valleys; Familists of Cape Order, etc. etc., of the Scattered Flock, etc. etc. Among doctrines, too wild and foul to be quoted, they held the lawfulness of occasional conformity with any predominant sect when it suited their convenience, of complying with the order of any magistrate, or superior power, however sinful. They disowned the principal doctrines of Christianity, as a law which had been superseded by the advent of David George—nay, obeyed the wildest and loosest dictates of evil passions, and are said to have practised among themselves the grossest libertinism. See Edwards's *Gangrana,* Pagitt s *Hercsiographia,* and a very curious work written by Ludovic Claxton. one of the leaders of the sect, called the *Lost Sheep Found,*— Small quarto, London, 1GC0. Scott.

Nevertheless, lest this person's occasional presence at the Lodge, which there were perhaps no means to prevent without exciting suspicion, should infer danger to the King's person, Rochecliffe, whatever confidence he otherwise reposed in him, recommended that, if possible, the King should keep always out of his sight, and when accidentally discovered, that he should only appear in the character of Louis Kerneguy. Joseph Tomkins, he said, was, he really believed, Honest Joe; but Honesty was a horse which might be overburdened, and there was no use in leading our neighbour into temptation.

It seemed as if Tomkins himself had acquiesced in this limitation of confidence exercised towards him, or that he wished to seem blinder than he really was to the presence of this stranger in the family. It occurred to Joceline, who was a very shrewd fellow, that once or twice, when by inevitable accident Tomkins had met Kerneguy, he seemed less interested in the circumstance than he would have expected from the man's disposition, which was naturally prying and inquisitive. "He asked no questions about the young stranger," said Joceline. "God avert that he knows or suspects too much!" But his suspicions were removed when, in the course of their subsequent conversation, Joseph Tomkins mentioned the King's escape from Bristol as a thing positively certain, and named both the vessel in which he said he had gone off, and the master who commanded her, seeming so convinced of the truth of the report, that Joceline judged it impossible he could have the slightest suspicion of the reality.

Yet, notwithstanding this persuasion, and the comradeship which had been established between them, the faithful under-keeper resolved to maintain a strict watch over his gossip Tomkins, and be in readiness to give the alarm should occasion arise. True, he thought, he had reason to believe that his said friend, notwithstanding his drunken and enthusiastic rants, was as trustworthy as he was esteemed by Dr. Rochecliffe; yet still he was an adventurer, the outside and lining of whose cloak were of different colours, and a high reward, and pardon for past acts of malignancy, might tempt him once more to turn his tippet1—For these reasons Joceline kept a strict, though unostentatious watch over Trusty Tomkins.

We have said, that the discreet seneschal was universally well received at Woodstock, whether in the borough or at the Lodge, and that even Joceline Joliffe was anxious to conceal any suspicions which he could not altogether repress, under a great show of cordial hospitality. There were, however, two individuals, who, for very different reasons, nourished personal dislike against the individual so generally acceptable.

One was Nehemiah Holdenough, who remembered, with great bitterness of spirit, the Independent's violent intrusion into his pulpit, and who ever spoke of him in private as a lying missionary, into whom Satan had put a spirit of delusion; and preached, besides, a solemn sermon on the subject of the false prophet, out of whose mouth came frogs. The discourse was highly prized by the Mayor and most of the better class, who conceived that their minister had struck a heavy blow at the very root of Independency. On the other hand, those of the private spirit contended, that Joseph Tomkins had made a successful and triumphant rally, in an exhortation on the evening of the same day, in which he proved, to the conviction of many handicraftsmen, that the passage in Jeremiah, "The prophets prophesy falsely, and the priests bear rule by their means," was directly applicable to the Presbyterian system of church government. The clergyman despatched an account of his adversary's conduct to the Reverend Master Edwards, to be inserted in the next edition of Gangrsena, as a pestilent heretic; and Tomkins recommended the parson to his master, Desborough, as a good subject on whom to impose a round fine, for vexing the private spirit; assuring him, at the same time, that though the minister might seem poor, yet if a few troopers were quartered on him till the fine was paid, every rich shopkeeper's wife in the borough would rob the till, rather than go without the mammon of unrighteousness with which to redeem their priest from sufferance; holding, according to his expression, with Laban, "You have taken from me my gods, and what have I more?" There was, of course, little cordiality To change sides. "*Revelation* xvi. 13. *Jeremiah* v. 31. See note in Chapter X. *Genesis* xxxi. 30. between the polemical disputants, when religious debate took so worldly a turn.

But Joe Tomkins was much more concerned at the evil opinion which seemed to be entertained against him, by one whose good graces he was greatly more desirous to obtain than those of Nehemiah Holdenough. This was no other than pretty Mistress Phoebe Mayflower, for whose conversion he had felt a strong vocation, ever since his lecture upon Shakspeare on their first meeting at the Lodge. He seemed desirous, however, to carry on this more serious work in private, and especially to conceal his labours from his friend Joceline Joliffe, lest, perchance, he had been addicted to jealousy. But it was in vain that he plied the faithful damsel, sometimes with verses from the Canticles, sometimes with quotations from Green's Arcadia, or pithy passages from Venus and Adonis, and doctrines of a nature yet more abstruse, from the popular work entitled Aristotle's Masterpiece. Unto no wooing of his, sacred or profane, metaphysical or physical, would Phoebe Mayflower seriously incline.

The maiden loved Joceline Joliffe, on the one hand; and, on the other, if she disliked Joseph Tomkins when she first saw him, as a rebellious puritan, she had not been at all reconciled by finding reason to regard him as a hypocritical libertine. She hated him in both capacities— never endured his conversation when she could escape from it—and when obliged to remain, listened to him only because she knew he had been so deeply trusted, that to offend him might endanger the security of the family, in the service of which she had been born and bred up, and to whose interest she was devoted. For reasons somewhat similar, she did not suffer her dislike of the steward to become manifest before Joceline Joliffe, whose spirit, as a forester and a soldier, might have been likely to bring matters to an arbitrement, in which the *couteau de chaste* and quarter-staff of her favourite would hare been too unequally matched with the long rapier and pistols which his dangerous rival always carried about his person. But it is difficult to blind jealousy when there is any cause of doubt; and perhaps the sharp watch maintained by Joceline on his comrade, was prompted not only by his zeal for the King's safety, but by some vague suspicion that Tomkins was not ill disposed to poach upon his own fair manor.

The Song of Solomon, in the Old Testament. The *Arcadia; or Menaphon* (1599; first published under the title *Menaphon* in 1589) of Robert Greene (1560?-1592) the dramatist, novelist and pamphleteer. An early poem by Shakespeare. This reference is obscure. It has been suggested that Scott had in mind the pamphlet *Aristotle's Legacy, or His Golden Cabinet of Secrets, with a Compleat Book of Riddles* (1090). *Othello,* I., 3, 146. "Hunting-knife.

Phoebe, in the meanwhile, like a prudent girl, sheltered herself as much as possible by the presence of Goody Jellicot. Then, indeed, it is true the Independent, or whatever he was, used to follow her with his addresses to very little purpose; for Phoebe seemed as deaf, through wilfulness, as the old matron by natural infirmity. This indifference highly incensed her new lover, and induced him anxiously to watch for a time and place, in which he might plead his suit with an energy that should command attention. Fortune, that malicious goddess, who so often ruins us by granting the very object of our vows, did at length procure him such an opportunity as he had long coveted.

It was about sunset, or shortly after, when Phoebe, upon whose activity much of the domestic arrangements depended, went as far as fair Rosamond's spring to obtain water for the evening meal, or rather to gratify the prejudice of the old knight, who believed that celebrated fountain afforded the choicest supplies of the necessary element. Such was the respect in which he was held by his whole family, that to neglect any of his wishes that could be gratified, though with inconvenience to themselves, would, in their estimation, have been almost equal to a breach of religious duty.

To fill the pitcher had, we know, been of late a troublesome task; but Joceline's ingenuity had so far rendered it easy, by repairing rudely a part of the ruined front of the ancient fountain, that the water was collected, and trickling along a wooden spout, dropped from a height of about two feet. A damsel was thereby enabled to place her pitcher under the slowly dropping supply, and without toil to herself, might wait till her vessel was filled.

Phoebe Mayflower, on the evening we allude to, saw, for the first time, this little improvement; and, justly considering it as a piece of gallantry of her silvan admirer, designed to save her the trouble of performing her task in a more inconvenient manner, she gratefully employed the minutes of ease which the contrivance procured her, in reflecting on the good nature and ingenuity of the obliging engineer, and perhaps in thinking he might have done as wisely to have waited till she came to the fountain, that he might have secured personal thanks for the trouble he had taken. But then she knew he was detained in the buttery with that odious Tomkins, and rather than have seen the Independent along with him, she would have renounced the thought of meeting Joceline.

As she was thus reflecting, Fortune was malicious enough to send Tomkins to the fountain, and without Joceline. When she saw his figure darken the path up which he came, an anxious reflection came over the poor maiden's breast, that she was alone, and within the verge of the forest, where in general persons were prohibited to come during the twilight, for disturbing the deer settling to their repose. She encouraged herself, however, and resolved to shew no sense of fear, although, as the steward approached, there was something in the man's look and eye no way calculated to allay her apprehensions.

"The blessings of the evening upon you, my pretty maiden," he said. "I meet you even as the chief servant of Abraham, who was a steward like myself, met Rebecca, the daughter of Bethuel, the son of Milcah, at the well of the city of Nahor, in Mesopotamia. Shall I not, therefore, say to you, set down thy pitcher that I may drink?"

"The pitcher is at your service, Master Tomkins," she replied, "and you may drink as much as you will; but you have, I warrant, drank better liquor, and that not long since."

It was, indeed, obvious that the steward had arisen from a revel, for his features were somewhat flushed, though he had stopped far short of intoxication. But Phoebe's alarm at his first appearance was rather increased when she observed how he had been lately employed.

"I do but use my privilege, my pretty Rebecca; the earth is given to the saints, and the fulness thereof. They shall occupy and enjoy it, both the riches of the mine, and the treasures of the vine; and they shall rejoice, and their *Genesis* xxiv. hearts be merry within them. Thou hast yet to learn the privileges of the saints, my Rebecca."

"My name is Phoebe," said the maiden, in order to sober the enthusiastic rapture which he either felt or affected.

"Phoebe after the flesh," he said. "But Rebecca being spiritualized; for art thou not a wandering and stray sheep?—and am I not sent to fetch thee within the fold?— Wherefore else was it said, Thou shalt find her seated by the well, in the wood which is called after the ancient harlot Rosamond?"

"You have found me sitting here sure enough,"said Phoebe; "but if you wish to keep me company, you must walk to the Lodge with me; and you shall carry my pitcher for me, if you will be so kind. I will hear all the good things you have to say to me as we go along. But Sir Henry calls for his glass of water regularly before prayers."

"What!" exclaimed Tomkins, "hath the old man of bloody hand and perverse heart sent thee hither to do the work of a bondswoman? Verily thou shalt return enfranchised; and for the water thou hast drawn for him, it shall be poured forth, even as David caused to be poured forth the water of the well of Bethlehem." 1

So saying, he emptied the water pitcher, in spite of Phoebe's exclamations and entreaties. He then replaced the vessel beneath the little conduit, and continued:— "Know that this shall be a token to thee. The filling of that pitcher shall be like the running of a sand-glass; and if within the time which shall pass ere it rises to the brim, thou shalt listen to the words which I shall say to thee, then it shall be well with thee, and thy place shall be high among those who, forsaking the instruction which is as milk for babes and sucklings, eat the strong food which nourishes manhood. But if the pitcher shall overbrim with water ere thy ear shall hear and understand, thou shalt then be given as a prey, and as a bondsmaiden, unto those who shall possess the fat and the fair of the earth."

"You frighten me, Master Tomkins," said Phoebe, "though I am sure you do not mean to do so. I wonder how you dare speak words so like the good words in the Bible, when you know how you laughed at your own master, and all the rest of them—when you helped to play the hobgoblins at the Lodge." 2 *Samuel* xxiii. 16.

"Think'st thou then, thou simple fool, that in putting that deceit upon Harrison and the rest, I exceeded my privileges?—Nay, verily. Listen to me, foolish girl. When in former days I lived the most wild, malignant rakehell in Oxfordshire, frequenting wakes and fairs, dancing around Maypoles, and shewing my lustihood1 at football and cudgel-playing—Yea, when I was called, in the language of the uncircumcised, Philip Hazeldine, and was one of the singers in the choir, and one of the ringers in the steeple, and served the priest yonder, by name Rochecliffe, I was not farther from the straight road than when, after long reading, I at length found one blind guide after another, all burners of bricks in Egypt. I left them one by one, the poor tool Harrison being the last; and by my own unassisted strength, I have struggled forward to the broad and blessed light, whereof thou too, Phoebe, shalt be partaker."

"I thank you, Master Tomkins," said Phoebe, suppressing some fear under an appearance of indifference; "but I shall have light enough to carry home my pitcher, would you but let me take it; and that is all the want of light I shall have this evening."

So saying, she stooped to take the pitcher from the fountain; but he snatched hold of her by the arm, and

Erevented her from accomplishing her purpose. Phoebe, owever, was the daughter of a bold forester, prompt at thoughts of self-defence; and though she missed getting hold of the pitcher, she caught up instead a large pebble, which she kept concealed in her right hand.

"Stand up, foolish maiden, and listen," said the Independent, sternly; "and know, in one word, that sin, for which the spirit of man is punished with the vengeance of Heaven, lieth not in the corporal act, but in the thought of the sinner. Believe, lovely Phoebe, that to the pure all acts are pure, and that sin is in our thought, not in our actions— even as the radiance of the day is dark to a blind man, but seen and enjoyed by him whose eyes receive it. To him who is but a novice in the things of the spirit, much is enjoined, much is prohibited; and he is fed with milk fit for babes,—for him are ordinances, prohibitions, and commands. But the saint is above these ordinances and restraints.— To him, as to the chosen child of the house, is given the pass-key to open all locks which withhold him from the enjoyment of his heart's desire. Into such pleasant paths will I guide thee, lovely Phoebe, as shall unite in joy, in innocent freedom, pleasures, which, to the unprivileged, are sinful and prohibited." Vigour. Compare Jooeline Joliffe's reminiscences of Philip Hazeldine, in Chapter III.

An allusion to the occupation of the Israelites during their period of slavery in Egypt.

"I really wish, Master Tomkins, you would let me go home," said Phoebe, not comprehending the nature of his doctrine, but disliking at once his words and his manner. He went on, however, with the accursed and blasphemous doctrines, which, in common with others of the pretended saints, he had adopted, after having long shifted from one sect to another, until he settled in the vile belief, that sin, being of a character exclusively spiritual, only existed in the thoughts, and that the worst actions were permitted to those who had attained to the pitch of believing themselves above ordinance. "Thus, my Phoebe," he continued, endeavouring to draw her towards him, "I can offer thee more than ever was held out to woman since Adam first took his bride by the hand. It shall be for others to stand dry-lipped, doing penance, like papists, by abstinence, when the vessel of pleasure pours forth its delights. Dost thou love money?—I have it, and can procure more—am at liberty to procure it on every hand, and by every means—the earth is mine and its fulness. Do you desire power?—which of these poor cheated commissioner-fellow's estates dost thou covet, I will work it out for thee; for I deal with a mightier spirit than any of them. And it is not without warrant that I have aided the malignant Rochecliffe, and the clown Joliffe, to frighten and baffle them in the guise they did. Ask what thou wilt, Phoebe, I can give, or I can procure it for thee— Then enter with me into a life of delight in this world, which shall prove but an anticipation of the joys of Paradise hereafter!"

Again the fanatical voluptuary endeavoured to pull the poor girl towards him, while she, alarmed, but not scared out of her presence of mind, endeavoured by fair entreaty to prevail on him to release her. But his features, in themselves not marked, had acquired a frightful expression, and he exclaimed, "No, Phoebe—do not think to escape—thou art given to me as a captive—thou hast neglected the hour of grace, and it has glided past—See, the water trickles over thy pitcher, which was to be a sign between us—Therefore I will urge thee no more with words, of which thou art not worthy, but treat thee as a recusant of offered grace."

"Master Tomkins," said Phoebe, in an imploring tone, "consider, for God's sake, I am a fatherless child—do me no injury, it would be a shame to your strength and your manhood—I cannot understand your fine words—I will think on them till to-morrow." Then, in rising resentment, she added more vehemently—" I will not be used rudely—stand off or I will do you a mischief." But, as he pressed upon her with a violence, of which the object could not be mistaken, and endeavoured to secure her right hand, she exclaimed, "Take it then, with a wanion to you!"— and struck him an almost stunning blow on the face, with the pebble which she held ready for such an extremity.

The fanatic let her go, and staggered backward, half stupified; while Phoebe instantly betook herself to flight, screaming for help as she ran, but still grasping the victorious pebble. Irritated to frenzy by the severe blow which he had received, Tomkins pursued, with every black

Eassion in his soul and in his face, mingled with fear lest is villany should be discovered. He called on Phoebe loudly to stop, and had the brutality to menace her with one of his pistols if she continued to fly. Yet she slacked not her pace for his threats, and he must either have executed them, or seen her escape to carry the tale to the Lodge, had she not unhappily stumbled over the projecting root of a fir-tree. But as he rushed upon his prey, rescue interposed in the person of Joceline Joliffe, with his quarterstaff on his shoulder. "How now? what means this?" he said, stepping between Phoebe and her pursuer. Tomkins, already roused to fury, made no other answer than by discharging at Joceline the pistol which he held in his hand. The ball grazed the under-keeper's face, who, in requital of the assault, and saying, "Aha! Let ash answer iron," applied his quarterstaff with so much force to the Independent's head, that lighting on the left temple, the blow proved almost instantly mortal.

A few convulsive struggles were accompanied with these broken words—" Joceline—I am gone—but I forgive thee —Doctor Bochecliffe—I wish I had minded more—Oh! —the clergyman—the funeral-service" As he uttered these words, indicative, it may be, of his return to a creed, which perhaps he had never abjured so thoroughly as he had persuaded himself, his voice was lost in a groan, which, rattling in the throat, seemed unable to find its way to the air. These were the last symptoms of life: the clenched hands presently relaxed—the closed eyes opened, and stared on the heavens a lifeless jelly—the limbs extended themselves and stiffened. The body, which was lately animated with life, was now a lump of senseless clay—the soul, dismissed from its earthly tenement in a moment so unhallowed, was gone before the judgment-seat.

"Oh, what have you-done?—-what have you done, Joceline!" exclaimed Phoebe; "you have killed the man!"

"Better than he should have killed me," answered Joceline; "for he was none of the blinkers 1 that miss their mark twice running.—And yet I am sorry for him. —Many a merry bout have we had together when he was wild Philip Hazeldine, and then he was bad enough; but since he daubed over his vices with hypocrisy, he seems to have proved worse devil than ever."

"Oh, Joceline, come away," said poor Phoebe, "and do not stand gazing on him thus;" for the woodsman, resting on his fatal weapon, stood looking down on the corpse with the appearance of a man half stunned at the event.

"This comes of the ale-pitcher," she continued, in the true style of female consolation, "as I have often told you —For Heaven's sake, come to the Lodge, and let us consult what is to be done."

"Stay first, girl, and let me drag him out of the path; we must not have him lie here in all men's sight—Will you not help me, wench?"

"I cannot, Joceline—I would not touch a lock on him for all Woodstock."

"I must to this gear myself, then," said Joceline, who, a soldier as well as a woodsman, still had great reluctance to the necessary task. Something in the face and broken words of the dying man had made a deep and terrific impression on nerves not easily shaken. He accomplished it, however, so far as to drag the late steward out of the open path, and bestow his body amongst the undergrowth of brambles and briers, so as not to be visible unless particularly looked after. He then returned to Phoebe, who had One who flinches when he fires a gun. *Richard* III., I., 4,158.

sat speechless all the while beneath the tree over whose roots she had stumbled.

"Come away, wench," he said, "come away to the Lodge, and let us study how this is to be answered for— the mishap of his being killed will strangely increase our danger.—What had he sought of thee, wench, when you ran from him like a madwoman?—But I can guess—Phil was always a devil among the girls, and I think, as Doctor Rochecliffe says, that, since he turned saint, he took to himself seven devils worse than himself.—Here is the very place where I saw him, with his sword in his hand raised against the old knight, and he a child of the parish—it was high treason at least—but, by my faith, he hath paid for it at last."

"But, oh, Joceline," said Phoebe, "how could you take so wicked a man into your counsels, and join him in all his plots about scaring the roundhead gentlemen?"

"Why look thee, wench, I thought I knew him at the first meeting, especially when Bevis, who was bred here when he was a dog-leader, would not fly at him; and when we made up our old acquaintance at the Lodge, I found he kept up a close correspondence with Dr. Rochecliffe, who was persuaded that he was a good King's man, and held consequently good intelligence with him The

Doctor boasts to have learned much through his means; I wish to Heaven he may not have been as communicative in turn."

"Oh, Joceline," said the waiting-woman, "you should never have let him within the gate of the Lodge!"

"No more I would, if I had known how to keep him out; but when he went so frankly into our scheme, and told me how I was to dress myself like Robinson the player, whose ghost haunted Harrison—I wish no ghost may haunt me!—when he taught me how to bear myself to terrify his lawful master, what could I think, wench? I only trust the Doctor has kept the great secret of all from his knowledge.—But here we are at the Lodge. Go to thy chamber, wench, and compose thyself. I must seek out Doctor Rochecliffe; he is ever talking of his quick and ready invention. Here come times, I think, that will demand it all."

Phoebe went to her chamber accordingly; but the strength arising from the pressure of danger giving way when the danger was removed, she quickly fell into a succession of hysterical fits, which required the constant attention of Dame Jellicot, and the less alarmed, but more judicious care of Mrs. Alice, before they even abated in their rapid recurrence.

The under-keeper carried his news to the politic Doctor, who was extremely disconcerted, alarmed, nay angry with Joceline, for having slain a person on whose communications he had accustomed himself to rely. Yet his looks declared his suspicion, whether his confidence had not been too rashly conferred—a suspicion which pressed him the more anxiously, that he was unwilling to avow it, as a derogation from his character for shrewdness, on which he valued himself.

Doctor Rochecliffe's reliance, however, on the fidelity of Tomkins, had apparently good grounds. Before the Civil Wars, as may be partly collected from what has been already hinted at, Tomkins, under his true name of Hazeldine, had been under the protection of the Rector of Woodstock, occasionally acted as his clerk, was a distinguished member of his choir, and, being a handy and ingenious fellow, was employed in assisting the antiquarian researches of Dr. Rochecliffe through the interior of Woodstock. When he engaged in the opposite side in the Civil Wars, he still kept up his intelligence with the divine, to whom he had afforded what seemed valuable information from time to time. His assistance had latterly been eminently useful in aiding the Doctor, with the assistance of Joceline and Phoebe, in contriving and executing the various devices by which the Parliamentary Commissioners had been expelled from Woodstock. Indeed, his services in this respect had been thought worthy of no less a reward than a present of what plate remained at the Lodge, which had been promised to the Independent accordingly. The Doctor, therefore, while admitting he might be a bad man, regretted him as a useful one, whose death, if inquired after, was likely to bring additional danger on a house which danger already surrounded, and which contained a pledge so precious.

Compare Phoebe's fear of Tomkins with Phoebe Pyncheon's fear of Judge Pyncheon in Hawthorne's *House of the Seven Gables.*

Might Scott have made the mortal combat between Tomkins and Joliffe more effective? Do you think Scott's imitators in romantic fiction at present would have made more oapital out of this incident?

CHAPTER THE THIRTIETH *Cassio.* That thrust had been my enemy indeed,
But that my coat is better than thou know'st.
Othello

On the dark October night succeeding the evening on which Tomkins was slain, Colonel Everard, besides his constant attendant Roger Wildrake, had Master Nehemiah Holdenough with him as a guest at supper. The devotions of the evening having been performed according to the Presbyterian fashion, a light entertainment, and a double quart of burnt1 claret, were placed before his friends at nine o'clock, an hour unusually late. Master Holdenough soon engaged himself in a polemical discourse against Sectaries and Independents, without being aware that his eloquence was not very interesting to his principal hearer, whose ideas in the meanwhile wandered to Woodstock and all which it contained—the Prince, who lay concealed there—his uncle—above all, Alice Lee. As for Wildrake, after bestowing a mental curse both on Sectaries and Presbyterians as being, in his opinion, never a barrel the better herring, he stretched out his limbs, and would probably have composed himself to rest, but that he as well as his patron had thoughts which murdered sleep.

The party were waited upon by a little gipsy-looking boy, in an orange-tawny doublet, much decayed, and garnished with blue worsted lace. The rogue looked somewhat stinted in size, but active both in intelligence and in limb as his black eyes seemed to promise their vivacity. He was an attendant of Wildrake s choice, who had conferred on him the *nom deguerre* of Spitfire, and had promised him promotion so soon as his young protege Breakfast, was fit to succeed him in his present office. It need scarce be said, that the menage was maintained entirely at the expense of Colonel Everard, who allowed Wildrake to arrange the household very much according to his pleasure. The page did not omit, in offering the company wine from time to time, to accommodate Wildrake with about twice the number of opportunities of refreshing himself which he considered it necessary to afford the Colonel or his reverend guest.

Mulled. *I.e.,* one as good as the other. Dull orange; the cavalier colour. 'Nickname,—name assumed by a knight on entering service.

While they were thus engaged, the good divine lost in his own argument, and the hearers in their private thoughts, their attention was about half past ten arrested by a knocking at the door of the house. To those who have anxious hearts, trifles give cause of alarm.

Even a thing so simple as a knock at the door, may have a character which excites apprehension. This was no quiet gentle tap, intimating a modest intruder;

no redoubled rattle, as the pompous annunciation of some vain person; neither did it resemble the formal summons to formal business, nor the cheerful visit of some welcome friend. It was a single blow, solemn and stern, if not actually menacing in the sound. The door was opened by some of the persons of the house; a heavy foot ascended the stair—a stout man entered the room, and drawing the cloak from his face, said, "Markham Everard, I greet thee in God's name."

It was General Cromwell.

Everard, surprised and taken at unawares, endeavoured in vain to find words to express his astonishment. A bustle occurred in receiving the General, assisting him to uncloak himself, and offering in dumb show the civilities of reception. The General cast his keen eye around the apartment, and fixing it first on the divine, addressed Everard as follows.

"A reverend man I see is with thee. Thou art not one of those, good Markham, who let the time unnoted and unimproved pass away. Casting aside the things of this world—pressing forward to those of the next—it is by thus using our time in this poor seat of terrestrial sin and care, that we may as it were But how is this?" he continued, suddenly changing his tone, and speaking briefly, sharply, and anxiously—" One hath left the room since I entered?"

Wildrake had, indeed, been absent for a minute or two, but had now returned, and stepped forward from a bay window, as if he had been out of sight only, not out of the apartment. "Not so, sir, I stood but in the background out of respect. Noble General, I hope all is well with the Estate, that your Excellency makes us so late a visit?— Would not your Excellency choose some"

"Ah!" said Oliver, looking sternly and fixedly at him —" Our trusty Go-between—our faithful confidant.—No, sir; at present, I desire nothing more than a kind reception, which, methinks, my friend Markham Everard is in no hurry to give me."

"You bring your own welcome, my lord," said Everard, compelling himself to speak.—" I can only trust it was no bad news that made your Excellency a late traveller, and ask, like my follower, what refreshment I shall command for your accommodation."

"The State is sound and healthy, Colonel Everard," said the General; "and yet the less so, that many of its members, who have been hitherto workers together, and proEounders of good counsel, and advancers of the public weal, ave now waxed cold in their love and in their affection for the Good Cause, for which we should be ready, in our various degrees, to act and do, so soon as we are called to act that whereunto we are appointed, neither rashly, nor over-slothfully, neither lukewarmly nor over-violently, but with such a frame and disposition, in which zeal and charity may, as it were, meet and kiss each other in our streets. Howbeit, because we look back after we have put our hand to the plough, therefore is our force waxed dim."

"Pardon me, sir," said Nehemiah Hqldenough, who, listening with some impatience, began to guess in whose company he stood—" Pardon me, for unto this I have a warrant to speak."

"Ah f ah!" said Cromwell. "Surely, most worthy sir, we grieve the Spirit when we restrain those pourings forth, which like water from a rock"

"Nay, therein I differ from you, sir," said Holdenough; "for as there is the mouth to transmit the food, and the profit to digest what Heaven hath sent; so is the preacher ordained to teach, and the people to hear; the shepherd to gather the flock into the sheepfold, the sheep to profit by the care of the shepherd."

"Ah! my worthy sir," said Cromwell, with much unction,

"methinks you verge upon the great mistake, which supposes that churches are tall large houses built by masons, and hearers are men—wealthy men, who pay tithes, the larger as well as the less; and that the priests, men in black gowns or gray cloaks, who receive the same, are in guerdon the only distributors of Christian blessings; whereas, in my apprehension, there is more of Christian liberty in leaving it to the discretion of the hungry soul to seek his edification where it can be found, whether from the mouth of a lay teacher, who claimeth his warrant from Heaven alone, or at the dispensation of those who take ordination and degrees from synods and universities, at best but associations of poor sinful creatures like themselves."

"You speak, you know not what, sir," replied Holdenough, impatiently. "Can light come out of darkness, sense out of ignorance, or knowledge of the mysteries of religion from such ignorant mediciners as give poisons instead of wholesome medicaments, and cram with filth the stomachs of such as seek to them for food?"

This, which the Presbyterian divine uttered rather warmly, the General answered with the utmost mildness.

"Lack-a-day, lack-a-day! a learned man, but intemperate; over-zeal hath eaten him up.—A well-a-day, sir, you may talk of your regular gospel-meals, but a word spoken in season by one whose heart is with your heart, just perhaps when you are riding on to encounter an enemy, or are about to mount a breach, is to the poor spirit like a rasher on the coals, which the hungry shall find preferable to a great banquet, at such times when the full soul loatheth the honey-comb. Nevertheless, although I speak thus in my poor judgment, I would not put force on the conscience of any man, leaving to the learned to follow the learned, and the wise to be instructed by the wise, while poor simple wretched souls are not to be denied a drink from the stream which runneth by the way.—Ay, verily, it will be a comely sight in England when men shall go on as in a better world, bearing with each other's infirmities, joining in each other's comforts.—Ay, truly, the rich drink out of silver flagons, and goblets of silver, the poor out of paltry bowls of wood— and even so let it be, since they both drink the same element. "

Here an officer opened the door and looked in, to whom Cromwell, exchanging the canting drawl, in which it seemed he might have gone on interminably, for the short brief tone of action, called out, "Pearson, is he come?"

"No, sir," replied Pearson; "we have inquired for him at the place you noted, and also at other haunts of his about the town."

"The knave!" said Cromwell, with bitter emphasis; "can he have proved false?—No, no, his interest is too deeply engaged. We shall find him by and by.—Hark thee hither.

While this conversation was going forward, the reader must imagine the alarm of Everard. He was certain that the personal attendance of Cromwell must be on some most important account, and he could not but strongly suspect that the General had some information respecting Charles's lurking place. If taken, a renewal of the tragedy of the 30th of January was instantly to be apprehended, and the ruin of the whole family of Lee, with himself probably included, must be the necessary consequence.

He looked eagerly for consolation at Wildrake, whose countenance expressed much alarm, which he endeavoured to bear out with his usual look of confidence. But the weight within was too great; he shuffled with his feet, rolled his eyes, and twisted his hands, like an unassured witness before an acute and not to be deceived judgeOliver, meanwhile, left his company not a minute's leisure to take counsel together. Even while his perplexed eloquence flowed on in a stream so mazy that no one could discover which way its course was tending, his sharp watchful eye rendered all attempts of Everard to hold communication with Wildrake, even by signs, altogether vain. Everard, indeed, looked for an instant at the window, then glanced at Wildrake, as if to hint there might be a possibility to escape that way. But the cavalier had replied with a disconsolate shake of the head, so slight as to be almost imperceptible. Everard, therefore, lost all hope, and the melancholy feeling of approaching and inevitable evil was only varied by anxiety concerning the shape and manner in which it was about to make its approach.

But Wildrake had a spark of hope left. The very instant Cromwell entered he had got out of the room, and down to the door of the house. "Back—back!" repeated by two armed sentinels, convinced him that, as his fears had anticipated, the General had come neither unattended nor unprepared. He turned on his heel, ran up stairs, and meeting on the landing-place the boy whom he called Spitfire, hurried him into the small apartment which he occupied as his own. Wildrake had been shooting that morning, and game lay on the table. He pulled a feather from a woodcock's wing, and saying hastily, "For thy life, Spitfire, mind my orders—I will put thee safe out at the window into the court—the yard wall is not high—and there will be no sentry there—Fly to the Lodge, as thou wouldst win Heaven, and give this feather to Mistress Alice Lee, if possible—if not, to Joceline Joliffe—say I have won the wager of the young lady. Dost mark me, boy?"

The sharp-witted youth clapped his hands in his master's, and only replied, "Done, and done."

Wildrake opened the window, and, though the height was considerable, he contrived to let the boy down safely by holding his cloak. A heap of straw on which Spitfire lighted rendered the descent perfectly safe, and Wildrake saw him scramble over the wall of the courtyard, at the angle which bore on a back lane; and so rapidly was this accomplished, that the cavalier had just re-entered the room, when, the bustle attending Cromwell's arrival subsiding, his own absence began to be noticed.

He remained during Cromwell's lecture on the vanity of creeds, anxious in mind whether he might not have done better to send an explicit verbal message, since there was no time to write. But the chance of the boy being stopped, or becoming confused with feeling himself the messenger of a hurried and important communication, made him, on the whole, glad that he had preferred a more enigmatical way of conveying the intelligence. He had, therefore, the advantage of his patron, for he was conscious still of a spark of hope.

Pearson had scarce shut the door, when Holdenough, as ready in arms against the future Dictator as he had been prompt to encounter the supposed phantoms and fiends of Woodstock, resumed his attack upon the schismatics, whom he undertook to prove to be at once soul-slayers, false brethren, and false messengers; and was proceeding to allege texts in behalf of his proposition, when Cromwell, apparently tired of the discussion, and desirous to introduce a discourse more accordant with his real feelings, interrupted him, though very civilly, and took the discourse into his own hands.

"Lack-a-day," he said, "the good man speaks truth, according to his knowledge and to his lights—ay, bitter truths, and hard to be digested, while we see as men see, and not with the eyes of angels.—False messengers, said the reverend man?—ay, truly, the world is full of such. You shall see them who will carry your secret message to the house of your mortal foe, and will say to him, 'Lo! my master is going forth with a small train, by such and such desolate places; be you speedy, therefore, that you may arise and slay him.' And another, who knoweth where the foe of your house, and enemy of your person, lies hidden, shall, instead of telling his master thereof, carry tidings to the enemy even where he lurketh, saying, 'Lo! my master knoweth of your secret abode—up, now, and fly, lest he come on thee like a lion on his prey.'—But shall this go without punishment?" looking at Wildrake with a withering glance. "Now, as my soul liveth, and as He liveth who hath made me a ruler in Israel, such false messengers shall be knitted to gibbets on the wayside, and their right hands shall be nailed above their heads, in an extended position, as if pointing out to others the road from which they themselves have strayed!"

"Surely," said Master Holdenough, "it is right to cut off such offenders."

"Thank ye, Mass-John," muttered Wildrake, "when did the Presbyterian fail to lend the devil a shove?"

"But, I say," continued Holdenough,

"that the matter is estranged from our present purpose, for the false brethren of whom I spoke are"

"Right, excellent sir, they be those of our own house," answered Cromwell; "the good man is right once more. Ay, of whom can we now say that he is a true brother, although he has lain in the same womb with us? Although we have struggled in the same cause, eat at the same table, fought in the same battle, worshipped at the same throne, there shall be no truth in him.—Ah, Markham Everard, Markham Everard!"

He paused at this ejaculation; and Everard, desirous at once of knowing how far he stood committed, replied, "Your Excellency seems to have something in your mind in which I am concerned. May I request you will speak it out, that I may know what I am accused of?"

"Ah, Mark, Mark," replied the General, "there needeth no accuser speak when the still small voice speaks within us. Is there not moisture on thy brow, Mark Everard? Is there not trouble in thine eye? Is there not a failure in thy frame? And who ever saw such things in noble and stout Markham Everard, whose brow was only moist after having worn the helmet for a summer's day— whose hand only shook when it had wielded for hours the weighty falchion?—But go to, man! thou doubtest over much. Hast thou not been to me as a brother, and shall I not forgive thee even the seventy-seventh time? The knave hath tarried somewhere, who should have done by this time an office of much import. Take advantage of his absence, Mark; it is a grace that God gives thee beyond expectance. I do not say, fall at my feet; but speak to me as a friend to his friend."

"I have never said anything to your Excellency that was in the least undeserving the title you have assigned to me," said Colonel Everard, proudly.

"Nay, nay, Markham," answered Cromwell; "I say not you have. But— but you ought to have remembered the message I sent you by that person" (pointing to Wildrake); "and you must reconcile it with your conscience, how, having such a message, guarded with such reasons, you could think yourself at liberty to expel my friends from Woodstock, being determined to disappoint my object, whilst you availed yourself of the boon, on condition of which my warrant was issued."

Everard was about to reply, when, to his astonishment, Wildrake stepped forward; and with a voice and look very different from his ordinary manner, and approaching a good deal to real dignity of mind, said, boldly and calmly, "You are mistaken, Master Cromwell; and address yourself to the wrong party here."

The speech was so sudden and intrepid, that Cromwell stepped a pace back, and motioned with his right hand towards his weapon, as if he had expected that an address of a nature so unusually bold was to be followed by some act of violence. He instantly resumed his indifferent posture; and, irritated at a smile which he observed on Wildrake's countenance, he said, with the dignity of one long accustomed to see all tremble before him, "This to me, fellow! Know you to whom you speak?"

"Fellow!" echoed Wildrake, whose reckless humour was now completely set afloat—"No fellow of yours, Master Oliver. I have known the day when Roger Wildrake of Squattlesea-mere, Lincoln, a handsome young gallant with a good estate, would have been thought no fellow of the bankrupt brewer of Huntingdon."

"Be silent!" said Everard; "be silent, Wildrake, if you love your life!"

"I care not a maravedi for my life," said Wildrake. "Zounds, if he dislikes what I say, let him take to his tools! I know, after all, he hath good blood in his veins; and I will indulge him with a turn in the court yonder, had he been ten times a brewer."

"Such ribaldry, friend," said Oliver, "I treat with the contempt it deserves. But if thou hast anything to say touching the matter in question, speak out like a man, though thou look'st more like a beast."

"All I have to say is," replied Wildrake, "that whereas you blame Everard for acting on your warrant, as you call it, I can tell you, he knew not a word of the rascally conditions you talk of. I took care of that; and you may take the vengeance on me, if you list."

"Slave! dare you tell this to *me?*" said Cromwell, still needfully restraining his passion, which he felt was about to discharge itself upon an unworthy object.

"Ay, you will make every Englishman a slave, if you have your own way," said Wildrake, not a whit abashed;— for the awe which had formerly overcome him when alone with this remarkable man, had vanished, now that they were engaged in an altercation before witnesses.—" But do your worst, Master Oliver; I tell you beforehand, the bird has escaped you."

"You dare not say so!—Escaped—So ho! Pearson! tell the soldiers to mount instantly Thou art a lying fool!—

Escaped?—Where, or from whence?"

"Ay, that is the question," said Wildrake; "for look you, sir—that men do go from hence is certain—but how they go, or to what quarter" "The better opinion seems to be that the business of brewing was carried on at some time by Robert Cromwell, or his wife and widow; though not by Oliver himself."— F. Harrison's *Cromwell,* p. 6. Neither Robert nor Oliver Cromwell was ever bankrupt, as far as is known. A Spanish coin of the smallest denomination.

Cromwell stood attentive, expecting some useful hint from the careless impetuosity of the cavalier, upon the route which the King might have taken.

"—Or to what quarter, as I said before, why, your Excellency, Master Oliver, may e'en find that out yourself."

As he uttered the last words he unsheathed his rapier, and made a full pass at the General's body. Had his sword met no other impediment than the buff jerkin, Cromwell's course had ended on the spot. But, fearful of such attempts, the General wore under his military dress a shirt of the finest mail, made of rings of the best steel, and so light and flexible that it was little or no encumbrance to the motions of the wearer. It proved his safety on this occasion, for the rapier sprung in shivers; while the owner, now held back by Everard and Holdenough, flung the hilt with passion on the ground, exclaiming, "Be damned the hand that forged thee!—To serve me so long, and fail me when thy true service would have honoured us both for ever! But no good could come of thee, since thou wert pointed, even in jest, at a learned divine of the Church of England."

In the first instant of alarm, and perhaps suspecting Wild rake might be supported by others, Cromwell half drew from his bosom a concealed pistol, which he hastily returned, observing that both Everard and the clergyman were withholding the cavalier from another attempt.

Pearson and a soldier or two rushed in—" Secure that fellow," said the General, in the indifferent tone of one to whom imminent danger was too familiar to cause irritation—" Bind him—but not so hard, Pearson;"—for the men, to shew their zeal, were drawing their belts, which they used for want of cords, brutally tight round Wildrake's limbs. "He would have assassinated me, but I would reserve him for his fit doom."

"Assassinated!—I scorn your words, Master Oliver," said Wildrake; "I proffered you a fair duello."

"Shall we shoot him in the street, for an example?" said Pearson to Cromwell; while Everard endeavoured to stop Wildrake from giving further offence.

"On your life harm him not; but let him be kept in safe ward, and well looked after," said Cromwell; while the prisoner exclaimed to Everard, "I prithee let me alone—I am now neither thy follower, nor any man's, and I am as willing to die as ever I was to take a cup of liquor.—And hark ye, speaking of that, Master Oliver, you were once a jolly fellow, prithee let one of thy lobsters here advance yonder tankard to my lips, and your Excellency shall hear a toast, a song, and a—secret."

"'Unloose his head, and hand the debauched beast the tankard," said Oliver; "while yet he exists, it were shame to refuse him the element he lives in."

"Blessings on your head for once," said Wildrake, whose object in continuing this wild discourse was, if possible, to gam a little delay when every moment was precious. "Thou hast brewed good ale, and that's warrant for a blessing. For my toast and my song, here they go together—

Son of a witch.

Mayst thou die in a ditch, With the butchers who back thy quarrels;
And rot above ground,
While the world shall resound
A welcome to Royal King Charles.

And now for my secret, that you may not say I had your liquor for nothing—I fancy my song will scarce pass current for much—My secret is, Master Cromwell—that the bird is flown—and your red nose will be as white as your winding-sheet before you can smell out which way."

"Pshaw, rascal," answered Cromwell, contemptuously, "keep your scurrile jests for the gibbet foot."

"I shall look on the gibbet more boldly," replied Wildrake, "than I have seen you look on the Royal Martyr's picture."

This reproach touched Cromwell to the very quick.— "Villain!" he exclaimed; "drag him hence, draw out a party, and But hold, not now—to prison with him— let him be close watched, and gagged, if he attempts to speak to the sentinels—Nay, hold—I mean, put a bottle of brandy into his cell, and he will gag himself in his own way, I warrant you—When day comes, that men can see the example, he shall be gagged after my fashion."

During the various breaks in his orders, the General was evidently getting command of his temper; and though he began in fury, he ended with the contemptuous sneer of one who overlooks the abusive language of an inferior. Something remained on his mind notwithstanding, for he continued standing, as if fixed to the same spot in the apartment, his eyes bent on the ground, and with closed hand pressed against his lips, like a man who is musing deeply. Pearson, who was about to speak to' him, drew back, and made a sign to those in the room to be silent.

Master Holdenough did not mark, or, at least, did not obey it. Approaching the General, he said, in a respectful but firm tone, "Did I understand it to be your Excellency's purpose that this poor man shall die next morning?" "Hah!" exclaimed Cromwell, starting from his reverie, "what say'st thou?" "I took leave to ask, if it was your will that this unhappy man should die to-morrow?

"Whom saidst thou?" demanded Cromwell: "Markham Everard—shall he die, saidst thou?"

"God forbid!" replied Holdenough, stepping back— "I asked whether this blinded creature, Wildrake, was to be so suddenly cut off?"

"Ay, marry is he," said Cromwell, "were the whole General Assembly of Divines at Westminster—the whole Sanhedrim of Presbytery—to offer bail for him."

"If you will not think better of it, sir," said Holdenough, "at least give not the poor man the means of destroying his senses—Let me go to him as a divine, to watch with him, in case he may yet be admitted into the vineyard at the latest hour—yet brought into the sheepfold though he has neglected the call of the pastor till time is well-nigh closed upon him."

"For God's sake," said Everard, who had hitherto kept Commonly called the Westminster Assembly, a convocation summoned by the Long Parliament to advise for the settling of the government and the liturgy of the Church of England. Most of its members were Presbyterians, and nearly all were Calvinists. It was in session from July, 1643, till February, 1649. The chief fruits of its labours were the Directory of Public Worship, the Confession of Faith, and the Larger and Shorter Catechisms, which were rejected in England, but established in Scotland.
The national council of the Jews. silence, because he knew Cromwell's temper on such occasions, " think better of what you do!"

"Is it for thee to teach me?" replied Cromwell; "think thou of thine own matters, and believe me it will require all thy wit.—And for you, reverend sir, I will have no father-confessors attend my prisoners—no tales out of school. If the fellow thirst after ghostly comfort, as he is much more likely to thirst after a quartern of brandy, there is Corporal Humgudgeon, who commands the *corps de garde,* will preach and pray as well as the best of ye.— But this delay is intolerable—Comes not this fellow yet?"

"No, sir," replied Pearson. "Had we not better go down to the Lodge? The news of our coming hither may else get there before ns."

"True," said Cromwell, speaking aside to his-officer, "but you know Tomkins warned us against doing so, alleging there were so many postern-doors, and sally-ports, and concealed entrances in the old house, that it was like a rabbit-warren, and that an escape might be easily made under our very noses, unless he were with us, to point out all the ports which should be guarded. He hinted, too, that he might be delayed a few minutes after his time of appointment—but we have now waited half an hour." "Does your Excellency think Tomkins is certainly to be depended upon?" said Pearson.

"As far as his interest goes, unquestionably," replied the General. "He has ever been the pump by which I have sucked the marrow out of many a plot, in special those of the conceited fool Rochecliffe, who is goose enough to believe that such a fellow as Tomkins would value anything beyond the offer of the best bidder. And yet it groweth late—I fear we must to the Lodge without him—Yet, all things well considered, I will tarry here till midnight.—Ah, Everard, thou mightest put this gear to rights if thou wilt! Shall some foolish principle of fantastic punctilio have more weight with thee, man, than have the pacification and welfare of England; the keeping of faith to thy friend and benefactor, and who will be yet more so, and the fortune and security of thy relations? Are these, I say, lighter in the balance than the cause of a worthless boy, who, with his father and his father's house, have troubled Israel for fifty years?"

"I do not understand your Excellency, nor at what service you point, which I can honestly render," replied Everard. "That which is dishonest I should be loath that you proposed." "Then this at least might suit your honesty, or scrupulous humour, call it which thou wilt," said Cromwell. "Thou knowest, surely, all the passages about Jezebel's palace down yonder?—Let me know how they may be guarded against the escape of any from within."

"I cannot pretend to aid you in this matter," said Everard; "I know not all the entrances and posterns about Woodstock, and if I did, I am not free in conscience to communicate with you on this occasion."

"We shall do without you, sir," replied Cromwell, haughtily; "and if aught is found which may criminate you, remember you have lost right to my protection."

"I shall be sorry," said Everard, "to have lost your friendship, General; but I trust my quality as an Englishman may dispense with the necessity of protection from any man. I know no law which obliges me to be spy or informer, even if I were in the way of having opportunity to do service in either honourable capacity."

"Well, sir," said Cromwell, "for all your privileges and qualities, I will make bold to take you down to the Lodge at Woodstock to-night, to inquire into affairs in which the State is concerned.—Come hither, Pearson." He took a paper from his pocket containing a rough sketch or groundplan of Woodstock Lodge, with the avenues leading to it. —"Look here," he said, "we must move in two bodies on foot, and with all possible silence—thou must march to the rear of the old house of iniquity with twenty file of men, and dispose them around it the wisest thou canst. Take the reverend man there along with you. He must be secured at any rate, and may serve as a guide. I myself will occupy the front of the Lodge, and thus having stopt all the earths, thou wilt come to me for farther orders— silence and despatch is all.—But for the dog Tomkins, who broke appointment with me, he had need render a good excuse, or woe to his father's son!—Reverend sir, be pleased to accompany that officer.—Colonel Everard, you are to follow me; but first give your sword to Captain Pearson, and consider yourself as under arrest." An allusion to Rosamond, under the name of the wicked wife of Ahab (1 *Kings* xvi., 31, etc.).
The hole or burrow where the fox is hidden.

Everard gave his sword to Pearson without any comment, and with the most anxious presage of evil followed the Republican General, in obedience to commands which it would have been useless to dispute.

Note that Cromwell's endeavour to capture Charles has not been referred to since his first hint to Wildrake. Can yon see any advantage in keeping Cromwell inactive in the background for so long?

CHAPTER THE THIRTY-FIRST

'' Were my son William here but now
He wadna fail the pledge."
Wi' that in at the door there ran
A ghastly-looking page—-
"I saw them, master, Oh! I saw,
Beneath the thornie brae,
Of black-mailed warriors many a rank,
Revenge!" he cried, "and gae"—

Henry Mackenzie.

The little party at the Lodge were assembled at supper, at the early hour of eight o'clock. Sir Henry Lee, neglecting the food that was placed on the table, stood by a lamp on the chimney-piece, and read a letter with mournful attention.

"Does my son write to you more particularly than to me, Doctor Rochecliffe*?"* said the knight. "He only says here, that he will return probably this night; and that Master Kerneguy must be ready to set off with him instantly. What can this haste mean? Have you heard of any new search after our suffering party? I wish they would permit me to enjoy my son's company in quiet but for a day."

"The quiet which depends on the wicked ceasing from troubling," said Doctor Rochecliffe, "is connected, not by days and hours, but by minutes.

Their glut of blood at Worcester had satiated them for a moment, but their appetite, I fancy, has revived."

"You have news, then, to that purpose?" said Sir Henry.

"Your son," replied the Doctor, "wrote to me by the same messenger: he seldom fails to do so, being aware of what importance it is that I should know everything that passes. Means of escape are provided on the coast, and Master Kerneguy must be ready to start with your son the instant he appears."

"It is strange," said the knight; "for forty years I have dwelt in this house, man and boy, and the point only was how to make the day pass over our heads; for if I did not scheme out some hunting match or hawking, or the like, I might have sat here on my arm-chair, as undisturbed as a sleeping dormouse, from one end of the year to the other; and now I am more like a hare on her form, that dare not sleep unless with her eyes open, and scuds off when the wind rustles among the fern."

"It is strange," said Alice, looking at Doctor Rochecliffe, "that the roundhead steward has told you nothing of this. He is usually communicative enough of the motions of his party; and I saw you close together this morning."

"I must be closer with him this evening," said the Doctor gloomily; "but he will not blab."

"I wish you may not trust him too much," said Alice in reply.—" To me, that man's face, with all its shrewdness, evinces such a dark expression, that methinks I read treason in his very eye."

"Be assured, that matter is looked to," answered the Doctor, in the same ominous tone as before. No one replied, and there was a chilling and anxious feeling of apprehension which seemed to sink down on the company at once, like those sensations which make such constitutions as are particularly subject to the electrical influence, conscious of an approaching thunder-storm.

The disguised Monarch, apprized that day to be prepared on short notice to quit his temporary asylum, felt his own share of the gloom which involved the little society. But he was the first also to shake it off, as what neither suited his character nor his situation. Gaiety was the leading distinction of the former, and presence of mind, not depression of spirits, was required by the latter.

"We make the hour heavier," he said, "by being melancholy about it. Had you not better join me, Mistress Alice, in Patrick Carey's jovial farewell?—Ah, you do not know Pat Carey—a younger brother of Lord Falkland's."

"A brother of the immortal Lord Falkland's, and write songs!" said the Doctor.

Note D. Patrick Carey. Scott. Lucius Cary, Viscount Falkland, a young man of great nobility and sweetness of character, Secretary of State in 1641, but forced by his sense of duty to abandon his friends of the Parliamentary party and to side with the King in 1642. Clarendon's account of his death at the battle of Newbury (Sept 20, 1643) is one of the most touching passages in the *History of the Rebellion* (Book VII.). See also Matthew Arnold's essay on Falkland in *Mixed Essays*.

"Oh, Doctor, the Muses take tithe as well as the Church," said Charles, "and have their share in every family of distinction. You do not know the words, Mistress Alice, but you can aid me, notwithstanding, in the burden at least—

Come, now that we're parting, and 'tis one to ten
If the towers of sweet Woodstock I e'er see agen,
Let us e'en have a frolic, and drink like tall men
While the goblet goes merrily round."

The song arose, but not with spirit. It was one of those efforts at forced mirth, by which, above all other modes of expressing it, the absence of real cheerfulness is most distinctly intimated. Charles stopt the song, and upbraided the choristers.

"You sing, my dear Mistress Alice, as if you were chanting one of the seven penitential psalms;1 and you, good Doctor, as if you recited the funeral service."

The Doctor rose hastily from the table, and turned to the window; for the expression connected singularly with the task which he was that evening to discharge. Charles looked at him with some surprise; for the peril in which he lived, made him watchful of the slightest motions of those around him—then turned to Sir Henry, and said, "My honoured host, can you tell any reason for this moody fit, which has so strangely crept upon us all?"

"Not I, my dear Louis," replied the knight; "I have no skill in these nice quillets of philosophy. I could as soon undertake to tell you the reason why Bevis turns round three times before he lies down. I can only say for myself, that if age and sorrow and uncertainty be enough to break a jovial spirit, or at least to bend it now and then, I have my share of them all; so that I, for one, cannot say that I am sad merely because I am not merry. I have but too good cause for sadness. I would I saw my son, were it but for a minute." The original song of Carey bears Wykeham, instead of Woodstock, for the locality. The verses are full of the bacchanalian spirit of the time. Scott. *Psalms* 6, 32, 38, 51, 102, 130, 142, so called from their penitential character; in Protestant Episcopal churches, appointed to be read during the services of Ash Wednesday, and in the Roman Catholic church on occasions of special humiliation.

Subtle distinctions. *Merchant of Venice*, I., 1, 47.

Fortune seemed for once disposed to gratify the old man; for Albert Lee entered at that moment. He was dressed in a riding suit, and appeared to have travelled hard. He cast his eye hastily around as he entered. It rested for a second on that of the disguised Prince, and satisfied with the glance which he received in lieu, he hastened, after the fashion of the olden day, to kneel down to his father, and request his blessing.

"It is thine, my boy," said the old man; a tear springing to his eyes as he laid his hand on the long locks, which distinguish the young cavalier's rank and principles, and which, usually combed and curled with some care, now hung wild and dishevelled about his shoulders. They remained an instant in this posture, when the old man suddenly started from it, as if ashamed of the emotion which he had expressed before so many witnesses, and passing the back of his hand hastily across his eyes, bid Albert get up and mind his supper, "since I dare say you have ridden fast and far since you last baited—and we'll send round a cup to his health, if Doctor Rochecliffe and the good company pleases—Joceline, thou knave, skink about—thou look'st as if thou hadst seen a ghost."

"Joceline," said Alice, "is sick for sympathy—one of the stags ran at Phoebe Mayflower to-day, and she was fain to have Joceline's assistance to drive the creature off—the girl has been in fits since she came home."

"Silly slut," said the old knight—" she a woodman's daughter!—But, Joceline, if the deer gets dangerous, you must send a broad arrow through him.

"It will not need, Sir Henry," said Joceline, speaking with great difficulty of utterance—" he is quiet enough now — he will not offend in that sort again."

"See it be so," replied the knight; "remember Mistress Alice often walks in the chase. And now fill round, and fill, too, a cup to thyself to over-red thy fear, as mad Will has it. Tush, man, Phoebe will do well enough—she only screamed and ran, that thou might'st have the pleasure to help her. Mind what thou dost, and do not go spilling the wine after that fashion.—Come, here is a health to our wanderer, who has come to us again." Serve the wine.
"Macbeth, V., 3, 15.

"None will pledge it more willingly than *I"* said the disguised Prince, unconsciously assuming an importance which the character he personated scarce warranted; but Sir Henry, who had become fond of the supposed page, with all his peculiarities, imposed only a moderate rebuke upon his petulance. "Thou art a merry, good-humoured youth, Louis," he said; "but it is a world to see how the forwardness of the present generation hath gone beyond the gravity and reverence which in my youth was so regularly observed towards those of higher rank and station—I dared no more have given my own tongue the rein, when there was a doctor of divinity in company, than I would have dared to have spoken in church in service time."

"True, sir," said Albert, hastily interfering, "but Master Kerneguy had the better right to speak at present, that I have been absent on his business as well as my own, have seen several of his friends, and bring him important intelligence."

Charles was about to rise and beckon Albert aside, naturally impatient to know what news he had procured, or what scheme of safe escape was now decreed for him. But Doctor Rochecliffe twitched his cloak, as a hint to him to sit still, and not shew any extraordinary motive for anxiety, since, in case of a sudden discovery of his real quality, the violence of Sir Henry Lee's feelings might have been likely to attract too much attention.

Charles, therefore, only replied, as to the knight's stricttire, that he had a particular title to be sudden and unceremonious in expressing his thanks to Colonel Lee—that gratitude was apt to be unmannerly—finally, that he was much obliged to Sir Henry for his admonition; and that quit Woodstock when he would, "he was sure to leave it a better man than he came there."

His speech was of course ostensibly directed towards the father; but a glance at Alice assured her that she had her full share in the compliment.

"I fear," he concluded, addressing Albert, "that you come to tell us our stay here must be very short."

"A few hours only," said Albert—" just enough for needful rest for ourselves and our horses. I have procured two which are good and tried. But Doctor Rochecliffe broke faith with me. I expected to have met some one down at Joceline's hut, where I left the horses; and finding no person, I was delayed an hour in littering them down myself, that they might be ready for to-morrow's work—for we must be off before day."

"I — I — intended to have sent Tomkins — but — but"hesitated the Doctor, "I"

"The roundheaded rascal was drunk, or out of the way, I presume," said Albert. "I am glad of it—you may easily trust him too far."

"Hitherto he has been faithful," said the Doctor, "and I scarce think he will fail me now. But Joceline will go down and have the horses in readiness in the morning."

Joceline's countenance was usually that of alacrity itself on a case extraordinary. Now, however, he seemed to hesitate.

"You will go with me a little way, Doctor!" he said, as he edged himself closely to Rochecliffe.

"How? puppy, fool, and blockhead," said the knight, "wouldst thou ask Dr. Rochecliffe to bear thee company at this hour?—Out, hound!—get down to the kennel yonder instantly, or I will break the knave's pate of thee."

Joceline looked with an eye of agony at the divine, as if entreating him to interfere in his behalf; but just as he was about to speak, a most melancholy howling arose at the hall-door, and a dog was heard scratching for admittance.

"What ails Bevis next?" said the old knight. "I think this must be All-Fools-day, and that every thing around me is going mad!"

The same sound startled Albert and Charles from a private conference in which they had engaged, and Albert ran to the hall-door to examine personally into the cause of the noise.

"It is no alarm," said the old knight toKerneguy, "for in such cases the dog's bark is short, sharp, and furious. These long howls are said to be ominous. It was even so that Bevis's grandsire bayed the whole livelong night on which my poor father died. If it comes now as a presage, God send it regard the old and useless, not the young, and those who may yet serve King and country!"

The dog had pushed past Colonel Lee, who stood a little while at the hall-door to listen if there were any thing stirring without, while Bevis advanced into the room where the company were assembled, bearing something in his mouth, and exhibiting, in an unusual degree, that sense of duty and interest which a dog seems to shew when he thinks he has the charge of something important. He entered, therefore, drooping his long tail, slouching his head and ears, and walking with the stately yet melancholy dignity of a war-horse at his master's funeral. In this manner he paced through the room, went straight up to Joceline, who had been regarding him with astonishment, and uttering a short and melancholy howl, laid at his feet the object which he bore in his mouth. Joceline stooped, and took from the floor a man's glove, of the fashion worn by the troopers, having something like the old-fashioned gauntlet projections of thick leather arising from the wrist, which go half way up to the elbow, and secure the arm against a cut with a sword. But Joceline had no sooner looked at what in itself was so common an object, than he dropped it from his hand, staggered backward, uttered a groan, and nearly fell to the ground.

"Now, the coward's curse be upon thee for an idiot!" said the knight, who had picked up the glove, and was looking at it—"thou shouldst be sent back to school, and flogged till the craven's blood was switched out of thee— What dost thou look at but a glove, thou base poltroon, and a very dirty glove, too?— Stay, here is writing— Joseph Tomkins? why, that is the roundheaded fellow— I wish he hath not come to some mischief—for this is not dirt on the cheveron, but blood—Bevis may have bit the fellow, and yet the dog seemed to love him well too—or the stag may have hurt him—Out, Joceline, instantly, and see where he is—wind your bugle."

"I cannot go," said Joliffe, "unless "—and again he looked piteously at Doctor Rochecliffe, who saw no time was to be lost in appeasing the ranger's terrors, as his ministry was most needful in the present circumstances.— "Get spade and mattock," he whispered to him, "and a dark lantern, and meet me in the wilderness."

Joceline left the room; and the Doctor, before following him, had a few words of explanation with Colonel Lee. His own spirit, far from being dismayed on the occasion, rather rose higher, like one whose natural element was intrigue and danger. "Here hath been wild work," he said, " since you parted. Tomkins was rude to the wench Phoebe—Joceline and he had a brawl together, and Tomkins is lying dead in the thicket, not far from Rosamond's Well. It will be necessary that Joceline and I go directly to bury the body; for besides that some one might stumble upon it, and raise an alarm, this fellow Joceline will never be fit for any active purpose till it is under ground. Though as stout as a lion, the under-keeper has his own weak side, and is more afraid of a dead body than a living one. When do you propose to start to-morrow?" i Stripes meeting at an angle, worn on the sleeve, or wrist of the glove, to indicate the rank of a non-commissioned officer.

"By daybreak, or earlier," said Colonel Lee; "but we will meet again— A vessel is provided, and I have relays in more places than one—we go off from the coast of Sussex; and I am to get a letter at, acquainting me precisely with the spot."

"Wherefore not go off instantly ?" said the Doctor.

"The horses would fail us," replied Albert; "they have been hard ridden to-day."

"Adieu," said Rochecliffe, " I must to my task—Do you take rest and repose for yours. To conceal a slaughtered body, and convey on the same night a king from danger and captivity, are two feats which have fallen to few folks save myself; but let me not, while putting on my harness, boast myself as if I were taking it off after a victory." So saying he left the apartment, and muffling himself in his coat, went out into what was called the Wilderness.

The weather was a raw frost. The mist lay in partial wreaths upon the lower grounds; but the night, considering that the heavenly bodies were in a great measure hidden by the haze, was not extremely dark. Doctor Rochecliffe could not, however, distinguish the under-keeper, until he had hemmed once or twice, when Joceline answered the signal by shewing a glimpse of light from the dark lantern which he carried. Guided by this intimation of his presence, the divine found him leaning against a buttress which had once supported a terrace, now ruinous. He had a pickaxe and shovel, together with a deer's hide hanging over his shoulder.

"What do you want with the hide, Joceline," said Dr. Rochecliffe, "that you lumber it about with you on such an errand?"

"Why, look you, Doctor," he answered, "it is as well to tell you all about it. The man and I—he there—you know whom I mean—had many years since a quarrel about this deer. For though we were great friends, and Philip was sometimes allowed by my master's permission to help me in mine office, yet I knew, for all that, Philip Hazeldine was sometimes a trespasser. The deer-stealers were very bold at that time, it being just before the breaking out of the war, when men were becoming unsettled. And so it chanced, that one day, in the Chase, I found two fellows, with their faces blacked, and shirts over their clothes, carrying as prime a buck between them as any was in the park. I was upon them in the instant—one escaped, but I got hold of the other fellow, and who should it prove to be but trusty Phil Hazeldine! Well, I don't know whether it was right or wrong, but he was my old friend and pot-companion, and I took his word for amendment in future; and he helped me to hang up the deer on a tree, and I came back with a horse to carry him to the Lodge, and tell the knight the story, all but Phil's name. But the rogues had been too clever for me; for they had flayed and dressed the deer, and quartered him, and carried him off, and left the hide and horns, with a chime, saying—

The haunch to thee,

The breast to me,

The hide and the horns for the keeper's fee.

And this I knew for one of Phil's mad pranks, that he would play in those days with any lad in the country. But I was so nettled, that I made the deer's hide be curried and dressed by a tanner, and swore that it should be his winding-sheet or mine; and though I had long repented my rash oath, yet now, Doctor, you see what it has come to—though I forgot it, the devil did not."

"It was a very wrong thing to make a vow so sinful," said Rochecliffe; "but it would have been greatly worse had you endeavoured to keep it. Therefore, I bid you cheer up," said the good divine; "for in this unhappy case, I could not have wished, after what I have heard from Phoebe and yourself, that you should have kept your hand still, though I may regret that the blow has proved fatal. Nevertheless, thou hast done even that which was done by the great and inspired legislator, when he beheld an Rhyme. Moses *(Exodus* ii. 11, 12).

Egyptian tyrannizing over a Hebrew, saving that, in the case present, it was a female, when, says the Septuagint, *Percussum Egyptium abscondit sabulo;* the meaning whereof I will explain to you another time. Wherefore, I exhort you, not to grieve beyond measure; for, although this circumstance is unhappy in time and place, yet, from what Phoebe hath informed me of yonder wretch's opinions, it is much to be regretted that his brains had not been beaten out in his cradle, rather than that he had grown up to be one of those Grindlestonians, or Muggletonians, in whom is the perfection of every foul and blasphemous heresy, united with such an universal practice of hypocritical assentation, as would deceive their master, even Satan himself."

"Nevertheless, sir," said the forester, "I hope you will bestow some of the service of the church on this poor man, as it was his last wish, naming you, sir, at the same time; and unless this were done, I should scarce dare to walk out in the dark again, for my whole life."

"Thou art a silly fellow—but if," continued the Doctor, "he named me as he departed, and desired the last rites of the church, there was, it may be, a turning from evil and a seeking to good even in his last moments; and if Heaven granted him grace to form a prayer so fitting, wherefore should man refuse it? All I fear is the briefness of time."

"Nay, your reverence may cut the service somewhat short," said Joceline; "assuredly he does not deserve the whole of it; only if something were not to be done, I believe I should flee the country. They were his last words; and methinks he sent Bevis with his glove to put me in mind of them."

"Out, fool! Do you think," said the Doctor, "dead men send gauntlets to the living, like knights in a romance; or, if so, would they choose dogs to carry their challenges? I tell thee, fool, the cause was natural enough. Bevis, questing about, found the body, and brought the glove to you to intimate where it was lying, and to require assistance; for such is the high instinct of these animals towards one in peril."

"Nay, if you think so, Doctor,"said Joceline—"and, doubtless, I must say, Bevis took an interest in the man— if indeed it was not something worse in the shape of Bevis, for methought his eyes looked wild and fiery, as if he would have spoken." He hid the slain Egyptian in the sand. Contemptuous term for Muggletonians.

As he talked thus, Joceline rather hung back, and, in doing so, displeased the Doctor, who exclaimed, "Come along, thou lazy laggard. Art thou a soldier, and a brave one, and so much afraid of a dead man? Thou hast killed men in battle, and in chase, I warrant thee."

"Ay, but their backs were to me," said Joceline. "I never saw one of them cast back his head, and glare at me as yonder fellow did, his eye retaining a glance of hatred, mixed with terror and reproach, till it became fixed like a jelly. And were you not with me, and my master's concerns, and something else, very deeply at stake, I promise you I would not again look at him for all Woodstock."

"You must, though," said the Doctor, suddenly pausing, —"for here is the place where he lies. Come hither deep into the copse; take care of stumbling— Here is a place just fitting, and we will draw the briers over the grave afterwards."

As the Doctor thus issued his directions, he assisted also in the execution of them; and while his attendant laboured to dig a shallow and misshapen grave, a task which the state of the soil, perplexed with roots, and hardened by the influence of the frost, rendered very difficult, the divine read a few passages out of the funeral service, partly in order to appease the superstitious terrors of Joceline, and partly because he held it matter of conscience not to deny the church's rites to one who had requested their aid in extremity.

This is a good example of a chapter designed to create a feeling of suspense in the reader. As a crisis is evidently approaching, it may be well to review the action and characters up to this point, determining the lines of character development, if any, and thus forecasting the final issue. From what you know of Scott's books, do you think their *denotement* is usually dictated by the laws that govern character, as in George Eliot's books, or do events outside of the characters decide the fate of the characters?

CHAPTER THE THIRTY-SECOND

Case ye, case ye,—on with your vizards.

Henby rv.

The company whom we had left in Victor Lee's parlour were about to separate for the night, and had risen to take a formal leave of each other, when a tap was heard at the hall-door. Albert, the vidette of the party, hastened to open it, enjoining, as he left the room, the rest to remain quiet, until he had ascertained the cause of the knocking. When he gained the portal, he called to know who was there, and what they wanted at so late an hour.

"It is only me," answered a treble voice.

"And what is your name, my little fellow *?"* said Albert.

"Spitfire, sir," replied the voice without.

"Spitfire?" said Albert.

"Yes, sir," replied the voice; "all the world calls me so, and Colonel Everard himself. But my name is Spittal for all that."

"Colonel Everard! arrive you from him?" demanded young Lee.

"No, sir; I come, sir, from Roger Wildrake, esquire, of Squattlesea-mere, if it like you," said the boy; "and I have brought a token to Mistress Lee, which I am to give into her own hands, if you would but open the door, sir, and let me in—but I can do nothing with a three-inch board between us."

"It is some freak of that drunken rakehell," said Albert, in a low voice, to his sister, who had crept out after him on tiptoe.

"Yet let us not be hasty in concluding so," said the young lady, "at this moment the least trifle my be of consequence.—What token has Master Wildrake sent me, my little boy?" Sentinel or scout.

"Nay, nothing very valuable neither," replied the boy; "but he was so anxious you should get it, that he put me out of window as one would chuck out a kitten, that I might not be stopped by the soldiers."

"Hear you?" said Alice to her brother; "undo the gate for God's sake."

Her brother, to whom her feelings of suspicion were now sufficiently communicated, opened the gate in haste, and admitted the boy, whose appearance, not much dissimilar to that of a skinned rabbit in a livery, or a monkey at a fair, would at another time have furnished them with amusement. The urchin messenger entered the hall, making several odd bows and conges, and delivered the woodcock's feather with much ceremony to the young lady, assuring her it was the prize she had won upon a wager about hawking.

"I prithee, my little man," said Albert, "was your master drunk or sober, when he sent thee all this way with a feather at this time of night?"

"With reverence, sir," said the boy, "he was what *he* calls sober, and what I would call concerned in liquor for any other person."

"Curse on the drunken coxcomb!" said Albert.— "There is a tester for thee, boy, and tell thy master to break his jests on suitable persons, and at fitting times."

"Stay yet a minute," exclaimed Alice; "we must not go too fast—this craves wary walking."

"A feather," said Albert; "all this work about a feather! Why, Dr. Rochecliffe, who can suck intelligence out of every trifle as a magpie would suck an egg, could make nothing of this."

"Let us try what we can do without him then," said Alice. Then addressing herself to the boy,—" So there are strangers at your master's?"

"At Colonel Everard's, madam, which is the same thing," said Spitfire.

"And what manner of strangers," said Alice; "guests, I suppose?"

"Ay, Mistress," said the boy, "a sort of guests that

NoteE. Signal of Danger by the Token of a Feather. Scott Salutes.
A name given to the shillings coined by Henry VIII., and to sixpences later. *Julius Ccesar,* II., 1, 15. make themselves welcome wherever they come if they meet not a welcome from the landlord—soldiers, madam.

"The men that have been long lying at Woodstock?" said Albert.

"No, sir," said Spitfire, "new comers, with gallant buffcoats and steel breastplates; and their commander—your honour and your ladyship never saw such a man—at least I am sure Bill Spitfire never did."

"Was he tall or short?" said Albert, now much alarmed.

"Neither one nor other," said the boy; "stout made, with slouching shoulders; a nose large, and a face one would not like to say No to. He had several officers with him. I saw him but for a moment, but I shall never forget him while I live."

"You are right," said Albert Lee to his sister, pulling her to one side, "quite right—the Archfiend himself is upon us!"

"And the feather," said Alice, whom fear had rendered apprehensive of slight tokens, "means flight—and a woodcock is a bird of passage."

"You have hit it," said her brother; "but the time has taken us cruelly short. Give the boy a trifle morenothing that can excite suspicion, and dismiss him. I must summon Rochecliffe and Joceline."

He went accordingly, but, unable to find those he sought, he returned with hasty steps to the parlour, where, in his character of Louis, the page was exerting himself to detain the old knight, who, while laughing at the tales he told him, was anxious to go to see what was passing in the hall.

"What is the matter, Albert?" said the old man; "who calls at the Lodge at so undue an hour, and wherefore is the hall-door opened to them? I will not have my rules, and the regulations laid down for keeping this house, broken through, because I am old and poor. Why answer you not? why keep a chattering with Louis Kerneguy, and neither of you all the while minding what I say?— Daughter Alice, have you sense and civility enough to tell me, what or who it is that is admitted here contrary to my general orders?"

"No one, sir," replied Alice; "a boy brought a message, which I fear is an alarming one."

"There is only fear, sir," said Albert, stepping forward,

"that whereas we thought to have stayed with you till tomorrow, we must now take farewell of you to-night."

"Not so, brother," said Alice, "you must stay and aid the defence here—if you and Master Kerneguy are both missed, the pursuit will be instant, and probably successful; but if you stay, the hiding-places about this house will take some time to search. You can change coats with Kerneguy too."

"Right, noble wench," said Albert, "most excellent— yes—Louis, I remain as Kerneguy, you fly as young Master Lee."

"I cannot see the justice of that," said Charles.

"Nor I neither," said the knight, interfering. "Men come and go, lay schemes, and alter them, in my house, without deigning to consult me! And who is Master Kerneguy, or what is he to me, that my son must stay and take the chance of mischief, and this your

Scotch page is to escape in his dress? I will have no such contrivance carried into effect, though it were the finest cobweb that was ever woven in Doctor Rochecliflie's brains.—I wish you no ill, Louis; thou art a lively boy; but I have been somewhat too lightly treated in this, man."

"I am fully of your opinion, Sir Henry," replied the person whom he addressed. "You have been, indeed, repaid for your hospitality by want of that confidence, which could never have been so justly reposed. But the moment is come, when I must say, in a word, I am that unfortunate Charles Stuart, whose lot it has been to become the cause of rain to his best friends, and whose present residence in your family threatens to bring destruction to you, and all around you."

"Master Louis Kerneguy," said the knight very angrily, "I will teach you to choose the subjects of your mirth better when you address them to me; and moreover, very little provocation would make me desire to have an ounce or two of that malapert blood from you."

"Be still, sir, for Godsake!" said Albert to his father. "This is indeed The King; and such is the danger of his person, that every moment we waste may bring round a fatal catastrophe."

"Good God!" said the father clasping his hands together, and about to drop on his knees, "has my earnest wish Saucy. been accomplished! and is it in such a manner as to make me pray it had never taken place!"

He then attempted to bend his knee to the King—kissed his hand, while large tears trickled from his eyes—then said, "Pardon, my Lord—your Majesty, I mean—permit me to sit in your presence but one instant till my blood beats more freely, and then"

Charles raised his ancient and faithful subject from the ground; and even in that moment of fear, and anxiety, and danger, insisted on leading him to his seat, upon which he sunk in apparent exhaustion, his head drooping upon his long white beard, and big unconscious tears mingling with its silver hairs. Alice and Albert remained with the King, arguing and urging his instant departure.

"The horses are at the under-keeper's hut," said Albert, "and the relays only eighteen or twenty miles off. If the horses can but carry you so far"

"Will you not rather," interrupted Alice, "trust to the concealments of this place, so numerous and so well tried—Rochecliffe's apartments, and the yet farther places of secrecy?"

"Alas!" said Albert, "I know them only by name. My father was sworn to confide them to but one man, and he had chosen Rochecliffe."

"I prefer taking the field to any hiding-hole in England," said the King. "Could I but find my way to this hut where the horses are, I would try what arguments whip and spur could use to get them to the rendezvous, where I am to meet Sir Thomas Acland and fresh cattle. Come with me, Colonel Lee, and let us run for it. The roundheads have beat us in battle; but if it come to a walk or a race, I think I can shew which has the best mettle."

"But then," said Albert, "we lose all the time which may otherwise be gained by the defence of this houseleaving none here but my poor father, incapable from his state of doing anything; and you will be instantly pursued by fresh horses, while ours are unfit for the road. Oh, where is the villain Jocelein!"

"What can have become of Doctor Rochecliffe?" said Alice; "he that is so ready with advice;—where can they be gone? Oh, if my father could but rouse himself!"

"Your father *is* roused," said Sir Henry, rising and stepping up to them with all the energy of full manhood in his countenance and motions—" I did but gather my thoughts—for when did they fail a Lee when his King needed counsel or aid?" He then began to speak, with the ready and distinct utterance of a general at the head of an army, ordering every motion for attack and defence—unmoved himself, and his own energy compelling obedience, and that cheerful obedience, from all who heard him. "Daughter," he said, "beat up dame Jellicot—Let Phoebe rise, if she were dying, and secure doors and windows."

"That hath been done regularly since—we have been thus far honoured," said his daughter, looking at the King —"yet, let them go through the chambers once more." And Alice retired to give the orders, and presently returned.

The old knight proceeded, in the same decided tone of promptitude and despatch—" Which is your first stage?" "Gray's—Rothebury, by Henley, where Sir Thomas Acland and young Knolles are to have horses in readiness," said Albert; "but how to get there with our weary cattle!"

"Trust me for that," said the knight; and proceeding with the same tone of authority—" Your Majesty must instantly to Joceline's lodge," he said, "there are your horses and your means of flight. The secret places of this house, well managed, will keep the rebel dogs in play two or three hours good—Rochecliffe is, I fear, kidnapped, and his Independent hath betrayed him—Would I had judged the villain better! I would have struck him through at one of our trials at fence, with an unbated weapon, as Will says.—But for your guide when on horseback, half a bow-shot from Joceline's hut is that of old Martin the verdurer; he is a score of years older than I, but as fresh as an old oak—beat up his quarters, and let him ride with you for death and life. He will guide you to your relay, for no fox that ever earthed in the Chase knows the country so well for seven leagues around."

"Excellent, my dearest father, excellent," said Albert; "I had forgot Martin the verdurer."

"Young men forget all," answered the knight—"Alas, that the limbs should fail, when the head which can best direct them—is come perhaps to its wisest!" A town on the Thames, 47 miles from Oxford, now famous for the annual boat races there. *'Hamlet*, IV., 7, 139. An officer who has charge of the trees and underwood in a forest.

"But the tired horses," said the King—"could we not get fresh cattle?"

"Impossible at this time of night," answered Sir Henry; "but tired horses may do much with care and looking to." He went hastily to the cabinet which stood in one of the oriel windows, and searched for something in the drawers, pulling out one after another.

"We lose time, father," said Albert, afraid that the intelligence and energy which the old man displayed had been but a temporary flash of the lamp, which was about to relapse into evening twilight.

"Go to, sir boy," said his father, sharply; "is it for thee to tax me in this presence!—Know, that were the whole roundheads that are out of hell in present assemblage round Woodstock, I could send away the Royal Hope of England by a way that the wisest of them could never guess.—Alice, my love, ask no questions, but speed to the kitchen, and fetch a slice or two of beef, or better of venison; cut them long and thin, d'ye mark me"

"This is wandering of the mind," said Albert apart to the King. "We do him wrong, and your Majesty harm, to listen to him."

"I think otherwise," said Alice, "and I know my father better than you." So saying, she left the room, to fulfil her father's orders.

"I think so, too," said Charles—"in Scotland the Presbyterian ministers, when thundering in their pulpits on my own sins and those of my house, took the freedom to call me to my face Jeroboam, or Rehoboam, or some such name, for following the advice of young counsellors— Oddsfish, I will take that of the gray beard for once, for never saw I more sharpness and decision than in the countenance of that noble old man."

By this time Sir Henry had found what he was seeking. "In this tin box," he said, "are six balls prepared of the most cordial spices, mixed with medicaments of the choicest and most invigorating quality. Given from hour to hour, wrapt in a covering of good beef or venison, a horse of spirit will not flag for five hours, at the speed of fifteen miles an hour; and, please God, the fourth of the time " 2 *Chronicles x.* places your Majesty in safety—what remains may be useful on some future occasion. Martin knows how to administer them; and Albert's weary cattle shall be ready, if walked gently for ten minutes, in running to devour the way, as old Will says—nay, waste not time in speech, your Majesty does me but too much honour in using what is your own. —Now, see if the coast is clear, Albert, and let his Majesty set off instantly— We will play our parts but ill, if any take the chase after him for these two hours that are between night and day— Change dresses, as you proposed, in yonder sleeping apartment—something may be made of that, too."

"But, good Sir Henry," said the King, "your zeal overlooks a principal point. I have, indeed, come from the under-keeper's hut you mention to this place, but it was by daylight, and under guidance—I shall never find my way thither in utter darkness, and without a guide— I fear you must let the Colonel go with me; and I entreat and command, you will put yourself to no trouble or risk to defend the house—only make what delay you can in shewing its secret recesses."

"Rely on me, my royal and liege Sovereign," said Sir Henry, "but Albert *must* remain here, and Alice shall guide your Majesty to Joceline's hut in his stead."

"Alice!" said Charles, stepping back in surprise— "why, it is dark night— and—and—and—" He glanced his eye towards Alice, who had by this time returned to the apartment, and saw doubt and apprehension in her look; an intimation, that the reserve under which he had placed his disposition for gallantry, since the morning of the proposed duel, had not altogether effaced the recollection of his previous conduct. He hastened to put a strong negative upon a proposal which appeared so much to embarrass her. "It is impossible for me, indeed, Sir Henry, to use Alice's services—I must walk as if bloodhounds were at my heels."

"Alice shall trip it," said the knight, "with any wench in Oxfordshire; and what would your Majesty's best speed avail, if you knew not the way to go?"

"Nay, nay, Sir Henry," continued the King, "the night is too dark—we stay too long—I will find it myself."

"Lose no time in exchanging your dress with Albert," said Sir Henry—" leave me to take care of the rest." 2 *Henry IV.,* I., 1, 47.

Charles, still inclined to expostulate, withdrew, however, into the apartment where young Lee and he were to exchange clothes; while Sir Henry said to his daughter, "Get thee a cloak, wench, and put on thy thickest shoes. Thou might'st have ridden Pixie, but he is something spirited, and thou art a timid horsewoman, and ever wert so—the only weakness I have known of thee."

"But, my father," said Alice, fixing her eyes very earnestly on Sir Henry's face, "must I really go along with the King? might not Phoebe, or dame Jellicot, go with us*?"*

"No—no—no," answered Sir Henry; "Phoebe, the silly slut, has, as you well know, been in fits to-night, and I take it, such a walk as you must take is no charm for hysterics—Dame Jellicot hobbles as slow as a broken-winded mare—besides, her deafness, were there occasion to speak to her—No—no— you shall go alone—and entitle yourself to have it written on your tomb, 'Here lies she who saved the King!' — And, hark you, do not think of returning to-night, but stay at the verdurer's with his niece—the Park and Chase will shortly be filled with our enemies, and whatever chances here you will learn early enough in the morning."

"And what is it I may then learn?" said Alice—" Alas, who can tell?—O, dearest father, let me stay and share your fate! I will pull off the timorous woman, and fight for the King, if it be necessary. But—I cannot think of becoming his only attendant in the dark night, and through a road so lonely.

"How!" said the knight, raising his voice; "do you bring ceremonious and silly scruples forward, when the King's safety, nay his life, is at stake! By this mark of loyalty," stroking his gray beard as he spoke, "could I think thou wert other than becomes a daughter of the house of Lee, I would"

At this moment the King and Albert interrupted him by entering the apartment, having exchanged dresses, and, from their stature, bearing some resemblance to each other, though Charles was evidently a plain, and Lee a handsome young man. Their complexions were different; but the difference could not be immediately noticed, Albert having adopted a black peruque, and darkened his eyebrows.

Albert Lee walked out to the front of the mansion, to give one turn around the Lodge, in order to discover in what direction any enemies might be approaching, that they might judge of the road which it was safest for the royal fugitive to adopt. Meanwhile the King, who was first on entering the apartment, had heard a part of the angry answer which the old knight made to his daughter, and was at no loss to guess the subject of his resentment. He walked up to him with the dignity which he perfectly knew to assume when he chose it.

"Sir Henry," he said, "it is our pleasure, nay our command, that you forbear all exertion of paternal authority in this matter. Mistress Alice, I am sure, must have good and strong reasons for what she wishes: and I should never pardon myself were she placed in an unpleasant situation on my account. I am too well acquainted with woods and wildernesses to fear losing my way among my native oaks of Woodstock."

"Your Majesty shall not incur the danger," said Alice, her temporary hesitation entirely removed by the calm, clear, and candid manner in which Charles uttered these last words. "You shall run no risk that I can prevent; and the unhappy chances of the times in which I have lived have from experience made the forest as well known to me by night as by day. So, if you scorn not my company, let us away instantly."

"If your company is given with goodwill, I accept it with gratitude," replied the monarch.

"Willingly," she said, "most willingly. Let me be one of the first to shew that zeal and that confidence, which I trust all England will one day emulously display in behalf of your Majesty."

She uttered these words with an alacrity of spirit, and made the trifling change of habit with a speed and dexterity, which shewed that all her fears were gone, and that her heart was entirely in the mission on which her father had despatched her.

"All is safe around," said Albert Lee, shewing himself; "you may take which passage you will—the most private is the best."

Charles went gracefully up to Sir Henry Lee ere his departure, and took him by the hand.—" I am too proud to make professions," he said, " which I may be too poor ever to realize. But while Charles Stuart lives, he lives the obliged and indebted debtor of Sir Henry Lee." "Say not so, please your Majesty, say not so," exclaimed the old man, struggling with the hysterical sobs which rose to his throat. "He who might claim all, cannot become indebted by accepting some small part."

"Farewell, good friend, farewell!'" said the King; "think of me as a son, a brother to Albert and to Alice, who are, I see, already impatient. Give me a father's blessing, and let me be gone."

"The God, through whom Kings reign, bless your Majesty," said Sir Henry, kneeling and turning his reverend face and clasped hands up to Heaven—" The Lord of Hosts bless you, and save your Majesty from your present dangers, and bring you in his own good time to the safe possession of the crown that is your due!"

Charles received his blessing like that of a father, and Alice and he departed on their journey.

As they left the apartment, the old knight let his hands sink gently as he concluded this fervent ejaculation, his head sinking at the same time. His son dared not disturb his meditation, yet feared the strength of his feelings might overcome that of his constitution, and that he might fall into a swoon. At length, he ventured to approach and gradually touch him. The old knight started to his feet, and was at once the same alert, active-minded, forecasting director, which he had shewn himself a little before.

"You are right, boy," he said, "we must be up and doing. They lie, the round-headed traitors, that call him dissolute and worthless! He hath feelings worthy the son of the blessed Martyr. You saw, even in the extremity of danger, he would have perilled his safety, rather than take Alice's guidance, when the silly wench seemed in doubt about going. Profligacy is intensely selfish, and thinks not of the feelings of others. But hast thou drawn bolt and bar after them? I vow I scarce saw when they left the hall."

"I let them out at the little postern," said the Colonel; "and when I returned, I was afraid I had found you ill."

"Joy—joy, only joy, Albert—I cannot allow a thought of doubt to cross my breast. God will not desert the descendant of an hundred kings—the rightful heir will not be given up to the ruffians. There was a tear in his eye as he took leave of me—I am sure of it. Wouldst not die for him, boy?"

"If I lay my life down for him tonight/' said Albert, "I would only regret it, because I should not hear of his escape to-morrow.

"Well, let us to this gear," said the knight; "think'st thou know'st enough of his manner, clad as thou art in his dress, to induce the women to believe thee to be the page Kerneguy?"

"Umph," replied Albert, "it is not easy to bear out a personification of the King, when women are in the case. But there is only a very little light below, and I can try."

"Do so instantly," said his father; "the knaves will be here presently."

Albert accordingly left the apartment, while the knight continued—" If the women be actually persuaded that Kerneguy be still here, it will add strength to my plot— the beagles will open on a false scent, and the royal stag be safe in cover ere they regain the slotl of him. Then to draw them on from hiding-place to hiding-place! Why the east will be gray before they have sought the half of them!—Yes, I will play at bob-cherry with them, hold the bait to their nose which they are never to gorge upon! I will drag a trail for them which will take them some time to puzzle out. —But at what cost do I do this?" continued the old knight, interrupting his own joyous soliloquy—" Oh, Absalom, Absalom, my son! my son!—But let him go; he can but die as his fathers have died, and in the cause for which they lived. But he comes—Hush! —Albert, hast thou succeeded? hast thou taken royalty upon thee so as to pass current?"

"I have sir," replied Albert; " the women will swear that Louis Kerneguy was in the house this very last minute."

"Right, for they are good and faithful creatures," said the knight, "and would swear what was for his Majesty's safety at any rate; yet they will do it with more nature and effect, if they believe they are swearing truth—How didst thou impress the deceit upon them?"

"By a trifling adoption of the royal manner, sir, not worth mentioning."

"Out, rogue!" replied the knight. "I fear the King's character will suffer under your mummery." Scent.

A child's play, consisting in catching with the teeth a cherry or other fruit hung upon a string. 2 *Samuel xix*. 4. "Umph," said Albert, muttering what he dared not utter aloud—" were I to follow the example close up, I know whose character would be in the greatest danger."

"Well, now we must adjust the defence of the outworks, the signals, etc. betwixt us both, and the best way to baffle the enemy for the longest time possible." He then again had recourse to the secret drawers of his cabinet, and pulled out a piece of parchment on which was a plan. "This," said he, "is a scheme of the citadel, as I call it, which may hold out long enough after you have been forced to evacuate the places of retreat you are already acquainted with. The ranger was always sworn to keep this plan secret, save from one person only in case of sudden death.—Let us sit down and study it together."

They accordingly adjusted their measures in a manner which will better shew itself in what afterwards took place, than were we to state the various schemes which they proposed, and provisions made against events that did not arrive.

At length young Lee, armed and provided with some food and liquor, took leave of his father, and went and shut himself up in Victor Lee's apartment, from which was an opening to the labyrinth of private apartments, or hiding-places, that had served the associates so well in the fantastic tricks which they had played off at the expense of the Commissioners of the Commonwealth.

"I trust," said Sir Henry, sitting down by his desk, after having taken a tender farewell of his son, "that Rochecliffe has not blabbed out the secret of the plot to yonder fellow Tomkins, who was not unlikely to prate of it out of school.— But here am I seated—perhaps for the last time, with my Bible on the one hand, and old Will on the other, prepared, thank God, to die as I have lived. —I marvel they come not yet," he said, after waiting for some time— "I always thought the devil had a smarter spur to give his agents, when they were upon his own special service."

Note the skilful heightening of suspense at the Lodge, by the revelation to Sir Henry of the real rank of his disguised guest; the quickening of interest in connection with the plan for Charles's escape; and the apparent development in character on the part of both Charles and Alice. Distinguish between scenes that test the moral fibre of a person when he is quite unconscious of any struggle (see almost every chapter of Scott) and scenes embodying a conscious moral or spiritual struggle,— which are very rare in Scott. Compare him with George Eliot and Hawthorne in this regard.

CHAPTER THE THIRTY-THIRD

But see, his face is black, and full of blood;

His eyeballs farther out than when he lived,

Staring full ghastly, like a strangled man;

His hair upreared—his nostrils stretched with struggling;

His hands abroad displayed, as one who grasped

And tugged for life, and was by strength subdued.

Henry VI. *Part I.*

Had those whose unpleasant visit Sir Henry expected come straight to the Lodge, instead of staying for three hours at Woodstock, they would have secured their prey. But the Familist, partly to prevent the King's escape, partly to render himself of more importance in the affair, had represented the party at the Lodge as being constantly on the alert, and had therefore inculcated upon Cromwell the necessity of his remaining quiet until he (Tomkins) should appear to give him notice that the household were retired to rest. On this condition he undertook, not only to discover the apartment in which the unfortunate Charles slept, but, if possible, to find some mode of fastening the door on the outside, so as to render flight impossible. He had also promised to secure the key of a postern, by which the soldiers might be admitted into the house without exciting alarm. Nay, the matter might, by means of his local knowledge, be managed, as he represented it, with such security, that he would undertake to place his Excellency, or whomsoever he might appoint for the service, by the side of Charles Stuart's bed, ere he had slept off the last night's claret. Above all, he had stated, that, from the style of the old house, there were many passages and posterns which must be carefully guarded, before the least alarm was caught by those within, otherwise the success of the whole enterprise might be endangered. He had therefore besought Cromwell to wait for him at the village, if he found him not there on his arrival; and assured him that the marching and countermarching of soldiers was at present so common, that even if any news were carried to the Lodge that fresh troops had arrived in the borough, so ordinary a circumstance would not give them the least alarm. He recommended, that the soldiers chosen for this service should be such as could be depended upon— no fainters in spirit—none who turn back from Mount Gilead for fear of the Amalekites, but men of war, accustomed to strike with the sword, and to need no second blow. Finally, he represented, that it would be wisely done if the General should put Pearson, or any other officer whom he could completely trust, into the command of the detachment, and keep his own person, if he should think it proper to attend, secret even from the soldiers.

All this man's councils Cromwell had punctually followed. He had travelled in the van of this detachment of one hundred picked soldiers, whom he had selected for the service, men of dauntless resolution, bred in a thousand dangers, and who were steeled against all feelings of hesitation and compassion, by the deep and gloomy fanaticism which was their chief principle of action—men to whom, as their General, and no less as the chief among the Elect, the commands of Oliver were like a commission from the Deity.

Great and deep was the General's mortification at the unexpected absence of the personage on whose agency he so confidently reckoned, and many conjectures he formed as to the cause of such mysterious conduct. Sometimes he thought Tomkins had been overcome by liquor, a frailty to which Cromwell knew him to be addicted; and when he held this opinion, he discharged his wrath in maledictions, which, of a different kind from the wild oaths and curses of the cavaliers, had yet in them as much blasphemy, and more determined malevolence. At other times he thought some unexpected alarm, or perhaps some drunken cavalier revel, had caused the family of Woodstock Lodge to make later hours than usual. To this conjecture, which appeared the most probable of any, his mind often recurred; and it was the hope that Tomkins would still appear at the rendezvous, which induced him to remain at the borough, anxious to receive communication from his emissary, and afraid of endangering the success of the enterprise by any premature exertion on his own part.

A mountainous district east of Palestine, the scene of frequent combats between the Israelites and the heathen. One chosen as the special object of divine mercy,—according to the doctrine of Calvin.

In the meantime, Cromwell, finding it no longer possible to conceal his personal presence, disposed of every thing so as to be ready at a minute's notice. Half his soldiers he caused to dismount, and had the horses put into quarters; the other half were directed to keep their horses saddled, and themselves ready to mount at a moment's notice. The men were brought into the house by turns, and had some refreshment, leaving a sufficient guard on the horses, which was changed from time to time.

Thus Cromwell waited with no little uncertainty, often casting an anxious eye upon Colonel Everard, who, he suspected, could, if he chose it, well supply the place of his absent confidant. Everard endured this calmly, with unaltered countenance, and brow neither ruffled nor dejected.

Midnight at length tolled, and it became necessary to take some decisive step. Tomkins might have been treacherous; or, a suspicion which approached more near to the reality, his intrigue might have been discovered, and he himself murdered or kidnapped, by the vengeful royalists. In a word, if any use was to be made of the chance which fortune afforded of securing the most formidable claimant of the supreme power, which he already aimed at, no farther time was to be lost. He at length gave orders to Pearson to get the men under arms—he directed him concerning the mode of forming them, and that they should march with the utmost possible silence; or as it was given out in the orders, "Even as Gideon marched in silence, when he went down against the camp of the Midianites, with only Phurah his servant. Peradventure," continued this strange document, "we too may learn of what yonder Midianites have dreamed."

A single patrol, followed by a corporal and five steady, experienced soldiers, formed the advanced guard of the party; then followed the main body. A rear-guard of ten men guarded Everard and the minister. Cromwell required the attendance of the former, as it might be necessary to examine him, or confront him with others; and he carried Master Holdenough with him, because he might *Judges* vii. 8-11.

escape if left behind, and perhaps raise some tumult in the village. The Presbyterians, though they not only concurred with, but led the way in the civil war, were at its conclusion highly dissatisfied with the ascendency of the military sectaries, and not to be trusted as cordial agents in any thing where their interest was concerned. The infantry being disposed of as we have noticed, marched off from the left of their line, Cromwell and Pearson, both on foot, keeping at the head of the centre, or main body of the detachment. They were all armed with petronels, short guns similar to the modern carabine, and, like them, used by horsemen. They marched in the most profound silence and with the utmost regularity, the whole body moving like one man.

About one hundred yards behind the rearmost of the dismounted party, came the troopers who remained on horseback; and it seemed as if even the irrational animals were sensible to Cromwell's orders, for the horses did not neigh, and even appeared to place their feet on the earth cautiously, and with less noise than usual.

Their leader, full of anxious thoughts, never spoke, save to enforce by whispers his caution respecting silence, while the men, surprised and delighted to find themselves under the command of their renowned General, and destined, doubtless, for some secret service of high import, used the utmost precaution in attending to his reiterated orders.

They marched down the street of the little borough in the order we have mentioned. Few of the townsmen were abroad; and one or two, who had protracted the orgies of the evening to that unusual hour, were too happy to escape the notice of a strong party of soldiers, who often acted in the character of police, to inquire about their purpose for being under arms so late, or the route which they were pursuing.

The external gate of the Chase had, ever since the party had arrived at Woodstock, been strictly guarded by three file of troopers, to cut off all communication between the Lodge and the town. Spitfire, Wildrake's emissary, who had often been a-bird-nesting, or on similar mischievous excursions in the forest, had evaded these men's vigilance by climbing over a breach, with which he was well acquainted, in a different part of the wall.

Between this party and the advanced guard of Cromwell's detachment, a whispered challenge was exchanged, according to the rules of discipline. The infantry entered the Park, and were followed by the cavalry, who were directed to avoid the hard road, and ride as much as possible upon the turf which bordered on the avenue. Here, too, an additional precaution was used, a file or two of foot soldiers being detached to search the woods on either hand, and make prisoner, or, in the event of resistance, put to death, any whom they might find lurking there, under what pretence soever.

Meanwhile, the weather began to shew itself as propitious to Cromwell, as he had found most incidents in the course of his successful career. The gray mist, which had hitherto obscured everything, and rendered marching in the wood embarrassing and difficult, had now given way to the moon, which, after many efforts, at length forced her way through the vapour, and hung her dim dull cresset1 in the heavens, which she enlightened, as the dying lamp of an anchorite does the cell in which he reposes. The party were in sight of the front of the palace, when Holdenough whispered to Everard, as they walked near each other—" See ye not—yonder flutters the mysterious light in the turret of the incontinent Rosamond? This night will try whether the devil of the Sectaries or the devil of the Malignants shall prove the stronger. 0, sing jubilee, for the kingdom of Satan is divided against itself!"

Here the divine was interrupted by a non-commissioned officer, who came hastily, yet with noiseless steps, to say, in a low stern whisper—" Silence, prisoner in the rear— silence, on pain of death."

A moment afterwards the whole party stopped their march, the word *halt* being passed from one to another, and instantly obeyed.

The cause of this interruption was the hasty return of one of the flanking party to the main body, bringing news to Cromwell that they had seen a light in the wood at some distance on the left.

"What can it be *?"* said Cromwell, his low stern voice, even in a whisper, making itself distinctly heard. "Does it move, or is it stationary?"

"So far as we can judge, it moveth not," answered the A light contained in a cup mounted on a pole or suspended from above. See *Marmion*, II., 18.
trooper. "Strange — there is no cottage near the spot where it is seen."

"So please your excellency it may be a device of Sathan," said Corporal Humgudgeon, snuffling through his nose; "he is mighty powerful in these parts of late."

"So please your idiocy, thou art an ass," said Cromwell; but, instantly recollecting that the corporal had been one of the adjutators or tribunes of the common soldiers, and was therefore to be treated with suitable respect, he said, "Nevertheless, if it be the device of Satan, please it the Lord we will resist him, and the foul slave shall fly from us. —Pearson," he said, resuming his soldier-like brevity, "take four file, and see what is yonder—No—the knaves may shrink from thee. Go thou straight to the Lodge— invest it in the way we agreed, so that a bird shall not escape out of it—form an outer and an inward ring of sentinels, but give no alarm until I come. Should any attempt to escape, Kill them."—He spoke that command with terrible emphasis.—"Kill them on the spot," he repeated, "be they who or what they will. Better so than trouble the Commonwealth with prisoners."

Pearson heard, and proceeded to obey his commander's orders.

Meanwhile, the future Protector disposed the small force which remained with him in such a manner, that they should approach from different points at once the light which excited his suspicions, and gave them orders to creep as near to it as they could, taking care not to lose each other's support, and to be ready to rush in at the same moment, when he should give the sign, which was to be a loud whistle. Anxious to ascertain the truth with his own eyes, Cromwell, who had by instinct all the habits of military foresight, which, in others, are the result of professional education and long experience, advanced upon the object of his curiosity. He skulked from tree to tree with the light step and prowling sagacity of an Indian bushfighter; and before any of his men had approached so near as to descry them, he saw, by the lantern which was placed on the ground, two men, who had been engaged in digging what seemed to be an ill-made grave. Near them lay extended something wrapped in a deer's hide, which greatly resembled the dead body of a man. They spoke together in a low voice, yet so that their dangerous auditor could perfectly overhear what they said.
" Representatives elected by each regiment of the Roundheads in 1647, to act in concert with the officers, in compelling Parliament to satisfy the demands of the army before disbanding it. "—*Diet. Eng. History.*

"It is done at last," said one; "the worst and hardest labour I ever did in my life. I believe there is no luck about me left. My very arms feel as if they did not belong to me; and, strange to tell, toil as hard as I would, I could not gather warmth in my limbs."

"I have warmed me enough," said Rochecliffe, breathing short with fatigue.

"But the cold lies at my heart," said Joceline; "I scarce hope ever to be warm again. It is strange, and a charm seems to be on us. Here have we been nigh two hours in doing what Diggen the sexton would have done to better purpose in half a one."

"We are wretched spadesmen enough," answered Doctor Rochecliffe. "Every man to his tools—thou to thy buglehorn, and I to my papers in cipher. —But do not be discouraged; it is the frost on the ground, and the number of roots, which rendered our task difficult.

And now, all due rights done to this unhappy man, and having read over him the service of the church, *valeat quantum,* let us lay him decently in this place of last repose; there will be small lack of him above ground. So cheer up thy heart, man, like a soldier as thou art; we have read the service over his body; and should times permit it, we will have him removed to consecrated ground, though he is all unworthy of such favour. Here, help me to lay him in the earth; we will drag briers and thorns over the spot, when we have shovelled dust upon dust; and do thou think of this chance more manfully; and remember, thy secret is in thine own keeping."

"I cannot answer for that," said Joceline. "Methinks the very night winds among the leaves will tell of what we have been doing—methinks the trees themselves will say, 'there is a dead corpse lies among our roots/ Witnesses are soon found when blood hath been spilled."

"They are so, and that right early," exclaimed Cromwell, starting from the thicket, laying hold on Joceline, and putting a pistol to his head. At any other period of Whatever it may be worth. his life, the forester would, even against the odds of numbers, have made a desperate resistance; but the horror he had felt at the slaughter of an old companion, although in defence of his own life, together with fatigue and surprise, had altogether unmanned him, and he was seized as easily as a sheep is secured by the butcher. Doctor Rochecliffe offered some resistance, but was presently secured by the soldiers who pressed around him.

"Look, some of you," said Cromwell, "what corpse this is upon whom these lewd sons of Belial have done a murder —Corporal Grace-be-here Humgudgeon, see if thou knowest the face."

"I profess I do, even as I should do mine own in a mirror," snuffled the corporal, after looking on the countenance of the dead man by the help of the lantern. "Of a verity it is our trusty brother in the faith, Joseph Tomkins."

"Tomkins!" exclaimed Cromwell, springing forward and satisfying himself with a glance at the features of the corpse—" Tomkins!—and murdered, as the fracture of the temple intimates!—dogs that ye are, confess the truth—You have murdered him because you have discovered his treachery—I should say his true spirit towards the Commonwealth of England, and his hatred of those complots in which you would have engaged his honest simplicity."

"Ay," said Grace-be-here Humgudgeon, "and then to misuse his dead body with your papistical doctrines, as if you had crammed cold porridge into its cold mouth. I pray thee, General, let these men's bonds be made strong."

"Forbear, corporal," said Cromwell; "our time presses. —Friend, to you, whom I believe to be Doctor Anthony Albany Rochecliffe by name and surname, I have to give the choice of being hanged at daybreak to-morrow, or making atonement for the murder of one of the Lord's people, by telling what thou knowest of the secrets which are in yonder house."

"Truly, sir," replied Rochecliffe, "you found me but in my duty as a clergyman, interring the dead; and respecting answering your questions, I am determined myself, and do advise my fellow-sufferer on this occasion"

"Remove him," said Cromwell; "I know his stiffneckedness of old, though I have made him plough in my furrow, when he thought he was turning up his own swathe—Remove him to the rear, and bring hither the other fellow.—Come thou here—this way—closer—closer. —Corporal Grace-be-here, do thou keep thy hand upori the belt with which he is bound. We must take care of our life for the sake of this distracted country, though, lack-aday, for its own proper worth we could peril it for a pin's point.—Now, mark me, fellow, choose betwixt buying thy life by a full confession, or being tucked1 presently up to one of these old oaks—How likest thou that?"

"Truly, master," answered the under-keeper, affecting more rusticity than was natural to him (for his frequent intercourse with Sir Henry Lee had partly softened and polished his manners), "I think the oak is like to bear a lusty acorn—that is all."

"Dally not with me, friend," continued Oliver; "I profess to thee in sincerity I am no trifler. What guests have you seen at yonder house called the Lodge?"

"Many a brave guest in my day, I'se warrant ye, master," said Joceline. "Ah, to see how the chimneys used to smoke some twelve years back! Ah, sir, a sniff of it would have dined a poor man."

"Out, rascal!" said the General, " dost thou jeer me? Tell me at once what guests have been of late in the Lodge—and look thee, friend, be assured, that in rendering me this satisfaction, thou shalt not only rescue thy neck from the halter, but render also an acceptable service to the State, and one which I will see fittingly rewarded. For, truly, I am not of those who would have the rain fall only on the proud and stately plants, but rather would, so far as my poor wishes and prayers are concerned, that it should also fall upon the lowly and humble grass and corn, that the heart of the husbandman may be rejoiced, and that as the cedar of Lebanon waxes in its height, in its boughs, and in its roots, so may the humble and lowly hyssop that groweth upon the walls flourish, and—and, truly—Understand'st thou me, knave?"

"Not entirely, if it please your honour," said Joceline; "but it sounds as if you were preaching a sermon, and has a marvellous twang of doctrine with it."

"Then, in one word—thou knowest there is one Louis Kerneguy, or Carnego, or some such name, in hiding at the Lodge yonder?" 1 Hanged. . 1 *Kings* iv. 33.

*"*Nay, sir," replied the under-keeper, "there have been many coming and going since Worcester-field; and how should I know who they are?—my service is out of doors, I trow."

"A thousand pounds," said Cromwell, "do I tell down to thee, if thou canst place that boy in my power."

"A thousand pounds is a marvellous matter, sir," said Joceline; "but I have more blood on my hand than I like already. I know not how the price of life may thrive —and, scape or hang, I have no mind to try."

"Away with him to the rear," said the General; "and let him not speak with his yoke-fellow yonder.—Fool that I am, to waste time in expecting to get milk from mules. —Move on towards the Lodge."

They moved with the same silence as formerly, notwithstanding the difficulties which they encountered from being unacquainted with the road and its various intricacies. At length they were challenged, in a low voice, by one of their own sentinels, two concentric circles of whom had been placed around the Lodge, so close to each other, as to preclude the possibility of an individual escaping from within. The outer guard was maintained partly by horse upon the roads and open lawn, and where the ground was broken and bushy by infantry. The inner circle was guarded by foot soldiers only. The whole were in the highest degree alert, expecting some interesting and important consequences from the unusual expedition on which they were engaged.

"Any news, Pearson?" said the General to his aide-decamp, who came instantly to report to his superior.

He received for answer, "None."

Cromwell led his officer forward just opposite to the door of the Lodge, and there paused betwixt the circles of guards, so that their conversation could not be overheard.

He then pursued his inquiry, demanding—" Were there any lights, any appearances of stirring—any attempt at sally—any preparation for defence?"

"All as silent as the valley of the shadow of death —Even as the vale of Jehoshaphat."

"Pshaw! tell me not of Jehoshaphat, Pearson," said Cromwell. "These words are good for others, but not for thee. Speak plainly, and like a blunt soldier as thou art. *Joel* iii. 2, 12.

Each man hath his own mode of speech; and bluntness, not sanctity, is thine."

"Well then, nothing has been stirring," said Pearson. —" Yet peradventure"

"Peradventure not me," said Cromwell, "or thou wilt tempt me to knock thy teeth out. I ever distrust a man when he speaks after another fashion from his own."

"Zounds! let me speak to an end," answered Pearson, "and I will speak in what language your Excellency will."

"Thy Zounds, friend," said Oliver, " sheweth little of face, but much of sincerity. Go to then—thou knowest love and trust thee. Hast thou kept close watch? It behoves us to know that, before giving the alarm."

"On my soul," said Pearson, "I have watched as closely as a cat at a mousehole. It is beyond possibility that anything could have eluded our vigilance, or even stirred within the house, without our being aware of it."

"'Tis well," said Cromwell; "thy services shall not be forgotten, Pearson. Thou canst not preach and pray, but thou canst obey thine orders, Gilbert Pearson, and that may make amends."

"I thank your Excellency," replied Pearson; "but I beg leave to chime in with the humours of the times. A poor fellow hath no right to hold himself singular."

He paused, expecting Cromwell's orders what next was to be done, and indeed, not a little surprised that the General's active and prompt spirit had suffered him during a moment so critical to cast away a thought upon a circumstance so trivial as his officer's peculiar mode of expressing himself. He wondered still more, when, by a brighter gleam of moonshine than he had yet enjoyed, he observed that Cromwell was standing motionless, his hands supported upon his sword, which he had taken out of the belt, and his stern brows bent on the ground. He waited for some time impatiently, yet afraid to interfere, lest he should awaken this unwonted fit of ill-timed melancholy into anger and impatience. He listened to the muttering sounds which escaped from the half-opening lips of his principal, in which the words, "hard necessity," which occurred more than once, were all of which the sense could be distinguished. "My Lord General," at length he said, "time flies." The expletive is a corruption of "God's wounds!" "Peace, busy fiend, and urge me not!" said Cromwell. "Think'st thou, like other fools, that I have made a paction with the devil for success, and am bound to do my work within an appointed hour, lest the spell should lose its force!"

"I only think, my Lord General," said Pearson, "that Fortune has put into your offer what you have long desired to make prize of, and that you hesitate."

Cromwell sighed deeply as he answered, "Ah, Pearson, in this troubled world, a man, who is called like me to work great things in Israel, had need to be, as the poet's feign, a thing made of hardened metal, immovable to feelings of human charities, impassible, resistless. Pearson, the world will hereafter, perchance, think of me as being such a one as I have described, 'an iron man, and made of iron mould.'—Yet they will wrong my memory—my heart is flesh, and my blood is mild as that of others. When I was a sportsman, I have wept for the gallant heron that was struck down by my hawk, and sorrowed for the hare which lay screaming under the jaws of my greyhound; and canst thou think it a light thing to me, that, the blood of this iad's father lying in some measure upon my head, I should now put in peril that of the son? They are of the kindly race of English sovereigns, and, doubtless, are adored like to demigods by those of their own party. I am called Parricide, Blood-thirsty Usurper, already, for shedding the blood of one man, that the plague might be stayed—or as Achan1 was slain that Israel might thereafter stand against the face of their enemies. Nevertheless, who has spoke unto me graciously since that high deed? Those who acted in the matter with me are willing that I should be the scapegoat of atonement—those who looked on and helped not, bear themselves now as if they had been borne down by violence; and while I looked that they should shout applause on me, because of the victory of Worcester, whereof the Lord had made me the poor instrument, they looked aside to say, 'Ha! ha! the Kingkiller, the Parricide—soon shall his place be made desolate.'—Truly it is a great thing, Gilbert Pearson, to be lifted above the multitude; but when one feeleth that his exaltation is rather hailed with hate and scorn than with love and reverencein sooth, it is still a hard matter for a mild, tender-con *Joshua* viii. 10-26. *Leviticus* xvi. 5-26.

scienced, infirm spirit to bear—and God be my witness, that, rather than do this new need, I would shed my own best heart's-blood in a pitched field, twenty against one." Here he fell into a flood of tears, which he sometimes was wont to do. This extremity of emotion was of a singular character. It was not actually the result of penitence, and far less that of absolute hypocrisy, but arose merely from the temperature of that remarkable man, whose deep policy, and ardent enthusiasm, were intermingled with a strain of hypochondriacal passion, which often led him to exhibit scenes of this sort, though seldom, as now, when he was called to the execution of great undertakings.

Pearson, well acquainted as he was with the peculiarities of his General, was baffled and confounded by this fit of hesitation and contrition, by which his enterprising spirit appeared to be so suddenly paralysed. After a moment's silence, he said, with some dryness of manner, "if this be the case, it is a pity your Excellency came hither. Corporal Humgudgeon and I, the greatest saint and greatest sinner in your army, had done the deed, and divided the guilt and the honour betwixt us."

"Ha!" said Cromwell, as if touched to the quick, "wouldst thou take the prey from the lion?"

"If the lion behaves like a village cur," said Pearson, boldly, "who now barks and seems as if he would tear all to pieces, and now flies from a raised stick or a stone, I know not why I should fear him. If Lambert' had been here, there had been less speaking and more action."

"Lambert! What of Lambert?" said Cromwell, very sharply.

"Only," said Pearson, "that I long since hesitated whether I should follow your Excellency or him—and I begin to be uncertain whether I have made the best choice, that's all."

"Lambert!" exclaimed Cromwell, impatiently, yet softening his voice, lest he should be overheard descanting on the character of his rival,—" What is Lambert?—a tulipfancying fellow, whom nature intended for a Dutch gardener at Delft or Rotterdam. Ungrateful as thou art, what could Lambert have done for thee?"

"He would not," answered Pearson, "have stood here hesitating before a locked door, when fortune presented the See note in Chapter XXVI.

means of securing, by one blow, his own fortune, and that of all who followed him."

"Thou art right, Gilbert Pearson," said Cromwell, grasping his officer's hand, and strongly pressing it. "Be the half of this bold accompt thine, whether the reckoning be on earth or heaven."

"Be the whole of it mine hereafter," said Pearson, hardily, "so your Excellency have the advantage of it upon earth. Step back to the rear till I force the door—there may be danger, if despair induce them to make a desperate sally."

"And if they do sally, is there one of my Ironsides who fears fire or steel less than myself?" said the General. "Let ten of the most determined men follow us, two with halberts, two with petronels, the others with pistols—Let all their arms be loaded, and fire without hesitation, if there is any attempt to resist or to sally forth—Let Corporal Humgudgeon be with them, and do thou remain here, and watch against escape, as thou wouldst watch for thy salvation."

The General then struck at the door with the hilt of his sword—at first with a single blow or two, then with a reverberation of strokes that made the ancient building ring again. This noisy summons was repeated once or twice without producing the least effect.

"What can this mean?" said Cromwell; "they cannot surely have fled, and left the house empty?"

"No," replied Pearson, "I will ensure you against that; but your Excellency strikes so fiercely, you allow no time for an answer. Hark! I hear the baying of a hound, and the voice of a man who is quieting him—Shall we break in at once, or hold parley?" *"1* will speak to them first," said Cromwell.—"Hollo! who is within there?"

"Who is it inquires?" answered Sir Henry Lee from the interior; "or what want you here at this dead hour?" ' We come by warrant of the Commonwealth of England," said the General.

"I must see your warrant ere I undo either bolt or latch," replied the knight; "we are enough of us to make good the castle: neither I nor my fellows will deliver it up but upon good quarter and conditions; and we will not treat for these save in fair daylight."

"Since you will not yield to our right, you must try our might," replied Cromwell. "Look to yourselves within, the door will be in the midst of you in five minutes."

"Look to yourselves without," replied the stout-hearted Sir Henry; "we will pour our shot upon you, if you attempt the least violence."

But, alas! while he assumed this bold language, his whole garrison consisted of two poor terrified women; for his son, in conformity with the plan which they had fixed upon, had withdrawn from the hall into the secret recesses of the palace.

"What can they be doing now, sir?" said Phoebe, hearing a noise as it were of a carpenter turning screw-nails, mixed with a low buzz of men talking.

"They are fixing a petard," said the knight, with great composure. "I have noted thee for a clever wench, Phoebe, and I will explain it to thee: "lis a metal pot, shaped much like one of the roguish knaves' own sugar-loaf hats, supposing it had narrower brims—it is charged with some few pounds of fine gunpowder. Then"

"Gracious! we shall be all blown up!" exclaimed Phoebe,—the word gunpowder being the only one which she understood in the knight's description.

"Not a bit, foolish girl. Pack old Dame Jellicot into the embrasure of yonder window," said the knight, "on that side of the door, and we will ensconce ourselves on this, and we shall have time to finish my explanation, for they have bungling engineers. We had a clever French fellow at Newark would have done the job in the firing of a pistol."

They had scarce got into the place of security when the knight proceeded with his description.—" The petard being formed, as I tell you, is secured with a thick and strong piece of plank, termed the madrier, and the whole being suspended, or rather secured against the gate to be forced —But thou mindest me not?"

"How can I, Sir Henry," she said, "within reach of such a thing as you speak of?—O Lord! I shall go mad with very terror—we shall be crushed—blown up—in a few minutes!"

"We are secure from the explosion," replied the knight, gravely, "which will operate chiefly in a forward direction into the middle of the chamber; and from any fragments The headquarters of Charles I. in the fall of 1645.
that may fly laterally, we are sufficiently guarded by this deep embrasure."

"But they will slay us when they enter," said Phoebe.

"They will give thee fair quarter, wench," said Sir Henry; "and if I do not bestow a brace of balls on that rogue engineer, it is because I would not incur the penalty inflicted by martial law, which condemns to the edge of the sword all persons who attempt to defend an untenable post. Not that I think the rigour of the law could reach Dame Jellicot or thyself, Phoebe, considering that you carry no arms. If Alice had been here she might indeed have done somewhat, for she can use a birding-piece."

Phoebe might have appealed to her own deeds of that day, as more allied to feats of *melee* and battle, than any which her young lady ever acted: but she was in an agony of inexpressible terror, expecting, from the knight's account of the petard, some dreadful catastrophe, of what nature she did not justly understand, notwithstanding his liberal communication on the subject.

"They are strangely awkward at it," said Sir Henry; "little Boutirlin would have blown the house up before now.—Ah! he is a fellow would take the earth like a rabbit—if he had been here, never may I stir but he would have countermined them ere now, and -'Tis sport to have the engineer

Hoist with his own petard, as our immortal Shakspeare has it."

"Oh Lord, the poor mad old gentleman," thought Phoebe—" Oh, sir, had you not better leave alone playbooks, and think of your end?" uttered she aloud, in sheer terror and vexation of spirit.

"If I had not made up my mind to that many days since," answered the knight, "I had not now met this hour with a free bosom—

As gentle and as jocund as to rest,
Go I to death—truth hath a quiet breast."

As he spoke, a broad glare of light flashed from without through the windows of the hall, and betwixt the strong iron stanchions with which they were secured—a broad discoloured light it was, which shed a red and dusky illumination on the old armour and weapons, as if it had been the reflection of a conflagration. Phoebe screamed aloud, and, forgetful of reverence in the moment of passion, clung close to the knight's cloak and arm, while Dame Jellicot, from her solitary niche, having the use of her eyes, though bereft of her hearing, yelled like an owl when the moon breaks out suddenly.
Fowling-piece. "*Hamlet,* III., 4, 207. *Richard II.,* I, 3, 95, 96.

"Take care, good Phoebe," said the knight; "you will prevent my using my weapon if you hang upon me thus. —The bungling fools cannot fix their petard without the use of torches! Now let me take the advantage of this interval.—Remember what I told thee, and how to put off time."

"Oh, Lord—ay, sir," said Phoebe, "I will say anything. Oh, Lord, that it were but over!—Ah! ah!"— (two prolonged screams)—" I hear something hissing like a serpent."

"It is the fusee, as we martialists1 call it," replied the knight; "that is, Phoebe, the match which fires the petard, and which is longer or shorter according to the distance."

Here the knight's discourse was cut short by a dreadful explosion, which, as he had foretold, shattered the door, strong as it was, to pieces, and brought down the glass clattering from the windows with all the painted heroes and heroines, who had been recorded on that fragile place of memory for centuries. The women shrieked incessantly, and were answered by the bellowing of Bevis, though shut up at a distance from the scene of action. The knight, shaking Phoebe from him with difficulty, advanced into the hall to meet those who rushed in, with torches lighted, and weapons prepared.

"Death to all who resist—life to those who surrender!" exclaimed Cromwell, stamping with his foot. "Who commands this garrison?"

"Sir Henry Lee of Ditchley," answered the old knight, stepping forward; "who, having no other garrison than two weak women, is compelled to submit to what he would willingly have resisted."

"Disarm the inveterate and malignant rebel," cried Oliver. "Art thou not ashamed, sir, to detain me before Men of war.
the door of a house which you had no force to defend? Wearest thou so white a beard, and knowest thou not, that to refuse surrendering an indefensible post, by the martial law, deserves hang*ing?"* "My beard and I," said Sir Henry, "have settled that matter between us, and agree right cordially. It is better to run the risk of being hanged, like honest men, than to give up our trust like cowards and traitors."

"Ha! say'st thou?" said Cromwell; "thou hast powerful motives, I doubt not, for running thy head into a noose. But I will speak with thee by and by. Ho! Pearson, Gilbert Pearson, take this scroll—Take the elder woman with thee—Let her guide you to the various places therein mentioned—Search every room therein set down, and arrest or slay upon the slightest resistance, whomsoever you find there. Then note those places marked as commanding points for cutting off intercourse through the mansion— the landing-places of the great staircase, the great gallery, and so forth. Use the woman civilly. The plan annexed to the scroll will point out the posts, even if she prove stupid or refractory. Meanwhile, the corporal, with a party, will bring the old man and the girl there to some apartment— the parlour, I think, called Victor Lee's, will do as well as another.— We will then be out of this stifling smell of gunpowder."

So saying, and without requiring any farther assistance or guidance, he walked towards the apartment he had named. Sir Henry had his own feelings, when he saw the unhesitating decision with which the General led the way, and which seemed to intimate a more complete acquaintance with the various localities of Woodstock than was consistent with his own present design, to engage the Commonwealth party in a fruitless search through the intricacies of the Lodge.

"I will now ask thee a few questions, old man," said the General, when they had arrived in the room; "and I warn thee, that hope of pardon for thy many and persevering efforts against the Commonwealth, can be no otherwise merited than by the most direct answers to the questions I am about to ask."

Sir Henry bowed. He would have spoken, but he felt his temper rising high, and became afraid it might be exhausted before the part he had settled to play, in order to afford the King time for his escape, should be brought to an end.

"What household have you had here, Sir Henry Lee, within these few days— what guests—what visitors? We know that your means of housekeeping are not so profuse as usual, so the catalogue cannot be burdensome to your memory."

"Far from it," replied the knight, with unusual command of temper; "my daughter, and latterly my son, have been my guests; and I have had these females, and one Joceline Joliffe, to attend upon us."

"I do not ask after the regular members of your household, but after those who have been within your gates, either as guests, or as malignant fugitives taking shelter?"

"There may have been more of both kinds, sir, than I, if it please your valour, am able to answer for," replied the knight.—" I remember my kinsman Bverard was here one morning—Also, I bethink me, a follower of his, called Wildrake."

"Did you not also receive a young cavalier, called Louis Garnegey?" said Cromwell.

"I remember no such name, were I to hang for it," said the knight.

"Kerneguy, or some such word," said the General; " we will not quarrel for a sound."

"A Scotch lad called Louis Kerneguy, was a guest of mine," said Sir Henry, "and left me this morning for Dorsetshire." "So late!" exclaimed Cromwell, stamping with his foot—"How fate contrives to baffle us, even when she seems most favourable!—What direction did he take, old man?" continued Cromwell—" What horse did he ride— who went with him?"

"My son went with him," replied the knight; "he brought him here as the son of a Scottish lord.—I pray you, sir, to be finished with these questions; for although I owe thee, as Will Shakspeare says,

Respect for thy great place, and let the devil
Be sometimes honoured for his burning throne,—' yet I feel my patience wearing thin." A county on the south-west coast.
Measure for Measure, V., 1, 293, 294.
Cromwell here whispered to the corporal, who in turn uttered orders to two soldiers, who left the room. "Place the knight aside; we will now examine the servant damsel," said the General.—" Dost thou know," said he to Phoebe, "of the presence of one Louis Kerneguy, calling himself a Scotch page, who came here a few days since?"

"Surely, sir," she replied, "I cannot easily forget him; and I warrant no well-looking wench that comes into his way will be like to forget him either."

"Aha," said Cromwell, "sayst thou so? truly I believe the woman will prove the truer witness—When did he leave this house?

"Nay, I know nothing of his movements, not I," said Phoebe; "lam only glad to keep out of his way. But if he have actually gone hence, I am sure he was here some two hours since, for he crossed me in the lower passage, between the hall and the kitchen."

"How did you know it was he?" demanded Cromwell.

"By a rude enough token," said Phoebe.—" La, sir, you do ask such questions!" she added, hanging down her head.

Humgudgeon here interfered, taking upon himself the freedom of a coadjutor. "Verily," he said, "if what the damsel is called to speak upon hath aught unseemly, I crave your Excellency's permission to withdraw, not desiring that my nightly meditations may be disturbed with tales of such a nature."

"Nay, your honour," said Phoebe, "I scorn the old man's words, in the way of seemliness or unseemliness either. Master Louis did but snatch a kiss, that is the truth of it, if it must be told."

Here Humgudgeon groaned deeply, while his Excellency avoided laughing with some difficulty. "Thou hast given excellent tokens, Phoebe," he said; "and if they be true, as I think they seem to be, thou shalt not lack thy reward.— And here comes our spy from the stables."

"There are not the least signs," said the trooper, "that horses have been in the stables for a month—there is no litter in the stalls, no hay in the racks, the corn-binns are empty, and the mangers are full of cobwebs."

"Ay, ay," said the old knight, "I have seen when I kept twenty good horses in these stalls, with many a groom and stable-boy to attend them."

"In the meanwhile," said Cromwell, "their present state tells little for the truth of your own story, that there were horses to-day, on which this Kerneguy and your son fled from justice."

"I did not say that the horses were kept there," said the knight. "I have horses and stables elsewhere."

"Fie, fie, for shame, for shame!" said the General; "can a white-bearded man, I ask it once more, be a false witness?"

"Faith, sir," said Sir Henry Lee, "it is a thriving trade, and I wonder not that you who live on it are so severe in prosecuting interlopers. But it is the times, and those who rule the times, that make grey-beards deceivers."

"Thou art facetious, friend, as well as daring, in thy malignancy," said Cromwell; "but credit me, I will cry quittance with you ere I am done. Whereunto lead these doors?"

"To bedrooms," answered the knight.

"Bedrooms! only to bedrooms?" said the Republican General, in a voice which indicated such was the internal occupation of his thoughts, that he had not fully understood the answer.

"Lord, sir," said the knight, "why should you make it so strange? I say these doors lead to bedrooms—to places where honest men sleep, and rogues lie awake."

"You are running up a farther account, Sir Henry," said the General; "but we will balance it once and for all."

During the whole of the scene, Cromwell, whatever might be the internal uncertainty of his mind, maintained the most strict temperance in language and manner, just as if he had no farther interest in what was passing, than as a military man employed in discharging the duty enjoined him by his superiors. But the restraint upon his passion was but

The torrent's smoothness ere it dash below.

The course of his resolution was hurried on even more forcibly, because no violence of expression attended or announced its current. He threw himself into a chair, with a countenance that indicated no indecision of mind, but a But mortal pleasure, what art thou in truth? The torrent's smoothness ere it dash below.

Campbell's Gertbude Of Wyoming. Scott.

determination which awaited only the signal for action. Meanwhile the knight, as if resolved in nothing to forego the privileges of his rank and place, sat himself down in turn, and putting on his hat which lay on a table, regarded the General with a calm look of fearless indifference. The soldiers stood around, some holding the torches which illuminated the apartment with a lurid and sombre glare of light, the others resting upon their weapons. Phoebe, with her hands folded, her eyes turned upwards till the pupils were scarce visible, and every shade of colour banished from her ruddy cheek, stood like one in immediate apprehension of the sentence of death being pronounced, and instant execution commanded.

Heavy steps were at last heard, and Pearson and some of the soldiers returned. This seemed to be what Cromwell waited for. He started up, and asked hastily, "Any news, Pearson? any prisoners—any malignants slain in thy defence?"

"None, so please your Excellency," said the officer.

"And are thy sentinels all carefully placed, as Tomkins' scroll gave direction, and with fitting orders?"

"With the most deliberate care," said Pearson.

"Art thou very sure," said Cromwell, pulling him a little to one side, "that this is all well, and duly cared for? Bethink thee, that when we engage ourselves in the private communications, all will be lost should the party we look for have the means of dodging us by an escape into the more open rooms, and from thence perhaps into the forest."

"My Lord General," answered Pearson, "if placing the guards on the places pointed out in this scroll be sufficient, with the strictest orders, to stop, and, if necessary, to stab or shoot, whoever crosses their post, such orders are given to men who will not fail to execute them. If more is necessary, your Excellency has only to speak."

"No—no—no, Pearson," said the General, "thou hast done well This night over, and let it end but as we hope, thy reward shall not be a wanting.—And now to business.— Sir Henry Lee, undo me the secret spring of yonder picture of your ancestor—Nay, spare yourself the trouble and guilt of falsehood or equivocation, and, I say, undo me that spring presently."

"When I acknowledge you for my master, and wear your livery, I may obey your commands," answered the knight; "even then I would need first to understand them."

"Avench," said Cromwell, addressing Phoebe, "go thou undo the spring—you could do it fast enough when you aided at the gambols of the demons of Woodstock, and terrified even Mark Everard, who, I judged, had more sense."

"Oh Lord, sir, what shall I do?" said Phoebe, looking to the knight; "they know all about it. What shall I do?"

"For thy life, hold out to the last, wench! Every minute is worth a million."

"Ha! heard you that, Pearson?" said Cromwell to the officer; then, stamping with his foot, he added, "Undo the spring, or I will else use levers and wrenching-irons— Or, ha!—another petard were well bestowed—Call the engineer."

"Oh Lord, sir," cried Phoebe, "I shall never live another peter—I will open the spring."

"Do as thou wilt," said Sir Henry; "it shall profit them but little."

Whether from real agitation, or from a desire to gain time, Phoebe was some minutes ere she could get the spring to open; it was indeed secured with art, and the machinery on which it acted was concealed in the frame of the portrait. The whole, when fastened, appeared quite motionless, and betrayed, as when examined by Colonel Everard, no external mark of its being possible to remove it. It was now withdrawn, however, and shewed a narrow recess, with steps which ascended on one side into the thickness of the wall. Cromwell was now like a greyhound slipped from the leash with the prey in full view. —"Up," he cried, "Pearson, thou art swifter than I—Up thou next, corporal." With more agility than could have been expected from his person or years, which were past the meridian of life, and exclaiming, "Before, those with the torches " he followed the party, like an eager huntsman in the rear of his hounds, to encourage at once and direct them, as they penetrated into the labyrinth described by Doctor Rochecliffe in the "Wonders of Woodstock."

Does Cromwell's fit of melancholy seem to you effectively portrayed? How would you compare it with the somewhat similar occurrence in Chapter VIII? Compare the account of the siege of the castle with similar sieges described in *Old Mortality, Ivanhoe, Quentin Durward, Peveril of the Peak,* and elsewhere.

CHAPTER THE THIRTY-FOURTH

The King, therefore, for his defence
Against the furious Queen,
At Woods: ock builded such a bower,
As never yet was seen.
Most curiously that bower was built,
Of stone and timber strong;
An hundred and fifty doors
Did to this bower belong:
And they so cunningly contrived,
With turnings round about,
That none but with a clew of thread
   Could enter in or out.
   Ballad Of Faik Rosamond.

The tradition of the country, as well as some historical evidence, confirmed the opinion that there existed within the old royal Lodge at Woodstock, a labyrinth, or connected series of subterranean passages, built chiefly by Henry II., for the security of his mistress, Rosamond Clifford, from the jealousy of his Queen, the celebrated Eleanor. Doctor Rochecliffe, indeed, in one of those fits of contradiction with which antiquaries are sometimes seized, was bold enough to dispute the alleged purpose of the perplexed maze of rooms and passages, with which the walls of the ancient palace were perforated; but the fact was undeniable, that in raising the fabric, some Norman architect had exerted the utmost of the complicated art, which they have often shewn elsewhere, in creating secret passages, and chambers of retreat and concealment. There were stairs, which were ascended merely, as it seemed, for the purpose of descending again—passages, which, after turning and winding for a considerable way, returned to the place where they set out—there were trapdoors and hatchways, panels and portcullises. Although Oliver was assisted by a sort of ground-plan, made out and transmitted by Joseph Tomkins, whose former employment in Doctor RocheclifEe's service had made him fully acquainted with the place, it was found imperfect; and, moreover, the most serious obstacles to their progress occurred in the shape of strong doors, party-walls, and iron grates—so that the party blundered on in the dark, uncertain whether they were not going farther from, rather than approaching, the extremity of the labyrinth. They were obliged to send for mechanics, with sledge-hammers and other instruments, to force one or two of those doors, which resisted all other means of undoing them. Labouring along in these dusky passages, where, from time to time, they were like to be choked by the dust which their acts of violence excited, the soldiers were obliged to be relieved oftener than once, and the bulky Corporal Grace-be-here himself puffed and blew like a grampus that has got into shoal water. Cromwell. alone continued, with unabated zeal, to push on his researches—to encourage the soldiers, by the exhortations which they best understood, against fainting for lack of faith—and to secure, by sentinels at proper places, possession of the ground which they had already explored. His acute and observing eye detected, with a sneering smile, the cordage and machinery by which the bed of poor Desborough had been inverted, and several remains of the various disguises, as well as private modes of access, by which Desborough, Bletson, and Harrison, had been previously imposed upon. He pointed them out to Pearson, with no farther comment than was implied in the exclamation, " The simple fools *I*" But his assistants began to lose heart and be discouraged, and required all his spirits to raise theirs. He then called their attention to voices which they seemed to hear before them, and urged these as evidence that they were moving on the track of some enemy of the Commonwealth, who, for the execution of his malignant plots, had retreated into these extraordinary fastnesses.

The spirits of the men became at last downcast notwithstanding all this encouragement. They spoke to each other in whispers, of the devils of Woodstock, who might be all the while decoying them forward to a room said to exist in the Palace, where the floor revolving on an axis, precipitated those who entered into a bottomless abyss. Humgudgeon hinted, that he had consulted the Scripture that morning by way of lot, and his fortune had been to alight on the passage, " Eutychus fell down from the third loft."1 *Acta* xx. 9.

The energy and authority of Cromwell, however, and the refreshment of some food and strong waters, reconciled them to pursuing their task.

Nevertheless, with all their unwearied exertions, morning dawned on the search before they had reached Doctor Rochecliffe's sitting apartment, into which, after all, they obtained entrance by a mode much more difficult than that which the Doctor himself employed. But here their ingenuity was long at fault. From the miscellaneous articles that were strewed around, and the preparations made for food and lodging, it seemed they had gained the very citadel of the labyrinth; but though various passages opened from it, they all terminated in places with which they were already acquainted, or communicated with the other parts of the house where their own sentinels assured them none had passed. Cromwell remained long in deep uncertainty. Meantime he directed Pearson to take charge of the ciphers, and more important papers which lay on the table. "Though there is little there," he said, "that I have not already known, by means of Trusty Tomkins. Honest Joseph, for an artful and thorough-paced agent, the like of thee is not left in England."

After a considerable pause, during which he sounded with the pommel of his sword almost every stone in the building, and every plank on the floor, the General gave orders to bring the old knight and Doctor Rochecliffe to the spot, trusting that he might work out of them some explanation of the secrets of this apartment.

"So please your Excellency, to let me to deal with them," said Pearson, who was a true soldier of fortune, and had been a buccanier in the West Indies, "I think that, by a whipcord twitched tight round their forehead, and twisted about with a pistol-but, I could make either the truth start from their lips, or the eyes from their head."

"Out upon thee, Pearson!" said Cromwell, with abhorrence; "we have no warrant for such cruelty, neither as Englishmen nor Christians. We may slay malignants as we crush noxious animals, but to torture them is a deadly sin; for it is written, 'He made them to be pitied of those who carried them captive.' Nay, I recall the order even for their examination, trusting that wisdom will be granted us without it, to discover their most secret devices. *Psalms* ovi. 46.

There was a pause accordingly, during which an idea seized upon Cromwell's imagination—" Bring me hither," he said, "yonder stool;" and placing it beneath one of the windows, of which there were two so high in the wall as not to be accessible from the floor, he clambered up into the entrance of the window, which was six or seven feet deep, corresponding with the thickness of the wall. "Come up hither, Pearson," said the General; "but ere thou comest, double the guard at the foot of the turret called Love's Ladder, and bid them bring up the other petard— So now, come thou hither."

The inferior officer, however brave in the field, was one of those whom a great height strikes with giddiness and sickness. He shrunk back from the view of the precipice, on the verge of which Cromwell was standing with com Elete indifference, till the General, catching the hand of is follower, pulled him forward as far as he would advance. "I think," said the General, " I have found the clew, but by this light it is no easy one. See you, we stand in the portal near the top of Rosamond's Tower; and yon turret, which rises opposite to our feet, is that which is called Love's Ladder, from which the drawbridge reached that admitted the profligate Norman tyrant to the bower of his mistress."

"True, my lord, but the drawbridge is gone," said Pearson.

"Ay, Pearson," replied the General; "but an active man might spring from the spot we stand upon to the battlements of yonder turret."

"I do not think so, my lord," said Pearson.

"What?" said Cromwell; "not if the avenger of blood were behind you with his slaughter-weapon in his hand?"

"The fear of instant death might do much," answered Pearson; "but when I look at that sheer depth on either side, and at the empty chasm between us and yonder turret, which is, I warrant you, twelve feet distant, I confess the truth, nothing short of the most imminent danger should induce me to try. Pah—the thought makes my head grow giddy!—I tremble to see your Highness stand there, balancing yourself as if you meditated a spring into the empty air. I repeat, I would scarce stand so near the verge as does your Highness, for the rescue of my life."

"Ah, base and degenerate spirit!" said the General; "soul of mud and clay, wouldst thou not do it, and much more, for the possession of empire!—that is, peradventure," continued he, changing his tone as one who has said too much, "shouldst thou be called on to do this, that thereby becoming a great man in the tribes of Israel, thou mightest redeem the captivity of Jerusalem—ay, and it may be, work some great work for the afflicted people of this land?"

"Your Highness may feel such calls," said the officer; "but they are not for poor Gilbert Pearson, your faithful follower. You made a jest of me yesterday, when I tried to speak your language; and I am no more able to fulfil your designs than to use your mode of speech."

"But, Pearson," said Cromwell, "thou hast thrice, yea, four times, called me your Highness."

"Did I, my lord? I was not sensible of it. I crave your pardon, said the officer.

"Nay," said Oliver, "there was no offence. I do indeed stand high, and I may perchance stand higher— though, alas, it were fitter for a simple soul like me to return to my plough and my husbandry. Nevertheless, I will not wrestle against the Supreme will, should I be called on to do yet more in that worthy cause. For surely he who hath been to our British Israel as a shield of help, and a sword of excellency, making her enemies be found liars unto her, will not give over the flock to those foolish shepherds of Westminster, who shear the sheep and feed them not, and who are in very deed hirelings, not shepherds."

"I trust to see your lordship quoit them all down stairs," answered Pearson. "But may I ask why we pursue this discourse even now, until we have secured the common enemy?"

"I will tarry no jot of time "—said the General; "fence the communication of Love's Ladder, as it is called, below, as I take it for almost certain, that the party whom we have driven from fastness to fastness during the night, has at length sprung to the top of yonder battlements from the place where we now stand. Finding the turret is guarded below, the place he has chosen for his security will prove a rat-trap, from whence there is no returning."

"There is a cask of gunpowder in this cabinet," said The Parliament is probably referred to.

Pearson; "were it not better, my lord, to mine the tower, if he will not render himself, and send the whole turret with its contents one hundred feet in the air?"

"Ah, silly man," said Cromwell, striking him familiarly on the shoulder; "if thou hadst done this without telling me, it had been good service. But we will first summon the turret, and then think whether the petard will serve our turn— it is but mining at last.—Blow a summons there, down below."

The trumpets rang at his bidding, till the old walls echoed from every recess and vaulted archway. Cromwell, as if he cared not to look upon the person whom he expected to appear, drew back, like a necromancer afraid of the spectre which he has evoked.

"He has come to the battlement," said Pearson to his General.

"In what dress or appearance *?"* answered Cromwell from within the chamber.

"A grey riding-suit, passmented1 with silver, russet walking-boots, a cut-band, a grey hat and plume, black hair."

"It is he, it is he!" said Cromwell; "and another crowning mercy is vouchsafed!"

Meantime, Pearson and young Lee exchanged defiance from their respective posts.

"Surrender," said the former, "or we blow you up in your fastness."

"I am come of too high a race to surrender to rebels," said Albert, assuming the air with which, in such a condition, a king might have spoken.

"I bear you to witness," cried Cromwell exultingly, "he hath refused quarter. Of a surety, his blood be on his head.—One of you bring down the barrel of powder. As he loves to soar high, we will add what can be taken from the soldiers' bandoleers.—Come with me, Pearson; thou understandest this gear.—Corporal Grace-be-here, stand thou fast on the platform of the window, where Captain Pearson and I stood but even now, and bend the point of thy partisan against any who shall attempt to pass. Thou art as strong as a bull; and I will back thee against despair itself."

"But," said the corporal, mounting reluctantly, "the Laced. Ornamented collar. Pike.

place is as the pinnacle of the Temple; and it is written, that Eutychus fell down from the third loft and was taken up dead."

"Because he slept upon his post," answered Cromwell readily. "Beware thou of carelessness, and thus thy feet shall be kept from stumbling.—You four soldiers, remain here to support the corporal, if it be necessary; and you, as well as the corporal, will draw into the vaulted passage the minute the trumpets sound a retreat. It is as strong as a casemate, and you may lie there safe from the effects of the mine. Thou Zerubbabel Robins, I know wilt be their lance-prisade."

Robins bowed, and the General departed to join those who were without.

As he reached the door of the hall, the petard was heard to explode, and he saw that it had succeeded; for the soldiers rushed, brandishing their swords and pistols, in at the postern of the turret, whose gate had been successfully forced. A thrill of exultation, but not unmingled with horror, shot across the veins of the ambitious soldier.

"Now—now!" he cried; "they are dealing with him!"

His expectations were deceived. Pearson and the others returned disappointed, and reported they had been stopped by a strong trapdoor of grated iron, extended over the narrow stair; and they could see there was an obstacle of the same kind some ten feet higher. To remove it by force, while a desperate and well-armed man had the advantage of the steps above them, might cost many lives. "Which, lack-a-day," said the General, "it is our duty to be tender of. What dost thou advise, Gilbert Pearson?" "We must use powder, my lord," answered Pearson, who saw his master was too modest to reserve to himself the whole merit of the proceeding—"There may be a chamber easily and conveniently formed under the foot of the stair. We have a sausage, by good luck, to form the train—and so"

"Ah!" said Cromwell, "I know thou canst manage such gear well—But, Gilbert, I go to visit the posts, and give them orders to retire to a safe distance when the retreat is sounded. You will allow them five minutes for this purpose."

" Lance-prisade," or "lance-brisade," a private appointed to a small command—a sort of temporary corporal. Scott. *Matthew* iv. 5. 'A linen bag filled with gunpowder.

"Three is enough for any knave of them all," said Pearson. "They will be lame indeed, that require more on such a service—I ask but one, though I fire the train myself."

"Take heed," said Cromwell, "that the poor soul be listened to, if he asks quarter. It may be, he may repent him of his hardheartedness, and call for mercy."

"And mercy he shall have,"—answered Pearson, "provided he calls loud enough to make me hear him; for the explosion of that damned petard has made me as deaf as the devil's dam."

"Hush, Gilbert, hush!" said Cromwell; "you offend in your language."

"Zooks, sir, I must speak either in your way, or in my own," said Pearson, "unless I am to be dumb as well as deaf!—Away with you, my lord, to visit the posts; and you will presently hear me make some noise in the world."

Cromwell smiled gently at his aide-de-camp's petulence, patted him on the shoulder, and called him a mad fellow, walked a little way, then turned back to whisper, "What thou dost, do quickly;" then returned again towards the outer circle of guards, turning his head from time to time, as if to assure himself that the corporal to whom he had intrusted the duty still kept guard with his advanced weapon upon the terrific chasm between Rosamond's Tower and the corresponding turret. Seeing him standing on his post, the General muttered between his mustaches,

"The fellow hath the strength and courage of a bear; and yonder is a post where one shall do more to keep back than an hundred in making way." He cast a last look on the gigantic figure, who stood in that airy position, like some Gothic statue, the weapon half levelled against the opposite turret, with the but rested against his right foot, his steel cap and burnished corselet glittering in the rising sun.

Cromwell then passed on to give the necessary orders, that such sentinels as might be endangered at their present posts by the effect of the mine, should withdraw at the sound of the trumpet to the places which he pointed out to them. Never, on any occasion of his life, did he display more calmness and presence of mind. He was kind, nay, facetious with the soldiers, who adored him; and yet he resembled a volcano before the eruption commences— all peaceful and quiet without, while an hundred contradictory passions were raging in his bosom.

Corporal Humgudgeon, meanwhile, remained steady upon his post; yet, though as determined a soldier as ever fought among the redoubted regiment of Ironsides, and possessed of no small share of that exalted fanaticism which lent so keen an edge to the natural courage of those stern religionists, the veteran felt his present situation to be highly uncomfortable. Within a pike's length of him arose a turret, which was about to be dispersed in massy fragments through the air; and he felt small confidence in the length of time which might be allowed for his escape from such a dangerous vicinity. The duty of constant vigilance upon his post, was partly divided by this natural feeling, which induced him from time to time to bend his eyes on the miners below, instead of keeping them rivetted on the opposite turret.

At length the interest of the scene arose to the uttermost. After entering and returning from the turret, and coming out again more than once, in the course of about twenty minutes, Pearson issued, as it might be supposed, for the last time, carrying in his hand, and uncoiling, as he went along, the sausage, or linen bag (so called from its appearance), which, strongly sewed together, and crammed with gunpowder, was to serve as a train betwixt the mine to be sprung, and the point occupied by the engineer who was to give fire. He was in the act of finally adjusting it, when the attention of the corporal on the tower became irresistibly and exclusively rivetted upon the preparations for the explosion. But while he watched the aide-de-camp drawing his pistol to give fire, and the trumpeter handling his instrument, as waiting the order to sound the retreat, fate rushed on the unhappy sentinel in a way he least expected.

Young, active, bold, and completely possessed of his presence of mind, Albert Lee, who had been from the loopholes a watchful observer of every measure which had been taken by his besiegers, had resolved to make one desperate effort for self-preservation. While the head of the sentinel on the opposite platform was turned from him, and bent rather downwards, he suddenly sprung across the chasm, though the space on which he lighted was scarce wide enough for two persons, threw the surprised soldier from his precarious stand, and jumped himself down into the chamber. The gigantic trooper went sheer down twenty feet, struck against a projecting battlement, which launched the wretched man outwards, and then fell on the earth with such tremendous force, that the head, which first touched the ground, dinted a hole in the soil of six inches in depth, and was crushed like an eggshell. Scarce knowing what had happened, yet startled and confounded at the descent of this heavy body, which fell at no great distance from him, Pearson snapped his pistol at the train, no previous warning given; the powder caught, and the mine exploded. Had it been strongly charged with powder, many of those without might have suffered, but the explosion was only powerful enough to blow out, in a lateral direction, a part of the wall just above the foundation, sufficient, however, to destroy the equipoise of the building. Then amid a cloud of smoke, which began gradually to encircle the turret like a shroud, arising slowly from its base to its summit, it was seen to stagger and shake, by all who had courage to look steadily at a sight so dreadful. Slowly, at first, the building inclined outwards, then rushed precipitately to its base, and fell to the ground in huge fragments, the strength of its resistance shewing the excellence of the mason-work. The engineer, as soon as he had fired the train, fled in such alarm, that he well-nigh ran against his General, who was advancing towards him, while a huge stone from the summit of the building, flying farther than the rest, lighted within a yard of them.

"Thou hast been over hasty, Pearson," said Cromwell, with the greatest composure possible—" hath no one fallen in that same tower of Siloe?' "Some one fell," said Pearson, still in great agitation, "and yonder lies his body half-buried in the rubbish."

With a quick and resolute step Cromwell approached the spot, and exclaimed, "Pearson, thou hast ruined me—the young man hath escaped.— This is our own sentinel— plague on the idiot! Let him rot beneath the ruins which crushed him!"

A cry now resounded from the platform of Rosamond's Tower, which appeared yet taller than formerly, deprived *Luke* xiii. 4. of the neighbouring turret, which emulated, though it did not attain to its height,—" A prisoner, noble General—a prisoner—the fox whom we have chased all night is now in the snare—the Lord hath delivered him into the hand of his servants."

"Look you keep him in safe custody," exclaimed Cromwell, "and bring him presently down to the apartment from which the secret passages have their principal entrance."

"Your Excellency shall be obeyed."

The proceedings of Albert Lee, to which these exclamations related, had been unfortunate. He had dashed from the platform, as we have related, the gigantic strength of the soldier opposed to him, and had instantly jumped down into Rochecliffe's chamber. But the soldiers stationed there threw themselves upon him, and after a struggle, which was hopelessly maintained against such advantage of numbers, had thrown the young cavalier to the ground, two of them, drawn down by his strenuous exertions, falling across him. At the same moment a sharp and severe report was heard, which, like a clap of thunder in the immediate vicinity, shook all around them, till the strong and solid tower tottered like the mast of a stately vessel when about to part by the board. In a few seconds this was followed by another sullen sound, at first low and deep, but augmenting like the roar of a cataract, as it descends, reeling, bellowing, and rushing, as if to astound both heaven and earth. So awful, indeed, was the sound of the neighbour tower as it fell, that both the captive, and those who struggled with him, continued for a minute or two passive in each other's grasp.

Albert was the first to recover consciousness and activity. He shook off those who lay above him, and made a desperate effort to gain his feet, in which he partly succeeded. But as he had to deal with men accustomed to every species of danger, and whose energies were recovered nearly as soon as his own, he was completely secured, and his arms held down. Loyal and faithful to his trust, and resolved to sustain to the last the character which he had assumed, he exclaimed, as his struggles were finally overpowered, "Rebel villains! would you slay your king?"

"Ha, heard you that!" cried one of the soldiers to the lance-prisade, who commanded the party. "Shall I not strike this son of a wicked father under the fifth rib, even as the tyrant of Moab was smitten by Ehud with a dagger of a cubit's length?"

But Robins answered, "Be it far from us, Merciful Strickalthrow, to slay in cold blood the captive of our bow and of our spear. Methinks, since the storm of Tredagh we have shed enough of blood—therefore, on your lives do him no evil; but take from him his arms, and let us bring him before the chosen Instrument, even our General, that he may do with him what is meet in his eyes."

By this time the soldier, whose exultation had made him the first to communicate the intelligence from the battlements to Cromwell, returned, and brought commands corresponding to the orders of their temporary officer; and Albert Lee, disarmed and bound, was conducted as a captive into the apartment which derived its name from the victories of his ancestor, and placed in the presence of General Cromwell.

Running over in his mind the time which had elapsed since the departure of Charles, till the siege, if it may be termed so, had terminated in his own capture, Albert had every reason to hope that his Royal Master must have had time to accomplish his escape. Yet he determined to maintain to the last a deceit, which might for a time insure the King's safety. The difference betwixt them could not, he thought, be instantly discovered, begrimed as he was with dust and smoke, and with blood issuing from some scratches received in the scuffle.

In this evil plight, but bearing himself with such dignity as was adapted to the princely character, Albert was ushered into the apartment of Victor Lee, where, in his father's own chair, reclined the triumphant enemy of the cause to which the house of Lee had been hereditarily faithful.

Tredagh, or Drogheda, was taken by Cromwell in 1649, by storm, and the governor and whole garrison put to the sword. Scott. *Judges* iii. 15-25. CHAPTER THE THIRTY-FIFTH

A barren title hast thou bought too dear;
Why didst thou tell me that thou wert a King?
Henry IV. *Part I.*

Oliver Cromwell arose from his seat as the two veteran soldiers, Zerubbabel Robins and Merciful Strickalthrow, introduced into the apartment the prisoner, whom they held by the arms, and fixed his stern hazel eye on Albert long before he could give vent to the ideas which were swelling in his bosom. Exultation was the most predominant.

"Art not thou," he at length said, "that Egyptian, which, before these days, madest an uproar, and leddest out into the wilderness many thousand men, who were murderers?—Ha, youth! I have hunted thee from Stirling to Worcester,—from Worcester to Woodstock, and we have met at last!"

"I would," replied Albert, speaking in the charactei which he had assumed, "that we had met where I could have shewn thee the difference betwixt a rightful King and an ambitious Usurper!"

"Go to, young man," said Cromwell; "say rather the difference between a judge raised up for the redemption of England, and the son of those Kings whom the Lord in his anger permitted to reign over her. But we will not waste useless words. God knows that it is not of our will that we are called to such high matters, being as humble in our thoughts as we are of ourselves; and in our unassisted nature frail and foolish; and unable to render a reason but for the better spirit within us, which is not of us.—Thou art weary, young man, and thy nature requires rest and refection,

being doubtless dealt with delicately, as one who hath fed on the fat, and drunk of the sweet, and who hath been clothed in purple and fine linen." *Acts* xxi. 38. Stirling Castle in Scotland was the headquarters of Charles II when Cromwell marched against him at the opening of the second civil war.

Here the General suddenly stopt, and then abruptly exclaimed—" But is this—Ah! whom have we here? These are not the locks of the swarthy lad Charles Stuart?—A cheat! a cheat!"

Albert hastily cast his eyes on a mirror which stood in the room, and perceived that a dark peruke, found among Doctor Kochecliffe's miscellaneous wardrobe, had been disordered in the scuffle with the soldiery, and that his own light-brown hair was escaping from beneath it."

"Who is this?" said Cromwell, stamping with fury— "Pluck the disguise from him."

The soldiers did so; and bringing him at the same time towards the light, the deception could not be maintained for a moment longer, with any possibility of success. Cromwell came up to him with his teeth set, and grinding against each other as he spoke, his hands clenched, and trembling with emotion, and speaking with a voice low-pitched, bitterly and deeply emphatic, such as might have preceded a stab with his dagger.

"Thy name, young man?"

He was answered calmly and firmly, while the countenance of the speaker wore a cast of triumph, and even contempt.

"Albert Lee of Ditchley, a faithful subject of King Charles."

"I might have guessed it," said Cromwell.—" Ay, and to King Charles shalt thou go, as soon as it is noon on the dial.—Pearson," he continued, "let him be carried to the others; and let them be executed at twelve exactly."

"All, sir?" said Pearson, surprised; for Cromwell, though he at times made formidable examples, was, in general, by no means sanguinary.

"All"—repeated Cromwell, fixing his eye on young Lee.—" Yes, young sir, your conduct has devoted to death thy

father, thy kinsman, and the stranger that was in thine household. Such wreck hast thou brought on thy father's house."

"My father, too—my aged father," said Albert, looking upward, and endeavouring to raise his hands in the same direction, which was prevented by his bonds. "The Lord's will be done!"

"All this havoc can be saved, if," said the General, "thou wilt answer one question—Where is the young Charles Stuart, who was called King of Scotland?"

"Under Heaven's protection, and safe from thy power," was the firm and unhesitating answer of the young royalist.

"Away with him to prison!" said Cromwell; "and from thence to execution with the rest of them, as malignants taken in the fact. Let a court-martial sit on them presently."

"One word," said young Lee, as they led him from the room.

"Stop, stop," said Cromwell, with the agitation of renewed hope—" let him be heard."

"You love texts of scripture," said Albert—"Let this be the subject of your next homily—' Had Zimri peace who slew his master?" "Away with him," said the General; "let him die the death!—I have said it."

As Cromwell spoke these words, his aide-de-camp observed that he became unwontedly pale.

"Your Excellency is overtoiled in the public service," said Pearson; "a course of the stag in the evening will refresh you. The old knight hath a noble hound here, if we can but get him to hunt without his master, which may be hard, as he is faithful, and"

"Hang him up!" said Cromwell.

"What—whom—hang the noble dog? Your Excellency was wont to love a good hound?"

"It matters not," said Cromwell; "let him be killed. Is it not written, that they slew in the valley of Achor, not only the accursed Achan,with his sons and his daughters, but also his oxen and his asses, and his sheep, and every live thing belonging unto him? And even thus shall we do to the malignant family of Lee, who have aided Sisera in his flight, when Israel might have been delivered of his trouble for ever. But send out couriers and patrols—Follow, pursue, watch in every direction—Let my horse be ready at the door in five minutes, or bring me the first thou canst find." 1 *Kings* xvi. 8-20. A stag-hunt.
See note in Chapter XXXIII *Judges* iv. The allusion is to Charles II.
It seemed to Pearson that this was something wildly spoken, and that the cold perspiration was standing upon the General's brow as he said it. He therefore again pressed the necessity of repose, and it would appear that nature seconded strongly the representation. Cromwell arose, and made a step or two towards the door of the apartment; but stopped, staggered, and, after a pause, sat down in a chair. "Truly, friend Pearson," he said, "this weary carcass of ours is an impediment to us, even in our most necessary business, and I am fitter to sleep than to watch, which is not my wont. Place guards, therefore, till we repose ourselves for an hour or two. Send out in every direction, and spare not for horses' flesh. Wake me if the court-martial should require instruction, and forget not to see the sentence punctually executed on the Lees, and those who were arrested with them."

As Cromwell spoke thus, he arose and half-opened a bed-room door, when Pearson again craved pardon for asking if he had rightly understood his Excellency, that all the prisoners were to be executed.

"Have I not said it?" answered Cromwell, displeasedly. "Is it because thou art a man of blood, and hast ever been, that thou dost affect these scruples to shew thyself tenderhearted at my expense? I tell thee, that if there lack one in the full tale of execution, thine own life shall pay the forfeit."

So saying, he entered the apartment, followed by the groom of his chamber, who attended upon Pearson's summons.

When his General had retired, Pearson remained in great perplexity what he ought to do; and that from no scruples of conscience, but from uncertainty whether he might not err either in postponing, or in too hastily and too literally executing, the instructions he had received.

In the meantime, Strickalthrow and Robins had returned, after lodging Albert in prison, to the room where Pearson was still musing on his General's commands. Both these men were adjutators in their army, and old soldiers, whom Cromwell was accustomed to treat with great familiarity; so that Robins had no hesitation to ask Captain Pearson, "Whether he meant to execute the commands of the General, even to the letter?" Number.

Pearson shook his head with an air of doubt, but added, "There was no choice left."

"Be assured," said the old man, "that if thou dost this folly, thou wilt cause Israel to sin, and that the General will not be pleased with your service. Thou knowest, and none better than thou, that Oliver, although he be like unto David the son of Jesse, in faith, and wisdom, and courage, yet there are times when the evil spirit cometh upon him as it did upon Saul, and he uttereth commands which he will not thank any one for executing."

Pearson was too good a politician to assent directly to a

E eposition which he could not deny—he only shook his ead once more, and said that it was easy for those to talk who were not responsible, but the soldier's duty was to obey his orders, and not to judge of them.

"Very righteous truth," said Merciful Strickalthrow, a grim old Scotchman; "I marvel where our brother Zerubbabel caught up this softness of heart?"

"Why, I do but wish," said Zerubbabel, "that four or five human creatures may draw the breath of God's air for a few hours more; there can be small harm done by delaying the execution,— and the General will have some time for reflection."

"Ay," said Captain Pearson, " but I in my service must be more pointedly obsequious, than thou in thy plainness art bound to be, friend Zerubbabel."

"Then shall the coarse frieze cassock1 of the private soldier help the golden gaberdine of the captain to bear out the blast," said Zerubbabel. "Ay, indeed, I can shew you warrant why we be aidful to each other in doing acts of kindness and long-suffering, seeing the best of us are poor sinful creatures, who might suffer, being called to a brief accounting."

"Of a verity you surprise me, brother Zerubbabel," said Strickalthrow; "that thou, being an old and experienced soldier, whose head hath grown gray in battle, shouldst give such advice to a young officer. Is not the General's commission to take away the wicked from the land, and to root out the Amalekite, and the Jebusite, and the Perizzite, and the Hittite, and the Girgashite, and the Amorite?1 and are not these men justly to be compared to the five kings, who took shelter in the cave of Makkedah, who were delivered into the hands of Joshua the son of Nun? and he caused his captains and his soldiers to come near and tread on their necks—and then he smote them, and he slew them, and then he hanged them on five trees, even till evening—And thou, Gilbert Pearson by name, be not withheld from the duty which is appointed to thee, but do even as has been commanded by him who is raised up to judge and to deliver Israel; for it is written, 'cursed is he who holdeth back his sword from the slaughter/" An outer cloak of coarse stuff.

'The reference is to the gilt insignia of rank worn upon the gaberdine, or outer coat.

Thus wrangled the two military theologians, while Pearson, much more solicitous to anticipate the wishes of Oliver than to know the will of Heaven, listened to them with great indecision and perplexity.

Heathen tribes exterminated by the Israelites. *Deuteronomy* vii. 1. *Joshua* x. 10. CHAPTER THE THIRTY-SIXTH

But let us now, like soldiers on the watch,
Put the soul's armour on, alike prepared
For all a soldier's warfare brings.
    Joanna Baillie.

The reader will recollect, that when Rocheclifffe and Joceline were made prisoners, the party which escorted them had two other captives in their train, namely, Colonel Everard and the Rev. Nehemiah Holdenough. When Cromwell had obtained entrance into Woodstock, and commenced his search after the fugitive Prince, the prisoners were placed in what had been an old guardroom and which was by its strength well calculated to serve for a prison, and a guard was placed over them by Pearson. No light was allowed, save that of a glimmering fire of charcoal. The prisoners remained separated from each other, Colonel Everard conversing with Nehemiah Holdenough, at a distance from Doctor Rochecliffe, Sir Henry Lee, and Joceline. The party was soon after augmented by Wildrake, who was brought down to the Lodge, and thrust in with so little ceremony, that, his arms being bound, he had very nearly fallen on his nose in the middle of the prison.

"I thank you, my good friend," he said, looking back to the door, which they who had pushed him in were securing—" *Point de ceremonie*—no apology for tumbling, so we light in good company.—Save ye, save ye, gentlemen all—What, *a la mort,* and nothing stirring to keep the spirits up, and make a night on't?—The last we shall have, I take it; for a make to a million, but we trine to the nubbing cheat f to-morrow.—Patron—noble patron, how goes it? This was but a scurvy trick of Noll, so far as you were concerned: as for me, why I might have deserved something of the kind at his hand." A halfpenny. Scott. f Hang-on the gallows. Scott.J

'No ceremony. 'At the point of death.
"Prithee, "Wildrake, sit down," said Everard; "thou art drunk—disturb us not."

"Drunk? I drunk?" cried Wildrake, "I have been splicing the main-brace, as Jack says at Wapping1—have been tasting Noll's brandy in a bumper to the King's health, and another to his Excellency's confusion, and another to the d n of Parliament—and it may be one or two more, but all to devilish good toasts. But I'm not drunk."

"Prithee, friend, be not profane," said Nehemiah Holdenough.

"What, my little Presbyterian Parson, my slender Mass John? thou shalt say amen to this world instantly"—said Wildrake; "I have had a weary time in't for one.—Ha, noble Sir Henry, I kiss your hand—I tell thee, knight, the point of my Toledo was near Cromwell's heart last night, as ever a button on the breast of his doublet. Rat him, he wears secret armour—He a soldier! had it not been for a cursed steel shirt, I would have spitted him like a lark.— Ha, Doctor Rochecliffe?—thou knowest I can wield my weapon."

"Yes," replied the Doctor, "and you know I can use mine."

"I prithee be quiet, Master Wildrake," said Sir Henry.

"Nay good knight," answered Wildrake, "be somewhat more cordial with a comrade in distress. This is a different scene from the Brentford storming party. The jade Fortune has been a very step-mother to me. I will sing you a song I made on my own ill-luck."

"At this moment, Captain Wildrake, we are not in a fitting mood for singing," said Sir Henry, civilly and gravely.

"Nay, it will aid your devotions— Egad, it sounds like a penitential psalm.

When I was a young lad, My fortune was bad,
If e'er I do well 't is a wonder.
I spent all my means Amid sharpers and queans;
Then I got a commission to plunder.
A quarter of London, on the north bank of the Thames, frequented by sailors. Women.

I have stockings, 't is true, But the devil a shoe,
I am forced to wear boots in all weather,
Be d d the boot sole, Curse ou the spur-roll,1
Confounded be the upper leather."

The door opened as Wildrake finished this stanza at the top of his voice, and in rushed a sentinel, who, greeting him by the title of a "blasphemous bellowing bull of Bashan, bestowed a severe blow, with his ramrod, on the shoulders of the songster, whose bonds permitted him no means of returning the compliment.

"Your humble servant again, sir," said Wildrake, shrugging his shoulders—" sorry I have no means of shewing my gratitude. I am bound over to keep the peace, like Captain Bobadil— Ha, knight, did you hear my bones clatter? that blow came twangingly off— the fellow might inflict the bastinado, were it in presence of the Grand Seignior—he has no taste for music, knight—is no way moved by the 'concord of sweet sounds.' I will warrant him fit for treason, stratagem, and spoil—Eh?—all down in the mouth— well—I'll go to sleep to-night on a bench, as I've done many a night, and I will be ready to be hanged decently in the morning, which never happened to me before in all my life—

When I was a young lad,
My fortune was bad—

Pshaw! This is not the tune it goes to. " Here he fell fast asleep, and sooner or later all his companions in misfortune followed his example.

The benches intended for the repose of the soldiers of the guard, afforded the prisoners convenience enough to lie down, though their slumbers, it may be believed, were neither sound nor undisturbed. But when daylight was but a little while broken, the explosion of gunpowder Such a soug. or something very like it. may be found in Ramsay's Teatable Miscellany, among the wild slips of minstrelsy which are there collected. Scott.
Spur rowel,—a spur made of a wheel with pointed teeth. *Psalms* xxii. 12. A boastful character in Ben Jonson's *Every Man in His Humour.*
«, '-*Merchant of Venice,* V., 1, 84.
which took place, and the subsequent fall of the turret to which the mine was applied, would have awakened the Seven Sleepers, or Morpheus himself. The smoke, penetrating through the windows, left them at no loss for the cause of the din.

"There went my gunpowder," said Rochecliffe, "which has, I trust, blown up as many rebel villains as it might have been the means of destroying otherwise in a fair field. It must have caught fire by chance."

"By chance? No," said Sir Henry, "depend on it, my bold Albert has fired the train, and that in yonder blast Cromwell was flying towards the heaven whose battlements he will never reach—Ah, my brave boy! and perhaps thou art thyself sacrificed, like a youthful Samson among the rebellious Philistines.—But I will not be long behind thee, Albert."

Everard hastened to the door, hoping to obtain from the guard, to whom his name and rank might be known, some explanation of the noise, which seemed to announce some dreadful catastrophe.

But Nehemiah Holdenough, whose rest had been broken by the trumpet which gave signal for the explosion, appeared in the very acme of horror—" It is the trumpet of the Archangel!" he cried—" It is the crushing of this world of elements—it is the summons to the Judgmentseat! The dead are obeying the call—they are with us— they are amongst us—they arise in their bodily frames— they come to summon us!"

As he spoke, his eyes were rivetted upon Doctor Rochecliffe, who stood directly opposite to him. In rising hastily, the cap which he commonly wore, according to a custom then usual both among clergymen and gownmen of a civil profession, had escaped from his head, and carried with it the large silk patch which he probably wore for the purpose of disguise; for the cheek which was disclosed was unscarred, and the eye as good as that which was usually uncovered.
Seven Christian youths who are said to have concealed themselves in a cavern near Ephesus during a persecution in the third century, and to have fallen asleep there, not awaking until two or three hundred years later, when Christianity had become the religion of the empire. 'In the later Roman poets, a god of dreams, son of sleep.
Colonel Everard, returning from the door, endeavoured in vain to make Master Holdenough comprehend what he learned from the guard without, that the explosion had involved only the death of one of Cromwell's soldiers. The Presbyterian divine continued to stare wildly at him of the Episcopal persuasion.

But Doctor Rochecliffe heard and understood the news brought by Colonel Everard, and relieved from the instant anxiety which had kept him stationary, he advanced towards the retiring Calvinist, extending his hand in the most friendly manner.

"Avoid thee—Avoid thee!" said Holdenough; "the living may not join hands with the dead."

"But I," said Rochecliffe, "am as much alive as yon are."

"Thou alive!—thou! Joseph Albany, whom my own eyes saw precipitated from the battlements of Clidesthrow castle?"

"Ay," answered the Doctor, "but you did not see me swim ashore on a marsh covered with sedges—*fugit ad salices*—after a manner which I will explain to you another time."

Holdenough touched his hand with doubt and uncertainty. "Thou art indeed warm and alive," he said, "and yet after so many blows, and a fall so tremendous— thou canst not be *my* Joseph Albany."

"I am Joseph Albany Rochecliffe," said the Doctor, "become so in virtue of my mother's little estate, which fines and confiscations have made an end of. "

"And is it so indeed!" said Holdenough, "and have I recovered mine old chum!"

"Even so," replied Rochecliffe, "by the same token I appeared to you in the Mirror Chamber—Thou wert so bold, Nehemiah, that our whole scheme would have been shipwrecked, had I not appeared to thee in the shape of a departed friend. Yet, believe me, it went against my heart to do it."

"Ah, fie on thee, fie on thee," said Holdenough, throwing himself into his arms, and clasping him to his bosom, "thou wert ever a naughty wag. How couldst thou play me such a trick?—Ah, Albany, dost thou remember Dr. Purefoy and Caius College?" 1 He fled to the willows. 'A college of the University of Cambridge (pronounced Kez).

"Marry, do I," said the Doctor, thrusting his arm through the Presbyterian divine's, and guiding him to a seat apart from the other prisoners, who witnessed this scene with much surprise. "Remember Caius College ?-" said Eochecliffe, "ay, and the good ale we drank, and our parties to Mother Huff cap's."

"Vanity of vanities," said Holdenough, smiling kindly at the same time, and still holding his recovered friend's arm enclosed and hand-locked in his.

"But the breaking the Principal's orchard, so cleanly done," said the Doctor; " it was the first plot I ever framed, and much work I had to prevail on thee to go into it." "Oh, name not that iniquity," said Nehemiah, "since I may well say, as the pious Master Baxter, that these boyish offences have had their punishment in later years, inasmuch as that inordinate appetite for fruit hath produced stomachic affections under which I yet labour."

"True, true, dear Nehemiah," said Rochecliffe, "but care not for them—a dram of brandy will correct it all. Mr. Baxter was,"—he was about to say "an ass," but checked himself, and only filled up the sentence with "a good man, I dare say, but over scrupulous."

So they sat down together the best of friends, and for half-an-hour talked with mutual delight over old college stories. By degrees they got on the politics of the day; and though then they unclasped their hands, and there occurred between them such expressions as, "Nay, my dear brother," and, "there I must needs differ," and, "on this point I crave leave to think;" yet a hue and cry against the Independents and other sectarists being started, they followed like brethren in full hollo, and it was hard to guess which was most forward. Unhappily, in the course of this amicable intercourse, something was mentioned about the bishopric of Titus, which at once involved them in the doctrinal question of Church Government. Then, alas! the floodgates were opened, and they showered on each other Greek and Hebrew texts, while their eyes kindled, their cheeks glowed, their hands became clenched, and they looked more like fierce polemics about to rend each other's eyes out, than Christian divines.
Richard Baxter (1615-1691), the noted Nonconformist divine, author of *The Saint's Everlasting Rest, A Call to the Unconverted,* etc. The friend of St. Paul, and first bishop of Crete. See Paul's *Epittte to Tititi.*

Roger Wildrake, by making himself an auditor of the debate, contrived to augment its violence. He took, of course, a most decided part in a question, the merits of which were totally unknown to him. Somewhat overawed by Holdenough's ready oratory and learning, the cavalier watched with a face of anxiety the countenance of Doctor Rochecliffe; but when he saw the proud eye and steady bearing of the Episcopal champion, and heard him answer Greek with Greek, and Hebrew with Hebrew, Wildrake backed his arguments as he closed them, with a stout rap upon the bench, and an exulting laugh in the face of the antagonist. It was with some difficulty that Sir Henry and Colonel Everard, having at length and reluctantly interfered, prevailed on the two alienated friends to adjourn their dispute, removing at the same time to a distance, and regarding each other with looks in which old friendship appeared to have totally given way to mutual animosity.

But while they sat lowering on each other, and longing to renew a contest in which each claimed the victory, Pearson entered the prison, and in a low and troubled voice, desired the persons whom it contained to prepare for instant death.

Sir Henry Lee received the doom with the stern composure which he had hitherto displayed. Colonel Everard attempted the interposition of a strong and resentful appeal to the Parliament, against the judgment of the courtmartial and the General. But Pearson declined to receive or transmit any such remonstrance, and with a dejected look and mien of melancholy presage, renewed his exhortation to them to prepare for the hour of noon, and withdrew from the prison.

The operation of this intelligence on the two clerical disputants was more remarkable. They gazed for a moment on each other with eyes in which repentant kindness and a feeling of generous shame quenched every lingering feeling of resentment, and joining in the mutual exclamation—"My brother — my brother, I have sinned, I have sinned in offending thee!" they rushed into each other's arms, shed tears as they demanded each other's forgiveness, and, like two warriors, who sacrifice a personal quarrel to discharge their duty against the common enemy, they recalled nobler ideas of their sacred character, and, assuming the part which best became them on an occasion so melancholy, began to exhort those around them to meet the doom that had been announced, with the firmness and dignity which Christianity alone can give.

The conduct of the doomed prisoners affords a good example of Scott's unforced method of character exhibition. Do you think the recognition scene between Holdenough and Rochecliffe foretells a happy ending of the story?
33 OHAPTEE THE THIRTY-SEVENTH
Most gracious prince, good Cannyng cried, Leave vengeance to our God,
And lay the iron rule aside,
Be thine the olive rod.
Ballad Of Sib Charles Bawdin.

The hour appointed for execution had been long past, and it was about five in the evening, when the Protector summoned Pearson to his presence. He went with fear and reluctance, uncertain how he might be received. After remaining about a quarter of an hour, the aide-de-camp returned to Victor Lee's parlour, where he found the old soldier, Zerubbabel Robins, in attendance for his return.

"How is Oliver?" said the old man, anxiously.

"Why, well,"answered Pearson, "and hath asked no questions of the execution, but many concerning the reports we have been able to make regarding the flight of the young man, and is much moved at thinking he must now be beyond pursuit. Also I gave him certain papers belonging to the malignant Doctor Rochecliffe."

"Then will I venture upon him," said

the adjutator; "so give me a napkin that I may look like a sewer, and fetch up the food which I directed should be in readiness."

Two troopers attended accordingly with a ration of beef, such as was distributed to the private soldiers, and dressed after their fashion—a pewter pot of ale, a trencher with salt, black pepper, and a loaf of ammunition bread. "Come with me," he said to Pearson, "and fear not— Noll loves an innocent jest." He boldly entered the General's sleeping apartment, and said aloud, "Arise, thou that art called to be a judge in Israel—let there be no more folding of the hands to sleep. Lo, I come as a sign to thee; wherefore arise, eat, drink, and let thy heart be glad within thee, for thou shalt eat with joy the food of him that laboureth in the trenches, seeing that since thou wert commander over the host, the poor sentinel hath had such provisions as I have now placed for thine own refreshment." A servant whose duty it was to wait upon the table. 'Such as was supplied to the soldiers.

"Truly, brother Zerubbabel," said Cromwell, accustomed to such acts of enthusiasm among his followers, "we would wish that it were so; neither is it our desire to sleep soft, nor feed more highly, than the meanest that ranks under our banners. Verily, thou hast chosen well for my refreshment, and the smell of the food is savoury in my nostrils."

He arose from the bed, on which he had lain down half dressed, and wrapping his cloak around him, sat down by the bedside, and partook heartily of the plain food which was prepared for him. While he was eating, Cromwell commanded Pearson to finish his report—" You need not desist for the presence of a worthy soldier, whose spirit is as my spirit."

"Nay, but," interrupted Robins, "you are to know that Gilbert Pearson hath not fully executed thy commands, touching a part of those malignants, all of whom should have died at noon."

"What execution—what malignants?" said Cromwell, laying down his knife and fork.

"Those in the prison here at Woodstock," answered Zerubbabel, "whom your Excellency commanded should be executed at noon, as taken in the fact of rebellion against the Commonwealth."

"Wretch!" said Cromwell, starting up and addressing Pearson, "thou hast not touched Mark Everard, in whom there was no guilt, for he was deceived by him who passed between us—neither hast thou put forth thy hand on the pragmatic Presbyterian minister, to have all those of their classes cry sacrilege, and alienate them from us for ever?"

"If your Excellency wish them to live, they live—their life and death are in the power of a word," said Pearson.

"Enfranchise them; I must gain the Presbyterian interest over to us if I can."

"Rochecliffe, the arch-plotter," said Pearson, "I thought to have executed, but"

"Barbarous man," said Cromwell, "alike ungrateful and impolitic—wouldst thou have destroyed our decoy-duck? This doctor is but like a well, a shallow one indeed, but something deeper than the springs which discharge their secret tribute into his keeping; then come I with a pump, and suck it all up to the open air. Enlarge him, and let him have money if he wants it. I know his haunts; he can go nowhere but our eye will be upon him—But you look at each other darkly, as if you had more to say than you durst. I trust you have not done to death Sir Henry Lee?" "No. Yet the man," replied Pearson, "is a confirmed malignant, and"

"Ay, but he is also a noble relic of the ancient English Gentleman," said the General. "I would I knew how to win the favour of that race. But we, Pearson, whose royal robes are the armour which we wear on our bodies, and whose leading staves are our sceptres, are too newly set up to draw the respect of the proud malignants, who cannot brook to submit to less than royal lineage. Yet what can they see in the longest kingly line in Europe, save that it runs back to a successful soldier? I grudge that one man should be honoured and followed, because he is the descendant of a victorious commander, while less honour and allegiance is paid to another, who, in personal qualities, and, in success, might emulate the founder of his rival's dynasty. Well, Sir Henry Lee lives, and shall live for me. His son, indeed, hath deserved the death which he has doubtless sustained."

"My lord," stammered Pearson, "since your Excellency has found I am right in suspending your order in so many instances, I trust you will not blame me in this also—I thought it best to await more special orders."

"Thou art in a mighty merciful humour this morning, Pearson," said Cromwell, not entirely satisfied.

"If your Excellency please, the halter is ready, and so is the provost-marshal."

"Nay, if such a bloody fellow as thou hast spared him, it would ill become me to destroy him," said the General. "But then, here is among Rochecliffe's papers the engagement of twenty desperadoes to take us off—some example ought to be made."

"My lord," said Zerubbabel, "consider now how often this young man, Albert Lee, hath been near you, nay, probably, quite close to your Excellency, in these dark passages, which he knew, and we did not. Had he been of an assassin's nature, it would have cost him but a pistol-shot, and the light of Israel was extinguished. Nay, in the unavoidable confusion which must have ensued, the sentinels quitting their posts, he might have had a fair chance of escape." The military officer charged with the management pf executions,

"Enough, Zerubbabel; he lives/' said the General. "He shall remain in custody for some time, however, and be then banished from England. The other two are safe, of course; for you would not dream of considering such paltry fellows as fit victims for my revenge."

"One fellow, the under-keeper, called Joliffe, deserves death, however," said Pearson, "since he has frankly admitted that he slew honest Joseph Tomkins."

"He deserves a reward for saving us a labour," said Cromwell; "that Tomkins was a most double-hearted villain. I have found evidence among these papers here, that if we had lost the fight at Worcester, we should have had reason to regret that we had ever trusted Master Tomkins—it was only our success which anticipated his treachery—write us down debtor, not creditor, to Joceline, an you call him so, and to his quarterstaff."

"There remains the sacrilegious and graceless cavalier who attempted your Excellency's life last night," said Pearson.

"Nay," said the General, "that were stooping too low for revenge. His sword had no more power than had he thrusted with a tobacco-pipe. Eagles stoop not at mallards, or wildrakes either."

"Yet, sir," said Pearson, "the fellow should be punished as a libeller. The quantity of foul and pestilential abuse which we found in his pockets makes me loath he should go altogether free. Please to look at them, sir."

"A most vile hand," said Oliver, as he looked at a sheet or two of our friend Wildrake's poetical miscellanies—"The very handwriting seems to be drunk, and the very poetry not sober—What have we here?
When I was a young lad,
My fortune was bad—
If e'er I do well, 't is a wonder—
Why, what trash is this?—and then again—
Now a plague on the poll
Of old politic Noll!
We will drink till we bring
In triumph back the King.
In truth, if it could be done that way, this poet would be a stout champion. Give the poor knave five pieces, Pearson, and bid him go sell his ballads. If he come within twenty miles of our person, though, we will have him flogged till the blood runs down to his heels."

"There remains only one sentenced person," said Pearson, "a noble wolf-hound, finer than any your Excellency saw in Ireland. He belongs to the old knight Sir Henry Lee. Should your Excellency not desire to keep the fine creature yourself, might I presume to beg that I might have leave?"

"No, Pearson," said Cromwell; "the old man, so faithful himself, shall not be deprived of his faithful dog.—I would / had any creature, were it but a dog, that followed me because it loved me, not for what it could make of me."

"Your Excellency is unjust to your faithful soldiers," said Zerubbabel, bluntly, "who follow you like dogs, fight for you like dogs, and have the grave of a dog on the spot where they happen to fall."

"How now, old grumbler," said the General, "what means this change of note?"

"Corporal Humgudgeon's remains are left to moulder under the ruins of yonder tower, and Tomkins is thrust into a hole in a thicket like a beast."

"True, true," said Cromwell, "they shall be removed to the churchyard, and every soldier shall attend with cockades of sea-green and blue ribbon—Every one of the non-commissioned officers and adjutators shall have a mourning-scarf; we ourselves will lead the procession, and there shall be a proper dole of wine, burnt brandy, and rosemary. See that it is done, Pearson. After the funeral, Woodstock shall be dismantled and destroyed, that its recesses may not again afford shelter to rebels and malignants."

The commands of the General were punctually obeyed, and when the other prisoners were dismissed, Albert Lee remained for some time in custody. He went abroad after his liberation, entered in King Charles's Guards, where he was promoted by that monarch. But his fate, as we shall see hereafter, only allowed him a short, though bright career.

We return to the liberation of the other prisoners from Woodstock. The two divines, completely reconciled to each other, retreated arm in arm to the parsonage-house, formerly the residence of Doctor Rochecliffe, but which he now visited as the guest of his successor, Nehemiah Holdenough. The Presbyterian had no sooner installed his friend under his roof, than he urged upon him an offer to partake it, and the income annexed to it, as his own. Dr. Rochecliffe was much affected, but wisely rejected the generous offer, considering the difference of their tenets on Church government, which each entertained as religiously as his creed. Another debate, though a light one, on the subject of the office of Bishops in the Primitive Church, confirmed him in his resolution. They parted the next day, and their friendship remained undisturbed by controversy till Master Holdenough's death, in 1658; a harmony which might be in some degree owing to their never meeting again after their imprisonment. Doctor Rochecliffe was restored to his living after the Restoration, and ascended from thence to high clerical preferment.

The inferior personages of the grand jail-delivery at Woodstock Lodge easily found themselves temporary accommodations in the town among old acquaintance; but no one ventured to entertain the old knight, understood to be so much under the displeasure of the ruling powers; and even the innkeeper of the George, who had been one of his tenants, scarce dared to admit him to the common privileges of a traveller, who has food and lodging for his money. Everard attended him unrequested, unpermitted, but also unforbidden. The heart of the old man had been turned once more towards him when he learned how he had behaved at the memorable rencontre at the King's Oak, and saw that he was an object of the enmity, rather than the favour, of Cromwell. But there was another secret feeling which tended to reconcile him to his nephew—the consciousness that Everard shared with him the deep anxiety which he experienced on account of his daughter, who had not yet returned from her doubtful and perilous expedition. He felt that he himself would perhaps be unable to discover where Alice had taken refuge during the late events, or to obtain her deliverance if she was taken into custody. He wished Everard to offer him his service in making a search for her, but shame prevented his preferring the request; and Everard, who could not suspect the altered state of his uncle's mind, was afraid to make the proposal of assistance, or even to name the name of Alice.

The sun had already set—they sat looking each other in the face in silence, when the tramping of horses was heard—there was knocking at the door—there was a light step on the stair, and Alice, the subject of their anxiety, stood before them. She threw herself joyfully into her father's arms, who glanced his eye needfully round the room, as he said in a whisper, "Is all safe?"

"Safe and out of danger, as I trust," replied Alice—*"I* have a token for you."

Her eye then rested on Everard—she blushed, was embarrassed, and silent.

"You need not fear your Presbyterian cousin," said the knight, with a good-humoured smile, "he has himself proved a confessor at least for loyalty, and ran the risk of being a martyr."

She pulled from her bosom the royal rescript, written on a small and soiled piece of paper, and tied round with a worsted thread instead of a seal. Such as it was, Sir Henry, ere he opened it, pressed the little packet with oriental veneration to his lips, to his heart, to his forehead; and it was not before a tear had dropt on it that he found courage to open and read the billet. It was in these words:—

"Loyal Our Much Esteemed Friend, And Our
Trusty Subject,

"It having become known to us that a purpose of marriage has been entertained betwixt Mrs. Alice Lee, your only daughter, and Markham Everard, Esq. of Eversly Chase, her kinsman, and by affiancy your nephew: And being assured that this match would be highly agreeable to you, had it not been for certain respects to our service, which induced you to refuse your consent thereto—We do therefore acquaint you, that, far from our affairs suffering by such an alliance, we do exhort, and, so far as we may, require you to consent to the same, as you would wish to do us good pleasure, and greatly to advance our affairs. Leaving to you, nevertheless, as becometh a Christian King, the full exercise of your own discretion concerning other obstacles to such an alliance, which may exist, independent of those connected with our service. Witness our hand, together with our thankful recollections of your good services to our late Royal Father as well as ourselves,

"C. R."

Long and steadily did Sir Henry gaze on the letter, so that it might almost seem as if he were getting it by heart. He then placed it carefully in his pocketbook, and asked Alice the account of her adventures of the preceding night. They were briefly told. Their midnight walk through the Chase had been speedily and safely accomplished. Nor had the King once made the slightest relapse into the naughty Louis Kerneguy. When she had seen Charles and his attendant set off, she had taken some repose in the cottage where they parted. With the morning came news that Woodstock was occupied by soldiers, so that return thither might have led to danger, suspicion, and inquiry. Alice therefore did not attempt it, but went to a house in the neighbourhood, inhabited by a lady of established loyalty, whose husband had been major of Sir Henry Lee's regiment, and had fallen at the battle of Naseby. Mrs. Aylmer was a sensible woman, and indeed the necessities of the singular times had sharpened every one's faculties for stratagem and intrigue. She sent a faithful servant to scout about the mansion at Woodstock, who no sooner saw the prisoners dismissed and in safety, and ascertained the knight's destination for the evening, than he carried the news to his mistress, and by her orders attended Alice on horseback to join her father.

There was seldom, perhaps, an evening meal made in such absolute silence as by this embarrassed party, each occupied with their own thoughts, and at a loss how to fathom those of the others. At length the hour came when Alice felt herself at liberty to retire to repose after a day so fatiguing. Everard handed her to the door of her apartment, and was then himself about to take leave, when, to his surprise, his uncle asked him to return, pointed to a chair, and giving him the King's letter to read, fixed his looks on him steadily during the perusal; determined that if he could discover aught short of the utmost delight in the reading, the commands of the King himself should be disobeyed, rather than Alice should be sacrificed to one who received not her hand as the greatest blessing earth had to bestow. But the features of Everard indicated joyful hope, even beyond what the father could have anticipated, yet mingled with surprise; and when he raised his eye to the knight's with timidity and doubt, a smile was on Sir Henry's countenance as he broke silence. "The King," he said, "had he no other subject in England, should dispose at will of those of the house of Lee. But methinks the family of Everard have not been so devoted of late to the crown as to comply with a mandate, inviting its heir to marry the daughter of a beggar."

"The daughter of Sir Henry Lee," said Everard, kneeling to his uncle, and perforce kissing his hand, "would grace the house of a Duke."

"The girl is well enough," said the knight proudly; "for myself, my poverty shall neither shame nor encroach on my friends. Some few pieces I have by Doctor Rochecliffe's kindness, and Jocelme and I will strike out something."

"Nay, my dear uncle, you are richer than you think for," said Everard. "That part of your estate, which my father redeemed for payment of a moderate composition, is still your own, and held by trustees in your name, myself being one of them. You are only our debtor for an advance of monies, for which, if it will content you, we will count with you like usurers. My father is incapable of profiting by making a bargain on his own account for the estate of a distressed friend; and all this you would have learned long since, but that you would not—I mean, time did not serve for explanation—I mean"

"You mean I was too hot to hear reason, Mark, and I believe it is very true. But I think we understand each other *now.* To-morrow I go with my family to Kingston, where is an old house I may still call mine. Come thither at thy leisure, Mark,—or thy best speed, as thou wilt—but come with thy father's consent."

"With my father in person," said Everard, "if you will permit."

"Be that," answered the knight, "as he and you will— I think Joceline will scarce shut the door in thy face, or Bevis growl as he did after poor Louis Kerneguy.—Nay, no more raptures, but good-night, Mark, good-night; and if thou art not tired with the fatigue of yesterday—why, if you appear here at seven in the morning, I think we must bear with your company on the Kingston road."

Once more Everard pressed the knight's hand, caressed Bevis, who received his kindness graciously, and went home to dreams of happiness, which were realized, as far as this motley world permits, within a few months afterwards.

Does Cromwell's sudden relenting in his stern purpose seem to you adequately prepared for and explicable through the previous delineation of his character, or do the exigencies of the story force the author to make Cromwell act in this way? What do you think of the fashion in which Scott usually marries his hero and heroine at the end of the story? After all that has happened, do you think the interposition of the King in the love affair shows delicacy of taste on the author's part f CHAPTER THE THIRTY-EIGHTH -My life was of a piece,

Spent in your service—dying at your feet.

Don Sebastian.

Years rush by us like the wind. We see not whence the eddy comes, nor whitherward it is tending, and we seem ourselves to witness their flight without a sense that we are changed; and yet Time is beguiling man of his strength, as the winds rob the woods of their foliage.

After the marriage of Alice and Markham Everard, the old knight resided near them, in an ancient manor-house, belonging to the redeemed portion of his estate, where Joceline and Phoebe, now man and wife, with one or two domestics, regulated the affairs of his household. When he tired of Shakspeare and solitude, he was ever a welcome guest at his son-in-law's, where he went the more frequently that Markham had given up all concern in public affairs, disapproving of the forcible dismissal of the Parliament, and submitting to Cromwell's subsequent domination, rather as that which was the lesser evil, than as to a government which he regarded as legal. Cromwell seemed ever willing to shew himself his friend; but Everard, resenting highly the proposal to deliver up the King, which he considered as an insult to his honour, never answered such advances, and became, on the contrary, of the opinion, which was now generally prevalent in the nation, that a settled government could not be obtained without the recall of the banished family. There is no doubt that the personal kindness which he had received from Charles, rendered him the more readily disposed to such a measure. He was peremptory, however, in declining all engagements during Oliver's life, whose power he considered as too firmly fixed to be shaken by any plots which could be formed against it. By Cromwell, in 1653.

Meantime, Wildrake continued to be Everard's protected dependent as before, though sometimes the connection tended not a little to his inconvenience. That respectable person, indeed, while he remained stationary in his patron's house, or that of the old knight, discharged manylittle duties in the family, and won Alice's heart by his attention to the children, teaching the boys, of whom they had three, to ride, fence, toss the pike, and many similar exercises; and, above all, filling up a great blank in her father's existence, with whom he played at chess and backgammon, or read Shakspeare, or was clerk to prayers when any sequestrated divine ventured to read the service of the Church. Or he found game for him while the old gentleman continued to go a-sporting; and, especially, he talked over the storming of Brentford, and the battles of Edgehill, Banbury, Round way-down, and others, themes which the aged cavalier delighted in, but which he could not so well enter upon with Colonel Everard, who had gained his laurels in the Parliament service.

The assistance which he received from Wildrake's society became more necessary, after Sir Henry was deprived of his gallant and only son, who was slain in the fatal battle of Dunkirk, where, unhappily, English colours were displayed on both the contending sides, the French being then allied with Oliver, who sent to their aid a body of auxiliaries, and the troops of the banished King fighting in behalf of the Spaniards. Sir Henry received the melancholy news like an old man, that is, with more external composure than could have been anticipated. He dwelt for weeks and months on the lines forwarded by the indefatigable Doctor Rochecliffe, superscribed in small letters, C. B., and subscribed Louis Kerneguy, in which the writer conjured him to endure this inestimable loss with the greater firmness, that he had still left one son (intimating himself), who would always regard him as a father.

These battles, as may be imagined, were either Royalist victories, or, as Edgehill, indecisive engagements. The port of Dunkirk, on the French side of the Channel, was, throughout the seventeenth century, the headquarters of pirates who preyed upon English commerce. When Cromwell allied himself with Louis XIV. against Spain, in 1657, it was agreed that Dunkirk should be besieged by a combined English and French force, and turned over to the English when captured. It fell in 1658, but was sold back to France by Charles II. in 1662 for five million livres.

But in spite of this balsam, sorrow, acting imperceptibly, and sucking the blood like a vampire, seemed gradually drying up the springs of life; and, without any formed illness, or outward complaint, the old man's strength and vigour gradually abated, and the ministry of Wildrake proved daily more indispensable.

It was not, however, always to be had. The cavalier was one of those happy persons whom a strong constitution, an unreflecting mind, and exuberant spirits, enable to play through their whole lives the part of a schoolboy— happy for the moment, and careless of consequences.

Once or twice every year, when he had collected a few pieces, the Cavaliero Wildrake made a start to London, where, as he described it, he went on the ramble, drank as much wine as he could come by, and led a *skeldering* life, to use his own phrase, among roystering cavaliers like himself, till by some rash speech, or wild action, he got into the Marshalsea, the Fleet, or some other prison, from which he was to be delivered at the expense of interest, money, and sometimes a little reputation.

At length Cromwell died, his son resigned the government, and the various changes which followed induced Everard, as well as many others, to adopt more active measures in the King's behalf. Everard even remitted considerable sums for his service, but with the utmost caution, and corresponding with no intermediate agent, but with the Chancellor himself, to whom he communicated much useful information upon public affairs. With all his prudence he was very nearly engaged in the ineffectual rising of Booth and Middleton in the west, and with great difficulty escaped from the fatal consequences of that ill-timed attempt. After this, although the estate of the kingdom was trebly unsettled, yet no card seemed to turn up favourable to the royal cause, until the movement of General Monk from Scotland. Even then, it was when at the point of complete success, that the fortunes of Charles seemed at a lower ebb than ever, especially when intelligence had arrived at the little Court which he then kept in Brussels, that Monk, on arriving in London, had put himself under the orders of the Parliament.

See Dickens's *Little Dorrit.* 'On September 3, 1658. »In May, 1659. George Booth and Sir Thomas Middleton headed a premature Royalist rising at Chester in August, 1659. They were defeated by the Parliamentary troops under Lambert.

'George Monk (1608-1670), first Duke of Albemarle, served first as a Royalist, and later under Cromwell, to whom, as well as to Richard Cromwell, he remained faithful. After the latter's death, and upon the expulsion of Parliament by Lambert in October, 1659, he advanced from Scotland, scattered Lambert's army, and entered London (Feb., 1660). When the new Parliament voted the Restoration, he met Charles II. at Dover (May 25, 1660).

It was at this time, and in the evening, while the King, Buckingham, Wilmot, and some other gallants of his wandering Court, were engaged in a convivial party, that the Chancellor (Clarendon) suddenly craved audience, and, entering with less ceremony than he would have done at another time, announced extraordinary news. For the messenger, he said, he could say nothing, saving that he appeared to have drunk much and slept little; but that he had brought a sure token of credence from a man for whose faith he would venture his life. The King demanded to see the messenger himself.

A man entered, with something the manners of a gentleman, and more those of a rakehelly debauchee—his eyes swelled and inflamed—his gait disordered and stumbling, partly through lack of sleep, partly through the means he had taken to support his fatigue. He staggered without ceremony to the head of the table, seized the King's hand, which he mumbled like a piece of gingerbread; while Charles, who began to recollect him from his mode of salutation, was not very much pleased that their meeting should have taken place before so many witnesses.

"I bring good news," said the uncouth messenger, "glorious news!—the King shall enjoy his own again!— My feet are beautiful on the mountains. Gad, I have lived with Presbyterians till I have caught their language —but we are all one man's children now—all your Majesty's poor babes. The Rump is all ruined in London—Bonfires flaming, music playing, rumps roasting, healths drinking, London in a blaze of light from the Strand to Botherhithe—tankards clattering"

"We can guess at that," said the Duke of Buckingham.

"My old friend Mark Everard sent me off with the news —I'm a villain if I've slept since. Your Majesty recollects me I am sure. Your Majesty remembers, sa—sa—at the King's Oak, at Woodstock?— *Isaiah* lii. 7.

The great east and west thoroughfare of London. A suburb on the south side of the Thames.

O, we'll dance, and sing, and play,
  For 't will be a joyous day
When the King shall enjoy his own again."

"Master Wildrake, I remember you well," said the King. "I trust the good news is certain?" "Certain! your Majesty; did I not hear the bells?— did I not see the bonfires?—did I not drink your Majesty's health so often, that my legs would scarce carry me to the wharf? It is as certain as that I am poor Roger Wildrake of Squattlesea-mere, Lincoln."

The Duke of Buckingham here whispered to the King, "I have always suspected your Majesty kept odd company during the escape from Worcester, but this seems a rare sample."

"Why, pretty much like yourself, and other company I have kept here so many years—as stout a heart, as empty a head," said Charles—" as much lace, though somewhat tarnished, as much brass on the brow, and nearly as much copper in the pocket."

"I would your Majesty would intrust this messenger of good news with me, to get the truth out of him," said Buckingham.

"Thank your Grace," replied the King; "but he has a will as well as yourself, and such seldom agree. My Lord Chancellor hath wisdom, and to that we must trust ourselves.—Master Wildrake, you will go with my Lord Chancellor, who will bring us a report of your tidings; meantime, I assure you that you shall be no loser for being the first messenger of good news." So saying, he gave a signal to the Chancellor to take away Wildrake, whom he judged, in his present humour, to be not unlikely to communicate some former passages at Woodstock, which might rather entertain than edify the wits of his court.

Corroboration of the joyful intelligence soon arrived, and Wildrake was presented with a handsome gratuity and small pension, which, by the King's special desire, had no duty whatever attached to it.

Shortly afterwards, all England was engaged in chorusing his favourite ditty—

Oh, the twenty-ninth of May,
It was a glorious day,
When the King did enjoy his own again.

On that memorable day, the King prepared to make his progress from Rochester to London, with a reception on the part of his subjects so unanimously cordial, as made him say gaily, it must have been his own fault to stay so long away from a country where his arrival gave so much joy. On horseback, betwixt his brothers, the Dukes of York and Gloucester, the Restored Monarch trode slowly over roads strewn with flowers—by conduits running wine, under triumphal arches, and through streets hung with tapestry. There were citizens in various bands, some arrayed in coats of black velvet, with gold chains: some in military suits of cloth of gold, or cloth of silver, followed by all those craftsmen, who, having hooted the father from Whitehall, had now come to shout the son into possession of his ancestral palace. On his progress through Blackheath, he passed that army, which, so long formidable to England herself, as well as to Europe, had been the means of restoring the Monarchy, which their own hands had destroyed. As the King passed the last files of this formidable host, he came to an open part of the heath, where many persons of quality, with others of inferior rank, had stationed themselves to gratulate him as he passed towards the capital.

"On Monday he went to Rochester, and the next day, being the nine and twentieth of May, and his birthday, he entered London: all the ways from Dover thither being so full of people, and acclamations, as if the whole Kingdom had been gathered. About or above Greenwich the lord mayor and aldermen met him, with all such protestations of joy as can hardly be imagined. And the concourse was so great, that the King rode in a crowd from the bridge to Temple bar; all the companies of the city standing in order on both sides, and giving loud thanks to God for his Majesty's presence. And he no sooner came to Whitehall, but the two Houses of Parliament solemnly cast themselves at his feet, with all vows of affection and fidelity to the world's end. In a word, the joy was so unexpressible, and so universal, that his Majesty said smilingly to some about him 'he doubted it had been his own fault he had been absent so long; for he saw nobody that did not protest, he had ever wished for his return.'"— Clarendon's *History,* Book xvi.

"A great open common in Kent, southeast of the city, crossed by the Dover road.
"

There was one group, however, which attracted peculiar attention from those around, on account of the respect shewn to the party by the soldiers who kept the ground, and who, whether Cavaliers or Roundheads, seemed to contest emulously which should contribute most to their accommodation; for both the elder and younger gentlemen of the party had been distinguished in the Civil War.

It was a family group, of which the principal figure was an old man seated in a chair, having a complacent smile on his face, and a tear swelling to his eye, as he saw the banners wave on in interminable succession, and heard the multitude shouting the long silenced acclamation, "God save King Charles!" His cheek was ashy pale, and his long beard bleached like the thistle down; his blue eye was cloudless, yet it was obvious that its vision was failing. His motions were feeble, and he spoke little, except when he answered the prattle of his grandchildren, or asked a question of his daughter, who sat beside him, matured in matronly beauty, or of Colonel Everard who stood behind. There, too, the stout yeoman, Joceline Joliffe, still in his silvan dress, leaned, like a second Benaiah, on the quarterstaff that had done the King good service in its day, and his wife, a buxom matron as she had been a pretty maiden, laughed at her own consequence; and ever and anon joined her shrill notes to the stentorian halloo which her husband added to the general exclamation.

Three fine boys and two pretty girls prattled around their grandfather, who made them such answers as suited their age, and repeatedly passed his withered hand over the fair locks of the little darlings, while Alice, assisted by Wildrake (blazing in a splendid dress, and his eyes washed with only a single cup of canary), took off the children's attention from time to time, lest they should weary their grandfather. We must not omit one other remarkable figure in the group—a gigantic dog, which bore the signs of being at the extremity of canine life, being perhaps fifteen or sixteen years old. But though exhibiting the ruin only of his former appearance, his eyes dim, his joints stiff, his head slouched down, and his gallant carriage and graceful motions exchanged for a stiff, rheumatic, hobbling 1 *Chronicles* xi. 22, 23.

gait, the noble hound had lost none of his instinctive fondness for his master. To lie by Sir Henry's feet in the summer or by the fire in winter, to raise his head to look on him, to lick his withered hand or his shrivelled cheek from time to time, seemed now all that Bevis lived for.

Three or four livery servants attended to protect this group from the thronging multitude; but it needed not. The high respectability and unpretending simplicity of their appearance gave them, even in the eyes of the coarsest of the people, an air of patriarchal dignity, which commanded general regard; and they sat upon the bank which they had chosen for their station by the way-side, as undisturbed as if they had been in their own park.

And now the distant clarions announced the Royal Presence. Onward came pursuivant1 and trumpet — onward came plumes and cloth of gold, and waving standards displayed, and swords gleaming to the sun; and at length, heading a group of the noblest in England, and supported by his royal brothers on either side, onward came King Charles. He had already halted more than once, in-kindness perhaps as well as policy, to exchange a word with persons whom he recognised among the spectators, and the shouts of the bystanders applauded a courtesy which seemed so well timed. But when he had gazed an instant on the party we have described, it was impossible, if even Alice had been too much changed to be recognised, not instantly to know Bevis and his venerable master. The monarch sprung from his horse, and walked instantly up to the old knight, amid thundering acclamations which rose from the multitudes around, when they saw Charles with his own hands oppose the feeble attempts of the old man to rise to do him homage.—Gently replacing him on his seat—" Bless," he said, "father—bless your son, who has returned in safety, as you blessed him when he departed in danger."

"May God bless—and preserve "—muttered the old man, overcome by his feelings; and the King, to give him a few moments' repose, turned to Alice—

"And you," he said, "my fair guide, how have you been employed since our perilous night walk? But I need not ask," glancing round—" in the service of King and Kingdom, bringing up subjects as loyal as their ancestors.—A fair lineage, by my faith, and a beautiful sight to the eye J A State messenger, or heraldic officer.

of an English King!—Colonel Everard, we shall see you, I trust, at Whitehall?" Here he nodded to Wildrake. "And thou, Joceline, thou canst hold thy quarter-staff with one hand sure?—Thrust forward the other palm."

Looking down in sheer bashfulness, Joceline, like a bull about to push, extended to the King, over his lady's shoulder, a hand as broad and hard as a wooden trencher, which the King filled with gold coins. "Buy a headgear for my friend Phoebe with some of these," said Charles; "she too has been doing her duty to Old England."

The King then turned once more to the Knight, who seemed making an effort to speak. He took his aged hand in both his own, and stooped his head towards him to catch his accents, while the old man, detaining him with the other hand, said something faltering, of which Charles could only catch the quotation—

Unthread the rude eye of rebellion,
And welcome home again discarded faith.

Extricating himself, therefore, as gently as possible, from a scene which began to grow painfully embarrassing, the good-natured King said, speaking with unusual distinctness to insure the old man's comprehending him, "This is something too public a place for all we have to say. But if you come not soon to see King Charles at Whitehall, he will send down Louis Kerneguy to visit you, that you may see how rational that mischievous lad is become since his travels. "

So saying, he once more pressed affectionately the old man's hand, bowed to Alice and all around, and withdrew; Sir Henry Lee listening with a smile, which shewed he comprehended the gracious tendency of what had been said. The old man leaned back on his seat, and muttered the *Nunc dimittis.* "Excuse me for having made you wait, my lords," said the King, as he mounted his horse; "indeed, had it not been for these good folks, you might have waited for me long enough to little purpose.—Move on, sirs."

The array moved on accordingly; the sound of trumpets and drums again arose amid the acclamations, which had *King John,* V., 4, 11, 12.
" Now lettest thou thy servant depart in peace;" *Luke* ii. 29-32. been silent while the King stopped; while the effect of the whole procession resuming its motion, was so splendidly dazzling, that even Alice's anxiety about her father's health was for a moment suspended, while her eye followed the long line of varied brilliancy that proceeded over the heath. When she looked again at Sir Henry, she was startled to see that his cheek, which had gained some colour during his conversation with the King, had relapsed into earthy paleness; that his eyes were closed, and opened not again; and that his features expressed, amid their quietude, a rigidity which is not that of sleep. They ran to his assistance, but it was too late. The light that burned so low in the socket, had leaped up, and expired, in one exhilarating flash.

The rest must be conceived. I have only to add that his faithful dog did not survive him many days; and that the image of Bevis lies carved at his master's feet, on the tomb which was erected to the memory of Sir Henry Lee of Ditchley.

It may interest some readers to know that Bevis, the gallant hound, one of the handsomest and active of the ancient Highland deer-hounds, had his prototype in a dog called Maida, the gift of the late Chief of Glengarry to the author. A beautiful sketch of him was made by Edwin Landseer, and afterwards engraved. I cannot suppress the avowal of some personal vanity when I mention that a friend, going through Munich, picked np a common snuff-box, such as are sold for one franc, on which was displayed the form of this veteran favourite, simply marked as Der lieblung hnnd von Walter Scott. Mr. Landseer's painting is at Blair-Adam, the property of my venerable friend, the Right Honourable Lord Chief-Commissioner Adam. Scott.

In the account of the King's return to England, note the genuineness of Scott's Jacobite enthusiasm. What do you think of a formal "round-up" of the characters at the close of a story, to enable the reader to know what happened "ever afterwards." compared with the method of leaving the reader to infer, through his knowledge of the characters, what their future history must be? Do you think the disposition of the characters in *Woodstock* exhibits poetic justice? See the close of Scott's introduction to *Ivanfioe,* where he comments nobly upon the "Virtue has had its reward" theory, as applied to fiction.

APPENDIX AUTHOR'S PREFACE TO FIRST EDITION

It is not my purpose to inform my readers how the manuscripts of that eminent antiquary, the Rev. J. A. Rochecliffe, D.

D., came into my possession. There are many ways in which such things happen, and it is enough to say they were rescued from an unworthy fate, and that they were honestly come by. As for the authenticity of the anecdotes which I have gleaned from the writings of this excellent person, and put together with my own unrivalled facility, the name of Dr. Rochecliffe will warrant accuracy, wherever that name happens to be known.

With this history the reading part of the world are well acquainted; and we might refer the tyro to honest Anthony a Wood, who looked up to him as one of the pillars of High Church, and bestows on him an exemplary character in the *Atherue Oxonienses,* although the Doctor was educated at Cambridge, England's other eye.

It is well known that Dr. Rochecliffe early obtained preferment in the Church, on account of the spirited share which he took in the controversy with the Puritans; and that his work, entitled *Malleus Hceresis,* was considered as a knock-down blow by all except those who received it. It was that work which made him, at the early age of thirty, Rector of Woodstock, and which afterwards secured him a place in the Catalogue of the celebrated Century White;—and worse than being shewn up by that fanatic, among the catalogues of scandalous and malignant priests admitted into benefices by the prelates, his opinions occasioned the loss of his living of Woodstock by the ascendency of Presbytery. He was Chaplain, during most part of the Civil War, to Sir Henry Lee's regiment, levied for the service of King Charles; and it was said he engaged more than once personally in the field. At least it is certain that Doctor Rochecliffe was repeatedly in great danger, as will appear from more passages than one in the following history, which speaks of bis own exploits, like Csesar, in the third person. I suspect, however, some Presbyterian commentator has been guilty of interpointing two or three passages. The manuscript was long in possession of the Everards, a distinguished family of that persuasion.

During the Usurpation, Doctor Rochecliffe was constantly engaged in one or other of the premature attempts at a restoration of monarchy; and was accounted, for his audacity, presence of mind, and depth of judgment, one of the greatest undertakers for the King in that busy time; with this trifling drawback, that the plots in which he busied himself were almost constantly detected. Nay, it was suspected that Cromwell himself sometimes contrived to suggest to him the intrigues in which he engaged, by which means the wily Protector made experiments on the fidelity of doubtful friends, and became well acquainted with the plots of declared enemies, which he thought it more easy to disconcert and disappoint than to punish severely.

Upon the Restoration, Doctor Rochecliffe regained his living of Woodstock, with other church preferment, and gave up polemics and political intrigues for philosophy. He was one of the constituent members of the Royal Society, and was the person through whom Charles required of that learned body solution of the curious problem, "Why, if a vessel is filled brimful of water, and a large live fish plunged into the water, nevertheless it shall not overflow the pitcher?" Doctor Rochecliffe's exposition of this phenomenon was the most ingenious and instructive of four that were given in; and it is certain the Doctor must have gained the honour of the day, but for the obstinacy of a plain, dull, country gentleman, who insisted that the experiment should be, in the first place, publicly tried. When this was done, the event shewed it would have been rather rash to have adopted the facts exclusively on the royal authority; as tho fish, however curiously inserted into his native element, splashed the water over the hall, and destroyed the credit of four ingenious essayists, besides a large Turkey carpet.

Doctor Rochecliffe, it would seem, died about 1685, leaving many papers behind him of various kinds, and, above all, many valuable anecdotes of secret history, from which the following Memoirs have been extracted, on which wo intend to say only a few words by way of illustration.

The existence of Rosamond's Labyrinth, mentioned in these pages, is attested by Drayton in the reign of Queen Elizabeth.

"Rosamond's Labyrinth, whose ruins, together with her Well, being paved with square stones in the bottom, and also her Tower, from which the Labyrinth did run, are yet remaining, being vaults arched and walled with stone and brick, almost inextricably wound within one another, by which, if at any time her lodging were laid about by the Queen, she might easily avoid peril It is hardly necessary to say, unless to some readers of very literal capacity, that Dr. Bochecliffe and his manuscripts are alike apocryphal.

imminent, and, if need be, by secret issues take the air abroad, many furlongs about Woodstock, in Oxfordshire."

It is highly probable, that a singular piece of phantasmagoria,-which was certainly played off upon the Commissioners of the Long Parliament, who were sent down to dispark and destroy Woodstock, after the death of Charles I. , was conducted by means of the secret passages and recesses in the ancient Labyrinth of Rosaniond, round which successive Monarchs had erected a Hunting-seat or Lodge.

There is a curious account of the disturbance given to those Honourable Commissioners, inserted by Doctor Plot, in his Natural History of Oxfordshire. But as I have not the book at hand, I can only allude to the work of the celebrated Glanville upon Witches, who has extracted it as a highly accredited narrative of supernatural dealings. The beds of the Commissioners and their servants were hoisted up till they were almost inverted, and then let down again so suddenly, as to menace them with broken bones. Unusual and horrible noises disturbed those sacrilegious intromitters with royal property. The devil, on one occasion, brought them a warming-pan; on another, pelted them with stones and horses' bones. Tubs of water were emptied on them in their sleep; and so many other pranks of the same nature played at their expense, that they broke up housekeeping, and left their intended spoliation only half completed. The good sense of Doctor Plot suspected that these feats were wrought by conspiracy and confederation, which Glanville of course endeavours to refute with all his might; for it could scarce be expected that ho who believed in so convenient a solution as that of supernatural agency, would consent to relinquish the service of a key, which will answer any lock, however intricate.

Nevertheless, it was afterwards discovered that Doctor Plot was perfectly right; and that the only demon who wrought all these marvels was a disguised royalist—a fellow called Trusty Joe, or some such name, formerly in the service of the Keeper of the Park, but who engaged in that of the Commissioners, on purpose to subject them to his persecution. I think I have seen some account of the real state of the transaction, and of the machinery by which the wizard worked his wonders; but whether in a book or a pamphlet I am uncertain. I remember one passage particularly to this purpose. The Commissioners having agreed to retain some articles out of the public account, in order to be divided among themselves, had entered into an indenture for ascertaining their share in the peculation, which they hid in a bowpot for security. Now, when an assembly of divines, aided by the most strict religious characters in the neighbourhood of Woodstock, were assembled to conjure down the supposed demon, Drayton's England's Heroical Epistles, Note A, on the Epistle, Rosamond to King Henry.

Trusty Joe had contrived a firework, which he let off in the midst of the exorcism, and which destroyed the bowpot; and, to the shame and confusion of the Commissioners, threw their secret indenture into the midst of the assembled ghost-seers, who became thus acquainted with their secret schemes of peculation.

It is, however, to little purpose for me to strain my memory about ancient and imperfect recollections concerning the particulars of these fantastic disturbances at Woodstock, since Doctor Rochecliffe's papers give such a much more accurate narrative than could be obtained from any account in existence before their publication. Indeed, I might have gone much more fully into this part of my subject, for the materials are ample;—but, to tell the reader a secret, some friendly critics were of opinion they made the story hang on hand; and thus I was prevailed on to be more concise on the subject than I might otherwise have been.

The impatient reader, perhaps, is by this time accusing me of keeping the sun from him with a candle. Were the sunshine as bright, however, as it is likely to prove; and the flambeau, or link, a dozen of times as smoky, my friend must remain in the inferior atmosphere a minute longer, while I disclaim the idea of poaching on another's manor. Hawks, we say in Scotland, ought not to pick out hawks' eyes, or tire upon each other's quarry; and therefore, if I had known that, in its date and its characters, this tale was likely to interfere with that recently published by a distinguished contemporary, I should unquestionably have left Doctor Rochecliffe's manuscript in peace for the present season. But before I was aware of this circumstance, this little book was half through the press; and I had only the alternative of avoiding any intentional imitation, by delaying a perusal of the contemporary work in question. Some accidental collision there must be, when works of a similar character are finished on the same general system of historical manners, and the same historical personages are introduced. Of course, if such have occurred, I shall be probably the sufferer. But my intentions have been at least innocent, since I look on it as one of the advantages attending the conclusion of Woodstock, that the finishing of my own task will permit me to have the Eleasure of reading Bbambletvehouse, from which I have itherto conscientiously abstained.

n AUTHOR'S INTRODUCTION—(1832)

The busy period of the great Civil War was one in which the character and genius of different parties were most brilliantly displayed, and, accordingly, the incidents which took place on either side were of a striking and extraordinary character, and afforded ample foundation for fictitious composition. The author had in some measure attempted such in Peveril of the Peak; but the scene was in a remote part of the kingdom, and mingled with other national differences, which left him still at liberty to glean another harvest out of so ample a store.

In these circumstances, some wonderful adventures which happened at Woodstock in the year 1649, occurred to him as something he had long ago read of, although he was unable to tell where, and of which the hint appeared sufficient, although, doubtless, it might have been much better handled if the author had not, in the lapse of time, lost every thing like an accurate recollection of the real story.

It was not until about this period, namely, 1831, that the author, being called upon to write this Introduction, obtained a general account of what really happened upon the marvellous occasion in question, in a work termed "The Every-day Book," published by Mr. Hone, and full of curious antiquarian research, the object being to give a variety of original information concerning manners, illustrated by curious instances, rarely to be found elsewhere. Among other matter, Mr. Hone quotes an article from the British Magazine for 1747, in the following words, and which is probably the document which the author of Woodstock had formerly perused, although he was unable to refer to the source of his information. The tract is entitled, "The Genuine History of the good Devil of Woodstock, famous in the world, in the year 1649, and never accounted for, or at all understood to this time."

The teller of this "genuine history" proceeds verbatim as follows:

"Some original papers having lately fallen into my hands, under the name of 'Authentic Memoirs of the Memorable

Joseph Collins of Oxford, commonly known by the name of Funny Joe, and now intended for the press,' I was extremely delighted to find in them a circumstantial and unquestionable account of the most famous of all invisible agents, so well known in the year 1649, under the name of the Good Devil of Woodstock, and even adored by the people of that place, for the vexation and distress it occasioned some people they were not much pleased with. As this famous story, though related by a thousand people, and attested in all its circumstances, beyond all possibility of doubt, by people of rank, learning, and reputation, of Oxford and the adjacent towns, has never yet been generally accounted for, or at all understood, and is perfectly explained, in a manner that can admit of no doubt, in these papers, I could not refuse my readers the pleasure it gave me in reading."

There is, therefore, no doubt that, in the year 1649, a number of incidents, supposed to be supernatural, took place at the King's palace of Woodstock, which the Commissioners of Parliament were then and there endeavouring to dilapidate and destroy. The account of this by the Commissioners themselves, or under their authority, was repeatedly published, and, in particular, is inserted as relation sixth of Satan's Invisible World Discovered, by George Sinclair, Professor of Philosophy in Glasgow, an approved collector of such tales.

It was the object of neither of the great political parties of that day to discredit this narrative, which gave great satisfaction both to the cavaliers and roundheads; the former conceiving that the license given to the demons, was in consequence of the impious desecration of the King's furniture and apartments, so that the citizens of Woodstock almost adored the supposed spirits, as avengers of the cause of royalty; while the friends of the Parliament, on the other hand, imputed to the malice of the fiend the obstruction of the pious work, as they judged that which they had in hand.

At the risk of prolonging a curious quotation, I include a page or two from Mr. Hone's Every-day Book.

" The honourable the Commissioners arrived at Woodstock manor-house, October 13th, and took up their residence in the King's own rooms. His Majesty's bedchamber they made their kitchen, the council-hall their pantry, and the presence-chamber was the place where they sat for despatch of business. His Majesty's dining-room they made their wood-yard, and stowed it with no other wood but that of the famous Royal Oak from the High Park, which, that nothing might be left with the name of the King about it, they had dug up by the roots, and bundled up into fagots for their firing.

"October 16. This day they first sat for the despatch of business. In the midst of their first debate there entered a large black dog (as they thought), which made a terrible howling, overturned two or three of their chairs, and doing some other damage, went under the bed, and there gnawed the cords. The door this while continued constantly shut, when, after some two or three hours, Giles Sharp, their secretary, looking under the bed, perceived that the creature was vanished, and that a plate of meat that the servants had hid there was untouched, and shewing them to their honours, they were all convinced there could be no real dog concerned in the case; the said Giles also deposed an oath, that, to his certain knowledge, there was not.

"October 17. As they were this day sitting at dinner in a lower room, they heard plainly the noise of persons walking over head, though they well knew the doors were all locked, and there could be none there. Presently after they heard also all the wood of the King's Oak brought by parcels from the dining-room, and thrown with great violence into the presencechamber, as also the chairs, stools, tables, and other furniture, forcibly hurled about the room, their own papers of the minutes of their transactions torn, and the ink-glass broken. When all this had some time ceased, the said Giles proposed to enter first into these rooms, and, in presence of the Commissioners, of whom he received the key, he opened the door and entered the room, their honours following him. He there found the wood strewed about the room, the chairs tossed about and broken, the papers torn, and the ink-glass broken over them all as they had heard, yet no footsteps appeared of any person whatever being there, nor had the doors ever been opened to admit or let out any person since their honours were last there. It was therefore voted *nem. con.,* that the person who did this mischief could have entered no other way than at the keyhole of the said doors.

"In the night following this same day, the said Giles, and two other of the Commissioners' servants, as they were in bed in the same room with their honours, had their bed's feet lifted up so much higher than their heads, that they expected to have their necks broken, and then they were let fall at once with such violence as shook them up from the bed to a good distance; and this was repeated many times, their honours being amazed spectators of it. In the morning the bedsteads were found cracked and broken, and the said Giles and his fellows, declared they were sore to the bones with the tossing and jolting of the beds.

"October 19. As they were all in bed together, the candles were all blown out together with a sulphurous smell, and instantly many trenchers of wood were hurled about the room; and one of them putting his head above the clothes, had not less than six thrown at him, which wounded him very grievously. In the morning the trenchers were all found lying about the room, and were observed to be the same they had eaten on the day before, none being found remaining in the pantry.

"October 20, This night the candles were put out as before; the curtains of the bed in which their honours lay, were drawn to and fro many times with great violence: their honours received many cruel blows, and were much bruised beside, with eight great pewter dishes, and three dozen wooden trenchers, which were thrown on the bed, and afterwards heard rolling about the room.

"Many times also this night they

heard the forcible falling of many fagots by their bedside, but in the morning no fagots were found there, no dishes or trenchers were there seen either; and the aforesaid Giles attests, that by their different arranging in the pantry, they had assuredly been taken thence, and after put there again.

"October 21. The keeper of their ordinary and his bitch lay with them: This night they had no disturbance.

"October 22. Candles put out as before. They had the said bitch with them again, but were not by that protected: the bitch set up a very piteous cry; the clothes of their beds were all pulled off, and the bricks, without any wind, were thrown off the chimney tops into the midst.

"October 24. The candles put out as before. They thought all the wood of the King's Oak was violently thrown down by their bedsides; they counted sixty-four fagots that fell with great violence, and some hit and shook the bed,—but in the morning none were found there, nor the door of the room opened in which the said fagots were.

'' October 25. The candles put out as before. The curtains of the bed in the drawing-room were many times forcibly drawn; the wood thrown out as before; a terrible crack like thunder was heard; and one of the servants, running to see if his master was not killed, found at his return, three dozen trenchers laid smoothly upon his bed under the quilt.

"October 26. The beds were shaken as before, the windows seemed all broken to pieces, and glass fell in vast quantities all about the room. In the morning they found the windows all whole, but the floor strewed with broken glass, which they gathered and laid by.

"October 29. At midnight candles went out as before, something walked majestically through the room and opened and shut the window; great stones were thrown violently into the room, some whereof fell on the beds, others on the floor; and about a quarter after one, a noise was heard as of forty cannon discharged together, and again repeated at about eight minutes' distance. This alarmed and raised all the neighbourhood, who, coming into their honours' room, gathered up the great stones, fourscore in number, many of them like common pebbles aud boulters, and laid them by, where they are to be seen to this day, at a corner of the adjoining field. This noise, like the discharge of cannon, was heard throughout the country for sixteen miles round. During these noises, which were heard in both rooms together, both the Commissioners and their servants gave one another over for lost, and cried out for help; and Giles Sharp, snatching Up a sword, had well-nigh killed one of their honours, taking him for the spirit as he came in his shirt into the room. While they were together, the noise was continued, and part of the tiling of the house, and all the windows of an upper room, were taken away with it.

"October 30. Something walked into the chamber, treading like a bear; it walked many times about, then threw the warming-pan violently upon the floor, and so bruised it, that it was spoiled. Vast quantities of glass were now thrown about the room, and vast numbers of great stones and horses' bones were thrown in; these were all found in the morning, and the floors, beds, and walls were all much damaged by the violence they were thrown in.

"November 1. Candles were placed in all parts of the room, and a great fire made. At midnight, the candles all yet burning, a noise like the burst of a cannon was heard in the room, and the burning billets were tossed all over the room and about the beds; and had not their honours called in Giles and his fellows, the house had assuredly been burnt. An hour after the candles went out, as usual, the clack of many cannon was heard, and many pailfuls of green stinking water were thrown on their honours in bed; great stones were thrown in as before, the bedcurtains and bedsteads torn and broken: the windows were now all really broken, and the whole neighbourhood alarmed with the noises; nay, the very rabbit-stealers that were abroad that night in the warren were so frightened at the dismal thundering, that they fled for fear and left their ferrets behind them.

"One of their honours this night spoke, and in the name of God asked what it was, and why it disturbed them so? No answer was given to this; but the noise ceased for a while, when the spirit came again, and as they all agreed, brought with it seven devils worse than itself. One of the servants now lighted a large candle, and set it in the doorway between the two chambers, to see what passed; and as he watched it, he plainly saw a hoof striking the candle and candlestick into the middle of the room, and afterwards making three scrapes over the snuff of the candle, to scrape it out. Upon this, the same person was so bold as to draw a sword; but he had scarce got it out, when he perceived another invisible hand had hold of it too, and pulled with him for it, and at last prevailing, struck him so violently on the head with the pommel, that he fell down for dead with the blow. At this instant was heard another burst like the discharge Probably this part was also played by Sharp, who was the regular ghost-seer of the party.

of the broadside of a ship of war, and at about a minute or two's distance each, no less than nineteen more such: these shook the house so violently that they expected every moment it would fall upon their heads. The neighbours on this were all alarmed, and, running to the house, they all joined in prayer and psalmsinging, during which the noise continued in the other rooms, and the discharge of cannon without, though nobody was there."

Dr. Plot concludes his relation of this memorable event with observing, that, though tricks have often been played in affairs of this kind, many of these things are not reconcilable with juggling; such as, 1st, The loud noises beyond the power of man to make, without instruments which were not there; 2d, The tearing and breaking of the beds; 3d, The throwing about the fire; 4th, The hoof treading out the candle; and, 5th, The striving for the sword, and the blow the man received from the pommel of it.

To shew how great men are sometimes deceived, we may recur to a tract, entitled "*The Secret History of the Good Devil of Woodstock,*" in which we find it, under the author's own hand, that he, Joseph Collins, commonly called Funny Joe, was himself this very devil;—that, under the feigned name of Giles Sharp, he hired himself as a servant to the Commissioners:—that by the help of two friends—an unknown trapdoor in the ceiling of the bedchamber, and a pound of common gunpowder—he played all these extraordinary tricks by himself;—that his fellow-servants, whom he kad introduced on purpose to assist him, had lifted up their own beds, and that the candles were contrived, by a common trick of gunpowder, to be extinguished at a certain time.

The dog who began the farce was, as Joe swore, no dog at all, but truly a bitch, who had shortly before whelped in that room, and made all this disturbance in seeking for her puppies; and which, when she had served his purpose, he (Joe Sharp, or Collins) let out, and then looked for. The story of the hoof and sword he himself bore witness to, and was never suspected as to the truth of them, though mere fictions. By the trapdoor his friends let down stones, fagots, glass, water, etc., which they either left there, or drew up again, as best suited his purpose; and by this way let themselves in and out, without opening the doors, or going through the keyholes, and all the noises described, he declares he made by placing quantities of white gunpowder over pieces of burning charcoal, on plates of tin, which, as they melted, exploded with a violent noise.

I am very happy in having an opportunity of setting history right about these remarkable events, and would not have the reader disbelieve my author's account of them, from his naming either white gunpowder exploding when melted, or his making the earth about the pot take fire of its own accord; since, how In his Natural History of Oxfordshire. ever improbable these accounts may appear to some readers, and whatever secrets they might be in Joe's time, they are now well known in chemistry. As to the last, there needs only to mix an equal quantity of iron filings, finely powdered, and powder of pure brimstone, and make them into a paste with fair water. This paste, when it hath lain together about twenty-six hours, will of itself take fire, and burn all the sulphur away with a blue flame and a bad smell. For the others, what he calls white gunpowder is plainly the thundering powder called by our chemists *pulvis fulminans.* It is composed of three parts of saltpetre, two parts of pearl ashes or salt of tartar, and one part of flower ot brimstone, mixed together and beat to a fine powder; a small quantity of this held on the point of a knife over a candle will not go off till it melt, and then it gives a report like that of a pistol; and this he might easily dispose of in larger quantities, so as to make it explode of itself, while he, the said Joe, was with his masters.

Such is the explanation of the ghostly adventures of Woodstock, as transferred by Mr. Hone from the pages of the old tract, termed the Authentic Memoirs of the memorable Joseph Collins of Oxford, whose courage and loyalty were the only wizards which conjured up those strange and surprising apparitions and works of spirits, which passed as unquestionable in the eyes of the Parliamentary Commissioners, of Dr. Plot, and other authors of credit. The *pulvis fulminans,* the secret principle he made use of, is now known to every apothecary's apprentice.

If my memory be not treacherous, the actor of these wonders made use of his skill in fireworks upon the following remarkable occasion. The Commissioners had not, in their zeal for the public service, overlooked their own private interests, and a deed was drawn up upon parchment, recording the share and nature of the advantages which they privately agreed to concede to each other; at the same time they were, it seems, loath to intrust to any one of their number the keeping of a document in which all were equally concerned.

They hid the written agreement within a flower-pot, in which a shrub concealed it from the eyes of any chance spectator. But the rumour of the apparitions having gone abroad, curiosity drew many of the neighbours to Woodstock, and some in particular, to whom the knowledge of this agreement would have afforded matter of scandal; as the Commissioners received these guests in the saloon where the flower-pot was placed, a match was suddenly set to some fireworks placed there by Sharp the secretary. The flower-pot burst to pieces with the concussion, or was prepared so as to explode of itself, and the contract of the Commissioners, bearing testimony to their private roguery, was thrown into the midst of the visitors assembled. If I have recollected this incident accurately, for it is more than forty years since I perused the tract, it is probable, that in omitting it from the novel, I may also have passed over, from want of memory, other matters which might have made an essential addition to the story. Nothing, indeed, is more certain, than that incidents which are real, preserve an infinite advantage in works of this nature over such as are fictitious. The tree, however, must remain where it has fallen.

Having occasion to be in London in October 1831, I made some researches in the British Museum, and in that rich collection, with the kind assistance of the Keepers, who manage it with so much credit to themselves and advantage to the public, I recovered two original pamphlets, which contain a full account of the phenomena at Woodstock in 1649. The first is a satirical poem, published in that year, which plainly shews that the legend was current among the people in the very shape in which it was afterwards made public. I have not found the explanation of Joe Collins, which, as mentioned by Mr. Hone, resolves the whole into confederacy. It might, however, be recovered by a stricter search than I had leisure for. In the meantime, it may be observed, that neither the name of Joe Collins, nor Sharp, occurs among the *dramatis personal* given in these tracts, published when he might have been endangered by anything which directed suspicion towards him, at least in 1649, and perhaps might have exposed him to danger even in 1660, from the malice of a powerful though defeated faction.

lit August, 1832.

Ill THE JUST DEVIL OF WOODSTOCK; OK,

A TRUE NARRATIVE OP THE SEVERAL APPARITIONS, THE FRIGHTS AND PUNISHMENTS, INFLICTED UPON THE RUMPISH COMMISSIONERS SENT THITHER TO SURVEY THE MANNORS AND HOUSES BELONGING TO HIS MAJESTIE.

London, printed in the year 1660. 4to.

The names of the persons in the ensuing Narrative mentioned, with others.

Captain Cockaine. Mr. Browne, the Surveyor.

Captain Hart. Their three Servants.

Captain Crook. Their Ordinary-keeper, and

Captain Carelesse. others.

Captain Roe. The Gate-keeper, with the

Mr. Crook, the Lawyer. Wife and Servants.

Besides many more, who each night heard the noise; as Sir Gerrard Fleetwood and his lady, with his family, Mr. Hyans, with his family, and several others, who lodged in the outer courts; and during the three last nights, the inhabitants of Woodstock town, and other neighbor villages.

And there were many more, both divines and others, who came out of the country, and from Oxford, to see the glass and stones, and other stuffe, the devil had brought, wherewith to beat out the Commissioners; the marks upon some walls remain, and many, this to testifie.

THE PREFACE TO THE ENSUING NARRATIVE.

Since it hath pleased the Almighty God, out of his infinite mercy, so to make us happy by restoring of our native King to us, and us unto our native liberty through him, that now the good may say, *magna temporum felicitas ubi sentire quce veils, et dieere* A doggerel, and, in parts, slightly indecent poem, entitled "The Woodstock Scuffle," which Scott introduced before this document, is omitted in this edition.

licet qua senlias, we cannot but esteem ourselves engaged, in the highest of degrees, to render unto him the highest thanks we can express. Although, srpris'd with joy, we become as lost in the performance; when gladness and admiration strikes us silent, as we look back upon the precipiece of our late condition, and those miraculous deliverances beyond expression. Freed from the slavery, and those desperate perils, we dayly lived in fear of, during the tyrannical times of that destestable usurper, Oliver Cromwell; he who had raked up such judges, as would wrest the most innocent language into high treason, when he had the cruel conscience to take away our lives, upon no other ground of justice or reason, (the stones of London streets would rise to witness it, if all the citizens were silent). And with these judges had such councillors, as could advise him unto worse, which will less want of witness. For should the many auditors be silent, the press (as God would have it), hath given it us in print, where one of them (and his conscience-keeper, too), speaks out, What shall we do with these men? saith he; *JEger intemperans erudelem facit medieum, et immedicabile vulnus ense reddendum.* Who these men are that should be brought to such Scieilian vespers, the former page sets forth—those which conceit *Vlopias,* and have their day-dreams of the return of, I know not what golden age with the old line. What usage, when such a privy councillor had power, could he expect, who then had published this narrative? This much so plainly shows the devil himself dislikit their doings (so much more bad were they than he would have them be), severer sure then was the devil to their Commissioners at Woodstock; for he warned them with dreadful noises, to drive them from their work. This councillor, without more ado, would have all who retain'd conceits of allegiance to their sovereign, to be absolutely cut off by the usurper's sword. A sad sentence for a loyal party to a lawful king. But Heaven is always just; the party is repriv'd, and do acknowledge the hand of God in it, as is rightly apply'd, and

as justly sensible of their deliverance: in that the foundation which the councillor saith was already so well laid is now turned up, and what he calls day-dreams are come to passe. That old line which (as with him) there seemed, *aliquid divini,* to the contrary is now restored. And that rock which, as he saith, the prelates and all their adherents, nay, and their master and supporter, too, with all his posterity, have split themselves upon, is nowhere to be heard. And that posterity are safely arrived in their ports, and masters of that mighty navy, their enemies so much encreased to keep them out with. The eldest sits upon the throne, his place by birthright and descent,

"Pacatumque regit Patriis virtutibus orbem;" upon which throne long may he sit, and reign in peace. That by his just government, the enemies of ours, the true Protestant Church, of that glorious martyr, our late sovereign, and of his royal posterity, may be either absolutely converted, or utterly confounded.

If any shall now ask thee why this narrative was not sooner published, as neerer to the times wherein the things were acted, he hath the reason for it in the former lines; which will the more clearly appear unto his apprehension, if he shall perpend how much cruelty is requisite to the maintenance of rebellion; and how great care is necessary in the supporters, to obviate and divert the smallest things that tend to the unblinding of the people; so that it needs will follow, that they must have accounted this amongst the great obstructions to their sales of his majestie's lands, the devil not joining with them in the security; and greater to the pulling down the royal pallaces, when their chapmen should conceit the devil would haunt them in their houses, for building with so ill got materials; as no doubt but that he hath, so numerous and confident are the relations made of the same, though scarce any so totally remarkeable as this (if it be not that others have been more concealed), in regard of the strange circumstances as long continuances, but especially the number of the persons together, to whom all things were so visibly both seen and done, so that surely it exceeds any other; for the devils thus manifesting themselves, it appears evidently that there are such things as devils, to persecute the wicked in this world as in the next.

Now, if to these were added the diverse reall phantasms seen at White-Hall in Cromwell's times, which caused him to keep such mighty guards in and about his bedchamber, and yet so oft to change his lodgings; if those things done at Saint James', where the devil so joal'd the centinels against the sides of the queen's chappell doors, that some of them fell sick upon it: and others, not taking warning by it, kild one outright, whom they buried in the place; and all other such dreadful things, those that inhabited the royal houses have been affrighted with.

And if to these were likewise added, a relation of all those regicides and their abettors the devil hath entred into, as he did the Gadarenes' swine, with so many more of them who hath fallen mad, and dyed in hideous forms of such distractions, that which hath been of this within these 12 last years in England (should all of this nature our chronicles do tell, with all the superstitious monks have writ, be put together), would make the greater volume, and of more strange occurrents.

And now as to the penman of this narrative, know that he was a divine, and at the time of those things acted, which are here related, the minister and schoolmaster of Woodstock; a person learned and discreet, not byassed with factious humours, his name Widows, who each day put in writing what he heard from their mouths (and such things as they told to have befallen them the night before), therein keeping to their own words; and, never thinking that what he had wiit should happen to be made publick, gave it no better dress to set it forth. And because to do it now shall not be construed to change the story, the reader hath it here accordingly exposed.

THE JUST DEVIL OP WOODSTOCK.

The 16th day of *October,* in the year of our Lord, 1649, the Commissioners for surveying and valuing his majestie's mannorhouse, parks, woods, deer, demesnes, and all things thereunto belonging, by name Captain Crook, Captain Hart, Captain Cockaine, Captain Carelesse, and Captain Roe, their messenger, with Mr. Browne, their secretary, and two or three servants, went from Woodstock town (where they had lain some nights before), and took up their lodgings in his majestie's house after this manner: The bed-chamber and withdrawing-room they both lodged in and made their kitchen; the presence-chamber their room for despatch of their business with all commers; of the council-hall their brew-house, as of the dining-room their wood-house, where they laid in the clefts of that antient standard in the High-Park, for many ages beyond memory known by the name of the King's Oak, which they had chosen out, and caused to be dug up by the roots.

October 17. About the middle of the night, these new guests were first awaked by a knocking at the presence-chamber door, which they also conceived did open, and something to enter, which came through the room, and also walkt about that room with a heavy step during half an hour, then crept under the bed where Captain Hart and Captain Carelesse lay, where it did seem (as it were) to bite and gnaw the mat and bed-coards, as if it would tear and rend the feather beds; which having done a while, then would heave a while, and rest; then heave them up again in the bed more high than it did before, sometime on the one side, sometime on the other, as if it had tried which captain was heaviest. Thus having heaved some half an hour, from thence it walkt out, and went under the servants' bed, and did the like to them; hence it walkt into a withdrawing-room, and there did the same to all who lodged there. Thus having welcomed them for more than two hours' space, it walkt out as it came in, and shut the outer door again, but with a clap of some mightie force. These guests were in a sweat all this while, but out of it falling into a sleep again, it became morning first before they spake their minds; then would they have it to be a dog, yet they described it more to the likenesse of a great bear; so fell to the examining under the beds, where, finding only the mats scracht, but the bed-coards whole, and the quarter of beef which lay on the floor untoucht, they entertained other thoughts.

October 18. They were all awaked as the night before, and now conceived that they heard all the great clefts of the King's Oak brought into the presence-chamber, and there thumpt down, and after roul about the room; they could hear their chairs and stools tost from one side of the room unto the other, and then (as it were) altogether josled. Thus having done an hour together, it walkt into the withdrawing-room, where lodged the two captains, the secretary, and two servants: here stopt the thing a while, as if it did take breath, but raised a hideous one, then walkt into the bed-chamber, where lay those as before, and under the bed it went, where it did heave and heave again, that now they in bed were put to catch hold upon bed-posts, and sometimes one of the other, to prevent their being tumbled out upon the ground; then coming out as from under the bed, and taking hold upon the bed-posts, it would shake the whole bed, almost as if a cradle rocked. Thus having done here for half an hour, it went into the withdrawing-room, where first it came and stood at the bed's feet, and heaving up the bed's feet, flopt down again a while, until at last it heaved the feet so high that those in bed thought to have been set upon their heads; and having thus for two hours entertained them, went out as in the night before, but with a great noise.

October 19. This night they awaked not until the midst of the night; they perceived the room to shake with something that walkt about the bedchamber, which having done so a while, it walkt into a withdrawing-room, where it took up a brasse warming-pan, and returning with it into the bedchamber, therein made so loud a noise, in these captains' own words, it was as loud and scurvie as a ring of five untuned bells rung backward; but the captains, not to seem afraid, next day made mirth of what had passed, and jested at the devil in the pan.

October 20. These captains and their company, still lodging as before, were wakened in this night with some things flying about the rooms, and out of one room into the other, as thrown with some great force. Captain Hart, being in a slumber, was taken by the shoulder and shaked until he did sit up in his bed, thinking that it had been one of his fellows, when suddenly he was taken on the pate with a trencher, that it made him shrink down into the bed-clothes, and all of them, in both rooms, kept their heads at least within their sheets, so fiercely did three dozen of trenchers fly about the rooms; yet Captain Hart ventured again to peep out to see what was the matter, and what it was that threw, but then the trenchers came so fast and neer about his ears, that he was fain quickly to couch again. In the morning they found all their trenchers, pots, and spits, upon and about their beds, and all such things as were of common use scattered about the rooms. This night there were also, in several parts of the room and outer rooms, such noises of beating at doors, and on the walls, as if that several smiths had been at work; and yet our captains shrunk not from their work, but went on in that, and lodged as they had done before.

October 21. About midnight they heard great knocking at every door; after a while the doors flew open, and into the withdrawing-room entered something as of a mighty proportion, the figure of it they knew not how to describe. This walkt awhile about the room shaking the floor at every step, then came it up close to the bedside, where lay Captains Crook and Carelesse; and after a little pause, as it were, the bed-curtains, both at sides and feet, were drawn up and down slowly, then faster again for a quarter of an hour, then from end to end as fast as imagination can fancie the running of the rings, then shaked it the beds, as if the joints thereof had crackt; then walkt the thing into the bed-chamber, and so plaied with those beds there; then took up eight peuter dishes, and bouled them about the room and over the servants in the truckle-beds; then sometimes were the dishes taken up and thrown crosse the high beds and against the walls, and so much battered; but there were more dishes wherein was meat, in the same room, that were not at all removed. During this, in the presence-chamber there was stranger noise of weightie things thrown down, and, as they supposed, the clefts of the Ring's Oak did roul about the room, yet at the wonted hour went away, and left them to take rest, such as they could.

October 22. Hath mist of being set down, the officers imployed in their work farther off, came not that day to Woodstock.

October 23. Those that lodged in the withdrawing-room, in the midst of the night were awakened with the cracking of fire, as if it had been with thorns and sparks of fire burning, whereupon they supposed that the bedchamber had taken fire, and listning to it farther, they heard their fellows in bed sadly groan. which gave them to suppose they might be suffocated; wherefore they called upon their servants to make all possible hast to help them. When the two servants were come in, they found all asleep, and so brought back word, but that there were no bed-clothes upon them; wherefore they were sent back to cover them, and to stir up and mend the fire. When the servants had covered them and were come to the chimney, in the corners they found their wearing apparel, boots, and stockings, but they had no sooner toucht the embers, when the firebrands flew about their ears so fast that away ran they into the other room for the shelter of their coverlids; then after them walkt something that stampt about the room as if it had been exceeding angry, and likewise threw about the trenchers, platters, and all such things in the room—after two hours went out, yet stampt again over their heads.

October 24. They lodged all abroad.

October 25. This afternoon was come unto them Mr. Richard Crook the lawyer, brother to Captain Crook, and now deputysteward of the manner, unto Captain Parsons and Major Butler, who had put out Mr. Hyans, his majestie's officer. To entertain this new guest the Commissioners caused a very great fire to be made, of neer the chimney-full of wood of the King's Oak, and he was lodged in the withdrawing-room with his brother, and his servant in the same room. About the midst of the night a wonderful knocking was heard, and into the room something did rush, which coming to the chimney-side, dasht out the fire as with the stamp of some prodigious foot, then threw down such weighty stuffe, what ere it was (they took it to be the residue of the clefts and roots of the King's Oak), close by the bedside, that the house and bed shook with it. Captain Cockaine and his fellow arose, and took their swords to go unto the Crooks. The noise ceased at their rising, so that they came to the door and called. The two brothers, though fully awaked, and heard them call, were so amazed, that they made no answer until Captain Cockaine had recovered the boldness to call very loud, and came unto the bedside; then faintly first, after some more assurance, they came to understand one another, and comforted the lawyer. Whilst this was thus, no noise was heard, which made them think the time was past of that night's trouble, so that, after some little conference, they applied themselves to take some rest. When Captain Cockaine was come to his own bed, which he had left open, he found it closely covered, which he much wondered at; but turning the clothes down, and opening it to get in, he found the lower sheet strewed over with trenchers. Their whole three dozen of trenchers were orderly disposed between the sheets, which he and his fellow endeavouring to cast out, such noise arose about the room, that they were glad to get into bed with some of the trenchers. The noise lasted a full half hour after this. This entertainment so ill did like the lawyer, and being not so well studied in the point as to resolve this the devil's law-case, that he next day resolved to be gone; but having not dispatcht all that he came for, profit and perswasions prevailed with him to stay the other hearing, so that he lodged as he did the night before.

October 26. This night each room was better furnished with fire and candle than before; yet about twelve at night came something in that dasht all out, then did walk about the room, making a noise, not to be set forth by the comparison with any other thing; sometimes came it to the bedsides, and drew the curtains to and fro, then twerle them, then walk about again, and return to the bed-posts, shake them with all the bed, so that they in bed were put to hold one upon the other, then walk about the room again, and come to the servants' bed, and gnaw and scratch the wainscot head, and shake altogether in that room; at the time of this being in doing, they in the bedchamber heard such strange dropping down from the roof of the room, that they supposed 'twas like the fall of money by the sound. Captain Cockaine, not frightened with so small a noise (and lying near the chimney), stept out, and made shift to light a candle, by the light of which he perceived the room strewed over with broken glass, green, and some of it as it were pieces of broken bottles; he had not long been considering what it was, when suddenly his candle was hit out, and glass flew about the room, that he made haste to the protection of the coverlets; the noise of thundering rose more hideous then at any time before; yet, at a certain time, all vanisht into calmness. The morning after was the glass about the room, which the maid that was to make clean the rooms swept up into a corner, and many came to see it. But Mr. Richard Crook would stay no longer, yet as he stopt, going through Woodstock town, he was there heard to say, that he would not lodge amongst them another night for a fee of £500.

October 27. The Commissioners had not yet done their work, wherefore they must stay; and being all men of the sword, they must not seem afraid to encounter with any thing, though it be the devil; therefore, with pistols charged, and drawn swords laied by their bedsides, they applied themselves to take some rest, when something in the midst of night, so opened and shut the window casements with such claps, that it awakened all that slept; some of them peeping out to look what was the matter with the windows, stones flew about the rooms as if hurled with many hands; some hit the walls, and some the beds' heads close above the pillows, the dints of which were then, and yet (it is conceived) are to be seen, thus sometime throwing stones, and sometime making thundering noise, for two hours space it ceast, and all was quiet till the morn. After their rising, and the maid come in to make the fire, they looked about the rooms; they found fourscore stones brought in that night, and going to lay them together in the corner where the glass (before mentioned) had been swept up, they found that every piece of glass had been carried away that night. Many people came next day to see the stones, and all observed that they were not of such kind of stones as are naturall in the countrey thereabout; with these were noise like claps of thunder, or report of cannon planted against the rooms, heard by all that lodged in the outer courts, to their astonishment, and at Woodstock town, taken to be thunder.

October 28. This night, both strange and differing noise from the former first wakened Captain Hart, who lodged in the bedchamber, who, hearing Boe and Browne to groan, called out to Cockaine and Crook to come and help them, for Hart could not now stir himself; Cockaine would faine have answered, but he could not, nor look about; something, he thought, stopt both his breath and held down his eye-lids. Amazed thus, he struggles and kickt about, till he had awaked Captain Crook, who, half asleep, grew very angry at his kicks, and multiplied words, it grew to an appointment in the field; but this fully recovered Cockaine to remember that Captain Hart had called for help, wherefore to them he ran in the other room, whom he found sadly groaning, where, scraping in the chimney, he both found a candle and fire to light it; but had not gone two steps, when something blew the candle out, and threw him in the chair by the bedside, when presently cried out Captain Carelesse, with a most pittiful voice, "Come hither, O come hither, brother Cockaine, the thing's gone of me." Cockaine, scarce yet himself, helpt to set him up in his bed, and after Captain Hart, and having scarce done that to them, and also to the other two, they heard Captain Crook crying out, as if something had been killing him. Cockaine snacht up the sword that lay by their bed, and ran into the room to save Crook, but was in much more likelyhood to kill him, for at his coming, the thing that pressed Crook went of him, at which Crook started out of his bed, whom Cockaine thought a spirit, made at him, at which Crook cried out "Lord help, Lord save me;" Cockaine let fall his hand, and Crook, embracing Cockaine, desired his reconcilement, giving him many thanks for his deliverance. Then rose they all and came together, discoursed sometimes godly and sometimes praied, for all this while was there such stamping over the roof of the house as if 1000 horse had there been trotting; this night all the stones brought in the night before, and laid up in the withdrawing-room, were all carried again away by that which brought them in, which at the wonted time left of, and, as it were, went out, and so away.

October 29. Their businesse having now received so much forwardnesse as to be neer dispatcht, they encouraged one the other, and resolved to try further; therefore, they provided more lights and fires, and further for their assistance, prevailed with their ordinary keeper to lodge amongst them, and bring his mastive bitch; and it was so this night with them, that they had no disturbance at all.

October 30. So well they had past the night before, that this night they went to bed, confident and carelesse; untill about twelve of the clock, something knockt at the door as with a smith's great hammer, but with such force as if it had cleft the door; then ent'red something like a bear, but seem'd to swell more big, and walkt about the room, and out of one room into the other, treading so heavily, as the floare had not been strong enough to bear it. When it came into the bedchamber, it dasht against the beds' heads some kind of glass vessell, that broke in sundry pieces, and sometimes would take up those pieces and hurle them about the room, and into the other room; and when it did not hurle the glasse at their heads, it did strike upon the tables, as if many smiths, with their greatest hammers, had been laying on as upon an anvil; sometimes it thumpt against the walls as if it would beat a hole through; then upon their heads, such stamping, as if the roof of the house were beating down upon their heads; and having done thus, during the space (as was conjectured) of two hours, it ceased and vanished, but with a more fierce shutting of the doors than at any time before. In the morning they found the pieces of glass about the room, and observed, that it was much differing from that glasse brought in three nights before, this being of a much thicker substance, which severall persons which came in carried away some pieces of. The Commissioners were in debate of lodging there no more; but all their businesse was not done, and some of them were so conceited as to believe, and to attribute the rest they enjoyed, the night before this last, unto the mastive bitch; wherefore, they resolved to get more company, and the mastive bitch, and try another night.

October 31. This night, the fires and lights prepared, the ordinary keeper and his bitch, with another man perswaded by him, they all took their beds and fell asleep. But about twelve at night, such rapping was on all sides of them, that it wakened all of them; as the doors did seem to open, the mastive bitch fell fearfully a yelling, and presently ran fiercely into the bed to them in the truckle-bed; as the thing came by the table, it struck so fierce a blow on that, as that it made the frame to crack, then took the warming-pan from off the table, and stroke it against the walls with so much force as that it was beat flat together, lid and bottom. Now were they hit as they lay covered over head and ears within the bed-clothes. Captain Carelesse-was taken a sound blow on the head with the shoulder-blade bone of a dead horse (before they had been but thrown at, when they peept up, and mist); Browne had a shrewd blow on the leg with the backbone, and another on the head, and every one of them felt severall blows of bones and stones through the bedclothes, for now these things were thrown as from an angry hand that meant further mischief; the stones flew in at window as shot out of a gun, nor was the bursts lesse (as from without) than of a cannon, and all the windows broken down. Now as the hurling of the things did cease, and the thing walkt up and down, Captain Cockaine and Hart cried out, In the name of the Father, Son, and Holy Ghost, what are you? What would you have? What have we done that you disturb us thus? No voice replied (as the Captains said, yet some of their servants have said otherwise), and the noise ceast. Hereupon Captains Hart and Cockaine rose, who lay in the bedchamber, renewed the fire and lights, and one great candle, in a candlestick, they placed in the door, that might be seen by them in both the rooms. No sooner were they got to bed, but the noise arose on all sides more loud and hideous than at any time before, insomuch as (to use the Captain's own words) it returned and brought seven devils worse than itself; and presently they saw the candle and candlestick in the passage of the door, dasht up to the roof of the room, by a kick of the hinder parts of a horse, and after with the hoof trode out the snuff, and so dasht out the fire in the chimnies. As this was done, there fell, as from the sieling, upon them in the truckle-beds, such quantities of water, as if it had been poured out of buckets, which stunk worse than any earthly stink could make; and as this was in doing, something crept under the high beds, tost them up to the roof of the house, with the Commissioners in them, until the testers of the beds were beaten down upon, and the bedsted-frames broke under them; and here some pause being made, they all, as if with one consent, started up, and ran down the stairs until they came into the Councel Hall, where two sate up a brewing, but now were fallen asleep; those they scared much with wakening of them, having been much perplext before with the strange noise, which commonly was taken by them abroad for thunder, sometimes for rumbling wind. Here the Captains and their company got fire and candle, and every one carrying something of either, they returned into the Presence-Chamber, where some applied themselves to make the fire, whilst others fell to prayers, and having got some clothes about them, they spent the residue of the night in singing psalms and prayers; during which, no noise was in that room, but most hideously round about, as at some distance.

It should "have been told before, how that when Captain Hart first rose this night (who lay in the bedchamber next the fire), he found their book of valuations crosse the embers smoking, which he snacht up and cast upon the table there, which the night before was left upon the table in the presence amongst their other papers; this book was in the morning found a handful burnt, and had burnt the table where it lay; Browne the clerk said, he would not for a 100 and a *1001.* that it had been burnt a handful further.

This night it happened that there were six cony-stealers, who were come with their nets and ferrets to the cony-burrows by Eosamond's Well; but with the noise this night from the Mannorhouse, they were so terrified, that like men distracted away they ran, and left their haies all ready pitched, ready up, and the ferrets in the cony-burrows.

Now the Commissioners, more sensible of their danger, considered more seriously of their safety, and agreed to go and confer with Mr. Hoffman, the minister of Wotton (a man not of the meanest note for life or learning, by some esteemed more high), to desire his advice, together with his company and prayers. Mr. Hoffman held it too high a point to resolve on suddenly and by himself, wherefore desired time to consider upon it, which being agreed unto, he forthwith rode to Mr. Jenkinson and Mr. Wheat, the two next Justices of Peace, to try what warrant they could give him for it. They both (as 't is said from themselves) encouraged him to be assisting to the Commissioners, according to his calling.

But certain it is, that when they came to fetch him to go with them, Mr. Hoffman answered, that he would not lodge there one night for 500/., and being asked to pray with them, he held up his hands and said, that he would not meddle upon any terms.

Mr. Hoffman refusing to undertake the quarrel, the Commissioners held it not safe to lodge where they had been thus entertained any longer, but caused all things to be removed into the chambers over the gatehouse, where they staid but one night, and what rest they enjoyed there, we have but an uncertain relation of, for they went away early the next morning; but if it may be held fit to set down what hath been delivered by the report of others, they were also the same night much affrighted with dreadful apparitions, but observing that these passages spread much in discourse, to be also in particulars taken notice of, and that the nature of it made not for their cause, they agreed to the concealing of things for the future; yet this is well-known and certain, that the gate-keeper's wife was in so strange an agony in her bed, and in her bedchamber such noise (whilst her husband was above with the Commissioners), that two maids in the next room to her, durst not venture to assist her, but affrighted ran out to call company, and their master, and found the woman (at their coming in) gasping for breath; and the next day said, that she saw and suffered that, which for all the world she would not be hired to again.

From Woodstock the Commissioners removed unto Euelme, and some of them returned to Woodstock the Sunday se'n night after (the book of Valuations wanting something that was for haste left imperfect), but lodged not in any of those rooms where they had lain before, and yet were not unvisited (as they confess themselves) by the devil, whom they called their nightly guest; Captain Crook came not untill Tuesday night, and how he sped that night the gate-keeper's wife can tell if she dareth, but what she hath whispered to her gossips, shall not be made a part of this our narrative, nor many more particulars which have fallen from the Commissioners themselves and their servants to other persons; they are all or most of them alive, and may add to it when they please, and surely have not a better way to be revenged of him who troubled them, than according to the proverb, tell truth and shame the devil.

There remains this observation to be added, that on a Wednesday morning all these officers went away; and that since then diverse persons of severall qualities, have lodged often and sometimes long in the same rooms, both in the presence, withdrawiugroom, and bedchamber belonging unto his sacred Majesty; yet none have had the least disturbance, or heard the smallest noise, for which the cause was not as ordinary as apparent, except the Commissioners and their company, who came in order to the alienating and pulling down the house, which is well-nigh performed.

A SHOET SURVEY OF WOODSTOCK, NOT TAKEN BY ANY OP THE BEFORE-MENTIONED COMMISSIONERS.

The noble seat, called Woodstock, is one of the ancient honours belonging to the crown. Severall mannors owe suite and service to the place; but the custom of the eountrey giving it but the title of a mannor, we shall erre with them to be the better understood.

The mannor-house hath been a large fabrick, and accounted among his majestie's standing houses, because there was alwaies kept a standing furniture. This great house was built by King Henry the First, but ampleyfied with the gate-house and outsides of the outer-court, by King Henry the Seventh, the stables by King James.

About a bow-shoot from the gate south-west, remain foundation signs of that structure, erected by King Henry the Second, for the security of Lady Rosamond, daughter of Walter Lord Clifford, which some poets have compared to the Dedalian labyrinth, but the form and circuit both of the place and ruins shew it to have been a house and of one pile, perhaps of strength, according to the fashion of those times, and probably was fitted with secret places of recess, and avenues to hide or convey away such persons as were not willing to be found if narrowly sought after. About the midst of the place ariseth a spring, called at present Eosamond's Well; it is but shallow, and shews to have been paved and walled about, likely contrived for the use of them within the house, when it should be of danger to go out.

A quarter of a mile distant from the King's house, is seated Woodstock town, new and old. This new Woodstock did arise by some buildings which Henry the Second gave leave to be erected (as received by tradition), at the suite of the Lady Rosamond, for the use of out-servants upon the wastes of the mannor of Bladon, where is the mother church; this is a hamlet belonging to it, though encreased to a market town by the advantage of the Court residing sometime near, which of late years they have been sensible of the want of; this town was made a corporation The Survey of Woodstock is appended to the preceding pamphlet.
in the 11th year of Henry the Sixth, by charter,-with power to send two burgesses to parliament or not, as they will themselves.

Old Woodstock is seated on the west side of the brook, named Glyme, which also runneth through the park; the town consists not of above four or five houses, but it is to be conceived that it hath been much larger (but very anciently so), for in some old law historians there is mention of the assize at Woodstock, for a law made in a Micelgemote (the name of parliaments before the coming of the Norman) in the days of King Ethelred.

And in like manner, that thereabout was a king's house, if not in the same place where Henry the First built the late standing pile before his; for in such days those great councils were commonly held in the King's palaces. Some of those lands have belonged to the orders of the Knights Templers, there being records which call them, *Terras quas Rex excambiavit cum Templariis.*

But now this late large mannor-house is in a manner almost turned into heaps of rubbish; some seven or eight rooms left for the accommodation of a tenant that should rent the Bang's meadows (of those who had no power to let them), with several high uncovered walls standing, the prodigious spectacles of malice unto monarchy, which ruines still bear semblance of their state, and yet aspire in spight of envy, or of weather, to shew, What kings do build, subjects may sometimes shake, but utterly can never overthrow.

That part of the park called the Highpark, hath been lately subdivided by Sir Arthur Haselrig, to make pastures for his breed of colts, and other parts plowed up. Of the whole saith. Roffus Warwicensis, in MS. Hen. I. p. 122, *Fecit iste Hex Parcum de Woodstock, cum Palatio infra praedictum Parcum, qui Parous eratprimus Parous Anglice, et continet in circuitu septem Miliaria; constructus erat A nno 14 kujus Regis, aut parum post.* Without the park the King's demesne woods were, it cannot well be said now are, the timber being all sold off, and underwoods so cropt and spoiled by that beast the Lord Munson, and other greedy cattle, that they are hardly recoverable. Beyond which lieth Stonefield, and other mannors that hold of Woodstock, with other woods, that have been aliened by former kings, but with reservation of liberty for his majestie's deer, and other beasts of forrest, to harbour in at pleasure, as in due place is to be shewed.

AUTHOR'S NOTES

Note A. Vindication Of The Book Of Common Prater, Against The Contumelious Slanders Of The Fanatic Party, Terming It Porridge.

The author of this singular and rare tract indulges in the allegorical style, till he fairly hunts down the allegory.

"But as for what you call porridge, who hatched the name I know not, neither is it worth the inquiring after, for I hold porridge good food. It is better to a sick man than meat, for a sick man will sooner eat pottage than meat. Pottage will digest with him when meat will not; pottage will nourish the blood, fill the veins, run into every part of a man, make him warmer; so will these prayers do, set our soul and body in a heat, warm our devotion, work fervency in us, lift up our soul to God. For there be herbs of God's own planting in our pottage as you call it—the Ten Commandments, dainty herbs to season any pottage in the world; there is the Lord's Prayer, and that is a most sweet potherb cannot be denied; then there is also David's herbs, his prayers and psalms, helps to make our pottage relish well; the psalm of the blessed Virgin, a good pot-herb. Though they be, as some term them, *cock-crowed* pottage, yet they are as sweet, as good, as dainty, and as fresh, as they were at the first. The sun hath not made them sour with its heat, neither hath the cold water taken away their vigour and strength. Compare them with the Scriptures, and see if they be not as well seasoned and crumbed. If you find any thing in them that is either too salt, too fresh, or too bitter, that herb shall be taken out and better put in, if it can be got, or none. And as in kitchen pottage there are many good herbs, so there is likewise in this church pottage, as you call it. For first, there is in kitchen pottage good water to make them so; on the contrary, in the other pottage there is the water of life. 2. There is salt to season them, so in the other is a prayer of grace to season their hearts. 3. There is oatmeal to nourish the body, in the other is the bread of life. 4. There is thyme in them to relish them, and it is very wholesome —in the other is the wholesome exhortation not to harden our heart while it is called to-day. This relisheth well. 5. There is a small onion to give it taste—in the other is a good herb, called Lord have mercy on us. These, and many other holy herbs are contained in it, all boiling in the heart of man, will make as good pottage as the world can afford, especially if you use these herbs for digestion.— The herb repentance, the herb grace, the herb faith, the herb love, the herb hope, the herb good works, the herb feeling, the herb zeal, the herb fervency, the herb ardency, the herb constancy, with many more of this nature, most excellent for digestion." *Oke! jam satis.* In this manner the learned divine hunts his metaphor at a very cold scent, through a pamphlet of six mortal quarto pages.

Note B. Dr. Michael Hudson.

Michael Hudson, the *plain-dealing* chaplain of King Charles I., resembled, in his loyalty to that unfortunate monarch, the fictitious character of Doctor Eochecliffe; and the circumstances of his death were copied in the narrative of the Presbyterian's account of the slaughter of his school-fellow;— he was chosen by Charles I., along with John Ashburnham, as his guide and attendant, when he adopted the ill-advised resolution of surrendering his person to the Scots army.

He was taken prisoner by the Parliament, remained long in their custody, and was treated with great severity. He made his escape for about a year in 1647; was retaken, and again escaped in 1648, and heading an insurrection of cavaliers, seized on a strong moated house in Lincolnshire, called Woodford House. He gained the place without resistance; and there are among Peck's Desiderata Curiosa several accounts of his death, among which we shall transcribe that of Bishop Kenneth, as the most correct and concise:—

"I have been on the spot," saith his Lordship, "and made all possible inquiries, and find that the relation given by Mr. Wood may be a little rectified and supplied.

"Mr. Hudson and his party did not fly to Woodford, but had quietly taken possession of it, and held it for a garrison, with a good party of horse, who made a stout defence, and frequent sallies, against a party of the Parliament at Stamford, till the colonel commanding them sent a stronger detachment, under a captain, his own kinsman, who was shot from the house, upon which the colonel himself came up to renew the attack, and to demand surrendry, and brought them to capitulate upon terms of safe quarter. But the colonel, in base revenge, commanded that they should not spare that rogue Hudson. Upon which Hudson fought his way up to the leads; and when he saw they were pushing in upon him, threw himself over the battlements (another account says, he caught hold of a spout or outstone), and hung by the hands as intending to fall into the moat beneath, till they cut off his wrists and let him drop, and then ran down to hunt him in the water, where they found him paddling with his stumps, and barbarously knocked him on the head."—Peck's *Desiderata Curiosa*, Book ix.

Other accounts mention he was refused the poor charity of coming to die on land, by one Egborough, servant to Mr. Spinks the intruder into the parsonage. A man called Walker, a chandler or grocer, cut out the tongue of the unfortunate divine, and shewed it as a trophy through the country. But it was remarked, with vindictive satisfaction, that Egborough was killed by the bursting of his own gun; and that Walker, obliged to abandon his trade through poverty, became a scorned mendicant.

For some time a grave was not vouchsafed to the remains of this brave and loyal divine, till one of the other party said, "Since he is dead, let him be buried."

Note C. Cannibalism Imputed To The Cavaliers.

The terrors preceding the civil wars, which agitated the public mind, rendered the grossest and most exaggerated falsehoods current among the people. When Charles I. appointed Sir Thomas Lunsford to the situation of Lord Lieutenant of the Tower, the celebrated John Lillburn takes to himself the credit of exciting the public hatred against this officer and Lord Digby, as pitiless bravoes of the most bloody-minded description, from whom the people were to expect nothing but bloodshed and massacre. Of Sir Thomas Lunsford, in particular, it was reported that his favourite food was the flesh of children, and he was painted like an ogre in the act of cutting a child into steaks and broiling them. The colonel fell at the siege of Bristol in 1643, but the same calumny pursued his remains, and the credulous multitude were told,

The post who came from Coventry,
Riding in a red rocket,
Did tidings tell how Lunsford fell,
A child's hand in his pocket.

Many allusions to this report, as well as to the credulity of those who believed it, may be found in the satires and lampoons of the time, although, says Dr. Grey, Lunsford was a man of great sobriety, industry and courage. Butler says, that the preachers

Made children with their lives to run for't,
As bad as Bloody bones or Lunsford.

But this extraordinary report is chiefly insisted upon in a comedy called the *Old Troop*, written by John Lacy the comedian. The scene is laid during the civil wars of England, and the persons of the drama are chiefly those who were in arms for the king. They are represented as plundering the country without mercy, which Lacy might draw from the life, having, in fact, begun his career as a lieutenant of cavalry in the service of Charles I. The troopers find the peasants loath to surrender to them their provisions, on which, in order to compel them, they pretend to be in earnest in the purpose of eating the children. A scene of coarse but humorous comedy is then introduced, which Dean Swift had not, perhaps, forgotten, when he recommended the eating of the children of the poor as a mode of relieving the distresses of their parents.

"*Lieutenant.* Second me, and I'll make them bring out all they have, I warrant you. Do but talk as if we used to eat children.—Why, look you, good woman, we do believe you are poor, so we'll make a shift with our old diet—you have children in the town?

"*Woman.* Why do you ask, sir?

"*Lieutenant.* Only have two or three to supper. Fleaflint, you have the best way of cooking children.

"*Fleaflint.* I can powder them to make you taste your liquor. I am never without a dried child's tongue or ham.

"*Woman.* O! bless me!

"*Fleaflint.* Mine's but the ordinary way; but Foodfarm is the man; he makes you the savouriest pie of a child chaldron that was ever eat.

"*Lieutenant.* A plague! all the world cannot cook a child like Mr. Kaggou a French cook or messman to the troop, and the buffoon of the piece.

"*Raggou.* Begar me think so; for vat was me bred in the King of Mogol's kitchen? dere we kill twenty shild of a day. Take you one shild by both his two heels, and put his head between your two knees, and take your knife and slice off all buttocks,—so fashion; begar, that make a de best Scots collop in de world.

"*Lieutenant.* Ah, he makes the best pottage of a child's head and feet, however; but you must boil it with bacon—Woman you must get bacon.

"*Woman.* O Lud—yes, sir!

"*Ford.* And then it must be very young.

"*Lieutenant.* Yes, yes—Good woman, it must be a fine squab child, of half a year old—a man child, dost hear?"—The Old Tboop, *Act III.*

After a good deal more to this purpose, the villagers determine to carry forth their sheep, poultry, etc., to save their children. In the meantime, the Cavaliers are in some danger of being cross-bit, as they then called it; that is, caught in their own snare. A woman enters, who announces herself thus:—

" *Woman.* By your leave, your good worships, I have made bold to bring you in some provisions.

"*Ford.* Provisions! where, where is this provision?

"*Woman.* Here, if it please you, I have brought you a couple of fine fleshy children.

"*Cornet.* Was ever such a horrid woman! what shall we do?

"*Woman.* Truly, gentlemen, they are fine squab children: shall I turn them up?—they have the bravest brawn and buttocks.

"*Lieutenant.* No, no; but, woman, art thou not troubled to part with thy children?

"*Woman.* Alas, sir, they are none of mine, they are only nurse children.

" *Lieutenant.* What a beast is this — whose children are they?

"*Woman.* A laundress that owes me for a year's nursing; I hope they'll prove excellent meat; they are twins too.

" *Raggou.* Aha, but! but begar we

never eat no twin shild, the law forbid that."—*Ibidem.*

In this manner the Cavaliers escape from the embarrassing consequences of their own stratagem, which, as the reader will perceive, has been made use of in the text.

Note D. Patrick Cabby.

"You do not know Patrick Carey," says King Charles in the novel; and, what is more singular, Patrick Carey has had two editors, each unknown alike to the other, except by name only. In 1771, Mr. John Murray published Carey's poems, from a collection said to be in the hands of the Rev. Mr. Pierspoint Crimp. A very probable conjecture is stated, that the author was only known to private friendship. As late as 1819, the Author of Waverley, ignorant of the addition of 1771, published a second quarto from an elaborate manuscript, though in bad order, apparently the autograph of the first. Of Carey, the second editor, like the first, only knew the name and the spirit of the verses. He has since been enabled to ascertain that the poetic cavalier was a younger brother of the celebrated Henry Lord Carey, who fell at the battle of Newbery, and escaped the researches of Horace Walpole, to whose list of noble authors he would have been an important addition. So completely has the fame of the great Lord Falkland eclipsed that of his brothers, that this brother Patrick has been overlooked even by genealogists.

Note E. Signal Of Dangeb By The Token Of A Featheb.

On a particular occasion a lady, suspecting, by the passage of a body of guards through her estate, that the arrest of her neighbour, Patrick Home of Polwarth, afterwards first Earl of Marchmont, was designed, sent him a feather by a shepherd boy, whom she dared not trust with a more explicit message. Danger sharpens the intellect, and this hint was the commencement of those romantic adventures which gave Grizzel Lady Murray the materials from which she compiled her account of her grandfather's escape, published by Mr. Thomas Thomson, Deputy Register of Scotland. The anecdote of the feather does not occur there, but the author has often heard it from the late Lady Diana Scott, the lineal descendant and representative of Patrick Earl of Marchmont.

THE END.

Longmans' English Classics. EDITED BY GEORGE RICE CARPENTER, A.B.,

Professor Of Rhetoric And English Composition In Columbia College.

LONGMANS' ENGLISH CLASSICS. EDITED BY GEORGE RICE CARPENTER, A.B.,

Professor of Rhetoric and English Composition in Columbia College.

This series is designed for use in secondary schools in accordance with the system of study recommended and outlined by the National Committee of Ten, and in direct preparation for the uniform entrance requirements in English, now adopted by the principal American colleges and universities.

Each Volume contains full Notes, Introductions, Bibliographies, and other explanatory and illustrative matter. Crown 8vo, cloth.

Books Prescribed for the 1896 Examinations. FOR READING.

Irving's Tales Of A Traveller. With an introduction by Professor Brander Matthews, of Columbia College, and explanatory notes by the general editor of the series. With Portrait of Irving. *Ready.*

George Eliot's Silas Marner. Edited, with introduction and notes, by Robert Herrick, A.B., Assistant Professor of Rhetoric in the University of Chicago. With Portrait of George Eliot. *Ready.*

Scott's Woodstock. Edited, with introduction and notes, by Bliss Perry, A. M., Professor of Oratory and Esthetic Criticism in the College of New Jersey. With Portrait of Sir Walter Scott. *Ready.*

Books Prescribed for 1896—Continued. Defoe's History Of The Plague In London. Edited, with introduction and notes, by Professor G. R. Carpenter, of Columbia College. With Portrait of Defoe. *Ready.*

Macaulay's Essay On Milton. Edited, with introduction and notes, by James Greenleaf Croswell, A.B., Head-master of the Brearley School, New York, formerly Assistant Professor of Greek in Harvard University. With Portrait of Macaulay. *Ready.*

Shakspere's A Midsummer Night's Dream. Edited, with introduction and notes, by George Pierce Baker, A.B., Assistant Professor of English in Harvard University. With Frontispiece.

Just Ready. FOR STUDY.

Webster's First Bunker Hill Oration, together with other Addresses relating to the Revolution. Edited, with introduction and notes, by Fred Newton Scott, Ph.D., Assistant Professor of Rhetoric in the University of Michigan. With Portrait of Daniel Webster. *Ready.*

Shakspere's Merchant Of Venice. Edited, with introduction and notes, by Francis B. Gummere, Ph.D., Professor of English in Haverford College, Member of the Conference on English of the National Committee of Ten. With Portrait.

Just Ready.

Milton's L'allegro, Ii Penseroso, Comus, And Lycidas. Edited, with introductions and notes, by William P. Trent, A.M., Professor of English in the University of the South. With Portrait of Milton. *Ready.*

'' I take great pleasure in acknowledging, if I have not waited too long, the receipt of the two beautiful volumes in your English Classics, Irving's ' Tales of a Traveller' and George Eliot's 'Silas Marner,' and in thanking you for them. They are not only thoroughly well edited, but excellent specimens of bookmaking, such books as a student may take pleasure in having, not merely for a task book but for a permanent possession. It is a wise project on your part, I think, to accustom young students to value books for their intrinsic worth, and that by the practical way of making the books good and attractive. I shall take great pleasure, as occasion arises, to recommend the series."

—Prof. John F. Genung, Amherst College.

"You are to be congratulated upon the excellence of the series of English Classics which you are now publishing, if I may judge of it by the three numbers I have examined.... Of these, the introductions, the suggestions to teachers, the chronological tables, and the notes are most admirable in design and execution. The editor-in-chief and his associates have rendered a distinct service to secondary schools, and the publishers have done superior mechanical work in the issue of this series."—Charles C. Ramsay, Principal of Durfee High School, Fall River, Mass.

"With the two (volumes) I have already acknowledged and these four, I find myself increasingly pleased as I examine. As a series the books have two strong points: there is a unity of method in editing that I have seen in no other series; the books are freer from objections in regard to the amount and kind of editing than any other series I know." — Byron Groce, Master in English, Boston Latin School.

"I am your debtor for two specimens of your series of English Classics, designed for secondary schools in preparation for entrance examinations to college. With their clear type, good paper, sober and attractive binding—good enough for any library shelves—with their introductions, suggestions to teachers, and notes at the bottom of the pages, I do not see how much more could be desired."

—Prof. D. L. Maulsby, Tufts College.

"Admirably adapted to accomplish what you intend—to interest young persons in thoughtful reading of noble literature. The help given seems just what is needed; its generosity is not of the sort to make the young student unable to help himself. I am greatly pleased with the plan and with its execution."—Prof. C. B. Bradley, University of California; Member of English Conference of the National Committee of Ten.

"Let me thank you for four more volumes of your excellent series of English Classics.... As specimens of book-making they are among the most attractive books I have ever seen for school use; and the careful editing supplies just enough information" to stimulate a young reader. I hope that the series may soon be completed and be widely used. "—Prof. W. E. Mead, Wesleyan University.

"The series is admirably planned, the 'Suggestions to Teachers' being a peculiarly valuable feature. I welcome all books looking toward better English teaching in the secondary schools."

—Prof. Katherine Lee Bates, Wellesley College.

"They are thoroughly edited and attractively presented, and cannot fail to be welcome when used for the college entrance requirements in English."— Prof. Charles F. Richardson, Dartmouth College.

Irving's 'Tales Of A Traveller.'

"I feel bound to say that, if the series of English Classics is carried out after the plan of this initial volume, it will contribute much toward making the study of literature a pure delight."

—Prof. A. G. Newcomer, Leland Stanford Jr. University.

"I have looked through the first volume of your English Classics, Irving's ' Tales of a Traveller,' and do not see how literature could bemade more attractive to the secondary schools."— Prof. Edward A. Allen, University of Missouri; Member of the English Conference of the National Committee of Ten.

"I have received your Irving's ' Tales of a Traveller' and examined it with much pleasure. The helpful suggestions to teachers, the judicious notes, the careful editing, and the substantial binding make it the most desirable volume for class use on the subject, that has come tomy notice."—Edwin Cornell, Principal of Central Valley Union: School, N. Y.

George Eliot's 'Silas Marner.'

"This book is really attractive and inviting. The introduction, particularly the suggestions to pupils and teachers, is a piece of real helpfulness and wisdom."

—D. E. Bowman, Principal of High School, Waterville, Me.

"The edition of 'Silas Marner' recently sent out by you leaves, nothing undone. I find the book handsome, the notes sensible and clear. I'm glad to see a book so well adapted to High School needs, and I shall recommend it, without reserve, as a safe and clean book toput before our pupils."

—James W. Mclane, Central High School, Cleveland, O.

Scott's ' Woodstock.'

"Scott's ' Woodstock,' edited by Professor Bliss Perry, deepens the impression made by the earlier numbers that this series, Longmans' English Classics, is one of unusual excellence in the editing, and will prove a valuable auxiliary in the reform of English teaching now generally in progress.... We have, in addition to the unabridged text of the novel, a careful editorial introduction; the author's introduction, preface and notes; a reprint of ' The Just Devil of Woodstock'; and such foot-notes as the student will need as he turns from page to page. Besides all this apparatus, many of the chapters have appended a few suggestive hints for character-study, collateral reading and discussions of the art of fiction. All this matter is so skillfully distributed that it does not weigh upon the conscience, and is not likely to make the: student forget that he is, after all, reading a novel chiefly for the pleasure it affords. The entire aim of this volume and its companions is literary rather than historical or linguistic, and in this fact their chief value is to be found." —*The Dial.*

'' I heartily approve of the manner in which the editor's work has been done. This book, if properly used by the teacher and supplemented by the work so clearly suggested in the notes, may be made of great value to students, not only as literature but as affording opportunity for historical research and exercise in composition."

—lillian G. Kimball, State Normal School, Oshkosh, Wis.

Defoe's 'history Of The Plague In London.'

"He gives an interesting biography of Defoe, an account of his works, a discussion of their ethical influence (including that of this 'somewhat sensational' novel), some suggestions to teachers and students, and a list of references for future study. This is all valuable and suggestive. The reader wishes that there were more of it. Indeed, the criticism I was about to offer on this series is perhaps their chief excellence. One wishes that the introductions were longer and more exhaustive. For, contrary to custom, as expressed in Gratiano's query, 'Who riseth from a feast with that keen appetite that he sits down?' the young student will doubtless finish these introductions hungering for more. And this, perhaps, was the editor's object in view, viz., that the introductory and explanatory matter should be suggestive and stimulating rather than complete and exhaustive!"—*Educational Review.*

"I have taken great pleasure in examining your edition of Defoe's 'Plague in London.' The introduction and notes are beyond reproach, and the binding and typography are ideal. The American school-boy is to be congratulated that he at length may study his English from books in so attractive a dress."—George N. Mcknight, Instructor in English, Cornell University.

"lam greatly obliged to you for the copy of the ' Journal of the Plague.' I am particularly pleased with Professor Carpenter's introduction and his handling of the difficult points in Defoe's life."—HamMond Lamont, A.B., Associate Professor of Composition and Rhetoric in Brown University.

Macaulay's 'Essay On Milton.'

"I have examined the Milton and am much pleased with it; it fully sustains the high standard of the other works of this series; the introduction, the suggestions to teachers, and the notes are admirable."

—William Nichols, The Nichols School, Buffalo, N. Y.

"I beg to acknowledge with thanks the receipt of Macaulay's 'Essay on Milton' and Webster's 'First Bunker Hill Oration' in your series of English Classics. These works for preparatory study are nowhere better edited or presented in more artistic form. I am glad you find it possible to publish so good a book for so little money." —Prof. W. H. Crawshaw, Colgate University.

"I am especially pleased with Mr. Croswell's introduction to, and notes at the bottom of the page of, his edition of Macaulay's ' Essay on Milton.' I have never seen notes on a text that were more admirable than these. They contain just the information proper to impart, and are unusually well expressed.

—Charles C. Ramsay, Principal of Fall River High School.

Webster's 'first Bunker Hill Oration,' Etc.

"Permit me to acknowledge with gratitude the receipt of Dr. Scott's edition of Webster's ' First Bunker Hill Oration ' and other addresses relating to the Revolution. I am greatly pleased with the volume, both in its externals and in the judicious helps that accompany the text. A faithful use of the suggestions herein offered would certainly make for genuine culture."—Ray Greene Huling, Principal of English High School, Cambridge, Mass.; Secretary of the New England Association of Colleges and Preparatory Schools; Member of the History Conference of the National Committee of Ten.

"' First Bunker Hill Oration' and the ' Essay on Milton ' seem in every way to be the handsomest and best edited edition on the market." —Theodore C. Mitchell, Secretary of the Schoolmasters' Association of New York and Vicinity.

Books Prescribed for the 189J Examinations. FOR READING.

Shakspere's As You Like It. With an introduction by Barrett Wendell, A.B., Assistant Professor of English in Harvard University, and notes by William Lyon Phelps, Ph.D., Instructor in English Literature in Yale University. *Ready.*

Defoe's History Of The Plague In London. Edited, with introduction and notes, by Professor G. R. Carpenter, of Columbia College. With Portrait of Defoe. *Ready.*

Irving's Tales Of A Traveller. With an introduction by Professor Brander Matthews, of Columbia College, and explanatory notes by the general editor of the series. With Portrait of Irving. *Ready. Books Prescribed for i8gy—Continued.*

George Eliot's Silas Marner. Edited, with introduction and notes, by Robert Herrick, A.B., Assistant Professor of Rhetoric in the University of Chicago. With Portrait of George Eliot.
Ready. FOR STUDY.

Shakspere's Merchant Of Venice. Edited, with introduction and notes, by Francis B. Gummere, Ph.D., Professor of English in Haverford College; Member of the Conference on English of the National Committee of Ten. With Portrait.
Just Ready.

Burke's Speech On Conciliation With America. Edited, with introduction and notes, by Albert S. Cook, Ph.D., Professor of the English Language and Literature in Yale University. With Portrait of Burke. *Preparing.* SCOTT'S Marmion. Edited, with introduction and notes, by Robert Morss Lovett, A.B., Instructor in Rhetoric in the University of Chicago. With Portrait of Sir Walter Scott.
Preparing.

Macaulay's Life Of Samuel Johnson. Edited, with introduction and notes, by the Rev. Huber Gray Buehler, of the Hotchkiss School, Lakeville, Conn. With Portrait of Johnson.
In the Press. Books Prescribed for the 1898 Examinations. FOR READING.

Milton's Paradise Lost. Books I. And II. Edited, with introduction and notes, by Edward Everett Hale, Jr., Ph.D., Professor of Rhetoric and Logic in Union College. With Portrait of Milton. *Preparing.*

Pope's Homer's Iliad. Books I., VI., XXII., And XXIV. Edited, with introduction and notes, by William H. Maxwell, A.M., Superintendent of Public Instruction, Brooklyn, N. Y.; Chairman National Committee of Fifteen; Member of English Conference of the National Committee of Ten. With Portrait of Pope. *Preparing. Books Prescribed for I8q8*—Continued.

The Sir Roger De Coverley Papers, from "The Spectator." Edited, with introduction and notes, by D. O. S. Lowell, A.M., of the Roxbury Latin School, Roxbury, Mass. With Portrait of Addison. *In the Press.*

Goldsmith's The Vicar Of Wakefield. Edited, with introduction and notes, by Mary A. Jordan, A.M., Professor of Rhetoric and Old English in Smith College. With Portrait of Goldsmith. *Preparing.*

Coleridge's The Rime Of The Ancient Mariner. Edited, with introduction and notes, by Herbert Bates, A.B., Instructor in English in the University of Nebraska. With Portrait of Coleridge. *Ready.*

Southey's Life Of Nelson. Edited, with introduction and notes, by Edwin L. Miller, A.M., of the Englewood High School, Illinois. With Portrait of Nelson. *In the Press.*

Carlyle's Essay On Burns. Edited, with introduction and notes, by Wilson Farrand, A.M., Associate Principal of the Newark Academy, Newark, N. J. With Portrait of Burns.

In the Press. FOR STUDY.

Shakspere's Macbeth. Edited, with introduction and notes, by John Matthews Manly, Ph.D., Professor of the English Language in Brown University. With Portrait. *Preparing.*

Burke's Speech On Conciliation With America. Edited, with introduction and notes, by Albert S. Cook, Ph.D. , Professor of the English Language and Literature in Yale University. With Portrait of Burke. *Preparing.*

De Quincey's Flight Of A Tartar Tribe. Edited, with introduction and notes, by Charles Sears Baldwin, Ph.D. , Instructor in Rhetoric in Yale University. With Portrait of De Quincey. *Preparing. % Other Volumes to follow.*

It has been the aim of the publishers to secure editors of high reputation for scholarship, experience, and skill, and to provide a series thoroughly adapted, by uniformity of plan and thoroughness of execution, to present educational needs. The chief distinguishing features of the series are the following: i. Each volume contains full "Suggestions for Teachers and Students," with bibliographies, and, in many cases, lists of topics recommended for further reading or study, subjects for themes and compositions, specimen examination papers, etc. It is therefore hoped that the series will contribute largely to the working out of sound methods in teaching English.

2. The works prescribed for *reading* are treated, in every case, as literature, not as texts for narrow linguistic study, and edited with a view to interesting the student in the book in question both in itself and as representative of a literary type or of a period of literature, and of leading him on to read other standard works of the same age or kind understandingly and appreciatively. 3. These editions are not issued anonymously, nor are they hackwork,—the result of mere compilation. They are the original work of scholars and men of letters who are conversant with the topics of which they treat. 4. Colleges and preparatory schools are both represented in the list of editors (the preparatory schools more prominently in the lists for 1897 and 1898), and it is intended that the series shall exemplify the ripest methods of American scholars for the teaching of English—the result in some cases of years of actual experience in secondary school work, and, in others, the formulation of the experience acquired by professors who observe carefully the needs of students who present themselves for admission to college. 5. The volumes are uniform in size and style, are well printed and bound, and constitute a well-edited set of standard works, fit for permanent use and possession—a nucleus for a library of English literature. LONGMANS, GREEN, & CO. 'S PUBLICATIONS. II ENGLISH HISTORY IN SHAKESPEARE'S PLAYS.

By Beverley E. Warner, M.A. With Bibliography, Chronological Tables, and Index. Crown 8vo, 331 pages, $1.75.

This volume had its origin in a course of lectures on the study of history as illustrated in the plays of Shakespeare. The lectures have been recast, pruned, and amplified, and much machinery has been added in the way of tables of contents, bibliography, chronological tables, and index. With such helps it is hoped that this book may effect a working partnership between the chronicle of the formal historian and the epic of the dramatic poet. They are addressed especially to those readers and students of English History who may not have discovered what an aid to the understanding of certain important phases of England's national development lies in these historical plays, which cover a period of three hundred years—from King John and Magna Charta to Henry VIII. and the Reformation.

"This unique book should be generally and carefully read. As a commentary upon the history in Shakespeare's plays, it is highly interesting; while the views of English History, shown through the medium of the great poet, are admirable. After reading the work, one should be a far more appreciative student of English History, and a more interested reader of Shakespeare."
—*Public Opinion,* New York.

"The work has been well done, and the volume will be a valuable aid to students, particularly the younger ones, and to the average reader, in connection with this interesting group of plays."— *Literary World,* Boston.

"Mr. Warner's book is thoroughly interesting, and really valuable. It calls special attention to the genuine historical value of the plays which he examines, whether they be genuine histories or not."—*The Churchman.*

"To read Mr. Warner's learned and interesting pages is to come back to Shakespeare with a new appreciation. "—*Book Buyer.* "Mr. Warner's book is full of suggestion gathered not merely from Shakespeare, but from the chronicles which he used and from the efforts of modern historians to restore the life of the period to which the plays relate."
— *Tribune,* New York.

"We take much pleasure in commending this volume to readers and students of the great dramatist. It presents in a systematic, intelligent, and very useful order a large amount of critical information as to the historical plays which adds enormously to their interest, and which without this aid can be obtained only at the cost of much searching of publications not easy to be had, such as the 'New Shakespeare Society's Transactions,' or T. P. Courtenay's 'Commentaries on the Historical Plays of Shakespeare.' This labor and much more in the way of the direct study of the dramas, and of the obscure and difficult history with which they are concerned, has been done by the author of this volume, and its results presented in a clear, condensed, and highly interesting form, which we have found to be so satisfactory as to be practically indispensable in a small working Shakespearian library."—*Independent,* New York.

"What the chronicle plays of Shakespeare have accomplished as a contribution to the understanding of English history is clearly set forth in Mr. Warner's solidly excellent book."—*Chatauquan.* LONGMANS, GREEN, & CO., 15 East Sixteenth Street, New York. 12 LONGMANS, GREEN, cV CO.'S PUBLICATIONS. PLAYS OF SHAKESPEARE.

Falcon Edition.
The following volumes, each with Introduction, Notes, and Glossary, are now ready. Price 35 cents each play:

Julius Caesar. By H. C. Beech-Ing, Rector of Yattendon, and late Exhibitioner of Balliol College, Oxford.

The Merchant of Venice. By H. C. Beeching.

King Henry IV. Part I. By Oliver Elton, late Scholar of Corpus Christi College, Oxford.

King Henry IV. Part II. By A. D. Innes, M.A, late Scholar of Oriel College, Oxford.

King Henry V. By A. D. Innes, M.A. King John. By Oliver Elton.

Twelfth Night. By H. Howard Crawley.

King Richard III. By W. H. Payne Smith, M.A., Senior Student of Christ Church, Oxford; and Assistant Master at Rugby School.

Much Ado About Nothing. By A. W. Verity, M.A., late Scholar of Trinity College, Cambridge.

Coriolanus. By H. C. Beeching.

Taming of the Shrew. By H, H. Crawley.

King Richard II. By E. K. Chambers, B.A.

The Tempest. By A. C. Liddell, M.A.

"*Julius Casar*" is prescribed for the entrance examinations of 1894, "*Twelfth Night" for* 1895, *and the "Merchant of Venice" for* 1894, 1895, *and* 1896, *at Harvard and other universities and colleges.* 'The only school edition of Shakespeare's plays, so far as I know, the notes of which are assthetic rather than linguistic, stimulant rather than dispiriting, is that called 'the Falcon.' From 'The Taming of the Shrew' in this edition, for example, a student could learn the use of the gallery over the stage, and so might get his eyes opened a little to the physical conditions of the theatre under Elizabeth—conditions which dominate the form of the Elizabethan drama." —Prof. Brander Matthews, in the *Educational Review,* April, 1892.

"The ' Falcon' Edition has earned a reputation for scholarship, taste, and judgment. The notes are in all cases excellent. Everything that is likely to present any difficulty is explained clearly, accurately, and not verbosely; and familiarity is shown both with the writings of the Elizabethans and with the Shakespearean scholarship of to-day. "—*Journal of Education.* "A particularly pure text, with introductory remarks, glossaries, and notes of an excellence for which this edition is renowned."—*Educational Times.*

"An edition now well known among teachers and students, and which offers much instruction and enjoyment to the thoughtful reader. The editing is characterized by conscientious care, judgment, and skill."—*Schoolmaster.*

"Mr. Beeching's *Julius Casar* is not only an excellent school-book, but a model of good Shakespeare editing for all readers; and his *Merchant of Venice* is no less."—*Academy.* LONGMANS, GREEN, & CO., 15 East Sixteenth Street, New York.

LONGMAN'S, GREEN, & CO:S PUBLICATIONS. ENGLISH HISTORY FOR AMERICANS.

By Thomas Wentworth Higginson, Author of "Young Folks' History of the United States," etc., and Edward Channing, Assistant Professor of History in Harvard University. With 77 Illustrations, 6 Colored Maps, Bibliography, a Chronological Table of Contents, and Index. 121110. Pp. xxxii-334. Teachers' price, f 1.20.

The name " English History for Americans," which suggests the keynote of this book, is based on the simple fact that it is not the practice of American readers, old or young, to give to English history more than a limited portion of their hours of study.... It seems clear that such readers will use their time to the best advantage if they devote it mainly to those events in English annals which have had the most direct influence on the history and institutions of their own land.... T he authors of this book have therefore boldly ventured to modify in their narrative the accustomed scale of proportion; while it has been their wish, in the treatment of every detail, to accept the best result of modern English investigation, and especially to avoid all unfair 01 one-sided judgments.... *Extracts from Author's Preface.* DR. W. T. HARRIS, U. S. COMMISSIONER OF EDUCATION.

"I take great pleasure in acknowledging the receipt of the book, and believe it to be the best introduction to English history hitherto made for the use of schools. It is just what is needed in the school and in the family. It is the first history of England that I have seen which gives proper attention to sociology and the evolution of political ideas, without neglecting what is picturesque and interesting to the popular taste. The device of placing the four historical maps at the beginning and end deserves special mention for its convenience. Allow me to congratulate you on the publication of so excellent a text-book." ROXBURY LATIN SCHOOL.

"... The most noticeable and commendable feature in the book seems to be its Unity.... I felt the same reluctance to lay the volume down... that one experiences in reading a great play or a well-constructed novel. Several things besides the unity conspire thus seductively to lead the reader on. The page is open and attractive, the chapters are short, the type is large and clear, the pictures are well chosen and significant, a surprising number of anecdotes told in a crisp and masterful manner throw valuable sidelights on the main narrative; the philosophy of history is undeniably there, but sugar-coated, and the graceful style would do credit to a Macaulay. I shall immediately recommend it for use in our school."—Dr. D. O. S. Lowell. LAWRENCEVILLE SCHOOL.

"In answer to your note of February 23d I beg to say that we have introduced your Higginson's English History into our graduating class and are much pleased with it. Therefore whatever endorsement I, as a member of the Committee of Ten, could give the book has already been given by my action in placing it in our classes."—James C. Mackenzie, Lawrenceville, N J.

ANN ARBOR HIGH SCHOOL. "It seems to me the book will do for English history in this country what the 'Young Folks' History of the United States' has done for the history of our own country—and I consider this high praise."
—T. G. Pattengill, Ann Arbor, Mich.
LONGMANS, GREEN, & CO., 15 East Sixteenth Street, New York. *LONGMANS, GREEN, & CO.'S PUBLICATIONS.*

A STUDENT'S HISTORY OF ENGLAND, from the Earliest Times to 1885. By Samuel Rawson Gardiner, M.A., LL.D., Fellow of AH Souls College, Oxford, etc.; Author of "The History of K.ngland from the Accession of James I. to 1642," etc. Illustrated under the superintendence of Mr. W. H. St. John Hope, Assistant Secretary of the Society of Antiquaries, and with the assistance in the choice of Portraits of Mr. George Scharf, C.B., F.S.A., who is recognized as the highest authority on the subject. In one Volume, with 378 Illustrations and full Index. Crown 8vo, cloth, plain, $3.00.

The book is also published in three Volumes (each with Index and Table of Contents) as follows: VOLUME I.—B.C. 5S-A.D. 1509. 410 pp. With 173 Illustrations and Index.
Crown 8vo, $1.20. VOLUME II.—A.D. 1509-1689. 332 pp. With 96 Illustrations and Index.
Crown Svo, $1.20. VOLUME III.—A. D. 1689-1885. 374 pp. With 109 Illustrations and Index.
Crown 8vo, $1.20.

'.Gardiner's "Student's History of England," through Part IX. (to 1789), is recommended by HARVARD UNIVERSITY as indicating the requirements for admission in this subject; and the ENTIRE work ie made the basis for English history study in the University.

YALE UNIVERSITY. "Gardiner's ' Student's History of England' seems to me an admirable short history.''—Prof. C. H. Smith, New Haven, Conn. TRINITY COLLEGE, HARTFORD.

"It is, in my opinion, by far the best advanced school history of England that I have ever seen. It is clear, concise, and scientific, and, at the same time, attractive and interesting. The illustrations are very good and a valuable addition to-the book, as they are not mere pretty pictures, but of real historical and archaeological interest."—Prof. Henry Ferguson.

"A unique feature consists of the very numerous illustrations. They throw light on almost every phase of English life in all ages.... Never, perhaps, in such a treatise has pictorial illustration been used with so good effect. The alert teacher will find here ample material for useful lessons by leading the pupil to draw the proper inferences and make the proper interpretations and comparisons.... The style is compact, vigorous, and interesting. There is no lack of precision; and, in the selection of the details, the hand of the scholar thoroughly conversant with the source and with the results of recent criticism is plainly revealed."—*The Nation,* N. Y.

"... It is illustrated by pictures of real value; and when accompanied by the companion ' Atlas of English History' is all that need be desired for its special purpose."—*The Churchman,* N. Y.

%*A prospectus and specimen pages of Gardiner's " Student's History of England" will be sent free on application to the publishers.* LONGMANS, GREEN, & CO., 15 East Sixteenth Street, New York.

CPSIA information can be obtained at www.ICGtesting.com
Printed in the USA
BVOW07s1724020614

355172BV00012B/245/P